THE PICTURES IN THE COLLECTION OF
HER MAJESTY THE QUEEN

Φ

THE LATER GEORGIAN PICTURES
BY OLIVER MILLAR
PHAIDON

THE LATER GEORGIAN PICTURES

IN THE COLLECTION OF

HER MAJESTY THE QUEEN

BY

OLIVER MILLAR

TEXT

PHAIDON

© 1969 PHAIDON PRESS LTD · 5 CROMWELL PLACE · LONDON SW7

PHAIDON PUBLISHERS INC · NEW YORK
DISTRIBUTORS IN THE UNITED STATES: FREDERICK A. PRAEGER INC
111 FOURTH AVENUE · NEW YORK · N.Y. 10003
LIBRARY OF CONGRESS CATALOG CARD NUMBER: 69–19807

*The reproduction in this Catalogue
of pictures and other works of art in the Royal Collection
and the use of material in the Royal Archives
are by gracious permission of Her Majesty The Queen*

SBN for complete set of two volumes: 7148 1397 4
SBN for this volume: 7148 1398 2

MADE IN GREAT BRITAIN
TEXT PRINTED BY WESTERN PRINTING SERVICES LTD · BRISTOL
PLATES PRINTED BY HUNT BARNARD AND COMPANY LTD · AYLESBURY

CONTENTS

PREFACE

THIS is the third part to be published of the new Catalogue Raisonné of the royal collection of pictures and the sequel to my volume on the Tudor, Stuart and early Georgian pictures, which was published in 1963. The items in it are numbered to follow the 649 pictures included in the earlier volume; the total of 1,238 pictures in the two parts represents the so-called British School in the royal collection from the early Tudors to the accession of Queen Victoria. This volume, almost as long as its predecessor, covers a shorter stretch of time. The artists have therefore been placed in alphabetical, instead of chronological, sequence. It is perhaps unfortunate that a catalogue dedicated to the British School should begin with Jacques-Laurent Agasse and end with Johann Zoffany, but, as in the earlier volume, I have included in this Catalogue the works painted in this country by visiting continental artists such as Hickel, Quadal, Robineau and Stroehling whose portraits represent amusing, if rather exotic, episodes in the history of royal patronage or in the development of the British royal portrait. Except in the case of Hickel[1] I have included in this Catalogue all the works by these painters in the royal collection, even though one or two were painted abroad. This volume includes all those painters who worked for George III, George IV and William IV. All the pictures by painters, such as R. B. Davis and Wilkie, who also worked for Queen Victoria have of course been included, even though some of them fall outside the chronological limits of the volume.[2] In the Introduction I have tried to produce a sketch for a full-dress account of the patronage of living painters by the Crown between 1760 and 1837.

The Catalogue is based on an inspection of the pictures themselves and an examination of the inventories of the royal collections and other related sources. Every picture has been carefully scrutinised and I have seen and measured the backs of all but a very small number of particularly large or inaccessible pictures. The first debt I must therefore acknowledge is to the Superintendents of Buckingham Palace and Windsor Castle, Mr. Stanley Williams and Mr. Stanley Lucking, who have always so readily made it possible for me to examine the pictures for this volume. Of those who actually got out, or took down, pictures for me I wish especially to thank Mr. W. J. Beatty, Mr. A. Benstead and the late Mr. R. Crisp at Windsor, and Mr. Cyril Taylor, Mr. S. L. Martin and Miss Joyce Leat at Buckingham Palace. Mr. E. J. Rainbow and Mr. W. Watson at Hampton Court, and Mr. H. G. White and Mr. W. L. Ross at Holyroodhouse, have been no less helpful.

The inventories of the royal pictures naturally provide information of fundamental importance for this Catalogue.[3] Other documentary material for the collections of George III and William IV is apparently scarce, but in the Public Record Office and, especially, in the Royal Archives at Windsor, there is a wealth of almost entirely unpublished documents dealing with the formation and maintenance of George IV's collection. These sources have formed the basis of this Catalogue. The history of many pictures can be traced in detail and only twenty-two, out of nearly 600, pictures appear without attribution. The acquisitions made by Queen Victoria and the Prince Consort are usually well documented, but there are nevertheless a number of pictures which came into the

1. Hickel's portrait of the Emperor Joseph II will be included in the volume of the Catalogue which will contain the German and Austrian pictures in the royal collection.
2. The pictures by Clarkson Stanfield have been held over for a possible volume on The Queen's Victorian paintings. His *Portsmouth Harbour* and *Opening of London Bridge* were painted for William IV, but his three other pictures in the royal collection were acquired by Queen Victoria and the Prince Consort, with whom Stanfield was also associated in the decoration of the garden pavilion at Buckingham Palace.
3. They are invs. Nos. 32–51 on pp. xlix–lii below.

collection, in circumstances which are at the moment obscure, between the death of George III and the drawing-up of Richard Redgrave's great inventory. Nor are the acquisitions made by King Edward VII, King George V or Queen Mary as well recorded as one would expect. Portraits were acquired, for example, at the Duke of Cambridge's sale in 1904 and it is probable that a number of family portraits had passed earlier into the royal collection from descendants of George III who were not in the direct line of succession.

In working on the pictures in this Catalogue one realises how much remains to be done on many painters, even in this illustrious period in the history of British painting. Important primary sources remain unprinted or are only available in unsatisfactory texts; Gainsborough and Lawrence are the only painters in this Catalogue of whom full and up-to-date catalogues exist; engravings still seem often to be undervalued as evidence of date and authorship. I am sure that further exploration in unpublished sources would bring to light more information about many of the pictures in this volume, although perhaps not much which would change attributions securely based on original sources. In particular, useful information must lie buried in the daily press and in the more serious periodicals, but I have only looked for specific details in these sources.[4] It would have been possible to delay publication of these volumes in the hope of finding more information; but 'information in hand, however imperfectly presented, is more important to the user than the promise of an ideally compiled work which may never be completed'.[5] I prefer to present the Catalogue as it is, so that the student who comes to work over the period 'in depth' may know what there is for him in the royal collection and in its own documentation in the Royal Archives.

The Catalogue has been compiled in exactly the same way as its predecessor. The biographies of artists have been kept as short as possible, but I have included information, usually from the Royal Archives, on a painter's work for the Crown, and on pictures by him formerly in royal possession, if it has not been possible to incorporate these facts into a particular entry in the Catalogue. The location of a painting appears below its title. This section of the entry can quickly become out of date. At Windsor and Hampton Court the numbers established in Redgrave's inventory are still in force and the relevant number is placed in brackets immediately after the location of the item; for items not at Windsor or Hampton Court I have placed Redgrave's number at an appropriate point in the section dealing with the picture's movements.

After the location of the item comes a note of the material on which it is painted and its size. Every picture in this Catalogue is in oil on canvas unless otherwise described. Measurements are given in inches and centimetres; if a picture has been enlarged, its present measurements, as stretched, are given and are followed by a note on the additions to them. Details of signatures, dates and inscriptions are followed by a description of the picture in which the terms 'right' and 'left' are from the spectator's point of view unless they refer to the stance or action of a sitter in a portrait.

There follows an account of the picture's history within the collection. Many pictures still hang in or near their original positions. I have stated where a picture was first placed and I have indicated episodes in a picture's history which throw light on the taste or affections of its owners. The principal literary references to a picture are set out below its history. In this section I have not attempted to list all the exhibitions to which it may have been lent, but have given only those

---

4. Mr. John Hayes has generously placed at my disposal the material on Gainsborough and Dupont which he has found in these sources. I have, of course, consulted the volumes of Press Cuttings in the library of the Victoria and Albert Museum and the Whitley MSS. in the Department of Prints and Drawings in the British Museum. There is also a good deal of information for this Catalogue in the unpublished sections of Farington's diary; the original diary and a complete transcription of it are in the Royal Library.

5. Sir Frank Francis in *The Times Literary Supplement*, 6 October 1966.

for which good catalogues were produced. After the literary references comes the main body of the entry, followed, in the case of a portrait, by a brief biography of the sitter. For royal sitters, however, the reader is referred to the Genealogical Table between pp. xliv and xlv, in which the parentage, dates of birth, marriage and death are recorded, where they are required, for all those of royal birth who appear in this volume.

The pictures in this part of the Catalogue Raisonné present special problems. They range from a comparatively small number which can be dealt with in a fairly summary fashion to portraits, groups and pictures of battles or ceremonies which demand a fuller treatment that the picture often does not deserve as a work of art. More sometimes has to be said about a picture by R. B. Davis, A. W. Devis or Stothard, for example, than needs to be said about a portrait by Gainsborough. In compiling entries for the state portraits by Ramsay (Nos. 996, 997) and Lawrence (see No. 919) it would be impossible to provide a definitive list of all the copies, versions and derivations of them that were produced; I have therefore given only an indication of the extent to which they were distributed. Where the royal collection only holds a copy of a popular portrait (e.g., Nos. 1033, 1034) I have only recorded the whereabouts of the original. I have tried to record the most important early engravings of royal—and other—portraits, but have not gone in detail into later derivations from them. Likewise it would be impossible to mention all the miniature copies of favourite royal portraits, especially those by Beechey and Lawrence, which were distributed widely within the circle of the royal family and their friends, often in richly jewelled lockets or in the lids of little boxes.

The ideal compiler of this volume, which contains so many pictures bought or commissioned for other than purely aesthetic reasons, would have a rare knowledge of the historical background of this period and special knowledge of social life, the sporting world and naval and military matters. I am very grateful to experts who have helped me to write accurately on these points, though I must naturally not make them responsible for anything that is printed here. Mr. Michael Robinson and Major N. P. Dawnay have patiently answered innumerable questions on naval and military problems and have added much to the value of many items in the Catalogue. Mr. Brian Vesey-FitzGerald has once again helped me to identify the breeds of the dogs which appear in so many portraits in this volume. Lt.-Col. John Miller and Mr. G. B. Corbet have helped in the same way with many of the pictures of horses and other animals. Mr. A. V. B. Norman has identified a number of weapons which are displayed in royal portraits; and my colleague Mr. Geoffrey de Bellaigue has identified some of the works of art found in the backgrounds of royal portraits and conversation pieces.

The condition of the pictures in this volume has been described where it affects the problem of authorship. I am once again indebted to Mr. Stephen Rees-Jones of the Courtauld Institute and his staff for carrying out investigations on pictures for me, and to the restorers who have worked on a number of the pictures in this volume and have provided me with information on their condition: the late Mr. Horace Buttery, Mr. Roy Vallance, Mr. Clifford and Mr. Gerald Freeman, Mr. Clifford Ellison and Miss Nancy Stocker.

I am very grateful to the owners of pictures and manuscripts, relating to the pictures in this Catalogue, which I have been allowed to see. I particularly wish to thank Mr. St. V. Beechey and Lt.-Col. John Leicester-Warren for the loan of documents in their possession, but it is impossible to list all those owners who have patiently answered questions about pictures in their possession. I am equally grateful to those scholars who have placed their special knowledge on particular painters at my disposal: Mr. Kenneth Garlick (Lawrence), Mr. John Hayes (Gainsborough and

Dupont), Mr. Basil Taylor (Stubbs) and Mary Webster (Zoffany). Mr. A. S. Marks has given me valuable information on Wilkie's sources, both visual and literary. Mrs. Mildred Archer has provided me with almost all the material for the pictures of Indian subjects. Mr. John Harris has identified architectural details in a number of backgrounds. Mr. Hugh Murray-Baillie has helped in identifying the orders worn in portraits. Dr. Richard Graewe and Dr. Hans Bleckwenn have provided me with information on German uniforms in certain portraits. Among those who have so kindly answered questions on special points, I particularly wish to thank: Mr. E. Archibald, Mr. Nicholas Barker, Dr. T. S. R. Boase, Dr. James Corson, Mr. Povl Eller, Mr. Brinsley Ford, the Rev. R. F. Griffiths, Dr. Mary Holbrook, Mr. Robin Hutchison, Mr. Harold Jennings, Dr. E. Launert, Mlle. Renée Loche, Prof. A. McLaren Young, Mr. Wright Miller, Mr. George Naish, Mr. Benedict Nicolson, Dr. E. Pelinck, Mr. J. D. Prown, Miss Elsa Scheerer, Mr. F. H. Stubbings, Mr. F. M. Underhill, Sir Anthony Wagner, Prof. Ellis Waterhouse and Drs. Hofmann and Handrick of the Coburger Landesstiftung and the Goethe-Nationalmuseum respectively. I have once again received unfailing kindness from my colleagues in the Royal Library, Mr. Robert Mackworth-Young and Miss Scott-Elliot; Miss Jane Langton, Miss Julia Gandy and Miss Sheila Russell have been endlessly patient in the Royal Archives.

I am grateful for permission to work in the library of the National Portrait Gallery and I have received much assistance in the Departments of Prints and Drawings and Coins and Medals in the British Museum; in the Public Record Office, the Witt Library and the libraries of the Society of Antiquaries and the Courtauld Institute; and from Messrs. Christie, Manson & Woods.

Mrs. Gilbert Cousland has typed every word of the Catalogue; I cannot express adequately my gratitude for her sustained interest in its progress. My wife has once again compiled the indexes and accompanied me on many happy excursions to gather the raw material for this volume.

1968   O.N.M.

INTRODUCTION

I. GEORGE III

'WE were so weary of our old King, that we are much pleased with his successor; of whom we are so much inclined to hope great things, that most of us begin already to believe them.'[1] Dr. Johnson's hopes were shared by those who saw in the young King George III an incipient interest in the fine arts which could not but be an improvement on the attitudes of the barbarous old grandfather whom he had succeeded, at the age of twenty-two, on 25 October 1760. The good-natured and dignified young King, so different from his grandfather who stood with 'his eyes fixed royally on the ground, and dropping bits of German news', was also a man of taste. Horace Walpole wrote to Sir Horace Mann on 1 November 1760 that the King liked medals; 'I imagine his taste goes to antiques too perhaps to pictures, but that I have not heard.'[2]

The accession of George III is a watershed in the history of the royal collection. Within a few months it was obvious that he was following the example of his father, Frederick, Prince of Wales, who at the time of his early death in 1751 had built up a fine collection of pictures and had shown promise of becoming, in Reynolds's words, 'a great Patron to Painters'. During the years of her widowhood, George III's mother, Augusta of Saxe-Gotha, had kept alive something of her husband's interest in the arts and had continued to commission portraits of her family. The most sensitive portrait of the young Prince George is the pastel by Liotard[3] in the series of portraits of herself and her children which were being drawn for the Princess of Wales in 1754. In the large family group, painted by Knapton for the Princess in 1751, the dead Prince of Wales looks down on his family, set in the manner of Van Dyck among a group of accessories which illustrate most clearly the future King's firm belief in 'a constitution of free and equal laws, . . . a constitution in fine the nurse of heroes, the parent of liberty, the patron of learning and arts, and the dominion of laws'.[4] Within a few years the young Prince, his mother, and their Households had come under the influence of 'The Favourite', Lord Bute, and his 'ornamental talents'. The Prince's own establishment, with Bute as Groom of the Stole, was set up in 1756. His emotional dependence on Bute lasted until after his accession and the formation of his tastes and his choice of painters for his service were inevitably influenced by the advice or example, of his 'dearest Friend', of whose judgement the young man professed 'the greatest opinion'.

It was to Bute that Walpole wrote, late in 1760 or early in 1761, after he had heard that the King 'was curious about his pictures'.[5] In his *Memoirs* Walpole drew a waspish picture of Bute endeavouring 'to give a loftier cast to the disposition of his pupil' and encouraging him to amuse his 'solitary hours' by giving countenance to art and artists. In Walpole's eyes the Scots Maecenas had little knowledge or taste and the young Augustus 'fell asleep over drawings and medals, which were pushed before him every evening';[6] but Maecenas was apparently involved in Richard Dalton's

1. *The Letters of Samuel Johnson*, ed. R. W. Chapman (1952), vol. I, pp. 133-4.
2. Horace Walpole, *Correspondence*, ed. W. S. Lewis, vol. IX (1941), p. 321; vol. XXI (1960), p. 449. It was probably from Walpole that Gray heard that the 'young monarch now on the throne is said to esteem and understand' the arts (letter to Algarotti, 9 September 1763; *Letters*, ed. D. C. Tovey (1912), vol. III, p. 25).
3. O. Millar, *The Tudor, Stuart and Early Georgian Pictures in the Collection of Her Majesty The Queen* (1963), No. 581.
4. *Ibid.*, No. 573; Sir L. Namier, *England in the Age of the American Revolution* (ed. of 1963), p. 84; E. K. Waterhouse, *Three Decades of British Art 1740–1770* (Philadelphia, 1965), p. 45.
5. *The Letters of Horace Walpole*, ed. Mrs. Paget Toynbee, vol. v (1904), p. 11.
6. Horace Walpole, *Memoirs of the Reign of King George the Third*, ed. G. F. Russell Barker (1894), vol. I, pp. 15–16.

purchase in Italy of pictures, drawings and other works of art for the King. The intensive buying of pictures in the 1760s and early 1770s, and above all the acquisition of Consul Smith's collection late in 1762,[7] were stimulated by the need to furnish Buckingham House which the King had bought for his newly-married consort and where they were established by the summer of that year. The King assembled the best pictures in the royal collection, which he had inherited from his grandfather in 1760, and many from his father's collection, at this new 'favourite mansion'. The 'stripping' of the older royal residences, to which Walpole referred when he wrote to George Montagu on 25 May 1762,[8] marks the end of the important part which Hampton Court and Kensington had played in the history of the royal collection since the time of William III.

During the 1760s the King was giving his patronage to a number of painters. The commission to Nathaniel Dance for his *Timon of Athens* (725)[9] may have been conveyed through Dalton to the painter in Rome. It is the first indication of the King's liking for neoclassical pictures; he hung the picture appropriately in the Library at Buckingham House. In 1764 Dalton was paid for three views of Florence which are presumably the three by Thomas Patch (Nos. 977–9) still in the royal collection. A lost caricature group by Patch had shown Edward, Duke of York, George III's younger brother, in Florence at the same period; two versions of Brompton's conversation-piece of the pleasure-loving Duke and his friends at Padua (689–90) passed later into the collection, but Brompton's portraits of the King's two eldest sons (687, 688), were given away to Lady Charlotte Finch. From early in his reign the new King was concerned to form a family portrait-gallery, as so many of his forbears had done since the time of the Tudors. Dance's portraits of the royal couple do not seem to have been painted for, or at least they were not kept by, the King and Queen;[10] but his portrait of the Duke of York (723) was probably intended by the King to form part of a projected series of family portraits in the Dining-Room at Buckingham House: 'The King intended to have portraits in that room of all his Brothers & Sisters, but on the marriages of the Dukes of Cumberland & Gloucester they were stopped'.[11] The Dance was only to be joined later by Gainsborough's great full-lengths (774, 775). At the same period the King's mother was commissioning portraits of her family. The large portrait (869) by Angelica Kauffmann of the Duchess of Brunswick and her son, and the double portrait by Francis Cotes of her sisters Louisa and Caroline (720), were painted in 1767 for the Dowager Princess of Wales who had them framed in 'very rich whole length Tabernacle Frames carved, and partly gilt in burnished gold', made by Bradburn and France. By 1794 these two family portraits, with versions of Allan Ramsay's new state portraits (see No. 996) in similar frames by Bradburn and France, were hanging at Carlton House. Francis Cotes received considerable patronage from the Crown in the 1760s. His pastels of members of the King's and Queen's families (e.g., *Figs.* I, II) were hung in the Blue Closet and the Bedchamber at Buckingham House.[12] The finest is perhaps the pastel (717) of the Queen with the infant Princess Royal in 1767, a more intimate version of the full-length in oil (718) of the same year. This large portrait, and the double portrait of the two Princesses (720), are good examples of the court style of the period: more harshly lit and stiffly articulated than Allan Ramsay's royal portraits and less sensitive in their handling of elaborate settings and attributes.

The artists patronised by the King and Queen in the 1760s were among those who had been exhibiting with the Society of Artists since 1760. To capture royal patronage was still regarded as a

7. M. Levey, *The Later Italian Pictures in the Collection of Her Majesty The Queen* (1964), pp. 28–35.
8. Horace Walpole, *Correspondence, op. cit.*, vol. X (1941), p. 33.
9. Numbers in brackets refer to the items in the Catalogue.
10. They are at Uppark.
11. Walpole, *Visits*, p. 79.
12. See p. 21 below. Queen Charlotte later had at Frogmore, in the State Bedroom, a pastel by Catherine Read of her two eldest sons with a large dog (Pyne, vol. I, *Frogmore*, p. 20). This was presumably the pastel engraved by J. Watson.

great prize. Dance, who had exhibited his *Death of Virginia* in 1761, when the King had noticed it, was excited at the prospect of the commission to paint *Timon of Athens* for him: 'if this is true, it will crown my wishes and I may then come home in triumph'.[13] In the choice of portrait-painters to record his family, however, the King continued to be influenced by the advice of Bute, and there seems little doubt that Zoffany and Allan Ramsay, the two most distinguished painters employed by the King and Queen in the 1760s, owed their place in the King's esteem to his 'dearest Friend'.

On 12 October 1757 Ramsay, whose Scottish origins no doubt endeared him to Bute, had made a drawing (*Fig.* III) at Kew of the Prince of Wales[14] on which he based a full-length (*Fig.* IV) for Lord Bute; in 1758 he was commissioned by the Prince to paint a full-length of Bute (*Fig.* V) which was eventually given by the King to Lord Mountstuart in 1783. The King, after his accession, 'was still pleased to honour' Ramsay with his employment and appointed him Principal Painter.[15] Ramsay embarked on the tasks which by ancient tradition belonged to the post. He provided a profile (*Fig.* VII) for the coinage of the new King, as Cooper and Kneller had done for Charles II, Anne and George I, and designed the new state portrait. Soon after the Coronation, Ramsay 'dressed in Coronation robes' a full-length of the King (see No. 996). Soon after her arrival in England, the Queen sat for a companion portrait (997). Ramsay's preliminary drawings for the hands and the crown survive. There are indications in the surface round the King's head in No. 996 that it was done from the life before the costume was painted; Ramsay himself wrote on 19 December 1761 that he had had two complete sittings from the King for the state portrait (of which a version was also being done for Bute), and that he was preparing to finish 'the posture of it, that it may have the advantage of being likewise painted from the life while I have the Royal robes set upon my figure'. For the rest of his working life Ramsay was to devote his energies to the production of a large number of repetitions of this new portrait and its companion. He was paid £84 for each copy. Carved and gilded frames were provided for them, usually by René Stone and Isaac Gossett.[16] The machinery for the quick repetition of the official royal portrait was established in Ramsay's studio in Soho Square, where the show-room was 'crowded with portraits of His Majesty in every stage of their operation'. It was probably more productive than Kneller's studio had been in making copies of the state portraits of William III and Mary II or than Lawrence's was to be in turning out the official likeness of George IV. It is remarkable how much of Ramsay's original quality is preserved through the reproduction of his state portraits. With the exception of Van Dyck's portrait of Charles I in robes of state in 1636,[17] Ramsay's is the most distinguished of all English state portraits. It is a sympathetic presentation of the shy and dignified young man whose appearance and manner had pleased Horace Walpole; it is elegantly staged in a sweeping rococo setting reminiscent of Nattier or of Louis Michel Van Loo's state portrait of Louis XV; and it is painted in a soft, powdered rococo range of colour. These qualities had been noticeable in Ramsay's first full-length of the King before his accession. In Van Loo's official portraits of the King's parents in 1742[18] there had been something of the elaborate Frenchified stage-craft and display of accessories which is developed in Cotes's large royal groups, but Ramsay's portraits are bathed in a softer atmosphere.

As a young man the King had hoped for a large family and looked forward to instilling high

13. B. Skinner in *Burl. Mag.*, vol. CI (1959), p. 346.
14. National Gallery of Scotland (D.242).
15. He shared the post with John Shackleton until the latter's death in 1767; Shackleton was being paid for portraits of the King and Queen up to 1765–6 (P.R.O., A.O.1, 419–21).
16. For an indication of the extent to which the portraits were distributed, see Nos. 996, 997. 'Peter Pindar' later wrote, in his *Lyric Odes for the Year 1785* (1787), that Ramsay had 'Left just nine rooms well stuff'd with Queens and Kings' designed for 'Viceroys, Ambassadors, and Plenipos'.
17. Millar, *op. cit.*, No. 145.
18. *Ibid.*, Nos. 536, 537 and p. 29.

principles and good sentiments into his children. During the 1760s the King and Queen lived a placid and devoted family life. Their small children dressed up and gave little theatrical performances. The parents 'have their Children always playing about them the whole time'; they were finally sent for again between six and seven o'clock '& play in the room with them till about 8'.[19] The domestic life at Buckingham House is evoked in Ramsay's group of the Queen with her two eldest sons (998) and in the portrait of the little Prince William beating a drum near a tea-table. (999). It is more vividly brought to life by Zoffany. His conversation-pieces develop ideas in the royal iconography which had been suggested earlier by such painters as Hogarth, Mercier, Wootton Du Pan and Richard Wilson. They record with a keen and sympathetic eye the royal family resting on a rustic seat (1207), playing with a dog in one of the fine new rooms at Buckingham House (1200) or grouped rather self-consciously in Van Dyck dresses and attitudes on a terrace (1201 The portrait of the Queen at her dressing-table (1199) with her two small sons in fancy dress is t most perfectly designed royal conversation-piece since the time of Van Dyck and is full of ger humour. It is also a valuable source for the appearance of one of the beautiful rooms in the Que apartments in the new house[20] and gives one a tantalising glimpse of walls hung with som Consul Smith's pictures in their pretty Venetian frames.

The same sensitivity and accuracy are seen, although in a different context, in the port of the optician and lens-maker John Cuff (1209). It was probably bought by, or painted for, King and Queen. Zoffany's skill at catching likenesses, and at putting together a number of fig in apparently spontaneously arranged groups, are displayed in the *Academicians* (1210). His a to stage-manage figures in conversation, his uncanny skill—and vigorous touch—in the reprod of objects in an interior and his capacity for hard work were stretched to the utmost in his mas piece, *The Tribuna of the Uffizi* (1211) which had been commissioned by the Queen after the collapse of Zoffany's plan to go to the South Seas with Captain Cook. 'Most of the likenesses strong' was one of Walpole's comments of Zoffany's *Academicians*; 'the likest Picture that ever was done', 'very like' and 'exactly him' are some of Lord Winchilsea's comments on the portraits in the *Tribuna*. To such practical and unpretentious patrons as George III and Queen Charlotte, Zoffany's skill in capturing a likeness must have been a strong recommendation. He painted a life-size portrait of Prince Ernest (1208) for Queen Charlotte's set of portraits of her family.[21] The portrait of the King (1195) that he exhibited at the Royal Academy in 1771 was described by Walpole as 'very like' and is perhaps the most sympathetic and revealing portrait of George III at this date; the companion portrait of the Queen (1196) is very close in its cold colour, rather steely surface and harsh light, to Francis Cotes's latest portraits.

In Ramsay's group of Queen Charlotte with her two eldest sons (998) there is perhaps a re-collection of Van Dyck's figures of the little Prince of Wales and of Queen Henrietta Maria holding the infant Princess Mary in Van Dyck's 'greate peece' of 1632 [22] which George III had hung in the Japan Room at Buckingham House; the recollection is stronger in one of Ramsay's preliminary drawings (*Fig.* 24) of the Queen and the baby in her arms. Two of the most popular Van Dycks in the royal collection look down on Zoffany's group of the same little boys playing with a dog (1200). From one of them, the *Villiers Boys* of 1635[23] come to life again as the same boys some years later

19. W. R. A. Geo. 15884–5, 15889–92.
20. There is a vivid account of the appearance of these rooms in 1767, with their 'finest Dresden and other china', cabinets of curiosities, pictures, miniatures and gilt toilet accessories in *Passages from the Diaries of Mrs. Lybbe Powys*, ed. Emily Climenson (1899), pp. 116–17.
21. Ramsay painted one portrait (1000) and probably another

(1001) for this set, which the Queen later arranged in the Eating-Room at Frogmore (Pyne, vol. 1, *Frogmore*, pp. 3–8), She also had at Frogmore Richard Wright's picture (1194) of her stormy passage to England under the escort of Lord Anson's squadron.
22. Millar, *op. cit.*, No. 150.
23. *Ibid.*, No. 153.

in the family group (1201); the two larger portraits of four of the royal children (1203, 1204) are unequivocally Van Dyckian. The King had brought many of his finest Van Dycks to Buckingham House and in 1765 he had bought Van Dyck's group of the *Five Eldest Children of Charles I*.[24] Yet the King was a severely practical collector, without the enthusiasm or improvidence of his father or his son. By the end of the 1760s Buckingham House was probably fully provided with pictures. On 16 January 1770 the King wrote to Lord Harcourt, the English Ambassador in Paris: 'I have, at least for the present, given up collecting pictures: therefore shall not trouble you with any commission for the Vandyke'. The Van Dyck which Lord Harcourt was offering to secure for the King was the portrait of Charles I *à la chasse*.[25] Only a collector whose emotions were rarely involved in his picture-buying could have rejected such a piece; one can imagine the delight with which Frederick, Prince of Wales, or George IV would have seized on the chance of purchasing it and the enthusiasm with which George IV would have recognised its significance for Gainsborough's portraits of himself and Colonel St. Leger (805) standing by their chargers.

Although George III had visited the exhibitions held by the Society of Artists, of which Joshua Kirby, his old teacher in perspective, was President, he seems to have determined from the beginning to give his support to schemes for the formation of the Royal Academy. The first approach to the King over this was probably arranged by William Chambers who had been appointed, under the influence of Lord Bute, architectural tutor to the King when he was Prince of Wales, had worked for the Prince's mother and was later to be successively Architect and Comptroller of the Works and ultimately Surveyor-General and Comptroller. He had also designed the State Coach which had first appeared before the public in 1762 (1193). With Benjamin West, Cotes and George Moser, Chambers presented to the King a petition in which he could learn of the effect of the strife within the Society of Artists; West and the King may also have discussed in private plans for the new Academy. On 28 November 1768 a Memorial was presented to the King in which he was begged to bestow his 'gracious assistance, patronage, and protection' in carrying into execution the 'useful plan' for establishing a 'Society for promoting the Arts of Design'. The Memorial was laid before the King by twenty-two artists, including the four who had signed the first petition and Dance, Cipriani, Zuccarelli, Angelica Kauffmann, Joseph Wilton, Paul Sandby, and Charles Catton, who had all worked for the King and his family. The King made it plain that he regarded the welfare of the arts as a matter of national concern and he promised his patronage and assistance. On 7 December a more detailed plan, drafted by Chambers, was shown to him. The King gave it his approval. The plan was written out in proper form as the new Academy's Instrument of Foundation, to which the King gave his signature on 10 December: 'I approve of this Plan; let it be put in execution'. In order that the King might have in an office where 'his interest is concerned' a person in whom he had full confidence, Chambers was appointed Treasurer of the new foundation.[26]

The King always followed with keen interest the affairs of his Academy; he probably commissioned Zoffany, whom he personally nominated a Royal Academician in 1769, to record its members grouped round the Academy's first Professor of Anatomy while he arranges a life-class (1210); the King and his family frequently visited the annual exhibition; he placed rooms in Old Somerset House at the disposal of the new society in 1771; but he was never on anything but

24. *Ibid.*, No. 152.
25. *Ibid.*, Fig. VII. *The Harcourt Papers*, ed. E. W. Harcourt, vol. III, p. 102. In 1783 Lord Northington sent to the King a copy of Cooper's engraving of Van Dyck's sketch (now at Belvoir) of the *Procession of the Knights of the Garter* and was

anxious to show the King the original, which was in his possession (*The Correspondence of King George the Third*, ed. Sir J. Fortescue, vol. VI (1928), p. 364).
26. S. C. Hutchison, *The History of the Royal Academy 1768–1968* (1968), ch. IV.

uncomfortable terms with the first President, Sir Joshua Reynolds, and he disliked his style. He bestowed a knighthood on Reynolds in 1769 on the eve of the first exhibition, but all dealings with the Sovereign on Academy matters were in the hands of Chambers, whom Reynolds described as 'Vice-roy over him'. The portrait which Reynolds had painted of the King before his accession (1011) bears a curious likeness to Liotard's portrait in pastel and has none of the sensitivity or grandeur of Ramsay's first full-length. It was still in Reynolds's hands at his death. So was the sketch (1012) which Reynolds made of the King's marriage. In 1763 the King paid £210 for Reynolds's enigmatic full-length of Lord Bute with his secretary, Charles Jenkinson (*Fig.* VI), but although his brothers and uncle (see Nos. 1009, 1013, 1017) sat to Reynolds, the King never seems to have given him another commission. When he and the Queen at last sat, in 1779–80, for the official portraits for the Royal Academy (see Nos. 1033, 1034) they found Reynolds's presence acutely uncongenial. The reversion to him in 1784 of Ramsay's post as Principal Painter brought Reynolds in his own eyes neither profit nor dignity; his classical portraits of ladies close to the Queen made no appeal to her or her husband; and Lord Eglinton, who had commissioned the portrait of Lord Bute with Jenkinson, is stated to have ceded the picture to the King and to have met the famous rebuff, when he asked the King to sit to Reynolds, that 'Mr. Ramsay is my painter, my Lord'.

In 1773 Catherine the Great, who already had versions of Ramsay's state portraits ('the best Originals from which Copys could be made'), wished Lord Cathcart to secure for her the best possible full-lengths of the King, Queen and their two eldest sons. Lord Cathcart hoped that the King would allow Reynolds to take these likenesses for the Empress, who knew of Reynolds's eminence, had read his *Discourses* and seen prints after his works, or that Reynolds should be commissioned by the King to paint the portraits as presents to the Empress. Lord Cathcart knew that it was difficult, if not impossible, for a painter to obtain sittings from the King and Queen, but pointed out to the King that Reynolds 'has now adopted another method of Colouring upon Principles of Duration upon which he and many other good Judges are of opinion he may absolutely depend, the Objection, not unjustly made to his former Pictures, being removed'.[27] Later the King's dislike of Reynolds may have been intensified by the knowledge that some of Reynolds's most consistent patrons were members of his own family with whom he had quarrelled or were the men whose political views he most despised: men who were leading his eldest son without difficulty from the paths of virtue and filial duty, were his champions in the Regency Crisis of 1788–9, and were filled with excited sympathy for the revolutionary movements in France.

The King's refusal to pretend to like something which he did not understand probably caused him to ignore Richard Wilson. Although Wilson had painted the King and his younger brother as little boys with their tutor[28] and was on friendly terms with Chambers, the King did not like two of Wilson's views of Kew Gardens which Chambers wanted him to buy. A cabal, probably formed by Richard Dalton, is stated to have pushed the claims of Zuccarelli, who had been lavishly patronised by Consul Smith and whose landscapes were bought by the King in large quantities, and to have encouraged the King to laugh at Wilson's pictures.[29] The King's uncle, the Duke of Cumberland, however, had the good taste to buy a superb version of Wilson's *Destruction of Niobe's Children* which he had seen exhibited at the Society of Artists in 1760; by 1790 it was in the collection

---

27. *The Letters of Sir Joshua Reynolds*, ed. F. W. Hilles (1929), pp. 112–13, 131, 133; W. T. Whitley, *Artists and their Friends in England 1700–99* (1928), vol. 1, pp. 252–7; E. K. Waterhouse, *op. cit.*, pp. 54–7; W.R.A., Geo. 1501; *The Correspondence of King George the Third*, ed. Sir J. Fortescue, vol. 11 (1927), pp. 452–3. 'Peter Pindar' in his *Lyric Odes for the Year 1785* (1787)

states that Dance, not Reynolds, received the commission to paint the King for the Empress.
28. W. G. Constable, *Richard Wilson* (1953), pp. 153–4.
29. W. G. Constable, *op. cit.*, pp. 49–50; E. K. Waterhouse, *op. cit.*, p. 57; M. Levey, *op. cit.*, pp. 29–31.

of the Duke of Gloucester.[30] The King, on the other hand, seems to have preferred in landscape-painting the superficialities of Zuccarelli or the finicky touch and conventional designs of such painters as John Taylor (1130, 1131) and Johan Jacob Schalch (1067, 1068).

It is perhaps strange that George III, so fond of animals, country life, farming and hunting gave, apparently, no commissions to any sporting or animal-painters. It is not even certain that he, and not his successor, commissioned the two pictures (1059, 1060) of his horses by Francis Sartorius. The touching portrait by Stubbs of the zebra which had been given to the King or to his consort and lived at Buckingham House, was not painted for them;[31] and the King seems to have had none of his uncle Cumberland's, or of his own eldest son's, keenness to have pictures of favourite or particularly interesting animals. Mary Moser produced, probably for Queen Charlotte, a series of flower-pieces (964–9), which are essays in the manner of Monnoyer, and is stated to have decorated a room for the Queen at Frogmore. But, except for the pictures they ordered from West, the King and Queen do not seem to have been much interested in genres other than the portrait. It was the portraits that always especially interested the King when he went round the summer exhibitions at the Royal Academy and even in his dealings with portrait-painters almost his sole concern was with likenesses of his family. Apart from them, the King and Queen seem only to have had on their walls portraits of some favourite clergymen (i.e., 726, 801, 802, 846) and Opie's portrait of Mrs. Delany (975) whom they had befriended.[32] With the family portraits by Cotes and Zoffany in the Bedchamber at Buckingham House hung 'A Lady at Tambour work' by Angelica Kauffmann, the portrait of Mrs. Delany and one of the Gainsboroughs (801 or 802) of Bishop Hurd.

George III was a brave and honest man who respected courage as much as he despised cowardice. Almost alone of the earlier Hanoverians he lived with his consort a domestic life untouched by scandal. He was patriotic and religious. He was obsessed with the evil, ingratitude, avarice and ambition which he saw in the world around him. At his accession he had issued a proclamation calling for the encouragement of piety and virtue and the punishment of vice, profanity and immorality. It is not therefore surprising that he admired the high-minded and vapid compositions of Benjamin West. Galt stated that George III's employment of West sprang partly from a sense of duty: 'it is the more deserving of applause, as it was rather the result of principle than of personal predilection'.[33] Between 1768 and 1780 the King paid over £4,000 to West; West's medieval subjects cost the King nearly another £7,000; and further works by West for the King cost £1,426. No other painter was employed on so generous a scale by George III.

West had been introduced to the King in 1768 by Robert Drummond, Archbishop of York, who showed the King a painting of *Agrippina landing with the Ashes of Germanicus* which he had painted for the Archbishop.[34] The King was so impressed with it that he commissioned the large painting of the *Departure of Regulus* (1152). This was exhibited, at the King's instructions, at the Royal Academy's first exhibition, in 1769. Plans for a set of classical pictures were forming in the King's mind. In 1770 West painted a companion picture, the *Oath of Hannibal* (1153), and in 1773 he produced the two smaller classical pieces (1154, 1155) which were hung with them in the Warm Room at Buckingham House. These canvases proclaim in dignified neoclassical terms the ancient virtues whose rule the King would have liked to re-establish. The types, the gestures, indeed even the mood and the texture in these four sombre paintings, are so clearly influenced by Poussin that they explain Zuccarelli's

30. It is now in the collection of Mr. and Mrs. Paul Mellon; exh., R.A., *Painting in England 1700–1850*, 1964–5 (301).

31. *Ibid.* (267).

32. There is no trace of the picture of a beggar and his dog which

the King is stated to have bought from Opie in 1782 (see below, p. 88).

33. Galt, part II, p. 33.

34. It is now in Yale University Art Gallery (D. Irwin, *English Neoclassical Art* (1966), p. 50).

remark: 'Here is a painter who promises to rival Nicolas Poussin'. They scarcely justify Zoffany's rejoinder: 'A figo for Poussin, West has already beaten him out of the field.'[35] In 1787 George III admired the *Sacraments* by Poussin which Reynolds had bought for the Duke of Rutland and was able to show to the King. He 'took much notice of the Poussins, more that I expected, as they are of a different kind from what he generally likes'.[36] In 1771 West painted for the King a replica (1167) of his *Death of Wolfe*; the King had apparently been put off buying the first version by hearing that the episode had been painted in contemporary terms. In 1772 and 1773 West completed his trilogy of heroic death in the Warm Room by joining Epaminondas (1156) and Bayard (1157) to Wolfe.

In 1776–9 West was at work on a set of portraits of the royal family, some of which were hung in the King's Closet at St. James's. The figures appear to be modelled in cardboard, but the portraits are not unsympathetic and the iconographical details are laboriously set down. The youngest children play with their dogs, toys and go-carts (1145, 1147), in one instance against the background of Kew Gardens and their grandmother's Great Pagoda; Prince William, a midshipman in the *Royal George* (Crabbe's 'princely tar'), points out the English Channel on a globe to Prince Edward who indicates a model of the *Royal George* securely resting on the white horse of Hanover (1144); the eldest sons (1143) are resplendent in Garter and Bath robes; their eldest sister sits tatting with her mother (1142) near a table on which is a bust of Minerva, a sheet of music and a folio of drawings by Raphael. The Queen herself (1139) stands in front of a group of her thirteen children (in 1779) with the Queen's Lodge at Windsor behind. This is the family as it was in its happy domestic life at Windsor—'in this our sweet retreat'—of which Mrs. Delany gives so charming a picture. It was also a period of crisis, when invasion was threatened and the French and Spanish fleets lay off Portsmouth. In West's portrait of the King (1138) he is in military dress, with the regalia on one side and his royal robe next to his martial hat. In the background are a detachment of the dragoons who were patrolling the coasts of Kent and Sussex and the fleet with the *Royal George* firing a salute. It is a convincing portrait, paradoxially by an American painter, of a brave King in a moment of national emergency, when the country rang aloud with rude alarms. The King holds a plan of the camps at which troops and militia were under canvas; one of the camps had been the scene of a review and a mock attack in front of the King and Queen in 1778, events recorded in Loutherbourg's two finely painted windswept scenes (932, 933). The royal visit to the fleet at Portsmouth in 1773 had been painted, presumably for the King, by Dominic Serres (1072–5); but the King did not apparently feel inclined to purchase the canvases by Paton which illustrate something of the spate of activity in the royal dockyards (980–4).[36a]

As early as 26 September 1762 Walpole had reported to Mann that the young Queen had been 'charmed' with Windsor. As the century drew to a close the royal family spent more and more of their time there. The Castle is seen under a lowering sky in the tragic postscript to West's portraits of the family: the *Apotheosis of Prince Octavius* (1149), whose death was such a grievous blow to his father. When the Queen and her daughters saw the picture at the Royal Academy in 1781, they were moved to tears. For the King's Audience Room at Windsor, which had for many years had associations with the Garter, West painted in 1787–9 a set of pictures (1158–64) illustrating the Institution of the Order and some of the exploits of the Black Prince, Edward III, the Founder of

35. H. Angelo, *Reminiscences* (1830), vol. I, pp. 360–1.
36. *Letters of Sir Joshua Reynolds*, ed. F. W. Hilles (1929), pp. 176–7.
36a. At the same period George III was assembling, with the help of Lord Sandwich, First Lord of the Admiralty, a set of painted perspective views of men-of-war including paintings by Joseph Marshall. Twenty-two of these were in the Model

Room at Buckingham House in 1819 (1010). They were later at Hampton Court. In 1864 Queen Victoria directed that they should be permanently transferred to the new Admiralty Museum. They are now in the Science Museum (information kindly supplied by Mr. B. W. Bathe).

the Order, and the original Knights, during the Hundred Years War. Something of the original arrangement of West's pictures in the Audience Room can be seen in Wild's watercolour, drawn for Pyne (*Fig.* VIII). Over the fireplace was a picture of St. George slaying the dragon (1151) which West had presumably painted specially for that position. Important as the series is for the development of medieval history painting in England and as an illustration of a fashionable taste in medieval subjects, West's canvases, especially the three (1162–4) on an enormous scale, are lifeless in texture and dull in colour. Although he is said to have taken pains over historical detail under the King's vigilant eye, the general effect is academic without being any more historically accurate than the figures grouped round the dying Epaminondas and Bayard.[37] Only in the smaller pictures in this series (e.g., No. 1158) does West bring off sometimes a genuinely exciting picture of a medieval clash of arms. But to George III West's paintings probably brought Edward III's famous victories 'into form and being, with a veracity of historical fact and circumstance which render the masquerades by Vario even a greater disgrace to St. George's Hall than they are to the taste of the age in which they were painted'.[38] The deterioration and destruction of so much of Verrio's lighthearted work at Windsor, especially of his *Triumph of the Black Prince* in St. George's Hall, are in tune with the King's preference for West's earnest efforts. The King's taste for Gothic, nurtured at Windsor, was perhaps seen most clearly in James Wyatt's designs for the castellated palace at Kew which evoked memories of Ariosto and Spencer in the minds of those who saw it. In 1803 the King was surprised at himself for having changed from Grecian to Gothic.[39]

Finally, about 1780, the King began to think of constructing a private chapel in Horn Court inside the Castle. West was to paint for this chapel thirty-five very large canvases illustrating the history of revealed religion. The project was abandoned by 1799, probably at the Queen's instigation, and West was not to begin any new pictures for the scheme. He had already completed or worked on a number of the pictures—he assessed what he had done on them at £21,705—and had received regular annual payments of £1,000. It is to the credit of George IV's good taste that the paintings were eventually returned to West. It seems that, even before the project was finally given over, West was losing his popularity at Windsor, possibly owing in part to the influence of Wyatt. His presence seems increasingly to have irritated the Queen, especially when the King was ill; and by 1804 West was being spoken of with contempt by the King's family. Even the King had ceased to think much of his work.[40] West's relations with other artists (such as Hoppner and Beechey), as well as with the royal family, must have been damaged by his determination to retain as much as he could of the King's favour and interest. The epitome of his royal service, and of the days when 'Peter Pindar' had called him 'George's idol', is the smooth, self-satisfied portrait which he painted of himself (*Fig.* IX) holding the Academy's Instrument of Foundation; under his other hand lies his own appointment as Reynolds's successor in the Presidency; between him and a bust of George III lie the Bible and Hume's *History of England*. Much of West's work for the King seems today dull and fustian stuff, but in patronizing him the King was encouraging those who hoped to see a flourishing school of history-painting in England: 'so that when Artists arise in the historical Line (of such acknowledged Merit as Mr. *West* and Signora *Angelica*) there can be no doubt of their

37. D. Irwin, *op. cit.*, pp. 95–6.

38. Galt, part II, p. 52. At some stage West had suggested that St. George's Hall should be ornamented with historical subjects by the most esteemed artists in England (V. & A., *Cuttings*, vol. II, p. 374). The projected decorations at Windsor by Matthew Wyatt included schemes devoted to St. George, with a set of full-lengths of the Sovereign and the Knights of the Garter, apparently the Founders of the Order, in armour

with surcoats in a new chapter room for the Order (W.R.A., Geo. Add. MS. 17, 1–6). See also Farington, *Diary*, vol. II, p. 180.

39. W.R.A., Geo. 16734.

40. See below, pp. 127–8. The only religious work by West in the royal collection is his *St. Peter Denying Christ* (1150) which he gave to the King.

being fully employed and amply rewarded'.[41] West himself, in a long letter written to the King on 22 June 1797, recalled the encouragement that every artist in England had felt when the King took the arts under his official patronage in 1768. 'Among that number, my humble efforts became distinguished by Your Majesty's Patronage, and under that Patronage my unceasing enthusiasm for carrying the higher department of Historical Painting into effect, have never ceased . . . from the Patronage so graciously afforded me, I have produced with the last Thirty years more extensive compositions and pictures of Magnitude than has fallen to the Lot of any one hand to produce in Europe, in the same Pireod.'[42]

By 1781, soon after West had completed his set of royal portraits and some years before he began to work at Windsor, Gainsborough's fame was 'quite established at Buckingham House . . . he is now, vice Mr. Zoffannii and other predecessors, the Apollo of the Palace'.[43] Queen Charlotte at her death owned twenty-two of his drawings, perhaps including ten of his twelve drawings in coloured chalks.[44] Whereas the King and Queen had been made uncomfortable by Reynolds, circumspect, cool and always on his dignity, the royal family seems to have enjoyed the company of his great rival, a 'natural gentleman' (as Northcote described him), easy, idiosyncratic and musical. The King and Queen clearly had no sympathy with the historical or classical mould in which many of Reynolds's most celebrated portraits were cast. Certainly the King would have shared Gainsborough's contempt for 'the foolish custom of painters dressing people like scaramouches and expecting the likeness to appear' and would have applauded him if he had heard him add, 'I have that regard for truth that I hold the finest invention as a mere slave in comparison.'[45] Even West's royal portraits had to be strictly contemporary in dress and accessories.

As early as 1770 Philip Thicknesse had regretted that no mark of royal favour had yet been shown to Gainsborough, but soon after Gainsborough's arrival in London from Bath in 1774 he received commissions from the King's brothers Gloucester and Cumberland. In 1777 he exhibited at the Royal Academy the full-lengths of the Duke and Duchess of Cumberland (793, 794). The portraits of the vicious little Duke, nervously fingering his George as he steals across the stage, and his raffish Duchess with her lovely eyes, are the most intelligent and amusing of all portraits bounded by the conventions of the state portrait. They are also, not even excepting Van Dyck's, the most beautifully painted of all English state portraits. The rich colour, set off by sparkling silvers, pinks and golds, the fluent handling of the draperies and the nervous, delicate modelling of the heads remind one of Gainsborough's devotion to the memory of Van Dyck. At Windsor, and presumably at Buckingham House, Gainsborough is said to have been 'rivetted' by the King's Van Dycks.[46]

In 1781 Gainsborough showed at the Royal Academy his great full-lengths of the King and Queen (774, 775). The portrait of the King, formal but sympathetic, was stated by one critic to be 'the most correct and graceful portrait ever given of him'; Walpole regarded it as 'very like, but stiff and raw'. The Queen's portrait was described as 'the only happy likeness we ever saw pourtrayed of her Majesty'. It is certainly the most sympathetic portrait painted of the Queen. The sympathy is matched, by Gainsborough's incomparable sensibility and skill, with tenderness, a

41. *Public Advertiser*, 2 May 1775.
42. W.R.A., Geo. 8523–4; *The Later Correspondence of George III*, ed. A. Aspinall, vol. II (1963), pp. 593–4.
43. Whitley, *Gainsborough*, p. 177.
44. Oppé, p. 11; twenty drawings by Gainsborough were in the Queen's sale at Christie's, 24 May 1819 (133–7), 25 May (117–21).
45. Whitley, *op. cit.*, p. 75. According to Farington (*Diary*, vol. I, p. 260) Gainsborough, adapting himself to his patrons'

humours, 'talked bawdy to the King, & morality to the Prince of Wales'.
46. H. Angelo, *op. cit.*, vol. I, p. 353; the portrait of Henrietta Maria which he particularly admired was probably Millar No. 147. Angelo's account of Gainsborough's conversations with the King should perhaps be treated with caution, but he is probably sound in his remarks on the royal family's liking for Gainsborough (pp. 219–20).

II. Francis Cotes: *Prince Ernest of Mecklenburg-Strelitz*. S.K.H. Prince Ernst August

I. Francis Cotes: *Princess Caroline*. S.K.H. Prince Ernst August

III. Allan Ramsay: *George III when Prince of Wales*.
National Gallery of Scotland

IV. Allan Ramsay: *George III when Prince of Wales*.
Marquess of Bute

V. Allan Ramsay: *John Stuart, 3rd Earl of Bute*.
Marquess of Bute

VI. Sir Joshua Reynolds. *The Earl of Bute with Charles Jenkinson*.
Marquess of Bute

VII. Allan Ramsay: *George III*. Marquess of Bute

VIII. C. Wild: *The King's Audience Chamber, Windsor Castle*. Royal Library, Windsor Castle

X. Sir Thomas Lawrence: *Queen Charlotte*. National Gallery

IX. Benjamin West: *Portrait of the Artist*. Society of Dilettanti

latent gaiety and a magic sense of poetry. It is in these four royal full-lengths that Gainsborough comes closest to Goya. Copies and derivations of the full-lengths of the King and Queen were made for distribution, though never in such quantities as the copies after Ramsay. In the same year, 1781, Prince William sat to Gainsborough at Buckingham House. The portrait (*Fig.* 10) was copied by Gainsborough when, down at Windsor in the autumn of 1782, he produced his set of fifteen ovals (778–92) of the King, Queen and their children: an important stage—and certainly the prettiest and most original—in the development of the royal iconography which meant so much to Gainsborough's patrons. They confirm Gainsborough's place as the most successful and eminent of the painters whom the King and Queen employed in their domestic, as opposed to their more official, capacity. At the end of the painter's life the King admired his *Cottage Children* or *Wood-Gatherers*.[47] In the last year of his life Gainsborough took his *Woodman* round to Buckingham House, where the King described it as 'a masterpiece of the pencil'. Although there were rumours after the painter's death that the King would buy it, he seems to have bought nothing of Gainsborough's after the ovals had been completed. Queen Charlotte had acquired the superb full-length of Karl Frederick Abel[48] but it was unfortunately sold after her death.[49]

The King's indecision in 1788 over the possible purchase of the *Woodman* should be attributed partly to the serious attack of 'the royal malady' which he suffered in that year and which, in the autumn, precipitated the Regency Crisis. During the last years of the century the choice of painters by the King and Queen was probably complicated as much by the King's increasingly wayward moods—and the agonising pain he suffered—as by the rivalries between the London portrait-painters after the death of Reynolds and Gainsborough. The King had always been, in his own words, 'apt to despise what I am not accustom'd to' and as he grew older became less receptive to new ideas and more attached to his old prejudices. Loyalty to Gainsborough's memory may have caused the King and Queen to order from his nephew, Gainsborough Dupont, revisions of his uncle's royal portraits (see Nos. 766, 767). In 1794 he thought Dupont's portrait of him 'the *best* likeness that had been painted' and in 1795 he took away from Hoppner the commission to paint his daughter-in-law in her wedding dress (768) and entrusted it to Dupont. The wedding ceremony was to be painted by Hamilton (827). The older he became, the more comfort the King derived from his quiet family life at Windsor and from the company of his children, especially his charming youngest daughters, Mary, Sophia and Amelia, whose sweetness and good looks fill the pages of Fanny Burney. As he had written to his eldest son in 1789: 'Where am I therefore to turn for comfort but into the bosom of my own family?' In 1785 the little girls were painted, probably at Windsor, by Copley (712). Everyone in the design was reported to have become thoroughly wearied by the tedium of sitting. Copley's riotously gay canvas is an exercise in the same iconographical theme as Du Pan's group of the King with his brothers and sisters in 1747.[50] It was attacked by Hoppner in the *Morning Post* of 5 May 1785: 'is this the fruit of your long studies and labours? . . . Is it because you have heard *fine feathers* make fine birds, that you have concluded *fine cloaths* will make Princesses? . . . Princesses, parrots, dogs, grapes, flowers, leaves . . . opposing, with hostile force, all attempts of our wearied eyes to find to repose'. Lawrence, however, had the intelligence to realise how much better it was than West's royal portraits. Hoppner was exhibiting at the same

---

47. Waterhouse, *Gainsborough*, No. 807.
48. *Ibid.*, No. 1.
49. With her eldest daughters the Queen visited Mrs. Gains-borough's exhibition in April 1789, when she bought some drawings (V. & A., *Cuttings*, vol. II, p. 472). It is stated in the same source that two pictures were set aside for the Queen at this exhibition.

There is some evidence that *c.* 1785 George III gave a commission to Gainsborough to paint a picture, possibly of Windsor or of the Water-walk at Richmond, with figures of ladies, comparable to his painting of *The Mall*. Mr. John Hayes associates with this project a group of drawings of ladies in fashionable dress (*Burl. Mag.*, vol. CXI (1969), pp. 28–31).
50. Millar, No. 572.

time his three charming portraits of the same Princesses (838–40) which he had also probably painted at Windsor. For some time Hoppner was a favourite with the King and Queen, but in 1795 his intemperate nature led him into an altercation with the King.[51] The King placed Copley's big picture at one end of the Queen's Ballroom at Windsor; at the other end was Ramsay's group of the young Queen with her two eldest sons.[52]

When the King visited the Royal Academy in 1795 he had 'condemned Hoppner's red and yellow trees'. Beechey he thought was 'first this year, Hoppner second'; on seeing Lawrence's Byronic full-length of Lord Mountstuart 'He started back with disgust'.[53] Lawrence had exhibited at the Royal Academy in 1789 his first full-length, a portrait of Lady Cremorne.[54] At Lady Cremorne's instigation, the Queen consented, not very willingly, to sit to Lawrence. In September 1789 the young painter was summoned to Windsor with his equipment and examples of his pictures in crayons and oil, in order to paint the Queen and her youngest daughter. He was advised by a friend that, although in the portrait of the Princess Lawrence had 'more scope for taste', he should concentrate, in painting the Queen, on 'individual likeness'. The portrait of the Princess (881) is far more spirited and accomplished than Hoppner's portraits of the little girls, but it does not seem to have been accepted by the King and Queen. The portrait of the Queen (*Fig.* X) was intended to be sent to Hanover. It is one of the most brilliant of all English royal portraits, the only portrait of the Queen worthy to hang in company with Gainsborough's; it was also regarded as 'a strong likeness'. But Lawrence had an unhappy time at the Castle. The Queen's sallow complexion was not thought to harmonise with the colour of her dress. There was difficulty over the choice of covering for the Queen's head which was finally left bare; this disgusted the King 'as her Majesty had never been so seen'. The Queen thought Lawrence presumptuous in suggesting she should talk with her daughters and thus animate her countenance; she preferred to listen to them reading to her. She finally refused to take the trouble to summon her dresser so that Lawrence could have a second sitting. Mrs. Papendiek had to sit for the bracelets and the brooch which held the scarf. West, who was at Windsor, was not anxious to encourage a promising young rival. It is to Lawrence's credit that he finished the portrait.[55] Although George III appointed Lawrence in 1792 to succeed Reynolds as Principal Painter, gave sittings to him for the fine full-length painted for the City of Coventry (see No. 871) and probably commissioned the version (875) of Lawrence's portrait of his little grand-daughter, he does not seem to have wished Lawrence to evolve a new state portrait. Until as late as *c.* 1815 Lawrence was turning out copies of Reynolds's official full-lengths. The King had paid little attention to Lawrence's *Satan* at the Academy in 1797, but Lawrence's portraits at the Royal Academy in 1799 pleased him highly. His portrait of Thurlow (914) met the King's idea of a portrait, 'being a true representation of the man without artificial fancies of dress &c.', but his portrait of Kemble as Hamlet[56] revived all the King's prejudices.

In 1793 Beechey became Portrait Painter to the Queen; in 1796 the King particularly noticed his portraits at the Academy; in 1798 he was knighted 'at the express intimation of the Queen'. In 1800 he exhibited at the Royal Academy his full-lengths of the King and Queen (658, 659): sober, commonsense portraits in contemporary dress and the last pair of portraits of the royal couple of

51. See below, p. 50. West was jealous of Hoppner's commission to paint the children, which he may have owed to the success of his *Miss Bailey* at the Royal Academy of 1784 (79) (W. T. Whitley, *Artists and their Friends in England 1700–99* (1928), vol. II, pp. 41–5).

52. Pyne, vol. I, pp. 100–1.

53. Farington, unpublished, 5 May 1795. The Lawrence is reproduced, Garlick, *Lawrence*, pl. 33.

54. Garlick, *op. cit.*, pl. 1.

55. Mrs. Papendiek's *Journals, Court and Private Life in the Time of Queen Charlotte*, ed. Mrs. V. Delves Broughton (1887), vol. II, pp. 130–4, 141–3.

56. Garlick, *op. cit.*, pl. 49; for *Satan* see *ibid.*, pl. 35.

which copies and derivations were distributed, including a number on a small scale, reminiscent of the days when Petitot, Hoskins or Boit had reproduced on a small scale royal portraits by Van Dyck and Kneller. They were placed in the King's Dining-Room at Kew with Beechey's full-lengths of Princess Augusta (672) and the Duke of Cumberland (673). In 1797–8 Beechey had been at work on his huge canvas of the King with his two sons at a review (660). He worked on it in the Octagon Room at Buckingham House. The Prince of Wales had been so 'irregular' in sitting that Beechey found it hard to get a good likeness, but the Duke of York was said to be 'very like' and the King 'a speaking likeness'. The scale is almost more than Beechey could manage, but the group contains sympathetic portraits of the warlike King and his brave—and favourite—son. It is not surprising that during his last illness George III was constantly reviewing troops in his imagination. Beechey's is the best of all the review pictures so dear to the Hanoverian heart. To that extent it takes up the Morier conventions, but it is also a not unsuccessful essay in the heroic baroque tradition of the *Pompa Introitus Ferdinandi*.

One of the copyists of Beechey's full-length of the King wrote in 1809 that it was the last portrait that the King ever sat for. Apart from the tragic likenesses taken during his incarceration at Windsor, this is probably true. In August 1804 Beechey had a terrifying reception from the King at Windsor.[57] He was told by the King that he did not understand colouring and that the King wanted no more of his pictures. Beechey had always treated his royal patrons with a rather ill-judged familiarity and there seems to have been a confusion in the King's mind as to what he had ordered from Beechey. In an effort to explain matters to the King, Beechey had met with a passionate outburst: 'West is an American, & Copley is an American, & You are an Englishman, and were you all at the D——l I should not care'. This caused Beechey to faint on a sofa in a Maid of Honour's apartment. When Hoppner some months later maliciously told the story to the Prince of Wales, he roared with laughter. The King's illness rendered him quite unpredictable in his dealings with anyone who crossed his path. A small matter could easily upset him. By the summer of 1806 George III had become so sick of sitting for his portrait that he vowed to turn out of his house anyone who asked for him to do so again. To Copley's tactless request, probably made in 1806, that he would sit to him he replied, 'Sit to you for a Portrait, What do you want to make a Show of me'. Henry Edridge, on the other hand, had been struck with the goodness of the King's disposition when he had been drawing the royal family at Windsor in 1802–3. He had talked with the King about art and artists. By 1806 the King's eyesight had become so bad that it was fruitless for him to go to the Academy's summer exhibition.[58]

II. GEORGE IV

THE PRINCE who laughed so uproariously at Hoppner's story of Beechey's discomfiture was a very different character from his father. It is easy to dismiss him by contrast as a gay, vain and charming voluptuary, idle, irresponsible and unreliable, hopelessly improvident, cowardly, self-centred and cold at heart; but some of these qualities are useful if one is to become so distinguished and sensitive as a connoisseur and patron of the arts as the Prince of Wales proved himself to be at an early age.

'In their dress, their table, their houses, and their furniture, the favourites of fortune united

57. See below, p. 5; it seems that West had endeavoured to abuse Beechey to the King.

58. Farington, *Diary*, vol. III, p. 251; vol. II, pp. 74, 118; vol. III, p. 204.

every refinement of conveniency, of elegance and of splendour, whatever could soothe their pride or gratify their sensuality.' Gibbon's account of the life of the Roman upper classes could be transposed with no loss of accuracy to describe the circles in which the young Prince shone. In his love of fine pictures and works of art he had inherited his grandfather's good taste and eye for quality. He had an unerring sense of how his pictures and furniture and other possessions could be harmonised in the decoration of a house or a single room. It is remarkable how many pictures, for example, at a given moment such as 1816, were in store, presumably because they did not fit into the latest arrangements at Carlton House: 'so magnificent just now, that it is well worth seeing', wrote Lady Sarah Spencer on 10 May 1810. 'He changes the furniture so very often, that one can scarcely find time to catch a glimpse at each transient arrangement before it is all turned off for some other.'[59]

Until he came of age the Prince of Wales lived on a tight rein under his parents' roof, but in 1783 he was given Carlton House which had belonged to his grandparents. By Christmas he had moved into it and was hard at work on improving it. He had also been given an annual income of £62,000. In 1784 his debts stood at nearly £150,000. Two years later he owed a quarter of a million pounds. In 1787 he was voted a sum towards the clearance of his debts, including £60,000 for the completion of his works at Carlton House; yet by 1792 his debts amounted to £400,000. The Prince's total disregard of any form of order or regulating principle in the handling of his finances was as much a cause of the miserable friction between himself and his father, who hated extravagance in any form, as were his shameful scrapes and love of dissipation.[60]

Artists and craftsmen found themselves swept away in the Prince's 'torrents of expense', to join the army of creditors who were instructed to send in details of work for the Prince for which they had not been paid.[61] George Simpson submitted in 1793 an account[62] for £275. 2s. 6d. for cleaning and repairing a very large number of pictures for the Prince, an account which incidentally provides an indication of the large number of pictures the Prince possessed by the time he was thirty. The bill was authorised by Richard Cosway, the foppish little miniaturist to whom the Prince had owed large sums of money since at least 1786 and who was perhaps consoled by being able to sign himself *Primarius Pictor* to the Prince and by exercising, it seems, some kind of surveyorship over his collections.[63] Loutherbourg, who had expended £420 on the Prince's behalf for a collection of ancient and foreign arms for the Armoury at Carlton House, sent in a bill (undated) for £2,500 for pictures ordered for the same room. They had been designed to fit the panels of the room and to be set over the four doors; one of the two largest pictures, which were for panels opposite the windows, was probably the huge *Banditti in a Landscape* (934), a spirited essay in the manner of Wilson. A series of such designs round the Armoury would have provided the Prince with a splendidly theatrical effect. John Russell's account with the Prince amounted only to £120. 15s.[64] His pastel of the Prince himself, of which a version is in the Fogg Museum of Art (*Fig.* XII), was later used by him in composing his full-length (1051) of the Prince buttoned tightly into the uniform of the Royal Society of Kentish Bowmen. Russell presents one of the most sympathetic portraits of his patron in this happy, harassed, time. It also seems to have been liked by the Prince himself, although Cosway's were the portraits of the Prince which were most lavishly distributed. Cosway's account for work done for the Prince, up to and just beyond May 1795, includes some thirty

59. *Correspondence of Sarah Spencer, Lady Lyttelton*, ed. Mrs. H. Wyndham (1912), pp. 103–4.

60. The best account of the Prince's early years and of his financial situation is to be found in Professor A. Aspinall's edition of *The Correspondence of George, Prince of Wales*, vol. I (1963), vol. II (1964).

61. This mass of (largely unsorted) material is in the P.R.O.; see below, p. li.

62. P.R.O., H.O. 73, 23.

63. See below, p. 21.

64. See below, p. 109.

portraits of his patron in various forms and guises. The most charming pastel done for the Prince by Russell, is, however, the portrait of Mrs. Fitzherbert (*Fig.* XI) which William IV sent back to her at Brighton after his brother's death. Russell's pastels recall the happy days when the Prince and Mrs. Fitzherbert were living at Brighton. There is a breath of Brighton's sea-air, and of the waves into which the Prince had first plunged in 1783, in the pastels he drew for the Prince of the 'Brighton Bather', Martha Gunn (1052), and her colleague 'Smoaker' Miles (1053).

Romney had never worked for George III, although, according to Farington, he hoped that he might succeed Reynolds as Principal Painter.[65] He was, however, one of the Prince's creditors to the extent of £351. 15s. He had painted for him a full-length of Mrs. Fitzherbert (£105) and a smaller portrait of her (£36. 15s.), which is probably the unfinished portrait at Thoresby Hall. He also painted for the Prince two full-lengths, each at £105, of Lady Hamilton: 'Mrs Hart . . . Historical'.[66] These are the two portraits of her which Romney stated on 7 July 1791 that he had begun for the Prince, the '*Calypso*, and a *Magdalene*, painted from her when Lady Hamilton, for the Prince of Wales'.[67] The *Calypso* is at Waddesdon (*Fig.* XV).[68] Of these four pictures, only one, the unfinished portrait of Mrs. Fitzherbert, was at Carlton House (in store) in 1816,[69] but it was sent to Mrs. Fitzherbert at Brighton by William IV on 5 October 1830.

The Prince regularly attended the Royal Academy's annual dinner. After his first appearance there in 1785 Reynolds wrote that he 'behaved with great propriety; we were all mightily pleased with him'.[70] From 1812 the Academy's business was submitted to the Prince instead of to his father. Unlike his father, the Prince had always admired Reynolds's work. Reynolds's executors submitted their account, for over £600, with the other creditors.[71] The most important items on the bill were the full-length of the Duke of Cumberland (probably No. 1017), a conventional princely portrait wholly lacking the wit of Gainsborough's portrait (793), and the magnificent full-length of the Prince (*Fig.* XIV) which had been shown at the Royal Academy in 1787 and was given to Lord Moira in 1810. The Prince sat to Reynolds on a number of occasions. At different periods he bought, or was given, portraits by Reynolds of his relations (e.g., 1009, 1010, 1013, 1014). In 1819 Lord Rivers gave him the grand equestrian portrait of Lord Ligonier which is now in the Tate Gallery. In 1810 the Prince was given by Lady Townshend the two large martial pieces of the heroes of the Seven Years War, Granby (1022) and Schaumburg-Lippe (1027), which he placed in the Crimson Drawing-Room at Carlton House. The full-lengths of Rodney (1026) and Keppel (1024), among the most moving of Reynolds's late full-lengths, were painted for the Prince, as was the superb—now ruined—full-length of that 'terrible brute', M. de Chartres (1025). He probably commissioned the sumptuous full-length (1018) of Frederick, Duke of York, newly returned from Germany to become his boon companion on the Turf and at the gaming-tables; at the Duke's sale in 1827 he bought the dashing full-length of Lord Hastings (1023). In 1810 Lord Erskine presented him with the portrait (1020) which shows off his elegant figure and charming face, and something of his 'gay and happy temperament, enjoying uninterruptedly a boyish flow of animal spirits'. In 1822 George acquired the portrait of Lord Southampton (1028) who had been so closely

65. *Diary*, vol. 1, p. 217.
66. P.R.O., H.O. 73, 24. Two unframed sketches of Lady Hamilton were sent by the Prince to Lord Hertford on 27 May 1810 (Jutsham, *R/D.*, f. 60).
67. *Memoirs of Lady Hamilton* (1815), p. 93; Rev. J. Romney, *Memoirs of the Life and Works of George Romney* (1830), pp. 180–2; he quotes (p. 217) a letter from Romney of 5 August 1790 in which he states that Prince William had sat to him and that the Prince of Wales, having admired 'a new picture

of Mrs. Fitzherbert', had promised to sit to him on returning from Brighton.
68. E. Waterhouse, Catalogue of the *Paintings* at Waddesdon (Office du Livre, Fribourg, 1967), pp. 97–8. The *Magdalen* was sold in the Earl of Inchcape's sale at Christie's, 28 July 1939 (112).
69. No. 249 in the inventory of that year.
70. *Letters, op. cit.*, pp. 124–5
71. See below, p. 98.

involved in the disagreements between him and his father over his debts. The unfinished Hogarthian portrait of Lord Eglinton (1019) was in the Prince's collection by 1816. Lord Yarmouth bought for the Prince at Burke's sale in 1812 the scintillating half-length of Garrick (1021). Among other portraits by Reynolds which the Prince owned for a time[72] was an unfinished full-length, later cut down to a half-length, of Mrs. Fitzherbert. Reynolds's niece, Lady Thomond, presented to the Prince in 1814 her uncle's *Cymon anf Iphigenia* (1030), which seems to link Correggio with Etty. In 1818 she gave him the large copy after Guido Reni's *St. Michael* (1031). At Lady Thomond's sale in 1821 George IV acquired the more celebrated *Death of Dido* (1029). She had given to the Prince in 1815 the portrait which Reynolds had painted of George III before his accession (1011) and which seems to have been unfavourably compared with Ramsay. Almost immediately after the Prince had bought from Burke's sale a copy of Reynolds's *Self-portrait* (1032), Lady Thomond presented him with the original (1008), 'the best portrait he ever painted of himself'. She remembered with gratitude 'The kind sentiments your Royal Highness was pleased to express for my late uncle'; 'it is his patron (and may I presume to say his friend) who thus honours his memory'.[73]

The amount of money due to Mrs. Gainsborough, for pictures painted by her late husband for the Prince of Wales, was £1,228. 10s. It is a testimony to the refinement of the Prince's tastes that he was patronising Gainsborough before he was twenty; it is perhaps no less a testimony to his charm that Gainsborough had been reluctant to acknowledge himself to be one of the Prince's creditors. Before sitting to Gainsborough in the autumn of 1782 (780) in the set of ovals painted for his parents, the Prince had commissioned portraits of himself from Gainsborough. The most important is the full-length with a horse (*Fig.* XIII), exhibited with its companion portrait of Colonel St. Leger (805) at the Royal Academy in 1782.[74] Smaller portraits of the Prince by Gainsborough, painted for friends and, in one instance, for despatch abroad, were probably based on this type. The one sent abroad was probably the Gainsborough sent to the Duke of York in 1782, 'reckoned by every body to be a remarkable strong likeness'. The Prince owned a full-length of himself in the uniform of the 10th Light Dragoons, of which Gainsborough had only painted 'The Head, and Sketch of part of the Body' (*Fig.* XVI). This he gave away to Lord Heathfield in 1810.[75]

Among the pictures ordered by the Prince from Gainsborough and no longer in the royal collection,[76] is a group of female portraits, which includes an unfinished portrait of Mrs. Fitzherbert (*Fig.* XVII) and the full-length of Perdita Robinson, for which the exquisite *modello* (804) is still in the collection. Of the two landscapes (*Figs.* XVIII, XIX) which were sent to Mrs. Fitzherbert in 1810 and may have been painted for her, one is dated 1784. These landscapes, although they were never taken up by the Prince, are perhaps more eloquent than any written testimony of the refinement which surrounded the Prince at this time of his life. The two landscapes were in the exhibition of Gainsborough's pictures at Schomberg House early in 1789, when the Regency Crisis was drawing to a close. Among the portraits left unfinished by Gainsborough and sold by Mrs. Gainsborough in 1797 was the pair of three-quarter-lengths (795, 796) of the Duke and Duchess of Cumberland who may have introduced their nephew to Gainsborough. They are valuable indications of the method used by fashionable portrait-painters in composing such portraits. The head and a small area of canvas around it are painted first, presumably in the presence of the sitter, and with almost no indication of the rest of the design. Then, as one sees in the portrait of the

---

72. See below, p. 98.

73. *Letters of George IV*, vol. I, 122. George IV honoured Reynolds's memory further by ordering a number of copies of his works in enamel by Henry Bone.

74. E. Waterhouse, *op. cit.*, pp. 36–9.

75. O. Millar, 'Gainsborough and George IV: A Lost Portrait', *Burl. Mag.*, vol. CIX (1967), pp. 531–2.

76. See below, p. 35.

Duchess, the dress and background are sketched in, to be filled out gradually in relation to the almost finished head. The Prince also acquired the deceptively idyllic portrait of the Cumberlands in a park with Lady Elizabeth Luttrell (797): a picture in a flawless state of preservation and a supremely poetic essay in the tradition of Zoffany's royal conversation-pieces and of Gainsborough's own early portraits in landscapes.

The Prince had ordered earlier Gainsborough's portrait of Lord Cornwallis (799) and the full-length of Colonel St. Leger (805); the latter, described by one critic as 'that enormous sign of the *Horse and Jockey*', contains splendid heads of the officer and his charger but is misunderstood as a whole; a comparison with the big portrait of Lord Granby (1022) reveals Reynolds's vast superiority in convincingly putting together such a design. The Gainsborough nostalgically reminds one, as so often, of Van Dyck; the Reynolds is soundly based on Rubens.[77] The elegant full-length of John Christian Fischer (800), given to the Prince by his brother Ernest in 1809, would have made a marvellous pendant to Queen Charlotte's portrait of Abel. In the sale of 1797 the Prince bought the *Diana and Actaeon* (806) which is perhaps a large oil sketch, startlingly modern in appearance, rather than an unfinished painting. It is as personal in its mood as Van Dyck's *Cupid and Psyche*[78] had been one hundred and fifty years earlier.

The Prince of Wales had apparently intended to hang the portraits of the Cumberlands (795, 796) in his 'State Room' at Carlton House. The lovely group of his three eldest sisters (798), which lost so much of its original colour-scheme and of the space around the sitters when it was barbarously cut down, had been specially painted for the Saloon in which the Prince planned to hang portraits of his family. The Prince shared to the full his family's enthusiasm for assembling portraits of their relations. In the West Ante-room at Carlton House in 1816 were hanging Reynolds's portraits of the two Cumberlands (1010, 1017) and Hoppner's full-length of the Duke of Clarence (835), with the portraits of M. de Chartres (1025), a full-length of Louis XV and portraits over the doors of George II and Queen Caroline.[79] The sumptuously decorated Ante-chamber, or Old Throne Room, contained the Ramsays of the Prince's parents (996, 997), his own portrait by Hoppner (834) and the Reynolds of the Duke of York (1018), all apparently in the frames made earlier by Bradburn and France.[80] In May 1784 the Prince had written to the Duke of York in Germany that he was keeping places in his house 'on purpose for Portraits of you & Billy'.[81] It is doubtful whether the 'State Room' or Saloon, in which the Gainsboroughs—of which only one was finished—

77. On an episode in the series of designs for the *History of Decius Mus* (R. Oldenbourg, *Rubens, Klassiker der Kunst*, Stuttgart, Berlin and Leipzig, 1921, pl. 145).

78. Millar, No. 166.

79. Inv. of 1816 (1–7); Pyne, vol. III, *Carlton House*, pp. 17–20, with a valuable plate (1819) by Wild.

80. *Ibid.* (15–18); Pyne, *op. cit.*, pp. 28–30 (plate (1816) by Wild). The frames on the Reynolds and the Hoppner had probably been taken off the Angelica (869) and the Cotes (720) which were in store at Carlton House in 1816. These four frames are today in the Throne Room at Buckingham Palace.

81. The letters of the royal family at this period contain information about the portraits they were sending to each other. When the Queen sent her portrait, presumably a miniature, to Prince William in 1782, she urged him: 'pray continue to look at it and let me have that inestimable pleasure to know, that my wishes are fulfilled in contributing to your happiness even when Absent from You, by the means of that Image, let it prevail upon You to become good . . .' (W.R.A., Geo. Add. 4, 17). The Duke of Kent, stationed

in Halifax in 1799, wrote to remind his mother of her promise to send him a half-length copy of her portrait by Beechey; he also hoped for a portrait of the King copied from the figure in Beechey's big *Review* (660). To the Prince of Wales he wrote hoping that a promised Hoppner of him would soon be sent out and asking him to remind Prince Ernest to grant a sitting on his behalf, 'but sitting is a thing he does not much like giving his time to'; he hoped the Duke of York would send him a copy of Beechey's portrait of the Duchess and another from the figure of the Duke in the *Review*. 'All our Sisters & Brothers at home, have engaged to send me out their pictures' (*ibid.*, Add. 7, 44, 45, 47). The Duke of York and Prince William sent portraits of themselves home from Germany in the 1780s. In 1817 the Princess Royal was asking the Prince of Wales to send her his portrait (see No. 780). Prince Augustus wrote plaintively to his eldest brother from Caserta in 1794, asking to be sent his portrait as a 'particular favour' (*Correspondence of George, Prince of Wales*, vol. II (1964), p. 531). In 1786 the Prince's uncle, the Duke of Gloucester, had written from Milan asking for 'a Good Head, to hang up at Gloucester House; I mean by that not to have the Expence

were to be placed, was ever completed as it had originally been planned, but it is the room later known as the Old Throne Room.[82]

The Prince's desire to collect portraits of his family led him also to commission from Beechey the set of portraits of 'the girls' (665–70) whom Beechey, like Gainsborough, Hoppner, Copley and Lawrence before him, painted at Windsor. Soon after Princess Amelia's death, the Beechey of her (670) was sent to Bone so that commemorative miniatures could be painted from it. Beechey's portrait of the Prince himself, in his sparkling Light Dragoon uniform, was painted for the Duke of Kent. The last set of family portraits is that by Stroehling (1093–9), which seems to have been painted for the Prince and contains some exaggerated neoclassical iconographical elements as well as a cruelly homely portrait of the Queen.

As well as his family, the Prince of Wales set himself to collect around him portraits of the men and women he respected or loved, 'the ministers of his serious business, and the companions of his looser hours'. His grandfather had commissioned conversation-pieces, indoors and out, of members of his gang,[83] but the Prince built up a far richer portrait-gallery. He owned portraits of Garrick (1021) and of 'La Bacelli' (769), the beautiful dancer and demirep, and of the musicians Abel (1048) and Fischer (800); he commissioned Hoppner to paint Haydn (843) for him; he acquired portraits of Reynolds (1008) and Wyatville (918); Lawrence's portrait of Scott (913) was specially painted for him. Among statesmen he owned portraits of Rockingham (1045), Pitt (908), Lord Kenyon (1090) and Spencer Perceval (868). In the Crimson Drawing-Room at Carlton House, with the two big canvases by Reynolds (1022, 1027), hung the incisive portraits of Thurlow (914) and Dr. Markham (847), by Lawrence and Hoppner, and the Reynolds of Erskine (1020). In the East Ante-room hung the Hoppners of Nelson (849), St. Vincent (851), Bedford (841) and Moira (842) and the Owen of Sir David Dundas (976).[84] Hoppner had been working for the Prince since about 1790 and in 1793 had become his Principal Painter.[85] He seems to have produced the chief portraits of the Prince until his likeness was officially entrusted to Lawrence. Of his early friends, the Prince owned portraits of Lord Spencer Hamilton (1173), Jack Payne (850), Sheridan (830), Fox (1042), the Duchess of Devonshire (1041), Perdita Robinson (804), Lady Melbourne (716), George Hanger (654), Colonel St. Leger (805) and, of course, of Mrs. Fitzherbert. Later in his life he added to his collection portraits of Sir William Curtis (894), the Duke of Devonshire (895) and Lord Eldon (896) by Lawrence and Corden's portrait of Sir Edmund Nagle (714).[85a] No other Prince or King in the history of the royal collection has ever assembled such a distinguished contemporary portrait-gallery; but no other Prince of Wales has been at the heart of such a galaxy of talent, charm and high spirits.

Like his father, the Prince of Wales loved outdoor pursuits. In a letter to his brother Frederick, in the autumn of 1781, he described hunting at 'yt. almost divine amusement'. 'I have plenty of excellent & beautiful horses, & ride ym. well up to ye [*sic*.] I have taken plenty of all ye rural amusements this autumn. I am become an exceeding good shot'.[86] He hunted until he became too heavy and in the closing years of the century he took on lease a succession of houses in Dorset and

of a full length; when a Good head shews the Character, and always preserves the likeness best . . .' (W.R.A., Geo. 54374).

82. See J. Hayes, 'An Unknown Gainsborough Portrait of Edward, Duke of Kent', *Burl. Mag.*, vol. CVIII (1966), pp. 362–5, for the portraits by Gainsborough which the Prince was planning in the 1780s to place together in one room.

83. e.g., Millar, Nos. 533, 535, 545–7 and 555.

84. Inv. of 1816 (8, 9, 11–14, 59–63); Pyne, *op. cit.*, pp. 20–4 (plate (1816) by Wild).

85. See below, p. 50.

85a. George IV also assembled marble busts of his contemporaries, including Gerard Lake, Fox, Pitt, the 5th and 6th Dukes of Bedford, Sheridan, Hastings, Ellenborough, Erskine, Lord Grenville, Markham, Thurlow, the Dukes of Devonshire and Wellington. He also acquired busts of Granby, William, Duke of Cumberland and Lord Ligonier (information from Mr. Geoffrey de Bellaigue).

86. *Correspondence of George, Prince of Wales*, vol. I (1963), p. 75.

XI. John Russell: *Mrs. Fitzherbert*. Lord Stafford

XII. John Russell: *George IV when Prince of Wales*.
Fogg Art Museum, Harvard University

XIII. Thomas Gainsborough: *George IV when Prince of Wales*.
National Trust, Waddesdon Manor

XIV. Sir Joshua Reynolds: *George IV when Prince of Wales*.
Duke of Norfolk

XV. George Romney: *Lady Hamilton as Calypso*. National Trust, Waddesdon Manor

XVI. Thomas Gainsborough: *George IV when Prince of Wales*
(detail). Sir George Tapps-Gervis-Meyrick, Bt.

XVII. Thomas Gainsborough: *Mrs. Fitzherbert*. California
Palace of the Legion of Honor, San Francisco

XVIII. Thomas Gainsborough: *Valley with a Shepherd and his Flock*. Private Collection

XIX. Thomas Gainsborough: *The Harvest Waggon*. Art Gallery of Toronto

XX. H. Meyer after Lawrence: *Lord Charles Stewart,*
later 3rd Marquess of Londonderry

XXI. Denis Dighton: *The Battle of Orthez*. Marquess of Anglesey

XXII. P. J. de Loutherbourg: *The Battle of First of June 1794.* National Maritime Museum

XXIII. J. M. W. Turner: *The Battle of Trafalgar.* National Maritime Museum

XXV. Sir Thomas Lawrence: *George IV.* National Gallery of Ireland, Dublin

XXIV. Sir Thomas Lawrence: *George IV.* Marquess of Londonderry

XXVII. Sir Thomas Lawrence: *Lady Maria Conyngham.* Metropolitan Museum, New York

XXVI. Sir Thomas Lawrence: *Lady Elizabeth Conyngham.* Gulbenkian Foundation, Lisbon

XXVIII. Sir David Wilkie: *Queen Victoria*. Lady Lever Art Gallery, Port Sunlight

Hampshire from which, as well as from Brighton, he could hunt. His chequered career on the Turf began in 1784, but the burden of his debts compelled him to sell his stud two years later. He was back on the Turf in 1788, but withdrew again temporarily in 1791 and sold his stud in 1792 after the scandal caused by Samuel Chifney's riding of Escape (see No. 1118). The Prince had a passion for horses and for driving smart vehicles. His debts in 1787 included nearly £29,000 on his Stable Account.

At this period the Prince was commissioning portraits of his horses from George Garrard, Sawrey Gilpin, Ben Marshall and Stubbs. By the end of 1792 Garrard had finished seven large pictures of the Prince's horses which, in frames made by Sefferin Nelson, were sent down to Kempshott.[87] It is possible, indeed, that the set of pictures painted for the Prince by Garrard and Stubbs, and perhaps even the set by Marshall, were originally hung at Kempshott House near Basingstoke or in another of the Prince's hunting-boxes.[88] Of Garrard's seven pictures, which had been painted at Aston Clinton, where the Prince's horses were in the care of Warwick Lake, only one survives, the portrait of Saltram (818). Sawrey Gilpin's most important commission from the Prince,[89] which seems to have cost him much effort, is lost. Many years earlier, one of his first patrons had been the Prince's great-uncle, William, Duke of Cumberland, who had kept him under his roof at Cumberland Lodge. His most mature picture for Cumberland was the group of Cypron with her brood in 1764 (819). Gilpin's stiff little portraits of Cumberland's horses (820–3), still very much in the Wootton tradition, were secured by the Prince of Wales. Ben Marshall's pictures of the Prince's horses (937–42) must be among his earliest works. They are still, though much freer in handling, influenced by Gilpin's presentations, although there is perhaps a new excitement in the dramatic lighting in the portrait of Lop (938) which seems connected with the more romantic vein which Gilpin reveals in his *Frightened Horses* (825). Far more important is the series of canvases, uniform in size and framed by Thomas Allwood, which Stubbs painted for the Prince in 1790–3:[90] portraits of the Prince himself, riding in Hyde Park (1109), and the notorious Lady Lade (1112), his grooms with favourite horses (1110, 1111), soldiers of his regiment mounting guard (1115), a riding-master in his school (1116), one of the Prince's dashing equipages (1117), two portraits of one of his greys (1122, 1123), pictures of favourite dogs (1124, 1125) and of a brace of red deer (1126). Other pictures by Stubbs were acquired by the Prince at different times, including, as the earliest Stubbs in his collection, the little portrait of Hollyhock (1119) in which the background was completed by Boucher and Claude-Joseph Vernet. A large picture which Stubbs painted for the Prince, perhaps as a companion to the lost Gilpin, has not been heard of since 1844.

During his later years on the Turf the Prince commissioned portraits of his horses from Henry Bernard Chalon who worked extensively for the royal family.[91] In 1808 Chalon painted at Newmarket portraits of Barbarossa (697), Orville (698), Selim (699) and Sir David (700). He charged twenty-five guineas for each horse and five guineas for each figure in his pictures. 'The very distressing Circumstances' in which the painter found himself led him to beg that too long a delay might not elapse between sending in his bill (on 8 May 1808) and being paid. He only had to wait five months. In 1817 he painted for the Prince Regent the hounds and huntsmen at the royal kennels on Ascot Heath (702). In 1814 Schwanfelder, who was, like Chalon, an official Animal Painter to the Prince Regent, painted three rather sombre portraits of his horses, including the Malcolm Arabian (1069). R. B. Davis, who grew up under royal patronage and whose brother Charles,

87. See below, p. 44.
88. For Kempshott House see Brig.-Gen. J. F. R. Hope, *A History of Hunting in Hampshire* (1950), ch. III; opp. p. 49 is a plan of the house showing the grand rooms on the front in which the pictures may have been hung.
89. See below, p. 45.
90. See below, p. 122.
91. See below, p. 15.

the famous Huntsman, appears in Chalon's *Unkennelling* as a young whipper-in, painted for George IV a portrait of Maria (736), the beautiful little horse who won a race for the King at the last race-meeting he attended. Abraham Cooper (710) and John Doyle (765) were also working for the King towards the end of his life.[92] The finest pictures of his horses painted for the King at this period are, however, the three by James Ward: Monitor (1135), Nonpareil (1136) and Soothsayer (1137). The King would not have appreciated the more wildly romantic aspects of Ward's style, but in these three pictures the latent energies of the animals are finely suggested and the landscapes have a feeling for light and wind far more impressive than the standard backgrounds used by Ward's contemporaries in the King's service. The King seems to have admired the painterly qualities of Ward's pictures, with their suggestions of Rubens or Teniers. Ward had worked intermittently for the royal family since at least 1794 and he hoped that he might be placed on the same footing with the Crown as Lawrence, Beechey and West had been. He hoped particularly that he might be given a room in which to work so that he could escape the discomfort and stench of working in the royal stables.[93]

From his father, and even more from William, Duke of Cumberland, George IV inherited an interest in wild animals. He maintained Cumberland's menagerie at Sandpit Gate in Windsor Great Park, a prototype of the zoos at Woburn and Whipsnade. When he was a very young man he bought animals and birds from Joshua Brookes, among them the red deer which Stubbs painted for him with such feeling in 1792 (1126). John Gould the naturalist was stuffing specimens for the King towards the end of his reign: the period when Agasse was painting for the King the only two pictures in his collection which are worthy to set beside his pictures by Stubbs, the White-tailed Gnus (652) and the beautiful, ill-fated Nubian Giraffe (651). Robert Home's picture of a rare White Leopard (833) in Lord Wellesley's menagerie at Barrackpore may have been given to George III. Some of the animals at Sandpit Gate are seen again in the picture (929), much influenced by Ward, by John Frederick Lewis who in his youth studied in the menageries at Exeter 'Change and at Windsor. George IV's love of yachting is recorded in J. T. Serres's picture (1079) of the *Royal George* at Portsmouth, painted in 1820, three years after the King had joined the Yacht Club.

George IV shared enthusiastically the passion for military matters which characterised the House of Brunswick. Passionately interested in military uniforms and equipment, William, Duke of Cumberland, had retained David Morier in his service and George IV acquired a large number of almost uniformly hideous martial portraits, some of which were placed in the Armoury at Carlton House, by this tireless painter of military scarecrows. Apart from a set of pictures of skirmishes (960–2), which had been in Cumberland's collection, all the portraits in the Morier manner in the royal collection were bought by George IV. He had admired and been given the huge Morier of George II[94] and had acquired smaller portraits of George II and Frederick, Prince of Wales.[95] At least nine portraits, of this type, of Cumberland (943–51) and four of George III (952–5), with portraits of other military sitters, were in George IV's collection. He also bought Quadal's picture of his father at a review (995) and the only equestrian portrait of Cumberland (1215) which is of some distinction and might have been painted in part by Brompton.

In addition to surrounding himself with portraits of his family on the battlefield or at seemingly unending reviews, George IV adored dressing up in uniform. He was passionately interested in clothes—in 1787 he owed his tailor nearly £17,000—and he spent huge sums on uniforms, weapons and equipment. This passion is recorded in his portraits: in Mather Brown's full-length (691) in an imaginary military uniform in which the Prince apes West's more serious image of his father in

92. See below. p. 32.   93. See below, p. 127.   94. Millar, No. 591.   95. *Ibid.*, Nos. 592–6.

1779 (1138), or in the Beechey (664) in the uniform of his beloved Light Dragoons. On the other hand he showed no wish to purchase the huge Copley of himself as a Field-Marshal on horseback (see No. 711), an overblown essay in the Van Dyck tradition.[96] Many years earlier Cosway had painted miniatures of the Prince in uniform or dressed as St. George, as well as in Van Dyck dress.[97] The Prince was an expert on how to wear a Van Dyck costume. He had taken great trouble in 1781 to send out to his brother Frederick a 'Vandyke dress' with careful instructions on how to arrange it. 'I flatter myself you will find all these things executed with yt dernier gout, wisdom & propriety you attribute to me in propria persona'. One Van Dyck dress for his brother was white and pink; another was to be 'white satting, with pink puffs and knots'. There may even have been a third, of lilac silk with pale buff puffs and knots.[98] Gainsborough, towards the end of his life, undertook to paint for Thomas Coke an equestrian portrait of the Prince, perhaps in armour or 'slight martial attire' with a Garter mantle, as a pendant to the portrait of the Duke of Arenberg at Holkham.[99] Even in his less riotous and less slender days the Prince sat to Stroehling for a small equestrian portrait which he gave to Lady Conyngham and got the artist to paint him as the Black Prince.[100] It would have hung happily in the Gothic Conservatory at Carlton House and reminds one how the Prince would have revelled in the Eglinton Tournament.

To the Prince's love of the military profession, to his desire to 'have his share of the glory that is going', was joined an increasingly deep interest in the great war in which his country was engaged. He would have been in no doubt that it was a war in defence of the ideal of monarchy and he gloried in its final victories. It was natural to him to surround himself with portraits of the great men of action of his day, successors to the heroes of the Seven Years War. Edward Wyatt made special frames—which survive—with dolphins, anchors, coral and sprigs of oak in the corners, for the full-lengths of Keppel (1024) and Rodney (1026) by Reynolds and the Hoppners of St. Vincent (851) and Nelson (849). These portraits of the last great men of the days of sail are in the tradition of the portraits painted earlier for James II and Queen Anne by Lely, Kneller and Dahl; their successors include Oswald Birley's series of portraits of the naval commanders of the Second World War. To the four full-lengths, George IV added a Hoppner of Lord Keith (845) and portraits of Sir David Dundas (976), Sir William Congreve (931) and Lord Hutchinson (987). Two pictures which came into the royal collection at a later date form a postscript to George IV's gallery of heroes. Stothard's almost unrecorded picture of the death of Sir Ralph Abercromby (1092) is a tentative essay in the tradition of West's *Death of Wolfe*; Arthur Devis's *Death of Nelson* (762) is a more competently arranged picture in exactly the same tradition. Sir John Moore, indeed, was surely thinking of George III's pictures by West when he spoke of Abercromby falling 'like Epaminondas and Wolfe, on the field of his victory'; and Nelson said that he could never pass a printshop which had on display the print after West's Death of Wolfe.[101]

In 1797 the Prince of Wales visited the exhibition of William Hodges's *Effects of Peace* and *Effects of War*. He is reputed to have said that a painting devoted to the horrors of war might unnecessarily

96. It derives ultimately from the Van Dyck of Charles I on horseback (see Millar, No. 144); the design had been used by Vanderbank in 1726 for George I (*ibid.*, No. 499).

97. P.R.O., H.O. 73, 18. Sketches by Cosway of the Prince in a Van Dyckian pose with a charger and as St. George in the same vein, were sold at Christie's, 1 February 1924 (83) and 12 December 1958 (162).

98. *Correspondence of George, Prince of Wales*, vol. 1 (1963), pp. 57, 62.

99. Whitley, *Gainsborough*, pp. 235, 257, 283.

100. See below, p. 119. In *The Examiner*, 9 August 1812, Stroeh-ling was attacked as an Israelite in practice and a mountebank in art. Can such a man, the writer asked, 'be the most fit object of patronage from the Prince Regent of England and the British Nobility'? Richard Westall had produced a design of the battle of Crécy for a painted window in the Conservatory at Carlton House (Jutsham, *R/D*, ff. 131, 148; Carlton House, 1816, No. 523).

101. Carola Oman, *Sir John Moore* (1953), p. 277, *Nelson* (1947), p. 598.

agitate the public mind.[102] The two large paintings by George Jones of the victories at Vittoria (865) and Waterloo (866), which originally hung in the Throne Room at St. James's on either side of Lawrence's portrait of George IV (873), are in a tradition that goes back to the Blenheim tapestries or to Van der Meulen's designs for the campaigns of Louis XIV in paint or tapestry, and can indeed be stretched back to Callot: a tradition in which the foreground is taken up with the victorious general and his staff and the fighting is relegated to the middle distance. On the other hand Denis Dighton, who provided the Regent with so much military material, gives a far more realistic account of the horrors of hand-to-hand combat in his *Battle of Orthez* (*Fig.* XXI), which the Regent gave to Lord Uxbridge[103] or in his two paintings of episodes during the battle of Waterloo which are still in the collection (763, 764). No detail is spared by Dighton's dry and careful brush in his effort to illustrate each moment in Sergeant Ewart's gruesome account of his capture of a French Eagle. In December 1823 Turner was beginning to collect material for his huge painting of Trafalgar (*Fig.* XXIII) for George IV. It hung in the Ante-room at St. James's, balancing Loutherbourg's *Glorious First of June* (*Fig.* XXII) on either side of Lawrence's portrait of George III (871), until August 1829 when both pictures were taken to Carlton House on their way to Greenwich Hospital.[104] The culmination of George IV's pride in the allied victories, his devotion to the monarchical ideal, admiration for his great contemporaries, and inherited enthusiasm for military affairs, is reached in the portraits painted for him by Sir Thomas Lawrence which are now in the Waterloo Chamber at Windsor.

On 22 June 1804 Lawrence had waited for four and a half hours for the Prince of Wales who was to have sat for a full-length to be given to Lord Fitzwilliam. Late in 1800 or early in 1801 Lawrence had painted the stagey full-length (874) of the Princess of Wales with her daughter, but this had been, it seems, designed as a present to Lady Townshend. The portrait of Thurlow (914), which had aroused George III's admiration at the Royal Academy in 1803, had been intended for the Princess, but the Prince made sure that it was sent to Carlton House after the exhibition was over. Instead of the promised full-length by Lawrence, Lord Fitzwilliam received one by Phillips,[105] and there seems to have been little contact between Lawrence and the Regent until the spring and early summer of 1814 which saw the fall of Paris and the Restoration of the Bourbons. On 2 May 1814 Lawrence received a letter from Lady Anne Barnard who ardently wished that his pencil should record these great events, 'the noblest . . . that the history of the world has to produce'. She had confidence in the Regent's taste and fine ideas on such an exalted scale, but nevertheless ventured to suggest themes for two large pictures, 'not inferior in size to that of West lately finished'. One was to show the restored Louis XVIII bestowing on the Regent the Order of the St. Esprit; the other was to include likenesses of the generals and sovereigns who were coming to London to meet the Regent. 'If the *present opportunity is lost*, its strength and force from collecting the countenances as they *now are*, will be lost to you for ever.' Lawrence, greatly excited ('extraordinary events produce unusual feelings'), sent the letter up to the Regent's Private Secretary, Sir John McMahon, on 5 June.[106] As early as 11 May Lawrence had told Farington that he had been talking

102. B. Smith, *European Vision and the South Pacific* (1960), p. 58.

103. See below, p. 31. Southey dedicated his *History of the Peninsular War* (1823–32) to George IV, to whose determination 'Great Britain is beholden for its triumph, and Europe for its deliverance'. In 1831–4 Thomas Heaphy was writing about a picture of Wellington and his generals in the Peninsula which the Regent had commissioned (W.R.A., Geo. 26743–9, 32831). In 1817 Hilton received part payment through Lawrence of 100 guineas for a picture of Wellington's entry into

Madrid (*ibid.*, 27088).

104. Jutsham, *Receipts*, f. 272; *The Literary Gazette*, 22 May 1824; W. T. Whitley, *Art in England 1821–37* (1930), pp. 62–4, 231–2. George III had apparently shown no desire to buy Copley's pictures of contemporary events (see below, p. 19); nor did George IV want to keep Bird's painting of the departure of Louis XVIII (see below, pp. 11–12).

105. See below, p. 91.

106. *Letters of George IV*, vol. 1, 438, 451.

with McMahon 'respecting a picture to be painted by Lawrence of the Emperor of Russia,—the King of Prussia, and the Prince Regent.'[107] The artist had sent a fine impression (*Fig.* XX) of Meyer's recently published mezzotint of his portrait of Lord Charles Stewart.[108] Lady Anne Barnard had called the print '*the finest thing I ever beheld*' and it must have impressed the Regent with Lawrence's unrivalled brilliance in painting such subjects.

Lawrence was, however, inexperienced in painting elaborate group portraits and proposed to paint single portraits which he could if necessary combine at a later stage. The idea of painting a group portrait of the distinguished visitors to London gradually developed into a simpler plan: a set of single portraits in the vein Lawrence had struck with his *Lord Charles Stewart*, but on a grander scale. Lawrence thus received a commission from the Prince to paint Blücher (886) and Platov (910) while they were in London; the sittings were arranged by Stewart. Lawrence also received sittings from Wellington (917) and began portraits of the King of Prussia (898) and the Emperor of Russia (883). In 1815 Lawrence was able to show at the Royal Academy his portraits of Blücher, Platov and Wellington with those of Metternich (see No. 905) and the Regent himself. Lord Charles Stewart had presented Lawrence to the Regent at a Levee on 28 July 1814; the Regent intended to visit Lawrence's studio to inspect his portraits; and by 21 August 1814 Lawrence had received four or five sittings for the full-length (*Fig.* XXIV) which is cast in the same mould as the portraits of Wellington and the Regent's distinguished visitors. Northcote told Lawrence that it was 'the *most like* & the best Portrait' of the sitter. At the Royal Academy in 1818 Lawrence showed his first full-length of the Regent in Garter robes (*Fig.* XXV) which is probably based on the same sittings. The Prince rests his hand lightly on the *Table des Grands Capitaines* which had been commissioned by Napoleon in 1806 and ultimately given to the Regent by Louis XVIII in 1817. The portrait clearly delighted the Regent[109] and it became his official portrait. After his accession in 1820 the plumed Garter hat was replaced by the new Imperial Crown. Lawrence, who had had much practice in turning out repetitions of Reynolds's portraits of the old King (see No. 1033), had now, like Ramsay before him, to organise the production of a new state portrait. In 1822 Lawrence stipulated to the Lord Chamberlain that he could not supply the portraits for less than £315 each, but he seems to have received as much as £525 and £630 for some of his repetitions. Even after the death of George IV and his painter a room in Kensington Palace was full of copies of the portrait.[110] In the royal collection there are four versions (919–22) and the variant (873) in Coronation robes which was being painted at the end of 1821 to hang over the fireplace in the Throne Room at St. James's between George Jones's big battle-pieces. Lawrence's presentation of George IV is as appropriate as Ramsay's had been of George III, a dashing, glittering display of robes and chains and of the florid, restless creature under them. Painted with unflagging panache, it was a perfect image of the hero of the alliance to be sent overseas. It was as happily in harmony with the King's environment, with the earthly paradise of ormulu in which he passed so much of his time, as Ramsay's portrait was with Buckingham House or the earlier rooms at Carlton House. At the end

107. *Diary*, unpublished, 11 May 1814. Nothing came of a scheme, put forward by John Bell, that, under the supervision of West, a set of portraits should be painted of the sovereigns, statesmen and commanders which could be issued in prints. Lawrence would have nothing to do with it (V. & A., *Cuttings*, vol. IV, pp. 940–1).

108. Garlick, *Lawrence*, pl. 72.

109. Neither Hoppner nor Phillips had produced a portrait of the Prince which could serve for long as the official likeness. William Owen had told Farington in 1812 that the Prince was going to sit for him and that copies of the portrait would be required (see below, pp. 88–9). To Owen's intense disappointment, and presumably owing to the Prince's appreciation of Lawrence's incomparable ability, the Prince did not sit to him and merely told Owen to copy Hoppner's portrait (834). Owen would have received small consolation from being asked to go with Lawrence to the Prince's Grand Fête at Carlton House.

110. See below, p. 60 and No. 919; William, 6th Duke of Devonshire, *Handbook to Chatsworth and Hardwick* (1845); P.R.O., L.C.1/72,7.

of his life Lawrence, rousing himself to work on the left sleeve in yet another portrait of the King, told Miss Croft that he had never ceased to find variety in his state portraits. He had never painted them precisely alike. 'If you could compare them, I hope you would find the last was still the best.'[111]

In July 1814 Lord Stewart, newly-appointed Ambassador to Vienna, had suggested to Lawrence that he should go to Vienna in order to seize the opportunity of painting for the Regent portraits of the sovereigns, statesmen and generals assembled for the Congress. The King of France was to be painted on the journey to or from Vienna.[112] Lawrence resolved to make the excursion and within a short time the arrangements were made. He planned to leave in January 1815, but on 1 March 1815 Napoleon landed in France. Lawrence's visit to Vienna is not mentioned again until 6 March 1816, when Stewart, knowing that Lawrence was still anxious to paint 'the Autocrat', suggested that he should go for sittings to St. Petersburg ('a tremendous journey') and that he should first paint in Vienna 'Schwarzenburg, Metternich, *Madame Murat*, and *Young* NAPOLEON'. But not until September 1818 did Lawrence depart, not for Vienna but for Aix-la-Chapelle, to paint the sovereigns, their ministers and generals, gathering there for the Congress. He was to receive 500 guineas for each full-length and £1,000 for expenses. He was by now on friendly terms with the Regent and his continental journey was 'felt as a very desirable circumstance by the chief members of Government.'[113] To Farington his friend seemed to be receiving 'a full reward for all your professional labours'. Still under the wing of Lord Stewart, Lawrence had sittings at Aix from the Emperors of Austria (897) and Russia (883), the King of Prussia (898), the Duke of Cambridge (878) and from the diplomats Hardenberg (900), Nesselrode (907) and Richelieu (911). At Aix Lawrence was slightly apprehensive of George Dawe, who had secured the patronage of Prince Leopold and was 'prowling' about nearby. Lawrence's practice was to make a careful drawing of the head of a sitter *ad vivum*; he took care to lock up his first drawing of the Emperor of Russia, but this did not prevent Dawe from ingratiating himself with the Autocrat. Lawrence gained 'increasing fame' from his work at Aix and was treated with great attention by his eminent sitters.

By the end of the year Lawrence was established in Vienna, where he painted the Emperor (897), the Archduke Charles (891), Schwarzenberg (912), the two Russian A.D.C.s Chernichev (892) and Uvarov (915), Count Capo d'Istria (888) and Gentz (899); at Aix and Vienna Lawrence was also painting Metternich (905). Lord Stewart was tireless in helping Lawrence and he filled his leisure hours with 'Comfortable Dinners and the Theatre—Splendid Dinners and High Society—Reviews and Court Fetes'. Something of the superb assemblies Lawrence witnessed, 'most beautifully splendid in Decoration, the most gorgeous in the magnificence of Dress', still sparkles in his portraits. North-cote, hearing of 'the high employment' Lawrence had enjoyed at Aix and Vienna, said 'there has been nothing like it except in the instances of Rubens & Vandyke . . . it wd. raise the credit of English Art abroad and make it more respected at Home'. Lawrence's skill and social address were no less successful in Rome. He arrived there from Vienna in May 1819 in order to paint the Pope (909) and Cardinal Consalvi (893). The portraits were greatly admired. 'It is pleasant on the Continent', he wrote to his brother in July, 'to be greeted by one's Countrymen, who have all seem'd to consider my presence, or rather my Works, as general advantage to the Character of England, in what relates to the progress of the Arts.' At every capital he received superb presents.

On 28 March 1820 Lawrence landed at Dover. Three days later Farington had a first sight of the

111. Williams, vol. II, p. 547.
112. Farington, *Diary*, unpublished, 21 September 1814.
113. He was closely involved with the Prince and Prince Leopold, and witnessed their grief, at the time of the death of Princess Charlotte, whom he had painted for her husband only a few weeks before her death (see No. 925).

portraits he had brought back with him, 'all proofs of his improved practise in his art'. All who saw them seemed filled with admiration. Wilkie thought them 'all in his finest manner, and The Emperor and The Pope decidedly beyond himself'. The King spoke of their being exhibited, 'but not at the Royal Academy'. Nor were the portraits ready to be exhibited. 'I shall not be quite easy', wrote Farington to Lawrence on 3 April, 'till I know that y^r pictures are *safely lodged upstairs*, to be brought down to your *painting room singly* for you to work upon them *privately and undisturbed*.' In the autumn Lawrence kindly took the invalid William Owen to Buckingham House, 'to show him his portraits of the foreign sovereigns he is now completing there'. Owen, no less kindly, praised them warmly. In the summer of 1821 the King seems to have been disturbed that they still had not been finished.

In 1818, before Lawrence left for Vienna, the Regent had expected that Lawrence would discuss with Nash how the portraits should eventually be arranged at Carlton House. In 1821 the King was proposing to construct a Gallery eighty feet long to receive the portraits. He was beginning to complain that, although he had paid for the portraits, they had not been delivered. The death of Lawrence on 7 January 1830 found the portraits in his studio and still not entirely finished and the death of the King on 26 June in the same year found them still without a permanent home. To the portraits painted in London, Aix and Vienna had been added those of Charles X (880) and the Duke of Angoulême (884) which Lawrence had painted in Paris in 1825, and the portraits, painted at various times in London, of the Duke of York (876), Castlereagh (889), Liverpool (903), Bathurst (885), Humboldt (901) and Count Münster (906).[114] At the end of January 1830 the portraits were delivered to the King. In the big commemorative exhibition of Lawrence's works at the British Institution later in the year the first twenty-one items were the portraits 'Painted by Order of His late Majesty FOR THE WATERLOO GALLERY AT WINDSOR'. At least four other items in the exhibition are now also in that room. William Seguier had been put on to getting the portraits ready for exhibition. From the bill he submitted on 10 April it is clear that he had done more than clean and varnish the canvases. He had to finish a number of backgrounds and work up 'hands and dress' in some of the portraits.[115] One can still see very clearly in many of them the aura round the head which marks the area in which Lawrence began the portraits when the sitter was in front of him.

The Waterloo Gallery or Chamber occupies the site of the former Horn Court. Thus the rather forbidding Valhalla which George IV planned for his heroes is on the site of the chapel of revealed religion on which West had set his heart. Wyatville's estimates for works at Windsor in 1829 included £18,000 for the Waterloo Chamber, but the room was not completed until the reign of William IV, 'to receive George IV's munificent gift to the nation'.[116] The original arrangement of the portraits in the Chamber was slightly simpler than the visitor to the Castle now sees. There was no second row of pictures and only three large portraits were placed in the galleries at the end of the room.[117] When Lawrence was off to Aix-la-Chapelle, *The Times* had applauded the Regent's

114. I have based this account of the formation of Lawrence's Waterloo series principally on Farington's *Diary*, vol. VII, pp. 242, 244, 257, 271–2, 279; vol. VIII, pp. 36, 172, 173, 211, 226–7; unpublished, 12, 21 December 1818, 31 December 1819, 31 March, 3, 8 April 1820; Williams, vol. I, pp. 337 et seq.; *Sir Thomas Lawrence's Letter-Bag*, ed. G.S. Layard (1906), pp. 96, 100–1, 133–54, 194–201; Cunningham, *Wilkie*, vol. II, pp. 30, 47. For the presents Lawrence collected, see Layard, *op. cit.*, p. 200, Williams, vol. II, pp. 427–8.

115. W.R.A., Geo. 26750.

116. W. H. St. John Hope, *Windsor Castle* (1913), vol. I, pp. 356, 363. In July 1831 the portraits were still deposited at Buckingham Palace (*Library of the Fine Arts*, vol. I (1831), p. 531).

See also J. D. Passavant, *Kunstreise* . . . (Frankfurt, 1833), p. 52.

117. Waagen, *Works of Art and Artists in England* (1838), vol. I, pp. 167–70; he saw the room in 1835, and at that time the Reynolds of Cumberland (1010) hung in the place now occupied by Charles X (890). The official *Guide* to Windsor of 1837 lists 28 portraits in the room; 7 more have been added in the *Visitants' Guide* of 1840. Queen Victoria's additions brought the number up to 42. From an early date the Waterloo Chamber contained portraits not by Lawrence, such as Nos. 1185, 1086 and 1087; later additions to the room included Nos. 988 and 902, 845, 850, 931, 976 and portraits of the Duke of Brunswick, the Prince of Orange and Von Alten.

scheme but entreated the artist 'to add to the merit of his beautiful portraits that essential one of resemblance. In general his portraits were scarcely a shadow of likeness.'[118] The courtly Lawrence found his sitters universally amiable. The Emperors, the French King and Dauphin, the Pope, the Cardinal and the Archduke, he found them but too gracious and benevolent, their faces and characters alike intelligent, noble and good. At Vienna he had been so courteous to his illustrious patrons that 'If the Empress of Austria made a remark upon a picture she found the next day that it had been attended to.'[119] This ingratiating mentality led inevitably to subtle flattery. Wilkie stated that 'those who knew and could compare the heads he painted with the originals, must have been struck with the liberties he would take in changing and refining the features before him'.[120] On seeing the Waterloo Chamber in June 1835, Sir William Knighton was disappointed 'in the Tone & Coloring of many of Sir Thomas Lawrence's Pictures . . . the Power He had of putting down on Canvass the most unexceptionable part of the Face & still preserving the likeness was very remarkable & hence the pleasure & satisfaction that all His Portraits gave to his employers.'[121] That this is true can be seen if Camuccini's portrait of the Pope or the portraits at Apsley House of the two Emperors by Einsle and Baron Gérard and of the King of Prussia by Herbig are compared with Lawrence's glamorous images.

Lawrence's portraits, as West generously remarked, 'rise to the dignity of history'. Haydon, who once thought Lawrence should have been called '*a Perfumer to his Majesty*', described the 'power that gave an air of fashion to the form and of beauty to the face, which enchanted his sitters & made them think higher of their own perfections'; but to him the Waterloo Gallery was inevitably 'a disjointed failure'. He would have liked something nearer Lady Anne Barnard's original conception, but 'they are seperate pictures . . . it is melancholy to see so total an absence in King & Painter & so little Comprehension of mind'.[122] Another critic had thought the King had erred in entrusting the entire commission to one painter.[123] Nevertheless Lawrence was by temperament one of the comparatively few painters of his time who could have risen with confidence to the challenging occasion offered to him by the Regent at the promptings of Lord Stewart. He created one of the most dazzling sets of portraits in the ancient tradition of the *Hommes Illustres*; and the finest of his Waterloo portraits are among the most brilliantly painted of the Romantic period.

After Lawrence had returned from Rome, George IV continued to bespeak portraits from him; some of them, such as Sir John McMahon, Angerstein, Benjamin West and Kemble as Hamlet, are no longer in the royal collection.[124] He commissioned the portraits of his sisters Mary (879) and Amelia (880); these dashingly painted portraits were for a time in the King's Bedroom at St. James's with Lawrence's portraits of Lady Conyngham and her daughter Maria. George IV's pictures of the two Conyngham girls (*Figs.* XXVI, XXVII) are delightful examples of Lawrence's gayest proto-Victorian manner towards the end of his career. The portrait of Lady Elizabeth is probably the one which Lawrence wanted to place himself at Royal Lodge early one morning before she and her mother came down, 'as its first impression on the spectators is a good deal affected by the situation and light in which it is first view'd'.[125] Prince George of Cumberland (882) was painted in a Sargent-like manner while he was in England in 1828. Canning (887), Sir William Curtis (894), 'the witless Falstaff to a hoary Hall', Devonshire (895), Eldon (896), the young Queen of Portugal (904) and

118. W. T. Whitley, *Art in England 1800–20* (1928), pp. 290–1.
119. Farington, *Diary*, vol. VIII, p. 236.
120. Cunningham, *Wilkie*, vol. III, p. 173.
121. W.R.A., Geo. 51237–8; see also *ibid.*, 51367, for Northcote's view, which Wellington shared, that 'there was no mind – no Character' in Lawrence's portraits.

122. *Diary*, ed. W. B. Pope, vol. III (Cambridge, Mass., 1963), pp. 70, 278, 412, vol. v (*ibid.*), p. 171.
123. *The Library of the Fine Arts*, vol. IV (1832), pp. 107–8.
124. See below, p. 60.
125. W.R.A., Geo. Add. 21, 96 (original at Slane Castle).

Sir Walter Scott (913) were painted for the King at this period. The portrait of Scott has only moved a few feet from where it was first placed by the King in the Corridor at Windsor. In the last year of the lives of the King and his painter Lawrence began the portrait of Wyatville (918) whose personality has left as firm an imprint as Lawrence's on Windsor and the age of the Regency.

In 1802 the Prince had become Patron of the short-lived British School, which had been set up to promote the exhibition and sale of works by British artists, alive or dead. He was successively Vice-Patron, President and Patron of the British Institution, which held its first exhibition in 1806, and he lent generously to its exhibitions.[126] In 1813 the Institution put on a commemorative Reynolds exhibition, the first of its kind ever to be held in England; the Prince lent pictures to the show and attended the inaugural dinner.[127] He talked a great deal about 'advancing the art in this country'. At the Academy dinner in 1811 he spoke of his pride as an Englishman 'that He might with confidence expect that as this country had risen superior to all others in Arms, in military & naval prowess, so it would in Arts'. The year before, he had talked to West of his desire to form a collection of the work of British artists; he was notoriously capricious,[128] but went some way towards making such a collection. In 1810 he bought at the Academy Bird's *Country Choristers* (685). West negotiated the purchase and gave to David Wilkie a commission from the Prince to paint a companion to it: *Blind-Man's-Buff* (1175) which in turn so delighted the Regent that Wilkie was asked to paint a sequel to it. This was the *Penny Wedding* (1176), freer in handling and richer in colour than *Blind-Man's-Buff* and perhaps more evocative of Teniers than of Adriaen van Ostade whose influence is felt in the tonality and the setting of the earlier picture. Wilkie certainly knew the etchings of David Deuchar which include, as well as scenes based on seventeenth-century genre paintings, scenes of peasant life in Scotland designed under their influence;[129] but Wilkie's paintings are more deeply influenced by Dutch and Flemish pictures in the Regency collections. In 1805 Wilkie, the young 'Scottish wonder', had seen pictures by Teniers 'which for clear touching certainly go to the height of human perfection in art'; and in 1807 Lord Mulgrave, discussing pictures which Wilkie had painted for him and Sir George Beaumont, 'believed Wilkie wd. go beyond Teniers, Ostade and all who had preceded Him, as He not only gave exquisitely the ordinary expressions of the human countenance but those of thought & abstraction'.[130] Even the form of Wilkie's signature in the *Penny Wedding*, as well as the crisply painted still-life, are affectionate pastiches of Teniers. There is with George IV, in his admiration of Wilkie considered in relation to his liking for Teniers and Ostade, the same connection in a patron's mind between his favourite earlier painters and his choice of contemporaries for his service as we saw earlier in Charles I's realisation of Van Dyck's debt to *their* mutual favourite, Titian.

George IV continued to admire Wilkie's manner after he had moved from his 'pan and spoon style'. On Wilkie's return in 1828 from his long tour on the Continent, the King bought his two pictures of Roman pilgrims (1177, 1178), which are in a fluent style in which Rubens's influence seems to predominate, and the three pictures (1179–81) of scenes from the Spanish guerrilla campaigns during the Napoleonic war. These three paintings, and the fourth (1182) which George IV commissioned to make up the set, illustrate in clear colour and confident brushwork, and with a vivid sense of romantic excitement, the heroic struggle of the motley personages who had been

126. He lent a number of his English pictures to the British Institution in 1814, 1826 and 1827. The two last exhibitions were made up entirely from his collection. William IV was no less generous in his loans to the B.I.

127. W. T. Whitley, *Art in England 1800–20* (1928), pp. 45–7, 206–7.

128. Farington, *Diary*, vol. II, pp. 233–4, vol. VI, pp. 89–90, 219, 264–5.

129. Deuchar's *Collection of Etchings after the Dutch and Flemish Schools* . . . was published in 1803. I am grateful to Mr. Arthur Marks for drawing my attention to them.

130. Cunningham, *Wilkie*, vol. I, pp. 79, 95, 152–3, 213–14, 267, 268, 289, 295, 298, 442; Farington, *Diary*, vol. IV, p. 101.

at that critical time for the alliance 'the only Continental allies of England'.[131] They are among the earliest illustrations of the interest that British artists and writers were beginning to feel in the art, history and appearance of the Spanish people.

In 1830 Wilkie exhibited at the Royal Academy the picture (1184), on which he had been at work since 1822, of the King entering Holyroodhouse during his visit to Scotland. Considering the time that had elapsed between Wilkie's two principal attacks on the picture, it is an exceedingly successful record, exactly appropriate in mood, of a moment in the famous northern trip by 'Fum the fourth, our royal bird'. In the big full-length (1183) of his patron in the dress he wore at his first Levee in Holyroodhouse, a latter-day Fergus MacIver in splendid new Highland garb, Wilkie provides one of the essential documents for the romantic revival of interest in Highland dress and in the clans whose chiefs had attended Prince Charles Edward Stewart at Holyrood 'sixty years since'.[132] Haydon was forced to admit that Wilkie's intercourse at court, his sittings from the King and his attendance at Levees had affected his old friend, 'though not much'.[133] Although Wilkie succeeded Lawrence as the King's Principal Painter, he was heavily defeated by Shee in the election for the Presidency of the Royal Academy.

George IV's purchase of one dull Northcote (974), the only picture in the royal collection of a Boydell-like quality, is unexpected; but his love of anecdote and fine quality in pictures explains his liking for William Collins and Mulready. Collins admired the technical skill of the Dutch painters so popular at that time, but disapproved strongly of their subjects, so often 'gross, vulgar and filthy'. He compared the tonality and colouring of Wilkie's *Penny Wedding* with Ostade, but praised the 'refined feelings, and exquisite humour' of the characters.[134] This refinement, and an infusion of 'those features which delight either in Nature or Poetry', can be seen in the *Scene on the Coast of Norfolk* (708), which had entranced the Regent at the Royal Academy in 1818 when Collins was all the cry, and the *Prawn Fishers* (709) which the King commissioned in 1824. In Mulready—in *The Wolf and the Lamb* (970), bought by the King in 1820, and the *Interior of an English Cottage* (971), acquired eight years later but closer in tone and design to Wilkie or Ostade—the refinements urged by Collins have acquired an almost Victorian flavour. In 1828 the King made one of his last, and most generous, purchases from a contemporary English painter: *The Mock Election* (829), almost the only picture by Haydon that would have appealed to the King.[135] In the same year Sir Everard Home presented to the King his brother Robert's picture (832) of the King of Oudh receiving tribute. George Place's portrait of the Nawab of Oudh (990) had probably been given to him by Pellegrin Treves. These two pictures would have formed a small Anglo-Indian group, with George III's portrait of the Nawab of the Carnatic (1192) and the picture (870), recently attributed to Tilly Kettle, of the Teshu Lama giving audience.

At the end of his life, when Carlton House had been given up and its furniture removed, and Buckingham Palace was still unfinished, the King spent more of his time at Windsor, at the King's

---

131. Cunningham, *op. cit.*, vol. II, pp. 506–7. When the Spanish pictures were shown to the King, Wilkie was 'pleased by the resemblance remarked to Rembrandt, to Murillo, and Velazquez. Nothing seemed to escape' (*ibid.*, vol. III, pp. 10–11).

132. In 1817 the Regent had become 'Chief of the Highland Society in London'; porters at Carlton House had on occasion been fitted up in Highland dress and the Prince himself had worn it as early as 1789 (information from Mr. A. V. B. Norman).

133. *Diary, op. cit.*, vol. III (1963), pp. 360–1.

134. W. Wilkie Collins, *Memoirs of the Life of William Collins* (1848), vol. I, pp. 112, 134.

135. Other English painters represented in George IV's collection were the amateurs Sir William Elford (770), Sir George Beaumont (656), Olivia Serres (1082, 1083) and John Taylor (1134). In 1827 the King paid £105. for John Harwood's painting of the interior of Henry VII's Chapel; it was sent down to Royal Lodge and is no longer in the collection (W.R.A., Geo. 26772; Jutsham, *Receipts*, f. 225). George IV also owned G. S. Newton's *The Duenna*, signed and dated 1828 ('Carleton Palace', No. 686; measurements given later as 24×20 in.) It was described by Sir Lionel Cust in 1901 as 'a hopeless wreck'.

(or Royal) Lodge as well as at the Castle. Sir Walter Scott saw in 1826 the improvements Wyatville was making at the Castle; some of the paintings he found fine; others, of Queen Charlotte's relations ('ill-coloured, ouran-outang-looking figures . . . in old-fashioned uniforms'), he found droll. In the autumn of 1828 Chantrey and Wilkie spent two days at Windsor helping the King to place pictures and statues.[136] In Wyatville's New Corridor or New Gallery the King placed some of his portraits by Hoppner, Gainsborough and Lawrence; he also presumably planned the sequence of state portraits in St. George's Hall, culminating in a version of his own likeness by Lawrence.[137] To Royal Lodge, he sent down his genre scenes by Bird, Collins, Mulready and Wilkie, many of his sporting pieces by Schwanfelder, Stubbs and Chalon, and family portraits by Stroehling. Lesser sporting pieces, and many of the Moriers, went to Cumberland Lodge.

When Sir William Hamilton, in 1788, had sent a colossal head in marble to George III, he had blamed the King's early education for his inability to appreciate the sublime. The throne, under George III, never became the 'altar of the Graces' as Walpole had described it in 1762.[138] Prejudice, parsimony and ill-health combined to prevent George III from being a generous and perceptive patron, but he helped to assemble one of the largest collections of English pictures in the world and if to them is added the continental pictures he bought, especially those from Consul Smith's collection, he can be accorded a very honourable place in the history of the royal collection. George IV, almost invariably easy and affable to the artists working for him and always ready to discuss artistic matters intelligently, enriched the collection with some of its finest English pictures. In 1824 John Young, Keeper of the British Institution, described him 'as one of the best monarchs this country ever knew, whose consummate taste and munificence has done more for the arts during his short reign, than could have been expected in a century'.[139] At the very end of his reign Peel told Lord Farnborough that the King stood high in the estimation of British artists and was universally admitted to be the greatest patron the arts had ever had in this country.[140] Caprice and a lack of concentration prevented him from composing a truly representative collection of the works of living British artists. No such collection could be complete which contained no picture by Constable or Turner. He would not have cared much for those 'other spirits' who stand apart 'Upon the forehead of the age to come'. His feeling for pictures, as collector and patron, reflected a good deal of 'what the world most prizes Turbans and Crowns and blank regality'. But if we place his British pictures, in our minds, alongside his seventeenth-century Dutch, French and Flemish pictures, if we consider the houses he built and decorated and the furniture and works of art with which he filled them, and if we do justice to his almost flawless and highly imaginative good taste, his position in the history of the royal collection is second only to that held by Charles I.

III. WILLIAM IV

ON 31 January 1794 Hoppner had told Farington that the Prince of Wales exceeded 'beyond comparison his other Brothers in manners'. He found the Duke of Clarence, whom he had already

136. *Journal* of Sir Walter Scott (ed. of 1939), vol. i, p. 252; *The Private Letter-Books of Sir Walter Scott*, ed. W. Partington (1930), p. 157.

137. Millar, p. 31.

138. *The Later Correspondence of George III*, ed. A. Aspinall, vol. i (1962), p. 372. Walpole's Preface to his *Anecdotes of Painting in England*.

139. D. Hall, 'The Tabley House Papers', *Walpole Society*, vol. xxxviii (1962), p. 108. I am grateful to Lt.-Col. J. L. B. Leicester-Warren for enabling me to read this letter *in toto*.

140. Quoted in W. T. Whitley, *Art in England 1821–37* (1930), p. 187.

painted at least twice, 'uncommonly illeterate'. At a sitting the Duke gave him on 22 January 1796, Hoppner observed the Duke's pleasure in 'mortifying' those he was with; but on 22 September 1799 Shee told Farington that he had been surprised to find the Duke 'conversible and well informed', although without taste and 'expressing a dislike to Poetry, and no feeling for painting'.[141] His eldest brother's taste for fine pictures he dismissed, after his own accession, as 'damned expensive'. He was touchingly anxious, even after he had left her, to collect '*all* the pictures of Mrs. Jordan' and he probably owned the large Hoppner (844) of her as the Comic Muse. He had the good fortune to be left by his aunt the full-lengths by Gainsborough (793, 794): 'as they represent the friends of his early youth they may recall . . . some happy days'. He had sat to Lawrence for a full-length (877) not long before his accession, and at the end of 1831 he gave sittings to Wilkie at Brighton for the full-length in Garter robes (1185), which was to be placed in the Waterloo Chamber and had presented Wilkie with the recurrent problem of combining a satisfactory likeness with 'the air of a state picture'. Copies of Wilkie's portrait were made for distribution, but it was Shee who seems to have had the greatest success with the King, who had admired his portrait of Lord Wellesley (1088). Shee had sittings at Brighton in 1833, where he achieved a likeness (1084) which Queen Adelaide said was 'the best by far that had ever been painted of the King'. In 1836 he was summoned to Windsor to paint the Queen (1085) who was insistent that the portrait should not flatter her; despite the difficulties this presented to him, Shee delighted his patrons. Shee was also commissioned to add portraits of Lord Anglesey (1086) and Sir Thomas Picton (1087) to the Waterloo Chamber. Shee enjoyed 'the courtly atmosphere' and had an agreeable time at Windsor; he had at first lodged at the Castle Hotel, but was soon summoned to stay at the Castle 'and form part of the royal circle'. The King and Queen were no less kind to the young George Chambers, who painted two pictures for Queen Adelaide (704, 705) and made a copy (706) for William IV of his picture of the *Capture of Bagur*.

   R. B. Davis was commissioned to paint the long frieze of the King's Coronation procession (728); it is almost a large version in paint of the early Victorian cut-outs or strip-cartoons of royal processions and ceremonies. The King, or more probably his consort, bought *The Orphan* from Sir William Allan. There are glimpses of the future in the King's and Queen's patronage of Stanfield and Landseer. But the King's principal interest, since he had been the 'little blasted seaman' of his brothers' letters, was the sea. He probably collected the sea-pieces which are first recorded at Hampton Court soon after his death, when they may have been taken to the newly-opened palace from Bushy Park;[142] and he commissioned from his Marine Painter, William John Huggins, three enormous canvases of incidents in the battle of Trafalgar (858–60).

IV. QUEEN VICTORIA

ON many ocasions when Queen Victoria's conversations with Lord Melbourne turned back to the days of his youth and his memories of his mother, they talked about painters. Lord Melbourne told the young Queen that her grandfather, 'though accused of the contrary, was excessively fond of the Arts'. They talked of George III's dislike of Reynolds and predilection for West. They had

141. These entries in Farington's *Diary* are unpublished. Seguier told Collins (*Memoirs, op. cit.*, vol. I, p. 340) on 16 July 1830 that 'our new sovereign has great views respecting the Arts'.
142. Among the pictures in this group are those by Cleveley (707), Elliott (772, 773), Paton (980–6), Pocock (991, 992) and J. T. Serres (1080, 1081). No. 657, by R. B. Beechey, had been given to William IV by Sir William Beechey.

much conversation about Cosway's 'sweet, lovely picture' of Melbourne's mother (716) which had belonged to George IV. She heard Lord Melbourne describe Gainsborough as 'a great artist, both in Landscape and Portrait'. After she had hung up the ovals (778–92) in her Audience Room at Windsor ('heads of all the Royal Family when young, and beautifully done'), she discussed them with Melbourne whose eyes filled with tears when he said 'I dare say it pleases them (the Family) your having them (the pictures)'. Princess Augusta had indeed been pleased to see the portraits so honourably displayed: 'it makes a great impression upon old People, who always think they are forgotten, as they generally are'.[143] After the Queen had visited Eton with Lord Melbourne in 1838, he found for her his own leaving portrait by Hoppner (848) which she was 'bold enough to ask Lord Melbourne to allow her to take possession of'.

As a little girl the Queen had sat to Beechey for the portrait (671) with her mother which had almost certainly been painted for her uncle Leopold I, King of the Belgians. In 1844 she received by bequest from Princess Sophia Matilda of Gloucester Beechey's portrait of the Duke of Gloucester (661) and the Reynolds of his Duchess (1015); in 1857 Mary, Duchess of Gloucester, left to the Queen the Beechey of Princess Sophia Matilda (662) with the portrait by Reynolds of the little Princess with a dog (1016). From the same bequest in 1857 came the Brompton (689) of the Duke of York with his friends, twelve years after Lady Holland had left her the version (690) which is perhaps the original of the design. Her uncle Leopold gave her in 1841 the Lawrence of himself (902) which his niece had always wanted.

The devotion felt by the Queen and the Prince Consort for their uncle led to the acquisition of a number of portraits of himself and Princess Charlotte. They owned versions of her portrait, and at least five versions of her husband's, by George Dawe who had captured the 'constant and liberal patronage' of the Coburgs soon after their marriage and had painted the standard portrait of the Queen's father (742, 743). Of Dawe's principal patron, Alexander I, the Queen and Prince Albert owned two portraits (745, 746) and the moving portrait (747) of his widow in mourning. In 1841 the Prince bought a version (749) of Dawe's portrait of his father and the Queen later secured the pretty portrait of her beloved half-sister Feodora (750); Wilkie's brilliant portrait of her half-brother Charles (1189) was probably given to the Queen by her mother. In 1870 the Count of Flanders had a copy painted for the Queen of Lawrence's portrait of Princess Charlotte (925). Leopold I, when he sent over to the Queen in 1845 the copy (1057) of Sanders's portrait of 'poor Aunt Charlotte's Picture', said that it was 'the likest that exists' and 'more Lady like than Mr. Daw's coarse paintings'. In 1843 the Queen acquired the Lawrence (874) of Princess Charlotte with her mother.

As the decoration of Buckingham Palace was completed the Queen arranged some of her family portraits in the State Apartments. By 1841 the two large Van Dyckian groups by Zoffany (1203, 1204) and the Ramsays (996, 997) of George III and Queen Charlotte had been placed in the Throne Room; in the Green Drawing-Room were portraits by Cotes (720), Dance (723), Ramsay (1002) and Copley (712); in the walls of the State Dining-Room were set state portraits by Lawrence (920), Gainsborough (774, 775, 793, 794), Van Loo, Shackleton and Kneller.[144] At a slightly later date the Queen built into the walls of the Principal Staircase the full-lengths of William IV (877) and Queen Adelaide (1085) by Lawrence and Shee, three portraits (743, 752, 755) by or

---

143. *The Girlhood of Queen Victoria*, ed. Lord Esher (1912), vol. II, p. 11; Journal, 23 September, 17 and 30 October, 8 November 1838. At the British Institution in 1833 (27 June) the Queen had admired works by Lawrence, West and Reynolds; at Hampton Court on 27 August 1836 she thought West's

portraits 'pretty' and the big Copley (712) 'very pretty'. She regarded the *Mock Election* (829), when she saw it at Windsor on 25 November 1838, as 'clever, but the colouring not English'.

144. Millar, Nos. 536, 537, 567, 345.

after Dawe, the Lawrence of Prince George (882), the Wilkie of her uncle Sussex (1186), a portrait of her mother by Hayter and the Beecheys (658, 659) of her grandparents.[145] During her widowhood the Queen bought a few earlier English pictures: sketches by Benjamin West (1165, 1166), the Serres of Windsor Bridge (1078) and the charming view of the Long Walk by Gilpin and Marlow (826); but the Prince Consort's death had destroyed all her early enthusiasm for buying pictures.

The Queen and her mother treated kindly her old drawing-master, Richard Westall, who had painted the liveliest portrait of her as a child (1170). Of the painters who had worked for her uncles, she continued to employ R. B. Davis to paint her horses (737, 738) until he was presumably outclassed in her eyes by Francis Grant and Landseer; she gave Shee sittings for a full-length for the Royal Academy. But Wilkie failed disastrously with the new Sovereign. As a little girl she had figured in an unfinished family group (1187). After her accession she recognised him as 'an early friend' and in October 1837 she gave him sittings at Brighton, where he developed his designs for his picture of the Queen's first Council (1188). At first the Queen liked the picture, and so did Lord Melbourne, but within a few months she was vexed that the likenesses were so bad, though she realised that it was a fine picture; by the end of 1847 she thought it 'one of the worst pictures I have ever seen, both as to painting & likenesses'. Wilkie was no more successful with his state portrait (*Fig.* XXVIII) which was shown at the Royal Academy in 1840 and in which he attempted to recapture the grandeur of a Genoese Van Dyck. The Queen thought it 'atrocious' and would have agreed with Melbourne's opinion that Wilkie 'never could paint portraits, and he never will'.[146] He had intended to give the Queen his portrait of the Sultan (1190), but long before he had left on his last journey he had been 'cut out' with the Queen by Hayter.[147]

V. MODERN TIMES

KING Edward VII bought in 1904 one of the best portraits of George IV (664) in the royal collection, was given a picture by Chalon (701) of a spaniel which may have belonged to George IV, and may have been given Singleton's little picture (1091) of the King's marriage. Otherwise his most important addition to the collection was perhaps the large landscape by West (1168) which shows that the painter occasionally relaxed in Windsor Great Park from the strains of preparing canvases for his Chapel. King George V was exceptionally fortunate in being left George Sanders's portrait of Byron (1056). Queen Mary was proud of being a great-granddaughter of George III. Any portrait, whatever its quality and scale or in whatever form it appeared, was of absorbing interest to her if it represented a member of 'the old Royal Family'. Her pleasure in the appearance of a brother or a daughter was enhanced if it reminded her of George III or his children.[148] She never bought a great picture, but could not resist the temptation of buying, for the royal collection, for King George V's collection or for her sons, portraits of her forbears even if the original was already safe in the royal collection. She also bought the very good Cotes of the Duke of Gloucester (719); good Beecheys of William Frederick, Duke of Gloucester (663), and of her grandmother the Duchess of Cambridge (674); a small version of Copley's equestrian *George IV* (711); the only

145. The most interesting of her other acquisitions, recorded in this Catalogue, are the huge Anglo-Indian piece by Casanova (695), the Devis (762) and Stothard (1092), and the Home of Wellington (831).

146. Journal, 4 April 1838.
147. B. R. Haydon, *Diary, op. cit.*, vol. IV (1963), p. 451.
148. J. Pope-Hennessy, *Queen Mary* (1959), p. 46.

Jackson (863) in the collection; a large group by Dawe (748); and one of West's portraits (1146) of the 'old Royal Family' which had escaped from the collection.

More recently King George VI and Queen Elizabeth brought into the collection the two Bromptons of the eldest sons of George III (687, 688) and the charming unfinished Wilkie (1187) of Princess Victoria surrounded by her family. The King was responsible for re-framing Gainsborough's ovals and for hanging them in accordance with the painter's injunctions; he had the same painter's mutilated group (798) of George IV's eldest sisters cleaned and beautifully framed to give him constant pleasure in his Audience Room at Buckingham Palace. Her Majesty the Queen has brought into the collection Marlow's *View of London Bridge* (936) and Zoffany's sketch (1202) for his Van Dyckian royal group. It appears at the moment to be the painter's only surviving oil sketch for one of his conversations.

GENEALOGICAL TABLE

This Table explains the relationship between royal sitters of whom portraits a**
the dates of relevant royal **

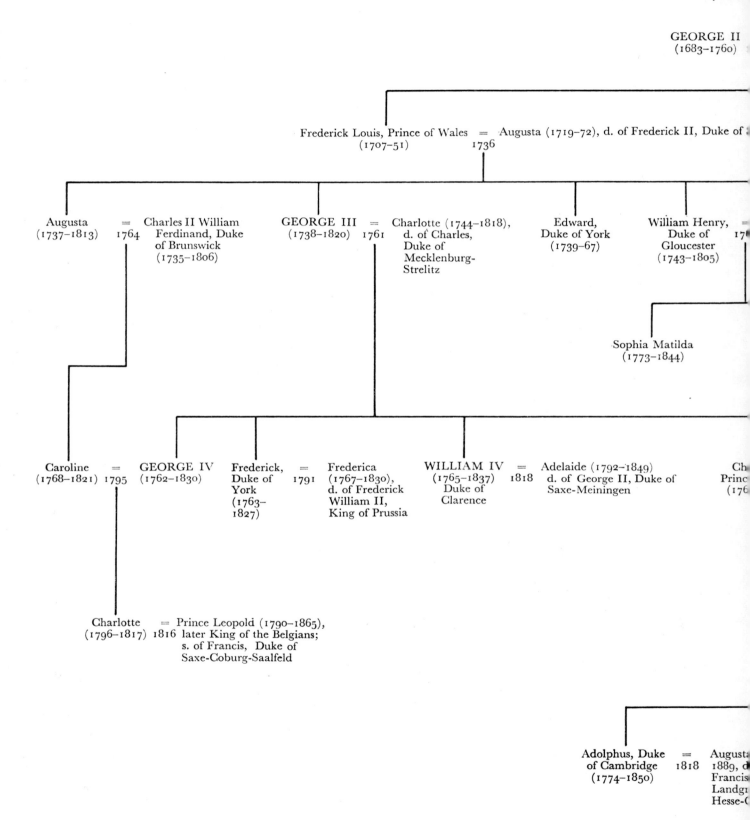

GEORGE II
(1683–1760)

Frederick Louis, Prince of Wales = Augusta (1719–72), d. of Frederick II, Duke of **
(1707–51)   1736

Augusta	=	Charles II William	GEORGE III	=	Charlotte (1744–1818),	Edward,	William Henry,	=
(1737–1813)	1764	Ferdinand, Duke of Brunswick (1735–1806)	(1738–1820)	1761	d. of Charles, Duke of Mecklenburg-Strelitz	Duke of York (1739–67)	Duke of Gloucester (1743–1805)	17

Sophia Matilda
(1773–1844)

Caroline	=	GEORGE IV	Frederick,	=	Frederica	WILLIAM IV	=	Adelaide (1792–1849)	Ch
(1768–1821)	1795	(1762–1830)	Duke of York (1763–1827)	1791	(1767–1830), d. of Frederick William II, King of Prussia	(1765–1837) Duke of Clarence	1818	d. of George II, Duke of Saxe-Meiningen	Princ (176

Charlotte = Prince Leopold (1790–1865),
(1796–1817) 1816 later King of the Belgians;
           s. of Francis, Duke of
           Saxe-Coburg-Saalfeld

Adolphus, Duke = Augusta
of Cambridge   1818 1889, d
(1774–1850)   Francis
                     Landg
                     Hesse-C

e to be found in the Catalogue and provides the dates of their births and deaths;
arriages have also been inserted.

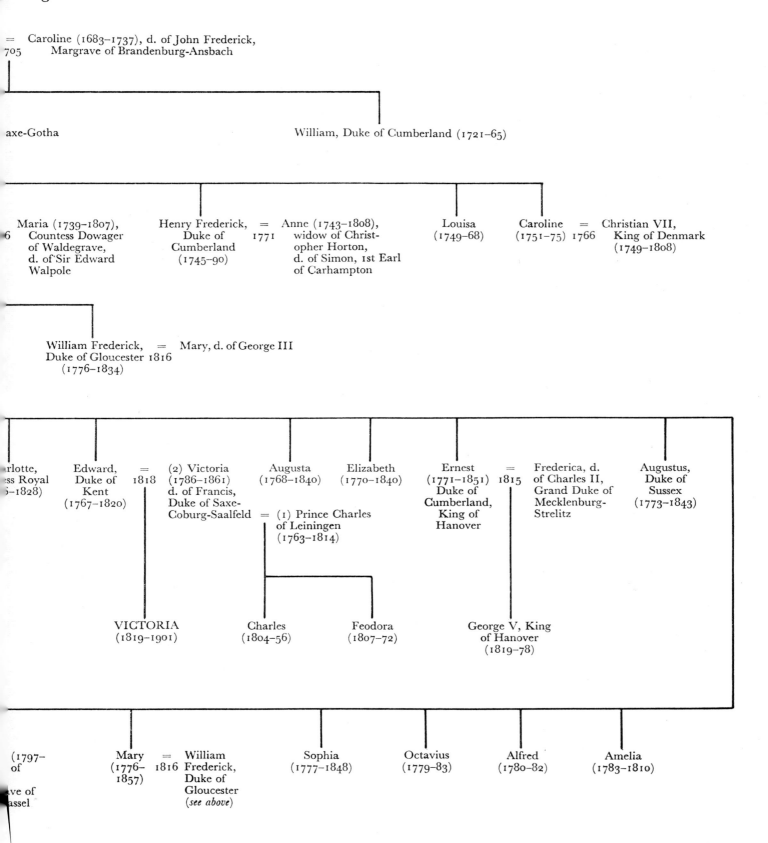

=   Caroline (1683–1737), d. of John Frederick,
705   Margrave of Brandenburg-Ansbach

axe-Gotha   William, Duke of Cumberland (1721–65)

Maria (1739–1807),   Henry Frederick,   =   Anne (1743–1808),   Louisa   Caroline   =   Christian VII,
6   Countess Dowager   Duke of   1771   widow of Christ-   (1749–68)   (1751–75) 1766   King of Denmark
of Waldegrave,   Cumberland   opher Horton,   (1749–1808)
d. of Sir Edward   (1745–90)   d. of Simon, 1st Earl
Walpole   of Carhampton

William Frederick,   =   Mary, d. of George III
Duke of Gloucester 1816
(1776–1834)

rlotte,   Edward,   =   (2) Victoria   Augusta   Elizabeth   Ernest   =   Frederica, d.   Augustus,
ss Royal   Duke of   1818   (1786–1861)   (1768–1840)   (1770–1840)   (1771–1851) 1815   of Charles II,   Duke of
5–1828)   Kent   d. of Francis,   Duke of   Grand Duke of   Sussex
(1767–1820)   Duke of Saxe-   Cumberland,   Mecklenburg-   (1773–1843)
                           Coburg-Saalfeld   =   (1) Prince Charles   King of   Strelitz
                                     of Leiningen   Hanover
                                     (1763–1814)

VICTORIA   Charles   Feodora   George V, King
(1819–1901)   (1804–56)   (1807–72)   of Hanover
                                               (1819–78)

(1797–   Mary   =   William   Sophia   Octavius   Alfred   Amelia
of   (1776–   1816   Frederick,   (1777–1848)   (1779–83)   (1780–82)   (1783–1810)
ve of   1857)   Duke of
assel   Gloucester
                     (*see above*)

BIBLIOGRAPHY

References to specialised art-historical and other works, and isolated references in documentary sources, will be found in the individual entries or groups of entries in the Catalogue. This Bibliography contains only the principal manuscript and printed sources that deal specifically with the growth of the royal collection. It has been considered useful to retain in it an account of the sources which relate to the history of the collection before the accession of George III.

I. INVENTORIES AND OTHER CLOSELY RELATED SOURCES

If the source is referred to in the Catalogue in an abbreviated from, the abbreviation is placed in brackets immediately after the title of the source.

THE TUDORS

1. Inventory of pictures etc. in the collection of Henry VIII in the Palace of Westminster, 1542.

MS. in P.R.O., in Vol. 160 of the Miscellaneous Books of the Augmentation Office. The occasion of the inventory was the appointment in 1542 of Sir Anthony Denny as Keeper of the Palace of Westminster; the inventory was drawn up by the Wardrobe clerk, N. Bristow, and is dated 24 April 1542. Only ff. 53–59, 106 v. and 135 were printed by W. A. Shaw (see below).

2. Inventory of pictures etc. in the collection of Edward VI at Greenwich, Westminster, Hampton Court, Oatlands, Nonesuch, The More, Richmond, Newhall and Bedington.

B.M., Harl. MS. 1419. Taken by virtue of a Commission dated 14 September 1547; only the entries for pictures were printed by Shaw.

3. Inventory of pictures etc. in the collection of Edward VI, 1549–50, at St. James's.

B.M., Harl. MS. 1419. The occasion of this sequel to the inventory of 1547 is obscure.

These three inventories were edited by W. A. Shaw, *Three Inventories of the Years 1542, 1547 and 1549–50 of Pictures in the Collections of Henry VIII & Edward VI* (1937).

An undated Tudor inventory, containing scattered references to pictures and drawn up *c.* 1560 by John Wolde, is among the MSS. at Glynde (see below).

JAMES I

4. Inventory of Anne of Denmark's pictures etc. at Oatlands, 1616.

MS. at Glynde Place, entitled 'An Inventory of her Ma^tyes stuffe in Otelands taken at her Ma^tyes remove in October 1616'.

5. Inventory of Anne of Denmark's pictures etc. at Oatlands, 1617.

MS. at Glynde Place, entitled 'An Inventory of hir Ma^ts owne stuffe in Oatelands taken ye day after remoove from thence being the 7th day of October 1617'.

These MSS., now the property of Mrs. Humphrey Brand, also include a copy of the 1617 inv., apparently made in 1618 and recording alterations and other amendments since October 1617, and miscellaneous notes of the period 1616–28. The MSS. have passed by descent from the Trevor family and should be associated with, and are partly in the hand of, Sir John Trevor, appointed Keeper of Oatlands on 31 August 1603.

CHARLES I

6. List of pictures in the possession of Charles I when Prince of Wales.

MS., probably drawn up *c.* 1624, entitled 'A note of all such pictures as your Highness hath at this present, done by several famous masters' own hands, by the life'; printed from the original in the P.R.O. by W. N. Sainsbury, *Original Unpublished Papers illustrative of the Life of Sir Peter Paul Rubens . . .* (1859), p. 355. The list is stated by Sainsbury to be partly in the hand of Sir Balthazar Gerbier; a copy is in the B.M., Stowe MS. 185, f. 219.

7. Catalogue of the collections of Charles I, drawn up by Abraham van der Doort.

MS. in Bodleian Library, MS. Ashmole 1514, entitled 'A Book of all such the kings Pictures As are by his Maiests. Especiall appoyntment placed at this present time remayning in Whitehall in the Severall . . . placees followeinge'.

Apparently the draft of a catalogue or 'Register' of the royal collections, concerned mainly with Whitehall, but including draft sections dealing with Nonesuch and Greenwich and copious annotations and amendments.

8. Catalogue of the contents of the Cabinet Room at Whitehall.

MS. in Royal Library. A fair copy, drawn up under Van der Doort's surveillance, of the section in MS. Ashmole 1514 that deals with the Cabinet Room.

9. Catalogue of the contents of the Cabinet Room at Whitehall.

MS. in Bodleian Library, MS. Ashmole 1513. A second fair copy, also drawn up under Van der Doort's surveillance, of the contents of the Cabinet Room.

10. Catalogue of the contents of the Chair Room at Whitehall.

B.M., Add. MS. 10112, entitled 'The Booke of the Kings: 40: Pictures and: 12: Statuas placed at this time in the Kings Chare roome . . .'. A fair copy, drawn up under Van der Doort's surveillance, of the section in his MS. that deals with the Chair Room.

These four MSS. (Nos. 7–10 above) were printed, and their relationship discussed, by O. MILLAR, 'Abraham van der Doort's Catalogue of the Collections of Charles I', *Walpole Soc.*, Vol. XXXVII (1960). Van der Doort was probably occupied with his 'Register' from at least 1637; the fair copies were probably written out in 1639; and some of Van der Doort's addenda are dated 1640. Of the copies of Van der Doort's catalogue, the most important is that by George Vertue, B.M., Harl. MS. 4718, probably the basis of the edition printed by William Bathoe in 1757 with an Advertisement by Horace Walpole. The copy made by Vertue for Frederick, Prince of Wales (see below, No. 30), is in the Surveyor's Office.

11. Catalogue of pictures etc. at Whitehall and in the Long Gallery at St. James's.

MS. in the Victoria and Albert Museum, MS. 86.J.13, entitled 'A CATALOGUE OF PICTURS'. Probably compiled in 1640, the MS. may have been written by Sir James Palmer and is not closely dependent on Van der Doort's work. It is printed in O. MILLAR, *op. cit.*

THE COMMONWEALTH

12. Valuations of the goods belonging to the royal family.

MS. in P.R.O., Miscellaneous Exchequer Auditors of Land Revenue, L.R.2, 124.
A resolution had been passed by the House of Commons on 23 March 1649 that the late King's goods should be inventoried, appraised and (a large part of them) sold, and on 4 July 1649 an Act was passed to this effect (*Acts and Ordinances of the Interregnum*, ed. C. H. Firth and R. S. Rait (1911), vol. II, pp. 160–8). Trustees were appointed, including Jan van Belcamp, to make detailed inventories and valuations of all royal goods in all royal residences; they were to make three copies of these 'appraisals' and the L.R. MS. is an almost complete set of original valuations by the Trustees, made between 27 August 1649 and 28 November 1651.

A more complete set of valuations formerly belonged to the Sebright family, but this is now missing; a typescript of it is in the Surveyor's Office.

13. Valuations of royal goods at Oatlands, Windsor, Wimbledon and Somerset House.

MS. in the possession of Lord Methuen at Corsham Court. The third set of original valuations for these parts of the royal collection.

A number of later copies of the valuations, loosely known collectively as the Commonwealth Sale Catalogue, are known. In one, B.M. Harl. MS. 7352, sent by Thomas Coke (see below) to the (2nd?) Earl of Oxford, the names of buyers and the prices they paid for royal goods are inserted. These appear to by reasonably accurate when they are compared with a bundle of original certificates to the Treasurers for the Sale recording the day by day sale of goods between 15 August 1649 and 1 February 1653 (P.R.O., S.P.29/447, 24, 1).
A mass of other material for the Sale is to be found among the State Papers in the P.R.O., *e.g.* in S.P. 28/282–5; 28/350 (9); 29/447,24; and in the S.P. Domestic in the printed *Calendars*.
Valuable documentary material on the formation and dispersal of the collection of Charles I is to be found in: A. LUZIO, *La Galleria dei Gonzaga venduta all'Inghilterra nel 1627–28* (Milan, 1913), and LE COMTE DE COSNAC, *Les Richesses du Palais Mazarin* (Paris, 1884).
The *Diary* of John Evelyn, ed. E. S. de Beer (1955), and the notebooks of Richard Symonds, especially B.M. Egerton MS. 1636, contain references to royal pictures in the hands of dealers and agents in the Interregnum.

THE RESTORATION

14. Declarations of former royal goods to the House of Lords Committee.

MSS. in House of Lords, calendared in H.M.C., *Seventh Report*, part 1 (1876), pp. 88–93.

A Committee of the Lords had been appointed on 9 May 1660 with full powers to recover as much as they could of the royal goods. On 12 May they issued an order that within seven days all in possession of any such goods should bring them to the Committee and between 10 and 28 May they received Declarations from those who held, or knew the whereabouts of, former royal possessions. Transcripts of the House of Lords material by Mr. Francis Needham were given to the Surveyor's Office.

15. Inventory of goods recovered by Colonel William Hawley.

B.M., Add. MS. 17916. The Colonel had been authorised by the Lords' Committee to receive information concerning royal goods, to seize and secure them and to deliver them to Whitehall; the MS. is, at least in part, a register of pictures etc. recovered by him and so delivered, and entries in it are dated between 1 June 1660 and 16 August 1661.

The Commissioners appointed to recover the King's goods were active until at least February 1673; there is material on their activities in the State Papers and in the *Calendar of Treasury Books*. A list of pictures and other works of art handed over by Lord Lisle on 8 and 10 September 1660 is in the National Library of Wales (MS. 6596D, 2nd part) and in the Penshurst MSS. (1160, 14).

THE LATER STUARTS

16. Inventory of Charles II's pictures etc. at Whitehall and Hampton Court.

MS. in Surveyor's Office, in two parts, entitled 'An Inventory of all his Maties Pictures in White-Hall' and 'An Inventory of all his Maties Pictures in Hampton-Court'. Probably drawn up *c.* 1666–7.

The documents dealing with the purchase of pictures by Charles II from William Frizell in 1660 and 1662, and lists of the pictures, are in B.M. Add. MS. 23199, the lists on ff. 28–31; these documents were published and discussed by B. READE, 'William Frizell and the Royal Collection', *Burl. Mag.*, vol. LXXXIX (1947), pp. 70–5.

The gift of pictures to Charles II by the States-General of Holland in November 1660 was discussed by D. MAHON, *ibid.*, vol. XCI (1949), pp. 303–5, 349–50, vol. XCII (1950), pp. 12–18, 238; a volume of engravings was issued in Amsterdam, VARIARUM IMAGINUM A CELEBERRIMIS ARTIFICIBUS PICTARUM CÆLATURÆ ELEGANTISSIMIS TABULIS REPRÆSENTATÆ, *Ipse Picturæ partim . . .* CAROLO II *. . . dono missæ sunt.* See also the exhibition, *Het Nederlandse Geschenk aan Koning Karel II van Engeland 1660*, Rijksmuseum, Amsterdam, 1965; and an unpublished paper, *Sammlung Gerrit und Jan Reynst*, by Fr. E. Reynst (1968).

17. Inventory of Henrietta Maria's goods at Colombes, 1669.

MS. in P.R.O., SP. 78/128, ff. 209–25, entitled, 'An inventory of all the Goods Plate, And Household Stuffe belonging to the late Queene the Kings Mother begun to bee taken att Colombe the last of October 1669, and finished the fifth of November 1669.'

Taken after the Queen's death in August 1669 to assist in establishing Charles II's claim to many of the pictures etc. in her possession. The negotiations were in the hands of Sir Leoline Jenkins, who presumably caused the inv. to be drawn up, and others who had been joined with him in a Commission of 27 September 1669 (*Cal. S.P.Dom.* (*1668–9*), pp. 503–4).

18. Inventory of the goods of James II, when Duke of York, at Culford Hall, 1671, and Whitehall, 1674.

MS. 891 in Bodleian Library. The two sections are entitled 'Goods of his Royall Highnesse the Duke of York at Culford hall in the charge of Maddam Elliott: 23 Octob^r 1671' and 'Goods of his Roy^ll Highnesse . . . in the custody and Charge of Phillip Kinnersley Yeom of his R^ll High^s. wardrobe of Beds: the first of June 1674'.

19. Inventory of James II's pictures in 1688 at Whitehall, Windsor, Hampton Court, and in the custody of the Queen Dowager, Catherine of Braganza, at Somerset House.

B.M., Harl. MS. 1890. An inventory of royal goods entitled 'INVENTORY OF HIS MAJESTYS GOODS 1688'. The first folio is dated 15 February 1688 (o.s.). Pictures and statues etc. occupy ff. 45–89, a section signed by William Chiffinch, Keeper of the King's Closet.

Vertue's copy of this MS. is in the B.M., MS. 15752; this served as the basis for the edition printed for W. Bathoe in 1758.

In the Surveyor's Office is a MS. closely dependent, and probably based, on James II's inv., drawn up in the reign of William III, who appears on f. 40 substituted for James II as the owner of the pictures at Windsor.

20. Inventory of William III's pictures etc. at Kensington, 1697.

B.M., Harl. MS. 7025, ff. 188–94, entitled 'A List of his Majesty's Pictures, as they are now placed in Kensington House. – 1697'.

21. Inventory of William III's pictures etc. at Kensington, 1700, and Hampton Court.

B.M., Harl. MS. 5150, the two sections entitled 'List of His Majesties Pictures as they are now Placed in Kensington House 1700' and 'Pictures in the Kings Private appartm^ts at Hampton-Court'.

References to pictures in William III's collection are scattered throughout the *Journal* of Constantijn Huygens the younger and in invs. of the furnishing of Kensington in 1697 and 1699/1700 (TH. H. LUNSINGH SCHEURLEER, 'Documents on the Furnishing of Kensington House', *Walpole Soc.*, vol. XXXVIII (1962), pp. 15–58).

22. Inventory of Queen Anne's pictures at Kensington, Hampton Court, Windsor, St. James's and Somerset House.

MS. in Surveyor's Office, entitled 'A LIST OF HER MAJESTIES PICTURES IN KENSIGTON HAMPTON COURT AND WINDSOR CASTLE'.

Drawn up by or for Peter Walton, Surveyor and Keeper of the pictures, probably between 1705 and 1710. Copious notes are added, apparently during the Queen's lifetime and probably *c.* 1710–12, by Thomas Coke, Vice-Chamberlain of the Household, recording later movements and rearrangements of the pictures.

An early copy of the section relating to Kensington is in the B.M., MS. 17917; a later copy of the whole is also in the B.M., MS. 20013. A list of pictures at Kensington in Vertue's MSS., B.M. MS. 19027, ff. 12–13, is close to relevant sections of No. 22.

23. Inventory of Queen Anne's pictures.

MS. in Surveyor's Office, entitled 'A list of the Pictures Belonging to the Crown, Taken By Mr. Walton when the Duke of Kent was Lord Chamberlain' [*i.e.*, 1704–10].
An early eighteenth-century MS., based on No. 22, with differences in detail, unaware of Coke's notes, and therefore perhaps derived from a copy of No. 22; on f. 9 v. is a reference to a picture being moved and replaced in 1728.

24. Inventory of Queen Anne's pictures.

MS. in Surveyor's Office, entitled as No. 23. A later eighteenth-century MS., very close to No. 23 and perhaps copied from it.

The MS. was given to Horace Walpole in 1775 by Topham Beauclerk. It contains annotations by Walpole, at one point dated 1776, and longer remarks by him, dated 1783, on the fly-leaves.

THE EARLY GEORGES

25. Inventory of pictures at Somerset House, 1714.

B.M., Add. MS. 19933, entitled 'The Pictures in the Store Rooms at Somerset House October: 28: 1714'. Still to some extent dependent on the numbering established in No. 22.

A list of pictures hanging in the Earl of Oxford's lodgings at St. James's, January 1715, is among the Lothian MSS. at Melbourne Hall (H.M.C., *Cowper MSS.*, vol. III (1889), pp. 112–13).

26. Inventory of pictures etc. at Windsor, 1724.

MS., in P.R.O., L.C.5,202 (ff. 323–33), entitled 'An Inventory of the Goods in the kings Royall Palace at Windsor – taken on ye 2^d Day of May Anno Dom. 1724. by Mrs Anne Marrott'. A perfunctory list, still dependent on No. 22.

27. Inventory of the pictures at Windsor.

MS. in B.M. Reading Room, Press Mark c.119 h.3, entitled 'A List of Pictures in Windsor Castle'. It closely follows Nos. 22 and 26 and appears to be a careless copy of an original inv. of the time of Queen Anne which had been annotated and amended over a number of years, at least up to 1736.

'A Catalogue of the Pictures in the Great Appartment of Windsor Castle', composed by Dr. Derham, Canon of Windsor 1716–35, was lent to Thomas Hearne in May 1733 and is printed in his *Remarks and Collections*, vol. XI, ed. Rev. E. H. SALTER, *Oxford Hist. Soc.*, vol. LXXII (1922), pp. 169–205. A MS. list of pictures at Windsor, of the same period, is in the Surveyor's Office.

28. Inventory of pictures etc. at Kensington, Hampton Court, Windsor and St. James's.

B.M., Stowe MS. 567, entitled 'Royal Pictures at Kensington Hampton Court Windsor & St James's.' MS. in French, probably drawn up early in the reign of George I, probably before 1723.

29. Inventory of George II's pictures at Kensington.

MS. in Surveyor's Office entitled 'A Catalogue taken of the Pictures, which are, in their Majesties Publick, and Private, Lodgings. in the Palace at Kensington.' References occur in the MS. to the removal of pictures in 1736.

30. Inventory of the pictures at Kensington, Hampton Court and Windsor.

MS. in Surveyor's Office, entitled 'The COLLECTIONS of PICTURES PAINTINGS &c. at KENSINGTON HAMPTON-COURT and in the CASTLE of WINDSOR 1750'.

The vol. is one of the three made by George Vertue (perhaps written by an amanuensis) for Frederick, Prince of Wales, apparently in 1750 (*Notebooks*, vol. I, p. 13): '. . . 3d book contain an account I had taken of all the pictures now at the palaces of Kensington. Hampton Court – and Windsor Castle, for all which I had visited and seen purposely by his Highnes order. and also had the assistance of the House-keepers books . . .'

The inv. is in three main sections:

I. 'A Catalogue taken of the Pictures . . . in the Publick and Private Lodgings of the Palace of Kensington. 1732. by Heny Lowman'. The catalogue was, however, made after the death of Queen Caroline in 1737 and was probably only based on the inv. of 1732.

II. 'Extract of an Inventory of his Majesty's Pictures at his Palace of Hampton Court. in the Charge of the Housekeeper 1750'.

III. 'At the Royal Palace and Castle, at Windsor. Pictures in the Appartments Described'. Probably also composed in 1750.

31. Vertue's inventory of the contents of Queen Caroline's Closet at Kensington.

B.M. MS. 15752 is Vertue's original draft (see No. 19), of which the last section is entitled '. . . an account of all the paintings, Limnings Drawings H. Holbein at Kingenton Palace in the Queen's Closet described by G.V. 1745'. This catalogue is printed at the end of Bathoe's edn. of James II's catalogue (1758), but it is stated at the end to have been 'taken at Queen CAROLINE's command, by Mr. VERTUE, in September, 1743'.

It is followed in Bathoe's volume by a short 'CATALOGUE OF THE Principal PICTURES, STATUES, &c. at Kensington Palace'.

In the Surveyor's Office are Horace Walpole's copies of Bathoe's two volumes on the collections of Charles I and James II. They contain annotations by Walpole and, at the end of the 1758 volume, very important addenda to the list of pictures at Kensington. These seem to be of varying dates; one section is dated 2 June 1763.

A volume of miscellaneous papers relating to Kensington Palace is in the B.M., MS. 20101; it contains references to pictures, 1728–61. Queen Caroline's Accounts in the Royal Archives contain a few references to pictures and artists.

The *Notebooks* of George Vertue (see below) contain very numerous references to the royal collection.

FREDERICK, PRINCE OF WALES

There is no formal inv. of the Prince's possessions. Descriptions of his collections are to be found in Vertue's *Notebooks* and lists of some of his pictures etc. in Vertue's miscellaneous papers, B.M. MS. 19027, especially ff. 20–24v. Pictures are mentioned in Sir William Chambers's description (see below) of Kew (1763).

Some of the Prince's payments to artists and craftsmen survive in the Royal Archives, but his expenditure, and that of his wife, is recorded in detail from 1728 onwards in a long series of volumes in the Duchy of Cornwall Office (abbr. as D. of Cornwall MSS).

GEORGE III

32. Inventory of pictures at Windsor.

Nos. 32–6 are in a MS. vol. in the Surveyor's Office, probably all in the same hand, but perhaps not all of the same date.

No. 32 occupies ff.1–29 and is entitled 'A Catalogue of the Pictures in His Majesty's Palace at Windsor taken in the Year 1776'. It is, however, very close indeed to Pote's account of 1749 (see below), or even to No. 30 (III), and probably still records the pictures as they were in the reign of George II or very early in the reign of George III.

33. Inventory of pictures at St. James's.

Occupying ff. 30v.–46 of the above, untitled. (abbr. as Geo. III, *St. James's*). Probably drawn up *c.* 1785.

34. Inventory of pictures at Buckingham House.

Occupying ff. 49–68 of the above, mutilated and untitled (abbr. as Geo. III, *Buck. Ho.*). Probably drawn up *c.* 1790–5; it agrees very closely with a list in the B.M., Add. MS. 6391, which is dated 8 November 1796 and was probably extracted from No. 34.

35. Inventory of pictures at Windsor.

Occupying ff. 69–100 v. of the above, untitled. The account is still close to Pote's of 1768 (see below) but variations from it seem to indicate that No. 35 records the pictures at Windsor *c.* 1780–6. A few pencil notes were added, probably nearer 1790.

36. Inventory of pictures at Hampton Court.

Occupying ff.101v.–135v. of the above, untitled (abbr. as Geo. III, *Hampton Court*). Probably of approximately the same date as No. 35; pencil notes were added slightly later.

37. Inventory of pictures at Kew.

MS. in Surveyor's Office, entitled 'A Catalogue of His Majesty's Pictures at Kew House' (abbr. as Geo. III, *Kew*). Probably drawn up *c.* 1800–5, but with slightly later pencil notes by the compiler of Nos. 47 and 48.

A MS. in the Surveyor's Office, entitled 'A Catalogue of the Pictures at Kew House', is probably a rough draft for No. 37.

38. Inventory of the pictures at Kensington.

MS. in Surveyor's Office, entitled 'A Catalogue of His Majesty's Pictures at Kensington Palace' (abbr. as Geo. III, *Kensington*). Probably drawn up *c.* 1785–90, but with later pencil notes.

39. Removals of pictures.

MS. in Surveyor's Office, entitled 'A Catalogue of Pictures sent from the Queen's Palace, St James's, Kensington & Hampton-Court Palaces, and Kew House, to His Majesty at Windsor Castle. 1804. & 1805' (abbr. as Geo. III, *Removals*).

The title probably only covers ff. 1–14 (except f. 9 v. which records moves on 24 July 1795); certainly ff. 17v.–20 v.

contain a separate list of pictures brought to Buckingham House from St. James's at the time of the fire, 25 January 1809.

40. Francis Legge's lists of pictures at Windsor, 1813, 1816.

MS. in Surveyor's Office in two volumes, the first entitled 'A Catalogue of His Majesty's collection of Paintings in Windsor Castle, according to the present arrangement . . . In two parts. compiled by F.L. 1813'.

The second volume is entitled 'A Catalogue of His Majesty's collection of Paintings in Windsor Castle, according to the present arrangement . . . compiled by F.L. 1816'. Both volumes also include a mass of biographical and other historical matter.

41. Inventory of pictures at Windsor.

Nos. 41 and 42 are in a MS. vol. in the Surveyor's Office, probably all written by the same hand.

No. 41 occupies ff. 84–109 and is entitled 'Now in Windsor Castle. from Mr. Legge's Catalogue'. It is closely based on the second volume of No. 40, but there are slightly later pencil annotations, including a passage on f. 109 which is signed with indecipherable initials.

42. List of pictures etc. bought by George III.

Occupying ff. 61–73 of the above, in three sections.

I. On ff. 61–73, entitled 'Catalogue of Paintings of the Italian School all in fine preservation, and in Carved Gilt Frames in modern & Elegant Taste. Bought by His Majesty in Italy, & now chiefly at Kew'.

II. On ff. 74–80, entitled 'Catalogue of the Flemish & Dutch Schools all in fine Preservation, in new gilt carved Frames. in Elegant Taste'.

III. On ff. 81–3, Addenda and Corrigenda to I and II.

These are the lists generally held to be of the pictures bought by George III with the collection of Consul Smith in 1762, but the lists are not original and must have been compiled from MSS. that are now lost. The Italian section was printed by Sir L. Cust in the *Burl. Mag.*, vol. xxiii (1913), pp. 150–62, 267–76, and the Dutch and Flemish lists by Sir A. Blunt, *Venetian Drawings . . . at Windsor Castle* (1957), pp. 19–23. The reader is also referred to Mrs. Frances Vivian's study of Smith as patron and collector.

The volume of which Nos. 41 and 42 form part also contains, ff. 1–60, a copy of James II's inv. (No. 19 above), probably based on the version of it drawn up in the reign of William III; later notes record collation between this text and the original Harl. MS. 1890 in the B.M.

43. Inventory of the pictures etc. at Kensington, 1818.

MS. in Surveyor's Office, entitled 'Catalogue of the Pictures in the Palace at Kensington. 1818'.

The volume forms, with Nos. 44 and 46, a set of catalogues, uniform in size, form and binding and all written by the same hand; the numbered items in No. 43 run from 1 to 658. Faulkner (see below) states (p. 357) that the catalogue was composed at the command of George, Prince of Wales (the future George IV), who ordered Benjamin West to make a survey of the whole collection. The three volumes should, therefore, be attributed to West in his official capacity as Surveyor of Pictures, a post which he held until his death in 1820, though William Seguier was also concerned at this date with royal catalogues. No. 43 contains later notes, some certainly dating from the reign of William IV.

44. Inventory of the pictures etc. at Buckingham House and St. James's Palace, 1819.

MS. in Surveyor's Office, dated 1819 on the cover, a sequel to No. 43, and entitled (items 659–1010) 'Catalogue of the Pictures at the Late Queens House Saint James's Park' and (for items 1011–1088) 'Catalogue of the Pictures at Saint James's Palace'. Clearly composed after the death of Queen Charlotte on 17 November 1818; in items No. 985–8, however, George III is described as 'His late Majesty', which implies that the catalogue, at least in part, was written after his death on 24 January 1820.

Material on the collection of George III is also to be found in the Royal Archives. In the Royal Library is a set of drawings to scale, indicating the arrangement of pictures on the walls of some of the rooms at Buckingham House early in the reign of George III. A later set of drawings, recording the disposition of pictures in certain rooms at Windsor, is also in the Royal Library.

Among the Cumberland Papers at Windsor is an inv. (Cumberland Papers, vol. I of misc. vols.) of the possessions of William, Duke of Cumberland. It is dated 1765 on a later binding and was presumably drawn up after his death.

GEORGE IV

45. Inventory of pictures etc. at Carlton House, 1816.

MS. in Surveyor's Office, entitled 'A CATALOGUE OF PICTURES, forming the Collection of HIS ROYAL HIGHNESS THE PRINCE-REGENT, in CARLTON-HOUSE. December, 1816'.

Drawn up by Michael Bryan, probably with advice from Sir Thomas Lawrence. In 1817 Bryan submitted an account for £105 'For making sundry Catalogues of the Collection, and for making a valuation of the same, in conjunction with Sir Thomas Lawrence'; the account was settled on 12 August 1819 (W.R.A., Geo. 27003).

Later 'Remarks' in the inv. include notes by Benjamin Jutsham (see below) on subsequent movements of the pic-
tures; many of these notes are dated and were made between 7 June 1817 and 1 November 1830. Jutsham also kept the inv. up to date by adding items 532–604, *i.e.*, up to and including acquisitions in the early part of 1823.

Various other later notes are scattered throughout the MS. Labels, written in the same hand as No. 45, giving the relevant number in the inv. and describing it as the New Catalogue of 1816, were fixed to the back of the pictures recorded in it; many of these labels survive.

46. Inventory of the pictures etc. at Carlton House, 1819.

MS. in Surveyor's Office, entitled 'Catalogue of The Prince Regents Pictures, in Carlton House, June 1819'.

The third of the volumes which made up (see Nos. 43 and 44) the survey initiated by the Regent. The items are numbered from 1 to 550, but there is a later continuation (see below) from 551 to 688.

47. Inventory of the pictures etc. at Carlton House.

MS. in Surveyor's Office, entitled 'CATALOGUE OF HIS MAJESTY'S PICTURES IN CARLETON PALACE'.

Drawn up very soon after the accession of George IV in 1820. It is compiled in very much the same way as No. 46, but the items run continuously from 1 to 688. The compiler of the catalogue added later notes recording movements of pictures etc. up to 1834. No. 47 is written in the same hand as No. 48; they were compiled by William Seguier who in 1820 had succeeded West in the Surveyorship and held the post until his death in 1843. The catalogue probably originally ended at No. 598; the later items are more briefly described but include purchases and movements from at latest May 1826 onwards and the latest entries, though probably all recording pictures belonging to George IV, were added after his death in 1830.[1]

Nos. 46 and 47 are closely connected. Doyne C. Bell,[2] using No. 47, copied the additional items 551–688 from it into No. 46. No. 46 had presumably been completed in June 1819 and very little had been added to it by the original compiler; and Bell seems to have had both texts in front of him in bringing No. 46 into line with No. 47.

Also in the Surveyor's Office is a secondary and untitled MS. drawn up by the same hand as No. 47, of the pictures at Carlton House. It appears to have been written immediately after the death of George IV (26 June 1830) and probably before 5 October 1830.

48. Inventory of the collection of George IV and William IV at Kensington, Buckingham Palace, St. James's, Kew and Hampton Court.

MS. in the Surveyor's Office, entitled 'CATALOGUE OF HIS MAJESTYS PICTURES'. Drawn up by the same hand and in the same form as No. 47 and perhaps complementary to it. The catalogue is divided into six sections:

I. Kensington Palace. Items running from 1 to 658, copied from No. 43 with occasional variations and with later notes recording movements of pictures between 2 October 1828 and 22 September 1838.

II. Buckingham Palace. Items running from 659 to 1010, copied from No. 44, but with later notes recording movements between 14 July 1824 and 17 December 1835.

III. St. James's Palace. Items running from 1011 to 1088, copied from No. 44, but with later notes recording movements between 6 July 1828 and 19 December 1835.

IV. Kew Palace. Items running from 1089 to 1223. Based on No. 37, which contains notes by the compiler of No. 48; later notes record movements between 12 July 1825 and 1835.

V. Hampton Court. Items running from 1224 to 1264, a continuation of the above, but incomplete and perhaps based on an earlier list.

Taken with No. 47 these five sections of No. 48, probably compiled *c*. 1825, provide a reasonably complete inv. of the royal collection with the exception of the pictures at Windsor. In sections I–IV No. 48 perpetuated an official numbering of the pictures; these numbers are still to be seen stamped on the back of royal pictures with the cipher of George IV.

VI. Hampton Court. An independent section, entitled 'Catalogue of His Majesty's Pictures 1835, Beginning in the Kings Guard Chamber, Hampton Court Palace'. Drawn up in the same manner as the remainder of the volume, but more perfunctorily; the inv. may be incomplete. It includes pictures taken to Hampton Court in December 1835, so the date in the title may be deceptive.

There are in the Surveyor's Office two copies of No. 48. The first is entitled 'CATALOGUE OF HER MAJESTY'S PICTURES. COPY 1844'. A pencil note at the beginning of the copy of section VI of No. 48 states that 'This Catalogue was made when the Parliament passed a vote for opening the Palace to the Public'.

The second copy is entitled 'CATALOGUE OF THE KING'S PICTURES. 1834'. The date is misleading as the volume is a complete copy of No. 48 and records events later than 1834.

The papers dealing with the King's debts as a young man, which include many references to pictures and painters, are in the P.R.O., H.O. 73.

There is a great deal of material on George IV's activities as a collector in the Royal Archives. The most important single source for his collections are the day-books (now in the Surveyor's Office) kept by Benjamin Jutsham in which are recorded the daily arrivals at, and despatchings from, Carlton House of works of art of all kinds. There are three volumes.

I. Volume entitled '1806 An Account of Furniture &c Received and Deliver'd By Benjamin Jutsham On Account of His Royal Highness The Prince of Wales at Carlton House' (abbr. as Jutsham, *R/D*). Recording the daily receipt of works of art etc. between 31 December 1806 and 21 June 1816, and the despatch of goods between 7 January 1807 and October 1820. Jutsham clearly had No. 45 at his elbow and annotated it frequently.

II. Volume entitled later 'INVENTORY OF FURNITURE ETC. GEORGE IV' (abbr. as Jutsham, *Receipts*). Recording the daily receipt of works of art etc. between 23 June 1816 and 7 December 1829.

III. Volume untitled (abbr. as Jutsham, *Deliveries*), recording the works of art etc. sent away from Carlton House between 23 October 1820 and 4 February 1830.

A copy was made by John Roberts in 1861 or 1867 of the references to pictures in these volumes; this was lent by Doyne Bell from the Lord Chamberlain's Office to J. Hollis who took another copy, dated 6 March 1875.

---

1. For these invs., see P.R.O., L.C.1/57, 65.

2. An official of the Privy Purse from 1851 to his death in 1888.

A fourth volume by Jutsham in the Surveyor's Office is a record of Privy Purse payments, entitled 'Bills on Account of Privy Purse for Expences of Armory &c' (abbr. as Jutsham, *PP*); it contains a few references to pictures.

Jutsham (*d.* 1836) is recorded as Inspector of Household Deliveries to George IV from 1803 to 1830 and continued until his death to serve William IV in the same capacity.

QUEEN VICTORIA

49. Acquisitions made by Queen Victoria and the Prince Consort.

A set of three MS. volumes in the Surveyor's Office:

I. Volume entitled 'CATALOGUE OF HER MAJESTY'S PRIVATE PICTURES, MINIATURES, ENAMELS &c. &c.' A detailed record of the Queen's acquisitions, whether by gift or purchase, between 1827 and Christmas, 1856.

II. Volume, untitled, continuing the record of the Queen's acquisitions between 1857 and Christmas, 1862.

III. Volume entitled 'List of Pictures presented to or purchased by His Royal Highness Prince Albert'. Drawn up in the same form as Nos. I and II, recording the Prince's acquisitions between 1839 and January 1847.

A fair copy of III was made by Thomas Cockerill in 1845, but only as far as item 188.

50. List of the Prince Consort's pictures at Windsor, 1862.

MS. in Surveyor's Office, entitled 'List of Pictures at Windsor Castle the property of His Royal Highness The Prince Consort—March 1862'.

51. The inventory of pictures in the collection of Queen Victoria.

The great survey in the Surveyor's Office (abbr. as *V.R. inv.*) of the entire royal collection of pictures, initiated by the Prince Consort, carried out by Richard Redgrave as Surveyor and, after 1882, continued by his successor, Sir J. C. Robinson.

The survey involved an accurate description of each picture on a separate sheet, with notes on its history and condition; to each sheet of the original of the survey was affixed a photograph[1] of the picture. Each sheet was signed by the Surveyor and Redgrave's successors continued to annotate and work on his original sheets; the results of Doyne Bell's researches on earlier invs. were added to them;

and the whole survey, with its new series of numberings, is a landmark in the history of the collection and Surveyorship. A copy of the original is also in the Surveyor's Office.

The individual sections of the original survey were made up as follows:

I. Windsor Castle. Nos. 1–1901, on sheets dated between January 1859 and 9 July 1879. The volumes of the copy bear the date 1878.

II. Buckingham Palace. Nos. 1–1643, on sheets dated between 8 October 1850 (*sic.*) and 1 June 1878. The volumes of the copy bear the date 1877.

III. Hampton Court. Nos. 1–1077, on sheets dated between February 1858 and 23 November 1876. The volumes of the copy bear the date 1872.

IV. St. James's Palace. Nos. 1–94, on sheets dated between March 1858 and 4 January 1871. The copy bears the date 1871.

V. Kew. Nos. 1–62. One sheet is dated 4 April 1863, the remainder in 1870; they are still in their original bound volume. There is also a copy in the Surveyor's Office.

VI. Stud Lodge. Nos. 1–27, on sheets dated 1868–9 and still in their original bound volume, dated by Redgrave 29 April 1870.

The format of Redgrave's survey was perpetuated in the following addenda to it:

VII. Holyroodhouse. Nos. 1–67, in their original volume, dated 1884; the entries are signed by Robinson. There is also a copy in the Surveyor's Office.

VIII. A copy of section VI with additional Nos. 28–52. The pictures had, however, by now been moved to Cumberland Lodge and the volume is entitled 'CUMBERLAND LODGE. CATALOGUE. 1896'.

IX. A bound volume of the pictures at Cumberland Lodge in 1896, closely dependent on section VIII.

In the Surveyor's Office is a Register, recording the receipt and removals of works of art belonging to the Crown in two volumes, running from 7 June 1879 to 13 May 1909; up to November 1887 it appears all to be in the hand of Doyne Bell. There is also in the Office a list of loans by the Queen to annual exhibitions of old masters at the R.A., 1870–81. Much material on the royal collection in and since the time of Queen Victoria is to be found in the Queen's Journal, in the Royal Archives, in the P.R.O. (Lord Chamberlain's papers), in the records of the Lord Chamberlain's Office and the Privy Purse, and in the notebooks of Sir George Scharf at the N.P.G.

An inv. of the pictures at Buckingham Palace was prepared for the Lord Chamberlain's Office in 1911 by Messrs. Trollope. A MS. inv. of the pictures at Marlborough House in 1925 is in the Surveyor's Office.

1. These were taken by Thurston Thompson, William Bambridge, William Johnson and E. Kemp.

II. PRINTED BOOKS

I. EARLY ACCOUNTS OF THE ROYAL COLLECTION

The following are the more important early catalogues of royal pictures and accounts of royal palaces containing references to the pictures.

For the Tudor collection, valuable lists of, or references to, works of art in royal palaces, extracted from the journals of distinguished visitors, are printed in:

RYE, W. B. *England as seen by Foreigners* (1865).
The following are also useful: the 'Journey through England and Scotland made by Lupold von Wedel', 1584–5, translated by G. von Bülow, *Trans. Roy. Hist. Soc.*, N.S., vol. IX (1895), pp. 223–70; *Thomas Platter's Travels in England 1599*, translated and ed. C. Williams (1937); 'Diary of the Journey of Philip Julius, Duke of Stettin-Pomerania, through England in the Year 1602', ed. G. von Bülow, *Trans. Roy. Hist. Soc.*, N.S., vol. VI (1892), pp. 1–67; *Queen Elizabeth and some Foreigners*, ed. V. von Klarwill (1928).

FIENNES, Celia. *Journeys through England*, ed. C. Morris (1947).

England in 1710. From the Travels of Z. C. von Uffenbach, trans. and ed. by W. H. Quarrell and Margaret Mare (1934).

DEFOE, D. *A Tour through England and Wales*, 3 vols. (1724–7), ed. G. D. H. Cole, 2 vols. (1928).

VERTUE, G. *Notebooks*, 6 vols. with index vol., *Walpole Soc.* vols. XVIII (1930), XX (1932), XXII (1934), XXIV (1936), XXVI (1938), XXIX (1947), XXX (1955).

BICKHAM, G. *Deliciæ Britannicæ; or, The Curiosities of Kensington, Hampton Court, and Windsor Castle . . .*, 2nd edn. (1742).

POTE, J. *The History and Antiquities of Windsor Castle . . .* (1749); and later editions.

DODSLEY, R. and J. *London and its Environs Described*, 6 vols. (1761).

CHAMBERS, SIR W. *Plans, Elevations, Sections, and Perspective Views of the Gardens and Buildings at Kew . . .* (1763).

WALPOLE, H. *Anecdotes of Painting* (1762–71), ed. J. Dallaway and R. N. Wornum, 3 vols. (1888).
— 'Journals of Visits to Country Seats, &c.', *Walpole Soc.*, vol. XVI (1928), pp. 9–80.

[MARTYN, T.] *The English Connoisseur*, 2 vols. (1766).

A Catalogue of the Pictures, &c. in His Majesty's Royal Apartments, Kensington Palace (1778).

PENNANT, T. *Some Account of London*, 3rd edn. (1793).

LYSONS, D. *The Environs of London . . .*, vol. III (1795), supplementary vol. (1800).

PYNE, W. H. *The History of the Royal Residences*, 3 vols. (1819), severally dedicated to the Queen, the Regent and the Duke of York. The original water-colour drawings for the plates, by such artists as C. Wild, Cattermole and Stephanoff, are in the Royal Library.

FAULKNER, T. *History and Antiquities of Kensington* (1820).

HAZLITT, W. *The Pictures at Windsor Castle* (1823), *Works*, ed. A. R. Waller and A. Glover, vol. IX (1903).

British Galleries of Art (1824).

WESTMACOTT, C. M. *British Galleries of Painting and Sculpture, . . .* (1824).

PASSAVANT, J. D. *Kunstreise durch England und Belgien* (Frankfurt-am-Main, 1833).

WAAGEN, G. F. *Works of Art and Artists in England*, 3 vols. (1838).
— *Treasures of Art in Great Britain*, 3 vols. (1854).
— *Galleries and Cabinets of Art in Great Britain* (1857).

JESSE, E. *A Summer's Day at Hampton Court . . . with an Illustrative Catalogue of the Pictures* (1839).

The Royal Gallery of Pictures, being a Selection of The Cabinet Paintings in Her Majesty's Private Collection at Buckingham Palace, published under the superintendence of John Linnell (1840).

[SEGUIER, W.] *Catalogue of Her Majesty's Pictures in Buckingham Palace* (1841).

JAMESON, MRS. *A Handbook to the Public Galleries of Art in and near London*, 2 vols. (1842).

A Descriptive Catalogue of the Pictures, Busts, Bronzes, &c. in the Corridor of Windsor Castle (1843).

A Descriptive Catalogue of the Pictures, . . . deposited in the Corridor of Windsor Castle (1845).

WAAGEN, G. F. *Descriptive Catalogue of a Collection of Byzantine, early Italian – German – and Flemish Pictures, belonging to His Serene Highness Prince Louis D'Ottingen Wallerstein* (1848).
— *Descriptive Catalogue of a Collection of Byzantine, early Italian, German, and Flemish Pictures, belonging to His Royal Highness Prince Albert . . .* (1854).

NASH, J. *Views of the Interior and Exterior of Windsor Castle* (1848). Some of the original water-colours survive in the Royal Library; those by, for example, Haghe, D. Morrison and J. Roberts illustrate pictures hanging on the walls of the interiors.[1]

---

1. Nineteenth-century photographs of royal interiors are a useful source; photographic illustrations were published, for example, by Disderi in *Windsor Castle* (1867) and B. B. Woodward, *Windsor Castle Picturesque and Descriptive* (1870).

GRUNDY, J. *The Stranger's Guide to Hampton Court Palace and Gardens* (1849).

UWINS, T. *Catalogue of The Pictures in Her Majesty's Gallery at Buckingham Palace, . . .* (1852).

LAW, E. *The History of Hampton Court Palace*, 3 vols. (1888–91).

HOPE, W. H. St. John. *Windsor Castle, An Architectural History*, 2 vols. (1913).

CUST, Sir L. *Notes on Pictures in the Royal Collection* (1911). Reprint of *Notes* i–xx on royal pictures published in the *Burlington Magazine*; Cust later published, up to 1918, a further twenty *Notes* in the same periodical.

SMITH, H. Clifford. *Buckingham Palace* (1930).

II. LATER CATALOGUES OF THE ROYAL COLLECTION

Catalogue of the Paintings, Sculpture, and other Works of Art, at Osborne (1876); a *Handbook* to Osborne, with a catalogue of the pictures, by A. I. Durrant (n.d.) was published in the reign of Edward VII.

[COLE, A. S.] *A Catalogue of the Works of Art at Marlborough House . . . and at Sandringham Norfolk belonging to Their Royal Highnesses the Prince and Princess of Wales* (1877).

LAW, E. *A Historical Catalogue of the Pictures in the Royal Collection at Hampton Court . . .* (1881).

[ROBINSON, SIR J. C.] *Catalogue of the Pictures in Her Majesty's Gallery and the State Rooms at Buckingham Palace* (1885).

Catalogue of Pictures in State Rooms, St. James's Palace (1894).

LAW, E. *The Royal Gallery of Hampton Court* (1898). This is very close in detail to Law's volume of 1881; thereafter Law produced a volume of illustrations, *Masterpieces of the Royal Gallery of Hampton Court* (1904) and a succession of official Guides to the Palace which include lists of the pictures (*e.g.*, in 1882, 1907, 1908, 1925, 1926, 1927).

LOGAN, Mary. *Guide to the Italian Pictures at Hampton Court* (1894).

LAW, E. *Kensington Palace . . . an Historical Guide . . .* (1899). Revised editions appeared in 1903, 1907 and 1926 and the material on pictures was incorporated into the author's Guide to *The London Museum at Kensington Palace . . .* (1912).

[CUST, Sir L.] *Catalogue of Paintings and Drawings in Buckingham Palace*, privately printed (1909).

Guide to . . . Windsor Castle, privately printed (1903), later revisions issued in 1906, 1907 and 1909.

CARTWRIGHT, Julia (Mrs. ADY). *Hampton Court* (1910).

Catalogue Raisonné of the Pictures in the possession of King George V in the Picture Gallery and the Royal Closet and on the Chapel Stairs at Buckingham Palace, privately printed (1920).

KONODY, P. G., CONWAY, Sir M., CUST, Sir L. *The King's Pictures*, 3 vols. (n.d., *temp.* George V).

Catalogue Raisonné of the Pictures in the possession of King George V in the State Apartments and Principal Private Apartments at Windsor Castle (1922).

LAW, E. *Kew Palace Illustrated, A Popular Guide . . . with a Catalogue of the Pictures* (1924).

BAKER, C. H. COLLINS. *Catalogue of the Pictures at Hampton Court* (1929).

— *Catalogue of the Principal Pictures in the Royal Collection at Windsor Castle* (1937).

Exhibition of The King's Pictures, R.A. (1946–7), with illustrated souvenir.

MILLAR, O. *The Tudor, Stuart and Early Georgian Pictures in the Collection of H.M. The Queen* (1963).

LEVEY, M. *The Later Italian Pictures in the Collection of H.M. The Queen* (1964).

I have made no attempt to list the more ephemeral Guide-Books to the royal palaces which have been issued from the eighteenth century to the present day and often contain lists of pictures. They are, on the whole, very unreliable compared with the inventories and should be used with caution. Miss Olwen Hedley compiled an invaluable check-list of the Windsor Guides issued in the eighteenth and nineteenth centuries.

Since 1962 catalogues issued of exhibitions in the Queen's Gallery, Buckingham Palace, have contained detailed information on aspects of the collection, especially: *Royal Children* (1963), *Italian Art* (1964), *George IV and the Arts of France* (1966), *Animal Painting* (1966–7), *Royal Review of the British Soldier* (1967–8), and *Van Dyck* (1968–9).

ABBREVIATIONS

Where an inventory is listed, a reference is given to the numbered description of inventories on pp. xlv–lii above.

Binyon	L. Binyon, *Drawings by British Artists of Foreign Origin working in Great Britain, in the British Museum* (1898–1907).
B.M.	British Museum.
Buckingham Palace, 1841, 1852, 1909, 1920	See the printed catalogues listed above, above, pp. liii–iv, under these dates
Burl. Mag.	*The Burlington Magazine.*
Carlton House, 1816	Inventory No. 45.
'Carleton Palace'	Inventory No. 47.
Chaloner Smith	J. Chaloner Smith, *British Mezzotinto Portraits,* 4 vols. (1878–83).
Collins Baker, *Hampton Court*	C. H. Collins Baker, *Catalogue of the Pictures at Hampton Court* (1929).
— *Windsor*	— *Catalogue of the Principal Pictures in the Royal Collection at Windsor Castle* (1937).
Correspondence of George, Prince of Wales	*The Correspondence of George, Prince of Wales,* ed. A. Aspinall, vols. I–V (1963–8).
Cunningham	A. Cunningham, *The Lives of the most Eminent British Painters* (1829–30), ed. and continued by Mrs. C. Heaton, 3 vols. (1879–80).
— *Wilkie*	— *The Life of Sir David Wilkie,* 3 vols. (1843).
D. of Cornwall MSS.	MSS. in the Duchy of Cornwall Office, see above p. xlix.
Eng.	Engraved.
Exh.	Exhibited.
Farington, *Diary*	Joseph Farington, *The Farington Diary,* ed. Sir J. Greig, 8 vols. (1923–8). Greig's edition is far from complete. The MS. of the entire diary is in the Royal Library.
Faulkner	T. Faulkner, *History and Antiquities of Kensington* (1820).
Galt	J. Galt, *The Life, Studies and Works of Benjamin West, Esq.* (1820).
Garlick, *Lawrence*	K. Garlick, *Sir Thomas Lawrence* (1954).
— *Catalogue*	— 'A Catalogue of the Paintings, Drawings and Pastels of Sir Thomas Lawrence', *Walpole Society,* vol. XXXIX (1964).
Geo. III, *Buck. Ho.*	Inventory No. 34.
— *Hampton Court*	Inventory No. 36.
— *Kensington*	Inventory No. 38.
— *Kew*	Inventory No. 37.
— *Removals*	Inventory No. 39.
— *St. James's*	Inventory No. 33.

Gilbey	Sir W. Gilbey, *Life of George Stubbs, R.A.* (1898).
Graves and Cronin	A. Graves and W. V. Cronin, *A History of the Works of Sir Joshua Reynolds,* 4 vols. (1899–1901).
Mrs. Jameson	Mrs. Jameson, *A Handbook to the Public Galleries of Art in and near London,* 2 vols. (1842).
Jutsham, *Deliveries*	Benjamin Jutsham's book of Deliveries, see p. li.
— *PP*	— book of Privy Purse Payments, see p. lii.
— *R/D*	— book of Receipts and Deliveries, see p. li.
— *Receipts*	— book of Receipts, see p. li.
Law, 1881, 1898	E. Law, *An Historical Catalogue of the Pictures in the Royal Collection at Hampton Court . . .* (1881) and *The Royal Gallery of Hampton Court* (1898).
— *Kensington*	— *Kensington Palace* (1899, 1903 etc.).
Leslie and Taylor	C. R. Leslie and T. Taylor, *Life and Times of Sir Joshua Reynolds,* 2 vols. (1865).
Letters of George IV	*The Letters of King George IV,* ed. A. Aspinall, 3 vols. (1938).
Levey	M. Levey, *The Later Italian Pictures in the Collection of H.M. The Queen* (1964).
McKay and Roberts	W. McKay and W. Roberts, *John Hoppner R.A.* (1909).
Manners and Williamson	Lady V. Manners and G. C. Williamson, *John Zoffany, R.A.* (1920).
Millar	O. Millar, *The Tudor, Stuart and Early Georgian Pictures in the Collection of H.M. The Queen* (1963).
Oppé	A. P. Oppé, *English Drawings . . . at Windsor Castle* (1950).
P.R.O.	Public Record Office.
Pyne	W. H. Pyne, *The History of the Royal Residences,* 3 vols. (1819).
Queen's House, 1819	Inventory No. 44.
R.A., *King's Pictures*	Royal Academy, *Exhibition of The King's Pictures* (1946–7).
Roberts	W. Roberts, *Sir William Beechey, R.A.* (1907)
Shaw Sparrow	W. Shaw Sparrow, *George Stubbs and Ben Marshall* (1929).
— *Sporting Artists*	— *British Sporting Artists* (1922).
V. & A.	Victoria and Albert Museum.

V. & A., *Cuttings* — *Cuttings from English Newspapers*, 7 vols., in the library of the Victoria and Albert Museum.

V.R. inv. Inventory No. 51.

Waagen (1838) G. F. Waagen, *Works of Art and Artists in England*, 3 vols. (1838).

— (1854) — *Treasures of Art in Great Britain*, 3 vols. (1854).

Walpole, *Anecdotes* H. Walpole, *Anecdotes of Painting*, ed. J. Dallaway and R. N. Wornum, 3 vols. (1888); vol. V, ed. F. W. Hilles and P. B. Daghlian (Yale University Press, 1937).

— *Visits* — 'Journals of Visits to Country Seats, &c.', *Walpole Soc.*, vol. XVI (1928), pp. 9–80.

Waterhouse, *Check List* E. K. Waterhouse, 'Preliminary Check List of Portraits by Thomas Gainsborough', *Walpole Society*, vol. XXXIII (1953).

— *Gainsborough* — *Gainsborough* (1958).

— *Painting in Britain* — *Painting in Britain 1530 to 1790* (1953).

— *Reynolds* — *Reynolds* (1941).

Whitley, *Gainsborough* W. T. Whitley, *Thomas Gainsborough* (1915).

Williams D. E. Williams, *The Life and Correspondence of Sir Thomas Lawrence*, 2 vols. (1831).

W.R.A., Geo. Georgian Papers in the Royal Archives at Windsor.

CATALOGUE

CATALOGUE

Jacques-Laurent Agasse

1767–1849. Swiss, born in Geneva; painter of animal subjects, portraits and scenes of town and country life; studied in Paris under David and Horace Vernet. He exhibited at the Royal Academy between 1801 and 1845.

He may have been introduced to George IV by Lord Heathfield (No. 650) or George Pitt, 2nd Lord Rivers (1751–1828). Agasse's account for pictures painted for the King includes, under 1827, one hundred guineas 'For a Portrait of Lord Rivers' (W.R.A., Geo. 26557; Agasse's receipt is dated 23 January 1829; the total payment also appears in W.R.A., Geo. 35791). This may have been the portrait of Lord Rivers which was engraved in 1827 by J. Porter. Portraits of Lord Rivers by Agasse are at Bramham Park, Hinton St. Mary and in the Musée d'Art et d'Histoire, Geneva. A set of paintings of animals by Agasse, sold at Sotheby's on 7 April 1965 (188–95), included one of tiger cubs inscribed as bred at Windsor in October 1824.

650. FRANCIS AUGUSTUS ELIOTT, SECOND BARON HEATHFIELD (1750–1813)

Windsor Castle (1412). 50⅜×41 in., 128×104 cm.

Riding on a roan horse, followed by a groom in livery.

In the collection of George IV. In March 1814 it was received at Carlton House from Lord Heathfield's nephew, Augustus Eliott-Fuller (Jutsham, *R/D*, f. 287: '. . . Portrait of The Late Lord Heathfield on Horseback—painted by Mʳ Agass—in a Rich Gilt Frame—the Frame made by Mʳ Smith'). Recorded in store at Carlton House in 1816 (381); sent to the King's Lodge on 31 May 1822 (Jutsham, *Deliveries*, f. 33).

Agasse painted a number of versions of this subject. The first was presumably the one exhibited at the Royal Academy in 1811 (529). In his 'Livre de Vérité' (Musée d'Art et d'Histoire, Geneva), three copies he had made of the portrait are recorded by Agasse under 15 January 1813, 15 May 1813 and 8 February 1814. Four versions do in fact survive: No. 650; a signed version which has passed by descent to Sir George Tapps-Gervis-Meyrick and is at Bodorgan (J. Steegman, *A Survey of Portraits in Welsh Houses*, vol. I (1957), p. 5); a very good signed version, on the art-market in London in 1952 and now in the Musée d'Art et d'Histoire; and an unsigned version, belonging to the Gottfried Keller Foundation and on loan (1967) to the Musée des Beaux-Arts at Lucerne.[1] The version shown at the Royal Academy in 1811 was probably the version at Bodorgan or the one at Geneva. No. 650 seems certainly to be by Agasse himself and his name is inscribed in a contemporary hand on the stretcher.

General, 1808, A.D.C. to the King, 1788–93, and Lord of the Bedchamber, 1812–13.

1. I am very grateful to Miss Renée Loche for consulting the 'Livre de Vérité' on my behalf.

651. THE NUBIAN GIRAFFE (*Plate* 284)

50⅛×40 in., 127,3×102 cm.

Signed: *JLA*

The giraffe is standing in a paddock near a shed. With it are the two Egyptian cows (see below), the two Arab keepers and Edward Cross.

Painted for George IV; recorded in the inventory of 'Carleton Palace' (643: 'Portrait of the Giraffe'); later at Windsor (1111). Lent to the Zoological Gardens in 1924.

Literature: R. Lydekker, 'On Old Pictures of Giraffes and Zebras', *Proceedings of . . . the Zoological Society of London* (1904, vol. II), pp. 339–42; B. Laufer, *The Giraffe in History and Art* (Chicago, 1928), p. 89; B. Taylor, *Animal Painting in England* (1955), pp. 36, 53; Arts Council, *The Romantic Movement*, 1959 (8); L. S. Lambourne, 'A Giraffe for George IV', *Country Life*, vol. CXXXVIII (1965), pp. 1498–1502; Detroit and Philadelphia, *Romantic Art in Britain*, 1968 (103).

Painted for George IV in October 1827. Agasse's account includes, under that year, two hundred guineas 'For a Picture of the Giraffe & Keepers. By command', and £18.17s. for the frame; his receipt is dated 23 January 1829 (W.R.A., Geo. 26557). In his 'Livre de Vérité' (Musée d'Art et d'Histoire, Geneva) Agasse records the picture under October 1827 and mentions a copy of it measuring 21×17 in.

In 1826 the giraffe had been captured when young with its brother on the plains of Senaar in the Sudan by some troops of Mehemet Ali, Pasha of Egypt. Having shot the calves' mother, they carried them back to Cairo, a journey of forty-five days, lashed to the backs of camels. The larger of the two creatures was presented by the Pasha to Charles X of France. The smaller was given to George IV and arrived at Waterloo Bridge on 11 August 1827; he had travelled from Alexandria to Malta, stayed there six months and sailed to England on the *Penelope*. He had travelled in company with his two Arab keepers and the 'two Egyptian cows (we believe in the character of wet nurses)'. On 13 August the party was taken by caravan to Windsor, where George IV was delighted with his present and constructed for it a spacious paddock in the menagerie at Sandpit Gate. A bill for eleven guineas to its keeper, William Mayor, covering the period 11 August to 26 October 1827, is at Windsor (W.R.A., Geo. 25593). The giraffe had, however, been seriously weakened by its long journey after capture and lost the use of its legs; an elaborate pulley was made for it by Mr. Bittlestone to enable it to stand up, but, in the summer or autumn of 1829, it died. The skin, stuffed by Gould and Tomkins, was given to the Zoological Society by William IV. When the Society's museum was dispersed in 1855, the stuffed skin was acquired by Dr. Crisp (L. S. Lambourne, *loc. cit.*). See Nos. 739, 1233.

Edward Cross was an importer of, and dealer in, foreign birds and beasts at the Royal Menagerie, Exeter 'Change. From 1824 onwards (and perhaps earlier) he had supplied

3

George IV with specimens. His account for work for the King, 1825–30, includes £100 for superintending the animals and birds at Virginia Water and Bears Rails; for superintending the menagerie at Sandpit Gate; for supervising the arrival of the giraffe, its journey to Cumberland Lodge and the construction and application of its steel support; and for staying with the giraffe for nearly six weeks during the period it remained out of doors (W.R.A., Geo. 25624–5). When Exeter 'Change was pulled down, Cross moved his animals first to the King's Mews in Charing Cross and then, in 1831, to the Surrey Gardens.

652. WHITE-TAILED GNUS (*Plate* 286)

50¼ × 40 in., 127,6 × 102 cm.

Signed: *JLA*.

Two animals standing in the foreground with a third lying down behind them. In the distance is a herd of them and, further away, a herd of zebras.

Painted for George IV; recorded at Windsor (1106) in 1879 (*V.R. inv.*). Lent to the Zoological Gardens in 1924.

Painted for George IV in September 1828. Agasse's account includes under September 1828 one hundred guineas 'For a Picture of the Gnus by command', and £18. 17s. for the frame; his receipt is dated 23 January 1829 (W.R.A., Geo. 26557). In his 'Livre de Vérité' (Musée d'Art et d'Histoire, Geneva) Agasse records the picture under September 1828. The account by Edward Cross (see No. 651) for his work for George IV (W.R.A., Geo. 25624–5) includes the money involved in fetching two gnus and a zebra from the *Slaney*, lying at Woolwich, and conveying them to Windsor by caravans early in June 1827; Cross also paid twelve shillings to the farrier who dressed the feet of the animals. In January 1828 a third gnu was secured. In No. 652 the animals are seen in spacious English country, probably the part of Windsor Great Park in which the gnus and zebras were kept.

Sir William Allan

1782–1850. Painter of historical and genre scenes, born in Edinburgh. President of the Royal Scottish Academy, 1838–50, and Wilkie's successor as Limner to the Queen in Scotland. He was a much-loved member of Sir Walter Scott's circle. He travelled in Russia as a young man and later in Asia Minor and on the Continent.

653. THE ORPHAN (*Plate* 283)

Buckingham Palace. Panel: 33½ × 28½ in., 85,7 × 72,4 cm.

Signed and dated: *William Allan Pinxt 1834*

In Sir Walter Scott's dining-room at Abbotsford, a girl (perhaps his daughter Anne (1803–33)) seated in deep mourning by Scott's empty chair, which stands beside a table on which his breakfast (?) is set out; a butler in black approaches with a tea-cup on a silver tray. There are portraits over the fireplace, Oriental armour in the corner and books and an Oriental vase in the foreground.

Recorded in the Picture Gallery at Buckingham Palace in 1841 (50: *V.R. inv.* (1876), No. 414), when it was stated to have been bought from the painter by William IV. In the *Athenaeum* (1850), p. 241, it is said, however, that Queen Adelaide had purchased it at the Royal Academy.

Exhibited at the Royal Academy in 1834 (169). On the back of the panel is a label by Allan: 'No 1 *The Orphan* / "Through the shadowy past / Like a Tomb-searcher, Memory ran, /

Lifting each shroud that time had cast / O'er buried hopes". / William Allan / 8 Scotland Street, Edin.' In August 1832, feeling that Scott's death was near and that Abbotsford might undergo changes, Lockhart had invited Allan to record the apartments as they had been when Scott lived in them. He executed a series of 'beautiful drawings, which may probably be engraved hereafter' (*Memoirs of the Life of Sir Walter Scott, Bart.*, vol. VII (1838), p. 393). Scott died on 21 September 1832. Some of Allan's drawings were engraved for Lockhart, but these drawings do not include one of the breakfast-room (National Gallery of Scotland, D.2700, 2704–6). Dr. James Corson states that the room is the dining-room, and not the breakfast-room at Abbotsford, despite the entry in the catalogue of 1841 (see above); but that the architectural details are inaccurately rendered. The figure of a girl does not apparently bear much resemblance to Anne Scott, but she is close in appearance to the figure of Anne Scott in Allan's picture (1844) of her with her father (Haddo). The chain-mail (which is still at Abbotsford) appears in Allan's sketch (1831) at Abbotsford of Scott in his study.

Thomas Beach

1738–1806. Portrait-painter. A pupil of Sir Joshua Reynolds, he worked for a time in Bath. He exhibited at the Society of Artists, 1772–83, and at the Royal Academy, 1785–97. In 1797 he showed (470) a portrait of the Prince of Wales, which is presumably the portrait at Breamore House, stated to have been given to the Prince's Equerry, Treasurer, and close friend, General (later Field-Marshal Sir Samuel) Hulse.

654. GEORGE HANGER, FOURTH LORD COLERAINE (1751–1824) (*Plate* 138)

Windsor Castle (778). 30 × 25 in., 76,2 × 63,5 cm.

Signed: *T. Beach p:*

Head and shoulders in the green uniform and feathered shako of Tarleton's Light Dragoons.

Presumably painted for George IV: recorded in store at Carlton House in 1816 (328: 'A half length of Major Hanger, now Lord Coleraine. Mr Beech'; the 1816 label is on the stretcher); taken to Windsor in April 1829.

Probably painted in 1782–3, when Hanger was a Major in Tarleton's regiment; his uniform is almost exactly identical with Colonel Tarleton's in Reynolds's portrait of 1782 in the National Gallery (5985).

Soldier and eccentric. He held a commission in the 1st Foot Guards, 1771–6, and served in the Hessian Jäger corps in America; he was imprisoned in the King's Bench for debt, 1798–9, and at one time traded as a coal-merchant. He sedulously refused to assume the title which he inherited in 1814. He was among the Prince of Wales's gay companions, 'but as the Prince advanced in life the eccentric manners of the Colonel became somewhat too free and coarse for the Royal taste'.

655. SIR RICHARD EDWARDS (*d.* 1794)

Windsor Castle (297). 30 × 25¼ in., 76,2 × 64,1 cm.

Head and shoulders in a painted oval, wearing a naval Captain's full-dress uniform.

In the collection of George IV; recorded in store at Carlton House in 1816 (292: 'A head of Admiral Edwards. Mr Beech'; Benjamin

Jutsham added under Beach's name in this inv.: 'Sir Joshua Reynolds', and in the inv. of 1819 the portrait appears (305) as by Reynolds); removed to the New Gallery at Windsor in May 1828.

It is tempting to associate with No. 655 an entry in Simpson's bill, under 5 March 1811, of five guineas 'To a ¾ Port: of the late Admiral Edwards' (W.R.A., Geo. 27830): an entry which may refer to the cleaning and restoration, but also possibly to the acquisition, of a portrait. In the *Catalogues* (1843, 1845) of the pictures in the Corridor at Windsor a suggestion was made that the sitter was Admiral Philips Cosby (1727(?)–1808) who commanded a squadron in the Mediterranean, 1785–9, and ended his career as Admiral of the White. Nathaniel Dance's portrait (1780) of Admiral Edwards in the National Maritime Museum, however, is conclusively of the same person as No. 654, which was painted presumably before Edwards became a flag officer in 1779; he had become a Captain in 1753. The attribution in 1816 to Beach is a reasonable one, though the portrait was clearly painted much under the influence of Reynolds.

Sir Richard Edwards, Commander-in-Chief in Newfoundland and at the Nore.

Sir George Beaumont

1753–1827. Famous as a collector and as a patron of writers and painters; amateur landscape painter.

656. A LANDSCAPE WITH FIGURES (*Plate* 259)

Windsor Castle (1129). 30½ × 25½ in., 77,5 × 64,8 cm.

Inscribed on the stretcher, probably by the artist: *Painted at Dunmow 1812* / [*Exhibited*] *1813. G. Beaumont* (initials in monogram).

A man and woman seated by the edge of a small river in a wooded landscape.

Presented to George IV by the artist's widow in April 1829; recorded in the inventory of 'Carleton Palace' (629).

Probably painted on the banks of the Chelmer near Sir George's house at Dunmow. If the inscription above is accurate, No. 656 could be one of the two landscapes exhibited by him at the Royal Academy in 1813 (7, 120).

Richard Brydges Beechey

1808–95. Sixth son of Sir William Beechey. Entered the Navy in 1822 and retired as Admiral in 1885. As an amateur painter of marine subjects he exhibited between 1832 and 1877.

657. THE *MADAGASCAR* AND *ETNA* STRUCK BY METEORIC BALLS

Windsor Castle (1020). 29 × 36 in., 73,7 × 91,4 cm.

The event is described in a contemporary inscription on the back: *In a very dark & rainy Night, off Corfu, The Madagascar & Ætna Bomb were set on fire in parts of the Rigging by Meteoric Balls. a very large one fell on the Deck of the Ætna & knock'd down 14 of her Crew. Painted by R. B. Beechey. 1830. 2d Lieut of the Ætna.*

Presented to William IV by Sir William Beechey on 18 June 1831 (*V.R. inv.*).

The *Etna*, on the left in No. 657, was a Bomb ship of 10 guns (Commander Robert Ingram), stationed in the Mediterranean; Beechey was one of her Lieutenants. The *Madagascar*, 46 guns, was under the command of Captain the Hon. R. C. Spencer. The episode recorded in the picture took place in the evening of 5 January 1830. The Captain of the *Madagascar* recorded in his Log: '8.25 PM Heavy rain thunder & lightening—8.30 felt the ship struck in several places by the lightening 8.35 observed the Mn Mast head on fire . . .' Next day he found that the main and mizen masts had been damaged by the lightning. Meanwhile on the *Etna* the lightning had struck the ship several times and at 8.20 one of the R.M. Artillerymen on board had been struck (P.R.O., Adm. 51/3023, 3276).

Sir William Beechey

1753–1839. Portrait-painter; exhibited at the Royal Academy from 1776 to 1838. He seems to have worked for the royal family from as early as 1793, when he became Portrait-Painter to the Queen. In 1795 the King thought that at the Academy 'Beechey was first' (Farington, unpublished, 5 May 1795); in 1796 he again 'particularly noticed Beechys' (*ibid.*, 22 April 1796). In 1797 Beechey painted the Prince of Württemberg at Windsor (Farington, *Diary*, vol. I, p. 209) and on 14 August of the same year he was being described by the King as '*the best painter*' (*ibid.*, p. 213). By the end of 1804, however, he had fallen from favour at court; he seems to have been the victim of an outburst at Windsor, when the King is alleged to have told him that he 'wanted no more of his pictures' (*ibid.*, vol. III, pp. 23, 33, 43, 62, 250). He continued to paint royal portraits until the 1830s and in 1813(?) he was appointed Painter to the Duke of Gloucester.

In 1801 the Prince of Wales appears to have been in Beechey's debt to the extent of £390. 12s. (W.R.A., Geo. 32221, 42950). The Duke of Kent's debts in 1819 included £400 owing to Beechey, and Beechey was listed in 1837 as one of his creditors to the extent of £346. 10s. (*ibid.*, Geo. Add. 7, 1434, 1485). Queen Adelaide paid Beechey £315 in 1831–1832 (W.R.A., Geo. 89601).

In addition to the portraits which are still in the royal collection, Queen Charlotte had at Frogmore (in the Green Pavilion) portraits by Beechey of the Dukes of Cambridge and Sussex and Princesses Augusta and Elizabeth (Pyne, vol. I, *Frogmore*, p. 14; see plate opposite p. 12) and, in the Eating Room, the portrait of Lady Louisa Georgina Bathurst ('Adoration'), which is stated to have been lent to George III because of its likeness to his youngest sons and to have been returned to Lord Bathurst after Queen Charlotte's death (*ibid.*, p. 8; Earl Bathurst, *Catalogue of the Bathurst Collection* (1908), p. 168). George IV also owned, if only for a short time, a version, painted in 1814, of Beechey's portrait of Spencer Perceval. Beechey sent in his account (£52. 10s.) for this in July 1816; it was sent to Carlton House; Beechey was paid on 28 August 1816 (W.R.A., Geo. 27055–8, 35503; Roberts, pp. 242, 245). During the reign of William IV Beechey was described as Principal Portrait-Painter to the King.

658. GEORGE III (*Plate* 157)

Buckingham Palace. 100 × 62¾ in., 254 × 159,4 cm.; there are additions on the right (5⅜ in.) and at the bottom (6¼ in.).

Full-length, standing, in the uniform of a General Officer with the Garter star on his coat, holding a stick in his right hand. Behind, his charger is held by a groom and in the distance is a troop of cavalry.

Painted for the King and placed with No. 659 in the King's Dining-Room at Kew (Geo. III, *Kew*: 'Portrait of the King'; measurements given as 96×56 in.; Beechey's name is included (No. 1212) in the later inv. of Kew, inv. No. 48, part IV, on p.li above). Removed to the State Apartments at St. James's on 24 October 1830, but later set up on the Principal Staircase at Buckingham Palace (*V.R. inv.*, 1864. No. 217; *Buckingham Palace*, 1909, p. 34).

Probably painted at Windsor in 1799–1800; exhibited at the Royal Academy in 1800 (69). It was stated (see Roberts, p. 70) that the horse was by Gilpin. The engraving of it by Benjamin Smith was published by Boydell in 1803 as the frontispiece to vol. I of his *Shakespeare* (the head was also engraved by Skelton, Cardon and others). In a copy at Hatfield, given by the King to the 1st Marquess of Salisbury (then Lord Chamberlain) the background is altered to a view of Hatfield House. A good copy is in the National Portrait Gallery (2502). Reduced copies and variants are not uncommon, i.e., with the Quadrangle at Windsor behind, sold at Christies, 12 December 1947 (139); and at Sotheby's, 6 November 1963 (228). A three-quarter-length variant is reproduced by Roberts, p. 106; a copy of the head, attributed to Hopkins, was sold with a pendant copy from No. 659 at Christie's, 17 October 1947 (163). A copy of the head was sold at Christie's, 20 May 1955 (13). A large enamel copy by Bone, signed and dated 1801, is at Windsor (2601); it was at Carlton House in 1816 (176). A copy by Bone of the head and shoulders, stated to be signed and dated 1807, was sold from Northwick Park, Christie's, 6 July 1965 (33). Also in the royal collection are miniature copies of the head by Grimaldi; one, signed and dated 1804, was presented to H.M. Queen Mary in 1936; another, painted in 1800, was at Carlton House in 1816 (197). A miniature copy of the head by Grimaldi is at Knole; a miniature copy of the head is in the Ashmolean Museum; another, by Shelley, was in the collection of Mr. F. W. Trimnell; another, attributed to Cosway, was in the collection of the King of Württemberg. A watercolour copy of the head by A. R. Burt, dated 1 May 1809, is in the Royal Library. On the back it is stated that the prototype was the last portrait for which the King sat.

659. QUEEN CHARLOTTE (*Plate* 156)

Buckingham Palace. 98¾×62⅝ in., 250,8×159,1 cm.; there are additions at the top (4 in.) and bottom (*c.* 2 in.) and on the left (5¼ in.).

Full-length, holding a Maltese dog in her arms and with two other dogs beside her, walking in the grounds of Frogmore House, which is seen in the distance.

Painted for the Queen and placed with No. 658 in the King's Dining-Room at Kew (Geo. III, *Kew*: 'Portrait . . . of the Queen'; measurements given as 96×56 in.; Beechey's name is included (No. 1213) in the later inv. of Kew, inv. No. 48, part IV, on p. li above). Later set up on the Principal Staircase at Buckingham Palace (*V.R. inv.*, 1864, No. 226; *Buckingham Palace*, 1909, p. 34).

Presumably the original of the design. The engraving by T. Ryder and T. Ryder jun., published in 1804, was done from the picture 'in his MAJESTY'S COLLECTION'; it was engraved as the frontispiece to vol. II of Boydell's *Shakespeare* (1803). The portrait was painted at Windsor in 1796. Farington records on 14 July 1796 that the King had told Yenn at Windsor 'that Beechy had painted the Queen, and Yenn saw the picture. The King, Queen &c. &c. are delighted with the picture. While the Queen was sitting, Yenn heard, Beechy had talked in his odd way.' On 16 January 1797 Farington called on Beechey and 'saw his whole length of

the Queen'. It was exhibited at the Royal Academy in 1797 (92). A version, given by the Queen to her Lord Chamberlain, the 16th Earl of Morton, is now in the Lee Collection, Courtauld Institute (35; *Catalogue* by P. Murray (1958), p. 18); another, at Upton Park, is said to be the version in Beechey's sale at Christie's, 11 June 1836 (68), and has the Round Tower in place of Frogmore in the background. A three-quarter-length copy (?) is reproduced by Roberts, p. 62; on 16 September 1799 the Duke of Kent wrote to his mother that she had promised him 'an half-length Copy of Your Picture by Beachy' (W.R.A., Geo. Add. 7, 44). A half-length copy was formerly at Burley-on-the-Hill. A copy of the head, attributed to Hopkins, was sold with a pendant copy from No. 658 at Christie's, 17 October 1947 (163). A large enamel copy by Bone, signed and dated 1799, is at Windsor (2600); Farington saw this at Bone's house on 21 September 1799; and on 28 September the Prince of Wales 'was much pleased with [it] & said He must have it'. It was at Carlton House in 1816 (177). A derivation by Grimaldi was also at Carlton House (198) and is now at Windsor (2539); a miniature copy of the head by Ferrière was sold at Christie's, 16 February 1965 (38); and a copy of the head in pastel, attributed to Russell, is at Knole. Harding's drawing at Windsor after No. 659 (Oppé, No. 290) probably served as the basis of the engraving by Bourlier, published in 1806.

660. GEORGE III AT A REVIEW (*Plate* 161)

Windsor Castle (3013). 163½×197½ in., 403,9×501,6 cm.

The King, mounted on a white horse, Adonis, and wearing a type of General's uniform with the star of the Garter, points towards a mock attack between the 3rd, or Prince of Wales's Own, Dragoon Guards and the 10th, or Prince of Wales's Own, Light Dragoons. Behind the King, brandishing his sabre, is the Prince of Wales in the uniform of Colonel of the 10th Light Dragoons. Following the King is Frederick, Duke of York, as Commander-in-Chief, wearing the star of the Garter on the uniform of a Field-Marshal; Lieutenant-General Sir David Dundas (1735–1820), Quartermaster-General; and Major-General Philip Goldsworthy (*c.* 1738–1801). In the foreground stands General Sir William Fawcett (1728–1804), Colonel of the 3rd Dragoon Guards, wearing the ribbon of the Bath, beside a charger held by a negro groom.

Literature: A. Watts, *The Cabinet of Modern Art* (1836), pp. 101–2; Law, 1881, 1898 (354); Roberts, pp. 57–63; W. T. Whitley, *Artists and their Friends in England 1700–99* (1928), vol. II, pp. 208, 217–19.

Painted for George III in 1797–8. The commission to paint the subject is stated to have been given by the King to Beechey after he had shown the King a sketch he had made of a scene he had witnessed on one of his journeys through Hyde Park. He had seen the King mounted on his favourite white horse, Adonis, reviewing the Household troops, attended by Generals Fawcett, Dundas and Goldsworthy (A. Watts, *loc. cit.*). The sketch may have been the signed sketch in the Victoria and Albert Museum (*Fig.* 1) which shows three mounted figures behind the Duke of York; in this sketch the military manoeuvres are taking place on flat ground and are watched by two figures on a bank; the uniforms are treated in a more general fashion than they are in an oil sketch, on the London art-market in 1937, in which only two mounted figures are seen on the right.[1] The oil

1. Mr. St. V. Beechey owns a sketchbook which contains studies of horses for the design, a slightly more detailed study for the figure and horse of the Duke of York and sketches for the left hand and reins of the King and for the turbaned groom.

sketch could have been the one shown by Beechey to Farington on 4 December 1797 ('He shewed me a sketch in Oil of large picture of the King on Horseback'); on 11 December Farington noted that the King 'is to sit to Beechy for his Portrait on Horseback on the 20th. inst' and on 22 December this sitting is recorded as having taken place. On 28 December Farington noted: 'I mentioned Beecheys case,—no pay, and to paint the King &c. on a Canvass 18 feet wide. He [West] said it was Beecheys own offer, which made a difference'.

It is clear from the preliminary sketches that the Prince of Wales was not part of Beechey's original design, but a story, preserved in the Beechey family, that the artist inserted the Prince in collusion with Queen Charlotte and that the King, on seeing what had been perpetrated, ordered the canvas to be torn from its stretcher and burnt, cannot be reconciled with what is known about Beechey's progress. On 2 February 1798 Farington records that Beechey was working on the picture in the Octagon Room in Buckingham House: 'Prince of Wales sat today'. Six days later, Beechey called on Farington: 'King has sat 3 times & head finished abt. an hour & half each time—Likeness very great—a speaking likeness. Duke of York very like. Prince so irregular in sitting & whole sitting made nothing of him yet'. According to Beechey (2 March), the King was anxious that the picture should be exhibited and, although Beechey was at one stage doubtful whether he could finish the picture in time, it was exhibited at the Royal Academy in 1798 (178: *His Majesty reviewing . . . attended by the Prince of Wales, the Duke of York . . .*). On 4 June Lawrence told Farington that Beechey had said 'that His Majesty had not paid Him £1200 as reputed' (these references from Farington's *Diary* are all unpublished); Beechey had apparently hoped that he would receive £1,000 and a knighthood for the picture (*Diary*, vol. V, p. 205). It was stated by one early source that the King's horse was painted by Charles Catton the Younger (Whitley, *loc. cit.*).

Perhaps partly owing to the extreme rapidity with which he must have worked on this enormous canvas, it began to deteriorate very early. On 2 September 1804 Farington recorded that Beechey had had to go to Windsor to restore the colours: 'the Scarlet Coats had lost their colour having been painted with red lead, or done in some glazing way' (*Diary*, vol. II, p. 282). In March 1812 West received the Prince of Wales's commands 'respecting Sir Wm. Beechey being permitted to have the large picture of the King at a Review from Windsor, in order to repair it, and afterwards to send it to Hampton Court'. In April West inspected the picture in the Queen's Library at St. James's. He found it 'in so ruinous a condition, so that makes it necessary to be lined before Sir William can make a restoration of it' (*Letters of George IV*, vol. I, 38, 59). Early in 1812 Beechey appears to have submitted a bill for £52. 10s. for lining and restoring the picture and adding to it fourteen inches of new canvas. Beechey refers to this work in a letter of 27 July 1816, from which it is not clear whether the bill had been settled. On this second occasion his account 'For Repairs of the large Picture' amounted to £105. He describes the picture as 'nearly destroyed'. He had had 'to repaint a great part of it', 'one of the Portraits was nearly destroyed', and owing to damage caused by the negligence of the servants at Windsor he had been compelled to replace the bottom of the canvas (i.e., the fourteen inches referred to above) (W.R.A., Geo. 26985, 27055-7); on 2 September 1817 Beechey received from the Lord Chamberlain's Office £105 for his work on the picture (Roberts, pp. 244-5). The picture was at that time at Windsor. Later it was at Hampton Court (166) and

Kensington, where it was cleaned by Mr. Horace Buttery in 1937 before being sent to Windsor, where it has since hung in the State Dining Room. Beechey's addition at the bottom of the canvas can still be discerned. There are slight *pentimenti* in the cavalry charging on the left in the mock encounter, in the off fore-foot of the King's charger, in the position of his stirrup and in the angle at which the Prince of Wales holds his sabre. The position of the Prince in relation to his horse is gravely misunderstood.

The picture was engraved by Ward and published on 1 June 1799 with a dedication to the Queen. A full-size copy of No. 660 is in the collection of Lord Anglesey. Small copies of No. 660 are not uncommon, e.g., on the art-market in London in 1923, and others were sold at Christie's on 5 March 1954 (113) and at Sotheby's on 25 July 1956 (54). A small copy was recorded in the Green Pavilion at Frogmore (Pyne, vol. I, *Frogmore*, p. 14). Copies of the head of the King also exist (see No. 675)[1] and painted and engraved derivations from this figure are very common (e.g., No. 676). At Somerley is a life-size derivation of this kind, in which the horse appears to be by Ward;[2] in Harlow's portrait of Beechey, in the same collection, the big picture appears in the background. The Duke of Kent, stationed in Halifax, where he was trying to assemble portraits of his family, wrote to the Queen on 16 September 1799 in the hope that the King would allow a copy to be made for him 'from that admirable likeness of His Majesty in Beachy's large Picture'; he also wrote, on 25 September, to the Duke of York, reminding him of his request for 'a half length Copy of your likeness as taken by Beachy in his large picture' (W.R.A., Geo. Add. 7, 44, 47).

For Sir David Dundas, see No. 976. Philip Goldsworthy, Lieutenant-General, 1799, was A.D.C. and first Equerry to the King; his sister Martha was sub-Governess to the King's daughters. Sir William Fawcett had served as an Ensign in the 'Forty-Five'; he became a General, 1796, and a Privy Councillor, 1799.

661. WILLIAM HENRY, DUKE OF GLOUCESTER (*Plate* 160)

Windsor Castle (467). 30 × 25 in., 76,2 × 63,5 cm.

Head and shoulders, in the uniform of Colonel of the 1st Foot Guards with the star of the Garter on his breast.

Bequeathed to Queen Victoria in 1844 by Princess Sophia Matilda of Gloucester (this is recorded by an inscription on the back of the canvas; in the MS. Catalogue of Queen Victoria's private pictures &c.; and in Queen Victoria's Journal for 28 December 1844: . . . 'the Princess left me a fine picture in oils (Kitcat) of her father, by Sir Wm. Beechey').

Literature: Collins Baker, *Windsor*, p. 11.

Probably painted not long before the Duke's death. He had been Colonel of the 1st Foot Guards since 1770. A copy was (1953) in the possession of Miss E. D. Ponsonby; another, at York House, is stated to have belonged to the Duke's Equerry, General White.

1. A miniature copy of the head by Bone is in the royal collection.
2. This is probably the derivation, then belonging to Lord Somerville, engraved by Ward and published on 1 February 1804; the horse was painted from life by Ward himself, the figure copied from Beechey by William Hopkins and the whole painted over and finished by Ward (C. R. Grundy, *James Ward* (1909), pp. 63-4). Henry Bone's enamel copy (October, 1817) from Lord Somerville's picture, was sold at Christie's, 25 June 1968 (73).

662. PRINCESS SOPHIA MATILDA OF GLOUCESTER *(Plate 169)*

Buckingham Palace. $56\frac{1}{4} \times 45\frac{1}{4}$ in., $142,9 \times 114,9$ cm.

Signed: *WB* (in monogram).

Three-quarter-length, leaning on a balustrade and resting her head on her right hand.

Formerly in the Dining-Room at Gloucester House; bequeathed by the sitter's sister-in-law, Mary, Duchess of Gloucester, to Queen Victoria in 1857: 'a picture of the Princess Sophia Matilda painted by Sir William Beechey' (will proved 5 June 1857); recorded in Buckingham Palace (564) in 1876 (*V.R. inv.*).

Literature: Roberts, p. 80.

Perhaps the portrait of the Princess exhibited at the Royal Academy in 1803 (129). The portrait was engraved by E. Scriven for *La Belle Assemblée* (1806). A version, formerly in the collection of Lord Ailwyn, was on the art-market in New York in 1926.

663. WILLIAM FREDERICK, DUKE OF GLOUCESTER

Buckingham Palace. $100\frac{1}{4} \times 72\frac{5}{8}$ in., $254,6 \times 184,5$ cm.

Full-length, standing in a landscape, in uniform as Colonel of the 3rd Foot Guards, with the star of the Garter; his hat is in his right hand and his left rests on his sword.

Acquired from the artist by Sir John Leicester; sold by C. Leicester Warren at Christie's, 12 June 1931 (64), and bought by H.M. Queen Mary for the King's private collection.

Literature: W. Carey, *A Descriptive Catalogue of a Collection of Paintings by British Artists, in the possession of Sir John Fleming Leicester* (1819), p. 119 (49); J. Young, *A Catalogue of Pictures by British Artists, in the possession of Sir John Fleming Leicester* (1825), p. 26 (55); Roberts, p. 119; D. Hall, 'The Tabley House Papers', *Walpole Soc.*, vol. XXXVIII (1962), pp. 65, 113.

Apparently a repetition by Beechey of a portrait which he had painted for the London Hospital. He received the final payment from the Hospital on 9 April 1808 (Roberts, p. 226); the portrait for the Hospital may have been the portrait exhibited at the Royal Academy in 1807 (93) and the source of the engraving by W. Say, published on 26 April 1807. Sir John Leicester paid Beechey for the second version in two instalments: £105 on 5 May 1810, when Beechey said that he was at work on the picture, and £106. 13*s.* on 22 February 1813. The portrait had been finished before 7 July 1812. Beechey's account included the sum paid for men for taking down the original picture at the London Hospital, bringing it to Beechey's studio in Harley Street and ultimately taking it back to the Hospital (Roberts, pp. 232, 237; MSS. sold with the portrait in 1931[1]). Beechey exhibited a portrait of the Duke at the Royal Academy in 1812 (157). An earlier head of the Duke, close in type to No. 663, was sold at Christie's, 3 June 1932 (41).

664. GEORGE IV WHEN PRINCE OF WALES *(Plate 162)*

Windsor Castle (2721). $50\frac{1}{2} \times 40$ in., $128,3 \times 102$ cm.

Three-quarter-length, standing, in the uniform of the 10th Light Dragoons, wearing the star of the Garter and resting his right hand on his sabre.

1. These MSS. included Beechey's correspondence with Sir John Leicester relating to No. 663. I have not seen the original MSS., which have apparently disappeared, but a copy of them is in the Surveyor's office.

Painted at the sitter's command (see below) for presentation to the Duke of Kent; presumably passed into the possession of George, Duke of Cambridge; sold in his sale at Christie's, 11 June 1904 (73), when it was bought by King Edward VII and placed in the Principal Corridor at Buckingham Palace (*Buckingham Palace*, 1909, p. 163).

Literature: Collins Baker, *Windsor*, p. 12.

No. 664 is a second version, painted by Beechey himself in 1803, of the portrait which had been his Diploma Work (1798) at the Royal Academy, where it still hangs (R.A., *Treasures of the Royal Academy*, 1963 (29); engraved by S. Bennet and T. Cheesman in 1805). On 5 September 1806 Beechey wrote to Robert Gray, the Prince of Wales's Vice-Treasurer, enclosing his account for £84 for the 'Portrait of His Royal Highness Bishop's Half length, painted for H.R.H. The Duke of Kent'; his receipt for this sum and for ten guineas for a frame, is dated 26 January 1807 (W.R.A., Geo. 26842–3). 'The Picture', according to Beechey, 'has been painted three or four years according to His Royal Highnesses Order from one in the Royal Academy'; when payment was made (*ibid.*, 89446) the portrait was stated to have been painted in 1803. Originally the portrait was to have been sent out to the Duke of Kent at Gibraltar, but it was in fact sent 'to accompany some other Pictures of the Royal Family at his Villa at Castle Hill'; Beechey wrote that 'The Prince did propose to sit to me for a trifling alteration of the Hair and when he has time and will honor me with his commands I shall be ever devoted to them'. It seems, from a comparison between No. 664 and the earlier version, as if Beechey made considerable, if subtle, alterations to bring the portrait up to date. A copy, from the collection of Lord Newton, was sold at Sotheby's, 17 July 1946 (65). A miniature copy by Bone is in the Royal Library.

665. CHARLOTTE, PRINCESS ROYAL *(Plate 163)*

Windsor Castle (2585). $36 \times 27\frac{1}{2}$ in., $91,4 \times 69,9$ cm.

Three-quarter-length, seated, wearing over her right shoulder the red ribbon of an order, possibly the Royal Order of the Golden Eagle of Württemberg or the Order of St. Catherine of Russia.

Painted for George IV; recorded in store at Carlton House in 1816 (361: 'A half length of the Queen of Wirtemberg. Sir William Beechey'); later at Buckingham Palace (847).

Literature: Collins Baker, *Windsor*, p. 12.

Nos. 665–70 constitute a set of portraits, painted for the Prince of Wales, of the daughters of George III. Beechey's account, dated 1800, for 'Pictures painted . . . by the Order of His Royal Highness the Prince of Wales' included a half-length of the Prince (at sixty guineas)[1] in the possession of Queen Charlotte at Frogmore, 'and six Portraits of the Princesses at forty guineas each—six frames for the same at seven guineas each'; his receipt is dated 12 February 1802 (W.R.A., Geo. 26806). Under the expenses incurred in this commission, Beechey included 'my expences to, from, & at Windsor', so it is probable that the portraits of the Prince's sisters were painted at Windsor. Nos. 666–8, 670 were exhibited at the Royal Academy in 1797. Some of the portraits in the series are severely cracked and had clearly been retouched at a very early date. When they were cleaned in 1963 Beechey's own varnish was not disturbed. The retouchings and the old varnish seem to indicate that the

1. Possibly the portrait exhibited, with Nos. 666–8, 670, at the R.A. in 1797 (91).

portraits began to deteriorate very early. On 6 January 1829 Nos. 666–70 were sent to Beechey 'to restore' at the King's command (note by Jutsham in *Carlton House*, 1816) and on 20 April 1831 Beechey submitted a bill for sixty guineas for 'restoring six Pictures of . . . The Princesses'; his receipts of payment from George IV's executors is dated 28 May 1831 (W.R.A., Geo. 26598, 32828–30, 32913; Jutsham, *PP.*, f. 165).

666. PRINCESS AUGUSTA (*Plate* 164)

Windsor Castle (2584). 36¼ × 28 in., 92,1 × 68,6 cm.

Three-quarter-length, seated, holding a sketch-book in her hands and wearing an enamelled anchor on her necklace; a classical bust (? Diana) is on a table beside her.

Painted for George IV; recorded with Nos. 667–70 in the South Ante-room at Carlton House in 1816 (37: 'A half length . . . of the Princess Augusta. Sir William Beechey'); four of this series were set in elaborate carved and gilded panels over the doors, and another was set over a pier glass, in this room; some can be seen therein in Wild's plate (1818) in Pyne, vol. III, *Carlton House*, p. 43; 'arranged to correspond with the general contour of the apartment' (No. 665 does not seem to have been placed in this room). The five panels were sent to Windsor on 15 March 1827 (Jutsham, *Deliveries*, f. 100). Later at Buckingham Palace (844).

Literature: Roberts, pp. 52–4; Collins Baker, *Windsor*, p. 13; R.A., *King's Pictures* (69).

See No. 665. Exhibited at the Royal Academy in 1797 (80).

667. PRINCESS ELIZABETH (*Plate* 165)

Windsor Castle (2586). 36½ × 28 in., 92,7 × 68,6 cm.

Half-length, seated at a table, wearing costume of a vaguely seventeenth-century design, about to start drawing with a crayon.

Painted for George IV; recorded with Nos. 666, 668–70 in the South Ante-room at Carlton House in 1816 (38: 'A half length portrait of the Princess Elizabeth. Sir William Beechey'); later at Buckingham Palace (848).

Literature: Roberts, pp. 52–4; Collins Baker, *Windsor*, p. 13.

See No. 665. Exhibited at the Royal Academy in 1797 (107).

668. PRINCESS MARY (*Plate* 166)

Windsor Castle (2589). 36¼ × 28 in., 92,1 × 68,6 cm.

Half-length, seated, holding on her lap a portfolio and a drawing of a child, based on a bust that stands on a table beside her.

Painted for George IV; recorded with Nos. 666–7, 669–70 in the South Ante-room at Carlton House in 1816 (39: 'A half length portrait of the Princess Mary. Sir William Beechey'); later at Buckingham Palace (842).

Literature: Roberts, pp. 52–4; Collins Baker, *Windsor*, p. 14; R.A., *King's Pictures* (67).

See No. 665. Exhibited at the Royal Academy in 1797 (106). An enamel miniature copy by Bone (signed) is in the Royal Library; it was recorded in the Prince's Old Bedroom at Carlton House in 1816 (200) and had presumably been commissioned by the Prince. An inscription on the back gives the date April 1797 for the copy or the original.

669. PRINCESS SOPHIA (*Plate* 167)

Windsor Castle (2588). 36½ × 28 in., 92,7 × 68,6 cm.

Half-length, seated, with her arms folded in her lap.

Painted for George IV; recorded with Nos. 666–8, 670 in the South Ante-room at Carlton House in 1816 (40: 'A half length portrait of the Princess Sophia. Sir William Beechey'); later at Buckingham Palace (846).

Literature: Collins Baker, *Windsor*, p. 14.

See No. 665. There are signs of alterations by the artist in drawing the right arm. A drawing by Harding after No. 669 is at Windsor (Oppé, No. 308); it presumably served as the basis of Cheesman's engraving, published in 1806. A copy is at Clarence House. A version, stated to have been in the collection of the Landgrave of Hesse, was in the Ober-Murlen sale, Frankfurt, 7–9 October 1920 (476). A miniature copy by Bone (February 1805) is at Windsor.

670. PRINCESS AMELIA (*Plate* 168)

Windsor Castle (2587). 36 × 28 in., 91,4 × 68,6 cm.

Half-length, seated, beside a table on which is a book or bundle of papers, with papers in her left hand.

Painted for George IV; recorded with Nos. 666–9 in the South Ante-room at Carlton House in 1816 (41: 'A half length portrait of the late Princess Amelia. Sir William Beechey'); later at Buckingham Palace (845).

Literature: Roberts, pp. 52–4; Collins Baker, *Windsor*, p. 15.

See No. 665. Exhibited at the Royal Academy in 1797 (73). It was presumably the half-length of the Princess which, on 5 December 1810, soon after her death, was sent from Carlton House to Bone 'to have Enamels taken from it' (Jutsham, *R/D*, f. 80). A drawing by Harding after No. 670 is at Windsor (Oppé, No. 309); it presumably served as the basis of Cheesman's engraving, published in 1806. A copy (formerly in the collection of the Landgrave of Hesse) was exhibited at Leggatt's in a summer exhibition, 1954 (10). Another is at Clarence House. On 27 July 1798 the Princess wrote to the Prince of Wales, 'You are always so good to me that I have taken the liberty to make use of your name & have sent word to Sir William Beechey that you had given me leave to have my picture copied by Cleaves for Dear Miny who is so anxious to have it . . .' (W.R.A., Geo. Add. 14, 6).

671. VICTORIA, DUCHESS OF KENT, WITH PRINCESS VICTORIA (*Plate* 170)

Buckingham Palace. 57 × 44½ in., 144,8 × 113 cm.

The Duchess is seated, three-quarter-length, on a sofa, holding a book on her lap, with an arm round the little Princess who is clutching a miniature of the Duke of Kent[1] which she has taken out of a case which rests on the sofa.

Probably painted for Prince Leopold (King Leopold I), in whose possession it was when it was engraved by Skelton (see below) in 1823; given to Queen Victoria in 1867 by King Leopold II and the Count of Flanders; in the White Drawing-Room at Windsor (798) in 1878.

Literature: Roberts, pp. 156–7, 252–4.

Painted in 1821 and exhibited at the Royal Academy in 1822 (66). On 6 June 1821 and 20 February 1822 payments of £110 and £110. 5s. respectively were made by the Duchess to Beechey. Beechey was summoned by the Duchess to Kensington Palace at one o'clock on 28 May 1821 for the first (?) sitting, which had been delayed as 'at this moment, The Princess Victoria has a slight cold' (MS. in possession of Mr. St. V. Beechey). William Skelton's engraving of No. 671

1. The miniature seems based on the portrait by Beechey (see No. 680).

was published in 1823. In April 1861 Queen Victoria purchased an enamel copy of No. 671 by Bone, possibly the copy exhibited by Bone at the Royal Academy in 1824 (432). A copy of No. 671 is at Belton.

672. PRINCESS AUGUSTA (*Plate* 159)

Buckingham Palace. 94⅜ × 58⅜ in., 239,7 × 148,3 cm.

Full-length, walking in a park with the turret of a castle on the right and the sea in the distance. She carries a parasol in her right hand and wears round her neck a pendant in the shape of an anchor, apparently the same as that worn in No. 666.

Presumably painted for George III; recorded in the King's Dining-Room at Kew (Geo. III, *Kew*); later at Frogmore (Windsor No. 1518).

Literature: R.A., *British Portraits*, 1956–7 (409).

Exhibited at the Royal Academy in 1802 (97).

673. ERNEST, DUKE OF CUMBERLAND

(*Plate* 158)

St. James's Palace. 94 × 58 in., 238,8 × 147,3 cm.

Full-length, standing, in the uniform of Colonel of the 15th Light Dragoons with the ribbon and star of the Garter, resting his left hand on his sabre.

Presumably painted for George III. Recorded in the King's Dining-Room at Kew (Geo III, *Kew*; Beechey's name is included (No. 1214) in the later inv. of Kew, inv. No. 48, part IV, on p. li above); later at Buckingham Palace (555).

Literature: W. T. Whitley, *Art in England 1800–20* (1928), p. 36.

Exhibited by Beechey at the Royal Academy in 1802 (61). Farington, in his 'Memorandum' for June 1802, said of Beechey 'His whole lengths common placed performances. —The Duke of Cumberland much the best'. The star of the Garter is clearly part of the original design, but the ribbon was painted over the Duke's tunic. A preparatory sketch (?) by Beechey for No. 673 is in the possession of H.R.H. the Duke of Gloucester. Fogg's engraving of this type was published on 19 May 1806; Scriven's engraving of the type, apparently from a version in the possession of Princess Elizabeth, made for *Le Beau Monde*, was published on 1 June 1807. A small copy was sold at Christie's on 12 December 1947 (140) with a small panel based on No. 658. The type is close to the three-quarter-length, formerly at Malahide Castle.

674. AUGUSTA, DUCHESS OF CAMBRIDGE

Buckingham Palace. 94 × 58¼ in., 238,8 × 147,9 cm.

Full-length, standing, resting her right arm on a ledge which is partly covered by an ermine-lined cloak upon which is her coronet.

Formerly in the possession of the Duchess's son, George, Duke of Cambridge (*d.* 1904); acquired by H.M. Queen Mary, the sitter's grand-daughter.

Literature: Roberts, pp. 148–9, 247.

Painted in 1818 for the Duke of Cambridge. On 4 August and in October 1818 Beechey received payments of £105 from the Duke for the portrait, which was exhibited at the Royal Academy in 1819 (87). From a letter written to Beechey on 12 July 1828, on behalf of the Duke, it seems that a copy of No. 674 was being painted, probably by George Beechey, for Mrs. Hastings.

After Sir William Beechey

675. GEORGE III

Holyroodhouse. 30⅛ × 25⅛ in., 76,5 × 63,8 cm.

Recorded at Kew in 1870 (*V.R. inv.*); transferred to Holyroodhouse in 1882.

A copy of the head of the King from No. 660; on the stretcher is an early label bearing the name of the Duke of York, which may indicate that No. 675 had belonged to Frederick, Duke of York.

676. GEORGE III

Windsor Castle (2384). 38⅜ × 32⅛ in., 97,5 × 81,6 cm.

Riding out of a wood on a golden dun horse.

Acquired by Queen Victoria. Stated on a label on the back to have been given by the King to Princess Elizabeth (*d.* 1840), to have been bought at the palace of Hesse-Homburg in 1868 by H. H. Nugent Bankes and to have passed to his daughter Mrs. John Acland.

The figure of the King is based on that in No. 660, but the horse and background are taken from Van Dyck's *modello* of Charles I (Millar, No. 144). Another version of this type of derivation from No. 660 is at Rockingham; another was sold at Christie's on 10 April 1953 (21); others are in the Belgian royal collection and at Althorp.

677. WILLIAM HENRY, DUKE OF GLOUCESTER

Kensington Palace. 30 × 25 in., 76,2 × 63,5 cm.

Head and shoulders in the undress uniform (?) of a Field-Marshal with the star of the Garter.

See No. 678; formerly at Buckingham Palace (416).

Probably a copy of a portrait of *c.* 1800, of which the original may have been that sold in the Duke of Cambridge's sale at Christie's on 11 June 1904 (?75) which in 1957 was in a private collection in Basel.

678. FREDERICA, DUCHESS OF YORK

Kensington Palace. 30 × 25 in., 76,2 × 63,5 cm.

Head and shoulders, looking to the right.

Nos. 677, 678, 682, 683, 1226, 1229 are stated (*V.R. inv.*) to have been bequeathed to Queen Victoria by the Duchess of Inverness. The Duchess died in 1873 and had inherited all the property of her husband, the Duke of Sussex; but her will (signed 11 March 1858; three codicils of 1864, 1866, 1872; proved 29 August 1873) contains no reference to these portraits; the portraits went from Kensington on 14 November 1873 (conceivably 1874) and are recorded at Buckingham Palace (No. 678 is No. 420) by 18 January 1876.

A copy from the three-quarter-length formerly in the Robinson collection and sold at Sotheby's on 20 November 1963 (100); the pattern was engraved by C. Knight in 1801 (published on 1 March 1802) and the original was probably the portrait exhibited at the Royal Academy in 1800 (68).

679. EDWARD, DUKE OF KENT.

Buckingham Palace. 94¼ × 58¾ in., 239,4 × 149,2 cm.

Signed: *Am. Faure d'après Sir Wm Beechey.*

Full-length, standing, wearing the undress uniform of (?) the 7th Regiment of Foot with the star of the Garter, resting his right hand on a stick and holding his hat in his left hand. In the background is a fortress over which flies the Union flag.

Presented to Queen Victoria by King Louis Philippe on her birthday, 24 May 1836 (MS. Catalogue of Queen Victoria's private pictures &c.); it was placed in the Red Drawing Room at Windsor (267), where it later served as a pendant to a full-length by Winterhalter of the Duchess of Kent.

A copy by Faure, apparently commissioned by King Louis Philippe as a present for Queen Victoria, from the portrait of which the original had hung at Castle Hill and had apparently belonged to Mme. de St. Laurent. It was given to the King in 1818 (W.R.A., Geo. Add. 7, 1318). W. Say's engraving, presumably of the original, was published on 14 July 1808. Princess Feodora of Leiningen wrote to Princess Victoria on 8 January 1836: 'It is very aimiable of the King of the French that he will send you that picture of your dear papa. You have no good one of him I believe. I know that they were great friends' (W.R.A., Vic. Y, 34, 40). The original was probably referred to by Louis Philippe when he thanked Queen Victoria on 12 April 1848 for a portrait of the Duchess of Kent which she had ordered to be copied for him: 'Il sera bientôt placé à Versailles à côté de celui du feu Prince Votre Père *in his younger days*, tel qu'il était quand je l'ai vû pour la première fois *en 1799*, à Halifax (Nova Scotia)' (*ibid.*, Y, 48, 47).[1] The original was probably the portrait which was later in the collection of the Duke of Vendôme, great-grandson of Louis Philippe, and was on the art-market in London in 1932. The fortress in the background is probably an allusion to the capture on 23 March 1794 of Fort Bourbon, Martinique, at which the Duke had distinguished himself. In the original the Union flag flies above the French flag, but in the copy the French flag is omitted.

680. EDWARD, DUKE OF KENT

St. James's Palace. 100 × 54¾ in., 254 × 139,1 cm.

Full-length, standing, in the uniform of Colonel of the 1st Foot, holding his sabre in his left hand and resting his right hand on his stick; he wears the ribbon and star of the Garter and the badge of St. Patrick.

Painted for Queen Victoria in 1845–6; recorded at Buckingham Palace in 1876 (*V.R. inv.*, No. 557).

A copy by Henry Le Jeune of the portrait in the Fishmongers' Hall; Skelton's engraving of this type was published on 1 November 1815 and the original was probably the portrait for which the Duke was sitting in September 1814[2] and which was exhibited at the Royal Academy in 1815 (159) (Roberts, pp. 129–30). Queen Victoria had applied on 25 September 1845 to the Fishmongers for the loan of the portrait; on 8 January 1846 Le Jeune wrote to thank them for the loan (Minute Books of the Company).

681. PRINCESS AUGUSTA

Windsor Castle (2615). 50⅜ × 40⅜ in., 127,9 × 102,5 cm.

Three-quarter-length, standing in a landscape, wearing a feathered hat and putting her glove on her right hand.

1. Another pair, composed of copies from the same sources, was sold by Stuker of Berne, 18 November 1966 (3982, 4147); this pair was stated to have come from the collection of Prince Frederick Leopold of Prussia.
2. The Duke informed Beechey that he would be with him on 21 September 'at the usual Hour, or as near it as possible, when I hope you will be able to forward the picture considerably, as I trust nothing will occur to prevent my giving you a full Hour and a halfs sitting' (MS. belonging to Mr. St. V. Beechey).

Recorded at Buckingham Palace (540) in 1876 (*V.R. inv.*).

A contemporary repetition, possibly not by Beechey himself, of the portrait which, when in the possession of the Duke of Gloucester, was engraved by S. W. Reynolds and S. Cousins (published on 8 March 1824) and was presumably the portrait exhibited at the Royal Academy in 1819 (97). The Duke of Gloucester's picture passed by descent to the Duke of Cambridge and was sold at Christie's on 11 June 1904 (70); it is now in the Museum of Fine Art, Baltimore.[1] A portrait of 'The Princess Augusta By Sir William Beechey', which had been bought at the Duke of York's sale, was sent from Carlton House to Windsor on 30 December 1828 (Jutsham, *Deliveries*, f. 216). It may conceivably have been No. 681.

682. PRINCESS AUGUSTA

Kensington Palace. 30⅛ × 25 in., 76,5 × 63,5 cm.

Half-length in a white dress with a rope of pearls round her waist.

See No. 678; formerly at Buckingham Palace (418).

Probably a copy of a portrait of *c.* 1815.

683. ERNEST, DUKE OF CUMBERLAND

Kensington Palace. 30 × 25 in., 76,2 × 63,5 cm.

Head and shoulders in a Hanoverian General's uniform with the star of the Garter.

See No. 678; formerly at Buckingham Palace (419).

Presumably a copy of a portrait of *c.* 1795.

684. ISABELLA CAROLINE, COUNTESS OF CAWDOR (1771–1848)

Windsor Castle (2725). 23¾ × 20 in., 60,3 × 50,8 cm.

Head and shoulders, wearing a gold bandeau round her head.

Recorded at Buckingham Palace in 1859 (796).

Formerly described as a portrait of Charlotte, Princess Royal, but in fact closely related to Beechey's full-length of Lady Cawdor which is now at Stackpole Court and was exhibited at the Royal Academy in 1795 (186); a version of No. 684 is also at Stackpole Court (J. Steegman, *A Survey of Portraits in Welsh Houses*, vol. II (1962), p. 202).

Daughter of the 5th Earl of Carlisle, she married in 1789 John Campbell, later 1st Lord Cawdor.

Edward Bird

1772–1819. Painter of subject-pictures and portraits, established in Bristol. In 1814 he went over from Dover to Calais in the yacht which conveyed Louis XVIII and the Duchess of Angoulême back to France. At Calais he painted portraits of them for inclusion in a picture of them on board with their suite and the accompanying English representatives. On 19 July 1814 he told Farington that he intended to paint two pictures of this subject: 'the Prince Regent desired to have the refusal of another'. On 25 May 1816 Bird told Farington that the picture was nearly finished and that the King of France had sat to him in the Tuileries (*Diary*, vol. VII, p. 269, vol. VIII, pp. 71–2). On 24 June 1816 Bird sent the picture for the Regent's inspection (Jutsham,

1. See K. Garlick in the Museum's *News*, vol. XXVI, No. 1 (1962), p. 13.

Receipts, f. 1). It appears as No. 280, in store, at Carlton House in 1816: 'The departure of Louis XVIII from Dover, with portraits of the Prince Regent, the Duke of Clarence, and many of the nobility. Mr Bird', measurements given as 43×68 in. Bird was apparently unable to get a decision from the Prince Regent, who eventually decided not to retain the picture. It was sent to Sir Charles Long on 15 May 1818 (Farington, *Diary*, vol. VIII, p. 99; Jutsham, *R/D*, f. 290). It is almost certainly the (signed) picture now at Burton Constable. Bird's difficulty in gaining sittings from some of the English noblemen whom he wished to include in the scene contributed to the melancholy which clouded his last years. His painting of *Chevy Chase* 'procured him the appointment of Historical Painter to the Princess Charlotte'. This was probably in 1813. The painter presented to his new patroness his *Surrender of Calais* (*Gentleman's Magazine*, vol. LXXXIX (1819), pt. ii, p. 470; Cunningham, vol. II, pp. 34–5, 37).

685. THE COUNTRY CHORISTERS (*Plate* 263)

Buckingham Palace. Panel: 24¾×36½ in., 62,9×92,7 cm.

Signed and dated: *E. Bird /1810*.

An interior with an elderly man conducting a rehearsal by rustic singers and musicians; a small child, in the arms of its mother, is being ordered out of the room. On the floor lies a book of anthems for country choirs.

Bought by George IV. Recorded in store at Carlton House in 1816 (214: 'The Country Choristers. Mr Bird'); in 1819 it was (154) in the Upper Ante-room; sent to the King's Lodge on 17 June 1824; later at Buckingham Palace (801).

Literature: Cunningham, vol. II, p. 29.

Exhibited at the Royal Academy in 1810 (100: *Village Choristers rehearsing an anthem for Sunday*), when the Prince of Wales, 'disposed to make a Collection of the Works of British Artists', expressed a wish through West to acquire the picture. The money for it (250 guineas) was given to West by the Prince who entrusted him with a commission to Wilkie to 'paint a companion to it', i.e., No. 1175 below (Farington, *Diary*, vol. VI, p. 89). Haydon stated that Wilkie had withdrawn a picture sent to the Academy in 1810 as he feared comparison with No. 685 (*Diary*, ed. W. B. Pope (Harvard University Press), vol. I (1960), pp. 151–2, 155).

John Boaden

d. 1839. Portrait-painter; exhibited at the Royal Academy from 1810 to 1833.

686. ALEXANDER I, EMPEROR OF RUSSIA (1777–1825)

Buckingham Palace. Oval: 30×25 in., 76,2×63,5 cm.

Inscribed on the back with the painter's name and the date 1814.

Head and shoulders in Field-Marshal's uniform with the ribbon and star of St. Andrew of Russia and the badge of St. George of Russia.

In the collection of George IV. Received at Carlton House from Colnaghi on 8 June 1814: 'A Half Length Portrait of Alexander Emperor of Russia—by J. Boaden—in A Gilt Frame' (Jutsham, *R/D*, f. 311); recorded in the Armoury at Carlton House in 1816 (454); later at Hampton Court and Windsor, but recorded at Buckingham Palace (482) in 1876 (*V.R. inv.*).

If the portrait was acquired on 8 June, it had presumably been painted before the Emperor's arrival in London on 6 June 1814. A drawing of the Emperor by Boaden, also dated 1814, is in the Royal Library (Oppé, No. 67); it was the source of Picart's engraving which was published by Colnaghi on 20 August 1814.

Richard Brompton

1734–88. Studied under Benjamin Wilson in London and Mengs in Rome. He was in Rome in 1757 and was befriended by Sir Horace Mann and the Earl of Northampton; he went to Venice in January 1763, was back in Rome by September 1764 and left in December 1765. He went to Russia *c.* 1778, under the protection of the Empress Catherine, and was appointed Court Painter at St. Petersburg. See also No. 1215.

687. GEORGE IV WHEN PRINCE OF WALES

Buckingham Palace. 78×57 in., 198,1×144,8 cm.

Inscribed: GEORGE. PRINCE OF WALES / AGED VIII YEARS & VI. MONTHS / FEBY MDCCLXXI. / Rᴰ BROMPTON Pinxᵗ

Full-length, standing, in Garter robes, holding in his right hand the plumed hat of the order. On the floor lie a breast-plate, helmet and gauntlet. On the left is the Prince's coronet on a table covered with a cloth decorated with the Prince of Wales's feathers. In the background is a view of Windsor.

Nos. 687–8 were given by Queen Charlotte to Lady Charlotte Finch and were placed at Burley-on-the-Hill in September 1771 (inv. of 25 May 1772 preserved with the MSS. at Burley-on-the-Hill); they remained there until the sale at Christie's, 20 June 1947 (8, 9), when they were bought by Her Majesty Queen Elizabeth the Queen Mother.

Literature (for the pair): Pearl Finch, *History of Burley-on-the-Hill* (1901), vol. II, p. 10 (as in the Saloon).

Nos. 687–8 were presumably painted for Queen Charlotte as a present for Lady Charlotte Finch. Edwards states (*Anecdotes of Painters* (1808), p. 175) that Brompton had painted the portraits for Lady Charlotte with whom he quarrelled over the price and that small copies were made for the engraver. Small versions on copper were exhibited at the Society of Artists in 1773 (42, 43), when Walpole described them as neatly painted, but extravagantly priced at £100 each. The engravings by J. Saunders of the two portraits were published on 10 May 1774.

688. FREDERICK, DUKE OF YORK

Buckingham Palace. 78×57 in., 198,1×144,8 cm.

Inscribed: FREDERICK. IIᴰ SON OF / GEORGE THE IIIᴰ / KING OF GREAT BRITAIN / BISHOP OF OSNABRUG / AGED VII YEARS & VI MONTHS / FEBY MDCCLXXI. / Rᴰ BROMPTON. Pinx.ᵗ

Full-length, standing, in the robes of the Bath and resting his right arm on a table on which are his coronet and the plumed hat of the order; over the table is a cloth, decorated with his arms and falling over a shield and helmet. In the background is a view of Westminster Abbey.

See No. 687.

689. EDWARD, DUKE OF YORK, WITH HIS FRIENDS IN VENICE (Plate 8)

Windsor Castle (1029). 48¼×63⅜ in., 122,5×161 cm.

Signed and dated: *R Brompton f | 1763* (see below).

The Duke, wearing the ribbon and star of the Garter, is seated in front of a classical vase, decorated with a relief of (?) Leda and the swan. On his right stand two members of his Household: Sir William Boothby (1721–87) (apparently in military dress) with his arm round the shoulders of Colonel Henry St. John (c. 1738–1818), beside two greyhounds, one wearing a collar inscribed with the Duke's name. The Duke is approached by John Murray (d. 1775); behind him are Lord Palmerston (1739–1802), leaning his arm on the Duke's seat, the Earl of Upper Ossory (1745–1818) and Topham Beauclerk (1739–80). On the left, behind Colonel St. John, is a ledge with the inscription (INCLITVS ANTEÑOR PATRIAM . . . CESV DO/MVS) composed by the humanist Lupato Lupati for the so-called Tomb of Antenor in Padua.

The Duke of York by will of 31 August 1763 (proved October 1767) left all his pictures to his brother, William Henry, Duke of Gloucester; No. 689 was bequeathed to Queen Victoria by Mary, Duchess of Gloucester, in 1857: 'a picture of my uncle the Duke of York surrounded by his friends painted by Zoffany' (will proved 5 June 1857). At Windsor by 1878 (*V.R. inv.*).

Literature: E. Edwards, *Anecdotes of Painters* (1808), p. 174; W. T. Whitley, *Artists and their Friends in England 1700–1799* (1928), vol. II, pp. 255–61; Collins Baker, *Windsor*, pp. 21–2; Brinsley Ford, 'The Letters of Jonathan Skelton', *Walpole Soc.*, vol. XXXVI (1960), p. 75.

Brompton seems to have made a mistake in the date inscribed on the canvas: the picture must have been painted in 1764. The Duke set off on a Mediterranean tour in the summer of 1763. He reached Genoa on 10 November, moved south in February 1764, went to Florence and Rome, and to Venice for the Feast of the Ascension. He arrived in Venice at the end of May and during his stay was entertained in the most splendid fashion; the highlight of the visit was the Regatta on Ascension Day, 31 May. Lord Palmerston estimated that each of the four Venetian noblemen deputed to receive and attend upon the Duke while he was in Venice must have spent three or four thousand pounds in the process.

The figures surrounding the Duke in No. 689 are those who made up his party during his stay in Venice, which lasted three weeks (B. Connell, *Portrait of a Whig Peer* (1957), pp. 50–1). The commission to Brompton to paint the Duke and his friends may have been arranged by Murray. The group was probably painted at Padua: after the Duke and his party had exhausted the entertainments at Venice and the patience of the Venetians 'we moved in a Body with our Prince and our Minister at our Head to Padua where the Fair was just beginning' (letter from Lord Palmerston to Mrs. Howe, 24 August 1764, in MSS. at Broadlands). In a letter of 13 June 1768 to Garrick, Brompton wrote . . . 'I think that at Padua I gave you my reasons for not waiting on you at Abano to finnish the picture, this I think was the only cause of shyness, & which was owing to Mr Murray's desire, that I might not loose the opportunity of painting The D: of York, since when I have had one constant [cause] to wish that honor had been conffir'd on any other person; but it was not possible to foresee that what Mr Murray intended to be of the utmost servis to me, shou'd be of so very contrary an Effect . . .' (V. & A., Forster Collection. 48 F. 25, vol. 29, letters in part cited by Whitley, *loc. cit.*). Brompton seems to have been immediately in difficulties over the payment for the original and for the copies that he was commissioned to produce: '. . . I am told that I am only to have 35 Zichines for Each Copy, & seventy only for the Orriginal . . .' He proposed to 'send [home] the picture for H.R: Highness [presumably No. 689; the Duke embarked at Genoa on 17 August] that the gentlemen may judge for them selves befor I make any Explainations . . . it will be eight months before I can have two of the pictures finnish'd which I must doo before I can send one to England . . .' (*ibid.*, letter to Garrick from Venice, 1 August 1764). On 9 October 1764 he wrote to Garrick from Rome 'Your Copy of Ld Ossory is finnish'd, when any opportunity presents itself I will send it, at present I am imploi'd upon the Copys of the Duke of Yorks picture, when I have finnish'd, three of them I shall probably Come to England to doo, the others . . .' (*ibid.*). Brompton still appears to have had the original in his possession on 8 June 1765 when Cardinal Albani wrote to Sir Horace Mann that 'Le Peintre Sr Brompton m'a fait voir le Tableau qu'il a fait pour S.A.R. le Duc de Yorck. je vous assure monsr que S.A. doit être bien contente de Lui, car Le Tableau est tres joli et tres gracieux et j'ai eu toute la satisfaction de le voir' (P.R.O., S.P. Foreign, 105/316, f. 135).[1] After his return to London, however, Brompton was disappointed in the hopes he had nourished of 'unlimited Commission & promisses' from those for whom he had worked before his arrival in England. A copy of No. 689 which he painted for Sir Lawrence Dundas resulted in the loss of 'several pounds' (*ibid.*). One of the versions, perhaps No. 690, was exhibited at the Society of Artists in 1767 (14), where it was noted by Walpole (*Walpole Soc.*, vol. XXVII (1939), p. 62); his identification of the sitters cannot be questioned, but he states that the group was painted in Venice. The version belonging to Consul Smith, sold in his sale at Christie's, 16 May 1776, 2nd day (98), may have belonged originally to Murray. There are indications in Brompton's letters that a version may have been made for Col. St. John. The repetition now at Fonmon Castle was probably produced for Sir William Boothby (*Country Life*, vol. CV (1949), p. 736; J. Steegman, *A Survey of Portraits in Welsh Houses*, vol. II (1962), p. 95); another was on the art-market in Edinburgh in 1956.

Sir William Boothby, 5th Bt., was Master of the Horse to the Duke and, with Colonel the Hon. Henry St. John, brother of the 2nd Viscount Bolingbroke and a Groom of the Bedchamber to the Duke, were in attendance on him during the tour; before they reached Venice the Colonel had 'been left ill at Rome, and Sir William Boothby so much out of order that he was unfit to go out of the house'. John Murray was Resident at Venice, 1754–66; his sister was Consul Smith's second wife. He was Ambassador to Turkey, 1766–75; Gibbon found him 'an honest plain man, and a very good companion who gives us most excellent dinners every other day', but to Lady Mary Wortley Montagu he was 'a scandalous fellow . . . not to be trusted to change a sequin . . . despised by this government for his smuggling, which was his original profession, and always surrounded with pimps and brokers'. Henry Temple, 2nd Viscount Palmerston, a minor Whig politician, was an enthusiastic patron and collector of works of art; he travelled 'more to inform, than to amuse himself, and few people take more pains to a better purpose'; he was a member of the Dilettanti Society and of the Literary Club and a close friend of Reynolds. John Fitzpatrick, 2nd Earl of Upper Ossory, was the husband of Horace Walpole's famous correspondent; Gibbon met him in Florence in 1764: 'Il est cependant grand

1. This reference was kindly given to me by Mr. Brinsley Ford.

amateur de la peinture. Il a un peintre dans sa suite'
(*Gibbon's Journey from Geneva to Rome*, ed. G. A. Bonnard
(1961), p. 222). Topham Beauclerk was a grandson of the
1st Duke of St. Albans; his friend Dr. Johnson said: 'How
little does travelling supply to the conversation of any man
who has travelled? how little to Beauclerk?'

690. EDWARD, DUKE OF YORK, WITH HIS FRIENDS IN VENICE

Kew (*Hampton Court* No. 1372). 48 × 63 in., 121,9 × 160 cm.;
the canvas has been enlarged all round and was originally
38½ × 50¼ in.

Bequeathed to Queen Victoria by Elizabeth Vassall Fox, Lady
Holland, in 1845 as by 'Brompton. Painted at Florence, 1764'
(MS. Catalogue of Queen Victoria's private pictures &c.); placed
at Windsor; recorded at Buckingham Palace (834) in 1876 (*V.R.
inv.*).

Literature: Norwich Castle Museum, *Eighteenth-Century Italy and the
Grand Tour*, 1958 (91).

A repetition, probably painted by Brompton, of his group
painted in 1764 (No. 689). It is possible that No. 690 is the
version painted for the Earl of Upper Ossory, whose sister
married the 2nd Lord Holland, father-in-law of the Lady
Holland who bequeathed the picture to Queen Victoria;
it could therefore probably be identified with the version
exhibited at the Society of Artists in 1767, which Walpole
said 'is now at Lord Ossory's at Ampthill'. In Lady Holland's will, 31 May 1845 (proved 16 March 1846) she
described the picture as 'the Picture of the Duke of York
surrounded by the British Residents and several English
Gentlemen when His Royal Highness was at Florence'. It is
possible that, if the enlargements to the canvas (see above)
were made by Brompton himself, No. 690 was the first
version of the design and that No. 689 was a repetition
painted for the Duke of York.

Mather Brown

d. 1831. Painter of portraits and subject-pictures. American,
born probably in Boston, he came to London at an early
age and became a pupil of Benjamin West. Exhibited at the
Royal Academy between 1782 and 1831. He was described
as Portrait-Painter to the Duke of York in 1789; he was also
described subsequently as Historical and Principal Painter
to the Duke and Duchess of York and to the Duke of
Clarence.

691. GEORGE IV WHEN PRINCE OF WALES

(*Plate* 132)

Buckingham Palace. 98⅜ × 71½ in., 249,9 × 181,6 cm. A later
addition of 6¾ in. at the top was removed in 1963.

Signed: *M. Brown—p.*

Full-length, standing, in a fancy military uniform (see
below), wearing the ribbon and star of the Garter and resting his left hand on a paper; on a table beside him are a
crown and the collar of the Garter and a state robe lined
with ermine; on the left lies the mantle of the Garter. In the
background is a fort with guns firing and warships at sea.

Recorded at Buckingham Palace (629) in 1876 (*V.R. inv.*).

On 5 March 1791 Mather Brown submitted to the Prince an
account for 140 guineas 'To a very large *extra-sized* Whole
Length of His Highness, painted two years ago, and pre-

sented to The Rt Hon. Ld Lougborough';[1] Brown's receipt
is dated 25 July 1791 (W.R.A., Geo. 26798). No. 691 could
have been painted in 1789 (Brown exhibited at the Academy in that year (93) a portrait of the Prince) and it is
tempting to identify it with the portrait given to Lord
Loughborough. The uniform is an imaginary concoction,
presumably designed by the Prince himself. The buttons
are those of a General Officer, although the Prince was not
at this date in the army. The buckle on the sword-belt is
embellished with the Prince of Wales's arms and feathers.
There are considerable *pentimenti*. The column was added
to the design; originally the sky continued behind the figure
of the Prince. There are amendments to the shape of the
coat, the position of the Garter badge and the direction of
the left arm. The papers under the Prince's hands were also
altered; at first they had on them traces of writing, apparently addressed to the Prince, and there are traces on the
scroll of a similar *Address*. The crown was at first placed
higher.

692. WILLIAM VON FREYTAG (1711–98)

Windsor Castle (1133). Oval: 28¾ × 23¾ in., 73 × 60,3 cm.

Signed and dated: *M. Brown | 1794* (the date is now very
obscure).

Head and shoulders in Hanoverian uniform.

Recorded at Windsor in 1879 (*V.R. inv.*).

Probably the portrait of the Field-Marshal by Brown which
Queen Charlotte saw on 13 February 1794, with his picture
of the battle of Famars (Diary in the Royal Library).

Field-Marshal, in command of the Hanoverian contingent
in the campaign against the French in the Low Countries.
He was closely associated with the royal family, but was
disliked by the eldest Princes. Prince William wrote from
Hanover to the Prince of Wales in 1785 that 'this son of
a bitch has taken a disliking to your regiment of Light
Dragoons in this service on account of your being upon bad
terms with the King'. Mather Brown also painted a picture
(engraved by S. W. Reynolds) of the rescue of the Field-
Marshal and Prince Adolphus after they had blundered into
a French picquet at Rexpoede on 6 September 1793.

Benjamin Burnell

Painter of landscapes, subject-pictures and portraits; exhibited at the Royal Academy from 1790 to 1828.

693. CHARLES FITZROY, FIRST LORD SOUTHAMPTON (1737–97)

Windsor Castle (773). 30 × 25⅛ in., 76,2 × 63,8 cm.

On the back of the lining canvas is the signature *Benjm Bur-
nell Pinxt*, presumably copied from the back of the original
canvas. The sitter's name is inscribed on the front. Head
and shoulders in peer's robes.

Probably painted for, or presented to, Queen Charlotte; recorded
in the Bow Drawing-Room by Pyne (vol. I, *Frogmore*, p. 19); on
10 May 1820 it was sent up by Princess Augusta from Frogmore
to Carlton House 'in a Gilt Frame' (Jutsham, *Receipts*, ff. 98–9)

1. Alexander Wedderburn, 1st Baron Loughborough and later 1st Earl
of Rosslyn (1733–1805), Chief Justice of the Common Pleas, 1780–93, and
Lord Chancellor, 1793–1801. He had been an adherent of the Prince of
Wales during the Regency crisis. One press report in 1789 states that
Brown's portraits of the Prince and the Duke of York had been painted
as presents for the Duke of Leinster (V. & A. *Cuttings*, vol. II, p. 467).

and it appears as No. 571 in the additions to the inv. of 1816; later at Windsor.

Probably painted *c.* 1785.
See No. 1028.

Joseph Cartwright

d. 1829. Marine painter. For some years Paymaster-General of the forces at Corfu. In 1828 he was appointed Marine Painter to the Duke of Clarence. He exhibited at the British Institution, 1823–9, and at the Royal Academy, 1823–8.

694. THE BATTLE OF THE NILE (*Plate* 232)

Buckingham Palace. 48⅛ × 72½ in., 122,2 × 184,1 cm.

Signed and dated: *JC 1801* (initials in monogram).

The scene at night (about 9.30 p.m.) near the end of the battle, which was begun in the evening of 1 August 1798. The French flagship *L'Orient* is seen on the left in flames and being rapidly abandoned before she blew up at about 10 p.m. On the right are ships under the command of Nelson who was at that time Rear-Admiral of the Blue; the nearest of them is probably Nelson's flagship, *Vanguard*, from which boats were sent across to rescue the crew of *L'Orient*.

Recorded at Buckingham Palace (541) in 1876 (*V.R. inv.*); later at Kensington.

The date, formerly read as 1826, is perhaps the earliest recorded on a picture by Joseph Cartwright, who exhibited at the British Institution in 1827 (384) a larger picture of the burning of *L'Orient*, a pendant to a view of the battle of Trafalgar.

A. Dufay de Casanova

fl. 1829–37. Painter of scenes of Indian life; also stated to have worked in miniature. He is recorded in Calcutta in 1829 and 1831 and in Lucknow in the early summer of 1834 and again in 1835–7. In the *Calcutta Literary Gazette* of 24 May 1834 he was described as 'a French gentleman of considerable knowledge of the art . . . not much known, and works so slowly and deliberately that his works are few.'

695. THE PUBLIC RECEPTION OF JOHN LOW (1788–1880) BY NĀSIR-UD-DIN HAIDAR, KING OF OUDH

Buckingham Palace. 60¾ × 112 in., 154,3 × 284,5 cm.

The King, seated under a rich canopy on a howdah on his elephant, receives John Low who is also in a howdah on an elephant with an umbrella behind. They are surrounded by a large crowd of spectators, attendants and officers, both British and Indian; in the background are British and Indian troops, cavalry, infantry and artillery, on the bank of the Gumti River; and in the distance is Lucknow with the palace of Farhat Bakhsh. In the foreground is the artist, sketching, beside a carriage containing three English ladies.[1]

Acquired at an auction in 1841 by Colonel Palmer; purchased by Queen Victoria in 1845 (*V.R. inv.*).

Literature: Sir W. Foster, 'Some Foreign European Artists in India', *Bengal Past and Present*, vol. XI (Oct.-Dec. 1930), pp. 81–2.

1. In Ursula Low, *Fifty Years with John Company* (1936), p. 156, two of them are identified as Low's wife Augusta (1809–93) and her sister Marianne Irvine (1816–91).

Nāsir-ud-din Haidar, son of the sitter in No. 832, succeeded his father in 1827 and died in 1837. John Low, soldier and administrator, who ended his distinguished career as a general and G.C.S.I., was British Resident at Lucknow, 1831–42. Sir Henry Lawrence said of the King that he was 'engaged in every species of debauchery', and that 'he added the natural fruits of a vicious education to those resulting from his protected position'. The interview recorded in No. 695 is stated to have taken place on 4 March 1834; Mrs. Mildred Archer has suggested that the occasion was the Id Festival, which sometimes occurs in March and was lavishly celebrated amongst Muslims. The rulers of Oudh made much of these festivals and held receptions during the celebrations.

Henry Bernard Chalon

1770–1849. Son of a Dutch etcher and musician, Jan Chalon. Animal-painter. He exhibited at the Royal Academy between 1792 and 1847 and at the British Institution between 1807 and 1849. In 1793 he appears as Animal-Painter to the Duchess of York[1] and many of his exhibited pictures were of birds, dogs, horses and ponies belonging to members of the royal family: George III, George IV, the Duke and Duchess of York, Princess Charlotte of Wales, William IV and Queen Victoria. In submitting his account for Nos. 697–700 below, Chalon referred to 'The very distressing circumstances under which I am impelled to the liberty of troubling you' (W.R.A., Geo. 26857, 32293, 88978).
On 18 January 1812 he submitted a further bill, amounting to £132. 6s. for four (?) paintings of ponies belonging to Princess Charlotte: £110. 5s. for 'Seven Ponies, five Greys & two Dark bays of Her Royal Highness the Princess Charlotte of Wales, at Fifteen Guineas Each'; £9. 9s. for 'Three Boys at three guineas Each'; and £12. 12s. for 'Four frames for Dº at three gnˢ Each' (W.R.A., Geo. 26904, 42917). In 1811 Chalon had exhibited at the Royal Academy three pictures of animals belonging to the Princess: (109) Little Bit and Gay, two of her favourite phaeton ponies; (178) Scorpion, a famous blood-horse; and (183) Pleasant and Spangle, two favourite ponies. In 1812 he exhibited (209) portraits of Stump and Hump, two of the Princess's favourite phaeton ponies. In the quarter ending April 1818 Chalon was paid £99. 17s. 6d. (*ibid.*, 35420). In 1820 he appears as Animal Painter to the King and to the Duke and Duchess of York. The Duke's sale at Christie's, 7 April 1827, included a number of pictures by Chalon.

696. MRS. JANE BAKER (1760–1835) WITH HER HUSBAND, WILLIAM BAKER

Buckingham Palace. Panel: 11⅞ × 15 in., 30,2 × 38,1 cm.

Signed and dated on the back: *H B Chalon pinxᵗ | 1800*.

Seated at a table over a decanter; Mrs. Baker apparently proposes a health; on the wall behind are crudely painted portraits of George III and Queen Charlotte.

Recorded at Buckingham Palace (683) in 1876 (*V.R. inv.*).

Jane Simpson, who married William Baker of Windsor, was Rocker to the Prince of Wales from 1762 and later to his brothers Frederick and William Henry. In 1804 she was appointed Necessary Woman to the Apartments of the Duke of Cambridge in St. James's Palace; in 1813–30 she was Housekeeper in the same establishment.

1. See Farington, *Diary*, vol. II, pp. 228–9. He was still so described in 1819–20.

697. BARBAROSSA

Windsor Castle (2313). 43¼ × 59⅝ in., 109,8 × 151,4 cm.

Signed and dated: *H. B. Chalon pinxit 1808 | Newmarket* (initials in monogram).

A bay horse standing in a paddock near a shed, with a distant view of a town (presumably Newmarket).

Painted for George IV; received with Nos. 698–700 at Carlton House from Chalon on 24 September 1813 (Jutsham, *R/D*, f. 267: '. . . Barbarossa by Sir Peter Bay . . .') and recorded in store at Carlton House in 1816 (409); sent to the King's Lodge on 31 May 1822; later at Stud Lodge (1155) and Cumberland Lodge.

On 8 May 1808 Chalon sent in his 'account for some Pictures which I had the honor of executing [presumably at Newmarket] for his Royal Highness the Prince of Wales'. The account came to £157. 10s.: £131. 5s. for the five horses at twenty-five guineas each, and £26. 5s. for the five figures, at five guineas each; Chalon's receipt is dated 25 October 1808 (W.R.A., Geo. 26857). On 4 April 1808 Colnaghi submitted an account for £64 for frames for the pictures: 'Burnished Gold frames with Golloss Tops, Shells in corners and Tablets . . .' (*ibid.*, 27739). Chalon exhibited No. 697 at the Royal Academy in 1808 (177: *Barbarossa, by Sir Peter, the property of H.R.H. the Prince of Wales*). The engraving of No. 697 by W. Ward was published on 2 December 1809. Redgrave stated in 1868 (*V.R. inv.*) that Chalon had originally painted a groom on the left of the picture, but that he had later painted him out and covered the area with the shed; this change is barely discernible.

Barbarossa was foaled in 1802, by Sir Peter out of Mule-spinner. In 1806 he won the Somerset Stakes at Brighton as well as races at Canterbury and Newmarket.

698. ORVILLE WITH FRANCIS SMALLMAN

Windsor Castle (2323). 43⅜ × 60¼ in., 111,1 × 153 cm.

Signed and dated: *H. B. Chalon pinxit 1808. | Newmarket* (initials in monogram).

A chestnut horse held by Smallman, a groom (in dark blue coat and red waistcoat), while being combed by a boy (in scarlet coat with dark blue collar and cuffs); in the background is the country near Newmarket with a rubbing-down house. On the ground are a saddle, cloth and bottle and a comb (?) which, like the one held by the boy, bears the initials TP.

Painted for George IV; received with Nos. 697, 699, 700 at Carlton House from Chalon on 24 September 1813 (Jutsham, *R/D*, f. 267: '. . . Orville by Bening. Chesnut . . .') and recorded in store at Carlton House in 1816 (410); sent to the King's Lodge on 31 May 1822; later at Stud Lodge (1154) and Cumberland Lodge.

See No. 697. 'Mr Smalman & a Boy' appear in Chalon's account among the figures whom he had painted in the pictures done for the Prince of Wales. No. 698 was exhibited at the Royal Academy in 1808 (167: *Orville, by Beningbrough, and Smallman, the groom, the property of H.R.H. the Prince of Wales*). W. Ward's engraving of No. 698 was published on 25 March 1809 with a dedication to the Prince of Wales.

Orville, a son of Beningborough out of Evelina, was bred by Lord Fitzwilliam in 1799; he stood over sixteen hands and had enormous strength. He won the St. Leger in 1802 and was bought by George IV in 1804; he was very successful, 1805–7, and was destroyed in 1826.

Francis Smallman was described in January 1803 as training groom to the Prince of Wales at Newmarket.

699. SELIM WITH WILLIAM EDWARDS AND MR. PERREN (*Plate 261*)

Windsor Castle (2312). 43½ × 60¼ in., 110,5 × 153 cm.

Signed and dated: *H. B. Chalon pinxit 1808 | Newmarket* (initials in monogram).

A sorrel horse ridden by William Edwards in royal colours (dark blue with gold lace, scarlet sleeves) on Newmarket Heath near a starting-post. In front rides Mr. Perren on the hack, Moonshine.

Painted for George IV; received with Nos. 697, 698, 700 at Carlton House from Chalon on 24 September 1813 (Jutsham, *R/D*, f. 267: '. . . Selim by Buzzard—Sorril . . .') and recorded in store at Carlton House in 1816 (411); sent to the King's Lodge on 31 May 1822; later at Stud Lodge (1153) and Cumberland Lodge.

See No. 697. 'Wm Ewards' [*sic*] and 'Mr Perren' appear in Chalon's account among the figures (of jockeys and grooms respectively) whom he had painted in the pictures done for the Prince of Wales; 'Moonshine a Hack' is included among the horses. W. Ward's engraving of No. 699 was published on 25 March 1809.

Selim, by Buzzard out of a mare by Alexander, was bred by General Sparrow in 1802 and bought by the Prince of Wales in 1805. When the Prince sold his horses, Selim was given to Colonel Leigh. He was successful over all distances and was 'full of quality, and so majestic altogether that no one would have suspected him to be the workman he was at all distances'. In 1808 he retired to stud.

For William Edwards see No. 736.

700. SIR DAVID WITH SAMUEL CHIFNEY (1786–1854)

Windsor Castle (2329). 34 × 42 in., 86,4 × 106,7 cm. Originally No. 700 was the same size as Nos. 697–9, but it was cut down to its present size in 1896. On the back of the stretcher is now fixed the portion of original canvas bearing the signature and date: *H. B. Chalon pinxit 1808. | Newmarket* (initials in monogram).

A chestnut horse with Sam Chifney up, wearing the royal colours, by a starting-post at Newmarket.

Painted for George IV; received with Nos. 697–9 at Carlton House from Chalon on 24 September 1813 (Jutsham, *R/D*, f. 267: '. . . Sir David by Trumpator—Chesnut . . .') and recorded in store at Carlton House in 1816 (412); sent to the King's Lodge on 31 May 1822; later at Stud Lodge (1152) and Cumberland Lodge.

See No. 697. 'Sam Chifney' appears in Chalon's account among the jockeys whom he had painted in the pictures done for the Prince of Wales. No. 700 was exhibited at the Royal Academy in 1808 (69). W. Ward's engraving of No. 700 was published on 12 August 1809 with a dedication to the Prince of Wales.

Samuel Chifney the younger, second son of Samuel Chifney (No. 1118), first rode for the Prince of Wales in 1802 at Stockbridge; he was, like his father, famous for the 'Chifney rush'. He maintained a training stable of his own at Newmarket.

701. A SPANIEL

Kew (Hampton Court No. 1461). 44¼ × 56¼ in., 112,4 × 142,9 cm. There is, in addition, a strip of wood at the bottom, 2 in. wide, on which the design is continued.

Signed and dated: *H. B. Chalon. pinxit 1812*; the initials are in monogram and the signature and date are inscribed on the addition to the canvas (see above).

Standing near the edge of a stretch of water, frightening mallards.

Sold by Willis, 26 July 1901; presented to King Edward VII on 16 November 1901 by Sir William Carington and placed at Windsor (2635).

When it was presented to King Edward VII, No. 701 was described as a portrait of a spaniel belonging to George IV.

702. UNKENNELLING THE ROYAL HOUNDS ON ASCOT HEATH (*Plate* 262)

Windsor Castle (1674). 40¾ × 51 in., 103,5 × 129,5 cm.

Signed and dated: *H. B. Chalon. pinxit 1817*.

A group of picked hounds are being unkennelled and are flocking round George Sharpe (1756–1830), Huntsman of the Royal or King's Hunt, on his favourite hunter, Flamingo; behind are three whippers-in, Charles Davis (1788–1866), John Mandeville or Manville and John Freeman; all the riders are in scarlet livery, laced with gold, with dark blue collars and cuffs.

Painted for George IV; recorded as an additional number (535) in the 1816 inv. of Carlton House; sent to the King's Lodge on 31 May 1822; later at Cumberland Lodge.

On 3 April 1818 Chalon submitted a bill for £100 for 'painting a picture representing the unkennelling of His Royal Highness the Prince Regent's Stag Hounds on Ascot Heath with a Likeness of Mr Sharpe His Royal Highness's Huntsman; also a frame for the above'; Chalon's receipt is dated 13 May 1818 (W.R.A., Geo. 27014, 35517). No. 702 was exhibited at the Royal Academy in 1817 (348).

George Sharpe had been the Prince's huntsman in the days when he had hunted in Hampshire; in 1825 the pack was taken over by his son-in-law, the famous Charles Davis (brother of R. B. Davis), who had become groom to the pack in 1816 and whipper-in in 1817. Davis's father had been huntsman to George III's harriers. The pack of hounds seen in No. 702 was presumably descended from the pack presented to George IV in 1813 by the Duke of Richmond. The hounds were kept in kennels on Ascot Heath. John Mandeville or Manville and John Freeman are recorded as whippers-in in 1816 and from 1816 to 1834 respectively. The figures are identified from a letter written by Charles Davis on (1?) February 1866 which is kept with No. 702; he states that 'the two whips came from Goodwood with the Hounds'.

Mason Chamberlin

d. 1787. Portrait-painter; exhibited at the Society of Artists, 1760–8, and at the Royal Academy, 1769–86 (see No. 1210). In 1771 he exhibited (31) whole lengths of Prince Edward and Princess Augusta; and a 'Portrait of Her late Majesty', attributed to him, is recorded in the Queen's Drawing-room at Kensington in 1818 (144; measurements given as 30 × 25 in.; Faulkner, p. 370 as 'a head'). It was moved to Hampton Court on 2 May 1833.

703. JOHN HUNTER (1728–93)

Windsor Castle (771). 36 × 27¾ in., 91,4 × 70,5 cm.

Half-length, seated, holding in his right hand a statuette of a man.

Recorded at Windsor in 1878 (*V.R.inv.*).

Probably painted *c.* 1780. In Chamberlin's portrait of William Hunter, presented by the painter to the Royal Academy in 1769 (R.A., *Treasures of the Royal Academy*, 1963, (23)), the sitter holds a slightly smaller version of the statuette.

Anatomist and surgeon, younger brother of William Hunter (see No. 1210). He was appointed Surgeon-Extraordinary to George III in 1776.

George Chambers

1803–40. Painter of marine subjects. Born at Whitby, the son of a seaman, Chambers began to draw and paint at sea at an early age and was employed by a house and ship painter. After he had settled in London his cabinet pictures attracted the notice of Admiral Lord Mark Kerr who in 1831 secured his introduction to William IV: 'who says he wants a picture or two, to try your skill'. The King bought, for fifty guineas, the painter's view of the opening of London Bridge, but later gave it to Sir Byam Martin. Chambers was invited to bring to Windsor sketches from which Queen Adelaide could 'choose her subjects'. On 17 October he went to Windsor, where the Queen selected the two sketches from which the artist worked up Nos. 704, 705. On 3 July 1832 the two pictures for the Queen were despatched to Windsor; Chambers was told by Sir Herbert Taylor that 'The Queen is extremely pleased with both pictures, and that they are highly approved of by others who have seen them . . . particularly that of Dover'. At the Queen's command Chambers received thirty guineas for each picture (J. Watkins, *Life and Career of George Chambers* (1841), pp. 40–8). In 1840 Queen Adelaide bought a drawing by Chambers of Dover; in 1839 a group of inhabitants of Whitby had unsuccessfully petitioned Queen Victoria to bestow her patronage upon him, possibly by appointing him her official Marine Painter (*ibid.*, pp. 135–41).

704. A VIEW OF GREENWICH (*Plate* 298)

Buckingham Palace. Panel: 19 9/16 × 28 in., 49,5 × 68,6 cm.

Signed and dated: *G. Chambers 1832*. The back of the panel is inscribed by the artist with the subject and date.

A view of the Thames at Greenwich, looking up the river at the river-front of Greenwich Hospital.

Painted for Queen Adelaide and bequeathed by her to Queen Victoria in 1849 (MS. Catalogue of Queen Victoria's private pictures &c.); later in Prince Leopold's Sitting-room at Osborne (584; Osborne *Catalogue* (1876), p. 350.)

Literature: J. Watkins, *Life and Career of George Chambers* (1841), pp. 43–8.

The subjects of Nos. 704, 705 were selected by Queen Adelaide from the sketches brought down to Windsor by Chambers for her inspection on 17 October 1831. The chosen sketches were marked by the Queen and Sir Herbert Taylor. The finished pictures were delivered at Windsor on 3 July 1832 and the artist received thirty guineas for each picture; the Queen also retained the frames so that Chambers received in all £80. 13s. (W.R.A., Geo. 89601). The sketch selected by the Queen may have been the watercolour (*Fig.* 2) now in the Laing Art Gallery, Newcastle. A version of No. 704, signed and dated 1835, is in the National Maritime Museum; a copy by John Paul (*c.* 1835) is in the London Museum. No. 704 was engraved by J. B. Allen for the *Royal Gallery of Art* (vol. IV, 11).

705. A VIEW OF DOVER (*Plate* 299)

Buckingham Palace. Panel: 19½ × 28 in., 49,5 × 68,6 cm.

Signed and dated: *G. Chambers. 1832*. The back of the panel is inscribed by the artist with the subject and date.

A view of Dover Castle with the town lying below it; in the foreground are fishermen and boats.

Painted for Queen Adelaide and bequeathed by her to Queen Victoria in 1849 (MS. Catalogue of Queen Victoria's private pictures &c.); later in Prince Leopold's Sitting-room at Osborne (582; Osborne *Catalogue* (1876), p. 350).

Literature: J. Watkins, *Life and Career of George Chambers* (1841), pp. 43–8.

See No. 704. No. 705 was engraved by T. A. Prior for the *Royal Gallery of Art* (vol. IV, 26).

706. THE CAPTURE OF BAGUR

Buckingham Palace. 24 × 33 1/16 in., 61 × 83,8 cm.

The *Hydra* is seen exchanging fire with a battery in the fort at the entrance to the harbour of Bagur or Begu; the landing party is seen putting off from the ship.

Painted for William IV; recorded at Buckingham Palace (766) in 1876 (*V.R. inv.*).

Literature: J. Watkins, *Life and Career of George Chambers* (1841), pp. 39–47.

Apparently a second version, painted in 1831–2 for William IV, of a picture painted by Chambers for the *Hydra's* Captain. The original had been seen by the King. On 11 October 1831 Chambers was told by Sir Herbert Taylor (through Lord Mark Kerr) that 'His Majesty also wishes to have a copy of the Hydra on the coast of Spain, as the one sent is sold.' The receipt of No. 706 was acknowledged on 12 March 1832: 'his Majesty begs to know what part of the coast of Spain is represented' and Chambers was summoned to St. James's Palace to provide this information and receive payment for the picture. An engraving of No. 706 by Gauci was published in 1833.

The capture of Bagur on the coast of Catalonia is described in the official despatch about his 'little enterprise' from the *Hydra's* captain, George Mundy (*Annual Register* for 1807, pp. 708–9). On the night of 6 August 1807 the *Hydra* chased into Bagur three armed polaccas. On the following morning, under fire from the battery and from a tower nearby, Captain Mundy anchored his ship (at 12.50 a.m.) and embarked a landing party of seamen and marines which silenced the enemy guns, captured the fort and seized the three boats.

John Cleveley

d. 1777.[1] A Deptford shipwright and marine painter, who exhibited at the Society of Artists from 1764 and at the Royal Academy from 1770. A number of his pictures illustrated moments when the King and Queen were afloat or visiting dockyards. In 1774 he exhibited at the Royal Academy (39, 40) two views of the review at Spithead recorded in more detail by Serres (Nos. 1072–5); he showed two more pictures of the review in 1775 (65, 66).

707. THE DOCKYARD AT DEPTFORD

Buckingham Palace. 35¼ × 59½ in., 89,5 × 151,1 cm.

Signed and dated: *Iohn | Cleveley | 1761*

1. I am grateful to Mr. Michael Robinson for informing me of his discovery of this date.

A view of Deptford from the north-west with the new church of St. Paul on the left, the Store-houses and Officers' Houses in the centre and the Boat Houses on the extreme right. A procession of state barges is coming up the river; a group of musicians is playing in one of them and a yacht is firing a salute.

Recorded at Hampton Court in 1849 (*The Stranger's Guide*, No. 930; later No. 999); later at Kensington.

Literature: Law, *Kensington*, 1903, p. 127.

The view of Deptford is very close to that drawn by Samuel and Nathaniel Buck and engraved in 1739. The passenger in the largest state barge is clearly a person of consequence; the steersmen wear scarlet livery decorated with the Prince of Wales's feathers.

William Collins

1788–1847. Painter of landscapes and genre scenes. In 1815 he first visited the coast of Norfolk which was to be the source of inspiration of many of his pictures: 'the impressions made upon his mind by the scenery of this place, seem to have lasted through life . . . many of the backgrounds to his coast pictures I can trace to sketches made in this locality'. In the following year he visited Hastings and intensively studied the coast and those who lived and worked there.
He had visited Scotland in 1818 and in 1822 he went with Wilkie on the occasion of George IV's visit to Edinburgh. He hoped to paint a picture recording an episode during the royal visit. He planned to paint the King's landing at Leith; he went on board the *Royal George* and made some sketches. Sir Charles Long, in a memorandum dated 29 November 1822 on the state of various projects, noted: 'Mr Collins has made Sketches representing His Majesty's Arrival in Scotland, and his Dis-embarkation at Leith, subject to His Majesty's Approval, when the Pictures are finished' (W.R.A., Geo. 22908–9). But Collins does not seem to have received a formal commission. George IV is stated to have wished to acquire Collins's *Taking out a Thorn*, shown at the Royal Academy in 1828 (86), which had been painted for J. Delafield (W. Wilkie Collins, *Memoirs of the Life of William Collins* (1848), vol. I, pp. 75–6, 91–3, 191–214, 306).

708. A SCENE ON THE COAST OF NORFOLK (*Plate* 292)

Windsor Castle (1079). 35¼ × 45⅜ in., 89,5 × 115,2 cm.

The beach at low tide with fishermen. In the foreground, by a fisherman's hut, are two boys with nets, fish and boats.

Purchased by George IV and recorded at Carlton House (inv. of 1816, additional No. 547: 'A Sea Coast—A Fisherman—& Two Boys—Near a Cottage with Fish—A Gray Horse with Panniers—Dog & Figures on the Beach. Collins'); sent to the King's Lodge on 17 June 1824 (Jutsham, *Deliveries*, f. 54);[1] later at Windsor, Buckingham Palace and St. James's.

Literature: Farington, *Diary*, vol. VIII, p. 175; W. Wilkie Collins, *Memoirs of the Life of William Collins* (1848), vol. I, pp. 118–20, 224, vol. II, p. 344.

Exhibited at the Royal Academy in 1818 (8). According to Wilkie Collins (*op. cit.*) the Earl of Liverpool (No. 903) had purchased the picture at the Royal Academy, but resigned it to the Prince Regent who 'had been so delighted

1. It was probably for this picture that Wyatt on 20 December 1825 provided a 'Large Carved Gilt Frame for a Picture, Painted by Collins—the Picture is at The Royal Lodge—Windsor' (Jutsham, *Receipts*, f. 210).

with the picture at the private view of the day before, that he desired to possess it'. On 10 July 1818 Collins was paid 150 guineas 'for his Picture of a View of the Coast of Norfolk—which HRH The Prince Regent was pleased to approve' (W.R.A., Geo. 27028). It was exhibited at the British Institution in 1819 (85) and engraved by A. Willmore.

709. PRAWN FISHERS AT HASTINGS (*Plate* 293)

Windsor Castle (1078). $35\frac{5}{8} \times 45\frac{1}{2}$ in., $90,5 \times 115,6$ cm.

Signed and dated: *W. Collins 1825*.

The beach at low tide, with children collecting prawns from a young fisherman; in the distance is a view of Hastings with the ruined castle on the cliff.

Painted for George IV and recorded in the inventory of 'Carleton Palace' (552: 'A Sea Shore with fishermen, painted as a companion to No. 309 [i.e., No. 708] Collins'); later at St. James's.

Literature: W. Wilkie Collins, *Memoirs of the Life of William Collins* (1848), vol. I, pp. 235–6, 252–4, 264, vol. II, p. 346.

Commissioned in 1824 by George IV, who chose the subject; as a result Collins spent part of the summer of 1824 at Hastings. The picture was painted at Hendon, where the painter spent the summer of 1825. When the picture was finished, Collins was summoned to Windsor to meet the King and 'superintend the hanging of his picture in the proper light' (Wilkie Collins, *op. cit.*). On 6 January 1826 Collins was paid 300 guineas, 'the price of a Picture I have recently had the honor to paint for His Majesty' (W.R.A., Geo. 26538). Engraved by A. Willmore.

Abraham Cooper

1787–1868. Painter of animals, battles and sporting subjects.

710. FLEUR-DE-LIS

Buckingham Palace. $27\frac{3}{4} \times 36$ in., $70,5 \times 91,4$ cm.

Signed and dated: *Fleur-de-lis | A Cooper RA. 1827*.

A bay mare, standing in an open landscape.

Painted for George IV. Recorded at Stud Lodge (1157) in 1868 (*V.R. inv.*); later at Marlborough House.

On 26 February 1828 Cooper was paid £52. 10s. for a portrait of Fleur-de-Lis and on 11 July 1829 J. Smith was paid £14. 9s. for the frame. Smith's account is dated 17 November 1827 (W.R.A., Geo. 26564, 35793); his trade-label is still on the frame. No. 710 is probably the picture shown by Cooper at the Royal Academy in 1827 (297: *Fleur de-lis, by Bourbon, the property of Sir M. W. Ridley, Bart., M.P.*). There are traces on the right of two figures standing near the horse's head; they were apparently painted out by the artist himself. J. Webb's engraving of the picture, published in the *Sporting Magazine*, vol. XXIV, New Series (October 1829), pp. 377–9, shows the picture in its present state; but T. Lupton's engraving, published on 1 July 1828, shows the two figures (a jockey and a trainer) still in the composition. By Bourbon out of Lady Rachel, Fleur-de-Lis was bred by Christopher Sykes in 1822, later sold to Sir Matthew White Ridley and by him sold to George IV in 1827. She won the Doncaster Cup in 1826 and the Goodwood Cup in 1829 and 1830. She thus won the splendid Goodwood Cup, made by Storr and Mortimer on the basis of a model approved by George IV, which still belongs to Her Majesty the Queen.

John Singleton Copley

1738–1815. Painter of portraits and historical subjects, many of them from contemporary history. Born, almost certainly in Boston, of Irish descent. He became the leading painter in the American colonies. In 1774 he came to London, where he finally settled in the following year. George III and his family went to private views of his big pictures: the *Death of Major Peirson* in May 1784, the *Siege of Gibraltar* in May 1791 and *Charles I in the House of Commons* in May 1795. On his arrival in London Copley had a commission from New England to paint the King and Queen; the King approved of Copley's plan (which came to nothing) for a picture of the Installation of the Order of St. Patrick in 1783, and promised that Prince Edward would sit; but in the summer of 1806 Copley was harshly rebuffed by George III when he asked the King if he would sit to him. In 1809 he took the Prince of Wales's name in vain in his effort to get his large equestrian portrait (see No. 711) hung at the Academy (Farington, *Diary*, vol. III, pp. 250–1, vol. V, p. 135; J. Prown, *John Singleton Copley* (Cambridge, Mass., 1966), vol. II, pp. 246, 296–7, 307, 331, 345).

711. GEORGE IV ON HORSEBACK

Windsor Castle (2961). $40\frac{1}{8} \times 33\frac{3}{4}$ in., $101,9 \times 85,1$ cm.

Riding in Field-Marshal's uniform with the ribbon and star of the Garter[1] and followed by a group of officers: General Lord Heathfield (1750–1813), Major-General Tomkyns Hilgrove Turner (?1766–1843), Lieutenant-Colonel Benjamin Bloomfield (1768–1846) and Adolphus Christian Frederick, Baron von Eben (1771–1832). In the distance are mounted troops of the 10th Light Dragoons and a camp.

Bought by H.M. Queen Mary from the Bowyer-Smith heirlooms at Christie's, 29 April 1932 (78).

Literature: J. D. Prown, *John Singleton Copley* (Cambridge, Mass., 1966), vol. II, p. 420).

A reduced version, probably by Copley himself, of the huge canvas exhibited by him at the Royal Academy in 1810 (58) and now in the Museum of Fine Arts, Boston. There is considerable freedom in the handling of the background and the mounted officers on the right, and the background is much simpler in detail and more atmospheric than in the larger version. Copley had begun to paint the big picture on his own initiative in 1804, having shown a sketch of it to the Prince who was pleased with it and promised to sit for 'the likeness'; the Prince did not, however, sit to Copley, and thus enable him to finish the picture, until August 1809. At the Academy in 1810 the picture was unfavourably criticised although the figures were recognised to be 'accurately drawn as to resemblances' (exh., Washington, New York, Boston, *John Singleton Copley*, 1965–6, pp. 130–3, 142; J. D. Prown, *op. cit.*, vol. II, pp. 374, 375, 378–9, 382, 403, 420–1). C. W. Turner's engraving of it was published by Copley on 1 January 1813 with a dedication to Princess Charlotte.

Copley had hoped that the Prince would buy the big picture. He wrote on 19 June 1813 to Colonel McMahon asking for the Regent's commands 'relative to the destination of the picture'[2] which he was anxious should be placed 'in a situation suitable to such a place' and which he priced at 1500

1. The Prince's sword has been identified by Mr. A. V. B. Norman at Windsor (766).
2. In his letter Copley includes, as well as the sitters listed above, 'Col. Quinton', presumably Colonel George Quentin of the 10th Light Dragoons; it is possible that he is the officer, in the group behind the Prince, who wears the uniform of this regiment; but perhaps more likely that he is the galloping officer nearest to the Prince in the background.

guineas. On 26 September 1814 he again wrote to Carlton House, stating that his account had 'long since' been sent to McMahon. On 20 October he was finally informed 'that H.R.H. never intended to purchase the Picture, having sat merely at the request of the Artist understanding it to be a Public work, like the Death of L. Chatham' (*Letters of George IV*, 290; W.R.A., Geo. 26951). At the Lyndhurst sale at Christie's, 5 March 1864, the big picture (lot 88) fetched five pounds.

For Lord Heathfield, see No. 650. Major-General (later Sir) Tomkyns Turner had been appointed Assistant Quarter-master-General to the forces in Britain, 1803, and Brigadier-General on the home staff, 1804; he was also Deputy Secretary at Carlton House under McMahon. Bloomfield (later 1st Lord Bloomfield) became a Major-General in 1814 and three years later succeeded McMahon as Keeper of the Privy Purse and Private Secretary to the Prince. Eben, a Major in Dillon's regiment, was an Equerry to the Prince, 1807–13.

712. THE THREE YOUNGEST DAUGHTERS OF GEORGE III (*Plates* 129, 130)

Windsor Castle (3126). 104½ × 73¼ in., 265,4 × 186 cm.

Signed and dated: *J. S. Copley R.A. 1785*

Princess Mary, shaking a tambourine and with two little spaniels and a springing spaniel at her feet, pulls along a little carriage in which sits Princess Amelia, clutching the hand of Princess Sophia who sits in the back of the carriage. The cart bears the monogram PA. Behind the group a vine grows round columns and above the children are two scarlet parrots pecking grapes. In the distance are Windsor Castle and the Queen's Lodge.

Painted for George III and Queen Charlotte. In 1804 or 1805 it was removed from the King of Denmark's staircase at Kensington (Geo. III, *Removals:* 'Their R: H:s the Princesses in a Chaise. Copley') to the Ballroom at Windsor (Francis Legge's lists, 1813, 1816; Pyne, vol. I, pp. 100–1). Recorded at Hampton Court in 1835 (531); by 1841 it was in the Green Drawing-Room at Buckingham Palace (*Buckingham Palace*, 1841 (195); later inv. No. 210); it was then in the frame which is now adapted for No. 1088, which now occupies its place in the Green Drawing-Room.

Literature: R. and S. Redgrave, *A Century of Painters of the English School* (1866), vol. I, pp. 229–30; R.A., *King's Pictures* (113); Waterhouse, *Painting in Britain*, p. 202; Washington, New York, Boston, *John Singleton Copley*, 1965–6, pp. 106–7, 140–1; J. D. Prown, *John Singleton Copley* (Cambridge, Mass., 1966), vol. II, pp. 313–17, 416–17.

According to C. R. Leslie (letter to William Dunlop, quoted in R. and S. Redgrave, *loc. cit.*) Copley obtained the commission to paint the King's youngest daughters through the good offices of Benjamin West; the sitters—dogs and parrots as well as children—grew 'equally wearied' during the painting of the picture; and complaints reached the King who in turn complained to West, who 'satisfied his Majesty that Mr. Copley must be allowed to proceed in his own way, and that any attempt to hurry him might be injurious to the picture, which would be a very fine one when done'. There are minor *pentimenti* in many places, revealing slight alterations to details as the design developed. A sheet of studies in the Museum of Fine Arts, Boston (*Fig.* 3; Prown, *Fig.* 471) may contain Copley's first ideas for the figure of Princess Mary. A drawing in the Victoria and Albert Museum (*ibid.*, *Fig.* 472) is certainly an original study for the design; but it is unlikely that another drawing in Boston (*ibid.*, 469) and a related drawing in Worcester,

Mass. (*ibid.*, 470) are associated with this design. A drawing at Windsor (Oppé, No. 136) is not by Copley, but is after either the painting or Bartolozzi's engraving from it, published in 1792. A small version of the design in a private collection in the U.S.A. is a copy after No. 712 rather than a sketch for it (exhibited at Detroit, *English Conversation Pieces of the Eighteenth Century*, 1948 (1); see A. T. Perkins, *A Sketch of the Life of J. S. Copley* (1873), p. 133; a copy of the section of No. 712 that includes Princesses Sophia and Amelia was (1955) in a private collection in Scotland. 'A highly finished sketch' for the picture was in the Lyndhurst sale, Christie's, 5 March 1864 (79). The picture was exhibited at the Royal Academy in 1785 (80). It was harshly criticised by Hoppner, reviewing the exhibition in the *Morning Post* of 5 May 1785 (Prown, *op. cit.*, pp. 315–16), and by other critics at the time.

After John Singleton Copley

713. WILLIAM II (1792–1849), KING OF HOLLAND, WHEN PRINCE OF ORANGE

Buckingham Palace. 50 × 39¾ in., 132,1 × 101 cm.

Three-quarter-length, standing in the uniform of an A.D.C. to a Commander-in-Chief, wearing the Peninsular Gold Medal and holding his sabre in his right hand.

Recorded at Buckingham Palace (459) in 1876 (*V.R. inv.*).

Literature: J. D. Prown, *John Singleton Copley* (Cambridge, Mass., 1966), vol. II, pp. 381–2, 428.

A copy of the portrait (of *c.* 1812) in the Wellington Museum at Apsley House. C. Turner's engraving of the portrait was published on 4 December 1813. The portrait is close in type to the figure of the Prince in Copley's *Battle of the Pyrenees* (painted in 1812–15 and now in Boston) and is traditionally stated to have been painted for presentation to Princess Charlotte who was, however, dissatisfied with it.

Son of William I, whom he succeeded in 1840. As a young man he had been a candidate for the hand of Princess Charlotte. At the end of 1813 she agreed to marry him, but in the summer of 1814 the engagement was broken off. He had served as an A.D.C. to Wellington in the Peninsula and commanded the Dutch and Belgian contingents in the Waterloo campaign, when he behaved with great gallantry and was wounded. In later life he did much to establish a constitutional monarchy in Holland.

William Corden

1797–1867. Portrait-painter, miniaturist and painter on china. He is stated to have secured the patronage of the royal family with a portrait of one of George IV's pages at Windsor in 1829.

Corden's bill of 1829 included, under 22 October, seven guineas 'To a Portrait of a Dog with a View of Virginia Water'. His account, dated 31 March 1830, included fifteen guineas for a copy of Lawrence's portrait of Lady Maria Conyngham (see below, p. 60; W.R.A., Geo. 26582, 26596). He was later employed as a copyist by Queen Victoria and the Prince Consort.

714. SIR EDMUND NAGLE (1757–1830)

Windsor Castle (359). 30 × 25¼ in., 76,2 × 63,8 cm.

Inscribed on the back of the canvas with the names of artist and sitter.

Head and shoulders, holding a paper in his hands, wearing the stars of the Bath and the Guelphic Order and the badge of the Bath.

Painted for George IV. Corden submitted a bill including, under 21 December 1829, ten guineas 'To a Portrait of Sir Edmund Negle', and an additional five guineas for a gilt frame. His receipt is dated 4 March 1830. On 31 March 1830 Corden submitted a bill including sixteen shillings, 'Balance of the Bill for Sir Edmᵈ Nagle pict'. (W.R.A., Geo. 26582, 26596). The engraving of No. 714 by W. J. Ward was published in 1830; it shows more space all round the figure and a table, with spectacles and a handkerchief, on the left.

Entered the Navy in 1770 and reached the rank of Admiral in 1819. In 1803 he was appointed to command the sea fencibles of the Sussex coast and he became a favourite with the Prince of Wales. In 1820 he was appointed a Groom of the Bedchamber.

Richard Cosway

1742–1821. Painter in oils and in miniature; he also drew a large number of portraits. He first exhibited in London in 1760. He quickly built up a very fashionable practice and became closely associated with the Prince of Wales at Carlton House. He was appointed (in or by 1785) Principal Painter to the Prince and constantly signed his works as *Primarius Pictor*. He produced many miniatures and portrait-drawings of the royal family, especially of George IV, and of Mrs. Fitzherbert. In 1788–9 Cosway was working on pictures for the ceiling of the grand saloon at Carlton House. The documents assembled when efforts were being made to settle the Prince's debts included a memorandum by Cosway of pictures painted by him for the Prince up to May 1795. The bill amounted to £1,625. 8s., which included £142. 6s. for 'Seven Pictures in compartments in Mrs Fitzherberts House Pall Mall' and some pictures which Cosway had bought for the Prince. Additional bills added a further £509. 15s. to the amount due to Cosway (P.R.O., H.O. 73, 18). Cosway also appears to have had an overall responsibility at this period for the Prince's growing collection of pictures. On 28 September 1795 he authorised George Simpson's account for work on many of the Prince's pictures (*ibid.*, H.O. 73, 23). As early as 1786 Cosway had been listed as a creditor to the Prince to the extent of £651 (W.R.A., Geo. 31910).

715. SIR WILLIAM ERSKINE (1769–1813)

Windsor Castle (362). Panel: 29 × 23⅝ in., 73,7 × 60 cm.
Signed on the back of the panel with the monogram RC.

Head and shoulders, in a carved painted oval, in General Officer's uniform.

In the collection of George IV; recorded in store at Carlton House in 1816 (291); removed to the New Corridor at Windsor on 6 August 1828.

Probably painted *c.* 1810. The mouldings on the painted oval, and (to a lesser extent) the uniform, are so thinly painted as to suggest that the portrait was not completely finished; there is a *pentimento* in the shape of the collar.

Entered the army in 1786, created a Baronet in 1791 and promoted Major-General in 1808; commanded a brigade of cavalry in the Peninsula. He later was in temporary command of the light division, but led it so recklessly as to bring it near to disaster. By now he was beginning to show signs of insanity, and after he had been ordered to leave the army he committed suicide at Lisbon.

716. ELIZABETH MILBANKE, VISCOUNTESS MELBOURNE (1752–1818)
(*Plate* 137)

Windsor Castle (326). Panel: 30 × 24¾ in., 76,2 × 62,9 cm.
Signed RC in monogram.

Head and shoulders in fancy seventeenth-century costume, wearing a feathered hat and holding a book in her left hand.

Probably painted for George IV (see below); recorded in store at Carlton House in 1816 (296: 'A head of Lady Melbourne. Mr Cosway'); in March 1838 brought from Hampton Court to Buckingham Palace for Queen Victoria's inspection and cleaned before being hung in Baroness Lehzen's room.

Literature: G. C. Williamson, *Richard Cosway, R.A.* . . . (1897), p. 117; Collins Baker, *Windsor*, p. 64.

Cosway's account for work done for the Prince of Wales, 1781–6, includes £31. 10s. for 'A Portrait of a Lady in Oil', painted in 1784 (W.R.A., Geo. 26792), which could be No. 716. Cosway appears to have altered the original position of the left arm and hand, which he at first placed lower and pointing downwards; the book was almost certainly an afterthought. The signature, the reference in the inventory of 1816 and the account submitted by Cosway correct the statement by W. M. Torrens (*Memoirs of . . . Melbourne* (1878), vol. I, p. 27) that the portrait was painted for the Prince by Maria Cosway. In 1838 Queen Victoria and Lord Melbourne discussed the portrait; the Queen sketched it (Journal, 22 February, 3, 4, 24, 31 March, 7 July 1838).

Daughter of Sir Ralph Milbanke, 5th Baronet; she married in 1769 the 1st Viscount Melbourne, a Gentleman, and later a Lord, of the Bedchamber to the Prince of Wales, whose mistress Lady Melbourne was reputed to have been. The mother of the great Lord Melbourne (No. 848), she was an enchanting creature, with a 'captivating manner and conversation', described by Lord Byron as 'not merely clever and engaging, but the most sagacious woman I ever knew'.

Francis Cotes

1726–70. Portrait-painter, originally a pupil of Knapton, working in oil and pastel. Exhibited at the Society of Artists, 1760–8, and Royal Academy, 1769–70.
In addition to the portraits that are still in the royal collection, three pastels are recorded at Buckingham House in the time of George III: 'The Prince of Wales and Bishop of Osnabourgh—in Crayons. Coates', measurements given as 32 × 26½ in. (in the Blue Closet); 'Prince Ernest' and 'The Queen of Denmark', both as by Cotes, measuring 24 × 18 in. and 24 × 19½ in. respectively, and hanging in the Bedchamber (Geo. III, *Buck. Ho.*). These two portraits are now in the collection of S.K.H. Prince Ernst August. That of the Queen of Denmark (see No. 720; *Fig.* I) is signed and dated 1766, the other (*Fig.* II) is signed and dated 1769. Pyne records (vol. I, *Frogmore*, p. 20) in the State Bedroom at Frogmore: '*Portrait of the Duchess of* ANCASTER—*Portrait of Lady* HOLDERNESS; painted in crayons by Francis Coates'. Princess Augusta's accounts include a receipt by Cotes, dated 3 November 1768, for £26. 5s. 'for the Picture' and three guineas for the frame (W.R.A., Geo. 55516) which it is not possible to attach with certainty to any particular picture.

717. QUEEN CHARLOTTE WITH CHARLOTTE, PRINCESS ROYAL

Buckingham Palace. Pastel on paper, oval: 38¾ × 33¼ in., 97,5 × 84,4 cm.

Signed and dated: *FCotes* (initials in monogram) *pxt | 1767*

Half-length, holding in her left arm the sleeping Princess; with her right hand she cautions the spectator against waking the child.

Presumably painted for the Queen; it is recorded in the King's Bedchamber at Buckingham House: 'The Queen and Princess Royal. Coates', measurements given as 38 × 32 in. (Geo. III, *Buck. Ho.*; B.M., Add. MSS. 6391, f. 123) and was seen in Buckingham House by Walpole: '. . . the present Queen & Princess royal asleep in her arms, by Cotes: the Queen gave a Duplicate of this to the late Duchess of Northumberland' (*Visits*, p. 79). It was removed to Windsor in 1804 or 1805 (Geo. III, *Removals*) and in 1813 is recorded in the King's Closet in the private apartments there (Francis Legge's lists; later inv. No. 465).

Literature: R.A., *King's Pictures* (91).

Exhibited at the Society of Artists in 1767 (32). Walpole noted in his catalogue: 'The Queen, fine; the Child, incomparable. The Duchess of Northumberland has the Original, given to her by the Queen . . . The Sleeping Child is equal to Guido . . .' In this early reference Walpole indicates that No. 717 is the second version and that the version still at Syon House, which is also signed and dated 1767, is the original one. In his later reference he describes the version at Syon as 'a Duplicate' (see above). The pastels may have preceded Cotes's repetition in oil (No. 718). The design was first drawn on a rectangular sheet of paper, 27 × 22¾ in., which Cotes made out to an oval. In a treatise on pastel painting, Cotes compiled a short list of 'The finest examples that are known in this branch of painting'; he ventured to include, 'if it will not be deemed too much presumption', some of his own portraits, among them 'her Majesty with the Princess Royal sleeping' (Whitley, *Artists and their Friends in England 1700–1799* (1928), vol. I, pp. 222, 268).

718. QUEEN CHARLOTTE WITH CHARLOTTE, PRINCESS ROYAL (*Plate 15*)

Windsor Castle (273). 94 × 58¼ in., 238,8 × 147,9 cm.

Signed and dated: *FCotes* (initials in monogram) *pxt 1767.*

Full-length, seated, with the sleeping child in her arms, raising her right hand to caution the spectator; her crown is on a carved table on the right.

Presumably painted for George III or Queen Charlotte; apparently at St. James's and then at Buckingham House (mutilated section of inv. No. 34 above: '. . . ess Royal F.St J's. Coats', measurements given as 88 × 58 in.); taken over by the Prince of Wales in or before 1794, when Simpson cleaned it for him (P.R.O., H.O. 73, 23). Recorded in store at Carlton House in 1816 (242), when, as in 1819 (344), the infant was identified with the Prince of Wales and the picture was attributed to Ramsay. Sent to Windsor on 30 December 1828; on this occasion Jutsham (*Deliveries*, f. 216) stated: 'I believe this Portrait has been reduced to a Half Length, by Command of His Majesty by orders given to Mr Seguier. N.B. the Canvas is only doubled Down behind the Frame'. In this state the portrait was recorded in the White Drawing-Room in 1861 (*V.R. inv.*; measurements, as stretched, given as 50¾ × 40½ in.); it was re-stretched to its present size in 1901.

Literature: E. Edwards, *Anecdotes of Painters* (1808), p. 34; Collins Baker, *Windsor*, p. 65.

No. 718 is virtually an extension, in a different medium, of No. 717; it is probable that the pastel preceded, and was the source of, the oil. The engraving of No. 718 by W. Wynne Ryland was published on 31 July 1770, when the original is stated to be in the King's possession; an engraving from the same source by Adlard was published in 1830 as of the Queen with the Prince of Wales. A drawing in the British Museum (L.B.3), in which a lady identified as the Duchess of Ancaster stands beside the Queen, was perhaps drawn after the picture and may not be a study for it.

719. WILLIAM HENRY, DUKE OF GLOUCESTER (*Plate 13*)

Windsor Castle (2971). Pastel on paper: 24 × 18 in., 61 × 45,7 cm.

Signed and dated: *FCotes pxt | 1769* (initials in monogram).

Head and shoulders in the uniform of Colonel of the 1st Foot Guards, wearing the ribbon and star of the Garter.

Sold from the collection of John Ambler at Christie's, 4 May 1933 (101), when it was bought by H.M. Queen Mary for the royal collection.

Literature: R.A., *King's Pictures* (78).

Presumably the portrait of the Duke 'in crayons' exhibited by Cotes at the Royal Academy in 1769 (27) and described by Walpole as 'Exceedingly like'. A miniature copy is at Windsor.

720. PRINCESS LOUISA AND PRINCESS CAROLINE (*Plate 14*)

Buckingham Palace. 104⅝ × 73½ in., 265,7 × 186,7 cm.

Signed and dated: *F Cotes. pxt 1767* (initials in monogram).

Full-lengths, Princess Louisa seated in front of a table with a raised music-stand, holding a book of music and a gittern or English guitar; her sister stands beside her chair, holding a roll of music, in front of an organ.

Probably painted for Augusta, Princess of Wales. Her accounts include payments to Bradburn and France for work in the six months ending on 1 April 1768; the payments include £125. 19s. for '2 very rich whole length Tabernacle Frames carved, and partly gilt in burnished Gold, for the Pictures of Her Majesty the Queen of Denmark . . .' (D. of Cornwall MSS., vol. LV (1); the other frame was for No. 869). Walpole records 'Two whole length pictures . . . and of the princesses Louisa and Caroline (queen of Denmark) in the other, are in the drawing-room of Melcomb House, Pall-Mall, belonging to the princess dowager of Wales' (*Anecdotes*, vol. V, p. 49, attributing both pictures to Angelica Kauffmann). Later at Carlton House: Simpson's work for the Prince of Wales in 1794 included six guineas for cleaning the picture and its frame (P.R.O., H.O. 73, 23). Recorded in store at Carlton House in 1816 (243: 'Whole length portraits of two of the Princesses, sisters to his Majesty. Ramsay'; measurements given as 108 × 71 in.); by 1841 it was in the Green Drawing-Room at Buckingham Palace (*Buckingham Palace*, 1841, p. 95; later inv. No. 215).

Literature: R.A., *King's Pictures* (109).

The head of Princess Caroline in No. 720 is very close to Cotes's pastel of her (*Fig.* I), signed and dated 1766, in the collection of S.K.H. Prince Ernst August (see above), and may have been derived from it. Another signed version of the pastel is at Frederiksborg on which the date has been read as 1765, 1766 and 1768. Another version of the head in pastel, but in a different costume, was sold at Christie's, 28 May 1948 (8b). A half-length portrait of Princess Louisa, closely related to No. 720, was sold at Christie's on 10 November 1950 (117) and is now at Clarence House.

Attributed to Francis Cotes

721. PORTRAIT OF A BABY (Plate 35)

Windsor Castle (1517). 50¼ × 40⅜ in., 127,6 × 102,5 cm.

Full-length, seated in a rocky landscape, as Cupid, holding a festoon of flowers in his hand; a basket of flowers and a quiver lie beneath his feet.

Recorded at Frogmore in 1872 (*V.R. inv.*).

Literature: Collins Baker, *Windsor*, p. 62.

Formerly attributed to Copley, and described as a portrait of George IV (*V.R. inv.*) as a baby or as a portrait of Adolphus, Duke of Cambridge (Collins Baker, *loc. cit.*). It can, however, be safely attributed to Cotes. The sitter is almost certainly one of the sons of George III and bears a resemblance to Prince Edward, later Duke of Kent. No. 721 could be the portrait of Prince Edward by 'Coats' which was recorded in the Presence Chamber at Kensington in 1778. A portrait of him by 'Coates' was also recorded in the Queen's Bedroom at Kew (Geo. III, *Kew*; later pencil note stating that this had gone to Windsor), but in the draft of this inventory it is described as 'in Crayons'. If No. 721 does represent Prince Edward, who was born on 2 November 1767, it was presumably painted late in 1768 or early in 1769. There are slight *pentimenti* in the draperies, where the flowers and the left hand are painted over them.

John Crome

1768–1821. Landscape painter, who worked for most of his life in and around Norwich, where he was born and where he died. In 1803 he formed, with a group of friends, the Norwich Society of Artists.

School of John Crome

722. A COTTAGE ON THE YARE

Buckingham Palace. 30⅜ × 25 in., 77,1 × 63,5 cm.

A cottage on the water with a rowing-boat tied up to some steps.

Formerly in the collections of Lockett Agnew and Mrs. Ruffer; in 1946 bequeathed by James Henly Batty to the royal collection.

Literature: Manchester City Art Gallery, *Works by Early British Masters*, 1909 (34), lent by Lockett Agnew; Castle Museum, Norwich, *Crome Centenary Exhibition*, 1921, not in catalogue, lent by Mrs. Ruffer; Agnew's, *Crome and Cotman*, 1958 (36).

Presumably painted by a follower of Crome in the Norwich School. The type of design probably derives from, for example, the *St. Martin's Gate* (?c. 1812) in the Castle Museum at Norwich. A variant of No. 722 was in the C. F. Blandy collection.

Nathaniel Dance, later Sir Nathaniel Dance-Holland

1735–1811. Painter of portraits and historical pieces. He exhibited at the Society of Artists, 1761–7, and at the Royal Academy from the first exhibition in 1769, where he showed (30, 31) full-lengths of the King and Queen which are now at Uppark. Dance is recorded in Italy, 1745–65. Farington (*Diary*, vol. I, p. 6) records in October 1793 Dance's reluctance to paint a portrait of the Prince of Wales.

In 1790 he retired from painting, entered parliament and, in 1800, become a Baronet.

723. EDWARD, DUKE OF YORK (Plate 17)

Buckingham Palace. 94¾ × 58½ in., 240,7 × 148,6 cm.

Full-length, standing, in Garter robes, with the plumed and jewelled hat of the order on a table beside him.

Recorded in the Dining-Room at Buckingham House, where it was seen by Walpole (Geo. III, *Buck. Ho.*; Walpole, *Visits*, p. 79); moved in 1804 or 1805 to Windsor, where it was hung in the King's Old State Bedchamber (Geo. III, *Removals*; Pyne, vol. I, *Windsor*, p. 155); later at Hampton Court, but by 1841 hanging in the Green Drawing-Room at Buckingham Palace (*Buckingham Palace*, 1841, p. 94; later inv. No. 213).

Perhaps painted for George III and intended by him to form part of the set of family portraits in the Dining-Room at Buckingham House (see above, p. xii). Walpole (*Anecdotes*, vol. V, p. 29) quotes a press report of 2 April 1764 that 'Mr. Dance, the celebrated English painter at Rome, ... has painted lately his royal highness the Duke of York'. The Duke was in Rome in the spring of 1764 (see No. 689) and had sat there to Batoni (Levey, No. 358), whose portrait of the Duke is very close to Dance's in the head. Dance may have brought the portrait back with him to England in 1765 in an unfinished state and completed the robes in London. The frame in which No. 689 is now placed is one of the fine tabernacle frames made for Carlton House (see Nos. 996, 997).

724. CHRISTIAN VII (1749–1808), KING OF DENMARK

Buckingham Palace. 30⅛ × 24¾ in., 76,5 × 62,9 cm.

Head and shoulders in a painted oval, wearing the ribbon of the Danish Order of the Elephant.

Painted for George III; recorded in the George II Closet at Kensington in 1818 (536); moved to Hampton Court (976) on 1 November 1833; later at Kensington.

Literature: Law, 1881, 1898 (34).

Presumably painted in the late summer or autumn of 1768 when the King—Walpole's 'little majesty'—was in London; he arrived on 11 August and left on 14 October. Fisher's engraving of the portrait, published on 1 April 1769, states that it was 'Done from the Original Picture painted by Mr Dance for the KING of GREAT BRITAIN', to whom the print was dedicated (Chaloner Smith, vol. II, p. 490).

Son of Frederick V (whom he succeeded in 1766) and Princess Louisa, youngest daughter of George II. In 1767 he married Princess Caroline, sister of George III. Through his favourite and physician, the Prussian Struensee, he initiated measures designed to strengthen the royal prerogative in Denmark, but in 1772 Struensee was executed on a charge of adultery with the Queen. A regency was established in 1784.

725. TIMON OF ATHENS (Plate 18)

Hampton Court (1261). 48 × 54 in., 121,9 × 137,2 cm.

The scene is an episode from Act IV. sc. 3 of Shakespeare's play. Timon, who has dug up gold outside his cave, is approached by Alcibiades 'in warlike manner' with Phrynia and Timandra; Timon bids the two ladies 'Hold up ... Your aprons mountant' and throws them the gold: 'There's more gold. Do you damn others, and let this damn you, And ditches grave you all.'

In the possession of George III by 1 June 1771 (see below) and recorded in the Library at Buckingham House (Geo. III, *Buck. Ho.*); taken to Windsor (later No. 836) in 1804–5 (Geo. III, *Removals*).

Literature: Collins Baker, *Hampton Court*, p. 60; R.A., *The First Hundred Years*, 1951–2 (3), *English Taste in the Eighteenth Century*, 1955–6 (356); exh., Rome, *Il Settecento a Roma*, 1959 (183); B. C. Skinner, 'Some Aspects of the Work of Nathaniel Dance in Rome', *Burl. Mag.*, vol. CI (1959), p. 346; Nottingham University Art Gallery, *Shakespeare in Art*, 1961 (21); Arts Council, *Shakespeare in Art*, 1964 (18); D. Irwin, *English Neoclassical Art* (1966), p. 79.

Painted for the King just before Dance's departure from Rome in 1765 or soon after his return to London. The commission may have been conveyed through the influence of Richard Dalton. Exhibited at the Society of Artists in 1767 (43; note by Walpole that it was 'now in the Queen's House'). On J. Hall's engraving, published by Boydell on 1 June 1771, No. 725 is stated to be in the King's collection. For earlier treatments of the subject by English illustrators of Shakespeare, see W. M. Merchant, *Shakespeare and the Artist* (1959), p. 176.

After Nathaniel Dance

726. JOHN THOMAS, BISHOP OF WINCHESTER (1696–1781)

Buckingham Palace. 32½ × 26 in., 82,5 × 66 cm.

Signed and dated: *T. Parkinson / Pt 1781* (initials in monogram).

Head and shoulders, seated, wearing Bishop's robes with his mantle and badge as Prelate of the Order of the Garter.

Painted for George III or Queen Charlotte and recorded in the Wardrobe in Buckingham House (B.M. Add. MS. 6391, f. 122; Geo. III, *Buck Ho:* 'The Bishop of Winchester, after Dance by Parkerson'); removed (1804–5) to Windsor (Geo. III, *Removals:* 'The Bishop of Winchester. Dr Thomas'), where it hung in the Council Room in the King's Private Apartments (Francis Legge's lists of 1813, 1816: '. . . (Dr Thomas) . . . Dance (a Copy)'). Later at Hampton Court (888) and Kensington.

Literature: Law, 1881, 1898 (374).

A copy by Parkinson from the three-quarter-length, signed and dated 1773, at Lambeth Palace. Since at least 1849 (*The Stranger's Guide*, No. 846) No. 726 has been identified with Brownlow North who succeeded John Thomas as Bishop of Winchester. The copy was presumably made at the time of Bishop Thomas's death.

Appointed a chaplain to George II, 1742; Bishop of Peterborough, 1747; in 1752 he was appointed Preceptor to George, Prince of Wales, and in 1757 he became Bishop of Salisbury and Clerk of the Closet. In 1761 he was translated to Winchester.

Richard Barrett Davis

1782–1854. Painter of animals and sporting subjects. Son of the Huntsman to the royal harriers and brother of the famous Huntsman, Charles Davis. He seems first to have been encouraged by George III (Farington, *Diary*, vol. II, p. 185). He exhibited regularly at the Royal Academy, 1802–53, and at the British Institution, 1808–51. He exhibited a number of pictures of animals belonging to the royal family and of hunting and sporting scenes in the Windsor district. He was Animal Painter to George IV and William IV.

727. THE FUNERAL PROCESSION OF QUEEN CHARLOTTE

Windsor Castle (3059). 15 × 33¼ in., 38,1 × 84,4 cm.

The procession has just passed the Guildhall at Windsor on its way up to the Castle. The late Queen's hearse, drawn by eight of her black horses, is followed by the coach of the Prince Regent as chief mourner drawn by six black horses. The procession is headed by a squadron of Horse Guards; immediately in front of the hearse are walking royal servants and grooms carrying lighted flambeaux.

Sold at Phillips, Son & Neale, 23 March 1954 (86), when it was purchased for the royal collection.

The Queen had died at Kew on 17 November 1818. She was buried in St. George's Chapel on the evening of 2 December. The funeral procession had left Kew soon after 9 a.m. that day and reached Frogmore at 7 in the evening; it then proceeded to the Castle. In No. 727 Davis probably gives an accurate impression of the last stage of the journey (see, for example, *Annual Register* for 1818, pp. 170–9).

728. THE CORONATION PROCESSION OF WILLIAM IV

Buckingham Palace. 28 × 1,540¾ in., 71,1 × 3,913 cm.

The frieze is now divided into a number of sections, but these do not apparently coincide with the artist's original divisions of his work.

The procession, with an escort of Household Cavalry and Lancers, moves across a background of plain sky in the following order. The two carriages of the Duke and Duchess of Gloucester, each drawn by six horses; the two carriages of the Duchess of Cambridge, each drawn by six horses; the carriage of the Duke of Sussex, drawn by six horses; the two carriages of the Duke and Duchess of Cumberland, each drawn by six horses; the King's Bargemaster and the King's forty-eight Watermen; ten carriages of the King and Queen, containing members of their Households and each drawn by six horses and attended by Grooms on foot; the King's Equerries and Aides-de-Camp on horseback, some of them seen riding beside the royal carriages; they are attended by mounted Grooms and Yeomen Riders and presumably include: Sir Philip Sidney, Sir Augustus d'Este (Equerries), Major-General Sir George Quentin (Equerry of the Crown Stable), Lieutenant-General Sir Robert Taylor (First and Principal A.D.C.) and Colonels Sir Charles Thornton, Sir Evan Murray MacGregor, Edward Gibbs, Sir C. Broke Vere, Hercules Pakenham, J. T. Jones, Sir George Scovell, Robert Henry Dick, Neil Douglas, Thomas Downman, William Elphinstone, Frederick Trench, T. W. Brotherton, William Wemyss, George Browne, Thomas Wood and John Le Couteur, Major-General John Gardiner (Deputy Adjutant-General), Major-General Sir Richard Jackson (Deputy Quartermaster-General), Colonel Sir Alexander Dickson (Deputy Adjutant-General of the Royal Artillery), Lieutenant-General Sir James W. Gordon (Quartermaster-General), Major-General John Macdonald (Adjutant-General) and Major-General Lord Fitzroy Somerset (Military Secretary); then come Thomas, Viscount Anson, Master of the Buckhounds, attended by two Grooms; six of the King's cream horses with rich trappings, each led by two Grooms; George Head, Deputy Knight Marshal, with Marshalmen in ranks of four; the Exon and Clerk of the Cheque of the Yeomen of the Guard, Henry Cipriani, T. H. Curteis, Charles Hancock, John Hancock and R. F. Fitzherbert, with one hundred Yeomen of the Guard; the Lieutenant and Ensign of the Yeomen of the Guard, John Gill and William Conyngham

Burton; twelve Footmen; the State Coach, drawn by eight cream horses, Yeomen of the Guard at each wheel, two Footmen at each door and four Grooms on either side of the horses; General Viscount Combermere, Gold Stick, and the Captain of the Yeomen of the Guard, Ulick de Burgh, Marquess of Clanricarde, riding on either side. The Queen was attended by the Duchess of Gordon and the Countess Brownlow, Lady of the Bedchamber.

Painted for William IV; recorded at Buckingham Palace (689) in 1875 (*V.R. inv.*).

No. 728 seems a fairly accurate record of the procession which formed down Constitution Hill at 9 a.m. on 8 September 1831 and arrived at Westminster Abbey at 11.15. It was under the orders of Lord Frederick Fitzclarence, Gentleman of the Horse to the King, assisted by R. W. Spearman, Chief Clerk of the Stables, who may be the two figures at the head of the procession (full descriptions of the procession are to be found in, for example, a special supplement to the *London Gazette* of 9 September 1831, published on 13 September; and on pp. 142–4 of the Chronicle in the *Annual Register* for 1831). Davis must have been given special facilities to see the procession and make sketches (Nos. 729–34 are six such sketches); there are *pentimenti* at certain points, where riders are painted in front of carriages; at least one sitter (Sir Augustus d'Este) has his name inscribed below him. Many of the figures, of all ranks, are clearly intended to be recognizable portraits.

Davis exhibited the first part of the picture at the Society of British Artists in 1832 (224), when at least one critic praised him for the way in which he had tackled so difficult a commission, for the 'great truth' shown in the horses and for the recognizable portraits (*Library of the Fine Arts*, vol. III (1832), pp. 448–9). In the same year Davis showed at the Royal Academy (148) a study of Lord Frederick Fitzclarence 'for a picture of the Coronation procession'. The critic in the *Gentleman's Magazine* (vol. CII (1832), pt. I, p. 349), however, reading that the exhibited section was only 'the first picture of a series', wondered if the King intended 'to build a national gallery for Mr. R. B. Davis's long-winded discourses' and advised the King 'to have them mounted on rollers and kept coiled up for state days and holidays' (see also *Athenaeum* (1832), pp. 196, 212).

729. DEW DROP

Buckingham Palace. 15¼ × 18¾ in., 38,7 × 47,6 cm.

Inscribed with the name of the horse and signed and dated: *Sketch'd by R. B. DAVIS. 1831.*

A white horse in Council harness decorated with red mane-dressing ribbons.

A study for one of the horses in No. 728, one in the team drawing the sixth of the King's and Queen's carriages.

730. RHESUS

Buckingham Palace. 15¼ × 18½ in., 38,7 × 47 cm.

Inscribed with the name of the horse and signed and dated: *Sketched by R. B. DAVIS. 1831.*

A black carriage-horse with red state harness.

A study for one of the horses in No. 728. Only six black carriage-horses with the red harness are seen in the procession: attached to the last of the ten carriages of the King and Queen.

731. STAR

Buckingham Palace. 13½ × 17⅛ in., 34,3 × 43,5 cm.

Inscribed with the name of the horse and signed and dated: *Sketch'd by R. B. DAVIS / 1831.*

A cream carriage-horse, wearing the blue state harness, ridden by a groom in royal livery.

A study for the leading horse of the eight drawing the State Coach in No. 728.

732. A CREAM HORSE

Buckingham Palace. 15¼ × 18⅝ in., 38,7 × 47,3 cm.

Signed and dated: *Sketch'd by R. B. DAVIS. 1831.*

A cream horse, with very rich trappings, walking in a landscape.

A study of one of the King's six cream horses which appear in No. 728.

733. A CARRIAGE-HORSE

Buckingham Palace. 15¼ × 18¾ in., 38,7 × 47,6 cm.

Inscribed, signed and dated: *White State Horse / [sketch'd] by R. B. DAVIS / 1831.*

A white horse with black state harness decorated with red mane-dressing ribbons.

A study for one of the horses in No. 728, one in the team drawing the ninth of the King's and Queen's carriages.

734. A CARRIAGE-HORSE

Buckingham Palace. 15 × 18⅝ in., 38,1 × 47,3 cm.

A bay carriage-horse with red state harness.

A study for one of the horses in No. 728. In the procession seven of the ten carriages of the King and Queen are drawn by bays with the red harness.

735. MALPEINADO

Buckingham Palace. 21¾ × 25 in., 55,2 × 63,5 cm.

Signed and dated: *R. B. DAVIS. / 1846.*

An Andalusian chestnut horse, standing in a yard with a mountainous landscape behind.

Painted for Queen Victoria; recorded at Buckingham Palace in 1876 (*V.R. inv.* (967) stating that the date, December 1846, was recorded on the back).

Two figures were originally included in the design, standing at the horse's head, one apparently in costume of a vaguely Spanish flavour; these were painted out, almost certainly by Davis himself, and are not visible in the photograph attached to the *V.R. inv.*

736. MARIA WITH WILLIAM EDWARDS AND JAMES ROBINSON (*b.* 1794)

Buckingham Palace. 25¾ × 36 in., 65,4 × 91,4 cm.

Signed and dated: *Maria / R.B.Davis / 1828*

A chestnut mare, held by William Edwards; Robinson the jockey, in royal colours, approaches with his whip and saddle.

Probably painted for George IV (see below), but not apparently recorded in later royal inventories; in the Billiard Room at Buckingham Palace by 1909 (p. 260 as by Ward) and 1911.

Possibly the picture for which Davis submitted his account for forty-five guineas (with £8 for the frame) in October

1828: 'A portrait of his Majesty's Racing Mare Maria, with Jockey &c'; his receipt is dated 20 and 27 March 1829 (W.R.A., Geo. 26565, 35794). A version of the picture, signed and dated 1828 and showing Maria in the same position, without Edwards and with the jockey up, was on the art-market in London in 1936.

Maria, by Waterloo out of Belvoirina, had been foaled at Hampton Court in 1824. She was bought by the Duke of York and, in 1827, sold to George IV. She was very successful at Ascot, 1827–8, and, ridden by Robinson, she won an exciting race at Egham in 1828, the last race-meeting attended by George IV. She was a beautiful little mare and a great favourite with the King; it was said that it would take twice round the Ascot Cup course at the very best pace before she would blow out a rushlight.

William Edwards, formerly a jockey (see No. 699), was later George IV's trainer after the King's return to the Turf in 1826. Jem Robinson had a very successful career, including the record number of winning rides in the Derby (six) and the 2,000 Guineas (nine).

737. JULIUS (Plate 295)

Buckingham Palace. 20¾×25¾ in., 52,7×65,4 cm.; stretched in lining.

Signed and dated: *R. B. DAVIS 1846*

A bay horse, standing in his stall; an ostler approaches with his saddle.

Painted for Queen Victoria; recorded at Buckingham Palace in 1876 (*V.R. inv.* (968), stating that the date, December 1846, was recorded on the back).

738. UXBRIDGE (Plate 294)

Buckingham Palace. 22¾×30½ in., 57,8×77,5 cm.

A chestnut horse, standing in a stable.

Painted for Queen Victoria in 1838 (MS. Catalogue of Queen Victoria's private pictures &c.) and recorded in 1876 in the Queen's Ante-room at Buckingham Palace (*V.R. inv.*, No. 279); later at Windsor Castle (2499).

Uxbridge had been bought by Queen Victoria from Lord Uxbridge (see No. 1086) in May 1838, when he was six years old. Writing to her uncle, Leopold I, on 10 April 1838 about her riding-horses, the Queen said: 'I have got *two Darlings* if I may use that word; they are both of them *quite perfect . . . very handsome,* full of *spirit,* delightful easy goers, very quiet & *never* shying at anything . . . Uxbridge . . . is a dark chestnut with a beautiful little Arabian Head' (W.R.A., Vic. Y, 89/7). The background is almost certainly unfinished. Uxbridge was given to Colonel Arbuthnot on 8 October 1845.

739. THE NUBIAN GIRAFFE (Plate 291)

35¼×27¾ in., 89,5×70,5 cm.

Signed and dated: *R. B. Davis. | Septr 1827.*

The giraffe is seen in two positions in the foreground; in the background giraffes are walking, lying down or browsing in the trees.

Painted for George IV; recorded at Windsor (1147) in 1879 (*V.R. inv.*). Lent to the Zoological Gardens in 1924.

Literature: R. Lydekker, 'On Old Pictures of Giraffes and Zebras', *Proceedings of . . . the Zoological Society of London* (1904, vol. II), pp. 341–2.

On 13 November 1827 Davis submitted his account for £84,

under September 1824, for a 'Picture of the Giraffe'. He sent the account to Sir William Knighton with a covering letter: 'I have finished for his Majesty a picture of Studies of the Giraffe and hope I am not wrong in enclosing to you the price of the Picture'; Davis's receipt is dated 27 November 1827 (W.R.A., Geo. 26556). It is clear from this letter that the animal painted by Davis was the famous giraffe (see No. 651) which had arrived in London in August 1827, and not, as Lydekker (*loc. cit.*) had suggested, a specimen of the now extinct Southern or Cape giraffe. No. 739 was exhibited at the British Institution in 1828 (306).

George Dawe

1781–1829. Painter of subject-pictures and portraits. He exhibited at the British Institution between 1806 and 1813 and at the Royal Academy between 1804 and 1818. Soon after the marriage of Princess Charlotte and Prince Leopold he was 'honoured with the constant and liberal patronage of the royal couple, of whom he painted a great number of portraits in a variety of costumes. Of her Royal Highness two only were exhibited, and both were placed at Claremont; but others were painted for her illustrious father and other members of the royal family. Of the Prince also he painted a number to correspond for the different branches of the royal family, and several for His Royal Highness's relatives on the Continent.' He exhibited portraits of his patrons at the Royal Academy in 1817 (62, 78) and 1818 (42, 78).[1] After the death of the Princess he secured the patronage of the Duke and Duchess of Kent. He went in the Duke's suite to Brussels, attended the review of allied troops at Cambray and proceeded to Aix-la-Chapelle, where in the autumn he was 'painting Emperors & Kings—employed by Prince Leopold'. He was invited by the Emperor Alexander I to go to St. Petersburg to paint a series of portraits of senior Russian officers. On his way he painted Goethe at Weimar (see No. 761) and Ernest I of Saxe-Coburg-Gotha (see No. 749) at Coburg. When he returned to England in 1828, he submitted many of his works to George IV in audience at Windsor. In September 1828 he set off again for Russia and in Berlin he painted a portrait of the Duke of Cumberland, probably that in the National Portrait Gallery (3309) (*Library of the Fine Arts*, vol. I (1831), pp. 9–17; Farington, *Diary*, vol. VIII, pp. 160, 202, 207–8).

Faulkner (p. 405) records, in the Dining Parlour of the Duke of Sussex at Kensington, 'The Apotheosis of her late Royal Highness the Princess Charlotte of Wales, three quarters.—Dawe'. The Duke of Kent's debts in 1819 included £320 owed to Dawe, who laid claims against the Duke's estate for £724. 10s. (W.R.A., Geo. Add. MSS. 7, 1434, 1485).

740. PRINCESS CHARLOTTE

Windsor Castle (791). Panel: 33⅜×15¾ in., 84,8×40 cm.

Signed and dated: *G Dawe RA | 1817*

Full-length, seated on a sofa, resting her right hand on a portfolio.

Recorded at Windsor in 1872 (*V.R. inv.*); later at Buckingham Palace.

The design is closely related to No. 751, with variations in the costume, which is less elaborate, and in the head which in No. 740 is covered with a cap. On the back of No. 740 is a paper label inscribed with the name of the Duke of York,

1. For them, see V. & A., *Cuttings*, vol. IV, pp. 1109, 1167.

which may indicate that it had been in the collection of Frederick, Duke of York.

741. LEOPOLD I, KING OF THE BELGIANS

Kensington Palace. Canvas, mounted on panel, oval: 8⅜ × 7¼ in., 21,3 × 18,4 cm.

Head and shoulders, with the ribbon and badge of the Garter.

On the back is an early, but partly damaged, label: '[Th]is Portrait of His Majesty [was painted] by G. Dawe R.A. in 1816. for the p[urpose] / of being engraved. Purchased by [me] / of his Brother H E Dawe. / Josia[h French. 1841]'[1] Stated (*V.R. inv.*) to have been bought by the Prince Consort in January 1847; later at Windsor (946).

The head, which may not have been painted *ad vivum*, is very close in type to the three-quarter-length, seated with a book under his left arm, in the Belgian royal collection; if Josiah French was correct in stating in 1841 that No. 741 was painted as the basis for an engraving, the plate in which the head comes very close to it is that by Hodgetts, published on 14 February 1818, which states, however, that the portrait had been painted in October 1817.

742. EDWARD, DUKE OF KENT (*Plate* 251)

Kensington Palace. 36¼ × 28 in., 92,1 × 71,1 cm.

Signed: *Geo. Dawe R. A. | Pinxt 1818*; the second line is now very obscure; the back of the original canvas was inscribed with the artist's name and the statement that the portrait was painted in 1818.

Half-length in the uniform of a Field-Marshal, with the ribbon of the Garter partly concealing the stars of the Garter and the Bath, and wearing his badge as G.C.B.

Purchased by Queen Victoria in 1839 and placed in the Bedroom at Buckingham Palace (MS. Catalogue of Queen Victoria's private pictures &c.; later inv. No. 313).

Literature: National Gallery of Canada, *A Pageant of Canada*, 1967 (137).

The portrait is very close in type to No. 743 and may have been the original portrait, from which other portraits were worked up and which would have been painted from sittings in 1818. The Duke had agreed to sit to Dawe on 20 April 1818, but the sitting was postponed for different reasons until later in the month; the Duke intended to give Dawe sittings, lasting from 7.30 or 8 until 10.45 a.m. on 9 and 10 May, 'but this the Duke fears will be the last, before he departs for the continent'. The Duke hoped to be able to sit to Dawe again on 25 August, but this sitting may have been cancelled; on that day Dawe was told that the Duchess of Kent (see No. 744) hoped to resume her sittings at a slightly later date 'as well as His Royal Highness to commence *his*, who has given up going to Castle Hill, so that Mr Dawe may now look forward with confidence, to some sittings from the Duke, after Saturday'; the Duke may in fact have sat on 26 August (Letters from Captain Harvey, Private Secretary to the Duke, to the artist, W.R.A., Geo. Add. 7, 6, 15–22). See Nos. 759, 760; another copy is in the Belgian royal collection. The type was engraved by J. Bacon and is also close to Dawe's three-quarter-length seated portrait of the Duke in civilian dress, engraved by T. Wright.

1. The gaps in the inscription have been inserted from the reading in the *V.R. inv.*

743. EDWARD, DUKE OF KENT

Buckingham Palace. 99½ × 55 in., 252,7 × 139,7 cm.; *c.* 5 in. have been turned over on the right. When the portrait was acquired in 1859 it was stated to measure 108 × 72 in.

Signed: *G DAWE. RA*

Full-length, in the uniform of a Field-Marshal with the ribbon and star of the Garter and his badge as G.C.B., standing beside a cannon on which he rests his right hand holding his plumed hat; his left hand rests on his sword; on the right are regimental colours inscribed with battle honours. In the distance are the town and fortress of Gibraltar.

Purchased by Queen Victoria from James Prendergast, nephew of George Dawe, for £120 in 1859. The portrait was offered to the Queen by Prendergast on 27 May and the purchase was completed by 7 June (W.R.A., Vic. Add. T, 32–35). Recorded on the Principal Staircase at Buckingham Palace in 1864 (*V.R. inv.* (220); *Buckingham Palace,* 1909, p. 35); it must have been considerably cut down in order to fit it into its present position.

Presumably painted to commemorate the Duke's years as Governor of Gibraltar, 1802–20. The type is, however, very closely related to No. 742, with slight variations in the arrangement of the Duke's orders, and was probably based on the same sittings given to the artist in 1818. James Prendergast, offering the portrait to the Queen (see above), stated that it had been 'painted in the year 1818 at the express command of His Royal Highness and was entirely approved of, it remained however in the possession of the artist till his death'. He later stated that the view of Gibraltar was 'taken from a sketch by Constable'. Dawe's relatives, moreover, were 'not aware of any other [full] length of the Duke by him'.

744. VICTORIA, DUCHESS OF KENT
(*Plate* 250)

Windsor Castle (587). 35½ × 28⅛ in., 90,2 × 71,4 cm.

Inscribed on the back with the names of sitter and artist.

Half-length, seated in a black dress.

Recorded in the collection of Queen Victoria (*V.R. inv.*, n.d.); probably inherited from Edward, Duke of Kent.

The type probably represents the companion portrait to No. 742. The Duchess hoped to give Dawe sittings, of one or two hours each, at Kensington Palace on five successive mornings in July 1818; she had later to cancel a sitting planned for 23 August and on 25 August had such bad toothache that she could not sit for three or four days; the sittings were probably resumed at the end of the month (W.R.A., Geo. Add. 7, 19–22). A version is in the Belgian royal collection. An engraving by J. Thomson and T. Woolnoth from this type (from a portrait then in the possession of the Duke of Kent and therefore probably No. 744) was published on 1 January 1820.

745. ALEXANDER I, EMPEROR OF RUSSIA
(1777–1825)

Windsor Castle (955). 23⅞ × 16¾ in., 60,6 × 42,5 cm.

Signed and dated: *Geo. Dawe/1817*

Full-length, standing in a landscape in uniform, holding his plumed hat in his left hand (for the uniform and orders see No. 746).

On the back is a label in the hand of the artist's brother, H. E. Dawe: 'This portrait of the Emperor Alexander was painted by my brother Geo. Dawe R.A. during his stay in Russia. and was brought by him to England sold to Mr J. French. 1844'; acquired by the Prince Consort in September 1844; recorded, as the Queen's private property, at Windsor in 1878 (*V.R. inv.*).

It seems that H. E. Dawe was wrong in stating that No. 745 was painted in Russia. It appears to be the earliest of Dawe's portraits of his patron. It was therefore painted before Lawrence completed No. 883 at Aix-la-Chapelle late in 1818 and before Dawe received the Tsar's invitation to go to Russia. It was presumably used by Dawe as the model for the portraits of the Tsar that he produced in Russia (e.g., No. 746).

See No. 883.

746. ALEXANDER I, EMPEROR OF RUSSIA (1777–1825) (*Plate* 248)

Kensington Palace. 94¾ × 60½ in., 240,7 × 153,7 cm.

Signed: *Geo. Dawe R.A. | Pinxt*

Full-length standing, holding his plumed hat in his left hand. The uniform is apparently the same as in No. 883 and the orders are also very close in disposition to those in the slightly earlier portrait: Sword of the Order of the Sword of Sweden, star of St. Andrew of Russia superimposed on the Garter, badges of St. George of Russia, (?) St. Andrew of Russia, Maria Theresa, (?) Polish Order of Military Merit and (?) St. Wlodomir.

Nos. 746, 747 were originally the property of Mrs. Pitt who had been a close companion of the Empress (No. 747); at her death(?) they were lent to her friend, Duchess Mary of Saxe-Coburg. After the Duchess's death on 24 September 1860 the portraits became the property of Mrs. Pitt's son, the Rev. Charles Whitworth Pitt. They arrived in England early in July 1861 in their 'massive gold frames' and were offered by Pitt to Queen Victoria 'As Memorials of two August Personages, whom it is impossible for me ever to forget, and as Relics of my poor Mother, by whom they were affectionately cherished.' The Queen bought the portraits for £190; on 26 July 1861 they arrived at Buckingham Palace (W.R.A., Vic. P.P., 7102, 8355). They were moved from Buckingham Palace (where No. 746 was No. 539) to Kensington in 1916.

Nos. 746, 747 were stated by the Rev. C. W. Pitt at the time of their purchase by Queen Victoria to have been painted at St. Petersburg. Colnaghi published Thomas Wright's engraving of the type on 1 March 1826 with a statement that it had been painted by Dawe from life. A life-size version, formerly at Londonderry House and now at Wynyard Park, is signed and dated at St. Petersburg, 1824; it was probably painted for the wife of the 3rd Marquess of Londonderry (H. Montgomery Hyde, *Londonderry House and its Pictures* (1937), p. 22, wrongly as painted in 1821); it is stated that Dawe requested Londonderry to agree that no copies should be made from it. A small version, signed and dated 1825, was in the Ranfurly sale at Christie's, 21 June 1929 (23). The type is, however, identical with that produced by Dawe as early as 1817 (see No. 745). In Martinov's view of Dawe receiving the Emperor in his studio (see No. 748), the Emperor's figure is of this type.

See No. 883.

747. ELIZABETH, EMPRESS OF RUSSIA (1779–1826) (*Plate* 249)

Kensington Palace. 94¾ × 60⅜ in., 240,7 × 153,3 cm.; originally *c.* 51½ × 42 in.

Full-length, standing, in widow's weeds with her hands clasped over her heart. Before her is a bust of the Emperor

Alexander I and in the background is a view of Taganrog on the Sea of Azov with the sun setting behind it.

See No. 746; at Buckingham Palace No. 747 was No. 542.

No. 747 was originally painted as a three-quarter-length, but was enlarged to a full-length, apparently by Dawe himself and presumably to turn it into a companion to No. 746 as a present to Mrs. Pitt. The view of Taganrog, where the Tsar had died, his bust and his widow's mourning attire indicate that No. 747 was painted soon after his death on 1 December 1825 and before the Empress's death on 16 May 1826. Their marriage had not been happy, but the last weeks of the Tsar's life were spent with his wife in great happiness at Taganrog.

Daughter of the Margrave Charles of Baden; she married the future Tsar in 1793. She was inconsolable at his death: 'Our angel has gone to heaven . . . Our dear deceased has resumed his look of benevolence; his smile proves to me he is happy, and that he gazes on brighter objects than exist here'.

748. CHARLOTTE (ALEXANDRA FEODOROVNA) (1798–1870), EMPRESS OF RUSSIA, WITH HER ELDEST CHILDREN, ALEXANDER (1818–81) AND MARIA (1819–76)

Buckingham Palace. 109 × 73 in., 276,9 × 185,4 cm.

Full-length on a settee, with the Prince at her knee and her right arm supporting the Princess.

Stated to have been in the possession of Adolphus Frederick, Duke of Cambridge, and to have hung in the apartments of Augusta, Duchess of Cambridge, in St. James's Palace until her death in 1889, when it was bought by the Grand Duke Paul Alexandrovitch of Russia for his residence in Leningrad; sold with the effects of his widow, Princess Palay at Christie's, 21 June 1929 (20), when it was acquired by H.M. Queen Mary.

Painted *c.* 1821, presumably in St. Petersburg. Thomas Wright's engraving of the group was published on 1 January 1826; the head was also engraved by Wright in a vignette. No. 748, or a version of it, is seen among other pictures in J. Bennet's aquatint, after A. Martinov, of Dawe receiving Alexander I in his studio in St. Petersburg.

Princess Charlotte of Prussia, daughter of Frederick William III, King of Prussia, married Tsar Nicholas I in 1817. The Tsar was succeeded by his son Alexander (II) in 1855; his daughter Maria married in 1839, as her first husband, Maximilian, Duke of Leuchtenberg.

749. ERNEST I (1784–1844), DUKE OF SAXE-COBURG-GOTHA

Buckingham Palace. 63¾ × 57 in., 161,9 × 144,8 cm.

Three-quarter-length, standing, in Field-Marshal's uniform with a scarlet cloak lined with ermine; he wears the collars of St. Andrew of Russia and the Order of the Crown of Saxony; he wears the ribbons of the Black Eagle of Prussia and St. Henry of Saxony; his stars include St. Andrew and (?) St. George of Russia; and his badges include the orders of St. Alexander Newski, (?) St. George and (?) St. Anne of Russia. In the background is a corner of Schloss Ehrenburg at Coburg and in the distance is the old Castle of Coburg.

Purchased by the Prince Consort for £50 in February 1841: 'Daw. 1818. Portrait of His Serene Highness Duke of Saxe Coburg & Gotha. unfinished half-length' (MS. 'Rough Catalogue' of the Prince's purchases, inv. No. 49 (III) above); later in the Prince's Writing-room at Buckingham Palace (*V.R. inv.*, No. 382).

A derivation, probably by Dawe himself, of the large full-length (*Fig.* 4; signed and dated as painted at Coburg in 1819) at Schloss Ehrenburg. Parts of the costume in No. 749 are perhaps in an unfinished state (see above), but the head and the upper part of the costume seem completely finished. On 13 May 1879 No. 749 was sent to Corden for a copy to be made; the copy was delivered at Windsor on 11 October 1879.

Son of Francis, Duke of Saxe-Coburg-Gotha; he was father of the Prince Consort and brother of the Duchess of Kent and Leopold I, King of the Belgians.

750. PRINCESS FEODORA OF LEININGEN
(1807–72) (*Plate* 252)

Windsor Castle (628). 23¾ × 18 in., 60,3 × 47,6 cm.

Signed: *Geo Dawe R A.*; inscribed on the back with the name of the artist and the date 1818.

Head and shoulders in a red dress; painted to be framed as an oval.

Almost certainly the portrait presented by the Duke of Kent to the Duchess, to whom he wrote from Kensington on 16 August 1819: 'Tu te rapelleras sans doute que le portrait peint par Monsieur Dawe a Amorbach au mois de Mars dernier, fait le *premier* de mes Cadeaux pour la journée si chere de demain, et je crois, que je n'en aurois pas pu trouver de plus cher a ton coeur, puisqu'en regardant la physiognomie de la chere Feodor, tu y liras tout l'attachement que te porte celui qui aujourdhui a depuis près de quinze mois le bonheur detre ton Epoux' (W.R.A., Vic. M, 3, 8). Later at Windsor.

The portrait was probably painted at the time indicated in the Duke's letter and not in 1818. The Princess herself wrote to Queen Victoria on 7 April 1862: 'You wished to know when those pictures of brother Charles and myself were painted by Daw? I think in the winter of 1819 at Amorbach' (W.R.A., Vic. Y,43, 20).

Daughter of the Duchess of Kent by her first marriage to Ernest Charles, Prince of Leiningen, and half-sister of Queen Victoria, who was devoted to her. In 1828 she married Ernest, Prince of Hohenlohe-Langenburg.

After George Dawe

751. PRINCESS CHARLOTTE

Windsor Castle (2876). 51¾ × 42¼ in., 131,4 × 107,3 cm.

Three-quarter-length, seated on a sofa, resting her right hand on a portfolio; on her breast she wears the star of St. Catherine of Russia.

Acquired by King Edward VII; formerly at Buckingham Palace (*Buckingham Palace*, 1909, p. 185, as by Haydon and as part of the private collection of King Edward VII); later at Marlborough House.

A copy in reverse of the portrait in the National Portrait Gallery (51) which, when it was purchased from Colnaghi in 1858, was stated by them to have been the first picture of the Princess painted from the life by Dawe, to have remained in Dawe's possession until his death and to have passed to his nephew, from whom it was acquired (MS., 10 July 1858, in archives of the Gallery). Engravings of this type by S. W. Reynolds and H. Dawe and T. Hodgetts were published on 10 March and 12 January 1818;[1] a full-length version is in the residence of the Belgian Ambassador,

36 Belgrave Square. A water-colour of the head of this type is at Windsor (2481), very close to that engraved by W. Say (published on 1 December 1817) as painted in October 1817. It may have been of this type that Leopold I was thinking when he wrote to Queen Victoria on 29 December 1843 of No. 1057: 'Though there are things which are not quite right, however it is more Lady like than Mr. Daw's coarse paintings' (W.R.A., Vic. Y,70, 27). At the time of her marriage the Princess had given to her husband a miniature of herself, based on Dawe, in a case inscribed with the date 16 December 1816. See also No. 740. The portrait of the Princess exhibited by Dawe at the Royal Academy in 1817 (78) was probably of this type.

752. PRINCESS CHARLOTTE

Buckingham Palace. 99½ × 64⅝ in., 252,7 × 164,1 cm.

Full-length, walking on a terrace at the head of a broad flight of steps, wearing a black dress and holding over her right shoulder an embroidered red shawl. On the right, at the base of an arch, stands a rose bush in a carved urn.

Recorded in the Large Drawing-Room in 1841 (*Buckingham Palace*, 1841, p. 97); later set up on the Principal Staircase (*V.R. inv.*, 1864 (224); *Buckingham Palace*, 1909, p. 36).

The portrait is of very little quality. It is presumably a copy of the full-length in the Belgian royal collection.[1] Another copy is at York House; and see No. 753.

753. PRINCESS CHARLOTTE

Buckingham Palace. Canvas on panel: 27⅝ × 16⅞ in., 70,2 × 42,9 cm.

Full-length, walking down a flight of steps into a garden and greeted by a dog.

See No. 754; formerly at Windsor (2919).

The design is derived from the same type as No. 752. No. 753 was presumably painted as a pendant to No. 754, but is less good and can hardly be by Dawe himself, though it seems to be contemporary or nearly contemporary with the pendant. The balustrade of the steps is not completely finished.

754. LEOPOLD I, KING OF THE BELGIANS

Buckingham Palace. Panel: 28 × 17¾ in., 71,1 × 45,1 cm.

Full-length, standing, in black, wearing the ribbon and star of the Garter and a block of badges of other orders on his coat; he holds his hat in his right hand and rests his left on a book on a table.

With No. 753 formed part of the private property of H.M. King George V; the pair were at Buckingham Palace until 24 January 1929, when they were sent to Windsor (2920).

Probably painted *c.* 1816–18; the head is close to Dawe's standard type for the Prince (e.g., No. 755), but is facing in the other direction.

755. LEOPOLD I, KING OF THE BELGIANS

Buckingham Palace. 99¼ × 55¼ in., 252,1 × 140,3 cm.; *c.* 8 in. at the top are a later addition.

Full-length, standing, in Field-Marshal's uniform, holding his hat in his left hand and resting his right hand on his sword. On a chair behind him lie the baton presented by

---

1. The later print is stated to have been engraved from a portrait in the possession of the Princess's husband.

1. This was probably the portrait exhibited by Dawe at the Royal Academy in 1818 (42).

the King to the Duke of Wellington and the King's mantles of the orders of the Garter and Bath. He wears the collars of the Garter, the Bath and the Guelphs; his badges include the orders of Maria-Theresa of Austria, St. George of Russia, St. Anne of Russia, St. Alexander Newski, (?)St. Joachim of Saxe-Coburg-Saalfeld and St. John of Jersualem.

Stated to have been painted for Queen Victoria in 1844, presumably to be set up on the Principal Staircase, where it was recorded in 1864 (*V.R. inv.* (225); *Buckingham Palace*, 1909, p. 35).

A copy by Corden at full-length of the same type as Nos. 756–8; there is a watercolour copy of the head of this type at Windsor (2480). The type is closely related, though there are differences in costume, accessories and setting, to the full-length in the Belgian royal collection, of which there is a copy at York House, and which was probably the portrait exhibited by Dawe at the Royal Academy in 1818 (78).

756. LEOPOLD I, KING OF THE BELGIANS
Buckingham Palace. $92\frac{1}{2} \times 56\frac{1}{2}$ in., $234,9 \times 143,5$ cm.

Recorded at Buckingham Palace in 1877 (*V.R. inv.* (1065); *Buckingham Palace*, 1909, p. 235).

A contemporary repetition of the same design as No. 755. There appear to be alterations in the position of the right hand and arm, and the head is rather more opaque in texture than the rest of the composition.

757. LEOPOLD I, KING OF THE BELGIANS
Buckingham Palace. $61\frac{1}{2} \times 50\frac{3}{4}$ in., $156,2 \times 128,9$ cm.
Three-quarter-length, standing.

Recorded in the Prince Consort's Writing-room at Buckingham Palace in 1868 (*V.R. inv.* (383)); it is probably the portrait by Corden after Dawe of 'The King of the Belgians half length in an English Field Marshal's Uniform' which the Prince had acquired for £40 in July 1844 (MS. 'Rough Catalogue' of the Prince's purchases, inv. No. 49 (III) above).

A copy from the same type as Nos. 755, 756.

758. LEOPOLD I, KING OF THE BELGIANS
St. James's Palace. 58×48 in., $147,3 \times 121,9$ cm.
Three-quarter-length, standing.

Recorded at Buckingham Palace (677) in 1876 (*V.R. inv.*).

A copy from the same type as Nos. 755, 756. In March 1842 the Prince Consort paid £45 for a copy, apparently painted by Schneider in 1817, of this type, but this copy was apparently given by the Prince to George Anson (MS. 'Rough Catalogue', *op. cit*).

759. EDWARD, DUKE OF KENT
$35\frac{3}{4} \times 28\frac{1}{8}$ in., $90,8 \times 71,4$ cm.

Formerly at Windsor (588); lent in 1955 to Earl Mountbatten of Burma.

A copy of No. 742.

760. EDWARD, DUKE OF KENT
$36\frac{1}{4} \times 28$ in., $92,1 \times 71,1$ cm.

Formerly at Frogmore (Windsor inv. No. 1550); lent in 1948 to the Kent House, Quebec.

A copy of No. 742.

761. JOHANN WOLFGANG GOETHE (1749–1832)
Osborne House. $28 \times 22\frac{1}{8}$ in., $71,1 \times 56,2$ cm.

Head and shoulders in a black coat, wearing round his neck the Order of Leopold of Austria and, on his breast, the stars of the White Falcon of Saxe-Weimar-Eisenach and St. Anne of Russia.

Bought by the Prince Consort in November 1853 and recorded at Buckingham Palace (392) in 1868 (*V.R. inv.*).

A copy by Melville of the portrait painted by Dawe at Weimar in May 1819 (see Goethe's references to the original in *Gedenkausgabe der Werke, Briefe und Gespräche*, ed. E. Beutler, Zürich and Stuttgart, vol. 21 (1951), pp. 330, 371–2, 441, 478 and *Tagebücher* (1964), pp. 371, 449). The original is now in the Goethe-Nationalmuseum at Weimar (*Gedenkausgabe*, *op. cit.*, vol. 26 (1949), frontispiece).

The greatest of German poets, who was also profoundly interested in the arts. Early in their married life the Prince Consort embarked on a course of readings aloud to Queen Victoria from Goethe.

Arthur William Devis

1762–1822. Painter of portraits and historical subjects; son of Arthur Devis. As a young man he spent a number of adventurous years in the East and in 1804 he was imprisoned for debt. He exhibited at the Royal Academy between 1781 and 1821, and at the British Institution between 1806 and 1819. He painted a picture of the *Apotheosis of Princess Charlotte* of which a version is now in the Belgian royal collection.

762. THE DEATH OF NELSON (*Plate* 231)
Kensington Palace. $37\frac{1}{4} \times 50\frac{3}{8}$ in., $94,6 \times 127,9$ cm.

The dying Nelson lies in the cockpit of the *Victory*. On his right, rubbing the dying man's breast, is the Chaplain, Alexander Scott (1768–1840); on Nelson's left, and holding his hand, is the Surgeon, William Beatty (*d.* 1842); looking up at Beatty is Nelson's Steward, Henry Lewis Chevalier, and above Nelson's left shoulder is the Purser, Walter Burke (*d.* 1815). Looking down on Nelson is Captain Thomas Hardy (1769–1839). In the right foreground, beside a wounded Marine, is Lieutenant (later Captain) George Bligh (*d.* 1834); behind him (see below) is Neil Smith (*d.* 1819), the Assistant Surgeon, and behind him, entering the cockpit, is the Carpenter, William Bunce. On the left, looking upwards, is Lieutenant (later Commander) John Yule (*d.* 1840); between him and the figure holding a lantern is Nelson's Neapolitan valet, Guitan (in profile) and, above him, Midshipman (later Commander) Francis Collingwood (1785–1835).

Offered by James Miller (of 2, Vassall Cottages, Addison Road) to Queen Victoria in September 1852; she commanded that it should be purchased for 500 guineas by the Lord Chamberlain; 'and it will be put up in the Gallery in Buckingham Palace' (W.R.A., P.P., Add. Vic., 46). Recorded in 1876 in the Princesses Corridor at Buckingham Palace (*V.R. inv.* (474)).

When No. 762 was purchased it was stated to be 'the original Sketch for the great picture of the death of Nelson'. Areas of the canvas are unfinished, with details summarily indicated, e.g., in the lower right corner and in the garments lying in the foreground, especially Nelson's coat. Comparison with the large finished picture, now in the National

Maritime Museum,[1] reveals minor differences in detail, e.g., in Nelson's hair; the figure of Smith in the finished picture is much older than the relevant figure in the sketch, who appears to be a young naval officer. The version of No. 762 which is in H.M.S. *Victory* is very close to No. 762 in quality, but may represent a slightly later stage in the development of the design; details such as Nelson's coat are more fully worked out than they are in No. 762.

W. Bromley's engraving of the finished picture was published by Boydell (who had bought the picture) on 2 March 1812 with a Key (on which the description above is based) and with a written account. According to this account Devis, in planning his picture, 'had many important advantages, which contemporary Painters could not attain; *he was the only Artist* who left the shores of ENGLAND to meet the VICTORY on her coming home, and three weeks passed on board, enabled him completely to acquaint himself with all the concomitant circumstances which attended the mournful event he had to represent. He saw, he conversed with the officers and crew, still impressed with the memorable and awful scene, and had access to the remains of the departed Hero. The Artist was allowed to have all the attendants at the Admiral's death grouped in the Cockpit, *exactly as they were there* at the moment when he expired; and *this very spot* of the ship he correctly copied from a miniature model made on board the Victory, so that the picture cannot fail to represent the scene as it was in reality.' Moreover 'All the spectators on the occasion sat to the Artist for their Portraits, which are not only faithful likenesses, but also marked with such feelings as were naturally displayed on the mournful catastrophe'. Devis presumably went on board the *Victory* after her arrival at Portsea on 4 December; he was certainly on board on 11 December, when William Beatty extracted the 'fatal ball' which 'in the exact state in which it was extracted' was drawn by Devis 'who was then on board' for a plate published in Beatty's *Authentic Narrative of the Death of Lord Nelson* (1807).[2] Farington had been told by Boydell as early as 4 December that he had offered £500 for the best picture to be painted of the death of Nelson and that '*Devis* . . . was painting a picture of that subject' (*Diary*, vol. III, p. 128). West admitted to Farington on 10 June 1807 that Devis's picture 'had much merit', but confirmed his opinion that such a subject required an epic representation (*ibid.*, vol. IV, p. 151). The finished picture was exhibited at the British Institution in 1809 (70).

Nelson was shot from the mizentop of the *Redoubtable* at about 1.15 p.m. on 21 October 1805. He was taken below into the cockpit (which Devis considerably heightened and enlarged)[3] and was supported on a makeshift bed by Alexander Scott and Walter Burke until his death at 4.30 p.m. In his last moments Scott rubbed his breast in an attempt to bring him relief from his pain. In Devis's picture Captain Hardy is seen, looking down on the dying Admiral, on his second and last visit to the cockpit; and William Beatty is apparently feeling Nelson's pulse just before he died.

For Nelson see No. 849. Hardy, who had entered the Navy in 1781 and was Captain of the *Victory* at Trafalgar, ended his career as Vice-Admiral and a Baronet. Dr. Scott had joined Nelson in the Mediterranean in 1803 and rendered

him invaluable service thereafter as private secretary and chaplain; in 1816 he was appointed Chaplain to the Prince of Wales. Beatty was Surgeon in the *Victory* with Smith as one of his assistants. Chevalier had entered Nelson's service in 1803. His master thought very highly of him—'I wonder he has not set up some hotel'—and Hardy sent him back to Lady Hamilton after Trafalgar with 'the last letters written by our most dear and ever to be lamented friend'. Burke was a relative of Edmund Burke. Bligh was wounded at Trafalgar. William Bunce was much respected by Nelson, who secured him in 1805 the post of Master-Shipwright at Gibraltar. Collingwood, with a fellow Midshipman, shot down the French marksman who had killed Nelson and later went on board the *Redoutable* to claim her as a prize.

Denis Dighton

1792–1827. Painter and draughtsman, specializing in military subjects. He was a protégé of the Prince of Wales and secured through him a commission in the 90th Regiment of Foot (Perthshire Volunteers). He only appears to have held this commission for a few months in 1811–12. In 1815 he was appointed military painter and draughtsman to the Prince Regent. He was making drawings on the field of Waterloo a few days after the battle. He exhibited at the Royal Academy, 1811–25.

George IV acquired from Dighton his large painting of the battle of Orthez (*Fig. XXI*). It was received at Carlton House on 2 July 1815, but was sent to Lord Anglesey as a present on 27 July 1815 (Jutsham, *R/D*, ff. 200, 349). It is still at Plas Newydd (it is signed and dated 1815).

For an introduction to his drawings and watercolours in the Royal Library, see A. E. Haswell Miller and N. P. Dawnay, *Military Drawings and Paintings in the Collection of H.M. The Queen*, vol. I (1966), pp. 15–17, pls. 300–55. He also made drawings of the Coronation of George IV (Oppé, Nos. 181, 182) and of episodes in the King's visit to Edinburgh in 1822.

763. THE BATTLE OF WATERLOO:
THE CHARGE OF THE SECOND BRIGADE
OF CAVALRY (*Plate 234*)

St. James's Palace. 47¾ × 60⅜ in., 121,3 × 163,3 cm.

Sergeant Charles Ewart (*d.* 1845) of the Scots Greys is seen capturing the Eagle and standard of the French 45th regiment which is breaking under the shock of the charge.

Recorded at Buckingham Palace (913) in 1876 (*V.R. inv.*).

Exhibited at the Royal Academy in 1817 (422) with a long descriptive note in the catalogue. The charge by the 1st (Household) and 2nd (Union) Brigade, the latter commanded by Major-General Sir William Ponsonby, took place between one and two o'clock; the 2nd Brigade was composed of the 1st (Royals), 2nd (Royal North British—the Scots Greys) and 6th (Inniskilling) Dragoons. In a few moments 15,000 French were flying in disorder and two field batteries were destroyed. Two thousand prisoners and two Eagles were captured (Marquess of Anglesey, *One-Leg* (1961), pp. 138–41). 'Such havoc', wrote Anglesey later, 'was rarely made in so few minutes.' Sergeant Ewart, of the right half-squadron of the Greys, and an outstanding swordsman, six foot four inches tall, captured the Eagle of the 45th French regiment of the line. He wrote later, 'I took the eagle from the enemy: he and I had a hard contest for it; he made a thrust at my groin, I parried it and cut him down through the head. After this a lancer came at me; I threw

---

1. G. P. B. Naish, *Nelson & Bronte* (National Maritime Museum, 1958), pl. 22. See also C. Mitchell, 'Benjamin West's "Death of Nelson"', in *Essays in the History of Art presented to Rudolf Wittkower* (1967), pp. 268–70, 273.
2. See J. Allen, *Life of Lord Viscount Nelson* (1857), pp. 295–6, for the account by Lt. Edward Williams of Devis's arrival and sojourn on board.
3. In the National Maritime Museum is Devis's drawing of the cockpit, 'sketched on board, at Portsmouth'.

the lance off by my right side, and cut him through the chin and upwards through the teeth. Next, a foot-soldier fired at me, and then charged me with his bayonet, which I also had the luck to parry, and then I cut him down through the head; thus ended the contest' (quoted in J. Naylor, *Waterloo* (1960), pp. 134–5). Dighton apparently illustrates the last stage in the contest for the Eagle. In the distance is the farm of La Haye Sainte; Count D'Erlon, commander of the French 1st Corps, is seen with his staff against the skyline on the left. On the right are the Royals, Inniskillings and the 8th and 9th Brigades of Infantry and Major Bull's troop of Royal Horse Artillery. Some French soldiers feigned death and fired in the backs of the British cavalry who had passed over them. One such soldier is cocking his musket in No. 763: 'they received no quarter'.

764. THE BATTLE OF WATERLOO: GENERAL ADVANCE OF THE BRITISH LINES (*Plate* 235)

St. James's Palace. 30⅛ × 48 in., 76,5 × 121,9 cm.

The Earl of Uxbridge, commander of the Allied cavalry, leading the cavalry in the final charge against the French columns.

Purchased by George IV and recorded in the Armoury at Carlton House in 1816 (493: 'The battle of Waterloo. Mr Dighton'); taken to Windsor in April 1829; later at Buckingham Palace (476).

Literature: W. Y. Carman, ' "The Battle of Waterloo" by Denis Dighton', *Journal of the Society for Army Historical Research*, vol. XLIII (1965), pp. 55–9.

On 7 November 1816 Dighton was paid £50 for 'A Painting of the Battle of Waterloo' (W.R.A., Geo. 26986, 35505). It is a smaller variant (perhaps specially painted for the Regent) of the large signed painting in the possession of the Marquess of Anglesey in which the action is set further back into the design and in which Wellington and his staff appear in the left foreground. Lord Anglesey's picture is assumed to be that exhibited at the Royal Academy in 1816 (206) with a long descriptive note in the catalogue. No. 764 shows the final stage in the battle under an evening light. On the right Lord Uxbridge (see No. 1086), in the uniform of a general officer of light cavalry, is leading the 5th and 6th Hussar Brigades, under Major-Generals Sir Colquhoun Grant and Sir Hussey Vivian, in the final charge against the broken remnants of the French cavalry, Cuirassiers and Lancers. On the left the 2nd or 3rd battalion of the 1st Foot Guards[1] is advancing upon Napoleon's Imperial Guards, encouraged in their last stand by a mounted French Marshal, presumably Ney. In the distance the Allied cavalry is advancing and the French are in retreat. As evening closed in, 'A panic seized the enemy in every direction, and they fled on all sides . . . each man thinking of his own preservation'. On the horizon to the left is La Belle Alliance, in front of which Napoleon and his staff are seen; on the right can be seen the Observatory. The catalogue of the Royal Academy in 1816 states that Lord Anglesey's picture was 'Painted from sketches made on the ground a few days after the action: and from information from the Duke of Wellington and Marquis of Anglesea's staffs, Royal Engineer department . . .' During this charge Lord Uxbridge was struck by a grape-shot on his right knee; the leg was amputated after the battle.

1. In Lord Anglesey's picture they are clearly men of the 2nd Battalion.

John Doyle

1797–1868. Painter and caricaturist. He came to London from Dublin in 1821 and later became famous as the caricaturist HB.

In addition to No. 765, George IV also received from Doyle, in May 1822, 'A Painting of a Gray Horse-Named-Cogniac with the Groom Charles Long hold him & part of Carlton House in the Back Ground—by Mr Doyle The Horse is Painted with a Side Saddle'. It was given away by the King (Jutsham, *Receipts*, f. 159). In the 1816 inv. of Carlton House, additional No. 596 was 'A Painting—A Grey Horse—Named—Perfection Doyle', which was given away, probably to Lady Conyngham, by the King. Jutsham, among sums paid to him between 12 November 1821 and 6 December 1822, received £1. 10s.: 'Paid Mr John Doyle—Artist—the Balance of an Account left unsettled by Sir Benjn Bloomfield for a Painting of Horses, as pr Mr Doyles account' (Jutsham, *PP.*, f. 79). There is in the Royal Archives a letter from Doyle to Sir William Knighton, 7 March 1830, in which he mentions his small equestrian portrait of the Duke of Wellington and seems to be soliciting patronage (W.R.A., Geo. 26594).

765. NONPAREIL

Buckingham Palace. 27⅛ × 34 in., 68.9 × 86,4 cm.

Signed and dated: *JDoyle, 1821*.

A bay horse, in a rich blue and gold harness, with a groom in royal livery leading him past a riding-school; on the right is a groom with a grey and a bay horse.

Acquired by George IV; received at Carlton House from Doyle on 29 May 1822 (Jutsham, *Receipts*, f. 161: '. . . a Portrait of a Horse Called Nonpareil—a Charger belonging to His Majesty . . . I furnished an Old Frame for it from the Stores'; 1816 inv., additional No. 598); later at Windsor (924).

For Nonpareil see No. 1136.

Gainsborough Dupont

1754–97. Nephew of Thomas Gainsborough, to whom he was apprenticed in 1772 and with whose work he was always closely associated. He exhibited at the Royal Academy between 1790 and 1797.

After his uncle's death he received commissions for a number of royal portraits. His undated bill (in the National Portrait Gallery) includes, in addition to pictures mentioned below, a pair of full-lengths of the King and Queen for the Duke of York, at £126, and a pair of half-lengths of them 'for Windsor Lodge', at £52. 10s. A portrait of the King, 'painted by Gainsborough Dupont', was recorded by Pyne in the Green Pavilion at Frogmore (vol. I, *Frogmore*, p. 13);[1] and a portrait of the Queen by him was among the pictures moved from the King's Closet, St. James's, to the Queen's House in 1809 (Geo. III, *Removals*). It was reported in the *Morning Herald* of 26 July 1796[2] that Dupont was at Windsor painting the Princesses, who intended to present the portraits to the Queen. There is no evidence that such portraits were ever painted by Dupont.

Between 1779 and 1793 Dupont issued a small number of very fine mezzotints after some of Gainsborough's portraits. See also Nos. 808, 809.

1. The portrait of the King may be the copy, in Lord Cottesloe's possession, from No. 774.
2. The references to Dupont from this source were most kindly given to me by Mr. John Hayes.

766. GEORGE III (*Plate* 107)

Windsor Castle (221). $94\frac{1}{4} \times 58$ in., $239,4 \times 147,3$ cm.

Full-length, standing, in robes of state, with the regalia on a table beside him.

Recorded in the King's Old State Bedchamber at Windsor in 1813 (Legge's lists: 'The King. in his Parliamentary Robes. Gainsbro' Dupont', measurements given as 93×57 in.); recorded in the *Royal Windsor Guide* (1832) in the sequence of royal portraits inserted, presumably by George IV, on the north wall of St. George's Hall.

Literature: W. T. Whitley, *Artists and their Friends in England 1700–99* (1928), vol. II, p. 184; Collins Baker, *Windsor*, p. 72.

No. 766 is closely based on Gainsborough's full-length of the King in Windsor uniform (No. 774), but the setting is an interior and the King is wearing his parliamentary robes. The head does not seem to be based on a fresh sitting. There is a *pentimento* in the left foot, which was originally placed further to the right. Dupont was paid £126 for a pair of full-lengths of the King and Queen for Windsor Castle (undated bill in archives of the National Portrait Gallery). No. 766 was probably the portrait of the King shown by Dupont at the Royal Academy in 1794 (85). Anthony Pasquin in his *Liberal Critique* of the exhibition refers to 'the glare of the scarlet drapery'. The *Morning Herald*, 29 April 1794, was more complimentary. Farington quotes a remark by the King to West 'that He thought Gainsborough Duponts portrait of him was the best likeness that had been painted' (*Diary*, vol. I, p. 45). The portrait was described at the Royal Academy as 'Similar to Gainsborough's whole-length with no hat, but with cloak over the shoulder'; the hat seems definitely to have been included in No. 767 in its first state, but not apparently in No. 766, in which the King's state robe could perhaps have been described as a 'cloak over the shoulder' (see also W. T. Whitley, *loc. cit.*). In the version of the same design which was finished by Dupont early in 1795 and presented by the King to Trinity House (*Morning Herald*, 23 April 1795) there is a view of a building on the right. There is a three-quarter-length variant of the same design as No. 766 in the Museum Naradowe, Warsaw (*Fig.* 9), in which the King's costume is blue and the collar of the Garter is omitted. This is apparently the portrait painted by Gainsborough in 1785 for the King of Poland on orders conveyed by the Polish ambassador in London. On 16 December 1788 Mrs. Gainsborough wrote to the King of Poland, claiming payment (Main Archives of Old Acts, Warsaw: Collection of the Popiel family, No. 185, Correspondance étrangère; reference kindly given to me by friends in the Museum Naradowe; T. Mankowski, *Galerja Stanislawa Augusta* (Lvov, 1932), p. 416 (1975), pl. 89)). It is possible, therefore, that Gainsborough himself evolved this type of derivation from No. 774. A full-length variant in robes of state, from the same source, is at Powis Castle. Queen Charlotte records in her Diary (in the Royal Library) that the King sat to Dupont 'for His Picture' on 29 March 1794 and that she sat to him 'for my Picture' on 9 August 1794.

767. GEORGE III

Windsor Castle (170). $95 \times 58\frac{1}{2}$ in., $241,3 \times 148,6$ cm.

Full-length, standing, in Garter robes with his hat in his left hand; his crown and sceptre are on a table beside him.

Painted for George IV and recorded in store at Carlton House in 1816 (235: 'A whole length of his Majesty, in the Windsor uniform'; measurements given as $94 \times 57\frac{1}{4}$ in. The 1816 label is still on the stretcher); later so altered (see below) as to fit it for the series of royal portraits set into the walls of the Throne Room at Windsor ('Carleton Palace', No. 347: 'Altered by Mr. Simpson, to the Robes of the Garter, now in the Throne Room Windsor Castle 1834'); it is still in the same position.

Literature: Collins Baker, *Windsor*, p. 72.

Presumably the full-length portrait of the King, painted for him as a present to the Prince of Wales, for which Dupont was paid £63 (undated bill in archives of the National Portrait Gallery); this was probably the full-length which was stated in The *Morning Herald* of 23 April 1795 to have been 'just conveyed by royal orders to *Carlton House*'. It was originally a straightforward derivation of No. 774 which Simpson turned into a Garter portrait. The left background is still presumably as left by Dupont, but the background on the right was apparently completely repainted by Simpson who added the crown and sceptre to the design. Traces of the original design of the figure are still very clear: e.g., the hat in the King's left hand, the original position of the legs and the gold lace on the Windsor uniform. The legs are now clearly based on those in Lawrence's portraits of George IV. See No. 766.

768. CAROLINE OF BRUNSWICK, PRINCESS OF WALES (*Plate* 106)

Buckingham Palace. 94×58 in., $238,8 \times 147,3$ cm.

Full-length, standing, wearing her wedding-dress (see below); she wears a coronet, and fastened at her breast is a miniature of the Prince of Wales.

Painted for George III. In 1804–5 'Portrait of Her Royal H. The Princess of Wales. Dupont' was among the pictures removed from the Queen's Apartment at St. James's to Windsor (Geo. III, *Removals*; later inv. No. 1521); recorded in Wyatt's Ceiling Room at Windsor, *c.* 1818 (inv. No. 41, p. 1 above); later at Frogmore.

Literature: W. T. Whitley, *Artists and their Friends in England 1700–99* (1928), vol. II, pp. 205–6; Collins Baker, *Windsor*, p. 73.

The King had intended that Hoppner should paint for him a portrait of the Princess in the dress she had worn at her wedding on 8 April 1795. On 17 April Hoppner attended on the Prince of Wales, 'who told him the King desired to have a whole length portrait of the Princess of Wales in the Robes in which she was married.' The King and the Prince agreed to entrust the commission to Hoppner, but when he waited on the King on 5 May 'to know the size and situation of the Princess of Wales's intended picture' he found that the King 'had not made up his mind about the picture'. On 12 August Yenn told Farington of Hoppner's unfortunate behaviour during his audience with the King, who had 'added He shd. not paint the Princess of Wales for him, but Gainsborough Dupont shd. do it' (Farington, *Diary*, vol. I (1923), pp. 96, 104, 206). The *Morning Herald* (12 June 1795) reported that the Princess was sitting to Dupont 'in her *Nuptial Robes*', and, on 30 December 1795 and 16 March 1796, that the portrait had been finished and was receiving its finishing touches. The portrait was rejected by the Royal Academy in 1796 because the frame was not ready (*Morning Herald*, 14 April, 21 April, 26 April); it was again submitted for exhibition at the Royal Academy in 1797, but, as the work of a deceased artist, was not accepted. A preliminary drawing by Dupont for the portrait (*Fig.* 5; J. Hayes in *Master Drawings*, vol. III, No. III (1965), p. 250) belongs to Mr. G. W. Leigh. There is a slight *pentimento* in the coronet in No. 768.

The Princess's dress was 'A royal robe; silver tissue petti-coat, covered with silver Venetian net and silver tassels;

body and train of silver tissue, festooned on each side with large cord and tassels; sleeves and tippet fine point lace, and the bands of the sleeves embroidered with plumes of feathers; a royal mantle of crimson velvet, silver cord and tassels, trimmed with ermine' (*The Gentleman's Magazine*, vol. LXV (1795), p. 430).

769. GIOVANNA ZANERINI, 'LA BACCELLI' (*d.* 1801)

Buckingham Palace. 29¾ × 24⅞ in., 75,6 × 63,2 cm.

Half-length, seated at a table, leaning on an open book.

Acquired by George IV and recorded in store at Carlton House in 1816 (330: 'A head of Signora Baccelli, with a book'); later at Windsor (472).

Literature: Buckingham Palace, 1909, p. 120; Waterhouse, *Check List,* p. 4; J. Hayes in *Connoisseur,* vol. CLXIX (1968), pp. 221–7.

Almost certainly painted by Gainsborough Dupont *c.* 1795. There is no evidence for the statement in the *Catalogue* of 1909 (*loc. cit.*) that No. 769 was among the unfinished pictures by Gainsborough bought by the Prince of Wales at Dupont's sale, 10, 11 April 1797. The lower part of the design seems to be unfinished.

A famous Venetian dancer—'noble, elegant and graceful'—who made her first appearance at the King's Theatre, Haymarket, on 19 November 1774; in the brilliant seasons of ballet in 1781 and 1782 she danced with Gaétan and Auguste Vestris and Charles Le Picq; she became the mistress of the 3rd Duke of Dorset, British Ambassador in Paris, and made her début at the Paris Opéra on 15 November 1782. Gainsborough painted for Dorset the famous full-length of her dancing (Waterhouse, *Gainsborough,* pl. 235).

Sir William Elford

c. 1748–1837. M.P. for Plymouth, 1796–1806, and Rye, 1807–8; Lieutenant-Colonel of the South Devon Militia; created a Baronet in 1800. As an amateur landscape-painter he exhibited regularly at the Royal Academy between 1774 and 1837. Many of his pictures were of scenes in Devonshire.

770. LANDSCAPE WITH A DISTANT COUNTRY HOUSE

Windsor Castle (1162). 34½ × 44¾ in., 87,6 × 113,7 cm.

Signed: *W. Elford Pt*

A view, across a river and wooded country under a stormy sky, towards a large country house and a church.

Presented by the artist to George IV in August 1819 (Jutsham, *Receipts,* f. 82; inscription on back of the canvas; additional No. 565 in Carlton House inv. of 1816); sent to Cumberland Lodge on 27 September 1823 (Jutsham, *Deliveries,* f. 47).

Presumably painted in South Devon, probably in the neighbourhood of Buckland Monachorum, near Sir William Elford's home.

William Elliott

d. 1792. Naval officer and amateur painter of marine subjects. He exhibited at the Royal Academy, 1784–9, as an honorary exhibitor, appearing on the first occasion as Lieutenant.

771. A NAVAL REVIEW

Buckingham Palace. 48⅛ × 73¼ in., 122,2 × 186 cm.

Signed and dated: *W. Elliott. f | 1790/17[?89].* The third line of the signature is obscure.

A squadron of warships sailing past a royal yacht flying the Royal Standard.

Probably acquired by George III. Recorded in the Music Room at Kew: 'Sea Piece. A Fleet commanded by Commodore Eliott. Pocock' (Geo. III, *Kew,* measurements later inserted as 48 × 72 in.); later at Buckingham Palace (1188) and Kensington.

The entry in the Kew inventory (above) is inexplicably misleading. No. 771 is admittedly close in style to Pocock, but is clearly signed by William Elliott. It is perhaps the picture exhibited by him at the Society of Artists in 1790 (87: 'His Majesty reviewing the Fleet on Board the Southampton Frigate off Plymouth'). The review took place on 18 August 1789, during the King's excursion to Weymouth and Plymouth after his recovery. He went on board the *Southampton* at about 8 a.m., and, after receiving a salute, witnessed a mock engagement between the two divisions of the fleet.

772. A VIEW OF PART OF THE BRITISH FLEET AT SPITHEAD

Buckingham Palace. 34¾ × 56 in., 88,3 × 142,2 cm.

Signed and dated: *T. Ell . . ./179[?1]*

Among the ships are probably the *Impregnable* (Vice-Admiral Sir Richard Bickerton), *Formidable, Gibraltar, Queen Charlotte, Victory* and *Royal George* (Admiral Samuel Barrington).

Nos. 772, 773 were recorded at Hampton Court in 1849 (*The Stranger's Guide,* Nos. 986, 990; No. 772 bears later No. 1017); both were later at Kensington.

Literature: Law, 1881, 1898 (893).

On the frame is a contemporary dedication to William Pitt of this view of the fleet which had secured to England the uninterrupted navigation of the Southern Ocean. The occasion recorded in No. 772 may be the assembly of ships for the review of 1790. Cleaning (1968) revealed the signature which is still hard to decipher, but in which the artist's initial is clearly T. It is possible therefore that Nos. 772 and 773 are not by William Elliott.

773. A VIEW OF PART OF THE BRITISH FLEET AT PORTSMOUTH

Buckingham Palace. 35⅜ × 55¾ in., 89,8 × 141,6 cm.

Among the ships is the *Royal William* (Rear-Admiral Robert Roddam); the others include a ship which is fitting out.

See No. 772 (No. 773 bears Hampton Court No. 1033).

Literature: Law, 1881, 1898 (903).

On the frame is a contemporary dedication of this view of the expeditious equipment of the British Fleet in 1790 to John Pitt, 2nd Earl of Chatham, First Lord of the Admiralty, 1788–94.

Thomas Gainsborough

1727–88. Painter of portraits and landscapes, who worked in Suffolk, Bath and London, where he exhibited regularly at the Society of Artists between 1761 and 1772 and at the Royal Academy, 1769–72, 1777–83. Soon after he had settled in London in 1774 Gainsborough painted the King's brothers and their wives and by 1781 was working for the King, Queen and Prince of Wales. In 1787 it was stated in the press that the Duke of York was going to sit to him (Whitley, *Gainsborough*, pp. 290–1). In the last year of Gainsborough's life he took his *Woodman* to Buckingham House, where it was admired by the King and his family; the King also admired, and may have considered buying, the *Cottage Children* or *Wood-Gatherers* (*ibid.*, pp. 292, 296, 323; Waterhouse, *Gainsborough*, No. 807).

Queen Charlotte owned a very important group of Gainsborough's drawings which were sold in 1819 (Oppé, p. 11). She also owned the full-length of Karl Friedrich Abel (Waterhouse, *Gainsborough*, No. 1) which is now in the Henry E. Huntington Library and Art Gallery, San Marino; it was sold on 25 May 1819 (93).

The documents assembled when efforts were being made to settle the Prince of Wales's debts include a list, possibly in the hand of the painter's widow (who died in December 1798) of 'Pictures painted by order of His Royal Highness The Prince of Wales by Thos Gainsborough' (P.R.O., H.O. 73, 19; a slightly differently worded version of this document is W.R.A., Geo. 26791). Apart from the pictures still in the collection, there are a number of pictures given away by the Prince. 'A full length with a Horse sent to Genll St. Leger' (£126) is now (*Fig.* XIII) at Waddesdon (Waterhouse, *Gainsborough*, No. 707); the 'Copy of Do delivered by order to Sir Tho: Dundass' (£126) is still at Aske Hall (*ibid.*, No. 708). Four smaller portraits of the Prince (each at £31. 10s.) are on the list, the first of them with the date 1781 beside it. They were delivered to 'Col: Leake' (i.e., Lake), Lord Lothian, Lady Courtown and 'abroad by particular orders'. The portraits painted for Lake and Lothian are now in private collections (*ibid.*, Nos. 704, 705); the one for Lady Courtown is the portrait in the National Gallery of Art, Washington. The one sent abroad is presumably the portrait sent to the Duke of York. On 1 March 1782 the Prince wrote to his brother: 'I have had painted for you a Picture ye same as one I have given Gerrard [i.e., Lake] it is a half length painted by Gainsberough & reckoned remarkably like by every [*sic*].'. On 15 October 1782 he again wrote that he was planning to send over the portrait: 'reckoned by every body to be a remarkable strong likeness, he is to pack it up himself it will be rol'd up & sent in a Tin case, you will therefore make yr servants take care how they unpack it.' On 20 December 1782 the Duke wrote to the Prince, with a thousand thanks 'for Your Picture which I think exceedingly like except the nose which is certainly not shaped like yours' (W.R.A., Geo. 43498–9, 43538, 43548–9; *Correspondence of George, Prince of Wales*, vol. I, pp. 83, 93, 96).

The list also includes (1) 'a Head of Mrs Elliot' at £31. 10s., perhaps the portrait now in the Frick Collection (Waterhouse, No. 240); this may be the 'Portrait of a Lady a ¾ by Gainsborough' which was lined and repaired by Simpson for the Prince in 1793 (P.R.O., H.O. 73, 23). (2) The full-length of Mrs. Robinson (see No. 804). (3) 'A Head of Mrs Fitzherbert delivered unfinished by His Highness's orders' (£31. 10s.). This was in store at Carlton House in 1816 (327, measurements given as 29½ × 24½ in.) and was sent to Mrs. Fitzherbert at Brighton on 5 October 1830. It is now (*Fig.* XVII) in the California Palace of the Legion of Honor (Waterhouse, No. 254). (4) Two landscapes, each at £105: 'A Large Landskip with a Cart & figures' and 'Do with Sheep &c.' They were in the exhibition at Schomberg House, March–May 1789 (74, 75) (*Burl. Mag.*, vol. LXXXIV–V (1944), pp. 107–10) and, in rich

gilt frames made by Wyatt, were sent to Mrs. Fitzherbert by the Prince's commands on 20 July 1810 (Jutsham, *R/D*, f. 68). They are now respectively in the Toronto Art Gallery (*Fig.* XIX; Waterhouse, No. 993) and (signed and dated 1784) in the collection of W. S. Constable Curtis (*Fig.* XVIII; Waterhouse, No. 992; Whitley, *Gainsborough*, pp. 229, 258–9, 325).[1] In the Prince's sale at Christie's, 29 June 1814, lot 21 was 'A large landscape with buildings and figures, *a genuine picture*', by Gainsborough (Jutsham, *R/D*, f. 164, measurements given as 74 × 61 in.) which is at Kinderhook, N.Y. (Waterhouse, No. 991). The Prince gave to Princess Sophia of Gloucester on 9 July 1816 a 'Whole Length Sketch by Gainsborough' of her father William Henry, Duke of Gloucester; it was sold at Christie's by the Earl of Waldegrave, 27 June 1958 (57). On 1 December 1810 he gave to Lord Heathfield (No. 650) 'The Head, and Scetch of part of the Body of His Royal Highness the Prince of Wales—painted by Gainsborough' which was finished by a later hand and is now at Bodorgan (*Fig.* XVI; *Burl. Mag.*, vol. CIX (1967), pp. 531–2).

The money due for pictures on the list cited above was £1,246. 10s. 6d. and it appears that some of the pictures remained in Mrs. Gainsborough's hands. The amount included £10. 13s. 6d. for the frame sent with the equestrian portrait to General St. Leger in 1789 and seven guineas for a frame with the picture sent to Lady Courtown. On 5 April 1793 Margaret Gainsborough was paid £246. 10s. 6d.; earlier a bond had been given for the remaining £1,000 (see also W.R.A., Geo. 32040, 32042, 32454, 88814). It is clear from a note by Farington in 1799 (*Diary*, vol. I, p. 262) that Gainsborough himself had been reluctant to join the Prince's creditors and had, as a result, never been paid by the Prince. The three pictures sent, by Gainsborough's family after his death, to the Prince to see if he wished to take them were perhaps the two landscapes and the portrait of Mrs. Fitzherbert.

774. GEORGE III (*Plate* 47)

Windsor Castle (2553). 94 × 62½ in., 238,8 × 158,7 cm.

Full-length, standing, in Windsor uniform with the ribbon and star of the Garter and the Garter round his knee; he holds his hat in his left hand.

Nos. 774, 775 are first recorded in the Dining-Room at Buckingham House: 'His Majesty . . . Her Majesty. Gainsborough'; measurements given as 79 × 61 in. (Geo. III, *Buck. Ho.*; B.M. Add. MSS. 6391, f. 123); in 1804–5 they were taken down to Windsor (Geo. III, *Removals*), but in the inv. of Buckingham House in 1819 they appear (822, 824) again in the Old Dining-Room (measurements given as 96 × 62). They remained in the State Dining-Room at Buckingham Palace (193, 195) until they were removed to Windsor in 1950.

Literature: Whitley, *Gainsborough*, pp. 173, 174, 176–7; R.A., *King's Pictures* (94), *First Hundred Years*, 1951–2 (89); Waterhouse, *Check List*, p. 48, *Gainsborough*, No. 309.

Exhibited at the Royal Academy in 1781 (146), when it received praise as a likeness (Whitley, *loc. cit.*). Copies of the pair were being distributed soon after. A pair by C. W. Hanneman, for the King of which he was paid in 1786, is at Audley End (R. J. B. Walker, *Audley End, Catalogue of the Pictures in the State Rooms* (1954), pp. 8, 36); another pair by the same artist, stated to have been presented by the sitters to the 2nd Earl Harcourt, was sold at Christie's, 11 June 1948 (109). A pair in the Town Hall at Worcester is said to have been given to the Earl of Coventry when the King and Queen visited Croome Court in 1788 (also in the Town

1. It was sold at Sotheby's on 26 June 1968 (34).

Hall is a derivation of the King in robes of state); other pairs are at Hatfield, Abingdon Town Hall (dated 1794), the Horse Guards, Schloss Marienburg and Schloss Ludwigsborg, near Stuttgart. Gainsborough Dupont published his mezzotint of No. 774 on 30 December 1790. Copies of the pair in pastel by De la Houlière were sold at Christie's, 31 March 1950 (25); miniature copies of the head from No. 774 are also recorded, e.g., by Richard Collins (1795) and Richard Crosse, sold at Sotheby's, 31 July 1961 (45, 70). A copy of the King alone belongs to the Royal Society of Musicians, to whom it is stated to have been presented by the sitter; a small copy is at Drummond Castle; and a pair of head and shoulders copies was in the Millais sale, Sotheby's, 19 November 1928 (59). A similar copy, of the King alone, in the collection of Lord Cottesloe and probably by Dupont, was in the collection of Sir Henry Halford, who stated in 1818 that it had belonged to Queen Charlotte and had been given to him at her death. Nos. 774, 775 were exhibited at the British Institution in 1820 (1, 6).

775. QUEEN CHARLOTTE (*Plate* 48)
Windsor Castle (2554). 94 × 62½ in., 238,8 × 158,7 cm.
Full-length, moving to the right, accompanied by a papillon and holding a fan in her right hand.

See No. 774.

Literature: Whitley, *Gainsborough*, pp. 173, 174, 176–7; R.A., *King's Pictures* (98), *First Hundred Years*, 1951–2 (94); Waterhouse, *Check List*, p. 19, *Gainsborough*, No. 130.

Exhibited at the Royal Academy in 1781 (168). Northcote told James Ward that 'the drapery was done in one night by Gainsborough and his nephew, Gainsborough Dupont; they sat up all night, and painted it by lamp-light' (*Conversations of James Northcote with James Ward on Art and Artists*, ed. E. Fletcher (1901), pp. 160–1). Dupont published his mezzotint of No. 775 on 4 June 1790 and it is possible that the small sketch of the design in the possession of H.R.H. Princess Alice, Countess of Athlone, (formerly in the collection of the Duke of Cambridge) is Dupont's preparatory sketch for the mezzotint. Another small version, which has been on the art-market in London on a number of occasions in the last thirty years, is finer and could be Gainsborough's original sketch for No. 775.
Copies of No. 775 were distributed with copies of the pendant (No. 774). A copy of No. 775 is at Herrenhausen and another is at Ludwigslust. A copy of the head is at Penshurst. A derivation, in a different costume, with the crown on a table behind the figure and a miniature of the King (based on No. 774) at her breast, is at Powis Castle; it is stated to have been given by the King to Lord Sidmouth (J. Steegman, *A Survey of Portraits in Welsh Houses*, vol. I (1957), p. 267). See Nos. 811, 812.

776. GEORGE III (*Plate* 76)
Windsor Castle (487). Oval: 16 × 13⅛ in., 40,6 × 33,3 cm.
Head and shoulders, in Windsor uniform, with the ribbon and star of the Garter, resting his right hand on the ribbon of the Order.

Perhaps acquired, with No. 777, by Queen Victoria; recorded at Windsor in 1859 (*V.R. inv.*).

Literature: Collins Baker, *Windsor*, p. 145.

A reduced copy from No. 774. There are alterations to the line of the shoulders and the quality of No. 776 and its companion seems good enough for them to be considered as reductions by Gainsborough himself.

777. QUEEN CHARLOTTE (*Plate* 77)
Windsor Castle (488). Oval: 16¼ × 13⅛ in., 41,3 × 33,3 cm.
Head and shoulders.

Perhaps acquired, with No. 776, by Queen Victoria; recorded at Windsor in 1859 (*V.R. inv.*).

Literature: Collins Baker, *Windsor*, p. 146.

As in the companion portrait (No. 776), the high quality suggests that No. 777 is a reduction by Gainsborough himself from No. 775; *pentimenti* in the flowers and lace with which the Queen's hair is dressed, and in the ribbons on the sleeve of her dress, support this attribution.

778–92. THE ROYAL FAMILY (*Plates* 49–63)
The series, painted for George III and Queen Charlotte, was probably commissioned by Queen Charlotte. The portraits were painted at Windsor in September and October 1782; on the backs of all but Nos. 779 and 792 was originally inscribed the date September 1782. During most of that month the royal family was at Windsor. On 14 September the *Morning Herald* wrote: '*Mr. Gainsborough* is now down at Windsor painting half length portraits of the whole Royal Family, by command of her Majesty, many of whom he has already finished, in that superior stile which has long distinguished his celebrated pencil.' On 30 October it was reported in the same paper that 'M𝓇 *Gainsborough* has just completed his painting of the whole Royal Family, at Windsor, sixteen in number, all of which are spoken of as highly-finished characteristic portraits of the illustrious personages who sat to him.' When the portraits were shown at the Royal Academy, those of the Prince of Wales and the three eldest Princesses were thought the best likenesses. Henry Angelo (see below) was therefore wrong in stating that his father, in attendance at Buckingham House, saw 'Gainsborough busily engaged in painting separate portraits of the royal children'; he recalled that the painter 'was all but raving mad with ecstasy in beholding such a constellation of youthful beauty'. The portraits were exhibited at the Royal Academy in 1783 (134, *en bloc*, as 'Portraits of the Royal Family . . .'). To the Hanging Committee Gainsborough wrote, presenting his compliments: 'and begs leave to *hint* to Them, that if The Royal Family, which he has sent for this Exhibition, (*being smaller than three quarters*) are hung above the line along with full lengths, he never more, whilst he breaths, will send another Picture to the Exhibition. This he swears by God.' In a letter to Newton, the Secretary of the R.A., he sent a little sketch (*Fig.* 14) in which he indicated how he wished the portraits to be hung: 'I w𝒹 beg to have them hung with the Frames touching each other, in this order, the Names are written behind each Picture.' (Both letters are preserved in the Library of the Royal Academy; printed, not very accurately, in *The Letters of Thomas Gainsborough*, ed. Mary Woodall (1963), p. 29). A writer in the *St. James's Chronicle* described the arrangement as 'a childish conceit and by no means worthy of Mr. Gainsborough'.
The portraits were hung by Queen Charlotte in the White or Queen's Closet at Buckingham House; they are recorded there in 1796 (B.M. Add. MSS. 6391, f. 122). In this reference, as in another early reference to them hanging there (Geo. III, *Buck. Ho.*; '. . . all by Gainsborough', measurements given as 23 × 17½ in.), the portrait of the Queen herself (No. 779) is not mentioned, perhaps by accident. In the

inventory of Buckingham House in 1819 all fifteen portraits are listed (700–14) in the Green Dressing-Room or Closet; the portrait of the Queen (714) is not described as an oval and its measurements are given as 30 × 25 in.[1] The portraits can be seen hanging in the room in their (original?) frames in Stephanoff's plate (1819) in Pyne, vol. II, *Buckingham House*, p. 22. It is clear, from the careless way in which the ovals are defined on the canvases, that the portraits were always intended to be framed as ovals; Nos. 790–2 have recently been stretched as ovals. In 1834 the portraits were removed to Kew from the Green Dressing-Room at Buckingham Palace. By 1838 they had been placed by Queen Victoria in the Queen's Audience Room in Windsor Castle (see above, pp. xl–i). They were arranged at the R.A. in 1946–47 (*King's Pictures* (87)) according to Gainsborough's original design and thereafter, in obedience to the commands of His Majesty King George VI, they were so displayed in the Corridor at Windsor, in frames of an eighteenth-century design. Many of the canvases have been slightly stretched in lining.

Literature (for the set): H. Angelo, *Reminiscences* (1828), vol. I, pp. 191–3; Whitley, *Gainsborough*, pp. 192–3, 195–7; Collins Baker, *Windsor*, pp. 138–9.

778. GEORGE III (*Plate* 49)

Windsor Castle (683). 23¼ × 17¼ in., 59 × 43,8 cm.

The back was originally inscribed with the date September 1782.

Head and shoulders, in a painted oval, wearing Windsor uniform with the ribbon and star of the Garter.

Literature: Collins Baker, *Windsor*, p. 134; Waterhouse, *Check List*, p. 48, *Gainsborough*, No. 310.

Early copies are recorded; the best are probably by Gainsborough Dupont. One was given by the King to Sir Herbert Taylor; another was in the Duke of Cambridge's sale at Christie's, 11 June 1904 (88). Another was at Schloss Arolsen.[2]

779. QUEEN CHARLOTTE (*Plate* 50)

Windsor Castle (684). 23½ × 17⅜ in., 59,7 × 44,1 cm.

Head and shoulders in a painted oval with a lace cap on her head and wearing a black lace shawl.

Literature: Collins Baker, *Windsor*, p. 134; Waterhouse, *Check List*, p. 19, *Gainsborough*, No. 132.

A very good autograph repetition (Waterhouse, *Gainsborough*, No. 133) is in the Metropolitan Museum, New York (Bache Collection). A copy is in the Victoria and Albert Museum (91–1879); another, traditionally said to have been given by the Queen to the Duke of Kent, was sold at Puttick & Simpson's, 31 May 1932 (56); another was with Sedelmeyer in 1901; a copy appeared in the King sale, American Art Association, New York, 31 March 1905 (20). A copy on enamel by Bone (1804) is in the Royal Library.

780. GEORGE IV WHEN PRINCE OF WALES (*Plate* 51)

Windsor Castle (686). 23⅜ × 17⅜ in., 59,4 × 44,1 cm.

The back was originally inscribed with the date September 1782.

Head and shoulders, in a painted oval, wearing Windsor uniform with the star of the Garter.

Literature: Collins Baker, *Windsor*, p. 134; Waterhouse, *Check List*, p. 111, *Gainsborough*, No. 703.

For a portrait of the Prince by Gainsborough of the same date, but of a different type, see above, p. 35. In 1817 the Princess Royal was entreating the Prince 'to be indulged with a Head in Oils of the same size as those Gainsborough painted for the Queen' (W.R.A., Geo. 51806–7; *Letters of George IV*, vol. II, 676).

781. PRINCE WILLIAM, LATER DUKE OF CLARENCE (*Plate* 52)

Windsor Castle (687). 23⅜ × 18⅜ in., 59,4 × 46,7 cm.

The back was originally inscribed with the date September 1782.

Head and shoulders, in a painted oval, in midshipman's uniform, with the ribbon and star of the Thistle.

Literature: Collins Baker, *Windsor*, p. 135, Waterhouse, *Check List*, p. 114, *Gainsborough*, No. 726.

In September 1782 the Prince was at sea. Gainsborough therefore presumably based this portrait on a half-length, now in the collection of Mrs. Etienne Boegner in New York (*Fig.* 10), which had passed by descent to the Duke of Cambridge and appeared in his sale at Christie's, 11 June 1904 (86). It had been engraved by Dupont and is thought to have been the portrait commissioned by George III in 1781 and for which the Prince sat twice at Buckingham House (Whitley, *Gainsborough*, p. 177). A small copy of No. 781 was sold at Sotheby's, 27 October 1965 (107). See No. 813.

782. CHARLOTTE, PRINCESS ROYAL (*Plate* 53)

Windsor Castle (689). 23¼ × 17¼ in., 59 × 43,8 cm.

The back was originally inscribed with the date September 1782.

Head and shoulders in a painted oval, wearing a fichu across her bosom.

Literature: Collins Baker, *Windsor*, p. 135; Waterhouse, *Check List*, p. 20, *Gainsborough*, No. 134.

783. PRINCE EDWARD, LATER DUKE OF KENT (*Plate* 54)

Windsor Castle (690). 23¼ × 17¼ in., 59 × 43,8 cm.

The back was originally inscribed with the date September 1782.

Head and shoulders, in a painted oval, wearing Windsor uniform.

Literature: Collins Baker, *Windsor*, p. 135; Waterhouse, *Check List*, p. 63, *Gainsborough*, No 406.

784. PRINCESS AUGUSTA (*Plate* 55)

Windsor Castle (691). 23⅜ × 17⅜ in., 59,4 × 44,1 cm.

The back was originally inscribed with the date September 1782.

Head and shoulders, in a painted oval, in a white dress with a gold band over her right shoulder.

Literature: Collins Baker, *Windsor*, p. 136; Waterhouse, *Check List*, p. 3, *Gainsborough*, No. 22.

---

1. It may therefore conceivably have been No. 811 below.
2. In her will, Charlotte, Princess Royal, bequeathed to Princess Elizabeth 'Das brüstbild Seiner Majestät des Königs von England in Oehl, von Gainsborough' (W.R.A., Geo. 51860); this may have been a portrait of George IV.

785. PRINCESS ELIZABETH (*Plate* 56)

Windsor Castle (692). 23⅜ × 17⅜ in., 59,4 × 44,1 cm.

The back was originally inscribed with the date September 1782.

Head and shoulders in a painted oval, with a fichu over her shoulders.

Literature: Collins Baker, *Windsor*, p. 136; Waterhouse, *Check List*, p. 36, *Gainsborough*, No. 238.

786. PRINCE ERNEST, LATER DUKE OF CUMBERLAND (*Plate* 57)

Windsor Castle (693). 23¼ × 17⅜ in., 59 × 44,1 cm.

The back was originally inscribed with the date September 1782.

Head and shoulders, in a painted oval, wearing Windsor uniform.

Literature: Collins Baker, *Windsor*, p. 136; Waterhouse, *Check List*, p. 25, *Gainsborough*, No. 175.

787. PRINCE AUGUSTUS, LATER DUKE OF SUSSEX (*Plate* 58)

Windsor Castle (694). 23⅜ × 17⅛ in., 59,4 × 43,5 cm.

The back was originally inscribed with the date September 1782.

Head and shoulders in a painted oval, wearing Windsor uniform and a white waistcoat.

Literature: Collins Baker, *Windsor*, p. 137; Waterhouse, *Check List*, p. 102, *Gainsborough*, No. 643.

788. PRINCE ADOLPHUS, LATER DUKE OF CAMBRIDGE (*Plate* 59)

Windsor Castle (696). 23⅜ × 17¼ in., 59,4 × 43,8 cm.

The back was originally inscribed with the date September 1782.

Head and shoulders in a painted oval, wearing Windsor uniform and a white waistcoat.

Literature: Collins Baker, *Windsor*, p. 137; Waterhouse, *Check List*, p. 16, *Gainsborough*, No. 109.

789. PRINCESS MARY (*Plate* 60)

Windsor Castle (697). 23¼ × 17⅜ in., 59 × 44,1 cm.

The back was originally inscribed with the date September 1782.

Head and shoulders in a painted oval.

Literature: Collins Baker, *Windsor*, p. 137; Waterhouse, *Check List*, p. 72, *Gainsborough*, No. 471.

790. PRINCESS SOPHIA (*Plate* 61)

Windsor Castle (685). Oval: 22¼ × 16⅝ in., 56,5 × 42,2 cm.

The back was originally inscribed with the date September 1782.

Head and shoulders.

Literature: Collins Baker, *Windsor*, p. 138; Waterhouse, *Check List*, p. 100, *Gainsborough*, No. 625.

791. PRINCE OCTAVIUS (*Plate* 62)

Windsor Castle (695). Oval: 22⅜ × 16⅝ in., 56,8 × 42,2 cm.

The back was originally inscribed with the date September 1782.

Head and shoulders in a buff coat and blue sash.

Literature: Collins Baker, *Windsor*, p. 138; Waterhouse, *Check List*, pp. 81–2, *Gainsborough*, No. 527.

Harding's drawing at Windsor after No. 791 (Oppé, No. 303) presumably served as the basis of the engraving by Cheesman, published in 1806. See Nos. 814–16. The sight of No. 791 at the Royal Academy in 1783 is said to have reduced the Queen and her daughters to tears (W. T. Whitley, *Artists and their Friends in England 1700–99* (1928), vol. I, p. 396).

792. PRINCE ALFRED (*Plate* 63)

Windsor Castle (688). Oval: 22⅜ × 16½ in., 56,8 × 41,9 cm.

Head and shoulders in a white dress with a pink sash.

Literature: Collins Baker, *Windsor*, p. 138; Waterhouse, *Check List*, p. 2, *Gainsborough*, No. 12.

Prince Alfred had died on 20 August 1782, just before Gainsborough's visit to Windsor; on the back of No. 792 was originally inscribed a note that it had been 'painted by remembrance'. The portrait was taken from the Queen's White Closet in Buckingham House to Windsor in 1804 or 1805 (Geo. III, *Removals*). Harding's drawing at Windsor after No. 792 (Oppé, No. 302) probably served as the basis of the engraving by Bourlier, published in 1806. See No. 817.

793. HENRY, DUKE OF CUMBERLAND (*Plate* 46)

Buckingham Palace. 93¾ × 56 in., 238,1 × 142,2 cm.

Full-length, in robes of state, fingering the collar of the Garter with his right hand and holding his coronet in his left.

Nos. 793, 794 were presented by the sitters to Elizabeth, Countess of Home (*d.* 1784), who placed them in her Ballroom—'my Capital Room'—at Home House (20, Portman Square) and apparently planned the decoration of the room around them. In her will (19 November 1783) the Countess requested permission of the Cumberlands to bequeath the portraits to the City of London, to hang in the Mansion House; but she provided that, if the Duke and Duchess disliked this idea, the Duke was to have the portraits and dispose of them in any way he chose. The Duke took possession of them. The Duchess, in her will (15 February 1808), bequeathed to William, Duke of Clarence, 'the two whole length portraits painted by Gainsborough of his late Royal Uncle and of myself as they represent the ffriends of his early youth they may recall to his Royal Highness's recollection some happy days.' The two portraits were placed, presumably after William IV's accession, in the State Dining-Room at Buckingham Palace (197, 191), where they are first recorded in the catalogue of 1841 (208, 209).

Literature: Whitley, *Gainsborough*, pp. 142–3; R.A., *King's Pictures* (104); Waterhouse, *Check List*, p. 25, *Gainsborough*, No. 176; L. Lewis, 'Elizabeth, Countess of Home, and her house in Portman Square', *Burl. Mag.*, vol. CIX (1967), pp. 443–53.

Exhibited at the Royal Academy in 1777 (131). *Pentimenti*, which became obvious during restoration in 1959, reveal that Gainsborough originally indicated a landscape background on the left, extending at least as far across the canvas as the Duke's right shoulder; there are also confusions in the area round the Duke's head. Robert Adam's drawing for a frame for the portrait when it was to be set up in Portman Square is in the Soane Museum (L. Lewis, *loc. cit., Fig.* 13). It is dated May 1773, when the portrait was still on show at the Royal Academy, and the frame is surmounted by an elaborate cresting in which the Duke's coronet and heraldic supporters are displayed above the collar of the Garter, to which attention had also been drawn by Gainsborough (see above). Home House had been begun in 1773 and the Countess moved in in 1776.

794. ANNE, DUCHESS OF CUMBERLAND
(*Plate* 45)

Buckingham Palace. 93¾ × 56 in., 238,1 × 142,2 cm.

Full-length, standing, in robes of state, resting her right arm on a ledge on which is her coronet.

See No. 793.

Literature: Whitley, *Gainsborough*, pp. 142–3; R.A., *King's Pictures* (102); Waterhouse, *Check List*, p. 26, *Gainsborough*, No. 180; L. Lewis, 'Elizabeth, Countess of Home, and her house in Portman Square', *Burl. Mag.*, vol. CIX (1967), pp. 443–53.

Exhibited at the Royal Academy in 1777 (132). During restoration by the late Mr. Horace Buttery in 1959 considerable confusions were revealed in the disposition of the state robe as it falls on either side of the figure. The arrangement of this robe had been altered at a very early date; Mr. Buttery re-established as far as possible the original arrangement. The portrait can be seen before restoration in Waterhouse, *Gainsborough*, pl. 182. The robe now falls from under the Duchess's right elbow in a more natural line; before the restoration a more ample sweep of robe came round from the shoulder at this point and partly concealed the coronet; the skirt now drops straight from her waist to the floor; and the lining of the robe under the right elbow has lost the flecks of ermine. On the other side of the figure, the Duchess's left hand, which used to hold up her robe as it fell down behind her, now rests on the edge of her skirt. Mr. Buttery also removed early additions to the Duchess's coiffure, which were perhaps made when the robes were altered: a *pentimento* shows that at one stage Gainsborough painted her coronet on her head.

795. HENRY, DUKE OF CUMBERLAND
(*Plate* 69)

Buckingham Palace. 29¼ × 23 in., 74,3 × 58,4 cm.; the canvas is now stretched to this size, but a large area of original canvas is turned over on the right (*c.* 7 in.) and at the bottom (*c.* 20 in.). A strip of original canvas must also have been removed from the left; Redgrave (*V.R. inv.*, March 1859) states that the canvas then measured 50 × 39½ in.; and his accompanying photograph shows the portrait in its original state.

Head and shoulders, probably in robes of state.

Nos. 795, 796 were left unfinished in Gainsborough's studio at his death. No. 795 was included among his unfinished portraits, the property of his widow, in Gainsborough Dupont's sale at Christie's, 10 April 1797 (25: *Duke of Cumberland, a head*); it was bought with No. 796 by Hammond for the Prince of Wales for £4. 6s. (*Walpole Soc.*, vol. V (1915–17), pp. 92, 102; No. 795 was described in the *Morning Herald* of that date as 'a head, on three-quarters canvas'). Recorded in store at Carlton House in 1816 (323) and 1819 (263; measurements given as 50 × 40 in.); later at Windsor (822).

Literature: Whitley, *Gainsborough*, pp. 210–11, 227, 346, 348; R.A., *King's Pictures* (86); Waterhouse, *Check List*, p. 25, *Gainsborough*, No. 177.

Nos. 795, 796 were being painted for the Prince of Wales late in 1783. They were intended presumably to be three-quarter-lengths in robes; there is an indication in No. 795 of the customary collar of plain fur on the sitter's robe of ermine and scarlet. In their unfinished condition they were shown with No. 798 in Gainsborough's exhibition at Schomberg House in July 1784: 'the three . . . pictures . . . intended for the Prince of Wales's State Room at Carlton House' (Whitley, *op. cit.*, p. 227). It is not known why the two portraits remained unfinished.

796. ANNE, DUCHESS OF CUMBERLAND
(*Plate* 65)

Windsor Castle (823). 50¼ × 40⅛ in., 127,6 × 101,9 cm.

Three-quarter-length, standing, wearing a coronet and robes of state.

Nos. 795, 796 were left unfinished in Gainsborough's studio at his death. No. 796 was included among his unfinished portraits, the property of his widow, in Gainsborough Dupont's sale at Christie's, 10 April 1797 (24: *Duchess of Cumberland, half length*); it was bought with No. 795 by Hammond for the Prince of Wales for £4. 6s. (*Walpole Soc.*, vol. V (1915–17), pp. 92, 102). Recorded in store at Carlton House in 1816 (254).

Literature: Whitley, *Gainsborough*, pp. 210–11, 227, 346, 348; R.A., *British Art*, 1934 (328), *Commemorative Catalogue* (1935), p. 59; Collins Baker, *Windsor*, p. 143; Waterhouse, *Check List*, p. 26; R.A., *European Masters of the Eighteenth Century*, 1954–5 (84); Waterhouse, *Gainsborough*, No. 181.

No. 796 was being painted, late in 1783, at the same time as No. 795; a report in November 1783 (Whitley, *op. cit.*, p. 210) stated erroneously that the portrait of the Duchess 'in her robes of State, with other paraphernalia of dignity', had been finished. It was shown with Nos. 795, 798 in Gainsborough's exhibition at Schomberg House in July 1784: 'The Duchess is pourtrayed in her State Robes with a ducal coronet on her head. The likeness is strong. The drapery and ground is in an unfinished state . . . intended for the Prince of Wales's State Room at Carlton House'. The face alone appears to have been almost finished.

797. HENRY, DUKE OF CUMBERLAND, WITH THE DUCHESS OF CUMBERLAND AND LADY ELIZABETH LUTTRELL (*d.* 1799)
(*Frontispiece and Plate* 73)

Windsor Castle (343). 64½ × 49 in., 163,8 × 124,5 cm. The composition was completed and is framed as an oval, *c.* 64 × 47½ in. When the canvas was lined at some period it was slightly stretched and was laid crooked on the new canvas; the two original joins in the canvas therefore run slightly upwards from left to right.

The Duke and Duchess are walking arm-in-arm in a park, accompanied by a cavalier spaniel; the Duke wears the ribbon and star of the Garter. Lady Elizabeth is seated behind them, apparently engaged in sketching them.

Presumably in Gainsborough's studio at the time of his death. It was among the pictures exhibited for sale at Schomberg House, 30 March–31 May 1789 (70: *Their Royal Highnesses the Duke and Duchess of Cumberland, and Lady Elizabeth Luttrell*, measurements given as 63½ × 47½ in., priced at fifty guineas). It remained unsold and appeared in Mrs. Gainsborough's sale at Christie's, 2 June 1792 (74). In store at Carlton House in 1816 (251: 'The late Duke and Duchess of Cumberland, with Lady Elizabeth Lutterel. Mr Gainsborough'); sent to Cumberland Lodge on 1 October 1823.

Literature: Whitley, *Gainsborough*, pp. 322, 327–8; R.A., *British Art*, 1934 (329), *Commemorative Catalogue* (1935), p. 59; Collins Baker, *Windsor*, p. 142; R.A., *King's Pictures* (82); Waterhouse, *Check List*, p. 25, *Gainsborough*, No. 178.

A late work, painted *c.* 1785–8. It had apparently been painted 'at the Duke's instance' and its appearance at Schomberg House in 1789 caused surprise. The Council of the Royal Academy, meeting in May 1789, resolved to offer Mrs. Gainsborough fifty guineas for it when her exhibition was over (Whitley, *loc. cit.*). It re-appeared, however, at Christie's in 1792 (see above), when it was probably bought by or for the Prince of Wales. A preliminary drawing by Gainsborough is in the British Museum (1902–6–17–6; *Fig.*

7). It is clear from the drawing that at an early stage Gainsborough conceived a rectangular design.[1] The areas at the corners of the canvas, now covered by the spandrels of the frame, are lightly painted with a continuation of the ground, sky and trees. These passages were thinly covered with brownish paint, presumably when Gainsborough decided on the oval shape. Whitley (loc. cit.) records a contemporary note that the setting is in the grounds of the Duke's Lodge (Cumberland Lodge) in Windsor Great Park.

Lady Elizabeth Luttrell, younger daughter of Simon Luttrell, 1st Earl of Carhampton, and sister of the Duchess of Cumberland 'shone with much splendour in the fashionable world', but she was a notorious gambler and was imprisoned in the King's Bench for debt. She died in Germany.

798. THE THREE ELDEST PRINCESSES: CHARLOTTE, PRINCESS ROYAL, AUGUSTA AND ELIZABETH (Plates 66–8)

Windsor Castle (2530). $51 \times 70\frac{3}{4}$ in., $129,5 \times 179,7$ cm.; there is an addition of c. $4\frac{1}{2}$ in. on the left.

The two eldest girls standing at three-quarter-length, Princess Augusta resting her arm within her elder sister's, beside a chair in which Princess Elizabeth is seated; Princess Augusta wears a miniature in a jewelled setting at her breast.

Painted for George IV, for Carlton House, where a special position was to be constructed for it; recorded in store there in 1816 (244: 'Whole length portraits . . . Mr Gainsborough', measurements given as 100×67 in.); later at Windsor and Buckingham Palace (201); taken to Windsor again in June 1901; at Buckingham Palace in the time of H.M. King George VI.

Literature: Whitley, *Gainsborough*, pp. 212, 213, 215, 216, 224–5, 226–7, 230, 258, 261, 349; Collins Baker, *Windsor*, pp. 140–1; Waterhouse, *Check-List*, p. 20; Arts Council, *Thomas Gainsborough*, 1953 (47); R.A., *European Masters of the Eighteenth Century*, 1954–5 (69); Waterhouse, *Gainsborough*, No. 135.

Finished early in 1784. Gainsborough intended to exhibit the group at the Royal Academy that year. Before it could be sent in, it had been sent to Buckingham House: 'The Frame of the Princesses', Gainsborough wrote, 'cannot be sent but with the Picture, as Their Majesties are to have a private View of the picture at Buckingham house before it is sent to the Royal Academy'. He asked the Hanging Committee at the Academy if, as he had painted the group in so tender a light, they would waive the regulations which governed the hanging of full-lengths as he could not allow it to be hung higher than five and a half feet from the ground; to hang it higher would, he argued, render the likenesses and work invisible. The Committee could not agree to this request and Gainsborough withdrew all his pictures and exhibited them later in the summer at Schomberg House (*The Letters of Thomas Gainsborough*, ed. Mary Woodall (1963), pp. 29–31; Whitley, *loc. cit.*). *The Three Princesses* are described and warmly praised in an account of Gainsborough's exhibition in the *Morning Herald* (Whitley, *op. cit.*, pp. 226–7). The picture was exhibited by Gainsborough at Schomberg House again in 1786, when it was stated (*ibid.*, p. 258) that it would remain in Gainsborough's hands until the Prince of Wales had completed the Saloon in Carlton House in which he intended to hang portraits of his family. The group is included, under June 1784, in the list of pictures painted for the Prince by Gainsborough: 'Picture for

Carleton House of Three Princesses, at £315' (W.R.A., Geo. 26791; P.R.O., H.O. 73, 19).

The group was originally a full-length; its appearance can be judged from the engraving by Dupont (*Fig.* 8), published in 1793, or from the small sketch-like copy, sometimes attributed to Dupont, in the Victoria and Albert Museum (136–1878). Sir Edwin Landseer told Redgrave on 25 November 1868 that early in the reign of Queen Victoria he had seen Saunders, an 'Inspector of Palaces',[1] cutting the canvas down so that it could be fitted into an overdoor; although Landseer spoke to the Queen about this, he was too late to save the discarded pieces of canvas from the flames (F. M. Redgrave, *Richard Redgrave, A Memoir* (1891), pp. 301–2). As well as cutting a large area of canvas from the bottom, Saunders took off a substantial strip at the top. The addition of c. $4\frac{1}{2}$ in. on the left was probably made at this time; this addition does not form part of the design as engraved by Dupont and the canvas is now wider than it was in 1816 (see above). At the end of the inventory of Kensington in 1818, in a section dealing with the Private Closet, are unnumbered items classed as drawings, among them: 'Portraits of the Princess Royal, Princess Augusta, and Princess Elizabeth. Gainsborough'. This was moved to Hampton Court on 12 September 1838, but cannot now be identified.

799. CHARLES, SECOND EARL AND FIRST MARQUESS CORNWALLIS (1738–1805) (Plate 70)

Buckingham Palace. 30×25 in., $76,2 \times 63,5$ cm.

Head and shoulders, in a painted oval, in the uniform of a Lieutenant-General.

Painted for George IV; not apparently in the inventory of Carlton House in 1816, but recorded in the Armoury at Carlton House in 1819 (495); moved to Windsor Castle in April 1829 and later in the Corridor (inv. No. 295).

Literature: Waterhouse, *Check List*, p. 24; Victoria Art Gallery, Bath, *Gainsborough*, 1951 (27); Waterhouse, *Gainsborough*, No. 167.

'A Head of Lord Cornwallis' appears, at £31. 10s., among the pictures painted by Gainsborough for the Prince of Wales (W.R.A., Geo. 26791; P.R.O., H.O. 73, 19). It is probably of the same period as the portrait in the National Portrait Gallery (281) which was exhibited at the Royal Academy in 1783 (45; see Whitley, *Gainsborough*, pp. 194–5). Both portraits were probably painted after Cornwallis's return to England in January 1782.

Gazetted Ensign in the Grenadier Guards, 1756; served in the Seven Years War and was A.D.C. to the King, 1765–6; in 1776 he was sent to America in command of seven regiments; he served with distinction until he capitulated at Yorktown in 1781; Governor-General and Commander-in-Chief in India, 1786–93 and 1805; Lord-Lieutenant and Commander-in-Chief in Ireland, 1798–1801. A friend of the Prince of Wales, to whom Gerard Lake described him as 'an officer so distinguished for his abilities & so universally ador'd by the Army'; Lord Cornwallis was, however, by 1789 so disgusted with the Prince's conduct that he was inclined to 'lament that I ever was acquainted with him'.

800. JOHANN CHRISTIAN FISCHER (1733–1800) (Plate 79)

Windsor Castle (3128). $90 \times 59\frac{1}{4}$ in., $228,6 \times 150,5$ cm.

Full-length, standing, leaning on a pile of music-books on a harpsichord-cum-piano inscribed *Merlin Londini fecit*, and

---

1. A drawing by Gainsborough, made at a slightly earlier stage in the development of the design, was sold at Christie's, 12 November 1968 (62), bt. by Her Majesty the Queen (*Fig.* 6). A drawing, after the painting and not by Gainsborough, was sold there on 16 July 1963 (96A).

1. This was, presumably, Henry Saunders, Inspector of Household Deliveries at Windsor Castle.

thus presumably made by Joseph Merlin; on the top of the instrument are an open book of music, an ink-well, snuff-box (?) and the musician's two-key oboe; in a chair behind him are his viola and bow and there is more music on the floor.

Presented to George IV by his brother, the Duke of Cumberland, in 1809: 'A whole Length Portrait of Mr Fisher in a Gilt Frame' was received from the Duke at Carlton House on 4 October 1809 (Jutsham, *R/D*, f. 101); recorded in store at Carlton House in 1816 (245); later at Hampton Court (747) and Buckingham Palace.

Literature: Waagen (1854), vol. II, p. 369; Law, 1881, 1898 (352); Whitley, *Gainsborough*, p. 167; R.A., *King's Pictures* (110); Waterhouse, *Check List*, p. 39, *Gainsborough*, No. 252.

Exhibited at the Royal Academy in 1780 (222). It is possible that it was painted for, or acquired by, Willoughby Bertie, 4th Earl of Abingdon (*d.* 1799) who was a talented amateur performer on the flute. It was sold by his successor, Montagu, 5th Earl of Abingdon, at Wytham Abbey in 1802; it was in B. Blackden's sale, 3 June 1803 (32), when it was bought by Morland. At one stage it is stated to have been exposed for several months in the shop of a picture-dealer in Catherine St., Strand (E. Edwards, *Anecdotes of Painters* (1808), p. 140).[1]

Composer and celebrated performer on the oboe. Born at Freiburg im Breisgau, he played for some years in the court band at Dresden and was thereafter in the service of Frederick the Great. He first appeared in London on 2 June 1768; thereafter he was a member of the Queen's Band and frequently played at court; his playing of the 4th Oboe Concerto during the Handel commemoration in 1784 particularly delighted the King; he failed, however, in 1786 to secure the post of Master of the King's Band. He was struck with paralysis while performing at court. Gainsborough, who admired his professional skill, disliked him. Mary Gainsborough and Fischer were married on 21 February 1780: 'as to his oddities and temper she must learn to like them as she likes his person'; the marriage soon came to grief.

801. RICHARD HURD (1720–1808), BISHOP OF WORCESTER (*Plate* 72)

Buckingham Palace. 29⅞ × 24¾ in., 75,9 × 62,9 cm.

Head and shoulders, in a painted oval, wearing rochet and chimere.

See No. 802. When both portraits of Hurd by Gainsborough were at Hampton Court, No. 801 bore *V.R. inv.* No. 887; later at Kensington.

Literature: Law, 1881, 1898 (367), *Kensington Palace* (1903), p. 111.

No. 801 is probably the portrait exhibited at the Royal Academy in 1781 (39), when it was stated to have been painted for the Queen and was warmly praised (Whitley, *Gainsborough*, pp. 173, 174, 177; 'finely executed', 'the warm truth of life'). This could have been the portrait mentioned by Fanny Burney in December 1786: 'He is, and justly, most high in [the Queen's] favour. In town she has his picture in her bedroom, and its companion is Mrs. Delany [i.e., No. 975]. How worthily paired! what honour to herself, such honour to them! There is no other portrait there but of royal houses' (*Diary and Letters of Mme. d'Arblay*, vol. III (1905), p. 138); this is confirmed in the relevant section of Geo. III, *Buck. Ho.*

1. There is a MS. note in the copy in the Royal Library: 'At a sale of Lord Abingdon's effects it did not produce £5.'

Cleaning (1964) revealed that No. 801 is an unquestionable original by Gainsborough which had been partly over-painted; there are *pentimenti* where the black robe goes over the left shoulder and in the outline of the wig beside the sitter's right cheek. Moreover, the version at Hartlebury Castle was stated by the Bishop's nephew, Richard Hurd, to have been copied by Gainsborough in 1788 from the original which he had painted in 1781; a copy by Dupont, commissioned by the Bishop in 1788, is thought to be the version sold from Viscount D'Abernon's collection at Christie's, 28 June 1929 (14) which was, in 1949, in the possession of Mrs. Hurd in New York (J. Nankivell, *The Collection of Portraits in Oils ... at Hartlebury Castle* (1953), p. 45).[1] Another version, with a red curtain in the background, is at Emmanuel College, Cambridge, and was almost certainly given (*c.* 1788) by the Bishop to Dr. Richard Farmer, Master of the College; although clearly painted in Gainsborough's studio it is unlikely that more than the face (and possibly not even that) is by Gainsborough himself (J. W. Goodison, 'Cambridge Portraits, III', *Connoisseur*, vol. CXLIII (1959), p. 87).

Scholar and critic; successively Archdeacon of Gloucester, 1767, Bishop of Lichfield and Coventry, 1774, and Bishop of Worcester and Clerk of the Closet, 1781. He was a favourite with the royal family and in 1776 succeeded William Markham (No. 847) as Preceptor to the Prince of Wales and Duke of York, whom he described as 'extremely promising'. In 1782 he built the Library at Hartlebury Castle, where he collected portraits of men of letters and earlier Bishops of Worcester and where, in 1788, he received the royal family when they attended the Three Choirs Festival. In 1783 he declined the Primacy. Walpole described him as 'a gentle, plausible man, affecting a singular decorum that endeared him highly to devout old ladies'. He was among those entrusted with drawing up the programme for West's series of paintings of the history of revealed religion for George III's private chapel at Windsor.

802. RICHARD HURD (1720–1808), BISHOP OF WORCESTER (*Plate* 71)

Windsor Castle (2614). 29⅝ × 24⅝ in., 75,2 × 62,5 cm.

Head and shoulders, seated and wearing rochet and chimere, with his left hand at his breast.

It is impossible to disentangle the provenances of Nos. 801, 802. The inventory of pictures at Buckingham House in the time of George III includes two portraits of the Bishop by Gainsborough, one in the Bedchamber, the other in the Wardrobe; the measurements of both are given as 30 × 25 in. (Geo. III, *Buck. Ho.*; B.M. Add. MSS. 6391, f. 122), and one of them was seen by Walpole: 'Bishop Hurd by Gainsborough, a head' (*Visits*, p. 79). In 1804 one of these portraits was moved from the King's Closet in Buckingham House to Windsor; it can probably be identified as the portrait recorded in the Council Room in the King's Private Apartments at Windsor in Francis Legge's lists of 1813, 1816 and with No. 802, which has on the back a label inscribed: 'from Windsor Castle 25 April 1832'. Both portraits were later at Hampton Court (e.g., *The Stranger's Guide* (1849), Nos. 847, 848), where No. 802 bore the *V.R. inv.* No. 889; they were later at Kensington. Taken to Windsor on 17 February 1906.

Literature: Law, 1881, 1898 (371), *Kensington Palace* (1903), p. 111; *Windsor*, 1922, p. 95; Collins Baker, *Windsor*, p. 143.

Considerable confusion surrounds the two portrait-types

1. I am very grateful to the Rev. R. F. Griffiths for checking the references given in this source to the Hurd MSS. in the care of the County Archivist at Worcester.

produced by Gainsborough of Bishop Hurd. Stylistic and documentary evidence combine to demonstrate that the original of both types is in the royal collection.

No. 802 may have been the later of the two portraits. J. Nichols stated that 'In 1783, an excellent likeness of Bishop Hurd was engraved by Hall, from an original by Gainsborough in the possession of his Majesty; intended for publication after his death' (*Literary Anecdotes of the Eighteenth Century*, vol. VI, part I (1812), p. 491). Hall's engraving is after No. 802 and it was used as the frontispiece to vol. I of Hurd's *Works* (1811), where it is described as 'From the Original Picture in the Possession of her Majesty'.

803. JAMES QUIN (1693-1766) (*Plate* 64)

Buckingham Palace. 25½ × 20 in., 64,8 × 50,8 cm.

A head, looking to the left.

Probably the unfinished portrait of Quin which had presumably remained in Gainsborough's studio until his death and was included among the unfinished portraits by Gainsborough, the property of his widow, in Gainsborough Dupont's sale at Christie's, 10 April 1797 (17), when it was bought (in) by Purce for six guineas (*Walpole Soc.*, vol. V (1915-17), pp. 92, 102; the notice of the sale in the *Morning Herald* of that date describes the portrait as 'Mr. Quin, Comedian, a head'). No. 803 is first recorded at Buckingham Palace (816) in 1876 (*V.R. inv.*); later at Windsor (2460).

Literature: Whitley, *Gainsborough*, pp. 38-40, 347, 348, 391; R.A., *King's Pictures* (85); Waterhouse, *Check List*, p. 89; Victoria Art Gallery, Bath, *Thomas Gainsborough*, 1951 (16); Waterhouse, *Gainsborough*, No. 568.

A study for the head of Quin in the full-length in the National Gallery of Ireland (565; Waterhouse, *Gainsborough*, pl. 69). The portrait was painted during Quin's retirement at Bath and the full-length was exhibited by Gainsborough at the Society of Artists in 1763 (41). Garrick, writing to Quin on 20 June 1763, told him that Hudson, who had painted Quin at an earlier date, was piqued by the success of 'the much, and deservedly, admired picture of you by Gainsborough . . . there is merit sufficient in that portrait to warm the most stoical painter'; Ozias Humphry, who stated, probably wrongly, that the portrait had been painted within a few months of Quin's death, described its popularity: 'The portrait . . . was of uncommon force and vigour, with a truth and animation beyond Mr. Gainsborough's usual performance' (Whitley, *op. cit.*, pp. 39, 391). In the final portrait Quin wears a dark blue coat, as opposed to the reddish-brown garment in No. 803. The type seems to have been used by Thomas King in designing the relief on the monument to Quin in the Abbey at Bath. There is a finished copy of No. 803 at the Garrick Club.

First appeared on the stage in Dublin, but by 1715 was acting in London; he gave his last performance (apart from subsequent benefits) in 1751; his greatest success was perhaps in the part of Falstaff. In January 1749 he directed the royal children in a performance of *Cato* before their parents in Leicester House; and he claimed to have given lessons in elocution to the young George III. In his will he left fifty pounds to Gainsborough.

804. MRS. MARY ROBINSON (1758-1800) (*Plate* 74)

Windsor Castle (772). 30 × 25 in., 76,2 × 63,5 cm.

Full-length, seated on a bank in a landscape with a Pomeranian beside her.

Presumably the 'small whole length of Mrs. Robinson' among the unfinished portraits by Gainsborough sold in Gainsborough Dupont's sale at Christie's, 10 April 1797 (7), when it was bought by Colonel Hamilton, presumably for the Prince of Wales (*Walpole Soc.*, vol. V (1917), pp. 93, 102); recorded in store at Carlton House in 1816 (329: 'An unfinished sketch for the large portrait of Mrs Robinson with a dog. Mr Gainsborough').

Literature: R.A., *British Art*, 1934 (256), *Commemorative Catalogue* (1935), pp. 55-6; Collins Baker, *Windsor*, p. 144; R.A., *King's Pictures* (83); Waterhouse, *Check List*, p. 92, *Gainsborough*, No. 580.

A *modello* for the life-size portrait in the Wallace Collection (42; p. 122 in *Catalogue* of 1968; Waterhouse, *Gainsborough*, No. 579) which was intended by Gainsborough to be exhibited at the Royal Academy in 1782. The portrait was, however, withdrawn, probably as a result of an article in which it was, as a likeness, compared unfavourably with portraits of Mrs. Robinson by Reynolds and Romney; the portrait by Reynolds was going to the same exhibition (Whitley, *Gainsborough*, pp. 180-4). At the sale of Mrs. Robinson's effects in 1785 the portrait is said to have been sold for thirty-two guineas. It was apparently bought by George IV: 'a full length of Mrs Robinson' at £105 is recorded among the pictures painted by Gainsborough for the Prince of Wales (W.R.A., Geo. 26791); it was in store at Carlton House in 1816 (234) and was sent to Lord Hertford by command of the Regent on 13 April 1818 (Jutsham, *R/D*, f. 282). In the life-size portrait Mrs. Robinson is holding a miniature, perhaps a portrait of the Prince.

Mary Darby, Mrs. Robinson, attracted the Prince of Wales's admiration by her performance as Perdita in *The Winter's Tale*, a part she first played at Drury Lane on 20 November 1779 and again, in front of the royal family, on 3 December. When the affair was over, George III had to pay £5,000 in order to get the Prince's love-letters back from Mrs. Robinson, who received in addition an annual pension of £500 from the Prince. In 1783 she was stricken with paralysis.

805. JOHN HAYES ST. LEGER (1765-1800) (*Plate* 75)

Buckingham Palace. 97½ × 74 in., 247,6 × 188 cm. (see below).

Full-length in a landscape, in the uniform of the 65th, 2nd Yorkshire North Riding, Regiment, holding his hat and sword in his left hand and in his right the bridle of his charger.

Painted for George IV; in store at Carlton House in 1816 (233: 'A whole length of Colonel St. Ledger, in his regimentals. Mr Gainsborough'); later at Hampton Court (733).

Literature: Law, 1881, 1898 (353); Whitley, *Gainsborough*, pp. 179, 185, 188-9, 190; R.A., *King's Pictures* (112); Waterhouse, *Check List*, p. 94, *Gainsborough*, No. 594.

Commissioned by the Prince of Wales from Gainsborough; on the list of pictures painted by Gainsborough for the Prince, No. 805 appears, at £126: 'A full length with a Horse of Col: St Leger' (W.R.A., Geo. 26791; P.R.O., H.O. 73, 19). On the same list, at the same price, is the full-length of the Prince 'with a Horse sent to Genll St Leger', the portrait (*Fig.* XIII) which was to some extent a companion piece to No. 805 and is now at Waddesdon Manor. No. 805 was exhibited at the Royal Academy in 1782 (58); the portrait of the Prince was shown at the same time (77). The elaborate saddle in No. 805, decorated with the star of the Garter, is the same as that in the portrait of the Prince. The Prince had given St. Leger the saddle and insisted that it should be shown in the picture (Whitley, *Gainsborough*, p. 189). The portrait was engraved by Dupont (Chaloner Smith, vol. I, p. 242; the print, dedicated to the Prince of Wales, was published on 4 May 1783). There are slight *pentimenti* in the lower part of the belt, in the facing on the right shoulder and on the left shoulder; in the saddle and back of the horse; in the horse's near hind leg which was at first nearer to the other leg; and in the foliage, which originally projected to the right of the horse's head. Gainsborough, moreover, enlarged the canvas in painting, presumably on finding that the horse was uncomfortably cramped: 6 in. on the left, 8 in. on the right and *c.* 4¼ in. on the top.

Gazetted Major in the 65th Regiment of Foot on 18 August 1780, Lieutenant-Colonel on 25 October 1782; Captain and Lieutenant-Colonel, 1st Foot Guards, 1787, Colonel, 1793; promoted Major-General on 25 February 1795, he died in India commanding the 80th Regiment of Foot. A boon companion of the Prince of Wales and the Duke of York, he was appointed Groom of the Bedchamber to the Prince in 1784. In 1782 the Prince described him as 'one of ye best fellows yt. ever lived'.

806. DIANA AND ACTAEON (*Plate* 78)

Windsor Castle (1027). 62¼ × 74 in., 158,1 × 188 cm.; the canvas has been considerably stretched in lining.

Actaeon, the stag's horns sprouting from his head, leans over a bank that overlooks a pool, at the foot of a waterfall in a wood, in which Diana and her nymphs are bathing.

Presumably in Gainsborough's studio at his death. Appeared, among pictures which were the property of his widow, in the sale of Gainsborough Dupont's possessions at Christie's, 10 April 1797 (43: *Diana and Actæon. T. Gainsborough*), when it was bought by Hammond for the Prince of Wales for £2. 3s. (*Walpole Soc.*, vol. V (1915–17), pp. 97, 103). Recorded in store at Carlton House in 1819 (342); later at Windsor and Buckingham Palace.

Literature: Whitley, *Gainsborough*, p. 348; R.A., *British Art*, 1934 (160), *Commemorative Catalogue* (1935), p. 59; R.A., *King's Pictures* (478); Arts Council, *Thomas Gainsborough*, 1953 (60); Waterhouse, *Gainsborough*, No. 1012; J. Hayes, 'Gainsborough's Later Landscapes', *Apollo*, vol. LXXX (1964), pp. 22–3.

A very late work, left unfinished by Gainsborough at his death and his only surviving painting of a mythological subject. It has the brilliance of a large sketch. The picture faithfully, but in a wistful and undramatic mood, records the story in Book III of Ovid's *Metamorphoses*: Actaeon, hunting in the mid-day heat through the sacred valley of Gargaphe, comes to the woodland cave with its 'spring of clear water, spreading out into a wide pool', where Diana and her nymphs were bathing; the goddess threw a handful of water into Actaeon's face, upon which he was transformed into a stag and consequently torn to pieces by his hounds. Three preparatory drawings survive. The earliest is probably that in the possession of the Marchioness of Anglesey (*Fig.* 11); the second is perhaps that formerly in the collection of Canon F. H. D. Smythe, now in the Huntington Library (*Fig.* 12); the third (*Fig.* 13), formerly in the Rudolf collection and now in the Cecil Higgins Museum, Bedford, brings to the composition a depth and a static quality which, as well as certain of the figures and a possible first suggestion of the waterfall, link the drawing most closely to the final painting (see J. Hayes in Arts Council, *Gainsborough Drawings*, 1960 (58).) For a suggestion that one of the nymphs is based on a lead statuette by Adriaen de Vries in the Victoria and Albert Museum, see G. Sawyer, 'A note on Thomas Gainsborough and Adriaen de Vries', *Journal of the Warburg and Courtauld Institutes*, vol. XIV, Nos. 1–2 (1951), p. 134. Redgrave claimed (*V.R. inv.*, March 1859) that No. 806 was signed with the letter G, but no trace of this can be found.

807. PORTRAIT OF AN OLD MAN
(*After Rembrandt*)

St. James's Palace. 30 × 25⅓ in., 76,2 × 63,8 cm.

Head and shoulders, wearing a flat black cap.

Apparently in Gainsborough's possession at the time of his death; included in the exhibition of his pictures at Schomberg House from 30 March to the end of May 1789 (93: 'A Man's Head, after Rembrandt'), when the sale of the pictures was arranged by Gainsborough Dupont by private contract ('Gainsborough's Collection of Pictures', *Burl. Mag.*, vol. LXXXIV–V (1944), pp. 107–10). No. 807 is recorded in the King's Closet at Windsor in 1813 (Legge's lists: 'A Head. (after Rembrandt) Gainsbro''), which indicates that it may have been acquired by Queen Charlotte. Later at Hampton Court (266) and Kensington.

Literature: Law, 1881, 1898 (366); Collins Baker, *Hampton Court*, p. 59; Waterhouse, *Gainsborough*, No. 1026; Guildhall, King's Lynn, *Artist to Artist*, 1962 (24).

A copy, perhaps painted *c.* 1770, of the picture by Rembrandt in the National Gallery (190) which was in the collection of the Duke of Argyll before 1781 (N. MacLaren, *The Dutch School*, National Gallery (1960), pp. 316–17). Gainsborough, incidentally, painted portraits of the 4th and 5th Dukes of Argyll (Waterhouse, *op. cit.*, p. 52).

After Thomas Gainsborough

808. GEORGE III

Buckingham Palace. 89 × 58¾ in., 226,1 × 149,2 cm.

Full-length, standing, in Windsor uniform, with the ribbon and star of the Garter, with his right hand on a stick and holding his hat in his left hand.

Nos. 808, 809 were bequeathed to Queen Victoria by Mary, Duchess of Gloucester (will proved, 5 June 1857). In her will the bequest appears as one picture: 'The full length Picture of King George the Third and Queen Charlotte painted by Gainsborough and Dupont given to me by George the Fourth and which hang up in the Great Drawing room at Gloucester House', but in the MS. volume of Queen Victoria's acquisitions both portraits are listed: 'Gainsborough. Full length portraits of George III & Queen Charlotte; had been given to the Duchess of Gloucester by George IV'. They were at Buckingham Palace (616, 617) in 1869 (*V.R. inv.*) and later at Windsor (2553, 2554). They are assumed to be the portraits recorded in the Queen's Bedroom at Kensington in 1818 (426, 427) and then stated to be by Dupont; measurements of both given as 88 × 57 in. In Faulkner's *History and Antiquities of Kensington* (1820), pp. 391–2, the portraits are said to be by Stewart. There is no evidence of their remaining in the collection and they could well have been given to the Duchess by George IV.

Literature: Collins Baker, *Windsor*, p. 145.

A variant of No. 774 in which the position of the King's right arm is altered and he wears boots in place of the shoes and stockings in the Gainsborough. There are also slight variations in the background. There is a *pentimento* in the position of the fingers of the right hand. Nos. 808, 809 may be the pair of full-lengths of the King and Queen which Dupont painted for £126 for Windsor Castle (undated bill in the National Portrait Gallery); Queen Charlotte's account-book (in the Royal Library) includes, under 13 October 1789, £130 'To Compton for Gainsborough Dupont the Painter'. The attribution of the pair to Dupont in the inventory of 1818 can presumably be accepted, but No. 808 is rather harder in texture and heavier in tone than No. 809 and is less close to Gainsborough in quality. There is the possibility that the pair was painted by Stewart.

A version of No. 808 is at Herrenhausen with a pendant close to the full-lengths (by Dupont) of Queen Charlotte in Abingdon Town Hall and at Stuttgart.

809. QUEEN CHARLOTTE
Buckingham Palace. 88 × 58¾ in., 223,5 × 149,2 cm.

See No. 808.

Literature: Collins Baker, *Windsor*, p. 145.

See No. 808. A very competent copy of No. 775, with only very slight variations in detail. In the case of No. 809, the attribution to Dupont seems plausible.

810. QUEEN CHARLOTTE
Windsor Castle (1592). 94 × 58 in., 238,8 × 147,3 cm.

Recorded in Wyatt's Ceiling Room at Windsor, *c.* 1818 (vol. of miscellaneous invs., f. 108: 'The Queen a Copy by Hopkins from Gainsborough').

A copy by Hopkins of No. 775 with the addition of the Queen's crown on a table on the right.

811. QUEEN CHARLOTTE
Buckingham Palace. 30 × 25¼ in., 76.2 × 64,1 cm.

Head and shoulders, in a painted oval.

Recorded at Buckingham Palace (1155) in 1876 (*V.R. inv.*), with indications that it had been in the royal collection for a number of years.

A slightly later copy from No. 775. It is conceivable that No. 811 is the portrait which was at Buckingham House in 1819 (714; see above, p. 37), but it is unlikely that so inferior a copy would have been hung with the set of ovals. A copy of the same type is at Penshurst.

812. QUEEN CHARLOTTE
Buckingham Palace. 30⅛ × 25 in., 76,5 × 63,5 cm.

Head and shoulders.

Formerly in the collection of G. Farrow; sold at Christie's, 11 June 1937 (127). Bought by H.M. Queen Mary for the royal collection.

A slightly later copy from No. 775.

813. PRINCE WILLIAM, LATER DUKE OF CLARENCE
Windsor Castle (2501). Millboard: 6 1/16 × 4⅞ in., 15,2 × 12,4 cm·
Head and shoulders, in a painted oval, in midshipman's uniform, with the ribbon and star of the Thistle.

In the collection of George IV; recorded in the Armoury at Carlton House in 1816 (490: 'The Duke of Clarence. (small.) Mr Gainsborough', measurements given as 5½ × 4 in.; the 1816 label is on the back); later at Kew and Buckingham Palace (1068).

Literature: Waterhouse, *Check List*, p. 114 (describing it as 'not traceable at present').

A contemporary repetition, on a small scale, of No. 781; despite the attribution in the inventory of 1816 (see above), it does not seem quite good enough to have been painted by Gainsborough himself.

814. PRINCE OCTAVIUS
Windsor Castle (1364). Millboard: 6 1/16 × 4⅞ in., 15,2 × 12,4 cm.
Head and shoulders, in a painted oval.

Formerly at Buckingham Palace.

An early copy, on a small scale, of No. 791; it is unlikely to be by Gainsborough himself.

815. PRINCE OCTAVIUS
Windsor Castle (834). 23⅝ × 19 in., 60 × 48,3 cm.

Head and shoulders, in a painted oval.

Recorded at Windsor in 1878 (*V.R. inv.*); on the stretcher, however, is the label applied in the time of Henry Saunders, Inspector of the Household at Windsor, 1828–45.

Literature: Collins Baker, *Windsor*, p. 146.

A slightly later copy of No. 791.

816. PRINCE OCTAVIUS
Kew (*Hampton Court* No. 1385). Oval: 23¼ × 17½ in., 59 × 44,5 cm.

Recorded at Frogmore in 1871 (*V.R. inv.*, Windsor No. 1546).

A copy of No. 791, probably painted in the nineteenth century and by the same hand as No. 817.

817. PRINCE ALFRED
Kew (*Hampton Court* No. 1386). Oval: 23 × 17 in., 58,4 × 43,2 cm.

Recorded at Frogmore in 1871 (*V.R. inv.*, Windsor No. 1543).

A copy of No. 792, probably painted in the nineteenth century and by the same hand as No. 816.

George Garrard

1760–1826. Painter of animals, sporting scenes, pictures of London and country life, and landscapes. A pupil of Sawrey Gilpin, he was also a competent sculptor. He exhibited regularly at the Royal Academy between 1781 and 1826. From as early as 1784 he was working for the Whitbread family and it was perhaps through the younger Samuel Whitbread that he secured the patronage of the Prince of Wales. On 5 January 1793 he was paid £630 by the Prince for 'Seven large Pictures of Horses painted at Aston Clinton'; his account is dated 6 November 1792 (P.R.O., H.O. 73, 19). On 19 May 1792 Sefferin Nelson had submitted a bill for £60. 12s. for 'Making Carving & Gilding in Burnished Gold Six Large Picture Frames for Paintings of Horses by Mr Garrat—to be sent to Kempshot 5 inch Moulding with 2 Members Carved with a French Strap leaf & a neat Ribbon & Stick the Six Measure 151 feet 6 at 8 Shillings pr foot'. In addition Nelson charged £1 for 'Porterage of the Frames to Mr Garrats & from thence to Carleton House'. On 25 August he submitted an account for £9. 18s. for a seventh frame 'for Painting of Horses as the former' and on 24 November 1792 he submitted an account for £4. 18s. 6d. for 'Making & Gilding Seven Tablets in Burnish'd Gold for ye above 7 Picture Frames sent to Kempshot, with ye Names of ye Horses painted on Each of them'. Nelson's work had been carried out 'by Order of Mr Gilpin, Horse Painter' (*ibid.*, 22; W.R.A., Geo. 32039).
Of these seven pictures, only one (No. 818 below) survives. The remainder were all recorded in store in the inventory of Carlton House in 1816: (442) 'A white arab. Mr Garrard', measurements given as 55 × 71 in. (443) 'Saltram. Mr Garrard', measurements given as the same. (447) 'Ulysses. Mr Garrard', measurements given as the same. (445) 'Virgo, a grey mare, Saltram's dam; a bay mare, Hardwick's dam; with Vamick at her foot. Mr Garrard', measurements given

as 55×82 in. (448) 'Calash, with Aston at her foot; and Whisky, a yearling, by Saltram. Mr Garrard', measurements given as 55×83 in. (446) 'Anvil. Mr Garrard', measurements given as 55×71 in. All seven pictures were sent to Cumberland Lodge on 31 May 1822 (Jutsham, *Deliveries*, f. 36) and they were all recorded there in January 1844 with the exception of the portrait of Anvil. This was at Windsor (1374) in 1879 but was in such bad condition by 1897 that it was burnt in that year. It was stated (*V.R. inv.*) to have been signed and dated 1792. The other five pictures have vanished.

No. 445 at Carlton House in 1816 had probably been the picture shown by Garrard at the Royal Academy in 1793 (30: *Mares and foals from H.R.H. the Prince of Wales's stud*). In 1794 he showed at the Royal Academy (73) a sketch of one of his pictures of mares and foals painted for the Prince (*Sporting Magazine*, vol. II (1793), p. 89; vol. IV (1794), p. 69).

818. SALTRAM (*Plate* 182)

Buckingham Palace. 56×72 in., 142,2×182,9 cm.

An inscription on the back, probably copied from an original inscription, states that No. 818 was painted in 1792.

A bay horse, held by a groom in royal livery and rearing outside a stable set in a wooded scene.

Painted for George IV; recorded in store at Carlton House in 1816 (444: 'Saltram, led by a groom. Mr Garrard'); sent to Cumberland Lodge on 31 May 1822; later at Windsor (1433).

One of the 'Seven large Pictures of Horses painted at Aston Clinton' for which Garrard submitted his account to the Prince of Wales on 6 November 1792 (see above) and which, in frames made by Sefferin Nelson in 1792, were sent to be hung at Kempshott.[1] There are *pentimenti* in the back and tail of the horse and, probably, in the position of its head which was at first apparently drawn in a lower position.
Saltram, son of Eclipse, was foaled in 1780 in the stud of General John Parker, later 1st Lord Boringdon. He won the Derby in 1783, was subsequently sold to the Prince of Wales and retired to stud after a few more races. In 1792 the Prince won £7,700 with Saltram's progeny.

Sawrey Gilpin

1733–1807. Younger brother of the Rev. William Gilpin. Painter of animals and birds, sporting scenes and historical and narrative scenes in which animals are involved. One of his earliest patrons was William, Duke of Cumberland, and at the time of the Duke's death he had a room on the Chamber Storey of Cumberland Lodge. He exhibited at the Society of Artists, 1762–83, and at the Royal Academy between 1786 and his death. At the Society of Artists in 1764 he showed (38) *Brood mares belonging to his Royal Highness the Duke of Cumberland*. Gilpin may have worked for George III: 'A Horse by Gilpin' appears in the Queen's Dressing-Room at Kensington (Geo. III, *Kensington*).
On 17 October 1804 Gilpin submitted a bill to the Prince of Wales for £200 'To the portrait of three Horses large size, Landscape &c.' He was paid on 31 October 1805 (W.R.A., Geo. 27277). On 4 April 1805 Benjamin Charpentier submitted his bill for a frame for the picture (*ibid.*, 26834; see also 32511, 89438, 89440). The picture was in store at Carlton House in 1816 (433): 'Three horses, a roan, a brown, and a white. Gilpin', measurements given as 64×84 in. It

1. The original frame of No. 818 is now on No. 870.

was sent to the King's Lodge on 31 May 1822 (Jutsham, *Deliveries*, f. 35) and was at Cumberland Lodge in January 1844. It has since vanished. It was presumably the picture exhibited at the Royal Academy in 1805 (205). Farington (*Diary*, vol. III, pp. 16–17) states that Gilpin had been 'arduously employed' in 1804 on the picture for the Prince. 'He came to town in April, & was indefatigable through the whole summer & autumn, coming from His residence at Brompton to Garrard's House in George St. Hanover Square every morning, & sometimes painting 10 hours in a day. The parts were many of them painted several times over as difficulties arose, or new ideas struck Him.'

819. CYPRON, KING HEROD'S DAM, WITH HER BROOD (*Plate* 20)

Windsor Castle (2317). 38¼×61⅞ in., 97,1×157,2 cm.

Signed and dated: *S: Gilpin 1764.*

Under a large oak tree stands Cypron with, lying down behind her, the yearling filly got by Regulus and, at her feet, Sejanus, her tenth foal; Thais; and the St. Quintin Mare with her colt Senlis. In the background are two horses, Drone and Dunce, clothed and ridden by grooms; in the distance on the right are Dapper, Dumpan (i.e., (?) Dumplin) and Doctor galloping and King Herod held by a groom.

Presumably painted for William, Duke of Cumberland. The inventory of the Duke's pictures at the Great Lodge in 1765 included, in the Old Dining-Room 'five paintings of Horses by Gilpin' (see Nos. 820–3); the *Guides* (1768, 1774) to Windsor and its environs mention, over the chimney-piece in this room, the Duke's collection of breeding mares, and Knight's *Windsor Guide* (1783) refers to 'his royal highness's stud, by Gilpin, 1764'. Later at Stud Lodge (1150) and Cumberland Lodge.

Literature: J. Wood, 'Artist of the Horse', *Country Life*, vol. CXXXIX (1966), p. 510.

Gilpin exhibited at the Society of Artists in 1765 (35), *King Herod's dam a capital stud mare in the possession of His Royal Highness the Duke of Cumberland, with all her brood, employed according to their ages*. Two other versions of the design are known; one, also signed and dated 1764, is at Scampston and was probably painted for Sir William St. Quintin; the other belongs to the Earl of Albemarle and was probably painted for George Keppel, 3rd Earl of Albemarle (1724–72), Lord of the Bedchamber to Cumberland. The indentification of the horses (above) is based on the early inscription on the Scampston version. No. 819 is certainly the earliest (though perhaps the least well-preserved) of the three as there are *pentimenti* in the head of Thais; in the position and stance of the St. Quintin mare and her colt; and in King Herod and his groom who were at first painted further to the left and in different positions. The painting of the trees and foliage is much thinner and less conscientious than in the picture (No. 826) in which Gilpin collaborated with Marlow, but is very similar to the same passages in Nos. 820–3. A drawing at Windsor of two horses galloping, though attributed to Paul Sandby, is very close to the horses on the right in No. 819 (Oppé, No. S.423).
The Duke of Cumberland had acquired Cypron in 1755; three years later she became the dam of King Herod (see No. 820); Dapper (see No. 822) and Dumplin had been sired by Scampston Cade. In May 1764 Dunce was a four-year-old, Drone a three-year-old, Doctor a two-year-old in the Duke's stud; the Duke was breeding from the St. Quintin mare in 1762. In 1764 Gilpin had exhibited at the Society of Artists (38) *Brood Mares belonging to his Royal Highness the Duke of Cumberland*.

820. KING HEROD

Windsor Castle (2310). 31 × 36¼ in., 78,7 × 92,1 cm.

Signed: *S. Gilpin*

A bay horse held by a groom in livery (scarlet coat with green cuffs) beside the rubbing-house at Newmarket.

Nos. 820–3 are presumably, with No. 819, 'five paintings of Horses by Gilpin' recorded in the Old Dining-Room in Windsor Great Lodge in the inventory of William, Duke of Cumberland's possessions in 1765 (W.R.A., Cumberland MSS., misc. vol. I); the four pictures were later at Cranbourne Lodge and Carlton House, where No. 820 was recorded in store in 1816 (428: 'King Herod, with a boy, in a crimson and green livery. Gilpin . . . from Cranburne lodge'; the 1816 label was noted on the stretcher in 1868 (*V.R. inv.*));[1] sent to Cumberland Lodge on 31 May 1822 (Jutsham, *Deliveries*, f. 34); later at Stud Lodge (1141).

Nos. 820–3 were presumably painted in the early 1760s, while Gilpin was in the service of the Duke of Cumberland. There are *pentimenti* in the legs of the groom and apparently in the foreground, where a saddle-cloth is loosely indicated. At the Society of Artists in 1765 Gilpin exhibited (36) a *Portrait of King Herod* which may be No. 820. King Herod, foaled in 1758, had been bred by the Duke; he was by Tartar out of Cypron and appears with his dam in No. 819. He was very successful for the Duke and continued to run until 1767 for Sir John Moore, who had bought him after the Duke's death; he died in 1780. His stud fee rose from ten to twenty-five guineas and 'his stock won over £200,000, 40 hogsheads of claret, 3 Cups, and the Whip' (D. Craig, *Horse-Racing* (1949), p. 38). A version of No. 820, stated to be dated 1766, was in the Durdans collection; in this version King Herod is held by a different groom and there is no cloth on the ground. Another version, signed and dated 1768, is at Scampston.

821. PORTRAIT OF A HORSE (*Plate 22*)

Windsor Castle (2308). 31 × 36 in., 78,7 × 91,4 cm.

Signed: *S. Gilpin*

A chestnut horse, standing in a glade, held by a groom in livery (scarlet coat with green cuffs and waistcoat).

See No. 820. No. 821 was in store at Carlton House in 1816 (429: 'A dark chesnut horse, with a groom, in the same livery. Gilpin . . . from Cranburne lodge'; the 1816 label was noted on the back in 1868 (*V.R. inv.*)); sent to Cumberland Lodge on 31 May 1822 (Jutsham, *Deliveries*, f. 35); later at Stud Lodge (1142).

See No. 820.

822. PORTRAIT OF A HORSE

Windsor Castle (2309). 31¼ × 31 in., 79,4 × 78,7 cm.

A light brown horse held in a wooded landscape by a groom in livery (scarlet coat with green cuffs).

See No. 820. No. 822 was in store at Carlton House in 1816 (431: 'A roan horse, with a groom, in the same livery. Gilpin . . . from Cranburne lodge'; the 1816 label was noted on the stretcher in 1868)); sent to Cumberland Lodge on 31 May 1822 (Jutsham, *Deliveries*, f. 35); later at Stud Lodge (1144).

See No. 820. It has been suggested that No. 822 is a portrait of Dapper of whom Gilpin exhibited a portrait at the Society of Artists in 1765 (37). Dapper, foaled in 1755, had been bred by Sir William St. Quintin of Scampston Hall; he was

1. The set had perhaps been received at Carlton House on 29 May 1814, when Jutsham recorded (*R/D*, f. 309) the receipt from Mrs. Villiers of three pictures of horses (including King Herod and Dapper) which had originally been at Cranbourne Lodge.

by Cade out of Cypron and is seen with his dam in No. 819. He was particularly successful at Ascot and Newmarket in 1759 and was one of the Duke of Cumberland's best horses.

823. PORTRAIT OF A HORSE

Windsor Castle (2311). 31¼ × 31¼ in., 79,4 × 79,4 cm.

A bay horse held by a groom in livery (scarlet coat with green cuffs) in a wooded landscape.

See No. 820. No. 823 was in store at Carlton House in 1816 (430: 'A bay horse, with a groom, in a crimson and green livery. Gilpin . . . from Cranburne lodge'); sent to Cumberland Lodge on 31 May 1822 (Jutsham, *Deliveries*, f. 35); later at Stud Lodge (1143).

See No. 820. It has been suggested that No. 823 is a portrait of Spiletta, a bay mare by Regulus out of Mother Western, foaled in 1749 and bred by Sir Robert Eden. In training in the Duke of Cumberland's stud, she apparently only raced once, but was used as a brood mare. In 1764 she became, by Marsk, the dam of the famous Eclipse, probably foaled in the paddocks at Cranbourne Lodge. She died in 1776. Gilpin's preliminary drawing for No. 823, signed and dated (or inscribed) *S. Gilpin 17* [ ], is at Windsor (Oppé, No. 272).

824. A BAY GELDING

Windsor Castle (1688). 28 × 35¾ in., 71,1 × 90,8 cm.

Signed and dated: *S. Gilpin 1800*.

Standing in a landscape near a barn.

Painted for George IV; recorded in store at Carlton House in 1816 (434); sent to the King's Lodge on 31 May 1822 (Jutsham, *Deliveries*, f. 35); later at Cumberland Lodge.

On 21 August 1800 Gilpin submitted an account for £31. 10s. for 'painting the portrait of a Horse 3 foot by 2–4' (W.R.A., Geo. 26805, annexing his receipt, dated 31 October 1801; 42948); on 28 February 1806 Colnaghi submitted an account for £3 for 'a Burnishd Gold Frame to a painting of a Horse—by Gilpin' (*ibid.*, 27332).

825. FRIGHTENED HORSES (*Plate 23*)

Windsor Castle (970). 35 × 45⅛ in., 88,9 × 114,6 cm.

Signed: *Sawrey Gilpin*.

Three startled horses, a grey and two darker horses, in a stormy landscape.

Recorded in the Cube Room at Kensington in 1818 (373); removed to Hampton Court on 13 September 1838; later at Cumberland Lodge.

Literature: R.A., *King's Pictures* (479).

Probably painted (*c.* 1780) for George III.

Sawrey Gilpin and William Marlow

826. THE DUKE OF CUMBERLAND VISITING HIS STUD (*Plate 21*)

Windsor Castle (2040). 41¾ × 55 in., 106 × 139,7 cm.

A view of the Long Walk, with the Duke of Cumberland, wearing a green coat with the star of the Garter, inspecting his mares and foals; his chaise stands on the Long Walk. In the distance is Windsor Castle with Queen Anne's Garden House and Burford House under the south wall of the Castle.

Stated to have been formerly in the Earl of Albemarle's collection and perhaps painted for or given to George Keppel, 3rd Earl of Albemarle (1724–72) (see No. 819). In the W. Angerstein sale at

Christie's, 24 February 1883 (264); bought by Queen Victoria on 3 March 1883 (P.R.O., L.C.1/405, 424).

Literature: R.A., *King's Pictures* (494), *The First Hundred Years*, 1951–2 (7); Virginia Museum of Fine Arts, *Sport and the Horse*, 1960 (31).

Probably painted *c.* 1764. No 826 is presumably the picture exhibited at the Society of Artists in 1771 (44), *His Royal Highness the late Duke of Cumberland visiting his stud, with a view of Windsor Castle from the great park, by Mr. Marlow.*[1] Although the landscape was formerly attributed to George Barret, there seems no reason to question this contemporary statement that Marlow collaborated with Gilpin. Almost all the landscape seems to be by Marlow in a most skilfully homogeneous work of collaboration.

The view of the Long Walk and the distant Castle is fairly close to the watercolour by Sandby in the Royal Library (A. P. Oppé, *The Drawings of Paul and Thomas Sandby . . . at Windsor Castle* (1947), No. 82); the mare standing in the ditch at the side of the Long Walk in No. 826, with the two horses and groom near the chaise, appear in a drawing in the same collection (*ibid.*, No. 388). It has been suggested that No. 826 was painted from a drawing by Sandby, in whose sale in 1817 was (62) a drawing of the Duke of Cumberland inspecting his stud in Windsor Great Park— 'animals by Gilpin'. But as Gilpin and the Sandbys were in the Duke's service it is perhaps unnecessary to suggest more than that they may have collaborated in designing so large an oil-painting and that there may have been stylistic affinities between the drawings of horses by the Sandbys and Gilpin. A variant of No. 826, in the possession of Mrs. Starkey (*Fig.* 16), is clearly by the same hands; fewer horses are shown and the Duke of Cumberland's chaise, probably containing the Duke, is proceeding towards the Castle. In the Angerstein sale (above) lot 263 was a companion picture of Virginia Water, with the Duke of Cumberland in his carriage, which Queen Victoria did not wish to acquire; it was attributed to Barret.

William Hamilton

1751–1801. Illustrator and painter of portraits and historical, biblical, literary and classical subjects.

827. THE MARRIAGE OF GEORGE, PRINCE OF WALES (*Plate* 172)

Buckingham Palace. 16 × 21 in., 40 × 53,3 cm.

The Prince with his bride standing with hands joined before the Archbishop of Canterbury, John Moore, in the Chapel Royal, St. James's Palace; near the altar stands the Bishop of London, Beilby Porteus. Under a gallery, in which the choir is placed, stand the Princess's bridesmaids; George III and Queen Charlotte are seated on either side of the bridal pair; and members of the royal family and household are grouped behind and around them. In the royal gallery is another group of figures.

Sold at Foster's, 25 February 1885 (66), attributed to Copley, and bought by Queen Victoria for £1. 15*s.* (P.R.O., L.C. 1/440,17); later at Windsor (2081).

An early nineteenth-century inscription on the back states that No. 827 is an original sketch for a large picture by H. D. Hamilton. It is, however, presumably a sketch for William Hamilton's picture of the marriage of the Prince of Wales. Farington recorded on 7 May 1795 that Hamilton,

who had been given a ticket to attend the ceremony,[1] had begun the picture. On 11 June he called on Hamilton. 'He has been lately employed in painting small portraits of the Nobility who were present at the Prince's marriage, for the picture intended to represent that subject. He told me the Princess Elizabeth first suggested the Idea of having a print of the subject to Tomkins the Engraver. The Duke of Dorset and the Marchioness of Bath, are the two persons who have hitherto refused to promise to sit for their portraits—The picture is to be 12 feet wide.' The commission to paint the scene may have come from Tomkins. On 16 July 1796 Farington noted that 'Hamilton is only to have £400 for the picture of the Prince of Wales' marriage of which Tomkins has only paid £100 & does not seem urgent to have the picture finished.' On 2 February 1797 he again called on Hamilton: 'Is finishing His picture of the Prince of Wales's marriage, but wants the Prince's coat, which, so unpleasant is the subject supposed to be, nobody will ask the Prince for it' (these references to Farington are unpublished). It is probable that the large picture was never finished and that Tomkins never issued his engraving.

The marriage took place in the evening of 8 April 1795 in the Chapel Royal, St. James's Palace. The Princess (for her costume see No. 768) was attended by four Maids of Honour (Miss Colman, Miss Erskine, Miss Poyntz and Miss Bruhl) and four bridesmaids (Lady Mary Osborne, Lady Caroline Villiers, Lady Charlotte Spencer and Lady Charlotte Legge). These eight figures, and the Princess's four attendants (Ladies Townshend, Jersey, Caernarvon and Cholmondeley), can be seen in Hamilton's sketch. The Prince was attended by the Dukes of Bedford (No. 841) and Roxburghe. The group on the right, behind and beside George III, probably includes the Dukes of Gloucester, York and Clarence, and, near the Sword of State, the Lord Chamberlain, the Marquess of Salisbury, and the Vice-Chamberlain, Charles Fulke Greville. Near the Queen during the ceremony stood her Lord Chamberlain, the Earl of Morton, her Vice-Chamberlain, William Price, and her Master of the Horse, Lord Harcourt. On the right in No. 827 are apparently the chairs of state, under a canopy, on which the King and Queen sat during the singing of an anthem after the marriage ceremony. The group in the royal pew or gallery probably includes the Prince of Orange (see No. 856) with his family. (Accounts of the ceremony are to be found in the *Annual Register*, vol. XXXVII (1795), pp. 15–16 of the Chronicle, and in *The Gentleman's Magazine*, vol. LXV (1795), pp. 429–31). See also No. 1091.

George Henry Harlow

1787–1819. Painter of portraits and historical subjects; a pupil of Lawrence. He visited Italy in 1818.

828. AUGUSTUS, DUKE OF SUSSEX (*Plate* 253)

Windsor Castle (2036). 30⅛ × 25⅛ in., 76,5 × 63,8 cm.

Head and shoulders, wearing the star of the Garter.

Acquired by the Lord Chamberlain in 1882 and recorded at Windsor in the following year.

Possibly the portrait of the Duke exhibited by Harlow at the Royal Academy in 1812 (280). The type was engraved by C. Warren as the frontispiece to vol. XXXVII (1820) of the *Transactions* of the Royal Society of Arts, of which the Duke was President. In the Preface to this volume the portrait is

1. For Walpole's comment see *Walpole Soc.*, vol. XXVII (1939), p. 66.

1. V. & A., *Cuttings*, vol. III, pp. 715, 726.

praised for the 'accuracy and happiness of the likeness'. At that time the original of the engraving belonged to T. Savory. The portrait was also engraved by W. J. Ward in 1825. There are extensive *pentimenti* in No. 828: in the collar and left shoulder, in the right arm which appears at first to have been painted considerably higher, and in the outlines of the cravat and the hair. A version is at York House.

Benjamin Robert Haydon

1786–1846. History-painter who seemed in his early days to be embarking on a successful career, but was ultimately driven by failure to suicide. After George IV had bought No. 829, Haydon was hopeful that the King would buy more pictures. He exhibited at the Western Exchange in March 1830 a group of pictures including his newly-finished *Punch* (now in the Tate Gallery, No. 682). The King had this sent down to Windsor on 6 March, but it was sent back two days later. Haydon remained convinced that the King had been influenced against him by the intrigues of William Seguier (*Diary*, ed. W. B. Pope, vol. III (Cambridge, Mass., 1963), pp. 308, 426–9, 456–61, 598).

829. THE MOCK ELECTION (*Plate* 297)

Kensington Palace. 57 × 73 in., 144,8 × 185,4 cm.

In the centre of the picture is the Lord High Sheriff (Jonas Alexander Murphy, an Irishman, released later after his friends had paid his debts) with curtain-rings round his neck for a chain and a mopstick with an empty 'strawberry-pottle' for a white wand; with his cocked hat he cautions one of the candidates (Joseph Paul Meredith, an Irishman firmly convinced that it was a genuine parliamentary election) who, in vaguely military dress, is urged on by the pugilist, Henry Josiah Holt (1792–1844), the 'Cicero of the Ring', in a striped dressing-gown. The 'member' wears an oilskin cap, a green coat and the red favour of his party. Opposite to him is the other member (Robert Stanton, of Colebrook House, Middlesex, M.P. for Penrhyn), wearing a yellow turban and the quilt from his bed; between him and the Sheriff is a Lord Mayor (Bourk or Birch, who later died of drink), holding a white wand with a blue and yellow bow. Below the Sheriff sits the head poll-clerk (Samuel Hart, the engraver), in a white jacket, swearing in the three burgesses. These are a dandy in a yellow silk dressing-gown, holding a very elaborate pipe; an 'exquisite', imprisoned three years, smoking a cigar, his toes staring through his shoes; and a typical character 'of middle age and careless dissipation' in a blue jacket and green cap. On the right of the poll-clerk is a figure—a head constable (Price)—with a mace, dressed in his red bed-curtain; another poll-clerk entering the names of the electors in a book; an assessor (Rook); and a man sticking a pipe into the quilted candidate.

In the right-hand group, sipping claret, sits 'a man of family and a soldier [a Major Campbell, who remained in prison until 1834], who distinguished himself in Spain'; he had been imprisoned in early life for running away with a ward in Chancery: 'one of the most tremendous heads I ever saw in nature, something between Byron and Buonaparte'; his mistress (Miss Corn?) is beside him; above him, an intoxicated elector (Charles Bennett) is clinging to a pump.

On the left is 'a good family in affliction': in mourning for their second boy, with their eldest child cheering the voters, their youngest in the arms of his nurse behind. The father holds a paper in his hand inscribed: *Debt, £26. 10s.*

Paid Costs, £157. 14s. [—*unpaid. Treachery, Squeeze and Co., Thieves Inn*].

Behind this family is a group of electors with flags, trumpets 'and all the bustle of an election'; flags bear the mottoes *LIBERTY of the SUBJECT* and *NO BAILIFFS*. On the ground lies a bill of exchange of the Hon. Henry Lawless, at 999 years' date, to Mr. Cabbage, tailor, of Bond St., for £1,562. 13s. 6d., 1827. In the background are the spiked wall and state house of the prison and, on the right, the prison with a party of electors listening to a speech under a red-striped blind.[1]

Bought by George IV in 1828 (see below) and recorded in the inventory of 'Carleton Palace' (623); Haydon noted on 5 June 1828 that the picture 'is moved to Windsor' where it was later in the Corridor (842); later at Buckingham Palace.

Literature: B. R. Haydon, *Explanation of the Picture of the Mock Election, which took place at the King's Bench Prison, July 1827* (1828); Cunningham, vol. III, p. 290; *Benjamin Robert Haydon: Correspondence and Table-Talk*, with memoir by F. W. Haydon (1876), vol. I, pp. 148–9, vol. II pp. 118–21; *The Autobiography and Memoirs of Benjamin Robert Haydon*, ed. T. Taylor (edn. of 1926), vol. I, pp. 414–27, vol. II, pp. 431–40; R.A., *King's Pictures* (482); *The Diary of Benjamin Robert Haydon*, ed. W. B. Pope, vol. III (Cambridge, Mass., 1963), pp. 211–72, 282–3.

In June 1827 Haydon had been imprisoned for debt in the King's Bench Prison. He was released at the end of July. During his sojourn in the prison he saw, in July 1827, a mock election. 'In the midst of this dreadful scene of affliction up sprung the masquerade election . . . I was perpetually drawn to the windows by the boisterous merriment of the unfortunate happy beneath me. Rabelais or Cervantes alone could do it justice with their pens. Never was such an exquisite burlesque. Baronets and bankers, authors and merchants, young fellows of fashion and elegance; insanity, idiotism, poverty and bitter affliction, all for a moment forgetting their sorrows at the humour, the wit, the absurdity of what was before them. I saw the whole from beginning to end. I was resolved to paint it, for I thought it the finest subject for humour and pathos on earth.' On 15 August he 'rubbed in' the picture. In his *Diary* he records the progress of his work upon it, occasionally jotting down in the *Diary* sketches of the figures he was at work on. He returned to the prison to collect details (e.g., on 17, 26, 31 August and 1 October). He began by working on the central group. By 23 August he had advanced far with the Sheriff ('The careless, Irish, witty look, the "abandon de gaieté" air of his head & expression was never surpassed by Hogarth'); on 24 August he was hard at work on the Member's head; two days later he sketched the head of a smuggler who carried the Union Jack; by the end of the month he was well advanced with the Lord Mayor, the other candidate ('I hit his likeness in a minute') and one of the poll-clerks. On 2 September he 'arranged the final colour & effect of the Election . . . I'll make this Picture a brilliant one.' By 5 September he had finished Holt the pugilist. On 7 September he was working hard on the Dandy seated on the right; Haydon had sketched him, and his mistress on 25 August. On 19 September he 'attacked the head Constable'; on 29 September he finished the central group. On 18 October, 'put in my new arrangement[2] & was delighted to find it so great an improvement this morning.' By 23 October he was far advanced with the 'good' family on the left; he finished the mother on 30

1. This description of the picture is based on Haydon's own account, printed in the *Autobiography and Memoirs, op. cit.*, vol. I, pp. 419–23, and in the account he himself published in 1828.
2. There are *pertimenti* in the lower right corner, including indications that the dandy was at first seated on a chair.

October; on 1 November he finished her son. He was hard at work on the buildings by the end of November and on 1 December finished the sky.

Haydon exhibited the *Mock Election* at the Egyptian Hall in January 1828, but to his distress it remained unsold. But on 18 April 1818 Seguier informed him that the King (probably encouraged by Haydon's friend, General Sir Thomas Hammond) wished to see the picture. He took the picture to St. James's Palace on the following day. On 21 April the King, who was delighted with the picture, paid Haydon five hundred guineas for it. In March 1828 Haydon had begun to paint his *Chairing the Member* as a sequel to the *Mock Election*; a number of the characters in No. 829 reappeared in the sequel and Haydon himself is seen looking out of his window in the prison. It was bought by a Mr. Francis and is now in the Tate Gallery (5644).

Karl Anton Hickel

1745–98. Portrait-painter, a pupil in Vienna of his brother Joseph. He worked in Munich, Mannheim, Switzerland and Paris and became Principal Painter to the Emperor Joseph II. He visited London and exhibited at the Society of Artists, 1791, and Royal Academy, 1792–6. In 1797 he left for Hamburg. See also above, p. vii.

830. RICHARD BRINSLEY SHERIDAN (1751–1816)

Buckingham Palace. 25½ × 21¼ in., 69,8 × 54 cm.; considerably stretched in lining; the original canvas is 23½ × 20 in.

Signed and dated: *K. Hickel p: | 1793*

Head and shoulders in a painted oval.

'A Half Length Portrait of The Late Mr Sherriden—Blue Coat & Buff Waistcoat' was received in a case at Carlton House on 22 November 1819, apparently from the Custom House (Jutsham, *Receipts*, f. 87; additional No. 569 in Carlton House inv. of 1816, with no artist's name and as an oval, perhaps indicating that it has been framed as an oval for many years); later at Hampton Court (891) and Kensington.

Literature: Law, 1881, 1898 (364), *Kensington* (1899), pp. 109–10.

Apparently a study from life for the figure of Sheridan in Hickel's painting in the National Portrait Gallery (745) of William Pitt addressing the House of Commons. The scene is the debate on war against France, held on 1 February 1793. The picture now in the National Portrait Gallery was formerly in the collection of the Emperor Francis I. A number of portraits by Hickel of other sitters in the group, painted in the same format as No. 830 and dated 1793 and 1794, are recorded. No. 830 may have remained in the artist's possession until his death.

Dramatist, Whig M.P., 1780–1812, and one of the most brilliant speakers of his time; Treasurer of the Navy, 1806–7. He was a close friend and adviser of the Prince of Wales, especially at the time of his marriage to Mrs. Fitzherbert. During Sheridan's last years he and the Prince did not meet, but the Prince gave or lent him £3,000, probably in order to pay his debts, and offered him asylum in Carlton House.

Robert Home

1752–1834. Painter of portraits and historical subjects. He exhibited at the Royal Academy between 1770 and 1789, but by January 1791 was in Madras, having gone without leave to India, where he had a most successful career. He went on Lord Cornwallis's campaign against Tippoo Sultan and in 1795 moved to Calcutta. In 1814 he went to Lucknow as painter to the Nawab of Oudh, a post he held until 1828.

831. ARTHUR WELLESLEY, LATER FIRST DUKE OF WELLINGTON (1769–1852)

St. James's Palace. 93 × 49½ in., 236,2 × 125,7 cm. There are in addition *c.* 5¼ in. turned over on the left and about the same amount on the right; the original width of the canvas was therefore *c.* 60 in.

Full-length, standing with his hand on his sword at the mouth of a tent, in the uniform of a Major-General with the ribbon and star of the Bath. In the background are soldiers of the Madras artillery and infantry.

Presented to Queen Victoria by the Maharajah of Mysore in 1862; recorded at Buckingham Palace (545) in 1876 (*V.R. inv.*).

Home produced a number of portraits of General Wellesley, who was in India, 1797–1805, and after his successful campaign against Tippoo Sahib was Governor of Seringapatam and Mysore, 1799–1805. William Hickey visited Home's studio in Calcutta late in December 1804 and saw two portraits 'as large as life of the Marquess Wellesley and his brother Arthur' (*Memoirs*, ed. A. Spencer, vol. IV (1925), pp. 304–5). In his own account book (now in the National Portrait Gallery) Home records that he began in September 1804 six portraits of Wellesley, all presumably based on one type. Among the six was one full-length at 2,000 rupees. Among four more portraits, listed under October 1804, was another full-length at 2,000 rupees 'for Penang', i.e., the East India Company. In August 1805 Home was paid 2,000 rupees by the Government for one of his full-lengths; this was probably the version still in Viceroy's House, Delhi, of which Charles Turner published an engraving at Calcutta on 15 March 1806. No. 831 is perhaps the full-length 'for a Native Prince' which is listed under March 1805 at 2,000 rupees. In the earlier versions the insignia of the Bath had to be added, but in No. 831 it seems part of the original design which must, therefore, have been painted after February 1805 when the news of Wellesley's appointment to the Bath reached Calcutta. Versions of the type, on a smaller scale, are in the National Portrait Gallery (1471), Apsley House and Stratfield Saye House; another was sold at Christie's, 8 March 1957 (109); a late copy is in the India Office (Sir W. Foster, 'British Artists in India, 1760–1820', *Walpole Soc.*, vol. XIX (1931), p. 46; Lord G. Wellesley and J. Steegman, *The Iconography of the Duke of Wellington* (1935), pp. 20–2).

See No. 917.

832. GHAZI-UD-DIN HAIDAR, KING OF OUDH (d. 1827), RECEIVING TRIBUTE (*Plate* 289)

95 × 61½ in., 241,3 × 156,2 cm.

The King, seated on his throne, under a canopy and attended by orderlies, receiving tribute from a man bowing in the foreground.

Presented to George IV by Sir Everard Home, 1st. Bt., brother of the painter, on 7 March 1828; recorded in the inventory of 'Carleton Palace' (613); later at Hampton Court (951), St. James's and Buckingham Palace. Lent by H.M. King George V to the Victoria Memorial Hall, Calcutta, in 1920 (*Illustrated Catalogue of the Exhibits*, Victoria Memorial, Calcutta (1925), No. 194).

Literature: Law, 1881, 1898 (360); Sir W. Foster, 'British Artists in India, 1760–1820', *Walpole Soc.*, vol. XIX (1931), p. 48.

Presumably painted *c.* 1820–5.

The Nawab Wazir of Oudh, who had succeeded his father (No. 990) in 1814, took the title of King in 1819, at the instigation of Lord Hastings (No. 1023), and assumed the style of Shah Zaman.

833. A WHITE LEOPARD

Kew (*Hampton Court* No. 1470). 54 × 73 in., 137,2 × 185,4 cm.

Lying in a dark and wooded jungle.

Recorded at Windsor (1278) in 1878 (*V.R. inv.*).

The animal is apparently a rare aberration of the common leopard[1] and was among the animals kept in Lord Wellesley's menagerie at Barrackpore in India. Home, in his account book (now in the National Portrait Gallery) records under August 1805 that he had begun a picture of 'A White Leopard Large', and under September 1805 that he had begun 'A White Leopard, large, sent to Marquis Wellesley'. Among the *Drawings illustrating the Quadrupeds of India*, made for Wellesley and now in the India Office Library, is one (N.H.D. 33, f. 1) which is a direct copy by an Indian artist of the animal in No. 833; another drawing (*ibid.*, f. 2) of the same animal bears an inscription by Wellesley: 'From Life sent from the Coast of Malabar. The Leopard spots are visible in a particular Light and are only Marked by a slight Elongation of the Hair. A similar one was killed at Nattore in Bengal'. It is possible that No. 833 was given by Lord Wellesley to George III, although there is no record of it in the royal collection before 1878 (see above); it was recently tentatively attributed to Stubbs, by whom the design is clearly influenced.

John Hoppner

1758(?)–1810. Portrait-painter, born in London of German parents. He was recommended to George III as 'a Lad of Genius'; the King placed him with John Chamberlaine, who was later Keeper of the royal drawings and medals. By 1785 Hoppner was working for the royal family. In the early 1790s he had passed a week with the Duke of Clarence and Mrs. Jordan (see No. 844). In 1795, when he was, with the approval of the King and Prince of Wales, to paint the portrait of the Princess of Wales which was later entrusted to Dupont (No. 768), the Queen was calling him 'a good young man'. By the late summer of that year Hoppner had quarrelled with the King who had 'condemned Hoppner's red and yellow trees, particularly the picture of Lady Charlotte Piercy'. This was No. 81 in the Royal Academy of that year, where the King admired Hoppner's *Duke of Rutland* (71) and *Lady Young* (141), but rated him below Beechey and 'had not made up his mind about the picture of the Princess'.

As early as *c.* 1790 Hoppner had painted Miss Maria Bover for the Prince of Wales and by 1793 he was the Prince's Principal Painter. In December 1799 he was painting the Princess of Wales and he was working for the Prince as late as 1807 (Farington, *Diary*, vol. I, pp. 39, 83–4, 96, 104, 206, 275; vol. III, pp. 43, 85; vol. IV, p. 131; unpublished, 2 and 5 May 1795.)

The account, dated 30 July 1810, sent in to the Prince of Wales by Hoppner's widow, included £52. 10*s.* for 'Half Length Portrait of HRH the Prince of Wales in Plain Clothes' and £105 for 'An Extra sized Half Length in the Robes of the Garter of HRH the Prince of Wales delivered to Sir Gore Ouseley to be taken to Persia' (W.R.A., Geo. 26877). The half-length in plain clothes had been received from Mrs. Hoppner on 14 June 1810 and was sent as a present to Lord Yarmouth on 31 August 1810 with a new frame made by Smith (Jutsham, *R/D*, ff. 70, 123); it is now in the Wallace Collection (563; Catalogue, *Pictures and Drawings* (1968), p. 154). The 'Extra sized' half-length could have been related to the full-length of which versions belong to the Marquess of Hertford and the Corporation of Liverpool. 'A whole Length Portrait of . . . The Prince of Wales with Negro Portrait' was received at Carlton House from Mrs. Hoppner on 7 April 1810 (Jutsham, *R/D*, f. 115); this could conceivably have been the Reynolds now at Arundel (see below, p. 98). The catalogue of pictures in the Corridor at Windsor in 1845 includes (p. 107) a portrait by Hoppner of the Duke of Wellington when Lieutenant-Colonel; this could conceivably be the portrait in the possession of the present Duke (Lord G. Wellesley and J. Steegman, *The Iconography of the First Duke of Wellington* (1935), p. 22). It is not clear from Pyne (vol. I, *Frogmore*, p. 19) whether or not Queen Charlotte owned a version of Hoppner's portrait of Pitt.

Among payments made on behalf of the Prince of Wales are (21 April 1806) £23. 6*s.* 4*d.* to J. Miles 'for Cleaning & repairing Pictures and Frames by order of Mr Hoppner' and (18 July 1806) £139. 18*s.* to Hoppner 'for cleaning & putting in order Pictures to 10 Octob 1805' (W.R.A., Geo. 32485, 89441, 89444). By 10 April 1793 the Prince of Wales owed Hoppner £352. By 9 March 1808 the debt stood at £651. At least part of the debt was cleared off, but £215. 5*s.* was still due to Hoppner's executors in 1812(?) (W.R.A., Geo. 32038, 32243, 32535, 89453, 89479). At the Hoppner sale at Christie's, 31 May 1823, the sketches (5, 30, 31) included the Prince of Wales and the Dukes of Clarence and Kent. In 1799 the Duke of Kent was writing to the Prince of Wales about 'the picture you were so good as to say, Hopner should do of you for me' (*ibid.*, Geo. Add. MSS. 7, 45).

834. GEORGE IV WHEN PRINCE OF WALES

Buckingham Palace. $94\frac{1}{2} \times 58\frac{1}{2}$ in., 240 × 148,6 cm.

Full-length, standing, in the robes of the Garter, with the plumed hat of the order in his right hand.

Presumably painted for the Prince. Recorded at Carlton House in 1816 (17), in the old Throne Room, where it can be seen in Wild's plate in Pyne (vol. III, *Carlton House*, p. 28); later at St. James's Palace.

Literature: McKay and Roberts, pp. 94–5.

Probably the portrait exhibited at the Royal Academy in 1796 (98); it seems to deserve, more than the portrait in the Wallace Collection (563), Anthony Pasquin's criticism (quoted in McKay and Roberts, *loc. cit.*). It is perhaps the portrait upon which Farington, on 25 January 1796, states that Hoppner was working (*Diary*, vol. I, pp. 137–8); he also states that the Prince desired the painter to make an alteration to it as it made him look like Mr. Lascelles of Harewood House. It was probably the portrait received from Mrs. Hoppner on 7 April 1810: 'A whole Length Portrait of His Royal Highness The Prince of Wales—Robed—' (Jutsham, *R/D*, f. 115). See No. 852. A copy is in the Ringling Museum of Art, Sarasota (394); another is in Freemasons' Hall.

1. I am grateful to Mr. G. B. Corbet for help in identifying the species.

835. WILLIAM IV WHEN DUKE OF CLARENCE

Buckingham Palace. 94¾ × 58¼ in., 240,7 × 147,9 cm.

Full-length, in Garter robes, standing by a table on which rests the plumed hat of the order and the mantle of the Thistle.

Painted for George IV. It was cleaned by Simpson in 1795 (P.R.O., H.O. 73, 23); recorded in the West Ante-room at Carlton House in 1816 (3: 'A whole length portrait of the Duke of Clarence. Mr Hoppner', with a note by Jutsham that it had been destroyed in the fire in this room on 8 June 1824). It was not, however, wholly destroyed and it was placed in store until 1874, when it was at Hampton Court (1144) and 'when it was restored, as far as possible by C. Buttery to retain some remains of a very fine work' (*V.R. inv.*).

Literature: Law, 1882 (950); McKay and Roberts, p. 52; *Buckingham Palace*, 1909, p. 146.

Probably the portrait exhibited at the Royal Academy in 1791 (98). Another portrait of the Duke was exhibited by Hoppner in 1792 (195), but the engraving of No. 835 by E. Hodges was published on 10 July 1792 (*Fig.* 15). The surface of No. 835 was so ruined by the fire of 1824 that nothing of the original quality of the portrait can be appreciated and almost all the detail has been obliterated. These are, however, preserved in the engraving, in which one can see, for example, that on the paper held in the Duke's right hand was a drawing of a man-of-war; there also appears to have been a drawing on the paper on the floor. A copy of the head and shoulders is at Clarence House.

836. EDWARD, DUKE OF KENT

Windsor Castle (364). 42 × 31¼ in., 106,7 × 79,4 cm.

Three-quarter-length, standing, in Lieutenant-General's uniform, holding his hat and sword in his right hand and wearing the star of the Garter.

Recorded at Windsor in 1859 (*V.R. inv.*).

Literature: McKay and Roberts, pp. 144–5; Collins Baker, *Windsor*, p. 173.

Presumably painted between 12 January 1796, when he was appointed Lieutenant-General, and 10 May 1799, when he was promoted General. The engraving by Cheesman after a drawing by Muller, published by Harding in 1806, appears to be based on No. 836; it is possible that Muller made a drawing, after the portrait by Hoppner, to assist the engraver. See No. 837; a copy of this type is at Clarence House.

837. EDWARD, DUKE OF KENT

Buckingham Palace. 29⅞ × 25 in., 75,9 × 63,5 cm.

Head and shoulders in General's uniform with the star of the Garter.

Formerly at Frogmore (Windsor inv. No. 1468) and stated to have belonged to the Duchess of Kent.

The head is very close to that in No. 836; the portrait seems to be by Hoppner himself, painted presumably after 10 May 1799, when the Duke had been promoted General, but based on the earlier type.

838. PRINCESS MARY (*Plate* 175)

Windsor Castle (275). 29¾ × 24¼ in., 75,6 × 61,6 cm. Later additions at top and bottom, bringing the height up to 36 in., were removed in 1964.

Half-length in a straw hat and a black shawl.

Presumably painted for George III and Queen Charlotte; probably the portrait in the King's Closet in the Private Apartments at Windsor in 1813, 1816 (Francis Legge's lists: 'H.R.H. Princess Mary', with no artist's name but with measurements given as 30 × 24 in.).

Literature: McKay and Roberts, p. 166; R.A., *British Art*, 1934 (431), *Commemorative Catalogue* (1935), p. 80; Collins Baker, *Windsor*, p. 167; R.A., *King's Pictures* (59); Canada and U.S., *British Painting in the Eighteenth Century*, 1957–8 (36).

Probably painted at Windsor. Exhibited at the Royal Academy in 1785 (222). The engraving by Caroline Watson was dedicated to Queen Charlotte and published on 1 March 1785.

839. PRINCESS SOPHIA (*Plate* 174)

Windsor Castle (274). 30 × 24½ in., 75,6 × 61,6 cm. Later additions at top and bottom, bringing the height up to 36 in., were removed in 1964.

Half-length in a straw hat with a pink ribbon, holding a bunch of flowers in her lap.

Presumably painted for George III and Queen Charlotte; probably the portrait in the King's Closet in the Private Apartments at Windsor in 1813, 1816 (Francis Legge's lists: 'H.R.H. The Princess Sophia', with no artist's name, but with measurements given as 30 × 24 in.).

Literature: McKay and Roberts, p. 240; Collins Baker, *Windsor*, p. 168 (wrongly as a copy after No. 854); R.A., *King's Pictures* (57).

Probably painted at Windsor. Exhibited at the Royal Academy in 1785 (220). The engraving by Caroline Watson, dedicated to the King and Queen, was published on 12 April 1786. There is a *pentimento* in the sash tied at the Princess's back; it was at first of a smaller shape. A copy was on the art-market in 1919. See No. 854.

840. PRINCESS AMELIA (*Plate* 173)

Windsor Castle (2724). 36 × 28 in., 91,4 × 71,1 cm.

Full-length, seated, with a drum on her lap and a little spaniel beside her.

Painted for George III and Queen Charlotte and recorded in the King's Gallery at Kensington (Geo. III, *Kensington* and No. 334 in inv. of 1818, as a portrait of the Princess Royal); moved to St. James's Palace on 2 February 1834; later at Buckingham Palace.

Literature: McKay and Roberts, p. 3; Collins Baker, *Windsor*, p. 168.

Probably painted at Windsor. Exhibited at the Royal Academy in 1785 (221). In the Royal Library is an unlettered impression of a very rare mezzotint after No. 840 (Chaloner Smith, vol. II, p. 644, where it is stated that the mezzotint was made by Hoppner himself); on the impression is an erroneous note that the portrait had been painted by Hoppner at the age of eighteen. See No. 855; another copy of No. 840 was on the art-market in 1919.

841. FRANCIS RUSSELL, FIFTH DUKE OF BEDFORD (1765–1802)

Buckingham Palace. 97¾ × 61¾ in., 248,3 × 156,8 cm.

Full-length, standing, in peer's robes, with his left hand on his hip and holding in his right a scroll of paper; in the background is a statue (? of Hercules) on a staircase leading down from a terrace.

Painted for George IV. It was received from Mrs. Hoppner on 7 April 1810 (Jutsham, *R/D*, f. 115) and placed in the East Ante-room at Carlton House (No. 60 in inv. of 1816: 'A whole length portrait of the late Duke of Bedford. M͡r Hoppner', measurements given as 93 × 57 in.); later at Hampton Court (961) and Kensington.

Literature: Law, 1881, 1898 (355); McKay and Roberts, pp. 17–18.

Hoppner's account, dated 6 January 1806 and receipted 18 January 1808, included £105 for 'The late Duke of Bedford'; Edward Wyatt's account for work on frames in 1811 included £2. 10s. 'To cutting and altering a large whole length frame for Painting (of the Duke of Bedford)' (W.R.A., Geo. 26829, 26890–1). There appears to be a *pentimento* in the right hand and paper, which were at first a few inches higher. Hoppner painted two full-lengths of the Duke. The earlier, probably that at Woburn, is perhaps the portrait exhibited at the Royal Academy in 1796 (248); the later, probably No. 841, may have been the one exhibited in the following year (79). Farington wrote on 12 May 1797 (*Diary*, vol. I, p. 207) that 'Hoppner has frequently much trouble with the people who sit to him.—The Duke of Bedford He has painted a second picture of, in room of the other'. The engraving by P. W. Tomkins of the head and shoulders of this type was published on 7 April 1802. The Duke of Bedford was among the sitters of whom unfinished paintings and sketches were in Hoppner's sale at Christie's, 31 May 1823 (40).

A Whig, a supporter of Fox and a friend of the Prince of Wales; he was one of the two Dukes who supported the Prince at his wedding, 8 April 1795. He carried out important agricultural research and development at Woburn and employed Henry Holland to build the south wing of the house. The Prince of Wales also possessed a bust (now at Windsor) of the Duke by Nollekens (1808).

842. FRANCIS RAWDON-HASTINGS, SECOND EARL OF MOIRA AND FIRST MARQUESS OF HASTINGS (1754–1826)

Buckingham Palace. 94½ × 58¾ in., 240 × 149,2 cm.

Full-length, standing, in military uniform with the ribbon and star of the Garter, beside a table on which he rests his left hand; in his right he holds a paper.

Painted for George IV. It was received from Mrs. Hoppner on 14 June 1810 (Jutsham, *R/D*, f. 123) and placed in the East Anteroom at Carlton House (No. 62 in inv. of 1816: 'A whole length portrait of Earl Moira. M͡r Hoppner', measurements given as 93 × 57 in.); removed to the New Corridor, Windsor Castle, on 30 April 1828, but brought back to 105 Pall Mall; later at Hampton Court (950) and Kensington.

Literature: Law, 1881, 1898 (358); McKay and Roberts, p. 172.

Exhibited at the Royal Academy in 1794 (66). In June 1812 the sitter was created Knight of the Garter and on 15 June the portrait had to be sent to Mr. (presumably Lascelles) Hoppner 'to add Ribbon & Star to it' (Jutsham, *R/D*, f. 116). J. Young's engraving of the portrait, described as belonging to the Prince of Wales, was published on 15 July 1805. A three-quarter-length version is at University College, Oxford.

See No. 1023.

843. FRANZ JOSEPH HAYDN (1732–1809) (*Plate* 176)

Windsor Castle (2986). 36¼ × 28¼ in., 92,1 × 71,7 cm.

Half-length, seated, holding a pen in his right hand and resting his left hand on papers.

Painted for George IV, but perhaps not delivered until after Hoppner's death. The portrait was received at Carlton House from Mrs. Hoppner on 14 June 1810; and the 'Account of Pictures delivered to His R.H. . . . by Phoebe Hoppner Widow and Executrix. . .', dated 30 July 1810, includes £31. 10s. for 'an Unfinished Portrait of D͡r Haydn' (Jutsham, *R/D*, f. 123; W.R.A., Geo. 26877). Recorded in Store at Carlton House in 1816 (363; the 1816 label is still on the back); later at Hampton Court (920) and Buckingham Palace.

Literature: Quarterly Review, October 1817; Law, 1881, 1898 (832); *Buckingham Palace*, 1909, p. 143; McKay and Roberts, pp. 117–18; H. C. Robbins Landon, *The Collected Correspondence and London Notebooks of Joseph Haydn* (1959), pp. 123, 272, 276.

Commissioned by the Prince of Wales during Haydn's first visit to London. In his notebooks Haydn records under 24 November 1791 that 'The Prince of Wales wants my portrait', and on 20 December 1791 he wrote from London to Maria Anna von Genzinger that 'The Prince of Wales is having my portrait painted just now, and the picture is to hang in his room'. Only the head and background in the portrait were finished; the remainder of the design is broadly indicated. The writer in the *Quarterly Review* (*loc. cit.*) states: 'The picture was not finished when Haydn left England [i.e., on 23 June 1792]; it was, however, so striking a likeness of this extraordinary man, that the Prince of Wales, for whom it was painted, would not permit Hoppner to touch it after his departure, and the portrait is now in His Royal Highness's possession'. The same writer describes Haydn's exemplary patience in sitting; 'but no birthday beauty was ever more solicitous to choose the favourable moment' and if, after protracted gazing in his looking-glass, he decided that he did not look his best, he would cancel a sitting. A copy of No. 843 by Mather Brown belongs to the Royal Society of Musicians. An engraving by Facius after No. 843 was published in 1807.

The celebrated composer paid two visits to London; both were highly successful and brought him into contact with the royal family. In 1791–2 he was presented at a court ball at St. James's and, on the following night, 19 January 1791, he attended a chamber concert at Carlton House. In the autumn he stayed with the Duke and Duchess of York at Oatlands and conducted his music. 'The Prince of Wales sat on my right side and played with us on his violoncello, quite tolerably. I had to sing too. The Prince . . . is the most handsome man on God's earth; he has an extraordinary love of music and a lot of feeling, but not much money'. Hadyn went to Ascot for the royal meeting in June 1792 and records the Prince's recipe for brewing punch. On the second visit, in 1794–5, he conducted his own works at a concert at York House on 1 February 1795, when the Prince presented him to the King and Queen; during this visit he played at twenty-six concerts at Carlton House and the Queen offered him apartments at Windsor for the summer.

844. MRS. JORDAN (1761–1816) AS THE COMIC MUSE

Buckingham Palace. 93¾ × 57½ in., 238,1 × 146 cm.

Full-length as Thalia, the muse of Comedy, holding her mask, flying to the arms of Euphrosyne from the advances of a satyr.

Perhaps acquired by William IV (see below); recorded at Hampton Court (704) in 1842 (Mrs. Jameson, vol. II, p. 414; later inv. No. 960); later at St. James's Palace.

Literature: Law, 1881, 1898 (359); McKay and Roberts, pp. 140–1.

Exhibited at the Royal Academy in 1786 (163): *Mrs.*

Jordan in the character of the Comic Muse, supported by Euphrosyne, who represses the advance of a satyr. Mrs. Papendiek records that she had seen Mrs. Jordan in her London début in 1785 and that she met her 'often afterwards at Höppner's', to whom she sat for Thalia, as being esteemed the greatest comic actress of the day' (*Journals*, ed. Mrs. V. Delves Broughton (1887), vol. I, p. 232). In May 1786 Hoppner advertised for subscriptions for an engraving of the picture; the engraving was made in mezzotint by Thomas Park and published on 1 August 1787 (Chaloner Smith, p. 959). Even after the Duke of Clarence had parted from Mrs. Jordan, he was anxious, in his own words, 'to have *all* the pictures of Mrs. Jordan, knowing and therefore admiring her public and private excellent qualities, the only two I had before; they are both at Bushy' (letter of 5 April 1813, quoted in *Mrs. Jordan and her Family*, ed. A. Aspinall (1951), pp. xvii–xviii.

Dorothy (Dora) Jordan was the daughter of Francis Bland and an actress, Grace Philipps. She began her career on the Dublin stage in 1779, but was seduced by the manager, Richard Daly, and fled to England. She made her début in London at Drury Lane on 18 October 1785 as Peggy in *The Country Girl*; she soon became unsurpassed as a comic actress, making her last appearance in London as Lady Teazle in 1814. Hazlitt described her as a 'child of nature, whose voice was a cordial to the heart . . . to hear whose laugh was to drink nectar . . . all exuberance and grace'. In 1790 she became the mistress of Prince William, later Duke of Clarence. They lived together in great happiness for twenty years and Mrs. Jordan bore the Duke ten children. In 1815 she retired to France, heavily in debt.

845. GEORGE KEITH ELPHINSTONE, LATER VISCOUNT KEITH (1746–1823) (*Plate* 179)

Windsor Castle (356). 50½ × 40½ in., 128,3 × 102,8 cm.

Three-quarter-length, standing, in the full-dress uniform of a flag officer, with the ribbon and star of the Bath, leaning against a rocky ledge.

Painted for George IV. It was received at Carlton House from Mrs. Hoppner on 7 April 1810 (Jutsham, *R/D*, f. 115); recorded in store at Carlton House in 1816 (259); removed to the New Gallery at Windsor in May 1828; still in the Corridor in 1878 (*V.R. inv.*), but thereafter placed in the Waterloo Chamber.

Literature: McKay and Roberts, p. 143; Collins Baker, *Windsor,* p. 169.

Probably painted in 1799, when the sitter was a Vice-Admiral; the cuffs of the uniform were altered after he had been promoted to full Admiral in 1801. A contemporary newspaper report (quoted in McKay and Roberts, *loc. cit.*) states that a proof-impression of S. W. Reynolds's mezzotint of No. 845, which was finally published on 2 April 1800, had been presented to the Prince of Wales, for whom Hoppner had painted the portrait 'a short time before the Noble Lord's departure to take Chief Command in the Mediterranean'. Keith had been ordered to the Mediterranean in November 1799 and reached Gibraltar early in December. In the mezzotint the cuffs are shown in their original, unaltered, form.

A younger son of the 10th Lord Elphinstone; entered the Navy in 1761; during a distinguished naval career he held command successively at Plymouth, the North Sea and East Channel and in the Channel and played a prominent part in putting down the mutinies at the Nore and Plymouth. He was Treasurer and Comptroller of the Household to the

Duke of Clarence who had served under him as a midshipman. See No. 1058.

846. CHARLES MANNERS-SUTTON (1755–1828), DEAN OF WINDSOR AND LATER ARCHBISHOP OF CANTERBURY

Windsor Castle (301). 50 × 40¼ in., 127 × 102,2 cm.

Three-quarter-length, standing, as Dean of Windsor, wearing the Dean's robes and insignia as Registrar of the Order of the Garter and holding a paper in his right hand; behind is a glimpse of the Garter stalls in the choir of St. George's Chapel, Windsor.

Probably painted for George III. Recorded in the Dining-Room in the King's private apartments at Windsor in 1813 ('The present Archbishop of Canterbury, when Dean of Windsor . . . Hopner').

Literature: McKay and Roberts, p. 248; Collins Baker, *Windsor,* p. 170.

Probably painted soon after Manners-Sutton's appointment to the Deanery at Windsor. George IV lent the portrait to the Archbishop's son, Charles Manners-Sutton, so that it could be engraved by C. Turner; it was received back on 23 October 1829 (Jutsham, *Receipts*, f. 278; 'it belonged to The Windsor Castle Collection of Pictures') and the mezzotint was published on 16 November. A sketch for the portrait was in Hoppner's sale, 31 May 1823 (5). A miniature copy of the head (1829) is in the Holbourne of Menstrie Museum of Art, Bath.

Grandson of the 3rd Duke of Rutland; appointed Dean of Peterborough, 1791, Bishop of Norwich, 1792, and, in 1794, Dean of Windsor. He and his wife were great favourites with the royal family and in 1805 he was appointed Archbishop of Canterbury. A prominent high churchman, he was described as 'a prelate whose amiable demeanour, useful learning, and conciliating habits of life particularly recommend his episcopal character'. See also No. 1222.

847. WILLIAM MARKHAM (1719–1807), ARCHBISHOP OF YORK (*Plate* 177)

Windsor Castle (309). 50½ × 40¾ in., 128,3 × 103,5 cm.

Three-quarter-length, seated, with a stick in his left hand and his hat in his right.

Probably painted for the Prince of Wales. On 20 November 1807 it was sent from Carlton House to Heath at 15 Russell Place 'to ingrave from' (see below); it was returned in April 1810 and on 16 June 1810 a gilt frame for it was received from Smith (Jutsham, *R/D*, ff. 16, 125). It was placed in the Crimson Drawing Room at Carlton House (No. 14 in inv. of 1816; Pyne, vol. III, *Carlton House*, p. 22, seen in plate), and removed to the New Gallery at Windsor on 8 August 1828.

Literature: Sir C. Markham, *A Memoir of Archbishop Markham* (1906), p. 92; McKay and Roberts, p. 165; Collins Baker, *Windsor,* p. 170.

Farington wrote on 12 November 1798 that 'The Archbishop of York is sitting to Hoppner'. The portrait was exhibited at the Royal Academy in 1799 (84), where it was warmly and justly praised as a portrait worthy of Reynolds. An enamel miniature copy by Bone, signed and dated 1800, was painted for the Prince of Wales and is still in the Royal collection. A copy of No. 847, painted by the sitter's granddaughter Lady Elizabeth Murray, is recorded at Becca by Sir C. Markham (*loc. cit.*) and another is in Westminster School; another copy is in the Bishop's House at Chester; a replica was stated by McKay and Roberts (*loc. cit.*) to be in the collection of the Earl of Mansfield. Impressions from the plate by Heath (see above) are exceedingly rare as the plate was destroyed after only fifteen impressions had been struck off (McKay and Roberts, *loc. cit.*).

A fine scholar, although as headmaster of Westminster, 1753–65, 'his business was rather in courting the great than attending to the school'; successively Dean of Rochester, Dean of Christ Church, Bishop of Chester and, 1777, Archbishop of York. In 1756 he had been appointed Chaplain to George II and from 1771 to 1776 he was Preceptor to George, Prince of Wales, and Prince Frederick. In 1774 Prince George wrote to him that 'your good instruction, your kindness, your good nature will never be effaced from my heart'; in 1800 he described himself to the Archbishop as 'your old and most gratefully attached pupil'.

848. WILLIAM LAMB, SECOND VISCOUNT MELBOURNE (1779–1848) (*Plate* 181)

Windsor Castle (325). 30×25 in., 76,2×63,5 cm.

Head and shoulders in Montem dress of a vaguely Tudor or Jacobean form, with a medal or badge suspended on a ribbon from his shoulders.

Presented by the sitter to Queen Victoria in September 1841: 'Hoppner, Portrait of Viscount Melbourne when 17. (unfinished.)', and placed in the Corridor at Windsor (MS. Catalogue of Queen Victoria's private pictures &c.); later at Buckingham Palace.

Literature: McKay and Roberts, p. 148; Collins Baker, *Windsor*, p. 171.

Lord Melbourne told Queen Victoria that Hoppner had painted two portraits of him when he left Eton (where he reached Sixth Form) in July 1796. When the Queen visited Eton 'for Montem' on 5 June 1838 Melbourne was in her party. They lunched with the Provost in a room, in the Queen's words, 'hung round with many portraits of the young men . . . who had been at Eton . . . Lord Melbourne's was not there, which it *ought* to have been'. Lord Melbourne stated that he had been painted by Hoppner for Dr. Langford, his master, but that the portrait, which can almost certainly be identified with No. 848, had been sold after the Doctor's death. He later told the Queen that it had been bought by his brother George Lamb and was at Melbourne Hall: 'the Provost was asking after it, and Lord M. said, "I know where it was. I could get it." Lord M. said it was very like, and "I think a very handsome boy",—which I'm sure it *is*, and he *was*; I regretted much there was no print of it' (*The Girlhood of Queen Victoria*, ed. Viscount Esher (1912), vol. I, pp. 343–4, vol. II, p. 82). On 8 September 1841 Melbourne wrote to the Queen that he had found the portrait in his house, 'in a case . . ., having been sent up in order to be cleaned and varnished, which it very much required'. He offered to send it to the Queen for her to see and it arrived at Windsor on 14 September; the next day the Queen wrote to Melbourne: 'it is a beautiful & spirited picture tho not quite finished and certainly in want of cleaning, but it is very like,—so much so that the Queen is bold enough to ask Lord Melbourne to allow her to take possession of it.—She believes Lord Melbourne has another of the same and if he wd. very kindly let her have this, she wd. have it cleaned and put up in the Gallery here . . .' Melbourne, 'proud and happy' at this suggestion, 'could hardly venture to offer it himself, but it gives him the [?highest] pleasure to think that Your Majesty is desirous of possessing it' (W.R.A., A.4(5), C.4(47, 51), C.6(2), A.4(11), C.6(3)). The costume and background are unfinished.

A Whig statesman of liberal views; Home Secretary in Lord Grey's ministry, 1830–34, and Prime Minister, 1834 and 1835–41. He was a devoted adviser to the young Queen Victoria, who wrote on his death: 'I sincerely regret him, for he was truly attached to me, and though not a firm Minister he was a noble, kind-hearted, generous being.'

849. HORATIO, FIRST VISCOUNT NELSON (1758–1805) (*Plate* 180)

St. James's Palace. 94×58¼ in., 238,8×147,9 cm.

Full-length, standing on a rocky shore in a Rear-Admiral's full-dress uniform. He wears the King's gold medals for St. Vincent and the Nile, the ribbon and star of the Bath, the ribbon and star of the Order of St. Ferdinand and Merit of Naples (1801) and the Turkish Order of the Crescent (1799). In the background is a view of the bombardment of Copenhagen.

Painted for George IV. Received at Carlton House from Mrs. Hoppner on 7 April 1810 (Jutsham, *R/D*, f. 115), but work on the frames of Nos. 849, 851, 1024, 1026 seems to have been carried out earlier (see No. 1024). Wyatt's bill for carving and gilding in Lady Day quarter, 1811, included £52. 10s. for 'richly Carving . . . 5 Coronets . . . for 4 Admiral frames (2 for Nelson Vict & Duke of Bronte)' (W.R.A., Geo. 26890–1). Recorded in the East Ante-room at Carlton House in 1816 (59: 'A whole length portrait of Lord Nelson Mr Hoppner'); taken to the New Gallery at Windsor on 24 July 1828, subsequently taken back to the Riding House and then removed to the State Apartments at St. James's in 1832.

Literature: McKay and Roberts, pp. 182–3; O. Warner, *A Portrait of Lord Nelson* (1958), pp. 219, 261–2, 363; Tate Gallery, *The Romantic Movement*, 1959 (212).

Hoppner's bill, dated 6 January 1806, for pictures painted for the Prince of Wales, included 'Lord Vist Nelson—whole-Length' at £147 (W.R.A., Geo. 26829). Farington noted on 24 March 1802 (*Diary*, vol. I, p. 342) that Hoppner was planning to send a whole length of Nelson to the Royal Academy. A preparatory sketch of the head, possibly painted at a slightly earlier date, is in the National Maritime Museum. Nelson presumably sat to Hoppner after his return to England on 1 July 1801 after the battle of Copenhagen on 2 April. In H. Meyer's engraving of No. 849, published on 21 December 1802, the background is the same as Hoppner's; but in C. Turner's immensely popular engraving of it, published on 9 January 1806, the background was re-designed to show the battle of Trafalgar. In No. 849 there are slight *pentimenti* in the disposition of Nelson's gold medals. No. 849 was exhibited at the British Institution in 1820 (55) and 1827 (157).

A number of copies exist. On 2 March 1806 Farington noted that Hoppner 'now has the picture from the Prince to make copies from it'; in September the Prince ordered Hoppner to enable Lane to make the copy for the Town Hall at King's Lynn. Shepperson's copy, begun on 9 November 1824, was sent to Greenwich on 9 March 1825 (Jutsham, *Deliveries*, f. 72). A copy is at Fyvie Castle. A three-quarter-length copy is at Holkham. A copy was in the Bryant sale at Christie's, 23 June 1865 (43); a so-called small study for the portrait was in the C. F. Huth sale, Christie's, 19 March 1904 (60). A three-quarter-length copy in miniature by Bone, signed and dated April 1805 and painted for the Prince of Wales, is at Windsor (2606); another, signed and dated 1808, was sold at Sotheby's on 31 March 1949 (119). A derivation with considerable variations is in H.M.S. *Mercury*. The effigy of Nelson by Catherine Andras in Westminster Abbey was based on sittings from Nelson, but was dependent to a considerable extent on Hoppner's presentation, which was regarded as a brilliant likeness.

Nelson went to sea as a midshipman at the age of twelve; in

1804 he became Vice-Admiral of the White. His heroic career, with its famous victories at the Nile, 1798, and Copenhagen, 1801, ended in his death at the moment of victory at Trafalgar, 21 October 1805.

850. JOHN WILLETT PAYNE (1752–1803)
(Plate 178)

Windsor Castle (362). 50×40 in., 127×101,6 cm.

Three-quarter-length, standing, in the full-dress uniform of a Rear-Admiral, and wearing the Gold Medal for the Battle of 1 June 1764.

Painted for George IV. Hoppner's account of 6 January 1806 includes £73 for 'Admiral Paine' (W.R.A., Geo. 26829); it was received at Carlton House from Mrs. Hoppner on 7 April 1810 (Jutsham, *R/D*, f. 115) and recorded in store at Carlton House in 1816 (256). It was removed to the New Gallery at Windsor in May 1828; in 1859 it was in the Castle (*V.R. inv.*), and was thereafter placed in the Waterloo Chamber.

Literature: McKay and Roberts, p. 199; Collins Baker, *Windsor*, p. 169.

Payne had been promoted to Rear-Admiral in 1799. A smaller version of the portrait, however, shows the sitter in the undress uniform of a Captain;[1] it is probable, therefore, that Hoppner produced the type *c.* 1795 and that either the uniform in No. 850 was altered after Payne's promotion in 1799 or that it was painted after the promotion and on the basis of an earlier portrait. In June 1812 a frame for it was received at Carlton House from Ashlin and Collins (Jutsham, *R/D*, f. 131). On 25 May 1813 the portrait was sent to Colnaghi 'to ingrave from' (*ibid.*, f. 132); this was presumably for the mezzotint (?by C. Turner) published by Colnaghi on 12 November 1813. 'Admiral Payne' was in the sale of unfinished paintings and sketches in oils by Hoppner, sold at Christie's, 31 May 1823 (14); this may conceivably be the version at Weston Park. McKay and Roberts (*loc. cit.*) mention a copy in enamel by Bone, sold in his sale, 30 June 1832 (3), probably that now in the National Maritime Museum.

Appointed in 1793 Keeper of the Privy Seal and Private Secretary to the Prince of Wales, of whom he was an intimate companion and adviser; appointed Auditor and Secretary of the Duchy of Cornwall in 1791; in 1795 he commanded the squadron that conveyed Princess Caroline of Brunswick to England.

851. JOHN JERVIS, BARON JERVIS AND EARL OF ST. VINCENT (1735–1823)

St. James's Palace. 94½×58¼ in., 240×147,9 cm.

Full-length, standing on the quarter-deck of the *Victory* (the name is written on the gun beside him), holding a telescope in both hands; he wears Admiral's full-dress uniform with the ribbon and star of the Bath and, round his neck, the King's gold St. Vincent medal.

Painted for George IV. It was received at Carlton House from Mrs. Hoppner on 7 April 1810 (Jutsham, *R/D*, f. 115: 'A whole Length Portrait of Lord Sᵗ Vincent'), but work on the frames of Nos. 849, 851, 1024, 1026 seems to have been carried out earlier by Wyatt (see No. 1024). Recorded in the East Ante-room at Carlton House in 1816 (63); removed to the New Gallery at Windsor on 24 July 1828, but, after returning to No. 105 Pall Mall, it was taken to St. James's in 1832.

Literature: McKay and Roberts, p. 229.

1. The portrait, in the possession of the Earl of Bradford at Weston Park, is reproduced in *The Correspondence of George, Prince of Wales*, vol. I (1963), p. 304.

Presumably the portrait exhibited at the Royal Academy in 1809 (170). It was described as 'an admirable likeness' of St. Vincent in his old age (McKay and Roberts, *loc. cit.*) and was engraved for Lodge's *Portraits* (1830) by H. J. Robinson. A copy by Shepperson, commissioned by George IV, was one of the copies (see No. 1026) by Shepperson sent down to Greenwich on 9 March 1825. It is now in the National Maritime Museum.

Entered the Navy in 1749; appointed successively Commander-in-Chief of the West Indies Station, 1793, the Mediterranean, 1795, and the Channel, 1800; Admiral of the Red, 1805, First Lord of the Admiralty, 1801, Admiral of the Fleet, 1821. On 14 February 1797 he defeated the Spanish fleet at Cape St. Vincent; in this engagement the *Victory* was his flagship and Nelson's pendant was flying in the *Captain*.

After John Hoppner

852. GEORGE IV WHEN PRINCE OF WALES

St. James's Palace. 94×58 in., 238,8×147,3 cm.

Full-length, standing, in the robes of the Garter.

Painted for George IV and received at Carlton House from Owen on 22 January 1823: '. . . after a Picture Painted by Mʳ Hoopner in His Majesty's Possession. This Portrait is not finished—Mʳ Owen not being in Health sufficient to allow him to finish it' (Jutsham, *Receipts*, f. 166; Carlton House inv. of 1816, additional No. 602). Later at Hampton Court (736).

Literature: Law, 1881, 1898 (356).

An unfinished copy by Owen of No. 834; the Prince of Wales had promised Owen that he would sit to him for his portrait, but ultimately asked the painter to make use of the existing portrait by Hoppner (see below, pp. 88–9).

853. GEORGE IV WHEN PRINCE OF WALES

Windsor Castle (2551). 30×25 in., 76,2×63,5 cm.

Head and shoulders in Garter robes.

At Windsor in or before 1905; probably acquired by King Edward VII.

Literature: Collins Baker, *Windsor*, p. 172.

A bad late copy of the head in No. 834; formerly described as a portrait of William IV when Duke of Clarence.

854. PRINCESS SOPHIA

Windsor Castle (2726). 30×25 in., 76,2×63,5 cm.

Recorded at Buckingham Palace (771) in 1876 (*V.R. inv.*).

Literature: Collins Baker, *Windsor*, p. 167.

An early copy of No. 839.

855. PRINCESS AMELIA

Buckingham Palace. 37¼×29¾ in., 94,6×75,6 cm.

Stated on a label on the back to have been bought by George Bankes of Kingston Lacy at the sale of the effects of Princess Sophia (d. 1848); to have been bought by Alfred de Rothschild from Mrs. Porteous, George Bankes's grand-daughter; and to have been presented by Alfred de Rothschild to King Edward VII on 27 June 1909.

A contemporary copy of No. 840, formerly described as a portrait of Prince Ernest and thought to be a copy after Hoppner by West.

856. WILLIAM V (1748–1806), PRINCE OF ORANGE

Buckingham Palace. Millboard: $13\frac{1}{4} \times 10\frac{1}{2}$ in., $33,6 \times 26,7$ cm.
Head and shoulders in a painted oval, wearing Windsor uniform with the ribbon and star of the Garter.

Nos. 856, 857 were probably acquired by Queen Victoria; they are recorded at Buckingham Palace (No. 856 as No. 1160) in 1876 (*V.R. inv.*).

An early, probably contemporary, copy, on a reduced scale, from the three-quarter-length exhibited at the Royal Academy in 1800 (190) and now in the collection of H.M. The Queen of the Netherlands at Het Loo (where there is also a second version). It is possible that the portrait was commissioned by the Prince of Wales. The Prince of Orange wrote to Hoppner on 22 August 1799 asking 'if he has received directions of His Royal Highness the Prince of Wales to paint the Portrait of the Prince of Orange' and suggesting that he make a start on it that day (B.M., Add. MSS. 24212, f. 114; McKay and Roberts, p. 189).
Nos. 856, 857 bear, on canvas mounted on the back, early nineteenth-century inscriptions in German giving the identity of the sitters. It is probable, therefore, that they came from a German, possibly a Prussian, source. An enamel miniature by Bone, after the original by Hoppner, is at Windsor (2605).

Son of William IV, whom he succeeded in 1751, and Anne, Princess Royal of England, aunt of George III. When French Republican troops entered Holland he fled to England in January 1795 with his family. According to Farington the Prince, who was a very heavy drinker, was ragged by the Prince of Wales, but always kindly treated by George III. He was an intelligent man and a distinguished collector of pictures. His collection now forms a large and important part of the Mauritshuis. For his son see No. 713.

857. WILHELMINA, PRINCESS OF ORANGE (1751–1820)

Buckingham Palace. Millboard: $13\frac{1}{4} \times 10\frac{1}{2}$ in., $33,6 \times 26,7$ cm.
Head and shoulders in a painted oval, wearing a fur-lined wrap.

See No. 856; No. 857 was recorded at Buckingham Palace (1161) in 1876 (*V.R. inv.*).

An early, probably contemporary, copy on a reduced scale, from the three-quarter-length portrait, now in the collection of H.M. The Queen of the Netherlands at Het Loo, which was presumably painted as a pendant to the original of No. 856 (McKay and Roberts, p. 189).

Daughter of Prince Augustus William of Prussia, sister of King Frederick William II and great-granddaughter of George I; in 1767 she married Prince William V of Orange, whom she accompanied into exile in England.

William John Huggins

1781–1845. Marine painter, who began life as a sailor in the East India Company's service and began to exhibit, at the Royal Academy, in 1817. He was Marine Painter to William IV.
A view of St. Helena by Huggins, stated to be signed and dated 1832, was formerly at St. James's Palace (*V.R. inv.*, 15 October 1862; measurements given as 13×32 in.) it was probably related to the watercolour of St. Helena by Huggins in the Royal Library (Oppé, No. 384).

858. THE BATTLE OF TRAFALGAR: I. THE BEGINNING OF THE ACTION: THE *VICTORY* BREAKING THE LINE

St. James's Palace. 97×120 in., $246,4 \times 304,8$ cm.

The *Victory* forcing her way, soon after mid-day on 21 October 1805, between the *Redoutable* (on the left) and the *Bucentaure*; on the left are seen the *Royal Sovereign*, *Temeraire*, *Santa Ana* (Spanish) and *Fougueux* (French); on the right, the *Santissima Trinidad* (Spanish) and *Neptune* (French).

Nos. 858–60 were painted for William IV. They were all later at Hampton Court (Mrs. Jameson, 418; *The Stranger's Guide*, Nos. 963–5); No. 858 (Hampton Court No. 963) was moved to St. James's by command of Queen Victoria in 1864 (*V.R. inv.*).

The engraving of No. 858 by E. Duncan was published in March 1837 with a dedication to the King by the painter; the print describes the moment in the battle which is illustrated in No. 858. It was from the mizentop of the *Redoutable* that the shot was fired, at about 1.15 p.m., which killed Lord Nelson (see No. 762). Huggins exhibited at Exeter Hall in the spring of 1834 two of the pictures (Nos. 858, 860) 'on which [he] has been for some time employed' (*Arnold's Library of the Fine Arts*, vol. III (N.S.) (1834), pp. 579–80).

859. THE BATTLE OF TRAFALGAR: II. THE CLOSE OF THE ACTION

Kensington Palace. 96×124 in., $243,8 \times 314,9$ cm.
Two shattered French ships and a British ship towards the end of the battle.

See No. 858; formerly at Hampton Court (1058).

Literature: Law, 1881, 1898 (899).

Apparently the last of the three pictures to be completed; it was shown at the British Institution in 1837 (375). A study, or reduced version, of No. 859 was in a private collection in 1966.

860. THE BATTLE OF TRAFALGAR: III. THE STORM AFTER THE BATTLE

Kensington Palace. 98×124 in., $248,9 \times 314,9$ cm.
The *Santissima Trinidad*, dismasted and rolling heavily; the *Victory* is under jury masts with Nelson's flag half-mast high; the *Royal Sovereign* is towed by the frigate *Euryalus*.

See No. 858; formerly at Hampton Court (1057).

Literature: Law, 1881, 1898 (898).

No. 860 illustrates an episode in the heavy storm which struck the fleets on 22 October 1805, the day after the battle of Trafalgar. The storm caused the loss of a number of French and Spanish ships which would otherwise have been held as prizes after the victory. The *Santissima Trinidad* was cleared and sunk.

Julius Caesar Ibbetson

1759–1817. Painter of landscapes and genre scenes. Many of his landscapes were painted in Wales and the Lake District.

Style of Julius Caesar Ibbetson

861. LANDSCAPE WITH A RIVER

Hampton Court (649). $16\frac{7}{8} \times 22$ in., $42,9 \times 55,9$ cm.

A river flowing between wooded banks; a group of men are hauling a tree across the river below a rocky waterfall.

Nos. 861, 862 were apparently in the royal collection by 1852 and were recorded at Hampton Court in 1859 (*V.R. inv.*).

Literature: Law, 1881, 1898 (439); Collins Baker, *Hampton Court*, p. 165.

Nos. 861, 862 are close in style to Ibbetson's late landscapes in oil, and are probably of subjects in the Lake District, but they do not seem of sufficiently good quality to have been painted by Ibbetson himself.

862. LANDSCAPE WITH A WATERFALL

Hampton Court (646). $17\frac{1}{4} \times 22\frac{1}{4}$ in., $43,8 \times 56,5$ cm.

A high waterfall pouring between steep hills; a shepherd's hut in the foreground.

See No. 861.

Literature: Law, 1881, 1898 (433); Collins Baker, *Hampton Court*, p. 165.

See No. 861.

John Jackson

1778–1831. Portrait-painter. He came to London in 1804 from Yorkshire and became a close friend of Wilkie and Haydon. He exhibited regularly at the Royal Academy between 1804 and 1830. He exhibited (principally subject-pictures) at the British Institution between 1808 and 1829. On 13 September 1807 Jackson submitted to the Prince of Wales a bill for twelve guineas for a portrait of 'the late Duke of Richmond', i.e., Charles Lennox, 3rd Duke (1735–1806); the receipt for payment was signed on 26 September 1808 (W.R.A., Geo. 26852).

863. FREDERICK, DUKE OF YORK

Buckingham Palace. 36×28 in., $91,4 \times 71,1$ cm.

Head and shoulders, wearing the star of the Garter and (?) the ribbon of the Bath under his coat.

Acquired by H.M. Queen Mary, perhaps *c.* 1900.

The type is close to that engraved after Jackson by S. W. Reynolds, published on 1 June 1825, which was close in turn to the head in the three-quarter-length in military uniform engraved by J. Wright (published 16 August 1822) from a portrait by Jackson in the painter's possession. Jackson had exhibited a portrait of the Duke at the Royal Academy in 1822 (127). A version of No. 863 is in the National Portrait Gallery (1615); another was on the art-market in London in 1921.

John Samuel Willes Johnson

1793–1857. Entered the navy in 1807 and acquired the rank of Captain in 1846. Among his last appointments was (1835) to the Coast Guard (W. R. O'Byrne, *A Naval Biographical Dictionary* (1849), pp. 585–6).

864. A STEAM YACHT OFF DOVER

Buckingham Palace. $28\frac{1}{2} \times 39\frac{3}{4}$ in., $72,4 \times 101$ cm.

Signed and dated: *Willes Johnson / 1830.*

A steam yacht, with a smaller yacht, off Dover, where the jetties are lined with spectators. In the bows of the smaller boat is a stout figure in a yachting-cap with the ribbon and star of the Garter (?).

Recorded at Windsor (1172) in 1879 (*V.R. inv.*).

The figure in the bows of the smaller boat is presumably intended to represent George IV or William IV.

George Jones

1786–1869. Painter of landscapes, genre scenes, battles, biblical and historical subjects and current events. He served in the Militia—he held a Captain's commission in the Montgomeryshire Militia—and joined the army of occupation in Paris after Waterloo. He 'has not only been a spectator of war, but an actor in its scenes' and George IV was impressed with his pictures of Waterloo and Vittoria (*Athenaeum* (1832), p. 505). He exhibited, at the Royal Academy and British Institution, between 1803 and 1870.

865. THE BATTLE OF VITTORIA (*Plate* 247)

St. James's Palace. $93\frac{3}{4} \times 127$ in., $238,1 \times 322,6$ cm.

Signed and dated: *G. Jones / [?1822].* The date is very hard to decipher.

The city of Vittoria lies in sunlight in the distance, surrounded by the Pyrenees. In the foreground on the left is the Marquess of Wellington surrounded by his staff; in front of him is a Hussar General, leading heavy cavalry and hussars. On the right is a General Officer riding beside an officer in the Horse Guards; beyond them are the Foot Guards advancing with the Rifle Brigade and other troops. In the distance can be seen the general advance upon the city.

Presumably acquired by or painted for George IV and hanging at St. James's by early 1824 (see No. 866). On 1 August 1829 it was received, with No. 866, at Carlton House from St. James's Palace, where both pictures had been hanging in the Throne Room; they were returned to St. James's in 1830 (Jutsham, *Receipts*, f. 272).

The battle was fought on 21 June 1813. Wellington, in command of the allied army of British, Portuguese and Spanish troops, inflicted a decisive defeat on the French under Joseph Bonaparte and Marshal Jourdan. No. 865 shows the scene in the early evening of the day, when Wellington was directing the final advance on the city and beyond. The victory marked the climax of the campaign in the Peninsula; the Prince Regent, in his congratulatory letter to Wellington, announced that he had created him a Field-Marshal. Joseph Bonaparte's losses included the pictures which he had stolen from the Spanish royal collection and which the King of Spain presented to Wellington. Jones had served in the Peninsula, but it does not seem to be known at what stage in his career he acquired the materials used in composing No. 865. A smaller version is at Petworth (198).

866. THE BATTLE OF WATERLOO

St. James's Palace. $99\frac{3}{4} \times 126\frac{1}{4}$ in., $238,1 \times 321,3$ cm.

On the right the Duke of Wellington, mounted on Copenhagen and attended by his staff, directing the final advance at the end of the day (see also No. 764); on the extreme right are Hussars charging. On the left the Union Brigade of Cavalry is advancing; further down in the centre the Foot Guards are moving forward. In the distance are seen Napoleon in the sunken road and (?) Marshal Ney attempting to rally the Imperial Guard. On the horizon in the distance is La Belle Alliance.

Presumably acquired by or painted for George IV. On 20 May 1824 Mrs. Arbuthnot saw it hanging at St. James's (*Journal*, ed. F. Bamford and Duke of Wellington (1950), vol. I, p. 313). On 1 August 1829 it was received, with No. 865, at Carlton House from St. James's Palace, where they had been hanging in the Throne Room; they were returned to St. James's in 1830 (Jutsham, *Receipts*, f. 272).

Painted as a pendant to No. 865. It is not apparently known when Jones began to collect material for his pictures of the battle but he was early obtaining information at the British army's headquarters. Some of his illustrations to *The Battle of Waterloo . . .* 'By a Near Observer' are dated 1816. At the British Institution he exhibited pictures relating to Waterloo in 1816 (149, 160, 163) and 1817 (207, 218, 219); in 1820 he exhibited there (48) the enormous picture which is now in the Royal Hospital and in 1822 he showed (43) a large diagram of the battle. On 27 April 1821 Jones told Farington (*Diary*, vol. VIII, p. 280) that he was at work on a picture of the battle, 15 feet wide, for Watson Taylor, in which many portraits of officers would be introduced. At the Royal Academy he showed in 1816 (23) a sketch for a large picture of 'Waterloo: Final defeat of the French . . . The View drawn on the spot'. In 1822 Jones exhibited at the Royal Academy (313) a picture of the battle which must, according to the catalogue, have been very close to No. 866, though with apparent differences in the figures grouped around Wellington. In 1827 Jones exhibited there (231) another picture of the close of the action, seen from the French side, and as late as 1853 (224) he was exhibiting pictures of the battle.

867. THE BANQUET AT THE CORONATION OF GEORGE IV (*Plate* 246)

Buckingham Palace. 43 × 35⅜ in., 109,2 × 89,8 cm.

The scene in Westminster Hall on the afternoon of 19 July 1821 at the moment of the entry of the King's Champion. The Champion, Henry Dymoke, mounted and in full armour and attended by his pages, is escorted by the Deputy Earl Marshal, Lord Howard of Effingham, and the Lord High Constable, the Duke of Wellington. In front of them a Herald reads the challenge. The King, robed and crowned, is seated on the throne under the south window of the hall, and raises his cup to drink to the Champion. He is attended by officers of state and others with the regalia; at the table are seated the Dukes of York, Sussex, Gloucester, Clarence and Cambridge and Prince Leopold of Saxe-Coburg. The King's Carver, the Earl of Denbigh, stands by the table. In the Royal Box on the right of the King are members of the royal family; opposite is the Foreign Ministers' Box; the two tiers of galleries down each side of the hall are filled with spectators, the peeresses in the lower tiers. A great crowd of peers and others is disposed on both sides of the steps leading up to the royal platform. The hall is lit by twenty-eight magnificent lustres suspended from the angels in the roof.

Purchased for the royal collection in 1911.

A large reproduction in colour of No. 867 is included in Robert Whittaker's *Ceremonial of the Coronation of . . . King George the Fourth* (1822). It is there stated that the painting had been commissioned by the Earl of Liverpool (No. 903) and was published by permission of Lady Liverpool (see also *Athenaeum* (1832), p. 505). It is apparently an accurate representation of the scene (see, for example, the full account in the *Annual Register* for 1821 (1822), Appendix to Chronicle,

pp. 328–89; and Haydon's *Diary*, ed. W. B. Pope (Harvard University Press), vol. II (1960), pp. 349–51); many of the spectators standing on the floor and steps of Westminster Hall are clearly recognisable portraits.

George Francis Joseph

1764–1846. Portrait and subject painter (principally), who is said to have been born in Dublin. He exhibited at the Royal Academy between 1788 and 1846, and at the British Institution between 1806 and 1834.

868. SPENCER PERCEVAL (1762–1812)

Kensington Palace. 29½ × 25 in., 74,9 × 63,5 cm.

Signed: *G. F. Joseph A.R.A. | Posthumous Portrait*

Head and shoulders, holding a paper in his left hand.

In the collection of George IV; received at Carlton House on 18 June 1814 from Mrs. Joseph (Jutsham, *R/D*, f. 311); in store at Carlton House in 1816 (285); later at Hampton Court (890).

Literature: Law, 1881, 1898 (373).

A good version of the posthumous portrait, based on a death-mask, produced by Joseph after Perceval's assassination. A three-quarter-length version belongs to the Earl of Harrowby; smaller versions are in the Houses of Parliament and the National Portrait Gallery (4); another was sold at Christie's, 2 July 1954 (96). An engraving of the design was published by C. Turner on 1 August 1812. It is possible, though perhaps unlikely, that No. 868 is the version recorded by Pyne (vol. I, *Frogmore*, pp. 18–19) in the Bow Drawing-Room at Frogmore. Queen Charlotte is stated to have been reduced to tears on seeing so faithful a likeness of the dead statesman when she visited Joseph's studio with some of the Princesses. Joseph exhibited a posthumous portrait of Perceval at the Royal Academy in 1813 (274).

Son of the 2nd Earl of Egmont; Solicitor-General, 1801, Attorney-General, 1802, Chancellor of the Exchequer, 1807; became Prime Minister in 1809, but was assassinated in the lobby of the House of Commons on 11 May 1812.

Angelica Kauffmann

1741–1807. Decorative painter and painter of portraits and of historical and classical subjects. Born in Switzerland, she studied and worked in Italy and came to London in 1766. She left England in 1781. In the Bedchamber at Buckingham House in the time of George III was: 'A Lady at Tambour work Angelico Koufman,' measurements given as 35 × 29 in. (Geo. III, *Buck Ho.*) which does not appear to be in the royal collection today.[1] See No. 1210.

869. AUGUSTA, DUCHESS OF BRUNSWICK, WITH HER SON CHARLES GEORGE AUGUSTUS (*Plate* 16)

Buckingham Palace. 106½ × 73¾ in., 270,5 × 187,3 cm.

Signed and dated: *Angelica Pinx: A:o 1767.*

Full-length, standing and supporting her infant son on a ledge which is decorated with a gilded ram's head and

---

1. It may have been a version of the so-called *Morning Amusement*, of which a version was exhibited at Kenwood in 1955 (6), or the portrait of Mary Townshend at her tambour, formerly in the collection of Lord Sidney and sold by Parke-Bernet, New York, 16 April 1949 (57) and measuring 36 × 28 in.

wreath; a trophy of arms is suspended from the upper left corner. In the foreground stands an urn decorated with a relief of Fame crowning the victor while Cupid draws roses from the womb of his consort, an allusion to the Brunswicks which is described in the inscription on the urn: *Carol. ILLE de Bruns. & Prin. Hered.* | *A: MDCCLX M. Jul. apud Emsdorff VICTORIA* | *et A. MDCCLXIV M. Jan. apud Britannos AMORE* | *Corona* [*tus*].

Presumably painted for Augusta, Princess of Wales. An account by Bradburn and France for work in the six months ending on 1 April 1768 included £125. 19s. for '2 very rich whole length Tabernacle Frames carved, and partly gilt in burnished Gold, for the Pictures of Her Majesty the Queen of Denmark [see No. 720] and Her Royal Highness, the Princess of Brunswick . . .'; their account for work done in the six months ending on 1 October 1767 had included £1 for one 'straining Room' [(?) = frame] for the picture of 'her Royal Highness the Princess of Brunswick p Mrs Jelicot'; and in their account for work in the six months ending on 1 April 1769 was 5s. for 'taking down the large Picture of the Princess of Brunswick, taking it out of the Frame (in order to be copied) and putting the Frame up out of the way' (D. of Cornwall MSS., vols. LIV (i), LV (i), LVI (i)). Presumably at Carlton House in 1794, when it was cleaned by Simpson (P.R.O., H.O. 73, 23). Recorded in store at Carlton House in 1816 (248); later at Hampton Court (603) and Kensington.

Literature: Waagen (1854), vol. II, p. 368; Law, 1881, 1898 (502); Lady V. Manners and G. C. Williamson, *Angelica Kauffmann* (1924), pp. 24, 193; Graves Art Gallery, Sheffield, *Famous British Women Artists*, 1953 (54).

Painted during a visit by the Princess to London, where she gave birth to a son at St. James's Palace on 8 February 1766. The inscription alludes presumably to the Hereditary Prince's victory at Emsdorff on 16 July 1760, when he was wounded, and to his marriage to the English Princess nearly four years later. No. 869 was engraved by Spilsbury with a dedication to the Princess of Wales from her 'most humble & most dutiful Servant, Angelica' (Chaloner Smith, p. 1324).

Tilly Kettle

1735–86. Portrait-painter. He exhibited at the Society of Artists between 1765 and 1776 and at the Royal Academy in 1777 and 1781–3. He was in India, 1769–76, and died on a second journey to the East.

Attributed to Tilly Kettle

870. THE TESHU LAMA (*d.* 1780) GIVING AUDIENCE

Windsor Castle (1373). 58 × 74⅝ in., 147,3 × 189,5 cm.

The Lama, with his attendants, receiving the offering of a white handkerchief.

Probably presented to George III; recorded by Pyne in the King's Drawing-Room at Hampton Court (vol. II, *Hampton Court*, p. 52; 'An Indian Subject, *an Asiatic Merchant exhibiting silk and other valuable merchandise to a Chinese Grandee*, painted by Kettle'); in the Hampton Court inv. of 1835, No. 870 is described (559) as 'The Introduction of Linen to the Great Mogul. Kettle'.

Mrs. Mildred Archer has identified the subject with the reception of George Bogle by the Teshu Lama at the monastery of Deshi-rib-gyal in southern Tibet on 8 November 1774. George Bogle (1746–81) was a young Scots merchant who had been Assistant Secretary to the Board of Revenue under the Governor of Bengal and later Secretary to the Select Committee. Warren Hastings appointed him, on 13 May 1774, Envoy to the Lama of Tibet. Details in Bogle's description of his first meeting with the Lama fit well with details in No. 870. The Lama's small apartment was 'hung round with different coloured silks', views of places in Tibet; the Lama (whose costume and appearance he describes) was seated cross-legged on his throne, attended by his physician and cup-bearer. Bogle, who may be the figure standing on the left in No. 870, laid the Governor's presents before his host, 'together with a white Pelong handkerchief on my own part, according to the custom of the country' (C. R. Markham, *Narratives of the Mission of George Bogle to Tibet . . .* (1876), pp. 83–4). Bogle was back in Calcutta in the early summer of 1775 and could have provided Kettle with the material and information necessary in compiling his picture. It is conceivable that Warren Hastings, who was exceedingly pleased with the success of Bogle's mission, ordered the picture and presented it to George III.

Sir Thomas Lawrence

1769–1830. Portrait-painter (principally), who showed at a very early age a facility for drawing and was earning money at Devizes, Oxford and Bath with portrait-drawings in pastel and pencil. In London in 1786 he was confident that only Reynolds could rival him 'for the painting of a head'. He began to exhibit pastels at the Royal Academy in 1787. In 1789 he exhibited there his first full-length, the portrait of Lady Cremorne (Garlick, *Lawrence*, pl. 1) who persuaded Queen Charlotte to sit to Lawrence in the autumn of that year (see above, p. 22). The portraits of Queen Charlotte (*Fig.* X) and Princess Amelia (No. 881) were exhibited at the Royal Academy in 1790. The King admired Lawrence's work at this period and in 1792 appointed him to succeed Reynolds as Principal Painter, a post he held until his death. In addition to his own portraits of George III (see Nos. 871, 872), he continued to produce copies, perhaps until as late as *c.* 1815, of Reynolds's official portraits of the King and Queen (see Nos. 1033, 1034). Farington was told by Hoppner on 5 May 1795 (unpublished) that when the King saw Lawrence's Byronic portrait of Lord Mountstuart (Garlick, *Lawrence*, pl. 33) at the Royal Academy in 1795 (86) he had 'started back with disgust'. He was, however, 'highly pleased' with Lawrence's works at the Academy in 1799. On 29 July 1801 Farington (unpublished) told Lawrence 'for his consideration what I had heard of the King's prejudice abt. the picture of Hamlet' (see below). The King greatly admired the portrait of Thurlow (No. 914).

Lawrence's name was among those linked, without foundation, to the Princess of Wales (No. 874) in the spreading of the scandals which led to the Delicate Investigation of 1806, during which Lawrence swore an affidavit on 24 September. As early as June 1804 the Prince of Wales was intending to sit to Lawrence, for a full-length for Lord Fitzwilliam (Farington, *Diary*, vol. II, p. 255); but Lawrence 'waited in vain 4 hours & a half' and does not seem to have been introduced to the Prince before 28 July 1814, when Lawrence was presented to him by Lord Stewart at a Levee (*ibid.*, unpublished, 29 July); by 21 August (*ibid.*) the Prince had sat '4 or 5 times for His Portrait to Lawrence at Lawrence's House'. On 22 April 1815 Lawrence was knighted by the Regent. In 1818–20 he was abroad on his delayed trip to paint the portraits now in the Waterloo Gallery: successively at Aix-la-Chapelle, Vienna and Rome. In 1825 he was in Paris to paint Nos. 884, 890. Lawrence had been employed to assist Michael Bryan in valuing the Regent's pictures and drawing up the inventory of pictures at Carlton House (see above, p. l, inv. No. 45) and gave help and advice to George IV on the formation of his collection.

Under No. 919 below (and above, pp. xxxiii–iv) is an indication of the extent to which versions and copies of Lawrence's portrait of George IV were distributed. In the Royal Archives are documents concerning the versions painted, c. 1823–9, for despatch to Scotland, probably for William Adam, the Lord Chief Commissioner, for Lord Eldon, Sir William Knighton, the Duke of Devonshire, Sir Charles Long, Lord Francis Conyngham, the Duke of Orléans, Lord Ravensworth, Cardinal Consalvi, John Nash and Sir William Curtis (W.R.A., Geo. 26530, 26533, 26545, 26558, 26579, 26583, 26645, 26656, 26664, 26686, 26687, 26752, 27041, 27043); the frames for a number of these were made by George Morant. The portrait for Curtis—'A Half Length Portrait of His Majesty in a Blue Coat & decoration with Orders, in a Gilt Frame'—was received at Carlton House from the Wardrobe and sent on 12 February 1825 to Lawrence, at Knighton's orders, for despatch to Curtis as a present from the King (Jutsham, Deliveries, f. 71, PP., f. 103). In addition to the portraits catalogued or mentioned below, George IV owned at one time other portraits by Lawrence. For a portrait of the Archduchess Charles, see below, No. 891. A half-length of Sir John McMahon (measurements given as 43½ × 34 in.) was received at Carlton House from Lawrence on 9 May 1815 (Jutsham, R/D, f. 339). It was in store at Carlton House in 1816 (379), but was given later, presumably by William IV, to Sir William Knighton (Garlick, Catalogue, p. 137). A portrait of Benjamin West, painted for £525 while Sir Benjamin Bloomfield was Keeper of the Privy Purse, was in the inventory of 'Carleton Palace' (666) but was given by William IV to the National Gallery in 1836 (now in the Tate Gallery (144), Garlick, op. cit., 195). The portrait of Angerstein, painted for £210 while Sir William Knighton was Keeper of the Privy Purse, was also recorded at 'Carleton Palace' (680) and given to the National Gallery (129) by William IV in 1836 (see M. Davies, Catalogue of The British School (1959), pp. 72–3; Garlick, op. cit., p. 19). George IV acquired, for £525, the portrait of Kemble as Hamlet which was at 'Carleton Palace' (656), was also given to the National Gallery by William IV in 1836 and is now in the Tate Gallery (142) (Garlick, op. cit., p. 116). When Sir Benjamin Bloomfield was Keeper of the Privy Purse, Lawrence painted for George IV half-lengths of Lady Conyngham and Lady Elizabeth Conyngham (Fig. XXVI) at £315 each, and a 'Kit Cat Portrait' of Lady Maria Conyngham at £210. The portraits of Lady Conyngham and Lady Maria (Fig. XXVII), in gilt frames, were placed by the King's commands in his bedroom at St. James's on 3 June 1826. On 30 December 1828 they were sent to Windsor, but they returned to St. James's on 25 April 1829. Corden submitted on 31 March 1830 his bill for fifteen guineas for a copy of the portrait of Lady Maria (W.R.A., Geo. 26596, 26643; Jutsham, Deliveries, ff. 81, 214, 215). The three portraits are probably those described by Garlick, Catalogue, pp. 58, 59. They appear to have belonged subsequently to the Conyngham family, but only the portrait of Lady Conyngham remains with the family.

George IV also owned the drawing of himself in armour which is in the Royal Library (Oppé, No. 412); in 1839 Queen Victoria purchased the pastel of Miss White of the Castle Inn, Devizes, drawn by Lawrence in 1784, which is now at Windsor (1359; Garlick, op. cit., p. 265).

Documents in the Royal Archives indicate that Lawrence received from the Crown over £7,000 for portraits of George IV and that the other portraits supplied to the King cost him over £17,500, excluding some £3,000 for expenses involved in Lawrence's visits to the Continent.

871. GEORGE III

Windsor Castle (179). 106 × 70 in., 269,2 × 177,8 cm.

Full-length, standing, in Garter robes, holding his glove in his left hand and resting his right on a table beside the plumed hat of the order; in the distance is a landscape with the Thames and the east end of Eton College Chapel.

Painted for George IV. Apparently placed over 'the Chimney Piece in the Anti Room to the Throne Room' at St. James's Palace, whence it was removed in June, and sent to Windsor on 13 July, 1829, 'I believe by the Command of His Majesty'; 'A whole Length Portrait of George The Third in a Carved & Gilt Frame, Festoon Carved & Gilt Ornaments, for Outside Ornaments, Crown &c Painted by Sir Thomas Lawrence' (Jutsham, *Receipts*, f. 269). Recorded at Hampton Court in 1835 (530), but in the Waterloo Chamber in 1837 (*Guide* to the Castle), already with the misleading attribution to Beechey.

Literature: Collins Baker, *Windsor*, p. 11; Garlick, *Lawrence*, p. 38, *Catalogue*, p. 85.

Although consistently attributed to Beechey since 1837 (e.g., *V.R. inv.* (1868);[1] Collins Baker, *loc. cit.*), No. 871 is undoubtedly by Lawrence. A 'Large Whole Length Portrait of The late King' is listed, at £525, among the portraits painted by Lawrence when Sir Benjamin Bloomfield was Keeper of the Privy Purse (i.e., 1818–23; W.R.A., Geo. 26642; *Letters of George IV*, vol. III, 1592). No. 871 appears to have been painted throughout by Lawrence himself, but it is based, with slight variations in costume, setting and accessories, on the portrait which he had painted for the City of Coventry (Garlick, *Lawrence*, pl. 7), and which had been exhibited at the Royal Academy in 1792 (65); a version of the Coventry portrait was formerly at Patshull. A version painted for the City of Liverpool, and received there in 1821, is very close to No. 871. In both No. 871 and the Liverpool version the head is fuller and broader than in the portrait of 1792; Lawrence may have revised the type but can hardly have had a fresh sitting from the King at this late date. A head and shoulders copy is at Schloss Marienburg; and see No. 872. No. 871 was exhibited at the British Institution in 1833 (35).

872. GEORGE III (*Plate* 188)

St. James's Palace. 67¾ × 46½ in., 172,1 × 118,1 cm.

Three-quarter-length, seated, in a richly carved chair, wearing robes of state with the collar of the Garter and holding a paper in his right hand; his crown is beside him.

Recorded at St. James's in 1871 (*V.R. inv.*).

Literature: Garlick, *Catalogue*, p. 85.

Possibly the portrait commissioned by George III as a present to Henry Addington, later 1st Viscount Sidmouth. The King had earlier sent a portrait of himself to hang in Addington's room at White Lodge, but in October 1804 it was reported that he 'proposes to send another in his full robes, to be placed in the great drawing-room there. Mr. Addington showed me the King's letter announcing this latter picture . . . it says "he has chosen to be painted in the royal robes, and in that state of ceremony in which he had been accustomed to hear the most honest and upright

---

1. Redgrave seems to have regarded it as by Lawrence, but to have altered the attribution in deference to current opinion.

Speaker whom the House of Commons had ever chosen" '
(*The Diary and Correspondence of Charles Abbott, Lord Colchester*,
ed. Lord Colchester, 3 vols. (1861) vol. I, p. 528). If the
King's intention was not fulfilled immediately, the promised
portrait could have been the 'Half length picture of the
King for the Speaker of the House of Commons' on which
Lawrence began work on 3 March 1809. He worked that
day on the portrait from 8 in the morning till 5.15 in the
evening and again from 10 p.m. till 1 a.m.; and on the next
day he worked from 5 a.m. to 4 p.m., 'when He sent the
picture to the Speakers who was to have a grand dinner that
evening' (Farington, *Diary*, vol. V, p. 123). The description
by Lord Colchester of the portrait of the King would fit
No. 872 and it is significant that Addington had been concerned in 1802 with Lawrence's portrait of the King for
Liverpool (unpublished, 13 and 17 February 1804). No. 872
is certainly entirely by Lawrence, although the head is very
close to his earlier portraits of the King (see No. 871), especially to the head in the full-length in Liverpool Town Hall.

873. GEORGE IV (*Plate* 216)

St. James's Palace. 114 × 79 in., 289,6 × 200,7 cm.

Full-length, standing, in Coronation robes, resting his right
hand on the same table as in No. 919 beside the Imperial
Crown; the King wears the collars of the Golden Fleece, the
Guelphic Order, the Bath and the Garter.

Painted for the King, probably to be placed over the fireplace in
the Throne Room at St. James's, where it still hangs.

Literature: R.A., *King's Pictures* (121), *Kings and Queens*, 1953 (254);
Garlick, *Lawrence*, p. 38, *Catalogue*, p. 87.

Apparently painted at the end of 1821. It was probably to
this portrait that Sir George Nayler was referring when
he wrote on 8 December 1821 asking for 'the use of His
Majesty's Portrait now painting by Sir Thomas Lawrence
to have a Plate engraven for the History of the Coronation
shewing the Full Dress of the Royal Robes at that great
solemnity' (W.R.A., Geo. Add. 3, 13). On 19 May 1830
Lord Farnborough wrote a request for the loan to the exhibition at the British Institution of the portrait of the King 'in
the Throne Room at St. James's' (*ibid.*, Geo. 26599). In
fact No. 873 is fundamentally a good version of Lawrence's
standard full-length of the King in Garter robes (see Nos.
919–22) over which the Coronation robes have been painted.
The collar of the 'Garter' portraits is visible above the ruff
of the Coronation robes; the edge of the folds of the original
Garter robes can still be seen on the floor in No. 873; so can
such details as the belt going round the waist. Copies of No.
873 are in the Royal Academy and the Walker Art Gallery,
Liverpool.
The sword seen in this portrait has been identified by Mr.
A. V. B. Norman at Windsor (34).

874. CAROLINE, PRINCESS OF WALES, AND PRINCESS CHARLOTTE (*Plate* 187)

Buckingham Palace. 119 × 80 in., 302,2 × 203,2 cm.

The Princess of Wales stands, tuning a large harp (on which
she was an accomplished performer), looking down at her
daughter who hands her a sheet of music entitled '[ ]MTION';
a portfolio of music lies at the child's feet.

Painted for Anne, Marchioness of Townshend (d. 1819), Mistress
of the Robes to the Princess of Wales.[1] Acquired by Queen Vic-

---

1. In a codicil (5 August 1821) to her will, the Princess had asked: 'I
give the large picture of myself and late daughter to the Cardinal
Albano.'

toria in 1843 for 200 guineas (MS. Catalogue of Queen Victoria's
private pictures &c.); subsequently at Windsor (454).

Literature: Williams, vol. I, pp. 253–9; W. T. Whitley, *Art in
England 1800-1820* (1928), pp. 18–19, 34; T. S. R. Boase, *English
Art 1800–1870* (1959), p. 11; Garlick, *Lawrence*, p. 31, *Catalogue*,
p. 51.

Painted at the Princess's residence at Montague House,
Blackheath, in circumstances described by Lawrence and by
the Princess of Wales during the Delicate Investigation into
her conduct (Williams, *loc. cit.*; letter, 27 March 1868, to Sir
George Scharf from Richard Evans (copy in archives of
Surveyor's office)). Princess Charlotte was living at that
time at Shooters Hill and came to Montague House in order
to sit to Lawrence. Lawrence stated in his affidavit of 24
September 1806 that he had stayed several nights at Montague House in 1801; the Princess, in a statement sent to
George III on 2 October 1806, stated that Lawrence
'began a large picture of me and of my daughter, towards
the latter end of 1800, or the beginning of 1801', and that
he had wished to stay at Montague House overnight so
that he could work on the picture early in the morning, before
the Princess and her daughter came for sittings. She added
that the picture had left her house by April 1801. Farington
was shown the picture by Lawrence on 12 March 1801;
Lawrence was unable to finish the picture in time for the
R.A. of 1801 ('He can plead the Princess having been too
unwell to sit') and the Princess of Wales was offended with
the Council of the R.A. for not granting him time to finish
a picture 'which is painted much to Her satisfaction'
(*Diary*, vol. I, pp. 304, 306, 307). It was exhibited at the
Royal Academy in 1802 (72). There is a *pentimento* in the
left outline of Princess Charlotte's dress, which was originally
further to the left; there are shadowy indications of a bust
of Minerva (?) on a ledge to the left of the Princess of
Wales. The figure of Princess Charlotte is closely related to
Lawrence's single portrait of her (No. 875). A drawing by
Lawrence in the collection of Sir Arundell Neave (*Fig.* 17)
is probably a preliminary study for No. 874. It shows the
Princess unwrapping her harp; the absence of a child may
indicate that it was not part of the Princess's first intention
that her daughter should be included in the design. An
oil-sketch, closely related to No. 874, was on the London
art-market in 1967; but the two heads are not those of the
Princess and her daughter and one may assume that
Lawrence's design was being exploited for another sitter.

875. PRINCESS CHARLOTTE

Windsor Castle (328). 30 × 25¼ in., 76,2 × 64,1 cm.

Half-length, seated, holding a birdcage in her left hand; a
bird is perching on her right hand.

Presumably painted for George III or Queen Charlotte (the
canvas has on the back the brand of George III's personal property); removed from the King's Sitting-room in Buckingham House
to Windsor in 1804–5 (Geo. III, *Removals*: 'Portrait of H.R.H. the
Princess Charlotte of Wales by Lawrence') and recorded in the
King's Closet in the Private Apartments at Windsor in 1813,
1816 (Legge's lists).

Literature: Garlick, *Lawrence*, p. 32, *Catalogue*, p. 54.

The design is closely related to the figure of the Princess in
No. 874, with bird and birdcage substituted for sheets of
music. It appears to be inferior in quality to No. 874 and
to have been copied from it. Bourlier's engraving of No. 875
was published by Harding on 19 May 1806; T. Garner's
was published in S. C. Hall's *Royal Gallery of Art* (1858).
Morant's bill includes, under 23 October 1826, seven

guineas 'To a Richly Ornamentᵈ Frame for a portrait Of the. Princess by order of Sir Thoˢ Lawrence' (W.R.A., Geo. 26545).

876. FREDERICK, DUKE OF YORK (*Plate* 197)

Windsor Castle (182). 108¼ × 70½ in., 274,9 × 179,1 cm.
Full-length, standing in Field-Marshal's uniform with the star of the Garter and the collars of the Garter and the Bath, holding across his body the mantle of the Garter and resting his left hand, with his baton. on a ledge beside the plumed hat of the order. He wears the Garter round his leg.

Painted for George IV; recorded in the inventory of 'Carleton Palace' (644: 'Full length Portrait of the late Duke of York. Lawrence. In the Waterloo Gallery, Windsor Castle').

Literature: Williams, vol. I, p. 358; Waagen (1838), vol. I, p. 168; Collins Baker, *Windsor*, p. 218; R.A., *King's Pictures* (122); Garlick, *Lawrence*, p. 64, *Catalogue*, p. 205.

Painted for George IV; Lawrence's account of 4 January 1817 included £420 for 'A Whole-length Portrait (large size) of H.R.H. The Duke of York' (W.R.A., Geo. 26634; *Letters of George IV*, vol. III, 1592). It had been exhibited at the Royal Academy in 1816 (61). It was in Lawrence's studio at his death and was claimed on 22 January 1830 (Garlick, *Catalogue*, p. 277); Seguier's account of 10 April 1830 includes four guineas for cleaning and varnishing the canvas (W.R.A., Geo. 26750). It was exhibited at the British Institution in 1830 (88); it had been engraved by W. T. Fry in 1822. A repetition, with variations in costume, was painted by Lawrence for the Merchant Taylors' Company, 1825–7 (F. M. Fry, *A Historical Catalogue of the Pictures . . . at Merchant Taylors' Hall* (1907), pp. 14–15). A version was recorded in the collection of the Grand Duke of Hesse Darmstadt. Enamels by Bone of the head of this type are at Slane Castle and Burghley; the head of this type was also used on a full-length, sold at Christie's, 22 April 1960 (173). A three-quarter-length of the Duke by Lawrence (*Fig.* 21), in the Ponce Museum of Art, Puerto Rico, is close to No. 876, with variations in the uniform and orders. It has been suggested —surely correctly—by Garlick (*Catalogue, loc. cit.*) that this may be the portrait exhibited at the Royal Academy in 1814 (64);[1] if so, Lawrence would have based his full-length of the Duke painted for George IV on his earlier portrait and may not have required a further sitting from the Duke. The earlier portrait was engraved by C. Turner in 1821. A portrait of the Duke in the Metropolitan Museum, attributed to Beechey, seems closely related to No. 876.

877. WILLIAM IV WHEN DUKE OF CLARENCE (*Plate* 229)

Buckingham Palace. 99¾ × 63¾ in., 253,4 × 161,9 cm.
Full-length, holding a paper in his right hand and his hat under his left arm, standing by a column, with a view of the sea-shore in the distance. He wears the star of the Garter on his coat and his badge as G.C.B. round his neck.

Recorded by 1864 (*V.R. inv.*, No. 222, as by Shee) on the Principal Staircase at Buckingham Palace.

Literature: Garlick, *Lawrence*, p. 32, *Catalogue*, pp. 198–9.

Presumably commissioned by the sitter. It was among the portraits in Lawrence's studio at the time of his death on 7 January 1830. The portrait, 'largest full length', had been

1. Farington records on 28 July 1813 (*Diary*, vol. VII, p. 194), that the Duke had been sitting to Lawrence for a half-length. The Ponce Museum also owns a miniature copy by Bone (1821) of its three-quarter-length.

finished in 1827 and was claimed by the Duke on 10 February 1830; it was delivered to him on 23 February and the Duke paid £630 for it. It was exhibited at the Royal Academy in 1829 (57) and at the British Institution in 1833 (36). Hodgetts's engraving of it was published in 1831. Lawrence's large preparatory drawing for the head (*Fig.* 19) is at Goodwood; this is probably the drawing in Lawrence's sale at Christie's, 19 June 1830 (406), engraved by F. C. Lewis in 1831 (Garlick, *Catalogue*, p. 248). A smaller drawing of this type was with the Folio Society in 1964; another was sold, as by Wilkie, at Sotheby's, 12 February 1964 (120). A version of No. 877, head and shoulders wearing the collar of the Prince of Wales's Lodge of Freemasons, belongs to the Lodge.

878. ADOLPHUS, DUKE OF CAMBRIDGE (*Plate* 196)

Windsor Castle (175). 106½ × 71 in., 301 × 180,3 cm.
Full-length, standing, in Field-Marshal's uniform, resting his hands on his sword and wearing the stars of the Garter and of the Black Eagle of Prussia.

Painted for George IV; recorded in the inventory of 'Carleton Palace' (645: 'Full length Portrait of H.R.H. The Duke of Cambridge. Lawrence. In the Waterloo Gallery, Windsor Castle').

Literature: Waagen (1838), vol. I, p. 168; Collins Baker, *Windsor*, p. 201; Garlick, *Lawrence*, p. 30, *Catalogue*, p. 47.

Begun at Aix-la-Chapelle in 1818; a 'Large Whole Length' of the Duke, at £525, was among the pictures painted for the King while Sir Benjamin Bloomfield was Keeper of the Privy Purse (W.R.A., Geo. 26642; *Letters of George IV*, vol. III, 1592). The portrait was in Lawrence's studio at his death and was claimed on 24 January 1830 (Garlick, *Catalogue*, p. 277); Seguier's account of 10 April 1830 includes four guineas for cleaning and varnishing it, and Morant's bill of 1830 includes the cost of a large frame for it (W.R.A., Geo. 26750, 26601). The portrait was exhibited at the British Institution in 1830 (86).

879. PRINCESS MARY, DUCHESS OF GLOUCESTER (*Plate* 228)

Windsor Castle (271). 55½ × 44 in., 141 × 111,8 cm.
Three-quarter-length, standing, wearing a plumed hat and holding a fan in her right hand. On her left shoulder she wears a jewelled miniature of George III or George IV.

Painted for George IV. On 7 October 1826 Morant was paid £51 for 'Two very richly Ornamented Frames', apparently completed by 4 April 1825, for Nos. 879, 880, which were to be conveyed to Buckingham House; but on 17 July 1827 he was paid the same sum for frames similarly described, apparently completed by 7 June 1826, which were conveyed to Carlton House (W.R.A., Geo. 26533, 26545). Recorded in the inventory of 'Carleton Palace' (682); deposited by the King's command in the King's Bedroom at St. James's in June 1826, sent to Windsor on 30 December 1828, but returned to St. James's on 25 April 1829 (Jutsham, *Deliveries*, ff. 81, 215). In the Green Drawing-Room at Windsor by (?) 1878 (*V.R. inv.*).

Literature: Williams, vol. II, p. 347; Collins Baker, *Windsor*, p. 191; Garlick, *Lawrence*, p. 39, *Catalogue*, p. 90.

Lawrence was painting the portrait at Buckingham House in April 1824; it was exhibited at the Royal Academy in 1824 (59). On 4 May 1824 Lawrence was paid £315 for a 'Bishops half Length Portrait of the Duchess of Gloucester', among the pictures painted at the King's command during Sir William Knighton's Keepership of the Privy Purse

(W.R.A., Geo. 26645; *Letters of George IV*, vol. III, 1591). There is a slight *pentimento* in the outline of the right cheek.

880. PRINCESS SOPHIA (*Plate* 227)

Windsor Castle (272). 55¾ × 44¾ in., 141,6 × 113,7 cm.

Three-quarter-length, seated, wearing on her left shoulder a miniature of George IV in a jewelled setting; an eye-glass is tucked into her waist.

Painted for George IV. See No. 879 for details of frames made for it by Morant. Recorded in the inventory of 'Carleton Palace' (683); deposited by the King's command in the King's Bedroom at St. James's in June 1826, sent to Windsor on 30 December 1828, but returned to St. James's on 25 April 1829 (Jutsham, *Deliveries*, ff. 81, 215). In the Green Drawing-Room at Windsor by (?) 1861 (*V.R. inv.*).

Literature: Collins Baker, *Windsor*, p. 191; R.A., *The First Hundred Years*, 1951–2 (173); Garlick, *Lawrence*, p. 58; R.A., *Sir Thomas Lawrence*, 1961 (41); Garlick, *Catalogue*, p. 179.

Exhibited at the Royal Academy in 1825 (57). It had been bespoken from Lawrence in 1825 and he had been paid £315 for it (W.R.A., Geo. 27042; *Letters of George IV*, vol. III, 1591; 'Bishop's half-length Portrait of Her Rl Highness The Princess Sophia'). There are *pentimenti* in the right arm and shoulder.

881. PRINCESS AMELIA (*Plate* 186)

Windsor Castle (832). Oval, 23¼ × 17¼ in., 59,0 × 43,8 cm. (see below).

Half-length, holding in her left hand a sprig of roses.

Painted for George III or Queen Charlotte. After it was shown at the Royal Academy in 1790 (see below) it is said to have been sent back to Windsor; but it does not appear in any contemporary inventories and it unaccountably appears in Foster's saleroom in 1825, when it was sold for a small sum. In return for a portrait of his wife by Lawrence, Foster got hold of the portrait of the Princess for him and in November 1825 Lawrence offered the portrait to George IV (W. T. Whitley, *Art in England, 1821–37* (1930), p. 111). Recorded at Windsor in 1859 (*V.R. inv.*).

Literature: Williams, vol. I, pp. 128, 136–7; Collins Baker, *Windsor*, p. 192; R.A., *King's Pictures* (80); Garlick, *Lawrence*, p. 24, *Catalogue*, pp. 17–18.

Painted at Windsor at the same time as the full-length of Queen Charlotte in the National Gallery (4257) (*Fig.* X). Lawrence received the Queen's commands to come down to Windsor on 27 September 1789 with his 'painting apparatus'; he was to be ready for a first sitting from the Queen on 28 September. Lawrence was advised by William Hamilton to be careful, in his portrait of the Queen, of 'individual likeness. In the princess you have more scope for taste, as the features will soon change from what they are at present' (*Sir Thomas Lawrence's Letter-Bag*, ed. G. S. Layard (1906), pp. 10–11). Lawrence unwittingly upset the child, and lost at least one sitting, by giving her only one of his drawings after giving two to each of her older sisters (Williams, *loc. cit.*). Lawrence was paid fifteen guineas for the portrait (Garlick, *Catalogue*, pp. 267, 268). It was exhibited at the Royal Academy in 1790 (26) and at the British Institution in 1833 (22). The portrait may have been originally designed on a rectangular canvas: it can be seen in that form in Bartolozzi's engraving (published 1790), but in a copy in Copenhagen, and in the photograph (1859) of No. 881 in *V.R. inv.*, where the measurements are given as 21 × 17 in., the figure is behind a painted oval. At a later date the canvas was converted into an oval; slight additions were made at

the sides and larger additions at the top (*c.* 1⅜ in.) and bottom (*c.* 1⅜ in.). Alterations had also been made to the composition. The naked piece of the Princess's right arm was almost entirely painted out; the right sleeve was widened; the sash was narrowed; and leaves were added under the flowers on the right. During restoration in 1963 these later alterations were corrected or removed; but comparison with Bartolozzi's engraving shows that the outline of the curtain originally went further to the right above the trees, and this has not been reconstituted.

882. PRINCE GEORGE OF CUMBERLAND, LATER KING GEORGE V OF HANOVER (*Plate* 223)

Buckingham Palace. 99½ × 54¼ in., 252,7 × 137,8 cm.; there is an addition at the bottom of *c.* 6¼ in.

Full-length, by a stream, leaning against a bank on which rests his cap; he wears on his breast the star of the Golden Lion of Hesse-Cassel. In the background is an extensive landscape with a castle.

Painted for George IV and recorded in the inventory of 'Carleton Palace' (672); later set up on the Principal Staircase at Buckingham Palace (*V.R. inv.*, 1864, No. 223).

Literature: Williams, vol. II, p. 490; Garlick, *Lawrence*, p. 34; *Catalogue*, p. 63.

Stated by Williams to have been painted in 1828 at Cumberland Lodge, 'where Sir Thomas staid for the purpose for six weeks'. The Prince returned to Germany in August 1828. The Castle in the background may therefore be intended for Windsor, as seen from the high ground near Cumberland Lodge. It was among the portraits in Lawrence's studio at the time of his death on 7 January 1830. It was claimed by the King on 22 January and delivered six days later; £420 was paid for it as it was only 'partly finished'; five hundred guineas would have been the price if it had been finished (W.R.A., Geo. 26675). Wyatt's account included, under 6 May 1830, £29. 17*s.* for a very rich frame for the portrait. In Lawrence's drawing of the head of the Prince (*Fig.* 20), in the collection of S.K.H. Prince Ernst August (Garlick, *Catalogue*, p. 223), the hair is differently arranged and the glance is towards the spectator.

883. ALEXANDER I, EMPEROR OF RUSSIA (1777–1825) (*Plate* 194)

Windsor Castle (199). 107½ × 70½ in., 273 × 179,1 cm.

Full-length, standing, in the uniform of a Russian Field-Marshal with his hands 'closely knit before him'; his military greatcoat and plumed hat are laid on a bank beside him. He wears the Sword of the Order of the Sword of Sweden and the star of St. Andrew of Russia superimposed on the Garter; his badges include that of the Order of St. George of Russia, the Iron Cross of Prussia and the Russian campaign medal of 1812.

Painted for George IV; recorded in the inventory of 'Carleton Palace' (652: 'Full length of the Emperor of Russia Lawrence. In the Waterloo Gallery, Windsor Castle').

Literature: Williams, vol. I, pp. 341–2, vol. II, pp. 109–10, 111–12, 114, 115–16, 117–18, 119, 127–8; *Sir Thomas Lawrence's Letter-Bag*, ed. G. S. Layard (1906), pp. 136–42; Collins Baker, *Windsor*, p. 198; R.A., *King's Pictures* (126); Garlick, *Lawrence*, p. 24; R.A., *Sir Thomas Lawrence*, 1961 (1); Garlick, *Catalogue*, pp. 16, 211.

Begun in London in 1814 and finished at Aix-la-Chapelle in 1818. The Tsar arrived in London on 7 June 1814 and sat to Lawrence at the Prince Regent's request. It is doubtful if Lawrence made much progress with the Tsar's portrait at this time, but at Aix-la-Chapelle, late in 1818, the Tsar gave Lawrence seven sittings, including two for a drawing with which the sitter was much satisfied. This drawing, probably finished in the first two sittings, was to be copied on to the large canvas in the Tsar's absence with his troops. When the sittings were resumed the Tsar came in the uniform he had worn at the battle of Leipzig; at the first sitting—of an hour and three-quarters—the portrait was considerably advanced. A further sitting took place on 8 November. At a fairly early stage, the Tsar's 'Aide de Camps, fine young Men, quite dance about the Picture, mad with Joy at its being so like him. The Figure is not sketch'd in, and they put themselves into Postures to shew me how he stands, not gracefully (as they say), but he stands so . . .' Later during the progress of the portrait Lawrence 'had to act decidedly against [the Tsar's] judgment and wishes, and to make a total alteration in the picture, changing entirely the action of the legs, and consequently of the trunk . . . He stands always resting on one leg—(you know what I mean, the other loose on the ground, like the figures of the antique) —and he stands either with his hat in his hand or with his hands closely knit before him. The first figure was thus [Lawrence presumably inserted a sketch at this point in his letter]. You perceive that he here seems to be shrinking and retiring from the object of his contemplation, determining at the same time to preserve and hold fast one certain good from the enemy, whatever be the issue of the battle. These were my objections, and the vexatious thing was, that, before an audience of his friends, I was to commence the alteration, by giving him *four* legs, and though gradually obliterating the two first; still their agreeable lines were remaining in most complicated confusion. What I expected took place: during almost the whole of it, the attendant generals complained, and the Emperor, though confiding in my opinion, was still dissatisfied. However, I accomplished the alteration, and the vessel righted.' Lawrence discerned 'great nobleness in the upper part of the countenance'.[1]

Both the Emperor and his mother (for whom the Emperor ordered Lawrence to paint the copy which is now in the Hermitage) were immensely pleased with the portrait; the Emperor gave Lawrence a superb diamond ring. On 3 January 1819 Lawrence wrote to Farington from Vienna, sending him his drawing of the Tsar; he had apparently used the drawing as a basis for the portrait, but when the latter had been completed, he finished the drawing from it, until it had become 'as perfect a resemblance as it was possible for me to make', with the characteristic ruddiness which the Tsar's constant journeyings in open carriages had given to his countenance (see also Layard, *loc. cit.*). Lawrence was paid £525 for the portrait (W.R.A., Geo. 26642; *Letters of George IV*, vol. III, p. 1592). It was in Lawrence's studio at his death and was claimed on 24 January 1830 (Garlick, *Catalogue*, p. 277); Seguier's account of 10 April 1830 includes four guineas for cleaning and varnishing the canvas (W.R.A., 26750). It was exhibited at the British Institution in 1830 (21). Lawrence's alterations to the figure are faintly discernible. There are also traces in the background of streaming flags; the background may first have shown a battle raging in the distance.

Son of the mad Tsar Paul I, whom he succeeded in 1801. At first the ally of Prussia and Austria, the Tsar came under Napoleon's spell at Tilsit in 1807, but was alienated from

1. On 18 November Metternich described the portrait as 'décent; il a des pantalons gris' (*Lettres . . . à la Comtesse de Lieven*, ed. J. Hanoteau (Paris, 1909), p. 10).

him before the disastrous Russian campaign of 1812. Caulaincourt wrote that 'underneath his appearance of goodwill, frankness and natural loyalty, there is a core of deep dissimulation which is the mark of an obstinacy which nothing can move.'

884. LOUIS-ANTOINE, DUKE OF ANGOULÊME (1775–1844) (*Plate* 202)

Windsor Castle (174). $106\frac{1}{2} \times 69\frac{1}{2}$ in., $270,5 \times 176,5$ cm.

Full-length, standing in a rocky landscape against a tempestuous sky, wearing military uniform with a cloak thrown over his left shoulder. His right hand is about to pick up his hat, his left clasps his sword. He wears the star of the St. Esprit on his breast with badges probably identifiable as those of: the Order of Saint-Lazare and of Notre-Dame-du-Mont Carmel; the Royal and Military Order of Saint Louis *or* the Institution of Military Merit; and the Royal Order of the Legion of Honour.

Painted for George IV; received with No. 890 at Carlton House on 9 May 1829: '. . . The Duke De Angouleme in a Gilt Frame. N.B. The Carved & Gilt Crowns to these Frames were ordered and made by Mr Wyatt; they were hung in the King's Closet at St. James's (Jutsham, *Receipts*, f. 267).

Literature: Collins Baker, *Windsor*, p. 199; Garlick, *Lawrence*, p. 25, *Catalogue*, pp. 21, 212.

Among the portraits bespoken from Lawrence by George IV in 1825 was a 'large whole length' of the Dauphin for £525; Lawrence's receipt (see also No. 890) for this sum is dated 16 December 1825 (W.R.A., Geo. 27042, 26688; *Letters of George IV*, vol. III, 1591). The portrait was begun in Paris. Charles X (see No. 890) had given Lawrence a sitting at St. Cloud on 27 August 1825 and commanded Lawrence to 'begin the Portrait of the Dauphin' on 30 August; the Dauphin was as gracious to Lawrence as his father had been; and on 2 November 1825 the Duke of Orléans wrote to Lawrence that he was availing himself of his kind offer to see the completed portraits at the Pavillon de Marsan (*Sir Thomas Lawrence's Letter-Bag*, ed. G. S. Layard (1906), pp. 197, 200, 201). The portrait was exhibited at the British Institution in 1830 (76). Lawrence's drawing for the head was sold in his sale at Christie's, 19 June 1830 (408); the head and shoulders were engraved by Billiard. A rapid sketch by Lawrence in the Royal Library, similar to the sketches for Nos. 910, 917, may represent Lawrence's first thought for the design. The left hand in No. 884 is unfinished. See No. 926.

Eldest son of Charles X (No. 890). During the Revolution he lived at Hartwell House with the other royal *émigrés*; in 1814 he joined Wellington's army in the Peninsula and, in the invasion of France, was active in proclaiming the Restoration. He was created Colonel-Général des Cuirassiers and Grand Amiral de France, but retired to Spain after Napoleon's landing. In 1823 he was put in command of the forces appointed to re-establish Ferdinand VII on the Spanish throne. After his father's accession he was in charge of all military matters, but was increasingly unpopular: 'emprunté, gauche, dépourvu de toute grâce, . . . certains tics le rendaient ridicule'. On 1 August 1830 his father and he abdicated jointly.

885. HENRY, THIRD EARL BATHURST (1762–1834) (*Plate* 206)

Windsor Castle (190). $51\frac{1}{2} \times 41\frac{1}{2}$ in., $130,8 \times 105,4$ cm.; *c.* $1\frac{1}{2}$ in. of original canvas are turned over at the top.

Three-quarter-length, seated, wearing the Garter round his

leg and the star of the order on his coat, and holding an eye-glass in his right hand.

Painted for George IV; recorded in the inventory of 'Carleton Palace' (660: 'Half length of Lord Bathurst. Lawrence. In the Waterloo Gallery, Windsor Castle').

Literature: Waagen (1838), vol. I, p. 169; R.A., *British Art*, 1934 (441), *Commemorative Catalogue* (1935), p. 93; Collins Baker, *Windsor*, p. 200; Garlick, *Lawrence*, p. 26; R.A., *Sir Thomas Lawrence*, 1961 (6); Garlick, *Catalogue*, p. 30.

Listed, at £315, with the pictures painted by Lawrence for George IV while Sir Benjamin Bloomfield was Keeper of the Privy Purse (W.R.A., Geo. 26642; *Letters of George IV*, vol. III, 1592). It was in Lawrence's studio at his death and was delivered on 26 January 1830 (Garlick, *Catalogue*, p. 278); Seguier's account of 10 April 1830 includes three guineas for cleaning, varnishing and 'new lining' the canvas (W.R.A., Geo. 26750). It was exhibited at the British Institution in 1830 (6). There are *pentimenti* in the hair, which was at first painted in a less dishevelled state, and in the column, which was originally further to the left.

Lord of the Admiralty, 1783–9, Lord of the Treasury, 1789–91, Commissioner of the Board of Control, 1793–1801, and Secretary for War and the Colonies, 1812–27. Greville, who was his private secretary, described him as 'a very amiable man and with a good understanding . . . a regular Tory of the old school . . . nervous and reserved, with a good deal of humour, and habitually a jester'.

886. FIELD-MARSHAL GEBHARDT VON BLÜCHER (1742–1819) (*Plate* 192)

Windsor Castle (189), 106¼ × 70¼ in., 269,9 × 178,4 cm.

Full-length, standing, in military uniform with his left hand on his sabre and pointing with his right. He wears a miniature of George IV in a jewelled setting,[1] over the ribbon of the Order of the Black Eagle; the Iron Cross of Prussia and the stars of the Orders of Maria Theresa of Austria, St. George of Russia and the Black Eagle. In the background is a Uhlan orderly mounting a charger.

Painted for George IV; recorded in the inventory of 'Carleton Palace' (654: 'Full length of Marshal Blucher. Lawrence. In the Waterloo Gallery Windsor Castle').

Literature: Williams, vol. I, pp. 341–2, 346; Waagen (1838), vol. I, p. 167; *Sir Thomas Lawrence's Letter-Bag*, ed. G. S. Layard (1906), pp. 255–8, 262; Collins Baker, *Windsor*, pp. 200–1; Garlick, *Lawrence*, p. 28; R.A., *Sir Thomas Lawrence*, 1961 (7); Garlick, *Catalogue*, pp. 38–9.

Painted in London in the summer of 1814. On 9 June Lawrence showed Farington a note from Sir Charles Stewart 'informing Him that the Prince Regent desired to have two whole length Portraits of General Blucher and Genl. Platoff and that he (Sir Charles) shd. bring Genl. Blucher to Lawrence to sit for His portrait at 12 o Clock on Friday the 10th. inst.' (Farington, *Diary*, vol. VII, p. 257). Miss Croft called on Lawrence when he was painting Blücher, perhaps at the first sitting. The Field-Marshal had been travelling all night, was 'evidently "half-seas-over"', and consequently falls asleep' as soon as Lawrence stopped talking to him. Miss Croft did her best to keep the old man awake. She said of the likeness 'that it struck me as perfect, with the exception of too much spirit about the lower part of the nose; he [i.e., Lawrence] replied that I was quite right, that from the loss

1. This is the miniature, in a rich jewelled setting and suspended on a blue ribbon, which the Regent presented to Blücher on his arrival in London.

of teeth and evident fatigue the corner of the mouth and nose seem'd to droop, but that, if I would begin talking of the Duke of Wellington, I should soon perceive it was no flattery of his.' Miss Croft on Lawrence's behalf requested Blücher to 'curl up his moustaches, so that they might not cover his lower as well as upper lip', which he did after 'putting his filthy fingers into his mouth . . . He wore a miniature of George the 4th. round his neck.' Lawrence at first painted the Uhlan with his wrong foot in the stirrup. The mob besieged Lawrence's house while the Field-Marshal was within (Layard, *loc. cit.*). Farington saw the portrait in Lawrence's studio on 21 July 1814. It was exhibited at the Royal Academy in 1815 (155), where it was greatly admired (e.g., Farington, *Diary*, vol. VIII, pp. 5, 14; Williams, vol. I, p. 346; 'the likeness excellent . . . the whole attitude and person of the man . . . expressive of his character'). Lawrence's account of 4 January 1817 includes £420 for the portrait (W.R.A., Geo. 26634; *Letters of George IV*, vol. III, 1592).

The portrait was in Lawrence's studio at his death and was claimed on 22 January 1830 (Garlick, *Catalogue*, p. 278). Seguier's account of 10 April 1830 includes four guineas for cleaning and varnishing the canvas; Morant's account in 1830 includes the price of a frame for it (W.R.A., Geo. 26750, 26601). It was exhibited at the British Institution in 1830 (7); it was engraved by Wagstaff in 1837 and Bromley in 1839. Lawrence's drawing of the head, of which F. C. Lewis published an engraving in April 1839, was in Lawrence's sale at Christie's, 18 June 1831 (119) (Garlick, *Catalogue*, p. 216).

A professional soldier who rose from the ranks to command the army of Silesia, which he led into Paris in 1814 beside the Bohemian army under the command of Schwarzenberg (No. 912); created Prince of Wahlstadt in that year. As Commander-in-Chief of the army of the Lower Rhine, he made the decisive intervention in support of Wellington at Waterloo. Wellington said of him later, 'He was a very fine fellow, and whenever there was any question of fighting, always ready and eager—if anything too eager.'

887. GEORGE CANNING (1770–1827)

Buckingham Palace. 94 × 58¼ in., 238,8 × 147,9 cm.

The back of the canvas is inscribed in chalk: *Sir Thos Lawrence R.A. | Nᵒ 1;* and in paint: *Right Honbe George Canning | Sir T Lawrence.* On the stretcher is a label: *Nᵒ 14 | Mr Canning | Painted by | Sir Thomas Lawrence*

Full-length, standing with arms folded in front of the empty benches of the House of Commons on which rests an open despatch box.

Painted for George IV; recorded in the inventory of 'Carleton Palace' (657; 'Full length of Mr Canning Lawrence'); later at Windsor (438).

Literature: Garlick, *Lawrence*, p. 30, *Catalogue*, p. 49.

Among the pictures bespoken from Lawrence by George IV in 1825 was 'Whole Length Portrait of the late Rt Honble George Canning' for £525; it was finished in March 1829 but Lawrence's receipt is dated 7 April 1828 (W.R.A., Geo. 26692, 27043; *Letters of George IV*, vol. III, 1591). It was presumably the full-length of Canning which was among the portraits in Lawrence's studio at his death and was claimed by the King on 24 January 1830 (Garlick, *Catalogue*, p. 278). Seguier's account of 10 April 1830 includes four guineas for cleaning and varnishing it (W.R.A., Geo. 26750).

No. 887 bears every sign of original quality and of being the first version of Lawrence's full-length of this sitter. The aura round the upper part of the figure, indicating the areas worked on when the sitter was in Lawrence's presence, can still be discerned and is very clearly seen in a photograph attached to the *V.R. inv.* (1859). There are extensive *pentimenti* in the right shoulder, the collar and cravat, in the fingers of the left hand, in the outline of the coat and in the position of the feet. The background, moreover, seems to have been extensively altered; there are indications that the present background replaced a more conventional arrangement of columns, curtains and a prospect of sky and trees. The version at Harewood House is generally held to be the original (T. Borenius, *Catalogue of the Pictures and Drawings at Harewood House* . . . (1936), No. 367; Garlick, *Catalogue, loc. cit.*), but it bears no trace of these confusions and must therefore have been painted *after* Lawrence had resolved them in the last stages of his work on No. 887. A version was exhibited at the Royal Academy in 1825 (83); No. 887 was also exhibited at the British Institution in 1830 (90). The engraving by C. Turner was published on 9 April 1829. Copies are in the Foreign Office and in the possession of Lord Allendale (both by M. Ayoub) and in the National Portrait Gallery (1338; by Evans). See No. 927.

Entered Parliament as M.P. for Newport in 1794 and in 1796–9 was Under Secretary for foreign affairs in Pitt's administration; in Lord Liverpool's administration he was appointed Foreign Secretary, September 1822; and in 1827 he was appointed Premier and Chancellor of the Exchequer by George IV.

888. JOHN, COUNT CAPO D'ISTRIA

(1776–1831) (*Plate* 213)

Windsor Castle (204). 50½ × 40½ in., 128,3 × 102,9 cm.

Three-quarter-length, seated, wearing a fur-lined cloak and a star, probably the Order of St. Alexander Newski, on his breast.

Painted for George IV; recorded in the inventory of 'Carleton Palace' (668: 'Half length of Count Capo D'Istria Lawrence. In the Waterloo Gallery, Windsor Castle').

Literature: Williams, vol. II, pp. 130, 134, 145; Waagen (1838), vol. I, p. 168; Collins Baker, *Windsor*, p. 203; R.A., *King's Pictures* (124); Garlick, *Lawrence*, pp. 30–1; R.A., *Sir Thomas Lawrence*, 1961 (13); Garlick, *Catalogue*, p. 50.

Painted in Vienna in 1818–19. On 3 January 1819 Lawrence wrote from Vienna, 'I have been successful in three finished resemblances painted here . . . and Count Capo d'Istrias'. A week later he wrote, 'Count Capo d'Istrias' . . . is the last portrait I have painted here, and fortunately is the best'. The portrait is listed, at £315, among the portraits painted by Lawrence while Sir Benjamin Bloomfield was Keeper of the Privy Purse (W.R.A., Geo. 26642; *Letters of George IV*, vol. III, 1592). It was in Lawrence's studio at his death and was claimed on 22 January 1830 (Garlick, *Catalogue*, p. 278); Seguier's account of 10 April 1830 included two guineas for cleaning and varnishing it (W.R.A., 26750). It was exhibited at the British Institution in 1830 (14).

Member of an ancient Corfiote family, he entered Russian service in 1807 and as a Secretary of State for foreign affairs was present as a Russian plenipotentiary at the Congress of Vienna. In 1827 he accepted the Presidency of the new Republic of Greece, but he was assassinated four years later at Apaulia. Lawrence described him as 'a man exceedingly popular from his known ability, fine wit, and talents, and society'.

889. ROBERT STEWART, VISCOUNT CASTLEREAGH, LATER SECOND MARQUESS OF LONDONDERRY (1769–1822)

Windsor Castle (181). 55½ × 43 in., 141 × 109,2 cm.

Three-quarter-length, wearing the ribbon and star of the Garter, standing by a table on which he rests his left hand, in which he holds a paper.

Painted for George IV; recorded in the inventory of 'Carleton Palace' (659: 'Half length of Lord Londonderry. Lawrence. In the Waterloo Gallery, Windsor Castle').

Literature: Waagen (1838), vol. I, p. 168; Collins Baker, *Windsor*, p. 203; R.A., *King's Pictures* (129); Garlick, *Lawrence*, p. 47, *Catalogue*, p. 130.

A replica, not of outstanding quality, painted by Lawrence from the portrait painted for the sitter, exhibited at the Royal Academy in 1814 (23) and still in the possession of Lord Londonderry. Lawrence's bill for work for George IV, dated 4 January 1817, included £157. 10s., later amended to £210, for a half-length of Castlereagh (W.R.A., Geo. 26634, 26641; *Letters of George IV*, vol. III, 1591). The portrait was in Lawrence's studio at his death and was claimed on 22 January 1830 (Garlick, *Catalogue*, p. 278); Seguier's account of 10 April 1830 includes two guineas for cleaning and varnishing the canvas (W.R.A., Geo. 26750). It was exhibited at the British Institution in 1830 (16). Other replicas are at Mount Stewart and Montalto; a copy is at Arniston House.

Chosen by Pitt as Chief Secretary for Ireland, 1799–1801, he was responsible for forcing the union with England through the Irish parliament in 1800; as Secretary for War, 1805, 1807–9, strongly supported Sir Arthur Wellesley; as Foreign Secretary, 1812–22, he was the senior British plenipotentiary at the Congress of Vienna.

890. CHARLES X (1757–1836), KING OF FRANCE (*Plate* 201)

Windsor Castle (205). 106 × 70½ in., 269,2 × 179,1 cm.

Full-length, standing, in dark blue uniform laced with silver, carrying his plumed hat on his left arm. He wears the stars of the Garter and St. Esprit, the Golden Fleece, and the ribbon of the St. Esprit. His other orders include the badges of St. Louis, the Legion of Honour and the Order of Fidelity and he wears the Garter round his leg. In the background is seen part of the Tuileries.

Painted for George IV; received with No. 884 from Lawrence at Carlton House on 5 May 1829: 'The Portrait of Charles The Tenth of France—Whole Length—in a Gilt Frame'; the portraits were hung in the King's Closet at St. James's (Jutsham, *Receipts*, f. 267).

Literature: Collins Baker, *Windsor*, pp. 204–5; R.A., *King's Pictures* (119); Garlick, *Lawrence*, p. 31; R.A., *Sir Thomas Lawrence*, 1961 (12); Garlick, *Catalogue*, pp. 53, 221.

Among the portraits bespoken from Lawrence by George IV in 1825 was 'a large whole length' of 'His Most Christian Majesty' for £525; Lawrence's receipt (see also No. 884) for this sum is dated 16 December 1825; and he received £1,000 in addition for his 'Expenses & time in Journey to & stay at Paris' (W.R.A., Geo. 27042, 26688; *Letters of George IV*, vol. III, 1591). The King gave Lawrence a sitting of about two hours at St. Cloud on 27 August 1825; on that occasion Lawrence found his countenance 'of striking Character with a peculiarly benevolent expression . . . It presents indeed some difficulty from its varying action; but not sufficient to make me doubtful of the result'. For much of the time the children of the Duke of Berry were romping round the King and the painter. To Mrs. Wolff, Lawrence described the King's high forehead, 'which with his wearing his Hair likewise high, gives peculiarity to the Head'. The King approved of the sketch Lawrence made at the first sitting and appointed a time for a second sitting. The portrait was not finished by 20 October 1825; its progress had been successful, but a substantial alteration, probably to the background, had been made since the King had last seen the portrait. By 2 November the two portraits were displayed for inspection in the Pavillon de Marsan (*Sir Thomas Lawrence's Letter-Bag*, ed. G. S. Layard (1906), pp. 197–201). Seguier's bill, 10 April 1830, included four guineas for cleaning and varnishing the portrait; Morant's bill, 30 December 1825, included £46. 10s. for 'an Extra large richly Ornamented frame in best Gold' for it (W.R.A., Geo. 26533, 26750). The portrait was exhibited at the British Institution in 1830 (19). The portrait was engraved by C. Turner (published on 10 May 1828) and S. Cousins. Lawrence's drawing for the head was in his sale at Christie's, 19 June 1830 (409); it was engraved by F. C. Lewis (1839). Lot 49 in the sale contained eight studies for accessories in the portrait. See No. 928.

Charles, Count of Artois, youngest brother of Louis XVI, succeeded Louis XVIII in 1824. During the Revolution and the Napoleonic Wars the Count had spent many years in exile in Britain. His reactionary policies precipitated the Revolution of 1830, when he abdicated and retired to Holyrood. In January 1825 he had created Lawrence Chevalier of the Legion of Honour and, after he had finished the two French royal portraits, presented him with a service of Sèvres porcelain. Lady Holland described him as 'a man of slender abilities with violent passions; before the revolution . . . weak and volatile . . . now weak and revengeful'.

891. CHARLES (1771–1847), ARCHDUKE OF AUSTRIA (*Plate* 198)

Windsor Castle (208). 106¼ × 70¼ in., 269,9 × 178,4 cm.

Full-length, standing in military uniform, resting his hands on his sword; he wears the Golden Fleece and the ribbon and star of the Order of Maria Theresa.

Painted for George IV; recorded in the inventory of 'Carleton Palace' (648: 'Full length of the Arch Duke Charles. Lawrence. In the Waterloo Gallery, Windsor').

Literature: Williams, vol. II, pp. 136, 145, 165–6, 175–6; Waagen (1838), vol. I, p. 167; Collins Baker, *Windsor*, p. 204; R.A., *King's Pictures* (127); Garlick, *Lawrence*, p. 31; R.A., *Sir Thomas Lawrence*, 1961 (18); Garlick, *Catalogue*, p. 53.

Painted in Vienna in 1819. In a letter of 10 January 1819 from Vienna, Lawrence described the Archduke: 'of small figure, and of dignified, pleasing manners, with a face of great strength of character, (peculiarly Austrian,) and a high, but not unmusical voice'. According to Lawrence, 'The Illness of the Arch-Duke Charles whose portrait I had begun. when it attacked him, detain'd me at Vienna till past the Holy Week, for I could not think of leaving it with the Picture of so distinguished a Personage unfinish'd. He gradually recover'd, and I had sittings from him which enabled me greatly to improve the resemblance, and complete the accurate drawings of his Person' (Williams, *op. cit.*; W.R.A., Geo. Add. 21, 37). Lawrence was paid £525 for the portrait, (W.R.A., Geo. 26642; *Letters of George IV*, vol. III, 1592); the portrait was in Lawrence's studio at his death, and was claimed on 24 January 1830; and Seguier's bill of 10 April 1830 includes four guineas for cleaning and varnishing the

portrait (W.R.A., Geo. 26750). It was exhibited at the British Institution in 1830 (20). The design of the figure is apparently based on Valentine Green's engraving, published on 15 January 1781, of Trumbull's portrait of George Washington.

The King had also apparently ordered from Lawrence a full-length portrait of the Archduchess Charles. Lawrence began this portrait in Vienna and it was claimed by the King on 24 January 1830 (Garlick, *Catalogue*, pp. 53–4, 277); only the head had been finished and only £262. 10s. was paid for the portrait. It was delivered to the King on 26 January 1830 (W.R.A., Geo. 26675), was recorded at 'Carleton Palace' (649), but was 'Sent by command of His Majesty, to Prince Esterhazy, to be by him forwarded to Vienna, Jany 1831'.

A younger brother of the Emperor Francis I (No. 897) and Commander-in-Chief of the Austrian armies; he was a brilliant and dashing commander.

892. ALEXANDER IVANOVITCH, PRINCE CHERNICHEV (1786–1857) (*Plate* 211)

Windsor Castle (197). 50½ × 40½ in., 128,3 × 102,9 cm.

Three-quarter-length, in military uniform, pointing with his left hand as if directing a charge in battle; he wears the ribbon of the Order of St. Alexander Newski and the badges of St. George of Russia and of the Order of Military Merit of Württemburg and the badge of Maximilian Joseph of Bavaria.

Painted for George IV; recorded in the inventory of 'Carleton Palace' (667: 'Half length of Tchernicheff. Lawrence. In the Waterloo Gallery. Windsor Castle').

Literature: Williams, vol. II, pp. 130, 145; Waagen (1838), vol. I, p. 168; Collins Baker, *Windsor*, p. 216; Garlick, *Lawrence*, p. 60; R.A., *Sir Thomas Lawrence*, 1961 (4); Garlick, *Catalogue*, p. 188.

Painted in December 1818 at Vienna, where the sitter was in attendance upon the Tsar; on 24 December 1818 Metternich wrote that Lawrence had just finished the portrait (*Lettres . . . à la Comtesse de Lieven*, ed. J. Hanoteau (Paris, 1909), pp. 82–3). On 3 January 1819 Lawrence wrote that he had been successful 'in three finished resemblances painted here. Two Russian generals, aide-de-camps to the Emperor, (Yarnicheff one) . . .'; and the portrait is listed by him with those that he had painted in Vienna. Lawrence himself described it as 'a strong likeness' (*Sir Thomas Lawrence's Letter-Bag*, ed. G. S. Layard (1906), p. 141). Lawrence was paid £315 for the portrait (W.R.A., Geo. 26642; *Letters of George IV*, vol. III, 1592); it was in Lawrence's studio at his death and was claimed on 22 January 1830 (Garlick, *Catalogue*, p. 278). Seguier's account of 10 April 1830 includes four guineas for cleaning and varnishing the canvas and 'the background finished' (W.R.A., Geo. 26750). The portrait was exhibited at the British Institution in 1830 (4).

Colonel of the Cossacks in 1811, and Russian Ambassador in Paris; from 1812 he served in the campaigns against the French and was present at the Conferences of Aix-la-Chapelle and Verona; Russian Minister of War, 1828, President of the Council, 1848; created a Prince in 1841.

893. ERCOLE, CARDINAL CONSALVI (1757–1824) (*Plates* 203)

Windsor Castle (194). 105¼ × 68¾ in., 267,3 × 174,6 cm.

There are two successive additions at the top, the first

(*c.* 10 in.) probably by Lawrence, the second (*c.* 3½ in.) of a slightly later date. There are also later additions on the right (3½ in.) and at the bottom (2½–3½ in.).

Full-length, seated in Cardinal's robes with his biretta and a document in his right hand; his left hand rests on a table on which is a paper inscribed: *Roma . . . 1812*(?); in the table lies a book entitled: *MOTO. PROPRIO / DELLA.SAN-TITA. D.N.S. / PAPA. PIO VII*, i.e., the new constitution granted by Pius VII in 1816 to the States of the Church. In the background is a view of the front of St. Peter's.

Painted for George IV; recorded in the inventory of 'Carleton Palace' (651: 'Full length of Cardinal Gonsalvi. Lawrence. In the Waterloo Gallery, Windsor Castle').

Literature: Williams, vol. II, pp. 152, 154, 167, 168, 177, 178, 186, 189, 193–4, 199, 200–2, 210, 219–20; Waagen (1838), vol. I, pp. 168, 169; *Sir Thomas Lawrence's Letter-Bag*, ed. G. S. Layard (1906), pp. 145–6; Collins Baker, *Windsor*, p. 205; R.A., *King's Pictures* (130); Garlick, *Lawrence*, p. 32; R.A., *Sir Thomas Lawrence*, 1961 (14); Garlick, *Catalogue*, p. 58.

Painted in Rome in 1819. On 17 May Lawrence was presented to the Cardinal, who arranged for Lawrence to put up in the Palazzo del Quirinale and to be provided with three rooms there for his painting and pictures. Lawrence described him as 'one of the finest subjects for a picture that I have ever had—a countenance of powerful intellect and great symmetry—his manners but too gracious . . . the expression of every wish was pressed upon me, and the utterance of every complaint', and later 'a very intelligent and noble character of countenance'. In a letter of 25 June, talking of the success of his portrait of the Pope (No. 909), he adds: 'I have been equally successful in the portrait of Cardinal Gonsalvi'; and on 29 June he wrote: 'Of the Cardinal's portrait I have made a very promising beginning.' In the beginning of July Lawrence was still occupied with 'a sitting from the Cardinal, and other employment on his picture . . . My portrait of the Cardinal is not so far advanced, for the hands are not painted from him, which they shall be . . . On the first day, I painted in the whole head, and very like him. He has a penetrating and pursuing eye, and I made him look directly at the spectator . . . The town artists are . . . surprised at the likeness, I have sketched in the whole figure; and from his taking precedence before any minister of other powers, I have painted him a small whole-length—a sitting figure of less dimensions than Sir William Grant's.' On returning to Rome from Naples he was again at work on the portrait; on 21 September he wrote that he had almost completed it and that it had been very successful (Williams, *loc. cit.*).

Lawrence was paid £525 for the portrait (W.R.A., Geo. 26642; *Letters of George IV*, vol. III, 1592). It was in Lawrence's studio at his death and was claimed on 24 January 1830 (Garlick, *Catalogue*, p. 277); the background was still unfinished: Seguier's account of 10 April 1830 includes five guineas for cleaning and varnishing the canvas and 'the back ground finished' (W.R.A., Geo. 26750). Morant's bill of 1830 includes the cost of a frame for the portrait (*ibid.*, 26601). The portrait was exhibited at the British Institution in 1830 (8) and engraved by Wagstaff in 1840. Lawrence's drawing of the Cardinal, given by the artist to the Duchess of Devonshire, who had been kind to him in Rome, is at Ickworth (Garlick, *Catalogue*, p. 222); it was engraved by F. C. Lewis in 1830. A drawing of the head is in the Marquess of Lansdowne's collection. A repetition of No. 893 was on the art-market in New York in 1950; a small version at Stansted House is probably a copy by J. Simpson; a three-quarter-length copy was sold at Sotheby's, 20 November 1963 (143).

A protégé of Cardinal York, appointed *cameriere segreto* to the Pope in 1783; he had been deported by French authorities in 1798, but after 1800 was Pope Pius VII's close adviser. Energetic and sociable, he was known as 'Monsieur Ubique', and he was the Pope's representative at the Congress of Vienna. He directed that after his death the proceeds of the sale of his presents should be given towards the cost of Thorwaldsen's monument to Pius VII in St. Peter's.

894. SIR WILLIAM CURTIS (1752–1829) (*Plate* 221)
Windsor Castle (434). 35¾ × 28¼ in., 90,8 × 71,7 cm.

Head and shoulders, seated, wearing an Alderman's scarlet robe lined with fur and with his shrieval gold chain over his shoulders.

Painted for George IV; recorded in the inventory of 'Carleton Palace' (681: 'Portrait of Sir Wᵐ Curtis Bart Lawrence'); at Windsor by 1828 (see below).

Literature: C. R. Leslie, *Memoirs of the Life of John Constable*, ed. A. Shirley (1937), p. 143; Collins Baker, *Windsor*, p. 192; R.A., *King's Pictures* (118); City Art Gallery, Bristol, *Sir Thomas Lawrence*, 1951 (30); R.A., *The First Hundred Years of the R.A.*, 1951–52 (196); Garlick, *Lawrence*, p. 34; R.A., *Sir Thomas Lawrence*, 1961 (40); Garlick, *Catalogue*, p. 63.

On 3 July 1823 Constable wrote to the Rev. John Fisher: 'We dined with Sir William Curtis; he is a fine old fellow, and is now sitting for his portrait to Lawrence for the king who desired it in these words, "D-n you, my old boy, I'll have you all in your canonicals, and then I can look at you every day". He is a great favourite,—birds of a feather' (C. R. Leslie, *loc. cit.*). The portrait was exhibited at the Royal Academy in 1824 (291). It was engraved by W. Say (1831). Morant's bill includes, under 10 November 1828, £12. 18*s.* for 'a Kit cat Frame . . . for a Portrait of Sir Wᵐ Curtis for Windsor' (W.R.A., Geo. 26558).

He inherited a business in sea-biscuits at Wapping, but became very prosperous: as banker, Alderman, Lord Mayor (1795–6), member of Parliament, Baronet and head of the Tory party in the City. George IV was very fond of him; he accompanied him in yachting trips and took him on the visit to Edinburgh in 1822, when the 'portentous apparition' of Sir William in full Highland dress 'cast an air of ridicule and caricature over the whole of Sir Walter's celtified pageantry'. In 1824 George IV bespoke from Lawrence (for £210) a 'Kit Cat Copy of His Majesty for Sir William Curtis' (W.R.A., Geo. 27041) which is still with Sir William's descendants (Garlick, *Catalogue*, p. 88).

895. WILLIAM CAVENDISH, SIXTH DUKE OF DEVONSHIRE (1790–1858) (*Plate* 224)
Windsor Castle (329). Panel: 30 × 24½ in., 76,2 × 62,2 cm.

Head and shoulders, wearing a fur-lined coat over Windsor uniform with the star of the Garter.

Painted for George IV; recorded in the inventory of 'Carleton Palace' (677: 'Portrait of the Duke of Devonshire. Lawrence. In the Corridor, Windsor Castle').

Literature: Collins Baker, *Windsor*, p. 193; R.A., *King's Pictures* (53); Garlick, *Lawrence*, p. 34, *Catalogue*, p. 68.

Among the portraits bespoken from Lawrence by George IV in 1825 was 'a Three Quarter's Portrait of the Duke of Devonshire' at £157. 10*s.* (W.R.A., Geo. 27043, with note:

'This price of a Three Quarter's Portrait stated by Sir T. L. 9.Dec.1828'); on 25 November 1828 Lawrence stated that it was finished and his receipt is dated 13 December 1828 (*ibid.*, 26662–3; *Letters of George IV*, vol. III, 1591, 1592). G. Morant's account for £25. 10s. for 'A richly ornamented Frame' for No. 895 is also dated 13 December; the frame still bears Morant's label. No. 895 is the latest of Lawrence's three surviving portraits of the Duke. The fur-lined coat may allude to his embassy to Russia; he had been created a Knight of the Garter in 1827.

Son of the famous Duchess (No. 1041). He bore the Orb at the Coronation of George IV, who regarded him as one of his 'personal and attached friends'. In 1826 he was sent as Ambassador Extraordinary to St. Petersburg for the Coronation of Tsar Nicholas I. Lord Chamberlain, 1827–8, 1830–4, he bore the Curtana at the Coronation of Queen Victoria. He was the 'model of the old English noble of his time. Very tall, very benignant, full of poetic spirit, delighting in doing good', he carried out extensive additions and alterations at Chatsworth in association with Wyatville (No. 918) and Joseph Paxton.

896. JOHN SCOTT, FIRST EARL OF ELDON
(1751–1838) (*Plate* 225)

Windsor Castle (357). Panel: 36 × 27½ in., 91,4 × 69,8 cm.
Half-length, seated, gazing at the spectator.

Painted for George IV; recorded in the inventory of 'Carleton Palace' (679: 'Portrait of the Earl of Eldon. Lawrence'). By 1838 it was in the Corridor at Windsor.

Literature: H. Twiss, *The Public and Private Life of Lord Chancellor Eldon* (1844), vol. III, pp. 313–14; Collins Baker, *Windsor*, p. 193; R.A., *King's Pictures* (132); Garlick, *Lawrence*, p. 35, *Catalogue*, p. 73.

Among the portraits bespoken from Lawrence by George IV in 1824 was a 'Kit Cat Portrait of the Lord Chancellor' at £210; Lawrence's receipt for this sum is dated 15 August 1826 (W.R.A., Geo. 27041, 26690; *Letters of George IV*, vol. III, 1591, 1592). On 15 July 1826 the portrait had been sent for by Lawrence to be varnished (Jutsham, *Deliveries*, ff. 81, 85). According to Lord Eldon's son, George IV had been much pleased with Lawrence's earlier portrait of Eldon when he had been Attorney-General, and desired that the portrait for himself should be 'in the same plain style of dress and general arrangement' (Twiss, *loc. cit.*). No. 896 is also very close in type to the portrait painted for Sir Robert Peel (R.A. 1825 (118), now at Cowdray Park). No. 896 is possibly the portrait exhibited at the Royal Academy in 1828 (463). A repetition, painted in Lawrence's studio, is in the National Portrait Gallery (464). No. 896 was engraved by Doo (1828), H. Robinson (1831) and others.

A Tory of the most reactionary nature, a lawyer of immense application, patience and justice, he was Solicitor-General, 1788–93, Attorney-General, 1793–9, and Lord Chancellor, 1801–27. Devoted to George III, he later was taken into the confidence of the Regent who nicknamed him 'Old Bags'.

897. FRANCIS I, EMPEROR OF AUSTRIA
(1768–1835) (*Plate* 193)

Windsor Castle (198). 106½ × 70¼ in., 270,5 × 178,4 cm.

Full-length, seated, in military uniform with his plumed hat on a table beside him. He wears the Garter round his leg and the ribbon and star of the order under a magnificent jewelled Golden Fleece; he also wears the stars of the Order of Leopold of Austria and of the Order of the Iron Crown of Austria.

Painted for George IV; recorded in the inventory of 'Carleton Palace' (647: 'Full length of the Emperor of Austria. Lawrence. In the Waterloo Gallery, Windsor Castle').

Literature: Williams, vol. II, pp. 110–11, 112, 113, 114, 117, 118, 119, 134, 145; Waagen (1838), vol. I, pp. 167–8, 169–70; Collins Baker, *Windsor*, p. 206; Garlick, *Lawrence*, p. 37; R.A., *Sir Thomas Lawrence*, 1961 (16); Garlick, *Catalogue*, p. 82.

Painted in 1818–19 at Aix-la-Chapelle and Vienna. The first sitting was probably given on or soon after 25 October 1818 (Prince R. de Metternich, *Mémoires . . . Prince de Metternich*, vol. III, Paris (1881), p. 129). On 5 November 1818 Lawrence wrote that the Emperor had sat to him in his new 'painting-room' at Aix, 'and the result has been, that, from the first sitting to the last completion of the likeness, (for it is finished,) I entirely succeeded, I may truly and accurately say, to the delight of his officers and attendants . . . Yesterday was his sixth sitting, and he sits to me once more for the hand, the face being entirely completed. 'I had some difficulties to encounter. His countenance is rather long and thin, and when grave, is grave to melancholy; but when he speaks, benevolence itself lights it up with the most agreeable expressions, and making it the perfect image of a good mind.' 'That expression', Lawrence later wrote, 'I have been happy enough to catch.' The Emperor seems to have sat again to Lawrence on 8 November; seven sittings were given in all. Copies were ordered by the Tsar and by the Emperor himself for the Town House at Aix. It seems that the Emperor intended that Lawrence should paint him again in Vienna and on 10 January 1819 he gave Lawrence the second of the fresh sittings, but it is not clear whether this was for an entirely different portrait or whether the large whole-length of the Emperor which Lawrence lists with his portraits done in Vienna is not in fact No. 897. Lawrence was paid £525 for the portrait (W.R.A., Geo. 26642; *Letters of George IV*, vol. III, 1592) which was still (unfinished) in Lawrence's studio at his death. It was claimed on 24 January 1830 (Garlick, *Catalogue*, p. 277); Seguier's account of 10 April 1830 includes ten guineas for cleaning and varnishing the canvas and 'The background and Accompaniments finished' (W.R.A., Geo. 26750). The portrait was exhibited at the British Institution in 1830 (18) and engraved by G. H. Phillips in 1837. Lawrence kept, and gave to Farington, 'the first accurate drawing—a canvass of the Emperor Francis' (Williams, vol. II, p. 131); F. C. Lewis's engraving of it was published in April 1839 (Garlick, *Catalogue*, p. 227). A watercolour copy of No. 897 is in the Musée Condé, Chantilly.

Eldest son of the Emperor Leopold II, whom he succeeded in 1792, and brother of the Archduke Charles (No. 891).

898. FREDERICK WILLIAM III, KING OF PRUSSIA (1770–1840) (*Plate* 199)

Windsor Castle (196). 106½ × 70¼ in., 270,5 × 178,4 cm.

Full-length, standing, in military uniform, holding his plumed hat in his right hand. He wears the badge of the Red Eagle of Prussia and the Iron Cross of Prussia, the star of the Black Eagle of Prussia superimposed on the Garter and the Sword of the Order of the Sword of Sweden.

Painted for George IV; recorded in the inventory of 'Carleton Palace' (653: 'Full length of the King of Prussia. Lawrence. In the Waterloo Gallery, Windsor Castle').

Literature: Williams, vol. I, pp. 341–2, vol. II, pp. 113, 117, 118,

119–20; Waagen (1838), vol. I, p. 168; Collins Baker, *Windsor*, p. 207; R.A., *King's Pictures* (123); Garlick, *Lawrence*, p. 37; R.A., *Sir Thomas Lawrence*, 1961 (9); Garlick, *Catalogue*, p. 83.

Begun in London in 1814 and finished at Aix-la-Chapelle in 1818. The King arrived in London on 7 June 1814 and sat to Lawrence at the Prince Regent's request; sittings were given at York House. At the end of 1818 the King gave Lawrence six sittings at Aix-la-Chapelle. Metternich wrote to Princess Lieven from Aix on 18 November that 'Le roi de Prusse est à peu près achevé et parfait' (*Lettres . . . à la Comtesse de Lieven*, ed. J. Hanoteau (Paris, 1909), p. 10). On 26 November Lawrence wrote that the King was taller than the Tsar (No. 883) or the Emperor of Austria (No. 897), 'but with more reserve of manner. He has good features, and is of a sincere and generous nature'. The King, and possibly the Tsar also, commissioned copies of the portrait (a repetition is recorded in Berlin). The Duke of Wellington had also asked Lawrence for a portrait of the King (*Sir Thomas Lawrence's Letter-Bag*, ed. G. S. Layard (1906), p. 134). The sitter presented Lawrence with a superb diamond ring with his initials in the centre.

Lawrence was paid £525 for the portrait (W.R.A., Geo. 26642; *Letters of George IV*, vol. III, 1592); it was in his studio at his death and was claimed on 24 January 1830 (Garlick, *Catalogue*, p. 277). Seguier's account of 10 April 1830 includes four guineas for cleaning and varnishing the canvas (W.R.A., Geo. 26750). It was exhibited at the British Institution in 1830 (17). A drawing of the King by Lawrence, sold in his sale at Christie's, 19 June 1830 (403), was engraved by F. C. Lewis in 1839 (Garlick, *Catalogue*, p. 227).

Succeeded his father, Frederick William II, in 1797; in 1813 he joined the Tsar Alexander I in alliance against Napoleon; in his later years he became increasingly reactionary in his views. For his wife, see No. 1103.

899. FREDERICK, BARON VON GENTZ (1764–1832) (*Plate* 218)

Windsor Castle (2459). 30⅜ × 24½ in., 77,2 × 62,2 cm

Head and shoulders in a fur-lined coat; of the two orders that he wears round his neck, the upper is the Red Eagle of Prussia and the lower may be the Iron Cross of Prussia; of the two badges worn in his buttonhole, the larger is that of St. Stephen of Austria and he wears the ribbon of the order across his breast.

Painted for George IV; recorded in the inventory of 'Carleton Palace' (663: 'Portrait of Gentz. Lawrence'); later at Hampton Court (936), but removed to Windsor in 1901.

Literature: Williams, vol. II, pp. 145, 168; Waagen (1838), vol. I, p. 169 (1854), vol. II, p. 413; Law, 1881, 1898 (363); Collins Baker, *Windsor*, p. 194; R.A., *King's Pictures* (79); Garlick, *Lawrence*, p. 38, *Catalogue*, pp. 85, 278.

No. 899 is listed, at £157. 10s., with the portraits painted for George IV during Sir Benjamin Bloomfield's Keepership of the Privy Purse: '[Half length] Three Quarters of Chevalier Gentz' (W.R.A., Geo. 26642; *Letters of George IV*, vol. III, 1592). Gentz met Lawrence in 1818 at Aix-la-Chapelle. On 29 October he went with Metternich to see the painter's 'herrlichen Portraits' and on 2 November, at dinner with Metternich, he met Lawrence 'der mein Portrait machen will'. Lawrence began the portrait in Vienna on 24 March 1819; on 27 March Gentz sat for six hours 'in welcher mein (für den Prinzen-Regenten von England bestimmtes) Portrait, in grosser Aehnlichkeit und Vollkommenheit so gut

als vollendet wird'; and on 31 March he gave the painter a further short sitting: 'mein Portrait der Gegenstand allgemeiner Bewunderung' (*Tagebücher von Friedrich von Gentz* (Leipzig, 1873), vol. II, pp. 278, 280, 314, 315). The portrait was not, however, finished by Lawrence and on 10 April 1830 William Seguier submitted an account for two guineas for cleaning and varnishing it and for 'The Dress finished' (W.R.A., Geo. 26750). The portrait was exhibited at the British Institution in 1830 (36) and 1833 (31). A replica was in the collection of Prince Metternich-Winneburg in Vienna. A good version was formerly in the collection of J. R. Saunders, London; a copy was in New York in 1927.

A leading writer on political and financial matters in the Revolutionary period; influenced in his youth by Kant, he entered the Prussian service, but in 1802 transferred himself to Vienna. In 1812 he became Metternich's secretary, and eventually his confidant; known as 'the Secretary of Europe', he acted as Secretary-General at the Vienna Congress and at a number of other Congresses. His early Liberalism, and sympathy with the French Revolution in its first stages, gave way to implacable opposition to Napoleon and a conservative approach to foreign and domestic problems.

900. CHARLES AUGUSTUS, PRINCE HARDENBERG (1750–1822) (*Plate* 209)

Windsor Castle (195). 56 × 44½ in., 142,2 × 113 cm.

Three-quarter-length, seated by a table on which he rests his left hand; his right holds his spectacles. He wears the Iron Cross of Prussia, the ribbon and star of the Black Eagle of Prussia and, round his neck, the ribbon and badge of the Red Eagle of Prussia.

Painted for George IV; recorded in the inventory of 'Carleton Palace' (671: 'Half length of Prince Hardenburg. Lawrence. In the Waterloo Gallery, Windsor Castle').

Literature: Williams, vol. II, pp. 112, 118; Waagen (1838), vol. I, p. 168; Collins Baker, *Windsor*, pp. 208–9; R.A., *King's Pictures* (128); Garlick, *Lawrence*, p. 41, *Catalogue*, p. 101.

Begun at Aix-la-Chapelle in 1818. When the Tsar (see No. 883) gave his first sitting to Lawrence early in November, the portrait of 'Prince Hardenburgh' was among those he saw. By 26 November Lawrence wrote that 'The ministers, in whose portraits I have equally succeeded, all request copies of them—Prince Hardenberg . . .' (Williams, *loc. cit.*). Lawrence was paid £315 for the portrait (W.R.A., Geo. 26642; *Letters of George IV*, vol. III, 1592). It was in Lawrence's studio at his death and was claimed on 22 January 1830 (Garlick, *Catalogue*, p. 278), when it was still unfinished: Seguier's account of 10 April 1830 includes five guineas for cleaning and varnishing it and 'the hands and dress finished' (W.R.A., Geo. 26750). It was exhibited at the British Institution in 1830 (13). A copy is at Arniston House; another was on the art-market in Lucerne in 1930.

Served at the courts of Hanover, Brunswick and Bayreuth; in 1791 he entered the Prussian service and became Foreign Secretary, 1804, and Chancellor, 1810.

901. CHARLES WILLIAM, BARON VON HUMBOLDT (1767–1835) (*Plate* 215)

Windsor Castle (185). 52¾ × 41½ in., 134, × 105,4 cm.

Three-quarter-length, standing, resting his left hand on papers.

Painted for George IV; recorded in the inventory of 'Carleton

Palace' (688: 'Portrait of the Baron d'Humboldt—Lawrence. The Head painted by Lawrence The rest by Evans'); placed later in the Waterloo Chamber.

Literature: Waagen (1838), vol. I, pp. 168–9; Collins Baker, *Windsor*, p. 209; Garlick, *Lawrence*, p. 43, *Catalogue*, p. 109.

Begun in London in 1828. On 21 July 1828 Lawrence wrote to the Duchess of St. Albans, regretting that he had been unable to go to her party on 18 July. 'It had happened that that Morning I had been oblig'd to take an early and very long sitting from Baron Humboldt, by His Majestys Command' (MSS. sold at Sotheby's, 2 March 1965 (469)). Only the head and cravat appear to be by Lawrence, although he may have indicated to some extent the remainder of the design. At Lawrence's death it was still in his studio. In his executors' list it is stated that the head only had been finished. It was delivered on 7 June 1830 and the executors received £157. 10s. for it on 12 June 1830 (Garlick, *Catalogue*, p. 279; W.R.A., Geo. 26680). Richard Evans had presumably finished the portrait before 3 June 1835, when Waagen (*loc. cit.*) saw it in the Waterloo Chamber. He found the likeness weak. He stated that the head had been painted by Lawrence, 'being pressed for time', on to a portrait begun by him of Lord Liverpool; he adds that the body had been finished, that Humboldt's head was added to it, but that the necessary alterations to the body were not carried out because of Lawrence's death. In fact the portrait adapted for this purpose was almost certainly a version of the portrait of Lord Melville, now at Dalmeny (Garlick, *Catalogue*, p. 141).

Founder of Berlin University in 1809; Prussian Minister in Rome, 1801, and a Prussian representative at the Congress of Vienna.

902. PRINCE LEOPOLD OF SAXE-COBURG, LATER LEOPOLD I, KING OF THE BELGIANS (*Plate* 217)

Windsor Castle (183) 106¼ × 71¾ in , 269,9 × 182,2 cm

Full-length, standing, in Garter robes, holding in his left hand the plumed hat of the order and clasping in his right hand a Field-Marshal's baton. He wears the collars of the Orders of the Guelphs, the Bath and the Garter.

Presented by the sitter to the Prince Consort on his birthday, 26 August 1841: '. . . Sir Thomas Lawrence . . . The King of the Belgians in the Robes of the Garter full length . . . (1828)' (MS. 'List of Pictures presented to or purchased by His Royal Highness Prince Albert').

Literature: Collins Baker, *Windsor*, p. 210; Garlick, *Lawrence*, p. 46, *Catalogue*, p. 125.

The portrait was begun in London in the summer of 1821. On 4 June 1821 Farington wrote in his *Diary* (vol. VIII, p. 286): 'Sir Thos. Lawrence told me that Prince Leopold sat to him yesterday for a whole length in Garter robes. He spoke of the Prince as being full of conversation.' The portrait was exhibited at the British Institution in 1830 (34); a second version (attributed to Winterhalter) is in the Royal Palace at Brussels; and the design was used for the figure of the Prince in the relevant plate in Sir George Nayler's projected *History of the Coronation of George IV* (1824, 1839). On 14 November 1834 the sitter wrote from Laeken to tell Princess Victoria that her portrait (probably the full-length by Hayter) 'will be suspended vis a vis of mine, painted by Lawrence, I can not disguise from you, that the size of your worthy Uncle somewhat overwhelms the Niece, who shines more by her virtues than her tallness' (W.R.A., Y.61/36).

On 22 August 1841 he wrote to the Prince Consort of his intention to let him have 'die schöne Lawrence' which he regarded as partly belonging to the Queen and which she had wished for; he expressed the hope that their children and children's children would glance at it now and again with a kindly eye; and, on 3 September, expressed his happiness in the pleasure the picture had given to the Prince: 'es ist auch als Kunstwerk nicht zu verachten' (*ibid.*, Y.144/53, 54). The Queen and Prince placed it in the Waterloo Gallery, where they went after luncheon on 15 September 1841 'to see the fine picture of Uncle Leopold by Lawrence which he has sent over as a birthday present to Albert to be placed there'. The paint has a noticeably smoother texture round the head than on the rest of the canvas.

903. ROBERT BANKS JENKINSON, SECOND EARL OF LIVERPOOL (1770–1828) (*Plate* 214)

Windsor Castle (176). 55 × 42¾ in., 139,7 × 108,6 cm. There are additions of 2⅝ in. at the top, *c* 2½ in. at the bottom, 1¼ in. on the left and 1½ in. on the right.

Three-quarter-length, standing by a table, wearing the ribbon and star of the Garter.

Painted for George IV; recorded in the inventory of 'Carleton Palace' (661: 'Half length of the Earl of Liverpool. Lawrence. In the Waterloo Gallery, Windsor Castle').

Literature: Waagen (1838), vol. I, p. 168; Collins Baker, *Windsor*, p. 210; Garlick, *Lawrence*, p. 47, *Catalogue*, p. 127.

A half-length of Lord Liverpool, at £315, was among the pictures painted by Lawrence (*c.* 1820) for George IV while Sir Benjamin Bloomfield was Keeper of the Privy Purse (W.R.A., Geo. 26642; *Letters of George IV*, vol. III, 1592). The portrait was in Lawrence's studio at his death and was claimed on 22 January 1830 (Garlick, *Catalogue*, p. 278); Seguier's account of 10 April 1830 includes two guineas for cleaning and varnishing it (W.R.A., Geo. 26750). C. Turner's engraving was published on 8 March 1827. The portrait was exhibited at the British Institution in 1830 (12). A replica, with slight variations, is at Ickworth.

Foreign Secretary, 1801–3; Home Secretary, 1804–6, in Pitt's second Ministry and again, 1807–9; Secretary for War and the Colonies, 1809–12; Prime Minister, 1812–27.

904. MARIA II, DA GLÓRIA, QUEEN OF PORTUGAL (1819–53) (*Plate* 226)

Windsor Castle (331). 36⅜ × 28¼ in., 92,4 × 71,8 cm.

Half-length, seated with her hands resting on the arm of her chair. She wears across her right shoulder the ribbons of the Portuguese Orders of Christ, St. Benedict d'Avis and St. James of the Sword; the stars on her breast include those of the Portuguese Order of the Conception and the Brazilian Orders of Pedro I, of the Cruzeiro and the Rose.

Painted for George IV; recorded in the inventory of 'Carleton Palace' (675: 'Half length of Donna Maria de Gloria. Lawrence'); it was hanging in the Closet at Windsor by 15 September 1838 (Queen Victoria, Journal for that day).

Literature: Williams, vol. II, pp. 513–14; Cunningham, *Wilkie*, vol. III, p. 28; Collins Baker, *Windsor*, p. 195; Garlick, *Lawrence*, p. 49, *Catalogue*, pp. 139, 279.

Among the portraits bespoken from Lawrence by George IV in 1825 was 'A Kit Cat Portrait of Her Majesty the Queen of Portugal' for £210; Lawrence had a final sitting from the Queen on 17 August 1829. Lawrence's receipt for payment is dated 9 September 1829 (W.R.A., Geo. 27043; *Letters of*

George IV, vol. III, 1591). In 1830 Edward Wyatt was paid £12. 16s. for a 'fully enrich'd Frame' for it and William Seguier was paid one guinea for cleaning and varnishing the portrait (*ibid.*, 26752, 26750). The back of the canvas is inscribed with the names of artist and sitter and the date 1827. It was exhibited at the British Institution in 1830 (52) and 1833 (34); it was engraved by R. Graves for *The Amulet* (1833), and by J. Lucas, 1836. A repetition is in the Museu Nacional de Arte Antiga, Lisbon, possibly the finished copy sold in Lawrence's sale at Christie's, 18 June 1831 (98).

Daughter of Pedro IV, King of Portugal, who had abdicated in 1826. She came to England in 1826 because of the civil disorders in Portugal. Greville records a dinner given by George IV on 28 May 1828 to the Dukes of Orléans and Chartres and the children's ball in the evening. 'It was pretty enough, and I saw for the first time the Queen of Portugal and our little Victoria. The Queen was finely dressed, with a riband and order over her shoulder, and she sat by the King. She is good-looking and has a sensible Austrian countenance . . . Our little Princess is a short, plain-looking child, and not near so good-looking as the Portuguese'. She left London in August 1829, but paid a second visit in 1833. Her second husband, Ferdinand of Saxe-Coburg, was Queen Victoria's and the Prince Consort's first cousin.

905. CLEMENS LOTHAR WENZEL, PRINCE METTERNICH (1773–1859) (*Plate* 207)

Windsor Castle (206). 50½ × 41 in., 128,3 × 104,1 cm.; in addition, the original painted surface has been turned over at the top (*c.* 2¼ in.), on the left (2½ in.), on the right (1 in.) and at the bottom (2½ in.).

Three-quarter-length, seated, wearing court uniform and holding a paper in his left hand. He wears three stars on his breast, the Golden Fleece, the ribbon of St. Stephen of Austro-Hungary (one of the three stars is the star of this order), and the Austrian Civil Cross of Honour.

Painted for George IV; recorded in the inventory of 'Carleton Palace' (662: 'Half length of Prince Metternick. Lawrence. In the Waterloo Gallery, Windsor Castle').

Literature: Williams, vol. II, pp. 112, 118, 122, 135, 136, 145; Waagen (1838), vol. I, p. 168; Collins Baker, *Windsor*, p. 211; Garlick, *Lawrence*, p. 50; R.A., *Sir Thomas Lawrence*, 1961 (15); Garlick, *Catalogue*, p. 142.

Lawrence had exhibited a portrait of Metternich at the Royal Academy in 1815 (76).[1] No. 905 is listed, at £315, among the pictures painted while Sir Benjamin Bloomfield was Keeper of the Privy Purse (W.R.A., 26642; *Letters of George IV*, vol. III, 1592); it was claimed from Lawrence's executors on 22 January 1830 (Garlick, *Catalogue*, p. 278), when it was probably still unfinished: Seguier's account of 10 April 1830 includes five guineas for cleaning and varnishing the portrait and 'the hands and dress finished' (W.R.A., Geo. 26750). It was exhibited at the British Institution in 1830 (3) and was engraved by S. Cousins (August 1829) and C. G. Lewis (1842).
In the autumn of 1818 and early in 1819, at Aix-la-Chapelle and Vienna, Lawrence was again at work on a portrait of Metternich; and it is possible that he was not painting a fresh portrait but re-working the earlier portrait. Lawrence's own list of the portraits he had painted at Vienna includes, under half-lengths: 'greatly altering, improving, and almost completing Prince Metternich'. On 1 October 1818 Metternich

1. A sitting in 1814 is recorded by Farington (*Diary*, vol. VII, p. 260).

wrote from Aix that Lawrence had nearly finished the portrait; on 11 November it was still not quite finished. On 18 November he wrote that he had been charmed 'd'y revoir mon portrait' and that he was going to sit to Lawrence on 19 November: 'je ferai ôter le trait méchant'. On 24 December, writing from Vienna, Metternich told Princess Lieven, 'Je vais faire terminer mon portrait. Lawrence lui-même m'a proposé de me rendre moins méchant, et je l'y ai autorisé.' Lawrence continued to be dissatisfied with the likeness—'below the character of his countenance'—and devoted a sitting of three hours on 11 January 1819 to finishing the right eye; on 12 February two hours were spent 'à ébaucher ma main droite'; and by now the portrait, no longer 'méchant', ran the risk in Metternich's eyes of being 'un peu trop *moutonné*'. On 10 March Metternich wrote that the portrait was finished except for two sittings which Lawrence had asked for in Rome, in which he wanted to complete Metternich's right calf; these sittings Metternich intended to refuse (Williams, *loc. cit.*; Prince R. de Metternich, *Mémoires* . . . *Prince de Metternich*, vol. III (Paris, 1881), pp. 129, 131; *Lettres du Prince de Metternich à la Comtesse de Lieven*, ed. J. Hanoteau (Paris, 1909), pp. 9–10, 82–3, 108, 130, 195, 240). The laboured quality of No. 905 is perhaps explained by these references, but it is possible that it is a second version, painted for the Regent, and that the original was that which in 1935 belonged to Prince Sandor Metternich. Other versions are in the Bundeskanzleramt, Vienna, and the Palais Esterhazy, Eisenstadt. In 1953 a small version, perhaps a preliminary sketch, belonged to Prince Lanckoronski. Metternich himself was anxious that the portrait should be copied and in January 1819 was planning to send to Princess Lieven 'une petite copie *bien cachée*'.

As a young man visited England, where he met Pitt, Fox and Burke and became a friend of the Prince of Wales; Austrian Minister at Dresden, 1803–6, and Berlin, 1806–9; Ambassador in Paris; Minister for Foreign Affairs, 1809–48. In the revolution of 1848 he took refuge in England, but he returned to Vienna and was kindly treated by the Emperor Franz Josef. To contemporaries Metternich appeared complacent, indolent, superficial ('a society hero and nothing more') and pompous; but his great influence as a statesman, in a very long career, rested in part on his attachment to the principal of equilibrium in European affairs and to his belief in the 'Concert of Europe'. He believed in 'the *Society* of States as the essential condition of the modern world'.

906. ERNEST FREDERICK, COUNT MÜNSTER (1766–1839) (*Plate* 210)

Windsor Castle (192). 52½ × 42 in., 133,3 × 106,7 cm.

Three-quarter-length, standing, wearing court uniform with the ribbon and star of the Royal Hanoverian Guelphic Order and holding a paper in his hands.

Painted for George IV; recorded in the inventory of 'Carleton Palace' (669: 'Half length of Count Munster. Lawrence. In the Waterloo Gallery, Windsor Castle').

Literature: Collins Baker, *Windsor*, p. 212; Garlick, *Lawrence*, p. 51, *Catalogue*, p. 148.

Garlick (*Catalogue, loc. cit.*) states that a letter, formerly in the possession of Canon Aston of Salisbury, referred to a sitting by Count Münster to Lawrence in London in 1820. The portrait was in Lawrence's studio at his death '½ finished' and was delivered to the King on 26 or 28 January 1830; £157. 10s. was to be paid for it (*ibid.*, p. 278; W.R.A., Geo. 26675). It was finished by Richard Evans who, on 1

July 1830, submitted his claim of fifty guineas on the late King's estate 'for finishing a portrait of Count Munster begun by the late Sir Tho<u>s</u> Lawrence'; his receipt for this sum is dated 14 July 1830 (W.R.A., Geo. 26600; 32824). little more than the head seems to be by Lawrence himself.

Hanoverian Minister of State from 1805 and Hanoverian representative at the Congress of Vienna. In March 1812 he was appointed one of three commissioners for protection and management of the King's private property. In 1818 he was employed in the negotiations for the marriage of the Duke of Clarence to Princess Adelaide of Saxe-Meiningen. He was often in England. In 1826 he was arranging for the despatch to Hanover of a version of Lawrence's official portrait of George IV (*Letters of George IV*, vol. III, 1255).

907. CHARLES ROBERT, COUNT NESSELRODE (1770–1862) (*Plate* 208)

Windsor Castle (200). 56 × 44¼ in., 142,2 × 112,4 cm.

Three-quarter-length, seated at a table on which he rests his left hand; he wears the ribbon of St. Alexander Newski, and the collar of the Order of the Annunciation.

Painted for George IV; recorded in the inventory of 'Carleton Palace' (664: 'Half length of Count Nesselrode. Lawrence. In the Waterloo Gallery, Windsor Castle').

Literature: Williams, vol. II, pp. 112, 118; Waagen (1838), vol. I, p. 168; Collins Baker, *Windsor*, p. 212; Garlick, *Lawrence*, p. 52, *Catalogue*, p. 151.

Painted at Aix-la-Chapelle late in 1818; when the Tsar (No. 883) gave his first sitting to Lawrence, his portrait of Nesselrode was among those he saw in his studio. Lawrence was paid £315 for the portrait while Sir Benjamin Bloomfield was Keeper of the Privy Purse (W.R.A., Geo. 26642; *Letters of George IV*, vol. III, 1592). It was unfinished and in Lawrence's studio at his death and was claimed on 22 January 1830 (Garlick, *Catalogue*, p. 278). Seguier's account of 10 April 1830 included four guineas for cleaning and varnishing the canvas and 'the hand and back ground, finished' (W.R.A., 26750). It was exhibited at the British Institution in 1830 (15). Nesselrode is stated to have asked Lawrence for a copy of the portrait (Williams, *loc. cit.*).

Foreign Minister to the Tsar Alexander I, a signatory of the Treaty of Fontainebleau in 1814 and a Russian plenipotentiary at the Congress of Vienna.

908. WILLIAM PITT (1759–1806) (*Plate* 190)

Windsor Castle (305). 59 × 48 in., 149,9 × 121,9 cm.

Three-quarter-length, standing by a table, resting his left hand on a paper inscribed: *Redemption | of the | National | Debt.*

Given to George IV by Angerstein in 1816 (see below); recorded in the inventory of 'Carleton Palace' (685: 'Portrait of Mr Pitt Lawrence'). Morant's bill, receipted 27 March 1829, includes, under 20 November 1828, £25. 10s. for 'A [richly ornamented Frame] for a Bishops ½ length Portrait of Mr Pitt. for Windsor Castle' (W.R.A., Geo. 26558). The portrait had been sent down to Windsor in November 1828.

Literature: Williams, vol. I, pp. 281–2, vol. II, p. 266; *Sir Thomas Lawrence's Letter-Bag*, ed. G. S. Layard (1906), pp. 46–7; Collins Baker, *Windsor*, p. 194; Garlick, *Lawrence*, p. 54, *Catalogue*, p. 161.

Painted posthumously for John Julius Angerstein from Angerstein's version of the bust of Pitt by Nollekens,[1]

1. A great many versions exist of Nollekens's bust of Pitt, which was based on a death-mask.

with assistance from the death-mask, but not from any other painted portrait. Lawrence does not seem to have painted Pitt in his lifetime, although on 5 October 1803 Farington had been told by Lawrence that he was to paint a full-length of him for the Princess of Wales and, on 6 September 1804, that Pitt had promised the Princess that he would sit to Lawrence for her (*Diary*, vol. II, pp. 158, 282); Pitt had also told Lawrence in 1804 that he would sit to him for a portrait for Lord Abercorn (*ibid.*, vol. III, p. 15, vol. V, pp. 57, 60), and Lawrence had studied Pitt's face when he was in his presence. On 7 May 1807 Farington 'Passed the whole morning with Lawrence whilst He painted a portrait of Mr. Pitt from Mr. Angerstein's Bust of Him by Nollekins & from his remembrance of Mr. Pitt.—I sat to Him to enable Him to judge of the colouring. He finished the head & I thought it an admirable likeness.' Farington again saw Lawrence at work on the portrait on 9 and 10 May; on 12 May he called on Lawrence '& sat to Him while He made a few alterations abt. the nose & mouth of Mr. Pitt's portrait which from recollection of His face, & from the Cast from it, He deemed necessary'; on 22 May Farington saw Lawrence at work on the background; and on 28 May Lawrence showed Farington a letter in which Dacre Adams expressed his desire to buy the portrait. On 11 June Farington stood to Lawrence 'while altering one of the Arms of the portrait . . ., at the suggestion of Sir N. Holland'. Lawrence told Farington, in two letters at this time, what visitors to his studio had thought of the portrait (Layard, *loc. cit.*). The coat, moreover, had originally been painted black; on 16 September Farington notes: 'Lawrence . . . had painted Mr. Pitt's Coat Crimson Lake colour instead of Black'; and on 25 September alterations to the background were being proposed. On 24 April 1808 Lawrence was still 'anxious abt. the alteration of the right arm of Mr. Pitt's portrait'. The portrait was exhibited at the Royal Academy in 1808 (95).

Farington records a number of comments upon the success of the portrait by those who saw it while it was being painted. The lower part of the face was thought to be the least successful part of the head, but on the whole it was warmly praised: the Marquess of Abercorn thought it 'very like'; Lady Chatham said it was 'beyond comparison the most like of anything that had been done'; West thought it a remarkably vivid likeness but very facile; and there were those who thought it less successful than Hoppner's portrait (*ibid.*, vol. IV, pp. 133, 135, 139, 152, 154, 164, 244, 252, vol. V, pp. 74, 77; unpublished, 26 May, 3 and 15 June, 20 July, 31 August 1807; see also W. T. Whitley, *Art in England 1800–20* (1928), p. 133). On 3 September 1816 Lawrence showed Farington the portrait that he had painted for Angerstein 'who had given it to the Prince Regent'; Lawrence was to make a copy of it for Angerstein (*ibid.*, vol. VIII, p. 89).[1] Angerstein's copy or replica is now in the possession of the Earl of Rosebery. No. 908 bears every sign of original quality and there are slight *pentimenti* in the left hand and in the papers on the right. The design was engraved by C. Turner and S. Cousins in 1837.

Younger son of the great Earl of Chatham. Chancellor of the Exchequer, 1782, Prime Minister, 1783; formed the three coalitions against France and devoted his life to the defeat of Napoleon; resigned in 1801 over Catholic Emancipation, but supported Addington's administration; returned to office, 1804, but died after the battle of Austerlitz had destroyed the third of the coalitions he had built up.

1. Copies had earlier been requested by Lords Aberdeen and Abercorn.

909. POPE PIUS VII (1742–1823) (Plate 204)

Windsor Castle (201). 106×70 in., 269,2×177,9 cm.

Full-length, seated on the papal throne on which he was carried at solemn ceremonies, holding a paper in his left hand inscribed: *Per | Anto Canova*.[1] In the background is a view of a sculpture gallery in the Vatican, in which are placed the *Apollo Belvedere, Laocoon* and *Torso Belvedere*.

Painted for George IV; recorded in the inventory of 'Carleton Palace, (650: . . . 'In the Waterloo Gallery, Windsor Castle').

Literature: Williams, vol. II, pp. 152–3, 159, 163, 166–7, 176–7, 186–7, 188–9, 193–6, 200, 209–10, 237; Waagen (1838), vol. I, p. 168; *Sir Thomas Lawrence's Letter-Bag*, ed. G. S. Layard (1906), pp. 144–6; Collins Baker, *Windsor*, p. 213; R.A., *King's Pictures* (131); Garlick, *Lawrence*, p. 54; T. S. R. Boase, *English Art 1800–70* (1959), pp. 12–13; R.A., *Sir Thomas Lawrence*, 1961 (5); Garlick, *Catalogue*, p. 162.

Painted in Rome in 1819. Lawrence was granted an audience with the Pope at the Palazzo del Quirinale on 18 May: 'He had a fine countenance—stoops a little—with firm yet sweet-toned voice . . . through all the storms of the past, he retains the jet black of his hair'. The Pope gave Lawrence nine sittings. In the first three, Lawrence 'painted . . . a very strong likeness of him. The face, however, is not finished; for the Pope being an old man, his countenance has a great deal of detail in it; and a good and cheerful nature, with a clear intellect, gives it variety of expression . . . He is a very fine subject, and it is probable that the picture will be one of the best that I have painted.' The portrait was greatly admired in Rome. On 25 June Lawrence wrote: 'No picture that I have painted has been more popular with the friends of its subject, and the public . . . and, according to my scale of ability, I have executed my intention: having given him that expression of unaffected benevolence and worth, which lights up his countenance with a freshness and spirit, entirely free (except in the characteristic paleness of his complexion) from that appearance of illness and decay that he generally has, when enduring the fatigue of his public functions.' The Pope himself took care that the correct ring should be represented on his right hand. By 18 and 29 June Lawrence could write of his complete success with the portrait: 'to the utmost of my expectation, and almost of my wishes'. He was particularly pleased at having, by rendering accurately the Pope's real character and 'with a good and true tone of colour' gained a victory over earlier portraits of the Pope by David and Camucini. 'The people of Rome', Lawrence wrote on 9 July, '. . . are delighted at seeing this venerable and good being so faithfully, and (though it is not in the least flattering) so favourably represented.'[2] By 15 July he had finished the likeness and greatly advanced with the rest. On 21 September he wrote to his sister that the portrait was finished. The Pope commissioned a copy from Lawrence for Rome.

Lawrence was paid £525 for the portrait (W.R.A., Geo. 26642; *Letters of George IV*, vol. III, 1592). It was in Lawrence's studio at his death and was claimed on 24 January 1830 (Garlick, *Catalogue*, p. 277). Seguier's account of 10 April 1830 includes four guineas for cleaning and varnishing the canvas (W.R.A., 26750). It was exhibited at the British Institution in 1830 (10) and engraved by S. Cousins in 1829. A small version is at Great Glen Hall; Garlick (*Catalogue*, p. 16) records two copies by Simpson of which the first may be the copy at Petworth (1). A drawing, now in

1. Perhaps the document by which Canova was created Marchese d'Ischia.
2. For Metternich's admiration for the portrait, see his *Mémoires*, vol. III (Paris, 1881), p. 218.

the Pierpont Morgan Library, is correctly described by Garlick (*ibid.*, p. 240) as after the painting (reproduced, *Burl. Mag.*, vol. XCV (1953), p. 356).

Luigi Barnaba Chiaramonti, a Benedictine, Bishop of Tivoli, 1782, and Cardinal Bishop of Imola, 1785; elected Pope in 1800. He had crowned Napoleon as Emperor in Notre-Dame in 1801, but excommunicated him after his annexation of the Papal States; arrested by the French, the Pope was taken to Fontainebleau. The version of Lawrence's portrait of George IV (see No. 919) which is now in the Vatican was sent to the Pope by the King in return for the Pope's portrait.

910. MATVEI IVANOVITCH, COUNT PLATOV (1757–1818) (Plate 191)

Windsor Castle (186). 106×70½ in., 269,2×179,1 cm. There are slightly later additions of 1½ in. on the left, 6½ in. on the right, *c.* 5 in. at the top and *c.* 4 in. at the bottom.

Full-length, standing, in the uniform of a Cossack general, resting his left hand with his hat upon the saddle of his charger and pointing with a baton in his left hand to the city of Paris (?) in a distant landscape. He wears the badges of the Orders of St. Anne and St. George of Russia, the Red Eagle of Prussia and St. John of Jerusalem; the stars of the Black Eagle of Prussia and St. George of Russia; the ribbon and star of St. Andrew of Russia; and a miniature of George IV in a jewelled setting.

Painted for George IV; recorded in the inventory of 'Carleton Palace' (655: 'Full length of the Hetman Platoff. Lawrence. In the Waterloo Gallery, Windsor Castle').

Literature: Williams, vol. I, pp. 345–6; Waagen (1838), vol. I, p. 167; *Sir Thomas Lawrence's Letter-Bag*, ed. G. S. Layard (1906), pp. 255–6, 258; Collins Baker, *Windsor*, p. 214; R.A., *King's Pictures* (120); Garlick, *Lawrence*, p. 54; R.A., *Sir Thomas Lawrence*, 1961 (3); Garlick, *Catalogue*, p. 163.

Painted in London in the summer of 1814. On 9 June Lawrence showed Farington a note from Sir Charles Stewart 'informing Him that the Prince Regent desired to have two whole length Portraits of General Blucher & Genl. Platoff' (*Diary*, vol. VII, p. 257). Platov sat to Lawrence in his house in Russell Square, which was guarded by mounted Cossacks. Farington saw the portrait in Lawrence's studio on 21 July 1814; the day before he had seen 'A Cossack . . . standing to Him for Him to paint part of the dress of Marshall Platoff' (*ibid.*, p. 269). Lawrence's account of 4 January 1817 included £420 for the portrait (W.R.A., Geo. 26634; *Letters of George IV*, vol. III, 1592) which was exhibited at the Royal Academy in 1815 (163): 'a capital portrait, and represented him with his long, oval, Asiatic face, and with a considerable expression of cunning, which was in fact his character' (Williams, *loc. cit.*). It was also much admired by Farington (*Diary*, vol. VIII, p. 5). It was in Lawrence's studio at his death and was claimed on 24 January 1830 (Garlick, *Catalogue*, p. 278). Seguier's account of 10 April 1830 includes four guineas for cleaning and varnishing the portrait; Morant's bill, in 1830, includes the price of a frame for it (W.R.A., Geo. 26750, 26601). The portrait was exhibited at the British Institution in 1830 (11). Four 'bold studies' for the portrait were in Lawrence's sale at Christie's, 17 June 1830 (47) (Garlick, *Catalogue*, p. 240). There are considerable *pentimenti* in and above the horse; the sitter's left hand was at first painted higher; and there are *pentimenti* in the orders. The design was perhaps influenced by No. 1022. A rapid preliminary drawing is in the Royal Library.

A 'common Cossack of the Don', he became their Hetman and distinguished himself in the pursuit of the French army from Moscow and in the Russian advance into France (see No. 1107). In London in 1814 he was 'so cursedly provoked at the fuss made that he won't accept an invitation to go out'. He was unable to speak a word of English or French, but is said to have persuaded two English women to return with him to Russia.

911. ARMAND EMMANUEL, DUKE OF RICHELIEU (1766–1822) (Plate 205)

Windsor Castle (209). $52\frac{1}{2} \times 42$ in., $133,3 \times 106,7$ cm.; the canvas has been enlarged all round; the original surface was $50 \times 39\frac{1}{2}$ in.

Three-quarter-length, standing, resting his left arm on a ledge and holding a paper in his left hand.

Presumably painted for George IV; recorded in the inventory of 'Carleton Palace' (670: 'Half length of the Duc de Richelieu. Lawrence. In the Waterloo Gallery, Windsor Castle').

Literature: Williams, vol. II, pp. 113, 118; Collins Baker, *Windsor*, pp. 214–15; R.A., *King's Pictures* (125); Garlick, *Lawrence*, p. 55; R.A., *Sir Thomas Lawrence*, 1961 (17); Garlick, *Catalogue*, pp. 9, 167.

Lawrence received sittings from Richelieu at Aix-la-Chapelle in November 1818. The sittings from the King of Prussia (No. 898) 'and the Duc de Richelieu (a fine subject for the pencil) will complete my list at this place'; and the Duke was among the ministers, 'in whose portraits I have equally succeeded', who requested copies of their portraits. The portrait does not appear in any of the documents concerning Lawrence in the Royal Archives. It was in Lawrence's studio at his death and was claimed on 22 January 1830 (Garlick, *Catalogue*, p. 278). There is a *pentimento* in the paper, which was originally held higher. A smaller variant, now in the Musée de Besançon, is the portrait exhibited at the Paris Salon, 1824 (1053).

Served as a volunteer in the Russian army; returned to France in 1814 and became Minister of Foreign Affairs in 1815.

912. CHARLES PHILIP, PRINCE SCHWARZENBERG (1771–1820) (Plate 200)

Windsor Castle (207). $123\frac{1}{2} \times 95\frac{1}{4}$ in., $315 \times 241,9$ cm.; enlarged in painting *c.* $22\frac{1}{2}$ in. on the right to include the subsidiary figure and the horse; there are enlargements of 15 in. at the bottom and *c.* 2 in. on the left.

Full-length, standing, in military uniform with a baton in his right hand. A Uhlan orderly holds his charger and helps him to put on his great-coat. The prince wears the Golden Fleece, the ribbon and star of the Order of Maria Theresa, the stars of the Bath, the Royal Hanoverian Guelphic Order (Military Division), and the Order of St. Stephen and the Sword of Sweden.

Painted for George IV; recorded in the inventory of 'Carleton Palace' (658: 'Full length of Prince Schwartzenburg. Lawrence In the Waterloo Gallery, Windsor Castle').

Literature: Williams, vol. II, pp. 119, 130, 135, 145; Waagen (1838), vol. I, p. 167; Collins Baker, *Windsor*, p. 215; Garlick, *Lawrence*, p. 57; R.A., *Sir Thomas Lawrence*, 1961 (8); Garlick, *Catalogue*, pp. 173, 242.

Painted in Vienna in 1819, perhaps begun late in 1818. Lawrence wrote from Aix-la-Chapelle on 26 November 1818 that he was setting off to Vienna '. . . to paint the portrait of Prince Schwartzenburgh'; by 3 January 1819 he was writing from Vienna that he had been successful 'in three finished resemblances painted here . . . and I have given, in one sitting, but that a very long one, a likeness of Prince Scwartzenburgh, that is greatly liked by all that have seen it'. He was paid £840 for it (Williams, *op. cit.*; W.R.A., Geo. 26642, '. . . with his Hulan and Horse'; *Letters of George IV*, vol. III, 1592). Seguier's bill of 10 April 1830 included ten guineas for cleaning and varnishing the portrait and for finishing 'the hand and dress' (W.R.A., 26750); the portrait was in Lawrence's studio at his death and was claimed on 22 January 1830. Wyatt's account includes, under 6 May 1830, £14. 15s. for a frame for the portrait (*ibid.*, 26752). It was exhibited at the British Institution in 1830 (89). There is a *pentimento* in the Uhlan's arm which Lawrence painted at first a little higher. There is a drawing for the figure of the Uhlan in the Ashmolean Museum (*Fig.* 18; R.A., *Sir Thomas Lawrence*, 1961 (81)). Lawrence informed Farington that he had, while in Vienna, made a drawing of Schwarzenberg (Williams, *op. cit.*, p. 146; Garlick, *Catalogue*, p. 242). A drawing of the head was on the art-market in New York in 1913; a (?less good) drawing, at half-length, was on the art-market in Munich in 1952.

Field-Marshal who had commanded the Austrian auxiliary corps in the Russian campaign of 1812. At the end of the Napoleonic Wars he was Commander-in-Chief of the allied Grand Army of Bohemia; Blücher was his principal subordinate. 'A soldier of great personal integrity but one whose natural diffidence was increased by an almost pathological terror of Napoleon.'

913. SIR WALTER SCOTT (1771–1832) (Plate 220)

Windsor Castle (393). $63\frac{3}{4} \times 52\frac{1}{2}$ in., $161,9 \times 133,3$ cm.

Three-quarter-length seated, with a pen in his right hand and a walking-stick, beside a table on which are an ink-stand, candle and manuscripts inscribed: *Waverley* and [*The Fair*] *Maid of Perth*.

Painted for George IV; recorded in the inventory of 'Carleton Palace' (678). Sent down to Windsor at the King's command in November 1828.

Literature: Williams, vol. II, pp. 265, 455–6; Cunningham, vol. III, p. 83; J. G. Lockhart, *The Life of Sir Walter Scott* (Edinburgh edn.), vol. VI (1902), pp. 182–5, vol. VII (1902), pp. 20–1, vol. X (1903), p. 234; W. T. Whitley, *Art in England 1821–37* (1930), p. 130; R.A., *British Art*, 1934 (468), *Commemorative Catalogue* (1935), p. 94; Collins Baker, *Windsor*, p. 196; R.A., *King's Pictures* (55), *The First Hundred Years of the Royal Academy*, 1951–2 (162); Garlick, *Lawrence*, p. 57, *Catalogue*, p. 173.

No. 913 is listed, at £315, with the portraits painted for George IV during Sir Benjamin Bloomfield's Keepership of the Privy Purse: 'Half Length Portrait of Sir Walter Scott' (W.R.A., Geo. 26643; *Letters of George IV*, vol. III, 1592). In April 1827 Morant made for it, for £30, 'A bold richly ornamented Frame' (W.R.A., Geo. 26559). There is some confusion over the dating of the portrait. On 9 March 1821 Farington records (*Diary*, vol. VIII, p. 276) that George IV had sent Bloomfield to Clarke, the King's librarian, 'for him to apply to Sir Walter Scott . . . to desire him to sit to Sir Thos. Lawrence for his Portrait to be placed in the Royal Collection'. Lockhart (*op. cit.*, vol. VI, pp. 182–3) states, however, that soon after Scott's arrival in London in March 1820 he sat to Lawrence for the King and that the head was finished before Scott left for Edinburgh at the end of April: 'to the perfect truth of the representation, everyone who ever surprised him in the act of composition at his desk, will bear witness'. But he regretted that, after Scott had left London, Lawrence had 'filled in the figure from a separate sketch'; he thought nothing could have been better than the head, 'as I first saw it floating on a dark sea of canvass', but that its effect had been impaired by the change of scale and faulty proportion shown in 'the rest of the person'.[1] Lawrence found it difficult to keep the talkative Scott, who liked sitting for his portrait at seven in the morning, in an appropriately solemn mood; he encouraged Scott to recite poetry in order to produce a sparkle in his eyes. On 20 March 1820 Scott wrote to his wife: 'My picture comes on and will be a grand thing but the sitting is a great bor[e]' (*Letters*, ed. H. J. C. Grierson, vol. VI (1934), p. 156). On 1 February 1822 Joanna Baillie saw the portrait, though in an unfinished state: 'the best likeness of you that I have ever seen' (*The Private Letter-Books of Sir Walter Scott*, ed. W. Partington (1930), p. 263). There appears to have been considerable delay in finishing the portrait. Not until 12 November 1826 did Scott go 'to sit to Sir T.L. to finish the picture for his Majesty, which every one says is a very fine one. I think so myself and wonder how Sir Thomas made so much out of an old weather-beaten block.' On 18 November 'I finished my sitting[s] to Laurence, and am heartily sorry there should be another picture of me . . . The person is remarkably like . . .'; he admired its lack of affectation (*The Journal of Sir Walter Scott, 1825–6*, ed. J. G. Tait (1939), pp. 273, 279). On 14 November 1826 Scott had written to Mrs. Scott of Harden, asking for 'an outline of Eildon hills to enable Lawrence to throw them into the back-ground of the portrait he has made of me for Windsor. Properly it should present them as seen from the west & if you have a sketch from that point I would prefer it . . . The portrait is a very fair one and makes me think I have been a very ill-used gentleman on former occasions' (*Letters*, ed. H. J. C. Grierson, vol. X (1936), pp. 129–30). Of the MSS. on the table, *Waverley* had been published in 1814; *The Fair Maid of Perth* was published in 1828 and its title must have been written on to the paper after the portrait had been finished. No. 913 was exhibited at the Royal Academy in 1827 (146) and the British Institution in 1833 (26) and engraved by J. H. Robinson (1833) and W. Humphrey (1844); in the latter, and in the engraving by Horsburgh (1854), the MSS. on the table include *The Lay of the Last Minstrel* with the two above.

Novelist and poet. In 1820 he was created a Baronet by George IV, who warmly admired him. In 1818 Scott had been one of the Commissioners appointed by the Regent to open the Crown Room in the Castle at Edinburgh and to bring to light the Honours of Scotland; the Waverley novels were regularly 'laid on His Majesty's table'. Scott was responsible to a great extent for the success of the King's visit to Scotland in 1822 and organised, down to the smallest detail, the programme of pageantry that enlivened it; he was greeted by the King at Leith as 'the man in Scotland I most wish to see'. See No. 1184.

914. EDWARD, FIRST LORD THURLOW (1731–1806) (*Plate* 189)

Windsor Castle (313). $50\frac{1}{2} \times 40\frac{1}{4}$ in., $128,3 \times 102,2$ cm.

Three-quarter-length seated, clasping the arm of his chair with his right hand.

Delivered to the Prince of Wales at Carlton House soon after the summer exhibition at the R.A. in 1803, and placed in the Crimson

Drawing Room (No. 11 in inv. of 1816; Pyne, vol. III, *Carlton House*, p. 23, seen in plate); removed to the New Corridor at Windsor on 30 April 1828.

Literature: Collins Baker, *Windsor*, p. 196; R.A., *King's Pictures* (47); City Art Gallery, Bristol, *Sir Thomas Lawrence*, 1951 (11); Garlick, *Lawrence*, pp. 10, 60, *Catalogue*, p. 186.

Farington recorded on 19 February 1803 that Lord Thurlow 'has lately been sitting to Lawrence', who found the old man 'disposed to converse'. On 7 April Farington dined with Lawrence: 'from 7 to 8 sat for a hand to complete the $\frac{1}{2}$ length picture of Lord Thurlow—the drapery of which He has begun & finished this day, as well as the hands'. Lawrence stated that he had worked for thirty-seven hours at a stretch on the portrait; by the end 'I could not distinguish one colour from another; remember, too, I was standing or walking all the while, for I never paint sitting' (Cunningham, vol. III, p. 102). When the portrait was shown at the Royal Academy in the summer of the same year (21) it was greatly admired. West told Farington that George III 'sd. it met his idea of a portrait being a true Representation of the man without artificial fancies of dress &c.'; Opie thought it the best portrait in the room; Fuseli seems to have regarded it as the best portrait exhibited by Lawrence that year; and Farington himself described it as 'the most complete performance in the room'. The portrait was at first intended for the Princess of Wales, but the Prince ensured that Thurlow delivered the portrait to him. Farington states that Lawrence had painted the drapery and both hands in one day ('on the *last day* of receiving pictures' for the R.A.) and that in the morning the entire lower part of the picture had been '*bare canvass*' (*Diary*, vol. II, pp. 83, 89, 94–6, 100, 158, 246). In April 1810 the frame was sent to Smith to be regilded (Jutsham, *R/D*, f. 56). On 5 June 1814 Lawrence wrote to Colonel McMahon that 'The greatest honor that I have ever receiv'd, after the gracious notice of His Majesty, is the having my picture of Lord Thurlow placed in his Royal Highnesses collection; and *so* placed as to fill me with the liveliest gratitude for such generous distinction' (*Letters of George IV*, vol. I, 451).

A lawyer of intensely conservative opinions, M.P. for Tamworth and successively Solicitor-General, 1770, Attorney-General, 1771, and Lord Chancellor, 1778–83, 1783–92. Although a firm supporter of George III and the royal prerogative, his dislike of Pitt led him, at the time of the Regency question in 1788, into clandestine negotiations with the Prince of Wales and the Whigs; in 1797 he attempted to mediate between the Prince and Princess of Wales. His solemn, imposing aspect 'proved him dishonest', in the words of Fox, 'since no man could *be* so wise as Thurlow *looked*'·

915. GENERAL THEODORE PETROVITCH UVAROV (1773/4–1824) (*Plate* 212)

Windsor Castle (211). $50 \times 40\frac{1}{4}$ in., $127 \times 102,2$ cm.

Three-quarter-length, standing, in military uniform with his plumed hat on his left arm. He wears three stars, including those of St. George of Russia and (?) St. Alexander Newski; his badges are those of Military Merit of Württemberg and (?) St. George of Russia; and his smaller badges include the Order of Maria Theresa of Austria, the campaign medal of 1812, St. Louis of France and (?) the Black Eagle.

Painted for George IV; recorded in the inventory of 'Carleton Palace' (665: 'Half length of Genl. Overoff. Lawrence. In the Waterloo Gallery, Windsor Castle').

Literature: Williams, vol. II, pp. 130, 145; Collins Baker, *Windsor*, p. 213; Garlick, *Lawrence*, p. 53, *Catalogue*, p. 155.

---

1. An exactly similar criticism is recorded in Cunningham, *loc. cit.*; a contemporary artist, who saw the canvas when only the head was finished, was very anxious that Lawrence should go no further with the portrait: 'The poet's frame, as *he will paint it*, will pull the sentiment out of the face'.

Painted at Vienna in December 1818; Metternich told Princess Lieven on 24 December that Lawrence had just finished the portrait (*Letters . . . à la Comtesse de Lieven*, ed. J. Hanoteau (Paris, 1909), pp. 82–3). On 3 January 1819 Lawrence wrote from Vienna that he had 'been successful in three finished resemblances painted here. Two Russian generals, aide-de-camps to the Emperor' (the other was No. 892); and his list of portraits painted in Vienna includes 'General Ovaroff'. The portrait is listed, at £315, with the portraits painted for the Regent while Sir Benjamin Bloomfield was Keeper of the Privy Purse (W.R.A., Geo. 26642; *Letters of George IV*, vol. III, 1592). It was in Lawrence's studio at his death and was claimed on 22 January 1830 (Garlick, *Catalogue*, p. 278); but it was still unfinished: Seguier's account of 10 April 1830 includes five guineas for cleaning and varnishing it and 'the hand and dress finished' (W.R.A., Geo. 26750). The costume and right hand, for example, do not seem good enough to have been painted by Lawrence himself. It was exhibited at the British Institution in 1830 (5).

A Russian cavalry general who led the cavalry in pursuit of the French in the retreat from Moscow in 1814.

916. RICHARD COLLEY WELLESLEY, MARQUESS WELLESLEY (1760–1842) (*Plate* 219)

Windsor Castle (311). 52 × 40¾ in., 132,1 × 103,5 cm.
Three-quarter-length, seated, wearing the Garter and the ribbon and star of the order.

Presented by the sitter to Queen Victoria and placed in the Corridor at Windsor (*A Descriptive Catalogue of the Pictures, . . . deposited in the Corridor . . .* (1845), pp. 78–82).

Literature: Collins Baker, *Windsor*, p. 197; Garlick, *Lawrence*, p. 61, *Catalogue*, p. 192.

Exhibited at the Royal Academy in 1813 (208); in a note to Farington, 12 August 1821, Lawrence had written that 'Lord Wellesley sits to me today' (W.R.A., Geo. Add. 15, 329). A replica or copy is at Stratfield Saye; others are at Eton, Ampleforth (formerly at Beningbrough), in the Castle, Dublin, in the Oriental Club and, from the collection of E. H. Riches, in the Foreign Office. Another, which had passed by descent from the sitter's widow, was presented to H.M. King George VI by Sir Algernon Law in 1940. The portrait was engraved by C. Turner (1815), S. Cousins (1842) and others. It is also the source of an Italian engraving by Zecchino.

Eldest brother of the 1st Duke of Wellington; Governor-General of Madras, 1797, and of Bengal, 1797–1805; Commander-in-Chief in India, 1800–5; Foreign Secretary, 1809–12, Lord-Lieutenant of Ireland, 1821–8 and 1833–4, Lord Steward, 1832–3, and Lord Chamberlain, 1835. He bore the Sceptre with Crown at the Coronation of George IV. Lawrence spoke of Wellesley to Farington on 8 April 1811 'as having ruined His fortune by His excessive expences on Women.—With all his abilities He has so great a share of vanity, that at the age of abt. 53 Lawrence has noticed when His Lordship sat to him for His Portrait, that His *Lips* were painted' (*Diary*, vol. VI, p. 258).

917. ARTHUR WELLESLEY, FIRST DUKE OF WELLINGTON (1769–1852) (*Plate* 195)

Windsor Castle (188). 124½ × 88¾ in., 317,5 × 225,4 cm.
Full-length, standing under an arch, in Field-Marshal's uniform. In his left hand he holds his plumed hat; in his right he holds the Sword of State, resting it on a draped ledge beside his baton and a letter addressed to him and signed *George P.R.* He wears the ribbon and collar of the Garter, and a richly jewelled Golden Fleece over the Garter ribbon; the star of the Order of the Tower and Sword of Portugal; the ribbon of the Order of Maria Theresa of Austria; and the Sword of Sweden. In the background is St. Paul's Cathedral on the occasion of the Thanksgiving Service on 7 July 1814, which Lawrence attended with Farington and at which the Duke carried the Sword of State.

Painted for George IV; recorded in the inventory of 'Carleton Palace' (646: 'Full length Portrait of the Duke of Wellington. Lawrence. In the Waterloo Gallery, Windsor Castle').

Literature: Farington, *Diary*, vol. VII, pp. 263, 264, 271–2; Williams, vol. I, pp. 346–7; Waagen (1838), vol. I, p. 167; *Sir Thomas Lawrence's Letter-Bag*, ed. G. S. Layard (1906), pp. 99, 287; Lord G. Wellesley and J. Steegman, *The Iconography of the First Duke of Wellington* (1935), p. 26; Collins Baker, *Windsor*, p. 217; Garlick, *Lawrence*, p. 62; R.A., *Sir Thomas Lawrence*, 1961 (2); Garlick, *Catalogue*, p. 194.

Painted in 1814–15 and exhibited at the Royal Academy in 1815 (109). Farington records that on 6 July 1814 the Duke came to sit for his portrait, 'a whole length for the Prince Regent. He came on Horseback attended by an Old Groom, and in the plainest manner; wearing a Blue Coat & a round Hat'. Farington saw the portrait in Lawrence's studio on 21 July 1814. On 17 February 1815 Lawrence wrote to Farington: 'I am glad to tell you that I succeed in the completion of Lord Wellington's Portrait. From its size and necessary accompaniments it has been a great Fag to me, and demanded more constancy of Labor, and vigilant attention than, I think, any Picture I have painted.' Miss Croft, who thought it the 'least agreeable likeness' of all Lawrence's portraits of the Duke, stated that the Duke wore, during the sittings 'a magnificent gold sash, striped in front with blue, red, and white'. Lawrence, finding this discordant, painted out the stripes in the Duke's absence. When he offered to replace them if they were of importance the Duke said 'Oh no, never mind, they merely constitute me Generalissimo of the Armies of Spain' (Layard, *loc. cit.*). The original striped sash can be clearly seen. A rapid preliminary drawing is in the Royal Library.

At the Academy in 1815 the portrait was criticised as a poor likeness (Farington, *Diary*, vol. VIII, p. 14; this reference is really under 27 June, not 26 June as printed) and as lacking any connection between the figure and the surrounding parts of the design (Williams, *loc. cit.*). Lawrence's account of 4 January 1817 includes £525 for the 'Triumphal Portrait (largest size)' of the Duke (W.R.A., Geo. 26634; the price was amended to £630 (*ibid.*, 26641); *Letters of George IV*, vol. III, 1592). The portrait was in Lawrence's studio at his death and was claimed on 24 January 1830 (Garlick, *Catalogue*, p. 277); Seguier's account of 10 April 1830 includes four guineas for cleaning and varnishing the canvas; and Wyatt's account, under 6 May 1830, includes £14. 10s. for a frame for it (W.R.A., 26750, 26752). The portrait was exhibited at the British Institution in 1830 (9). The engraving by W. Bromley was published on 18 June 1818 and (with J. Murray) in 1825. The first, published by Bowyer, was authorised by the Prince Regent, whose permission Lawrence had received from Colonel McMahon. He had written to him on 24 August 1814 that 'Application has been made to me respecting them, particularly for this portrait of Lord Wellington which is now very greatly improv'd; (and I may fairly say admir'd)'. The plate would be executed under Lawrence's 'immediate direction', dedicated to the Prince, 'and the distinction . . . mention'd of Lord W.'s sitting to me at H.R.H. desire' (*Letters of George IV*, vol. I, 478); on the print it is stated that Wellington is shown as he appeared on the day of public thanksgiving at St. Pauls'.

Lady Mornington's 'ugly boy Arthur ... fit food for powder', purchased a major's commission in the 33rd Foot in 1793 and served in the Low Countries. In India, 1796–1805, achieved distinction as commander and administrator; in command of a British force in Portugal in 1808; victorious in the Peninsular War, he finally drove the French out of Spain in 1813 and defeated them at Orthez and Toulouse in 1814. Later in the year was Ambassador to France and in 1815 replaced Castlereagh at the Congress of Vienna. In 1815 he was appointed to command the Anglo-Netherland and Hanoverian forces in Europe and on 18 June defeated Napoleon at Waterloo. The Duke entered politics in 1818; Lord High Constable at the Coronations of George IV, William IV and Queen Victoria; Prime Minister, 1828–30. He was venerated by Queen Victoria, who chose him as godfather to Prince Arthur, later Duke of Connaught. See also No. 831.

918. SIR JEFFRY WYATVILLE (1766–1840) (*Plate 222*)

Windsor Castle (1). $56\frac{1}{2} \times 44$ in., $143,5 \times 111,8$ cm.

Three-quarter-length, seated at a table with two plans under his hands, one inscribed: *Principal Story | ROUND TOWER | 1830*, the other inscribed: *King George IV ... Gateway 1824*. In the background is a view of Windsor Castle from the south-east, clearly showing the Round Tower and the Gateway.

Painted for George IV. On the back is an inscription: 'Sir Jeffrey Wyatville / one of the last works of / Sir Thomas Lawrence / President of the Royal Academy / Painted by Command of His Majesty / George Fourth 1829 / Placed in Windsor Castle Sept. 1835 / by King William 4th'. Earlier the portrait had been recorded at 'Carleton Palace' (674).

Literature: Garlick, *Lawrence*, p. 64, *Catalogue*, p. 204.

Among the portraits bespoken from Lawrence by George IV in 1825 was 'A Bishop's Half-Length Portrait of Jeffrey Wyatville Esq.' at £315 (W.R.A., Geo. 27043); on 20 September 1828 Lawrence said that the portrait had been 'commenc'd' (*ibid.*, 26657–8); and on 28 January 1830 it was delivered to the King (*ibid.*, 26675; Garlick, *Catalogue*, p. 279). Seguier's account of 10 April 1830 includes five guineas for cleaning and varnishing the portrait and for 'the back ground and dress finished'; and Wyatt's bill for £18. 17s. 6d. for a rich frame for it is dated 6 May 1830 (W.R.A., Geo. 26750, 26752). The portrait was exhibited at the British Institution in 1830 (79); H. Robinson's engraving was published in 1834 and states that the portrait was by Evans. An unfinished head of Wyatville, of the same date but looking to the right, is recorded in the Camille Groult collection in Paris.

Nephew and pupil of James Wyatt, who had been surveyor of works at the Castle, 1796–1813. The younger man began to carry out his alterations to the Castle in the summer of 1824, after his schemes had been preferred to those submitted by Smirke and Nash. The King laid the first stone of the work on 12 August 1824 and on the same day Wyatt was authorised to change his surname. His original estimates soon ceased to tally with the actual cost of the work. £25,000 for the Round Tower was included in the estimates for 1828; in June 1830 King George IV's Gateway was among the works that had been completed (W. H. St. John Hope, *Windsor Castle* (1913), vol. I, pp. 355–68).

Studio of Sir Thomas Lawrence

919. GEORGE IV

Windsor Castle (222). $98\frac{3}{4} \times 62$ in., $250,8 \times 157,5$ cm. The canvas has clearly been cut at top, bottom and on both sides in order that it should fit into its present position.

Full-length, standing, in Garter robes, resting his right hand on a paper which lies under his new Imperial Crown upon the *Table des Grands Capitaines*; the King wears the collars of the Golden Fleece, the Guelphic Order, the Bath and the Garter.

Recorded in the *Royal Windsor Guide* (1832) at the end of the sequence of royal portraits inserted, presumably by George IV, on the north wall of St. George's Hall.

Literature: Collins Baker, *Windsor*, p. 219; Garlick, *Lawrence*, p. 38, *Catalogue*, pp. 86–7.

Lawrence exhibited at the Royal Academy in 1818 (61) his original portrait of George IV in Garter robes, now in the National Gallery of Ireland (*Fig. XXV*), which was closely dependent on the portrait exhibited in 1815 (65) (*Fig. XXIV*; see above, No. 873 and pp. xxxiii–iv). Thereafter a very large number of versions and copies were produced in Lawrence's studio; the portrait became, after the King's accession in 1820, the official portrait; and after the accession the crown replaced the plumed hat of the Order of the Garter on the table beside the King. The best versions, after the original, are probably those in the Vatican (commissioned by Pius VII in 1819), at Slane Castle (painted for Lady Conyngham) and in the Town Hall at Windsor. On 4 August 1821 Byfeld submitted a bill for £67. 10s. for making a frame for the portrait for Dublin and £10. 8s. for making a case and packing the portrait; on 4 March 1823 he submitted a bill for the same sums for the frame and case for the portrait for the Mayor of Windsor; he was paid on 6 July 1824 (Jutsham, *PP.*, f. 84; W.R.A., Geo. 26513). While Sir Benjamin Bloomfield was Keeper of the Privy Purse (1818–23) £787. 10s. was paid to Lawrence for 'Large Whole Length Portrait of His Majesty in the Garter Robes for The Royal Palace Windsor' and £525 was paid to him for a 'Large Whole length Portrait of His Majesty' (W.R.A., Geo. 26643; *Letters of George IV*, vol. III, 1592). The two portraits are probably Nos. 919, 920. No. 919 appears to be a good, freshly painted, version of the design, clearly painted in the studio under Lawrence's eye. He may have painted the head which is of a slightly heavier texture than the remainder of the surface. It is difficult to be certain which of the versions of this design in the royal collection was the portrait shown by Lawrence at the Royal Academy in 1822 (77: 'for the Royal Palace of Windsor').

George IV's accounts contain payments for whole-lengths of the King, which were presumably all of this design, for the University of Oxford (£630)[1] during Bloomfield's Keepership; for the City of Dublin (630) during Knighton's Keepership; and for the Duke of Wellington (£525 paid on 23 February 1825), and Count Münster for Hanover (£525 paid on 27 November 1826) (W.R.A., Geo. 26530, 26641, 26642, 26686, 26691, 27041, 27042, 27066–7; *Letters of George IV*, vol. III, 1592).

In addition to the versions of No. 919 mentioned above, there are versions in the Houses of Parliament, Drapers' Hall, Brighton Art Gallery, at Coventry (St. Mary's Guildhall), Chatsworth, Goodwood, Sandhurst, Stratfield Saye House, Wynyard Park, and in the Baltimore Museum of Art. The version in the National Portrait Gallery (2503) is

1. Mrs. R. L. Poole, *Catalogue of Portraits* ..., vol. I (1912), p. 145.

in the British Embassy in Vienna. A version was formerly in the Russian Imperial collection; a version stated to have been originally in the Hanoverian royal collection was in Vienna in 1938; and a version was formerly at Highcliffe Castle. Reduced versions also exist. The type of head was used, for example, in the head and shoulders painted for Sir William Knighton, now in the Scottish National Portrait Gallery (139). A large enamel copy by Bone is at Somerley. Hodgetts's engraving, based on an early version of the design, was published in June 1829. See above p. 60.

920. GEORGE IV

Buckingham Palace. 113¾ × 71¼ in., 288,9 × 181 cm.; *c.* 3 in. of original canvas has been turned over on the left, *c.* 3 in. on the right and *c.* 1½ in. at the top.

Recorded in the State Dining-Room at Buckingham Palace in 1841 (No. 203 in catalogue of that year; later inv. No. 194).

Literature: Garlick, *Catalogue*, p. 87.

A good version of the same design as No. 919. It was presumably one of the earlier of the versions as it is painted throughout with considerable freedom. Lawrence probably himself worked on the head and cravat; the face has a markedly heavier texture than the rest of the canvas. There is also apparently a *pentimento* in the outline of the collar against the King's left cheek.

921. GEORGE IV

Windsor Castle (180). 107 × 74¾ in., 271,8 × 189,9 cm.

A portrait of George IV was seen in the Waterloo Chamber by Waagen on 3 June 1835 ((1838), vol. I, p. 168) and is recorded in *The Royal Windsor Guide* for 1837.

Literature: Collins Baker, *Windsor*, p. 208; Garlick, *Catalogue*, p. 87.

A copy, painted in Lawrence's studio, of the same design as No. 919, but of inferior quality. No. 921 may have been the version which was cleaned and varnished by Seguier at a charge of four guineas (his account of 10 April 1830, W.R.A., Geo. 26750).

922. GEORGE IV

Windsor Castle (169). 113 × 66½ in., 287 × 168,9 cm.; in addition there is *c.* 6½ in of original canvas turned over on the left, *c.* 7½ in. on the right and *c.* 2½ in. at the top.

Recorded in the Throne Room, where it still is, in the *Royal Windsor Guide* (1837).

Literature: Collins Baker, *Windsor*, p. 219; Garlick, *Catalogue*, p. 87.

A copy, coarse in texture and with no trace of Lawrence's own hand, of the same design as No. 919.

923. PRINCESS MARY, DUCHESS OF GLOUCESTER

Buckingham Palace. 27 × 22 in., 68,6 × 55,9 cm.

Head and shoulders in a white dress, with a richly jewelled chain over her left shoulder.

Probably passed by descent to the Duke of Cambridge; in his sale at Christie's, 11 June 1904 (93), when it was bought by Agnew's; bought in 1905 by the 9th Duke of Marlborough.

Literature: Garlick, *Catalogue*, p. 90.

A repetition, probably painted in Lawrence's studio but not by Lawrence himself, of the portrait exhibited at the Royal

Academy in 1817 (72). The original had been given by the Duchess to her lady-in-waiting, Miss Adams, and passed by descent to Major David Fisher-Rowe. Another version was sold at Christie's on 5 July 1902 (49). No. 923 has been for a long time framed as an oval, a format exactly identical with J. E. Coombs's engraving of this type, published on 1 October 1841. It is possible that the engraving was based on No. 923 and not on the original.

After Sir Thomas Lawrence

924. GEORGE IV

Buckingham Palace. Panel: 23¾ × 16¼ in., 60,3 × 41,3 cm.

Full-length, seated on a sofa, wearing the Garter, the star of the order and the Golden Fleece.

Acquired in 1899 from A. R. Barber of Windsor; thereafter at Buckingham Palace and Windsor (2395).

Literature: Buckingham Palace, 1909, p. 110.

An early copy, on a small scale, of the full-length in the Wallace Collection (559) painted in 1822 (Garlick, *Lawrence*, pl. 95, *Catalogue*, pp. 87–8) of which a number of reductions and derivations are recorded. Lawrence delivered to George IV on 28 January 1830 'A small whole length of his Majesty' at £126; Wyatt's bill includes under 6 May 1830 a rich frame for small whole length of George IV measuring 3' 9¼" × 2' 7½"; for exhibition at the British Institution in 1830, Lord Farnborough secured 'the small Picture of His Majesty sitting upon the Sofa'. All these references (W.R.A., Geo. 26599, 26675, 26752) probably refer to an autograph replica, painted for the King, of the original in the Wallace Collection, which had been painted for Lady Conyngham.

925. PRINCESS CHARLOTTE

Windsor Castle (574). 36½ × 28½ in., 92,7 × 72,4 cm. In addition there is a large area of original canvas turned over: *c.* 6¼ in. at the top, *c.* 7 in. at the bottom, *c.* 5 in. on the left and *c.* 7½ in. on the right.

Half-length in a black dress, holding a scarf in her right hand; her left, wearing elaborate rings on the third finger, rests on her bosom.

Literature: R.A., *Kings & Queens,* 1953 (263); Garlick, *Lawrence,* p. 32, *Catalogue,* p. 54.

A slightly simplified copy of the portrait that was painted at Claremont in October 1817 and exhibited at the Royal Academy in 1821 (70). The original, painted for the Princess as a birthday present to her husband, is still in the Belgian royal collection (Garlick, *Lawrence,* pl. 91). The Princess died on 6 November 1817 and the portrait was sent to Carlton House. Both her father and her husband wished to keep the portrait and Lawrence was anxious to paint a copy of the portrait ('which I was certain I could make both in closeness of resemblance and merit as a picture, fully equal to the original') as a present to the Regent. Eventually on 16 December, Lawrence took the original portrait back to Claremont (*Letters of George IV,* vol. II, 713, 716, 722; Farington, *Diary,* vol. VIII, pp. 148, 150–2, 155–6, 160–1; unpublished 21 November, 14, 17 December). The Regent is stated to have ordered from Lawrence a full-length copy and Prince Leopold seems also to have commissioned from Lawrence a full-length of the Princess (Farington, *Diary,* vol. VIII, pp. 156–7). A 'Whole Length Portrait of the late Princess Charlotte', at £420, was among the portraits painted by Lawrence for George IV during Sir Benjamin Bloomfield's Keepership of the Privy Purse (i.e., 1818–23; W.R.A., Geo. 26642; *Letters of George IV*, vol. III, 1592); this was recorded at 'Carleton Palace' (673) and at Hampton Court in 1835 (549); it was in Lawrence's studio at his death and was claimed on 22 January 1830 (Garlick, *Catalogue*, p. 279; *Sir Thomas Lawrence's Letter-Bag*, ed. G. S. Layard (1906), p. 276). No. 925 could conceivably be this copy, cut down, but it is the same size as the original in the Belgian royal collection and, as the private property of Queen Victoria, is more likely to be the copy painted from 'le portrait de la Princesse Charlotte par Lawrence' by command of the Count of Flanders for Queen Victoria in 1870; the copy was finished by 29 August 1870 and on 30 December 1870 the Count wrote of his pleasure in Queen Victoria's satisfaction with the portrait (W.R.A., Vic. Y.163, 31–2 a). R. Golding's engraving of the type was published on 1 January 1822; W. T. Fry's engraving was published in 1829. Lawrence's drawing of this type, sold at Christie's, 18 June 1831 (133), was also engraved by Golding (Garlick, *Catalogue*, p. 221); it is presumably the drawing in the possession of H.M. The King of the Belgians. Garlick (*loc. cit.*) records a copy of No. 925 formerly in the collection of the Earl of Ilchester; another version was on the art-market in Paris in 1906.

926. LOUIS-ANTOINE, DUKE OF ANGOULÊME (1775–1844)

Holyroodhouse. 39¼ × 28¼ in., 99,7 × 71,8 cm.

See No. 928. No. 926 remained at Buckingham Palace (658) until 1965.

927. GEORGE CANNING (1770–1827)

Windsor Castle (187). 52 × 41½ in., 131,1 × 104,5 cm.

Three-quarter-length, standing with folded arms beside the Foreign Secretary's despatch-box.

Noticed by Waagen in the Waterloo Chamber on 3 June 1835 (Waagen (1838), vol. I, p. 169; *V.R. inv.*, 22 October 1868).

Literature: Collins Baker, *Windsor*, p. 202; Garlick, *Lawrence*, p. 30, *Catalogue*, p. 49.

A three-quarter-length variant from the full-length design (No. 887). No. 927 does not seem to be by Lawrence himself and does not appear to have been commissioned by George IV. It may have been painted for William IV so that Canning could take his place in the Waterloo Chamber, for which the full-length would not have been suitable. Another half-length copy was sold at Christie's, 6 November 1953 (19).
See No. 887.

928. CHARLES X (1757–1836), KING OF FRANCE

Holyroodhouse. 39 × 28¼ in., 99,1 × 71,8 cm.

Nos. 926, 928 are half-length copies by Corden from the full-lengths by Lawrence (Nos. 884, 890). They were painted for Queen Victoria in the summer of 1847 (for seven pounds each) to be hung in the series of Bourbon portraits in the Bourbon room in the suite at Buckingham Palace which was being fitted up for a visit by the King and Queen of the Belgians (Queen Victoria, Journal for 22 June 1847; Catalogue of Her Majesty's Private Pictures . . .). No. 928 remained at Buckingham Palace (657) until 1965.

John Frederick Lewis

1805–76. Painter, principally in watercolour, of Italian, Spanish and Oriental subjects. In his early years, however, he showed great talent as an animal painter and he studied in the menagerie at Exeter 'Change and among George IV's animals at Windsor. In 1826 he exhibited at the Royal Academy (529) a picture of Rattler, one of the King's favourite staghounds, and at the British Institution (202) a group of the King's staghounds.

929. JOHN CLARK(E) WITH THE ANIMALS AT SANDPIT GATE (*Plate* 290)

Windsor Castle (841). Panel: 32⅝ × 30¾ in., 82,9 × 78,1 cm.

Standing outside Sandpit Gate with a bowl of food and surrounded by some of the animals and birds in his charge: small deer, a gazelle, wallaby and pony, a humped ox; peacocks, an emu, a macaw and a cockatoo.

Stated to have been painted for George IV; recorded at Windsor in 1878 (*V.R. inv.*).

Probably painted by Lewis at the same period as his *Buck-Shooting in Windsor Great Park*, painted in 1825, and now in the Tate Gallery (4822). The old man with the animals can possibly be identified with John Clark who died at the age of sixty-five on 8 October 1827 and was buried at Old Windsor.

James Lonsdale

1777–1839. Portrait-painter; exhibited at the Royal Academy from 1802 and was active in the formation of the Society of British Artists.

930. AUGUSTUS, DUKE OF SUSSEX

Buckingham Palace. 30 × 25 in., 76,2 × 63,5 cm.

Head and shoulders, wearing the ribbon and star of the Garter.

Purchased by Queen Victoria in February 1857 and recorded at Buckingham Palace (568) in 1876 (*V.R. inv.*).

Probably the portrait exhibited by Lonsdale at the Royal Academy in 1823 (567). It (or another version) was engraved by Skelton 'from a Portrait by Jaˢ Lonsdale in 1824 in the Possession of T. J. Pettigrew Esqʳ' as frontispiece to Pettigrew's *Bibliotheca Sussexiana* (1827). Pettigrew, who died in 1865, had been Surgeon to the Duke, the Duke and Duchess of Kent and Princess Victoria, and Librarian to the Duke of Sussex.

931. SIR WILLIAM CONGREVE (1742–1814) (*Plate* 257)

Windsor Castle (354). 50½ × 40½ in., 128,3 × 102,9 cm.

Three-quarter-length, standing, in his dress uniform as Colonel-Commandant of the Royal Artillery; in the background is a river on which is a pontoon carrying light field-guns; on the bank of the river a gunner stands with surveying instruments beside a pile of cases on which rests a paper inscribed *R:M.* [i.e., Royal Military] *REPOSITORY / 1776.*

Painted for George IV. Recorded in store at Carlton House in 1816 (257: 'A half length of General Sir Wᵐ Congreve. Mr Lonsdale'; the remains of the 1816 label are on the back); moved to the New Gallery at Windsor on 24 July 1828; in the Corridor in 1878 (*V.R. inv.*) and thereafter placed in the Waterloo Chamber.

Literature: Collins Baker, *Windsor*, p. 231.

Probably painted *c.* 1805-10. Formerly identified (e.g., by Collins Baker, *loc. cit.*) as Sir William Congreve, 2nd Bt. (1772-1828) and inventor, who was, however, never a soldier and who, in 1816, was not therefore a General (see above); nor can No. 931 represent someone born in 1772. In 1808 Lonsdale exhibited at the Royal Academy (4) a portrait of the younger man.

Lieutenant-General. Appointed, 1803, Colonel-Commandant of the Royal Artillery; was also Comptroller of the Royal Laboratory at Woolwich and superintendent of military machines.

Philipp Jakob, or Philip James de, Louterbourg

1740-1812. Painter of landscapes, subject-pictures, battles and scenes of military and pastoral life. Born in Fulda, of Polish origin. Worked in Germany and Paris and came in 1771 to London, where he became Garrick's chief designer of scenery at Drury Lane. He exhibited at the Royal Academy between 1772 and 1812. In 1793 he accompanied the Duke of York's expedition to the Netherlands.
Jutsham records the receipt at Carlton House from the Ante-room at St. James's on 1 August 1829 of 'A Painting of Lord Howe's Victory of June 1st 1794 By Loutherberg'. With Turner's picture of Trafalgar (see above, p. xxxii), it was sent to be stored in the Riding House and 'thence sent to Greenwich Hospital by Command of His Majesty' (Jutsham, *Receipts*, f. 272). It is signed and dated 1795 and is now in the National Maritime Museum (*Fig. XXII*).

932. WARLEY CAMP: THE MOCK ATTACK (*Plate* 83)
Buckingham Palace. 48 × 72½ in., 121,9 × 184,1 cm.
Signed and dated: *P J. De Loutherbourg 1779*

An attack, in hilly wooded country, by troops converging on forces drawn up in square. The attack is being watched in the distance by the King who is stationed with his staff by a small observatory.

Presumably painted, with No. 933, for George III; recorded in the Music Room at Kew (Geo. III, *Kew*; George IV, No. 1089); moved to Windsor (323) in 1835.

Exhibited at the Royal Academy in 1779 (182): *A Landscape, in which are represented the manœuvres of an attack performed before their Majesties on Little Warley Common, under the command of Gen. Pierson, on the 20th of October, 1778.* The King and Queen had travelled from Buckingham House to Thorndon Place, the residence of Lord Petre, on 19 October. On the following day, attended by his suite and by Lord Amherst (see No. 995), the King reviewed the troops stationed at the militia camp at Warley. After the march past seen in No. 933, the Light Infantry and Grenadiers 'marched with the artillery through the woods towards Little Warley (followed by the whole line in two columns), where, as well as in the adjacent woods, several batteries were placed, and many manœuvres of attack and defence were performed, with the continued firing of musquetry and cannon, to which the situation and variety of the ground were very favourable and afforded much pleasure to the numerous spectators' (M. D. Petre, *The Ninth Lord Petre* (1928), pp. 44-8; J. W. Burrows, *The Essex Militia* (1929), pp. 169-71; information from Mr. F. G. Emmison, who has suggested that No. 932 was composed looking east about three-quarters of a mile

north-west of Childerditch church). The King and Queen watched the manœuvres from a stand erected for them by Lord Petre 'in the centre of the scene'. Among De Loutherbourg's sketches in the British Museum (201, C.5) are studies of uniforms, drawings of helmet-caps, of Light Infantry and militia caps and of guns, all relevant to, though not directly connected with, the details in Nos. 932, 933.
The writer of the *Candid Review* of the exhibition at the Royal Academy in 1780 says of No. 933 that it was 'intended as a present to his Majesty, from General *Pierson* and Officers of the Camp'.

933. WARLEY CAMP: THE REVIEW (*Plate* 84)
Buckingham Palace. 47¾ × 72¼ in., 121,3 × 183,5 cm.
Signed and dated: *P. I. De Loutherbourg 1780*

In front of the camp is the King, with his staff, reviewing an artillery train which is moving up to file past; spectators are running up to watch the parade.

Presumably painted, with No. 932, for George III; recorded in the Music Room at Kew (Geo. III, *Kew*; George IV, No. 1090); moved to Windsor (321) in 1835.

Painted as a companion to No. 932 and exhibited at the Royal Academy in 1780 (15: *The troops at Warley-camp reviewed by his Majesty, 1778*). On the morning of 20 October, before the mock attack shown in No. 932, the King had witnessed the march past of infantry and artillery. There are *pentimenti* where De Loutherbourg painted out a driver at the head of the leading horse of the artillery train in the foreground, and where he sketched in two dogs, which he later painted out, in the foreground.
It has been suggested by the staff of the Essex Record Office that the view in No. 933 is looking north-east towards Brentwood, and includes (with some artistic licence) the tower of old St. Thomas's Chapel on the left, Thorndon Hall behind the trees on the right and the windmill on Ingrave Common on the extreme right.

934. BANDITTI IN A LANDSCAPE
Buckingham Palace. 98 × 146¼ in., 248,9 × 372,1 cm.
Signed and dated: *P. I. de Loutherbourg. R.A / 1804*

Banditti drinking and resting, with their women, children and dogs, on the rocky bank of a foaming river in a mountainous landscape; on the opposite bank is a ruined castle.

Painted for George IV. Set up in the Front Room at Carlton House in 1806 (see below); at Carlton House in 1816 (529: 'A large landscape (Canarvon Castle,) with figures. Mr Loutherbourg', measurements given as 98 × 146); at Buckingham Palace (489) by 1862 (*V.R. inv.*).

On 22 February 1806 De Loutherbourg submitted a bill for £1,000 'for a large Picture, 12 feet 2 inch by 7 feet 2 inch which he has had the Honor of painting for H:R:H: the Prince of Wales, & which at present is at Carlton House, according to H:R:Highness's Commands'. Payment, which was completed on 23 January 1807 (W.R.A., Geo. 26830), is recorded in the settlement of the Prince's debts (*ibid.*, 32486 ('a Large Picture of Banditti'), 89441, 89444, 89447). Robert Cribb & Son submitted a bill for £160. 4s. 6d. for making a frame, fitting it up at Carlton House, placing the picture into it and hanging it up 'over the Chimney in the Front Room next to the Hall' (19, 20 July 1806; W.R.A., Geo. 26839). It is possible that No. 934 was one of a set of large pictures painted by De Loutherbourg for the Armoury Room at Carlton House. An undated bill drawn up by him, 'for Pictures Orderd by His Royal Highness for the armory Room Carleton House', amounts to £2,500, including £1,200 for 'Two Pictures for the large panels opposite the windows. Size 12 feet 3 inch = by 8 feet 1½ in' (P.R.O., H.O. 73, 23). The castle in the background bears only a generic resemblance to Caernarvon Castle (the picture is said to have given its name to the Carnarvon Room at Buckingham Palace) and it could equally well be intended to suggest Harlech or Conway; both castles figured in pictures exhibited by De Loutherbourg at the Royal Academy.

Robert McInnes

fl. 1841–66, when he exhibited at the Royal Academy portraits, subject-pictures and landscapes.

935. SIR JAMES KEMPT (1764–1854) (*Plate* 256)
Windsor Castle. (184). 50×39¾ in., 127×101 cm.

Three-quarter-length, standing, in general's uniform, holding his plumed hat in his right hand. He wears the ribbon and star of the Bath and the star of the Royal Hanoverian Guelphic Order and the Peninsular Gold Cross; his medals and badges are: the Legion of Honour, the Waterloo Medal, the medal of Maria Theresa, the Military Medal of William of the Netherlands and the Order of St. George of Russia.

Stated (*V.R. inv.*) to have been exchanged for a portrait of Kempt by Pickersgill which was sent to Sir George Cooper in 1855 and had been painted for the Waterloo Chamber, where it had been since at least 1837 (*Guide* to the Castle). It probably came into Queen Victoria's possession with No. 1092.

Literature: Collins Baker, *Windsor*, p. 233.

Stated to have been painted in 1836; exhibited at the Royal Academy in 1841 (130). The engraving by S. Bellin was published on 1 April 1841.

Gazetted Ensign in the 101st Regiment of Foot in 1783; served in the Low Countries, Egypt and the Peninsula, where he commanded a brigade under Picton. At Waterloo he commanded the 8th Brigade and took over the command of Picton's division when Picton was killed. Governor-General of Canada, 1828–30, and Master-General of the Ordnance, 1834–8.

William Marlow

1740–1813. Topographical painter, who specialised in views of London, but also worked in France and Italy. See also No. 826.

936. A VIEW OF LONDON BRIDGE (*Plate* 12)
Buckingham Palace. 40×49¾ in., 101,6×126,4 cm.

The north end of the bridge with, in the foreground, figures with horses, carts and merchandise on a wharf below the church of St. Magnus the Martyr. Beyond the bridge can be seen Fishmongers' Hall, St. Paul's Cathedral, the spire of St. Antholin and the tower of St. Michael, Cornhill.

Purchased by Her Majesty the Queen, when Princess Elizabeth, in November 1947.

Literature: Guildhall Art Gallery, *William Marlow*, 1956 (2).

Marlow exhibited a picture of this subject at the Society of Artists in 1762 (56: *A view of a wharf, St. Magnus's Church and a part of London Bridge*). A version of the design is in

the collection of Lady Lucas; another (signed) is at Scampston Hall; a third, which appeared at Christie's on 12 May 1950 (58), was bought by the London Museum.

Benjamin Marshall

1768–1835. Painter of sporting subjects and portraits. In his early days he was a schoolmaster and, in his later years, a sporting writer. He exhibited at the Royal Academy between 1800 and 1819.

937. CURRICLE WITH A HUNTSMAN (*Plate* 184)
Windsor Castle (2315). 34×39¾ in., 86,4×101 cm.

Signed: *B. Marshall pˢ / for G.P.W.*

A black horse, with saddle and bridle, led by a huntsman in royal livery (scarlet coat, blue collar and cuffs) in a landscape with a steep wooded hill on the left and riders (?huntsmen) on the right.

Presumably painted for George IV; recorded at Stud Lodge (1148) in 1868 (*V.R. inv.*); later at Cumberland Lodge.

Literature: Shaw Sparrow, p. 50, *Sporting Artists*, p. 174; R.A., *King's Pictures* (489).

Curricle, by Trentham out of a sister to Gay, was bred as a racehorse by the 3rd Duke of Richmond; he was a fine hunter and was bought by the Prince of Wales who declared that he 'was not only the finest but the best horse he ever saw, and that the best runs he ever witnessed were from the back of his "DEAR CURRICLE"' (note accompanying Romney's engraving of No. 937 in the *Sporting Magazine*, 2nd series, vol. IV (April 1832), pp. 401–2). Curricle appears as one of the hunters kept by the Prince of Wales at Kempshott in 1791, when he was often ridden by John Gascoigne (see No. 1111) and No. 937 was probably painted *c.* 1794.

938. LOP (*Plate* 183)
Windsor Castle (2328). 43⅛×40¼ in., 86,8×102,2 cm.

Signed: *B. Marshall pˢ / for G.P.W.*

A grey horse walking in an enclosure, with a stable on the left, under a stormy sky in an apparently mountainous landscape.

Presumably painted for George IV; on Whessel's plate (see below) of 1802 the picture is stated to be in the possession of the Prince of Wales; recorded at Stud Lodge (1147) in 1868 (*V.R. inv.*); later at Cumberland Lodge.

Literature: Shaw Sparrow, *Sporting Artists*, p. 174; R.A., *King's Pictures* (487).

Probably painted *c.* 1794. The horse can be identified as Lop from Whessel's engraving, published on 1 January 1802, in which the animal is seen against a different, and simpler, background. He was bred by Sir John Rous, foaled in 1791, by Crop. Sold in 1795 to Colonel Chalton and in 1797 to Mr. Howorth, he ended his career as a stallion in the Duke of Beaufort's stud.

939. MISTAKE
Windsor Castle (2325). 34¼×40¼ in., 87×102,2 cm.

Signed: *B. Marshall pˢ / [for GPW]*

A brown gelding hack, standing in an open landscape.

Presumably painted for George IV; recorded at Stud Lodge (1165) in 1869 (*V.R. inv.*); later at Cumberland Lodge.

Literature: Shaw Sparrow, *Sporting Artists*, p. 174.

Probably painted *c.* 1794.

940. TIGER

Windsor Castle (2327). 34 × 40¼ in., 86,4 × 102,2 cm.

Signed: *B. Marshall p.ᵗ | for G.P.W.*

A light chestnut hack, with white saddle-marks, standing by a tree beside a fence.

Presumably painted for George IV; recorded at Stud Lodge (1163) in 1868 (*V.R. inv.*); later at Cumberland Lodge.

Literature: Shaw Sparrow, *Sporting Artists*, p. 174; Leicester Museums, *Ben Marshall. . . .*, 1967 (15).

Probably painted *c.* 1794. Tiger was a favourite hack of the Prince of Wales although he was 'light below the knee' for a rider of his weight. In 1793 he appears as one of the hunters kept by the Prince at Kempshott. A small version, almost certainly a copy, is in the collection of Mr. and Mrs. E. Berger.

941. A BLACK HORSE

Windsor Castle (2326). 34 × 40¼ in., 86,4 × 102,2 cm.

Signed: *B. Marshall p.ᵗ | for G.P.W.*

A black horse, with white saddle-marks, standing in an open landscape near a gate through which comes a groom in royal livery (scarlet coat with dark blue collar).

Presumably painted for George IV; recorded at Stud Lodge (1158) in 1868 (*V.R. inv.*); later at Cumberland Lodge.

Literature: Shaw Sparrow, *Sporting Artists*, p. 174; R.A., *King's Pictures* (490).

Presumably one of the Prince of Wales's hunters; probably painted *c.* 1794.

942. A ROAN HACK (*Plate* 185)

Buckingham Palace. 35 × 40 in., 88,9 × 101,6 cm.

Signed: *B. Marshall P.ᵗ | for G.P.W.*

Standing, saddled and bridled, under the colonnade of Carlton House. Behind are houses in Pall Mall and two porters (?) in a box.

Presumably painted for George IV; recorded at Stud Lodge (1146) in 1868 (*V.R. inv.*); later at Cumberland Lodge and Windsor (2314).

Literature: Shaw Sparrow, p. 49; R.A., *King's Pictures* (492); Virginia Museum of Fine Arts, *Sport and the Horse*, 1960 (46).

Probably painted *c.* 1794. A variant, sold at Christie's on 3 July 1964 (66), showed the horse in the same position against a different background. This variant design was engraved for the *Sporting Magazine* for November 1802 (vol. 21, p. 56), when the horse, the property of the Prince of Wales, was said to have been formerly the property successively of Lord Egremont and Mr. Tattersall; and to be ridden constantly by the Prince who had once trotted him for six miles in 21½ minutes.

David Morier

1705?–1770. Painter of military and sporting subjects. For his portraits of George II and Frederick, Prince of Wales, see Millar, pp. 191–2, Nos. 591–6. It is clear that Nos. 597, 599 and 600 can also be attributed to Morier. He was officially recorded as 'Limner' to the Duke of Cumberland, with an annual salary of £100, between 1752 and 1764. For his paintings of military uniforms, see A. E. Haswell Miller and N. P. Dawnay, *Military Drawings and Paintings in the Collection of H.M. the Queen* (1966), pp. 8–9, 221, pls. 23–124.

It is not possible with safety to attach to any of the portraits below references to a portrait of the Duke of Cumberland 'at the Battle of Preston Pans', bought from Cutter by George IV in or before July 1812 (Jutsham, *R/D*, f. 213), or to a portrait of George III 'on a Brown Horse attended by the Marquess of Granby and other Officers', recorded in store at Carlton House in 1819 (356) and sent to Cumberland Lodge on 1 October 1823. In 1762 Morier had exhibited at the Society of Artists (71) a portrait of the King on horseback. *Lloyd's Evening Post*, 17 July 1764, records that a painting of George III, attended by Lord Ligonier, reviewing a regiment of horse in Hyde Park, had been fixed up at Buckingham House in the previous week (information from Mrs. Frances Vivian). No artist's name is given, but the painting could be No. 952 or a version of it.

943. WILLIAM, DUKE OF CUMBERLAND

Kew (Hampton Court No. 1370). 49⅜ × 39¼ in., 125,4 × 99,7 cm.

On horseback in a scarlet military state coat with blue facings and gold lace, wearing the ribbon and star of the Garter and holding a baton in his right hand. In the background is a landscape with a fortified town.

Recorded at Cumberland Lodge in 1873 (*V.R. inv.*, Windsor No· 1676). It is possible that No. 943 had been acquired by George IV, but it is impossible to relate it with certainty to any of the many references, in his inventories and related material, to portraits of the Duke of this type. 'A small whole length of William, Duke of Cumberland', recorded in store at Carlton House in 1816 (281, measurements given as 49 × 38), was sent to Cumberland Lodge on 1 October 1823.

The design probably dates from *c.* 1743. The head and cravat seem to have been painted by a better hand than the rest of the canvas. A copy, formerly in the collection of Sir Lyonel Tollemache, was sold at Christie's on 23 December 1954 (199).

944. WILLIAM, DUKE OF CUMBERLAND

Windsor Castle (1414). 49¾ × 39¾ in., 126,4 × 101 cm.

Riding on a rearing bay horse in a scarlet military state coat with the ribbon of the Garter. The battle in the background presumably alludes to the Jacobite rebellion of 1745.

In the collection of George IV. Possibly one of the two pictures of Cumberland ('His R.H. Duke of Cumberland at the Battle of Preston Pans' or 'Dᵒ at Culloden') acquired by the King from Cutter on 14 April 1818 (Jutsham, *PP.*, f. 41; W.R.A., Geo. 27015). No. 944 is possibly additional No. 542 in the 1816 inv. of Carlton House ('Portrait of William Duke of Cumberland Mounted upon a Bay Horse—at the Battle of Preston Pans'; measurements given as 43½ × 39½ in.) which was sent to Cumberland Lodge on 1 October 1823.

The type presumably dates from *c.* 1745–50.

945. WILLIAM, DUKE OF CUMBERLAND

Windsor Castle (1349). 20 × 16 in., 50,8 × 40,6 cm.

Riding on a rearing grey horse, wearing the frock uniform of the 1st Guards, a breastplate and the ribbon and star of the Garter; he brandishes a sword in his right hand. A battle is raging in the background.

In the collection of George IV. Probably one of the 'Three Paintings King of Prussia Duke of Cumberland &c' bought from Colnaghi for fifteen guineas on 18 July 1808; in the following month they were varnished and repaired and their frames were regilded (W.R.A., Geo. 27463). No. 945 was in the Armoury at Carlton House in 1816 (458; the 1816 label is still on the back) and was later at Kew.

The type probably dates from *c.* 1745–50.

946. WILLIAM, DUKE OF CUMERBLAND

Windsor Castle (445). 50 × 40 in., 127 × 101,6 cm.

Riding on a bay horse in a scarlet military state coat, with the ribbon and star of the Garter and the badge of the Bath. In the background is a battle in which Hungarian cavalry are engaged.

Acquired by George IV from Phillips. Jutsham (*R/D*, f. 305) noted under 18 May 1814 that 'these Portraits have been some months in the House under consideration but not determined on till this day'. They included 'William Duke of Cumberland on a Bay Horse—not any Frame'. Nos. 593, 595 above were acquired with it. Recorded in store at Carlton House in 1816 (264; the 1816 label is still on the back).

The type probably dates from *c.* 1745–50.

947. WILLIAM, DUKE OF CUMBERLAND

Windsor Castle (1413). 64 × 60 in., 162,6 × 152,4 cm.

Riding on a bay horse, wearing a scarlet military state coat over a breastplate and the ribbon and star of the Garter. The battle raging in the background seems to refer to the Duke's continental campaigns.

Acquired by George IV for twelve guineas from Cutter on 14 April 1818 (Jutsham, *PP.*, f. 41; W.R.A., Geo. 27015; additional No. 541 in Carlton House inv. of 1816); sent to Cumberland Lodge on 27 September 1823.

The type probably dates from *c.* 1745–50.

948. WILLIAM, DUKE OF CUMBERLAND

Kew (*Hampton Court* No. 1370A). 50¼ × 40 in., 127,6 × 101,6 cm.

On horseback in a scarlet military state coat with blue facings and gold lace, wearing the ribbon of the Garter and the badge of the Bath and holding a baton in his right hand. Behind him rides John, 1st Earl Ligonier, wearing the uniform of Colonel of the 7th Regiment of Horse and the ribbon of the Bath; in the foreground sits a soldier, probably a Pandour, from one of the continental regiments under Cumberland's command. In the background is a review.

Acquired by George IV. No. 948 may be the picture bought by General Hammond for the Prince and received at Carlton House on 16 August 1812: '. . . William Duke of Cumberland mounted on a Gray Horse—Gilt Frame' (Jutsham, *R/D*, f. 219). No. 948 was recorded in store at Carlton House in 1816 (262: 'William, Duke of Cumberland, on a white horse, with Lord Ligonier; an encampment in the background'); sent to Cumberland Lodge on 1 October 1823 (later Windsor No. 1672).

Probably painted *c.* 1749. The modelling and texture are harder than, for example, No. 952; No. 948 is close in quality, particularly in the horse, to the portraits of George II and Frederick, Prince of Wales, in this convention (Millar, Nos. 594, 595). A copy of No. 948 was sold at Christie's on 20 July 1956 (124). There is a version at Aske Hall with different accessories in the background.

949. WILLIAM, DUKE OF CUMBERLAND

Buckingham Palace. 29¾ × 25 in., 75,6 × 63,5 cm.

Riding a rearing horse, holding a baton in his right hand and wearing a military state coat with the ribbon of the Garter. In the background, under a lowering sky, a battle, presumably Culloden, is taking place against the Jacobite insurgents; a wounded Highlander crouches in the lower right corner of the canvas.

In the collection of George IV; probably the picture recorded in store at Carlton House in 1816 (261: 'William, Duke of Cumberland, on a bay horse, with troops drawn up in the background', measurements given as 27 × 24 in.; the 1816 label is still on the back); sent to Cumberland Lodge on 1 October 1823 (Jutsham, *Deliveries*, f. 44); later at Windsor (999; in the *V.R. inv.* the measurements are given as 50 × 39 in.; this is almost certainly a mistake, although it is possible that the canvas has since been slightly reduced).

Probably painted *c.* 1750.

950. WILLIAM, DUKE OF CUMBERLAND

Buckingham Palace. 24 × 19⅞ in., 61 × 50,5 cm.

On horseback, wearing a military state coat (possibly as Colonel of the 1st Foot Guards) with the ribbon of the Garter and holding a baton in his right hand. Behind him rides an officer and in the background the troops under Cumberland's command are routing the Jacobite insurgents at (presumably) Culloden.

Among the pictures offered to George IV by Benjamin Louis Vulliamy, as from his father's property, in a letter of 28 February 1812 (*Letters of George IV*, vol. I, 20: Vulliamy's name is inscribed on the stretcher); it was received from Vulliamy on 9 November 1812 ('by Morea'), sent to Simpson to be cleaned two days later and sent from the Armoury at Carlton House on 23 May 1820 for exhibition at the British Institution (Jutsham, *R/D*, ff. 122, 231, 354); recorded in the Armoury at Carlton House in 1816 (481); later at Kew and Windsor (1081).

Presumably painted *c.* 1750.

951. WILLIAM, DUKE OF CUMBERLAND

Buckingham Palace. 30 × 25 in., 76,2 × 63,5 cm.

Full-length, standing, in a military state coat over a breastplate with the ribbon and star of the Garter and the badge of the Bath. In his right hand he supports a baton on a table; in the background is a view of a parade-ground on which is drawn up a detachment of Foot Guards.

In the collection of George IV; recorded in store at Carlton House in 1816 (260); sent to Windsor (later No. 982) from the King's Lodge on 2 October 1823 (Jutsham, *Deliveries*, f. 44).

Probably painted *c.* 1750. At some date the canvas was damaged, perhaps deliberately slashed; the two cuts intersect at a point above the Duke's heart. A small version was on the London art-market, *c.* 1960.

952. GEORGE III

Kew (*Hampton Court* No. 1376). 50 × 39⅝ in., 127 × 101 cm.

On horseback in a scarlet military coat, laced with gold, and wearing the ribbon and star of the Garter. Behind the King rides John, 1st Earl Ligonier, wearing a scarlet coat laced with silver, probably an early form of staff uniform, with the star of the Bath; and two officers, one of whom, in scarlet with blue flashes, is probably an A.D.C. In the background is a review with, among the spectators, three mounted figures seen from behind; one of these is a woman and may be intended for the Queen.

In the collection of George IV, but conceivably painted for George III as it was received from Kensington at Carlton House on 7 August 1812: 'His Present Majesty . . . at a Review attended by

Lord Ligonier—by Morea' (Jutsham, *R/D*, f. 217); recorded in store at Carlton House in 1816 (268); sent to the King's Lodge on 27 September 1823; later at Windsor (1411) and Cumberland Lodge.

Probably painted *c.* 1760-5. It is possible that the four heads were painted by another hand. The composition was engraved by Peter Mazell as by David Morier. A version belongs to Mr. Donald Nicholas.

For Lord Ligonier see No. 957.

953. GEORGE III

Windsor Castle (1080). 20 × 16 in., 50,8 × 40,6 cm.

Riding on a bay horse, in a scarlet military coat laced with gold, with the ribbon and star of the Garter; two mounted officers follow behind. In the distance troops are drawn up for review.

In the collection of George IV. Probably the picture received on 22 July 1811 from Troup from General Hammond: 'A Small Painting—Portrait of George the Third on Horseback—Bay Horse—' (Jutsham, *R/D*, f. 171). A frame for it was received from Smith on 21 January 1812 (*ibid.*, f. 183). No. 953 was in the Armoury at Carlton House in 1816 (462).

The type probably dates from *c.* 1762.

954. GEORGE III

Windsor Castle (1678). 50¼ × 39¾ in., 127,6 × 101 cm.

Riding on a grey horse in a scarlet military coat laced with gold, with the ribbon of the Garter. In the background cavalry are drawn up for a review.

Both Nos. 954, 955 were in the collection of George IV, but it is not possible accurately to disentangle the references to them in the inventories of his collection. No. 954 is probably No. 269 in the inv. of 1816 (in store): 'His Majesty, on a grey horse, with troops in the background', measurements given as 49 × 40 in. This was sent to the King's Lodge on 2 October 1823 and to Cumberland Lodge in January 1844. It was recorded at Cumberland Lodge in 1873 (*V.R. inv.*).

A version of the same design as No. 955. The type presumably dates from *c.* 1765.

955. GEORGE III

Windsor Castle (447). 50 × 40 in., 127 × 101,6 cm.

Riding on a grey horse in a scarlet military coat laced with gold, with the ribbon of the Garter. Cavalry are drawn up in the background.

See No. 954. Redgrave noted the name of Vulliamy on the back in 1878 (*V.R. inv.*) and No. 955 is probably the portrait of George III from the set of seven such portraits offered to the Regent by Benjamin Lewis Vulliamy on 28 February 1812 and received at Carlton House on 9 November 1812: '. . . George The Third on Horseback—Gray Horse—in Gilt Frame—by Morea' at ten guineas (*Letters of George IV*, vol. I, 20; Jutsham, *R/D*, f. 231). It was sent to be cleaned by Simpson on 11 November (Jutsham, *loc. cit.*, f. 122). No. 955 is probably the picture recorded in store at Carlton House in 1816 (479: 'His Majesty, on a grey horse'; measurements given as 48 × 39 in.). No. 955 was recorded at Windsor in 1878 (*V.R. inv.*).

A version of the same design as No. 954.

956. JOHN MANNERS, MARQUESS OF GRANBY (1721-70)

Windsor Castle (1082). 24 × 19⅞ in., 61 × 50,5 cm.

Riding on a rearing grey horse in the uniform of Colonel of the Royal Regiment of Horse Guards, with a breastplate. A battle is being fought in the distance and two Light Dragoons are galloping towards it.

In the collection of George IV. One of the set of such pictures offered to the Regent by Benjamin Lewis Vulliamy on 28 February 1812 and received at Carlton House on 9 November 1812: 'The Marquis of Granby mounted on a Horse', at five guineas (*Letters of George IV*, vol. I, 20; Jutsham, *R/D*, f. 231). It was sent to be cleaned by Simpson on 11 November (Jutsham, *loc. cit.*, f. 122). Recorded in the Armoury at Carlton House in 1816 (482); later at Kew.

The type probably dates from *c.* 1760.

See No. 1022.

957. JOHN, FIRST EARL LIGONIER (1680-1770)

Windsor Castle (1677). 50¼ × 40¾ in., 127,6 × 103,5 cm.

Riding on a rearing bay horse, in a dark blue coat, presumably as Master-General of the Ordnance, with the ribbon of the Bath, a breastplate and a sword in his right hand. In the background a battle, probably in the Low Countries, is taking place in which the Horse Guards are prominent; William, Duke of Cumberland, is seen on horseback, talking to another officer.

In the collection of George IV. Possibly one of the paintings of this type acquired from Cutter on 14 April 1818 (W.R.A., Geo. 27015) and possibly to be identified with additional No. 544 in the Carlton House inv. of 1816: 'A Portrait of An Officer—Unknown— Mounted upon a Chesnut Horse—in Review—or Battle', measurements given as 55½ × 39 in.; it was sent to Cumberland Lodge on 1 October 1823 and may in turn be identical with No. 360 in the inv. of 1819: 'Portrait of an Officer upon a Chesnut Horse at a Review', measurements given as 55 × 39 in. and sent to Cumberland Lodge on the same day. No. 957 was recorded at Cumberland Lodge in 1873 (*V.R. inv.*).

The type probably dates from *c.* 1760. There are *pentimenti* in the ribbons of the order worn by the officer conversing with Cumberland in the background.

Born in France; served under Marlborough, commanded the British foot at Fontenoy, was Commander-in-Chief in the Austrian Netherlands, 1746-7, and was appointed Commander-in-Chief, 1757; became a Field-Marshal in 1766. George IV owned the equestrian portrait of him by Reynolds (see below, p. 98).

958. JAMES MONTAGU(E)

Windsor Castle (1372). 50 × 40 in., 127 × 101,6 cm.

Riding a grey horse in a riding-school; his uniform (?) is dark blue with gold lace over a red waistcoat with gold lace. The flag of St. George and the Red Ensign are suspended from two posts in the school.

In the collection of George IV (additional No. 603 in the Carlton House inv. of 1816; the Carlton House label is still on the back); it may have been presented to him by the sitter.

Painted, probably *c.* 1765, in the style of the equestrian portraits usually associated with Morier.

Appointed Yeoman Rider to George III; Clerk to the King's Mews and, 1790-1812, Equerry to His Majesty's Crown Stable. He was also Clerk of the Stables, 1778-87, to the Prince of Wales, who retained an affection for him and granted him an annual persion. He was still alive in 1804.

959. HENRY HERBERT, TENTH EARL OF PEMBROKE (1734-94)

Windsor Castle (980). 29½×35½ in., 74,9×90,2 cm.

Riding on a cream horse in the uniform of Colonel of the 1st Dragoons; troops are drawn up in the background.

In the collection of George IV. One of the set of such pictures offered to the Regent by Benjamin Lewis Vulliamy on 28 February 1812 and received at Carlton House on 9 November 1812: 'The Late Earl of Pembroke mounted on a Horse ... by Morea', at seven guineas (*Letters of George IV*, vol. I, 20; Jutsham, *R/D*, f. 231). It was sent to be cleaned by Simpson on 11 November (Jutsham, *loc. cit.*, f. 122). Recorded in store at Carlton House in 1816 (439). Sent to the King's Lodge on 27 September 1823.

The type probably dates from soon after his appointment in 1764 as Colonel of the 1st Dragoons.

An Aide-de-Camp to George II and Lord of the Bedchamber to George III, who adored his charming Countess. He commanded the Cavalry Brigade in Germany, 1761-3, became a Major-General in 1761 and a General in 1782. He was greatly interested in the managing of horses ('horse mad' in his own words) and in 1761 published his *Method of Breaking Horses*. Paintings at Wilton, illustrating the horsemanship of the Earl, his family and friends, are associated traditionally with Morier.

960. A SKIRMISH BETWEEN ENGLISH AND FRENCH CAVALRY

Windsor Castle (1284). 24×39⅞ in., 61×101,3 cm.

Dragoons skirmishing with a party of *Mousquetaires du Roi* on the edge of a cavalry action.

Nos. 960-2 and Millar No. 599 were in the collection of William, Duke of Cumberland; they are recorded at Cranbourne Lodge in 1765, No. 960 probably as 'A Skirmish between some English Dragoons and french Gens d'Armes'; the four pictures were in General Taylor's room at Buckingham House in 1819 (865-8).

The set of four paintings were presumably painted for Cumberland to show troops of different nationalities in action.

961. HUSSARS ATTACKING A BAGGAGE WAGON

Windsor Castle (1283). 24×39¾ in., 61×101 cm.

A detachment of Austro-Hungarian Hussars attacking a French baggage wagon.

See No. 960; in the 1765 inv. of Cranbourne Lodge No. 961 appears as 'A painting of Hussars attacking the ffrench Baggage'.

See No. 960.

962. AN ENGAGEMENT BETWEEN FRENCH TROOPS AND A DETACHMENT OF THE 'FREE COMPANY'

Windsor Castle (1286). 23¾×39½ in., 60,3×100,3 cm.

A hand-to-hand combat between French infantry and men of the Austrian 'Vreie Compagnien'.

See No. 960; in the 1765 inv. of Cranbourne Lodge No. 962 appears as 'A Skirmish of the ffree Company with a Part of French'.

See No. 960.

Mary Moser

1744-1819. Flower-painter and one of the original members of the Royal Academy (see No. 1210), where she exhibited, 1769-92, as Miss Moser and, after her marriage, as Mrs. Hugh Lloyd, 1797-1802.

According to J. T. Smith (*Nollekens and his Times*, 2nd ed. (1829), vol. I, p. 65), Queen Charlotte 'took particular notice of Miss Moser, and for a considerable time employed her at Frogmore, for the decoration of one chamber, which her Majesty commanded to be called Miss Moser's Room, and for which the Queen paid upwards of 900l.'

963. A VASE OF FLOWERS

Windsor Castle (1529). 114¼×79¼ in., 290,2×201,3 cm.

An urn, decorated with a relief of Britannia, standing on a base decorated with the star of the Garter and a lion's head in relief; this is in turn supported on a base, decked with Garters and oak-leaves and decorated with the royal arms in relief. The base is supported by the lion and unicorn; a harp rests against it; and there are swathes of roses and thistles at its foot. At the top of the canvas are suspended Garter collars and a medallion of St. George; and the design is filled out with swags and festoons of flowers.

The canvas is inserted into the panelling of the room at Frogmore House which is traditionally associated with Mary Moser (see above). In quality it is very close to the four hanging swags painted on the walls of the room and to the painted floral decoration of the ceiling. No. 963 and these related decorations are also close in quality to Nos. 964-9. It is not known when the canvas was set up at Frogmore, and the emphasis on the Garter which it contains may indicate that it was originally connected in some way with the decoration of the King's Audience Chamber at Windsor (see above, pp. xviii-xix).

964. A BUNCH OF FLOWERS

Windsor Castle (1528). 33¾×30⅞ in., 85,7×78,4 cm.; framed as an oval.

Nos. 964-9 are traditionally stated (e.g., *V.R. inv.*, October 1871) to have been painted by Mary Moser for Queen Charlotte for the decoration of the room in Frogmore House where they hang and which was decorated by Mary Moser with wall paintings which seem to be by the same hand (see also No. 963). Nos. 964, 965 are painted against a plain grey background and are clearly designed to be framed as ovals, possibly over the doors of this room.

965. A BUNCH OF FLOWERS

Windsor Castle (1523). 33⅞×30¾ in., 86×78,1 cm.; framed as an oval.

See No. 964.

966. A VASE OF FLOWERS

Windsor Castle (1524). 25⅞×25¾ in., 65,7×65,4 cm.

See No. 964; Nos. 966-9 were probably designed as free-standing pictures, to hang in, but not to be built into, the room entrusted to Mary Moser by Queen Charlotte. In No. 966 the flowers are primarily among those that flower in spring.

967. A VASE OF FLOWERS

Windsor Castle (1525). 25¾×26⅛ in., 65,4×66,4 cm.

See No. 964; in No. 967 the flowers are primarily among those that flower in summer.

968. A VASE OF FLOWERS (*Plate* 11)

Windsor Castle (1527). $26\frac{1}{8} \times 25\frac{3}{4}$ in., $66,4 \times 65,4$ cm.

Signed: *Mary Moser / R A.*

See No 964; the flowers in No. 968 are primarily those that flower in summer.

969. A VASE OF FLOWERS

Windsor Castle (1526). $25\frac{5}{8} \times 25\frac{1}{4}$ in., $65,1 \times 64,1$ cm.

Signed: *Mary Moser A R* [*sic*]

See No. 964.

William Mulready

1786–1863. Painter of genre scenes; also illustrated books. He came to London as a child from his native County Clare and exhibited regularly at the Royal Academy from 1804 to 1862.

970. THE WOLF AND THE LAMB (*Plate* 281)

Buckingham Palace. Panel: $23\frac{5}{8} \times 20\frac{1}{8}$ in., $60 \times 51,1$ cm.

Redgrave records a signature, *Wm Mulready*, on the brass plate attached to the gate-post (*V.R. inv.*, October 1858); it is now not easy to discern this, but it appears to read [?*W*] *MULREADY*.

A boy, on his way to school, and his little dog have been set upon by another boy; a little girl is summoning help from the victim's mother, apparently a widow, in a neighbouring house. According to Redgrave (*loc. cit.*) the background is a part of Kensington Mall.

Bought by George IV. It was received at Carlton House in May 1821: '. . . Gilt Frame . . . This Painting was bought of Mʳ Mulready by His Majesty—it had been some Months in His Majesty's Apartments' (Jutsham, *Receipts*, f. 135; *Carlton House*, 1816, additional No. 582); sent to the King's Lodge on 17 June 1824 (Jutsham, *Deliveries*, f. 55); later in the Queen's Dressing-Room at Windsor, but sent to Buckingham Palace (186) on 3 May 1858.

Literature: R. and S. Redgrave, *A Century of Painters* (1866), vol. II, p. 312; F. G. Stephens, *Memorials of William Mulready* (1890), pp. 54, 82–4, 89; W. T. Whitley, *Art in England 1800–20* (1928), pp. 316–17; City Art Gallery, Bristol, *William Mulready*, 1964 (11).

Exhibited at the Royal Academy in 1820 (106) and bought by George IV; Mulready's receipt for £210 is dated 7 December 1820 (W.R.A., Geo. 26764). On 8 October 1823 No. 970 was sent, at Sir William Knighton's instructions, to Mulready's studio at Kensington Gravel Pits in order that it might be engraved (Jutsham, *Deliveries*, f. 48); the picture was brought back to Carlton House by Seguier on 30 December 1825. The engraving was made by J. H. Robinson and published on 5 March 1828. Mulready gave to the Artists' Fund the rights in this engraving, of which George IV bought three 'Choice Proofs' for £23. 2s. on 16 December 1828 (W.R.A., Geo. 26572–3, 35684). A later engraving was made by C. W. Sharpe.

No. 970 was one of the very few pictures in which Mulready had yielded to 'the seductive powers of asphaltum' (Stephens, *op. cit.*, p. 89). At some date it had been returned to Mulready who had 'cut out certain portions of the injured parts and repainted them from the ground'. It had been chosen for exhibition in Paris in 1855 (893) and Bentley had attempted to repair the extensive damage that the asphaltum had caused. It again fell into a deplorable state and was entrusted in 1861 to Mulready himself who reported, after having it for three months, that he could do nothing to repair it 'short of the entire removing the injured parts and repainting'. In 1864, after Mulready's death and with Queen Victoria's permission, Redgrave entrusted it to Buttery who stopped the damages most successfully (note, 20 December 1864, by Redgrave in *V.R. inv.*; letter from Redgrave to Col. Biddulph, 9 March 1861, in Surveyor's office). The frame bore traces of the wax dropped from the candles held near the picture by George IV whenever he explained the story of No. 970 to his friends (Whitley, *loc. cit.*). A copy of the two boys belonged in 1957 to Mrs. Strange.

971. THE INTERIOR OF AN ENGLISH COTTAGE (*Plate* 280)

Buckingham Palace. Panel: $24\frac{1}{2} \times 19\frac{7}{8}$ in., $62,2 \times 50,5$ cm.

Signed and dated: *William Mulready. 1828.*

A young mother, seated at the window of a cottage, awaits the return of her husband who is hailing her from the back of his horse in the distance; a girl is asleep at her mother's knee and a small boy sleeps in his cot by the fireside.

Bought by George IV; it was received at Carlton House from Mulready on 30 October 1828 and sent on Sir William Knighton's orders to Royal Lodge on 4 November 1828 (Jutsham, *Receipts*, f. 264; 'Carleton Palace', No. 620); at Buckingham Palace (185) by 25 January 1861 (*V.R. inv.*).

Literature: R. and S. Redgrave, *A Century of Painters* (1866), vol. II, pp. 314–16; R.A., *King's Pictures* (488), *The First Hundred Years.* 1951–2 (244).

Exhibited at the Royal Academy in 1828 (127) and bought by George IV; Mulready's receipt for £315 is dated 28 October 1828 (W.R.A., Geo. 26567–8, 35802). The payment was made through Lawrence and authorised by Sir William Knighton (*Memoirs* (1838), vol. II, pp. 29–30). No. 971 was engraved by C. Cousen as 'The Home-Expected'. A sketch by Mulready for No. 971 is in the Tate Gallery (1797) and a cartoon in the Victoria and Albert Museum.

John Nash

1752–1835. Architect and speculative builder. In 1798 he exhibited at the Royal Academy (1022) a design for a conservatory for the Prince of Wales and in the same year married Mary Anne Bradley, who may have been involved in an affair with his patron. Thereafter Nash was associated with the Prince in the creation of Regent's Park, the remodelling of the Royal Pavilion at Brighton and the reconstruction of Buckingham House. The death of George IV marked the end of Nash's career as a public architect and he was deprived of any responsibility for Buckingham Palace.

972. A CLASSICAL DESIGN FOR CARLTON HOUSE

Buckingham Palace. Pen on paper, later mounted on canvas and partly worked over in oil: $27\frac{1}{2} \times 56$ in., $69,8 \times 142,2$ cm.

The front of a large classical palace with troops drawn up for review in the foreground. In the distance on the left is a glimpse of the statue of Charles I at Charing Cross.

Recorded at Buckingham Palace (1128) in 1876 (*V.R. inv.*).

Literature: J. Summerson, *John Nash* (1935), p. 147.

Nos. 972, 973 were presumably drawn *c.* 1814, at the time Nash was working at Carlton House, and were perhaps connected with the Prince Regent's ideas (which came to nothing) for building an entirely new palace. In No. 972 the classical palace is seen at the end of Waterloo Place, but this is shown much wider than it actually is and the drawing must have been composed before Waterloo Place was built (1815 onwards). At a very early date, perhaps to give the Regent a more vivid impression of his architect's designs, Nos. 972, 973 were overpainted in oil: in No. 972 the sky, foreground and figures are all in this medium. Under the present surface it is impossible to determine whether Nash had used wash or pencil as well as ink in his original drawings.

973. A GOTHIC DESIGN FOR CARLTON HOUSE

Buckingham Palace. Pen on paper, later mounted on canvas and partly worked over in oil: $27\frac{1}{2} \times 56\frac{1}{8}$ in., $69,8 \times 142,6$ cm.

The front of a large Gothic palace from the garden; the church of St. Martin in the Fields is seen in the distance on the right.

Recorded at Buckingham Palace (1129) in 1876 (*V.R. inv.*).

Literature: J. Summerson, *John Nash* (1935), p. 147.

See No. 972. Presumably designed to be submitted to the Prince Regent as a design for a Gothic palace. Nash's additions to Carlton House had included a Gothic dining-room and a Gothic library. As in No. 972, the original drawing was heavily overpainted in oil (with sky, garden, trees and figures) up to, and partly over, the drawing of the building.

James Northcote

1746–1831. Painter of portraits, subject-pictures and scenes from history, especially from the Wars of the Roses. He worked in Reynolds's studio from 1771 to 1776.

974. THE MARRIAGE OF RICHARD, DUKE OF YORK

Buckingham Palace. 83×58 in., $210,8 \times 147,3$ cm.

Signed and dated: *James Northcote. | pinx.t 1821.*

The little couple standing at the altar while their hands are joined by an Archbishop; a Cardinal addresses them; on the altar is an open book in which is inscribed: *The MARRIAGE on the 15th of Jany 1477 | of Richard Duke of York second son of | King Edward IV.th with the Lady Ann Mowbray | Daughter and sole heir of John Lord Mowbray | Duke of Norfolk.*

Acquired by George IV and recorded in the inventory of 'Carleton Palace' (631); recorded at Buckingham Palace (993) in 1877 (*V.R. inv.*).

Presumably the picture exhibited at the Royal Academy in 1821 (217); Say's engraving of No. 974 was published on 4 May 1821. On 6 December 1828 Northcote was paid £105 'for a Picture' (W.R.A., Geo. 35803); Edward Wyatt's bill included, under 22 March 1830, £24. 15s. for a 'Large rich frame' for No. 974. A version is at Kitley.
Richard, Duke of York (1473–?84), younger son of Edward IV, was married on 15 January 1478 to Ann, daughter and heiress of John Mowbray, 4th Duke of Norfolk. The ceremony took place in St. Stephen's Chapel, Westminster, in the presence of the King, Queen and other royal ladies (presumably the group behind in No. 974 represents the royal party) and was conducted by James Goldwell, Bishop of Norwich. The Cardinal may be intended for Thomas Bourchier, Archbishop of Canterbury. The literary source used by Northcote may have been the account of the ceremony in Francis Sandford's *A Genealogical History of the Kings and Queen of England* (1707), pp. 415–17.

John Opie

1761–1807. Painter of portraits and subject-pictures. He came to London from the West Country in 1783 as the protégé of Dr. John Wolcot. The success of No. 975 and the influence of Mrs. Boscawen, led to Opie's introduction, accompanied by Wolcot, to the King and Queen in 1782. He showed them a group of pictures, from which the King selected a picture of a beggar and his dog. The King ordered West, who was present at the audience, to pay Opie for the picture. At that time Opie had a commission to paint the Duke and Duchess of Gloucester (J. J. Rogers, *Opie and his Works* (1878), pp. 21–3, 24–5; A. Earland, *John Opie and his Circle* (1911), pp. 31–7; W. T. Whitley, *Artists and their Friends in England 1700–99* (1928), vol. I, pp. 377–8).

975. MARY GRANVILLE, MRS. DELANY
(1700–88) (*Plate* 135)

Windsor Castle (3134). $30\frac{1}{8} \times 25$ in., $76,5 \times 63,5$ cm.

Head and shoulders, in a painted oval, in widow's dress, wearing on a black ribbon a heart-shaped locket on which is the monogram CR or GR under a crown.

Painted for George III and Queen Charlotte and placed in the Bedchamber at Buckingham House (Geo. III, *Buck. Ho.*); later at Hampton Court (944) and Kensington.

Literature: J. J. Rogers, *Opie and his Works* (1875), pp. 20–4, 88–9; Law, 1881, 1898 (375); A. Earland, *John Opie and his Circle* (1911), pp. 33, 36–7, 273; Royal Institution of Cornwall, *John Opie and Henry Bone*, 1951 (20).

Probably painted early in 1782. On 14 February 1782 Walpole wrote to Mann about Opie: 'He has done a head of Mrs. Delany for the King—*oui vraiment*, it is pronounced like Rembrandt, but as I told her, it does not look older than she is, but older than she does' (*Letters*, ed. Mrs. P. Toynbee, vol. XII (1904), p. 166). Lady Bute persuaded Mrs. Delany to sit again to Opie for a portrait in the same dress and pose; this second version is now in the National Portrait Gallery (1030) in a frame specially designed for it by Horace Walpole (*The Autobiography and Correspondence of . . . Mrs. Delany*, ed. Lady Llanover; 2nd series (1862), vol. III, p. 497; Arts Council, *John Opie*, 1962–3 (15)). A third version, with slight variations, is in the possession of Mrs. Granville; it is inscribed on the back as painted in 1782.

Daughter of Bernard Granville, married first to Alexander Pendarves and later to Patrick Delany, Dean of Down (*d.* 1768). She met the royal family on their visits to the Dowager Duchess of Portland at Bulstrode Park. The King and Queen became very fond of her; they were intrigued by the paper mosaics which she made of flowers and plants and sent her specimens to copy from Kew; and after the Duchess's death in 1785 they gave her a house near the Queen's Lodge at Windsor and a private pension of £200 per annum. Her letters provide a delightful picture of the family life of the royal family 'in this our sweet retreat' at this period.

William Owen

1769–1825. Portrait-painter. He succeeded Hoppner as Portrait-Painter to the Prince of Wales, 1810–20(?), and on 24 October 1812 told Farington that the Prince had promised to sit to him and that several copies of the portrait would be required (*Diary*, vol. VII, p. 123). Owen had been introduced to the Prince after painting a portrait of Cyril Jackson, Dean of Christ Church; the Prince had been pleased with his portrait of Sir David Dundas (No. 976); but never fulfilled his promise to sit to Owen himself. Instead, presumably because he was by now patronising Lawrence, the Prince told Owen to copy Hoppner's portrait (see Nos. 834, 852), a commission which ended in failure (W.R.A., Geo. 26509-12).

976. SIR DAVID DUNDAS (1735-1820) (*Plate* 255)

Windsor Castle (358). $54\frac{1}{2} \times 44\frac{1}{4}$ in., $138,4 \times 112,4$ cm.

Three-quarter-length, standing, in the uniform of a general, wearing the ribbon and star of the Bath, and holding his plumed hat in his right hand and his sword under his left arm.

Painted for George IV. It was received, in a gilt frame, at Carlton House from Owen on 27 June 1812 (Jutsham, *R/D*, f. 209) and placed in the East Ante-room (No. 61 in inv. of 1816). It was removed to the New Gallery, Windsor Castle, on 6 August 1828; in 1878 it was in the Corridor (*V.R. inv.*); and thereafter it was placed in the Waterloo Chamber.

Literature: Collins Baker, *Windsor*, p. 248.

Exhibited at the Royal Academy in 1813 (136). In his remonstrance of 16 January 1823, addressed to Sir William Knighton, Owen stated that, after he had waited on the Regent at Carlton House, 'Lady Dundas called on me to say that Sir David had received his Royal Highnesse's commands to sit to me for his portrait for him. This was done with success, and when Sir David and myself attended to present the picture, it was received with the most flattering expressions of approbation. His Royal Highness immediately pointed out a distinguished place for the picture, and superintended the hanging of it; speaking to all about him and to myself, in terms of the highest commendation . . .' (W.R.A., Geo. 26509-10). A head and shoulders version is in the possession of Sir Robert Whyte Melville Dundas.

Gazetted Lieutenant-fireworker in the Royal Artillery, 1754, and Lieutenant in the 56th Regiment of Foot two years later. He served in the Seven Years War; partly as a result of his studies in Germany, became an expert on military tactics, regulations and drill; Quartermaster-General, 1795; commanded the camps at Weymouth and Windsor, which brought him into contact with George III; particularly praised by the Duke of York for his services in the expedition to the Helder, 1799. Governor of Chelsea Hospital, 1805, and Commander-in-Chief, 1809-11. See also No. 660.

Thomas Patch

c. 1725-1782. Painter of topographical subjects and caricatures, working in Florence from 1755 until his death. He figures prominently in Zoffany's *Tribuna* (No. 1211).

977. A DISTANT VIEW OF FLORENCE
(*Plate* 10)

Kensington Palace. $46 \times 91\frac{1}{4}$ in., $116,8 \times 231,8$ cm.

A panoramic view of Florence from the high ground to the west, probably from a point near Bellosguardo, with shepherdesses, flocks and sportsmen in the foreground.

Nos. 977-9 may be the 'three Views of Florence' for which Dalton was paid £44 by George III in 1764 (W.R.A., Geo. 17114). No.

977 was in the Queen's Dressing-Room at Kensington in 1818 (222); taken to Hampton Court on 12 September 1838; later at Buckingham Palace (778) and York House.

Literature: F. Watson, 'Thomas Patch', *Walpole Soc.*, vol. XXVIII (1940), pp. 38-9.

Probably painted *c.* 1763. Versions, with variations in the foreground and conceived as painted from a point slightly nearer the city, are in the Royal Albert Memorial Museum, Exeter, and the Norton Simon Foundation, California. A large version, close to No. 977 in scale, but with variations in the foreground and signed and dated 1767, was sold by Mr. Fred Beddington at Christie's, 22 March 1968 (107). It seems that Patch evolved one distant view of Florence and thereafter repeated it with variations in the foreground.

978. A VIEW OF THE ARNO IN FLORENCE BY DAY

St. James's Palace. $34\frac{1}{2} \times 69\frac{1}{4}$ in., $87,6 \times 175,9$ cm.

Signed and dated: *T PATCH | 1763* (initials in monogram)

A view from the Lungarno Guicciardini, looking down the Arno towards the Ponte alla Carraia and across the river to the Palazzo Corsini, with groups of figures in the street and in boats on the water.

See No. 977. No. 978 was recorded at St. James's in 1819 (1087) and was later at Hampton Court (653), York House and Kensington.

Literature: Law, 1881, 1898 (519); F. J. B. Watson, 'Thomas Patch', *Walpole Soc.*, vol. XXVIII (1940), p. 38.

A signed variant of No. 978, sold in the Currie sale at Christie's, 27 March 1953 (61), is now in the Museum of Art, University of Kansas (see their *Register*, 7 (May, 1956), pp. 25-8); another (also signed) was sold from the collection of Lord Clifden at Sotheby's, 23 November 1966 (4).

979. A VIEW OF THE ARNO IN FLORENCE BY NIGHT

St. James's Palace. 35×69 in., $88,9 \times 175,3$ cm.

A view from the Lungarno Guicciardini, looking up the Arno towards the Ponte a Sta. Trinita, with the Ponte Vecchio beyond; on the right, near the bridge, is the Palazzo dei Padri delle Missioni; across the river are the tower of Sta. Trinita and, in the distance, the Campanile, the Duomo and the Palazzo Vecchio with fireworks blazing from its tower; facing the spectator, across the river, is the Palazzo Gianfigliazzi.

See No. 977. No. 979 was recorded at St. James's in 1819 (1086) and was later at Hampton Court (642), York House and Kensington.

Literature: Law, 1881, 1898 (520); F. J. B. Watson, 'Thomas Patch', *Walpole Soc.*, vol. XXVIII (1940), p. 38.

Presumably painted as a companion to No. 978. The fireworks are presumably those which were let off as part of the celebrations on the annual festival of S. Giovanni Battista on 24 June. A picture very like No. 979 is included in his conversation piece at Malahide Castle, which may be intended to represent the interior of Sir Horace Mann's house in Florence. Patch painted a number of versions of this view by daylight (e.g., in the Ilchester collection); it is possibly related to, but is not (as is stated by Watson, *op. cit.*) closely dependent, on pl. VI in Giuseppe Zocchi's *SCELTA di XXIV Vedute delle principali Contrade, Piazze, Chiese, e Palazzi della Città di Firenze* (1754).

Richard Paton

1716?–1791. Marine painter, stated to have been taken to sea by his protector, Sir Charles Knowles. He exhibited at the Society of Artists, 1762–70, and the Royal Academy, 1776–80.

The inventory of William, Duke of Cumberland's, possessions in 1765 includes 'A Sea fight without a frame (by Patten) a Dᵒ by Moonlight by Dᵒ'

980. THE DOCKYARD AT DEPTFORD
(*Plate* 86)

Buckingham Palace. 40×58 in., 101,6×147,3 cm.

A view of the dockyard, looking down the river towards the church of St. Alphege and Greenwich Hospital. A royal yacht is firing a salute and a barge, flying the Royal Standard, is apparently returning to it.

Mrs. Jameson records at Hampton Court in 1842 (p. 419, No. 743) four views of Deptford, Woolwich, Chatham and Sheerness; No. 980 was recorded at Hampton Court in 1849 (*The Stranger's Guide*, No. 931; later No. 1000); later at Kensington.

Literature: Law, 1881, 1898 (934).

Walpole records (*Anecdotes*, vol. V, pp. 105–6) a newspaper report that on 17 February 1775 Paton had waited on the King at Buckingham House with some of his pictures, including 'two . . . being views of the royal dockyards at Deptford and Chatham [see No. 981]; also prints finely engraved from the last-mentioned pictures by Messrs. Woollett and Canot. His majesty was pleased to honour the artist with his approbation, and to express satisfaction at his performances.' Woollett's engraving of No. 980 was published on 14 February 1775 with a dedication to the King and the statement that the figures had been painted by John Hamilton Mortimer. Paton exhibited views of Deptford at the Royal Academy in 1776 (220) and 1779 (233). On the first occasion the picture was described as *A view of his Majesty's Dockyard at Deptford and the royal Hospital at Greenwich, with the procession of the Trinity Masters, being part of a set of views of the royal dock yards.*

In the summer of 1770 Thomas Jones records that 'About this time Paton was engaged in painting Views of the principal Dockyards, and Mortimer had undertaken to paint the figures—for this purpose, on the 27th of this month [July], They both set off for Portsmouth' (see No. 984) ('Memoirs of Thomas Jones', ed. A. P. Oppé, *Walpole Soc.*, vol. XXXII (1951), p. 22). Edwards states (*Anecdotes of Painters* (1808), p. 166) that Paton 'painted some views of the Dockyards, by permission both of his Majesty and from the Admiralty; but his original scheme was never completed. The figures in these pictures were also painted by Mortimer.'

981. THE DOCKYARD AT CHATHAM (*Plate* 85)

Buckingham Palace. 40¾×58⅞ in., 103,5×149,5 cm.

A view of the dockyard with the Royal Standard flying on the quay and the King's (?) coach drawn up.

See No. 980. Recorded at Hampton Court in 1849 (*The Stranger's Guide*, No. 969; later No. 1062); later at Kensington.

Literature: Law, 1881, 1898 (937); Eastbourne and Kenwood, *John Hamilton Mortimer*, 1968 (110).

See No. 980. P. C. Canot's engraving of No. 981 was published on 1 July 1793 with the statement that the figures had been painted by Mortimer; there is a picturesque group of men, women and marine genre in the foreground. No. 981 is probably the picture exhibited by Paton at the Royal Academy in 1778 (227: *View of his Majesty's dockyard at Chatham, and part of the river Medway, in the county of Kent*).

982. THE DOCKYARD AT WOOLWICH

Buckingham Palace. 40×58¼ in., 101,6×147,9 cm.

A view of the dockyard with the Royal Standard flying on an uncompleted ship.

See No. 980. Recorded at Hampton Court in 1849 (*The Stranger's Guide*, No. 971; later No. 1066); later at Kensington.

Literature: Law, 1881, 1898 (938).

Presumably painted *c.* 1775–80. The figures in the small boats in the foreground are presumably by Mortimer.

983. THE DOCKYARD AT SHEERNESS

Buckingham Palace. 40½×58¼ in., 102,9×147,9 cm.

A view of the dockyard from the sea in a high wind.

See No. 980. Recorded at Hampton Court in 1849 (*The Stranger's Guide*, No. 957; later No. 1055); later at Kensington.

Literature: Law, 1881, 1898 (936).

The engraving of No. 983 by W. Watts was published on 1 March 1803.

984. THE DOCKYARD AT PORTSMOUTH

Buckingham Palace. 40×58¼ in., 101,6×147,9 cm.

A view of the dockyard with the Royal Standard and the Admiralty flag flying on a large ship under construction.

See No. 980. Recorded at Hampton Court in 1849 (*The Stranger's Guide*, No. 955; later No. 1051); later at Kensington.

Literature: Law, 1881, 1898 (935).

The figures in the foreground are probably by Mortimer. See No. 980.

985. SIR CHARLES KNOWLES'S ATTACK ON PORT LOUIS

Buckingham Palace. 33½×41 in., 85,1×104,1 cm.

Inscribed by the artist: *Fort St Louis | 8 March 1747/8.*

Admiral Knowles, in the *Canterbury*, with seven two deckers attacking the fort; on the left Spanish fireships are being towed clear.

Recorded at Hampton Court in 1849 (*The Stranger's Guide*, No. 929; later No. 998); later at Kensington.

Literature: Law, 1881, 1898 (866).

Charles Knowles (d. 1777), Rear Admiral of the White, arrived off Port Louis in Hispaniola on 8 March 1748. Although the fort was strongly constructed and well defended, it was silenced after a cannonade lasting three hours. The Admiral destroyed the fortifications.

Nos. 985, 986 were presumably painted *c.* 1770. Thomas Jones records that about the beginning of 1769 he was 'engaged in painting backgrounds for Paton the Ship painter—They were distant views on the Coast of Cuba and Hispaniola—The pictures were, I believe, painted for Admiral Sr Charles Knowles, and I went to Sr Charles's house to copy the various Trees of that Climate from a picture which he had procured in the West Indies' ('Memoirs of Thomas Jones', ed. A. P. Oppé, *Walpole Soc.*, vol. XXXII (1951), p. 15). A replica of No. 985 is in the

National Maritime Museum; it was formerly attributed to Samuel Scott.

986. SIR CHARLES KNOWLES'S ENGAGEMENT WITH THE SPANISH FLEET OFF HAVANA

Buckingham Palace. 33 × 56 in., 83,8 × 142,2 cm.

The action between Admiral Knowles's squadron and the Spaniards at the moment when the *Cornwall* lost her main topmast.

Recorded at Hampton Court in 1849 (*The Stranger's Guide*, No. 933; later No. 1002); later at Kensington.

Literature: Law, 1881, 1898 (867).

See No. 985. The action took place on 1 October 1748. Knowles, by now Rear Admiral of the Red, fell in with the Spanish squadron some four leagues off Havana. Knowles succeeded in compelling the Spanish ships to retreat, captured the *Conquistadore* and destroyed the *Africa* flagship, but was found at a subsequent court-martial to have been negligent in not bringing more of his squadron to bear upon the enemy in the beginning of the action and in not shifting his flag from the *Cornwall* as soon as she had been disabled.

Thomas Phillips

1770–1845. Portrait-painter (principally). As a young man he worked as a glass-painter, and at one period was employed under West's aegis in St. George's Chapel, Windsor. He exhibited at the Royal Academy between 1792 and his death.

Phillips's account, dated 17 April 1806, includes £52. 10s. for a portrait of the Prince of Wales, £20 for a frame for it and fifteen guineas for a portrait of William Battine (W.R.A., Geo. 26831–2). On 10 August 1809 Phillips submitted a bill for £126 for a portrait of the Prince of Wales in Garter robes, given to Lord Fitzwilliam; his receipt is dated 21 January 1811 (*ibid.*, Geo. 26869–70, 89471). In 1811 Phillips was writing about an account 'for a Picture I have recently painted for His R Hss the Prince Regent' (*ibid.*, 26882), which was possibly No. 987.

987. JOHN HELY-HUTCHINSON, FIRST BARON HUTCHINSON AND SECOND EARL OF DONOUGHMORE (1757–1832)

Kensington Palace. 50 × 40 in., 127 × 101,6 cm.

Three-quarter-length, in the uniform of a Lieutenant-General with the ribbon and star of the Bath, holding in his left hand a map of Egypt; by him on a table are writing materials and a letter addressed to him as Lord Hutchinson.

Painted for George IV and recorded in store at Carlton House in 1816 (258) as by Beechey; this is corrected to Phillips in the inventory of 'Carleton Palace' (328); lent on 2 November 1818 to Moody (=Mudie) for the purpose of designing a medal from it;[1] on 24 April 1827 it was sent with the King's permission to Col. Hely-Hutchinson in order that a copy might be made from it (Jutsham *R/D*, f. 304, *Deliveries*, f. 103); removed to the New Gallery at Windsor on 24 July 1828; later at Hampton Court (872).

Literature: Law, 1881, 1898 (368).

On 20 May 1811 Phillips submitted a bill for £84 for 'a Portrait of the Rt Honl Lord Hutchinson' (W.R.A., Geo.

1. The medal by Webb, issued by James Mudie, entitled 'Egypt Delivered' (J. Mudie, *An Historical and Critical Account of a Grand Series of National Medals* (1820), IX).

26896, 42917). The type is very close to the engraving, published on 9 June 1809, by K. Mackenzie from a drawing by W. Evans from a portrait in Lord Hutchinson's possession. Copies are in the possession of the Earl of Donoughmore and the Hon. David Hely-Hutchinson, and at the Army and Navy Club.

Entered the army in 1774. In 1801 he commanded the first division in Abercromby's army in Egypt; after Abercromby's death in the battle of Alexandria (see No. 1092) he succeeded to his command, captured Cairo and Alexandria and totally defeated the French in Egypt. A friend of George IV, he was entrusted in 1820 with a mission to Queen Caroline.

Henry William Pickersgill

1782–1875. Portrait-painter (principally), who exhibited at the Royal Academy between 1806 and 1872.

988. ROWLAND, FIRST VISCOUNT HILL (1772–1842) (*Plate* 254)

Windsor Castle (203). 50 × 40 in., 127 × 101,6 cm.

Three-quarter-length, standing, in General's uniform, holding a telescope and with his plumed hat beside him; he wears the ribbon and star of the Bath and the stars of the Royal Hanoverian Guelphic Order, the Tower and Sword of Portugal and St. George of Russia; and the Peninsular Gold Cross with four clasps, the Waterloo Medal and the badges of St. George of Russia, Maria Theresa and the Military Medal of William of the Netherlands.

Presumably painted for William IV to hang in the Waterloo Chamber, where it is recorded in 1840 (*Visitants' Guide*).

Literature: Collins Baker, *Windsor*, p. 256.

Engraved by Mote. A half-length copy was on the art-market in 1922. The type is very close to the full-length in the United Services Club, probably the portrait exhibited at the R.A. in 1832 (15).

Gazetted Ensign in the 38th Regiment of Foot in 1790; commanded the 90th Regiment in the Egyptian campaign of 1801; in 1808 was placed in command of a brigade in the force sent out under Wellesley to Portugal and rendered distinguished service in the Peninsula and at Waterloo. A great favourite with George IV, he bore the Royal Standard at his Coronation; appointed Commander-in-Chief in 1828.

989. SIR GEORGE ADAM WOOD (1767–1831)

Buckingham Palace. 59 × 40⅛ in., 127 × 101,9 cm.

Three-quarter-length, standing, in the uniform of a staff officer of Artillery, holding his sword in both his hands. He wears the star and badge of the Order of the Guelphs; his badges include the Order of Maria Theresa, the Military Order of William of Orange and the Orders of St. Louis (?) and St. Wlodomir; he also wears the Waterloo medal.

Recorded at Buckingham Palace (460) in 1876 (*V.R. inv.*).

Probably painted *c.* 1825.

Commissioned in the Royal Artillery in 1781, Wood rose to the rank of Major-General in 1825; he had served under the Duke of York in Flanders and in the Peninsula, and he commanded the artillery in the Waterloo campaign. He was appointed A.D.C. to the King in 1814 and ended his career as Governor of Carlisle.

George Place

d. 1805. Portrait-painter, born in Dublin, who went to Lucknow in 1798. As a miniature painter he had exhibited at the Royal Academy between 1791 and 1797.

990. SA'ADAT ALI KHAN, NAWAB OF OUDH (d. 1814)

Windsor Castle (1025). 45⅛ × 31¼ in., 114,6 × 79,4 cm.; the canvas is stretched on a mahogany stretcher of unusual construction. On the back are early labels giving Mather Brown as the artist and describing the sitter as the Nawab of Arcot.

Full-length, standing, in Indian costume, resting his hand on a table on which are papers and writing-materials. In the background is a view of a palace.

In the collection of George IV by January 1800. Recorded at Carlton House in 1816 (305: 'A portrait, supposed to be that of the Nabob of Arcot'; the name of Mather Brown is added later); in the inv. of 1819 the portrait appears (215) as 'supposed that of the Nabob of Oude' without the name of an artist; in 1878 (*V.R. inv.*) the portrait is given to Mather Brown.

Mrs. Mildred Archer has pointed out that the portrait is identical with Say's engraving at three-quarter-length (*Fig. 22*) of the portrait of the Nawab by Place. The engraving was published on 1 January 1800; on the plate the portrait is stated to have been painted at Lucknow for Pellegrin Treves the younger and to be in the possession of the Prince of Wales. Treves was a friend of the Prince of Wales, to whom he presumably presented No. 990. He had secured an appointment in the Bengal Civil Service, through the Prince's influence, in 1784; he was in retirement in England, 1802–6.

Ruled as Nawab of Oudh from 1798. An ally of the British, to whom he was forced to cede a large part of his territory. He was much influenced by western tastes and was the patron of such artists as Home and Place. His son and successor was Ghazi-ud-din Haidar (No. 832).

Nicholas Pocock

1741?–1821. Painter of marine subjects, especially naval battles. He went early to sea as captain of vessels belonging to Richard Champion, a Bristol merchant. He settled in London in 1789 and remained there until he moved to Bath in 1817. He exhibited at the Royal Academy between 1782 and 1815 and at the British Institution, 1806–10.

991. SIR ROBERT CALDER'S ACTION OFF CAPE FINISTERRE

Buckingham Palace. 40 × 61 in., 101,6 × 154,9 cm.

Signed and dated: *N. Pocock | 1812*

An English ship, possibly the *Hero*, attacking three Spanish ships; in the distance on the right are more English ships.

Possibly in the collection of William IV; recorded at Hampton Court in 1849 (*The Stranger's Guide*, No. 946), later inv. No. 1038; later at Kensington.

Literature: Law, 1881, 1898 (878).

No. 991 illustrates the action off Cape Finisterre on 22 July 1805, when Rear-Admiral Sir Robert Calder (1745–1818), under orders to intercept the combined French and Spanish fleets returning from the West Indies, fell in with the enemy and, in an action lasting four hours, cut off and **destroyed** two Spanish ships, the *St. Raphael* and *El Firme*.

992. SIR RICHARD STRACHAN'S ACTION OFF FERROL (*Plate 233*)

Buckingham Palace. 40½ × 61 in., 102,9 × 154,9 cm.

Signed and dated: *N Pocock 1812*

A severely damaged English ship alongside shattered French ships.

Possibly in the collection of William IV; recorded at Hampton Court in 1849 (*The Stranger's Guide*, No. 945), later inv. No. 1037; later at Kensington.

Literature: Law, 1881, 1898 (877).

No. 992 illustrates the close of the action on 4 November 1805, when Sir Richard Strachan (1760–1828) fell in with four French ships of the line which had escaped from Trafalgar under the command of Rear-Admiral Dumanoir. In the ensuing action off Ferrol the French ships—the *Formidable*, *Duguay-Trouin*, *Mont Blanc* and *Scipion*—were severely damaged and taken. Strachan himself was in the *Caesar*. 'The enemy suffered much', he wrote, 'but our ships not more than is expected on these occasions.'

993. SHIPS IN A GALE

Windsor Castle (998). 19⅛ × 29⅛ in., 48,6 × 74 cm.

An English frigate before the wind; on the right is a Dutch ship and on the left three English ships.

Stated in an inscription on the stretcher to have been bought by the Prince Consort from Mr. St. Croix in 1844.

On grounds of style the attribution to Pocock seems reasonable; there is a comparable picture in the National Maritime Museum.

James Pollard

1792–1867. Sporting artist, active in all fields, but a specialist in coaching scenes.

994. THE DUKE OF YORK'S MOSES WINNING THE DERBY IN 1822

Buckingham Palace. 28 × 44 in., 71,1 × 111,8 cm.

Signed and dated: *J. Pollard Pinxt | 1822*.

Moses, ridden by Thomas Goodisson, passing the post, followed by Mr. Batson's Figaro and the Duke of Grafton's Hampden.

Probably acquired by King Edward VII.

Moses, a bay son of a Gohanna mare by Whalebone, was bred by the Duke of York in 1819. In 1823 he won the Claret Stakes at Newmarket. In 1816 the Duke had won the Derby with his Prince Leopold. In the Derby of 1822 Moses started as third favourite at 6 to 1 and beat Figaro by a head. Up to Tattenham Corner the running had been made by the Earl of Egremont's Wanton, but from that point the three leaders drew away from the rest of the field. Moses later went to the stud at Hampton Court; he was bought by the Duke of Richmond for 1,100 guineas when the Duke of York's horses were sold in 1827. Goodisson was the Duke of York's favourite jockey.

Martin Ferdinand Quadal

1736–1808. Painter of portraits, genre scenes and animals. A native of Moravia, he studied in Vienna and Paris and exhibited in London, 1772–3, 1791–3. He is stated to have been in Dublin in 1779 and in 1779–80 he was painting for the Duke of Buccleuch. He was later in Holland and at St. Petersburg.

995. GEORGE III AT A REVIEW

Windsor Castle (1679). 71¼×86¼ in., 181×219,7 cm.

Signed and dated: *J. M. Quadal 1772*

The King is seen in military uniform at the head of a mounted party of General Officers, raising his hat to an artillery officer, probably Colonel Thomas Ord(e); in the distance are troops drawn up and artillery firing. Beyond the King are Lord Granby (bare-headed) and Jeffrey, Lord Amherst (1717–97); behind the King are William Henry, Duke of Gloucester, and, nearer the spectator, George, 4th Viscount and 1st Marquess Townshend (1724–1807); behind them is (?) Colonel Tonyn.

Acquired by George IV. It was received at Carlton House in April 1812 from Cutter of Warwick St: 'A Painting—with Portraits on Horseback—Viz. . . . George III Marquis of Granby Lord Amherst Duke of Gloucester Lord Townshend Col. Tonyn. on View' (Jutsham, *R/D.*, f. 191); recorded in store at Carlton House in 1816 (277; the 1816 label is still on the back); sent to the King's Lodge on 27 September 1823 and to Cumberland Lodge in January 1844. On 27 September 1822 it had been sent to Seguier for repair; a frame had fallen against it while it was in the 'Temporary Room' (Jutsham, *Deliveries*, ff. 39, 47).

Probably the picture exhibited by Quadal at the Royal Academy in 1773 (224: *His Majesty reviewing the artillery, on horseback*).[1] On the stretcher is an old piece of canvas on which is inscribed 'The King receiving Major General . . . / Colonel Orde Poullett . . . / on Blackheath 1772'. The review, of the 3rd and 4th battalions of the Royal Regiment of Artillery, took place on 24 August 1772. 'That fine corps went through their different evolutions with great exactness, though greatly incommoded by the weather.' In the Carlton House inventory of 1819 the picture (No. 339) is described as by 'J. M. Quadel and Zoffanii . . . The Heads by Zoffanii and admirable'. It appears conceivable that the heads of the King and the Duke of Gloucester were painted by another and a better hand than Quadal's. On the other hand, Quadal's group, signed and dated 1788, in the Army Museum at Vienna, of Joseph II at a review, is closely comparable to No. 995 and there is no suggestion of dual authorship.

For Lord Granby see No. 1022; the Duke of Gloucester was promoted in 1772 from Lieutenant-General to General and in 1770 had been appointed Colonel of the 1st Foot Guards. Lord Amherst, Commander-in-Chief in North America, 1758–64, Lieutenant-General of H.M. Ordnance, 1772–82 (and see No. 1138), wears in No. 995 the uniform of Colonel of the Buffs; Lord Townshend was Lieutenant-General, 1763–7, and Master-General, 1772–82, 1783, of the Ordnance; Thomas Orde, then Lieutenant-Colonel, was promoted Colonel in the artillery, 1771 and became Colonel Commandant of the 4th Battalion, Royal Artillery; Colonel Tonyn was presumably Patrick Tonyn, lately Lieutenant-Colonel of the 104th Regiment of Foot and later appointed Governor of East Florida.

1. Walpole's note is 'Bad'; in the same exhibition No. 225 was *His Majesty reviewing the artillery on horseback, in a Roman dress* by Quadal, on which Walpole's comment was 'worse'.

Allan Ramsay

1713–84. Portrait-painter, born in Edinburgh, who settled in London in 1738 after his return from the first of his continental tours. In 1757 he was introduced to the Prince of Wales by Lord Bute, for whom he painted a full-length of the Prince (*Fig.* IV) for which the preparatory drawing (*Fig.* III) was made at Kew on 12 October 1757. After the accession of the Prince, Ramsay was appointed Principal Painter, but he was compelled to share the post with John Shackleton until the latter's death in 1767 (see above, p. xiii). The production of countless replicas of his official portraits of the new King and Queen (see Nos. 996, 997) placed a great strain on Ramsay and 'knowing that the full exertion of all my abilities was not more than sufficient for what I was *called upon* to undertake, I took a very extraordinary step, which had never been taken by any of my predecessors, and refused to paint any more for the public'. Although he did not adhere to this resolution, Ramsay painted very little after 1766 except replicas of the royal portraits.

In 1758 Ramsay was commissioned by the Prince to paint a full-length of Lord Bute. This was given by the King to Lord Mountstuart in 1783 and is now at Mount Stuart (*Fig.* V; Kenwood, *Paintings and Drawings by Allan Ramsay* (1958 (18)).

996. GEORGE III (*Plate* 1)

Buckingham Palace. 98×64 in., 248,9×162,6 cm.; including apparent, but early, additions of *c.* 2¼ in. at the top, *c.* 3 in. at the bottom, *c.* 3½ in. on the left and *c.* 3½ in. on the right.

Full-length, standing in coronation robes over gold coat and breeches, with his right hand on his hip and his left on a table on which rests his crown (? St. Edward's).

Nos. 996, 997 are probably the pair recorded in the Old Throne Room at Carlton House in 1816 (15: 'A whole length portrait of his Majesty. Ramsay' and 16: ' A whole length portrait of her Majesty. Ramsay', measurements of both given as 97×63 in.). They had been in Carlton House at least since 1795, when Simpson cleaned and varnished them (P.R.O., H.O. 73, 23), are mentioned by Pyne, vol. III, *Carlton House*, p. 30, and can be discerned in Wild's plate (1816). Their frames (see below) are now on other pictures at Buckingham Palace. Nos. 996, 997 are certainly the pair which was in the Throne Room at Buckingham Palace by 1841 (*Buckingham Palace*, 1841, p. 92; later inv. Nos. 206 (Queen Charlotte) and 207 (George III)). A pair is also recorded in the King's Presence Chamber at Windsor in 1813 (Francis Legge's list; as by Ramsay, with measurements of each given as 93×57 in.; possibly discernible in Stephanoff's plate (1818) in Pyne, vol. I, *Windsor*, p. 170, but not mentioned in the text).

Literature: A. Smart, *The Life and Art of Allan Ramsay* (1952), pp. 104, 111–12, 119–24, 210, 218; R.A., *Paintings and Drawings by Allan Ramsay*, 1964 (51).

Almost certainly the prime original of Ramsay's state portrait of George III. There are signs in the surface of the paint round the head which indicate that it was painted on to the canvas from life, before the figure and background were completed, a phenomenon that would perhaps not be apparent in a copy. Ramsay had painted for Lord Bute a full-length of the King before his accession (see above, p. xiii). In Ramsay's own words: 'When his Majesty came to the Crown he was still pleased to honour me with his employment, and I painted, from the life, a whole length picture of him for Hanover,[1] a profil for the coinage, and another whole length, which after the Coronation, I, by his

1. S.K.H. Prince Ernst August of Hanover owns a single three-quarter-length version of the portrait of George III and versions of the pair of full-lengths.

Majesties orders, dressed in Coronation robes. Soon after her Majesty's arrival, she likewise did me the honour to sit to me; and these two pictures in coronation robes are the originals from which all the copies ordered by the Lord Chamberlain are painted' (Letter of 10 January 1766 to the Duke of Portland, Lord Chamberlain; R. W. Goulding, *Catalogue of the Pictures ... at Welbeck Abbey ...* (1936), pp. 470–2). No. 996, therefore, is apparently a version of a full-length, painted between the King's accession on 25 October 1760 and his coronation on 22 September 1761; the original of the design may have been the portrait painted for Hanover; and in this type the King was at first wearing a costume which he later commanded Ramsay, in the version which was to remain in London, to alter to coronation robes. From a letter written by Ramsay to Lord Bute on 19 December 1761 it seems that Ramsay was himself at work, from the life, on two versions of the portrait, one for Bute and the other for the Crown.

'His Majesty has been pleased to bestow two compleat sittings upon that picture intended for your Lordship, and I am now making all the preparations for finishing the posture of it, that it may have the advantage of being likewise painted from the life while I have the Royal robes set upon my figure. I should, therefore, be glad to know if you would chuse to have it of the same size with that intended for St. James's,[1] which is 3 inches higher, and 5 broader than the ordinary size of whole lengths, or if you would have it of the same size with those already hung up in your dining room. Altho you should determine upon having the ordinary height preserved in this picture, yet I shall beg leave to extend it 2 or 3 inches in the breadth, as the manner I have chosen to expand the robes makes such an addition of canvas in some measure necessary ...' (Letter in Bute MSS.; in the same letter Ramsay refers to the 'picture I am new-painting for Hanover', to which he was anxious to 'be allowed to add a couple of inches').

Walpole records (*Anecdotes*, vol. V, p. 56) in March 1762 that 'Ramsay has done another whole length of the king, better than that he did for Lord Bute, ... when the king was Prince of Wales. This has more air, and is painted exactly from the very robes which the king wore at his coronation. The gold stuff and ermine are highly finished; rather too much, for the head does not come out so much as it ought. He had drawn the queen too, but it is much flattered, and the hair vastly too light.' Presumably, soon after the satisfactory completion of the state portrait, the companion portrait of Queen Charlotte (No. 997) was painted. There are references in royal sources to versions of the portraits perhaps designed to be hung in royal residences. Augusta, Princess of Wales's, accounts for work in the 'Pall Mall Apartmᵗˢ', in the year January 1767–January 1768 included, in payments to John Bradburn and William France, £2 paid 'For 2 straining Rooms [*sic*] for the Picture of the King, and Queen p Mʳ Ramsay' and £113. 15s. for '2 very rich whole Lenth Tabernackle Frames, carved, and gilt, part burnished (for the Pictures of their Majesties)' (D. of Cornwall MSS., vol. LIV (i)).[2] On 3 February 1769 Ramsay was paid from the King's Privy Purse £84 each for 'a Picture of Your Majesty at full Length' and 'Dᵒ of the Queen'; on 2 September 1769 he was paid from the same source 'for two Pictures of your Majesties put up at Carlton House at 80 Guineas each' (W.R.A., Geo. 17216, 17226). Ramsay thereafter was responsible for producing a very large number of repetitions, at £84 each, of these official

1. This, which may be No. 996, should be the whole length which Ramsay 'by his Majesties orders dressed in Coronation robes'.
2. The frame for the King is almost certainly that now on No. 1002.

portraits for the King's and Queen's friends and relations, for official institutions and for fellow-sovereigns and the King's representatives overseas. The accounts of the Treasurer of the Chamber, for example, include copious payments to Ramsay. In the year October 1762–October 1763 he was paid £1,409. 18s. 6d. for 'several whole Length Pictures of their Majesties' (P.R.O., A.O.1, 420, 200); October 1763–October 1764, £2,816. 5s. 'for thirty Pictures of their Majesty's at whole length: for several of the Nobility Ambassaders and Governors of Provinces' (*ibid.*, 201); October 1764–October 1765, £2,161. 5s. 3d. 'for several whole Length Pictures of their Majesty's (*ibid.*, 202); October 1765–October 1766, £753. 3s. 'for several whole Length Pictures of their Majestys' (*ibid.*, 203); October 1766–October 1767, £1,880. 3s. 'for several whole Length Pictures of their Majesties' (*ibid.*, 204); October 1767–October 1768, £564. 17s. 3d. 'for several whole Length Pictures of their Majesties' (*ibid.*, 205); October 1768–October 1769, £376. 11s. 6d. 'for several whole Length Pictures of their Majestys' (*ibid.*, 206); October 1769–April 1770, £112. 8s. 9d. 'for their Majesties Pictures at whole length for his Excellency Thomas Shirley Governor of the Bahama Islands', and £223. 19s. 6d. 'for two Pictures of his Majesty and two Pictures of the Queen at whole Length for the Earl of Du[n]more as Governor of New York, and his Excellency Peter Chester as Governor of West Florida' (*ibid.*, 207); April 1770–April 1771, £1,128. 17s. 3d. 'for several whole length Pictures of their Majesties' (*ibid.*, 208); April 1771–April 1772, £376. 11s. 6d. 'for several whole Lenght pictures of their Majesty's' (*ibid.*, 209); April 1772–April 1773, £845. 18s. 9d. 'for several whole Length Pictures of their Majesty's' (*ibid.*, 210); October 1773–October 1774, £376. 11s. 'for several whole Length Pictures of their Majesties' (*ibid.*, 211); October 1775–October 1776, £1,127. 17s. 'for several whole Length Pictures of their Majesties' (*ibid.*, 213); October 1777–October 1778, £376. 11s. 6d. 'for two whole Length Pictures of their Majesties' (*ibid.*, 215); April 1779–October 1780, £564. 17s. 6d. 'for three whole Length Pictures of their Majesties' (*ibid.*, 217); October 1780–October 1781, £188. 5s. 9d. 'for two whole Length pictures of their Majesties' (*ibid.*, 218). These payments include sums for extraordinary, unspecified work.

During the period covered by these payments, rich carved and gilded frames were made for Ramsay's state portraits by René Stone and Isaac Gossett. Payments to these craftsmen for the frames are to be found in the same accounts and the destination of portrait and frame is sometimes specified therein. For example: the account for October 1769–April 1770 includes payments to Stone for frames for a portrait of the King for the Great Mogul and for the portraits for Lord Dunmore and Peter Chester; October 1774–October 1776, Gossett was paid for frames for portraits sent to the Governor of the Bahamas, the Governor of the Province of Massachusetts Bay, and the Governors of Grenada, Tobago, St. Vincent, Senegambia etc.; October 1776–October 1777, Gossett was paid for frames for portraits for the Governors of Jamaica and Quebec (*ibid.*, 214); April 1779–October 1780, he was paid for frames for portraits 'sent to Governors Abroad' (*ibid.*, 217); October 1780–October 1781, he was paid for frames for portraits sent to William Browne, Governor of the Bermuda Islands.

It is not surprising that Joseph Moser, visiting Ramsay's studio in Soho Square, found 'his show-room crowded with portraits of His Majesty in every stage of their operation. The ardour with which these beloved objects were sought for by distant corporations and transmarine colonies was astonishing; the painter with all the assistance he could procure could by no means satisfy the diurnal demands that were made in Soho Square upon his talents and industry, which was probably the reason why some of these pictures were not so highly finished as they ought to have been.' Ramsay was compelled to employ assistants in the mass production of the state portrait. David Martin was working under Ramsay on the state portraits in the 1760s and in 1776 Philip Reinagle succeeded Martin as Ramsay's principal assistant (A. Smart, *op. cit.*, pp. 121–2, with names of other assistants). At the end of Ramsay's life Reinagle was probably almost entirely responsible for the state portraits; of the earlier copies Ramsay may have painted the heads at least.

It would be impossible to list all the copies of the two state portraits. Particularly good copies of the pair are in the Scottish National Portrait Gallery (216, 217), in the Guildhall (1764), Chelsea Hospital, in the Town Hall at Huntingdon, in Glasgow, in the National Gallery of Victoria; at Marlborough House, Petworth (473, 474), Knole, Goodwood, Ickworth, Bramshill (formerly), Badminton (despatched by Ramsay on 13 December 1764), Paultons Park, Ragley, Glynde Place, Firle, Grimsthorpe, Littlecote, Blickling, Ampleforth, Port Eliot, in the possession of the Marquesses of Bute and Lansdowne, and formerly at Stoke Park (said to have been given to Sir George Howard). Copies were sold from the collection of the Duke of Bedford at Christie's, 19 January 1951 (131) and from that of Earl Amherst at Sotheby's, 29 January 1964 (11, 12); copies also appeared at Christie's, 8 February 1929 (24), 17 May 1946 (57, 58), 15 February 1957 (103) and 5 April 1957 (117). Copies given by George III to William I, Elector of Hesse-Cassel, are at Wilhelmshöhe; copies are in the British Embassy at Washington, in the Governor's Palace at Colonial Williamsburg and in the Herron Museum of Art, Indianapolis. See also Nos. 1004, 1005. Three-quarter-length versions are in the National Portrait Gallery (223, 224); another pair was sold at Christie's, 15 May 1953 (140). A head and shoulders copy is in the Wallace Collection. Copies of the King alone are in the Foreign Office and at Somerset House, at Lanhydrock, Stratfield Saye (painted for Lord Rivers for the Embassy in Turin), in the Examination Schools and St. John's College, Oxford, formerly at Hinchingbrooke (sold at Sotheby's, 4 December 1957 (187)), and at Copenhagen (562). See also No. 1003. Ramsay's preliminary drawings of the King's hands are in the National Gallery of Scotland (D.2117 and 2119 (*Fig.* 28)); in the same collection (D.255) is his drawing of the crown (*Fig.* 23). The engraving by W. Wynne Ryland, published in 1767, is stated to have been from the original in possession of the Queen, presumably No. 996.

997. QUEEN CHARLOTTE (*Plate 2*)

Buckingham Palace. 98 × 63½ in., 248,9 × 161,3 cm., including apparent, but early, additions of *c.* 1¾ in. at the top, *c.* 2½ in. at the bottom, *c.* 4 in. on the left and *c.* 3¼ in. on the right.

Full-length, standing in robes of state, in front of a richly carved and gilded chair decorated with the crown, sceptres, cipher and royal supporters, resting her left hand on her crown (perhaps intended for her Nuptial Crown) which rests on a cushion beside her two sceptres.

See No. 996.

Literature: R.A., *King's Pictures* (95); A. Smart, *The Life and Art of Allan Ramsay* (1952), pp. 124, 208; R.A., *Paintings and Drawings by Allan Ramsay*, 1964 (47).

The Queen sat to Ramsay soon after her arrival in England (see above) and No. 997 is the prime original of the portrait painted as a companion to the state portrait of the King (see No. 996). It is finer in quality than the pendant and far more sensitive—not only in colour—than even the best of the repetitions of it and is the only version in which the Queen's head is dressed and placed in this way. Walpole (see above) described the portrait as 'much flattered, and the hair vastly too light'. In all the repetitions the Queen's head is turned more to her left, the expression is different and the hair is darker and differently treated. These modifications would have required a fresh sitting. A short inscription on the back ('Princess of Wales') recorded in an addendum to the *V.R. inv.* (1876) perhaps indicates that No. 997 was painted for, or temporarily held by, Augusta, Princess of Wales. Ramsay's preliminary drawing for the Queen's right arm is in the National Gallery of Scotland (D.2111; *Fig.* 30). While No. 997 was being painted, the Queen's jewels and regalia were in Ramsay's studio and a guard was posted day and night round the building. A three-quarter-length copy of the final state portrait of the Queen is in Queen Charlotte's Hospital; a full-length belongs to the Marquess of Lansdowne; another is in the Louvre (1818); a variant is in the Queen's College, Oxford.

998. QUEEN CHARLOTTE WITH HER TWO ELDEST SONS (*Plate 3*)

Buckingham Palace. 98 × 63¾ in., 248,9 × 161,9 cm.

Full-length group: the Queen is seated with Prince Frederick, later Duke of York, on her lap; she leans against a piano on which is a work-box and a copy of *Some Thoughts concerning Education* (1693) by John Locke; at her knee stands Prince George, holding a bow; behind him is a drum.

Recorded in the King's Gallery at Kensington in 1778; removed to Windsor in 1804 or 1805 (Geo. III, *Removals:* 'Portrait of Her Majesty the P. of Wales & D. of York when Young. Ramsay') and placed at the end of the Ballroom, a position in which it can be seen in Wild's plate (1817) to Pyne (vol. I, *Windsor*, p. 98). Later at Hampton Court (627), St. James's and Buckingham Palace and Windsor (3127).

Literature: R.A., *King's Pictures* (97); A. Smart, *The Life and Art of Allan Ramsay* (1952), pp. 129–30.

Payments to Ramsay from the Privy Purse on 3 February 1769 included £210 for a picture 'of the Queen with Prince of Wales & Prince Frederick'[1] (W.R.A., Geo. 17216). There may have been delays in settling Ramsay's account for this group or he may have been slow in finishing it. From the apparent ages of the children the group could be dated 1764. The three sitters are painted on three separate, inserted and contiguous pieces of canvas, the Queen's head on a rectangular canvas (13½ × 21⅜ in.) and the children on irregular shaped pieces. A later source suggests that only one of the Queen's sons, at different ages, is represented. He states improbably that Ramsay was so slow in finishing the portrait of Prince George that by the time he had completed it the child had grown into the 'sturdy boy' inserted by the Queen's side (Rev. G. Croly, *The Personal History of . . . George IV*, 2nd ed. (1841), pp. 252–3). Pyne (*op. cit.*, vol. I, p. 100) describes George IV's version of this story, which indicates that he had changed so much in the time Ramsay had taken to complete the design 'that it was then determined to introduce his royal highness in another position in the same composition'. It is possible that Ramsay's surgery on the canvas

1. In the inv. of Kensington in 1778 the children are described as Princes William and Edward.

was caused by his having to recast the design in order to take account of the elder Prince's rapid growth. A drawing by Ramsay in the National Gallery of Scotland (D.251; *Fig.* 24) may be Ramsay's first idea for the figures of the Queen with Prince Frederick; there is also a study for the whole composition (D.2149). There are also studies for her two hands and arms (D.2087, 2097), a study for the figure of Prince George (D.245; *Fig.* 25) in which the position of the figure is different from (perhaps younger than) the final design, and studies for arms (D.2065; *Fig.* 29) which may be connected with the same figure. D.1997, 1998 are not wholly convincing as studies for the head of Prince George. The head of the Queen in No. 998 is based on a separate sitting from those that served for her state portraits. Copies of No. 998 are at Badminton and in the possession of the Marquess of Lansdowne; another was on the art-market in 1923.

999. PRINCE WILLIAM, LATER DUKE OF CLARENCE (*Plate* 6)

Windsor Castle (1516). $50\frac{1}{2} \times 38\frac{1}{2}$ in., $128,3 \times 97,8$ cm., including an addition on the right of *c.* $1\frac{1}{2}$ in.

Full-length, standing in 'coats', beating a little drum on which is the royal cipher; the drum rests on a stool over which is draped an ermine-lined mantle; behind the Prince is a table on which are tea-cups, a cream-jug and a gilt vase.

Presumably painted for George III or Queen Charlotte. Formerly at Frogmore and probably to be identified with a portrait recorded in the Bow Drawing-Room there: '*Portrait of his Royal Highness the Duke of* CLARENCE, *when a child, painted by Ramsay*' (Pyne, vol. I, *Frogmore*, p. 19).

Literature: Collins Baker, *Windsor*, p. 331, as Zoffany; R.A., *King's Pictures* (66); *British Painting in the Eighteenth Century*, Montreal-Toledo, 1957–8 (51).

Probably painted in 1767; the Prince had been born on 21 August 1765 and appears to be about two years old. Formerly attributed to Zoffany and identified as Prince Edward, later Duke of Kent; but the reference in Pyne (see above) is almost certainly to this portrait. It is indubitably by Ramsay and a charming example of his late manner. The figure was painted on a canvas *c.* $29\frac{1}{2} \times 24\frac{1}{2}$ in., which was enlarged by the painter. Among the drawings in the National Gallery of Scotland, catalogued under Ramsay and Vanhaecken are two (D.2003, 2004; *Fig.* 26) which are studies for a portrait of a child in 'coats' beating a drum; although the setting and pose do not, especially in D.2004, bear a very close resemblance to No. 999, they could represent Ramsay's ideas for the portrait. Payment for it may have been included in the £152. 5*s.* which Ramsay was paid on 3 February 1769 'for other Portraits' (W.R.A., Geo. 17216). A small copy of No. 999 was sold at Sotheby's, 27 October 1965 (107).

1000. PRINCE GEORGE AUGUSTUS OF MECKLENBURG-STRELITZ (1748–85) (*Plate* 5)

Windsor Castle (1533). 50×40 in., $127 \times 101,6$ cm.; the head and shoulders are painted on a separate piece of canvas *c.* $26\frac{1}{2} \times 22\frac{1}{2}$ in., which the artist set into a larger canvas.

Three-quarter-length, in Austrian military uniform (see below), holding his hat in his right hand and resting it on a ledge.

Presumably painted for Queen Charlotte. Pyne recorded a portrait of Prince George in the Eating Room at Frogmore (vol. I, *Frogmore*, pp. 7–8, and plate by Wild (1819) opposite p. 2), stating

that it had been painted abroad.[1] No. 1000 may have been for a time at Hampton Court, but was at Frogmore in 1871 (*V.R. inv.*, as by Ziesenis) and was taken up to the Castle in 1924.

Literature: R.A., *Paintings and Drawings by Allan Ramsay*, 1964 (49).

A late work, painted during one of the Prince's visits to London. The Prince was in London between November 1768 and August 1769, which could well be the date of this portrait. The recent attribution of the portrait to Ramsay is supported by the preparatory drawing (*Fig.* 27) in the National Gallery of Scotland (D.2043). The drawing indicates that, although Ramsay painted the head on a smaller canvas, the portrait was always intended to be a three-quarter-length. Payment for it may have been included in the £152. 5*s.* which Ramsay was paid on 3 February 1769 'for other Portraits' (W.R.A., Geo. 17216). There are slight *pentimenti* down the far side of the figure and in the position of the right hand.

Younger brother of Queen Charlotte. In June 1769 he was begging George III to effect his transfer from the Austrian to the British forces. He attained the rank of Major-General in the Austrian army. In No. 1000 the Prince is wearing the uniform of an officer of Cuirassiers, of the 4th Regiment of Austrian-Salzburg Dragoons—'Serbellonis'—of which he was later (1778–86) Colonel.

Attributed to Allan Ramsay

1001. ELIZABETH ALBERTINA, PRINCESS OF MECKLENBURG-STRELITZ (1713–61) (*Plate* 4)

Kew (*Hampton Court* No. 1389). $50\frac{1}{8} \times 40$ in., $127,3 \times 101,6$ cm.

Three-quarter-length, seated by a table, holding a fan in both her hands.

Probably painted for Queen Charlotte (see below) and perhaps the portrait ('Her Majesty's Mother') recorded in the King's Gallery at Kensington in the reign of George III (Geo. III, *Kensington*). It was later at Hampton Court, presumably one of the two portraits of Queen Charlotte's mother recorded in the inv. of 1835 (627, 629); thereafter at Frogmore (*V.R. inv.*, 1871, Windsor No. 1537).

Both the sitter and artist of No. 1001 have been in doubt. It has been attributed variously (and wrongly) since 1871 to Ziesenis and Woge, but it seems to be a very pretty example of Ramsay's late style; in technique and colour the portrait is very close to his other royal portraits of the 1760s. The sitter has been identified as Princess Christiana, sister of Queen Charlotte. But the head is clearly based on a German portrait in the royal collection (Windsor No. 1544, now at Kew) which is almost certainly of Queen Charlotte's mother. The jewel in the hair and the black scarf tied round the head are taken over from the earlier portrait, in which there is also a carved table with an ermine-lined red robe lying across it. There is also a general similarity between the costumes in the two portraits. The Queen's mother had died in 1761, just before Queen Charlotte's departure for London. It seems probable that the Queen commissioned Ramsay to compose a posthumous portrait of her mother which could hang alongside the other portraits on this scale of her relations, among them Nos. 1000, 1208. A drawing by Ramsay (*Fig.* 31) in the National Gallery of Scotland (D.2076 a) is a study of two hands holding a fan in exactly the same position as in No. 1001; on the verso is a study for a portrait

---

1. See below, p. 148, for a possible reference to No. 1000 as by Zoffany at Buckingham House.

of Princess Augusta of 1769, which could therefore also be the date of No. 1001. The pose of No. 1001 bears some relation to Ramsay's portrait of Mrs. Martin of 1761 (R.A., *Allan Ramsay*, 1964 (63)); in the preliminary drawing for this portrait (*ibid.* (119)) the fan is held in two gloved hands, but in the painting the upper hand is concealed in a muff.

Daughter of Ernest Frederick, Duke of Saxe-Hildburghausen; married in 1735 Prince Charles Louis Frederick I of Mecklenburg-Strelitz.

Studio of Allan Ramsay

1002. AUGUSTA, PRINCESS OF WALES

Buckingham Palace. 94¾ × 58¼ in., 240,7 × 147,9 cm.

Full-length, walking in a garden, wearing a black lace shawl over her head and shoulders and holding a parasol; behind her is a large carved urn (now on the East Terrace at Windsor) on a pedestal.

Recorded in store at Carlton House in 1816 (237: 'A whole length of the late Princess of Wales. Ramsay'; the 1816 label is still on the stretcher); by 1841 it was in the Green Drawing-Room at Buckingham Palace (*Buckingham Palace*, 1841, p. 94, as a portrait of the Princess of Brunswick; later inv. No. 211).

Literature: A. Smart, *The Life and Art of Allan Ramsay* (1952), pp. 54, 111, 125.

A copy, probably painted in Ramsay's studio, of a portrait in the collection of the Marquess of Bute. The original, which is a late work, was presumably painted for the 3rd Earl of Bute. A study for the portrait is in the National Gallery of Scotland (D.2046). The setting for the portrait is sometimes described as Carlton House, but it is more probable that it is intended for Kew. Another full-length version, formerly in the collection of H.M. Queen Mary, is now at Clarence House. A version of the head and shoulders was sold at Christie's, 13 February 1948 (67). On 31 May 1769 Ramsay was paid fifty guineas by the Princess 'for a half length picture of her Royal Highness sent to Brunswick' (W.R.A., Geo. 55588). No. 1002 has been adapted to fit one of the magnificent tabernacle frames which were made for royal portraits in the Old Throne Room or Ante-Chamber at Carlton House; it has the 1816 label (No. 15) and is therefore the frame made for No. 996.

1003. GEORGE III

Buckingham Palace. 98 × 59½ in., 248,9 × 151,1 cm.

Inscribed later: *KING GEORGE the THIRD | by ALLAN RAMSAY*

Formerly, with Nos. 344, 362 above, in the Old South Sea House; sold at Phillip's, 22 May 1894 (146) and bought by Edward VII when Prince of Wales (P.R.O., L.C. 1/605, II, 96); recorded at Buckingham Palace in 1909 (p. 254).

A very good version, on which Ramsay himself presumably worked at least in part, of the state portrait (No. 996).

After Allan Ramsay

1004. GEORGE III

Buckingham Palace. 84½ × 60½ in., 214,6 × 153,7 cm.

Nos. 1004, 1005 were formerly the property of the 1st Marquess of Cambridge (*d.* 1927), brother of H.M. Queen Mary, by whom they were presumably acquired.

Nos. 1004, 1005 are bad copies of the state portraits (Nos. 996, 997).

1005. QUEEN CHARLOTTE

Buckingham Palace. 91½ × 57½ in., 232,4 × 146,0 cm.

See No. 1004.

John Rand

fl. 1840. Portrait-painter.

After John Rand

1006. AUGUSTUS, DUKE OF SUSSEX

Buckingham Palace. 36 × 28½ in., 91,4 × 72,4 cm.

Head and shoulders, wearing a skull cap and the star of the Garter, with the ribbons of the Garter and the Bath partly concealed under his coat.

Bought in September 1891 from the executors of Charles Wilde, 2nd Lord Truro (*d.* 1891), by Dr. James Edmunds, who presented it in May 1897 to the Duchess of York, later H.M. Queen Mary.

The type is close to that engraved by W. Walker after John Rand; the engraving was published in July 1840. The quality is very coarse and No. 1006 is probably a copy of Rand's portrait, presumably painted for the Duke of Sussex's daughter, Augusta Emma D'Este, who had married Thomas Wilde, 1st Baron Truro (1782–1855).

Maria, Lady Ravensworth

1773–1845. Daughter of John Simpson of Bradley Hall. In 1796 she married Sir Thomas Liddell who in 1821 was created Baron Ravensworth. Her daughter, Lady Bloomfield, wrote that 'She painted admirably both in oils and water colours, so that her copies of the old masters are almost equal to the originals' (*Reminiscences of Court and Diplomatic Life* (1883), vol. I, p. 13).

1007. LANDSCAPE WITH A SHEPHERD AND HIS FLOCK

Windsor Castle (1156). 27⅛ × 20¾ in., 68,9 × 52,7 cm.

A shepherd resting on a bank near cows, sheep and goats.

Presented by the painter to George IV. Jutsham recorded that it was hung up in the Ante-room to the Regent's Bedroom in October 1816: '. . . in a Gilt Frame . . . this Picture, I understand, was presented to the Prince Regent by Lady Liddell many Months past' (*Receipts*, f. 6; No. 157 in inv. of 1816).

A copy of a signed picture by Dirck van den Bergen, which was sold at Sotheby's on 7 July 1954 (111).

Sir Joshua Reynolds

1723–92. Portrait- and history-painter, born at Plympton and apprenticed to Thomas Hudson in London in 1740. In 1749 he went to Italy and after his return in 1752 he set up in London. In 1768 he became the first President of the Royal Academy; in the following year he was knighted; and in 1784 he succeeded Ramsay as Principal Painter to the King, who was, however, never kindly disposed towards him. 'The King and Queen could not endure the presence of him; he was poison to their sight.' George III's Privy Purse accounts include, in the Christmas quarter of 1763, £210 'To Mr Reynolds for Lord Bute's Picture', the large full-length with Charles Jenkinson which belongs to Lord Bute (*Fig.* VI; W.R.A., Geo. 17111). The payment occurs also in vol. I of the Ledgers in the Fitzwilliam Museum, under 7 December 1763: 'Lord Bute & Mr Jenkinson paid by the King.' It was later given by George III to Lord Mount-stuart (see above, pp. xv–xvi).

The documents assembled when efforts were being made to settle the Prince of Wales's debt include an account submitted by Reynolds's executors for £682. 10s. The pictures in this account include a portrait of the Duke of Cumberland (see No. 1017); 'a Portrait of Your Royal Highness with a Black Servant' at £262. 10s., which had been exhibited at the Royal Academy in 1787 (90), was given by the Prince to Lord Moira in April 1810 (Jutsham, *R/D*, f. 56) and is now at Arundel Castle (*Fig.* XIV); 'a Copy of Do' at £131. 5s.;[1] 'a Copy of a Portrait of Your Royal Highness in Robes Single Figure' at £105; and 'a Copy of a Head' at £26. 5s. (P.R.O., H.O. 73, 21). In May and June 1789 the Prince again sat to Reynolds (Sitter-book at R.A.). This may have been in connection with a full-length which was sent to Simpson on 25 February 1811 to be cleaned, varnished, repaired and newly stretched (at ten guineas), was returned to Carlton House on 19 March and finally sent by the York wagon as a present to the Hon. Lawrence Dundas on 4 May 1811 (Jutsham, *R/D*, ff. 84, 86; W.R.A., Geo. 27830). This may have been the source of the copy mentioned above and was presumably the whole length of the Prince, at two hundred guineas, which was still unfinished in April 1788 'the head of which was copied from Mr. Braddyll's picture' (W.R.A., Geo. 26793–6). Mr. Braddyll's picture (1785) is now in the National Gallery (890; see M. Davies's *Catalogue, British School* (1959), pp. 82–3). On 22 April 1788 Reynolds also had 'a Head of His Royal Highness intended for Count Kegeneck'[2] at fifty guineas and, at £315, a portrait of the Prince with a horse, which was given by the Prince to Lord Melbourne and is now at Brocket Hall (W.R.A., Geo. 26793–6).

On 21 June 1819 Lord Rivers gave to the Prince the equestrian portrait of Lord Ligonier (Jutsham, *Receipts*, f. 78) which is recorded as additional No. 560 in the Carlton House inventory of 1816, but was given to the National Gallery by William IV in 1836 and is now in the Tate Gallery (143). The Prince of Wales had owned since 1792 a full-length of Charles Manners, 4th Duke of Rutland. It had been delivered to Simpson to be cleaned and revarnished on 12 October 1810, when it was 'in bad Condt.'; it was in store at Carlton House in 1816 (238, measurements given as 94×58 in.), but when the Prince heard that a portrait of the Duke by Reynolds had been burnt in the fire at Belvoir Castle on 26 October 1816, he sent the portrait in his own possession, on 7 June 1817, as a present to the Duke of Rutland (Jutsham, *R/D*, ff. 72, 260; W.R.A., Geo. 26878–9; Graves and Cronin, vol. II, pp. 849–50).

On 1 May 1813 the Prince presented to Lord Melbourne 'A Half Length Portrait by Sir Joshua Reynolds—of Mrs Eliot—not Framed' (Jutsham, *R/D*, f. 132). In the Carlton House inventory of 1816, additional No. 553 was 'A Half Length Portrait of Lady Maynard—Dressed in a Crimson Gown—Blue Sash—& Blue Mantle over the Left Shoulder. Sir Joshua Reynolds', measurements given as 36×28 in.

This may have been the portrait of Lady Maynard by Reynolds for which the Prince paid fifteen guineas on 2 June 1819. On 20 May 1819 it was 'taken by The Prince Regent in his Carriage—I do not know where it was taken to' (W.R.A., Geo. 27091; Jutsham, *Receipts*, f. 42, *R/D*, ff. 302, 318). It was certainly given away by the Regent.

On 22 April 1788 Reynolds reported that he had on hand for the Prince an unfinished full-length of Mrs. Fitzherbert at two hundred guineas (W.R.A., Geo. 26793–6). This is probably the portrait which appears, as an unfinished half-length, in store at Carlton House in 1816 (362, measurements given as 36×27½ in.), was sent to Brighton for Mrs. Fitzherbert by William IV on 5 October 1830 and is now in the possession of the Earl of Portarlington. Reynolds's account with the Prince is set out in the Ledgers, vol. II, in the Fitzwilliam Museum.

1008. PORTRAIT OF THE ARTIST (*Plate* 105)

Windsor Castle (2861). Panel: 29⅝×24⅞ in., 75,2×63,2 cm.

Head and shoulders, wearing spectacles.

Originally in the possession of the artist's niece, Mary Palmer, Marchioness of Thomond (d. 1820). On 20 June 1812 she wrote to George IV, offering the portrait to him, and on 29 June it was received at Carlton House (*Letters of George IV*, vol. I, 122; Jutsham, *R/D*, f. 209: 'not any Frame. presented to The Prince Regent'); recorded in store at Carlton House in 1816 (295). Later at Buckingham Palace (179, *Buckingham Palace*, 1909, p. 141), and recorded in the Gallery there in 1841 (1: 'Painted for his private Collection. . .').

Literature: Waagen (1838), vol. II, p. 376, (1854), vol. II, p. 24; Graves and Cronin, vol. II, pp. 804–5; Collins Baker, *Windsor*, p. 270; Waterhouse, *Reynolds*, p. 80; R.A., *King's Pictures* (89).

Painted in 1788. When she presented the portrait to George IV, Lady Thomond described it as 'the best portrait he ever painted of himself'. Boswell wrote of it as 'The last picture Sir Joshua Reynolds did of himself. It has a sort of *pulled up* look, and not the placid gentleness of his smiling manner; but the features, though rather too largely and strongly limned, are most exactly portrayed; and the dress in every respect being such as he usually wore, I think it the best representation of my celebrated friend' (*Portraits of Sir Joshua Reynolds*, ed. F. W. Hilles (1952), p. IX). It was exhibited at the British Institution in 1820 (30), 1826 (4) and 1827 (67). The type was engraved by Caroline Watson (1789), S. W. Reynolds and G. Clint (1799).

Many copies exist. A repetition formerly in the collection of the Duke of Leeds was sent by Reynolds to the 5th Duke on 4 October 1790 with a suitable letter; Malone described it as 'a duplicate' of the original: 'The last portrait which he painted of himself (with spectacles), in 1788, is extremely like him, and exhibits him exactly as he appeared in his latter days, in domestick life' (*Letters of Sir Joshua Reynolds*, ed. F. W. Hilles (1929), p. 207). Among others, the most important are those at Belton, Kitley, Petworth (308), Dulwich (104), Kenwood (29; stated to have been painted for Edmund Malone in 1788), in the Wellington Museum, Apsley House (1533), and in Berlin. A copy was also in the Sidney sale at Christie's, 10 December 1937 (144), as from the collection of Sir George Beaumont; another, stated to be by Marchi, was sold there, 22 December 1949 (19); and another was sold there in the Hon. Arthur Guinness sale, 10 July 1953 (72). Good copies belong to Mr. Walter Leake (1948), Mr. Julian Gardiner (1950), and Senator E. A. McGuire (1957). Others are in Toledo and the Peabody Institute, Baltimore, and many lesser copies and derivations are recorded. See also No. 1032. An enamel

1. This was intended for Lord Charlemont.
2. This was Count Kegeneck, envoy extraordinary and minister plenipotentiary from Austria and Germany, 1782–6.

copy by Bone (October 1809) and another by Grimaldi are in the Royal Library. A chalk drawing of the head, stated to have been given by Lady Thomond to E. Dayes, was sold at Christie's, 19 June 1953 (14), and is now in Mr. Paul Mellon's collection; another drawing of the head in chalk was sold at Christie's, 24 October 1958 (56), with a statement by William Cribb that it had been given to his father by Sir Joshua in 1790. A third such copy is in the Plymouth Art Gallery and another is in the Heywood-Lonsdale collection. No. 1008 is covered with bituminous cracking, but it is of very good quality and clearly by Reynolds himself.

1009. WILLIAM, DUKE OF CUMBERLAND

Windsor Castle (279). 36×28 in., 91,4×71,1 cm.

Half-length, wearing the robes of the Garter with the collar of the order and pointing with his right hand to the front.

Presented to George IV by Sir William Keppel (*d.* 1834) in 1829 and recorded in the inventory of 'Carleton Palace' (632: 'Portrait of William Duke of Cumberland Sir J. Reynolds').

Literature: Graves and Cronin, vol. I, p. 216; Collins Baker, *Windsor*, p. 267.

The Duke sat to Reynolds on 6 and 20 March 1758 and again in January 1761 (Sitter-books at R.A.). From the first sitting Reynolds presumably derived the type seen in No. 1009 and in full-lengths (see No. 1010). Three-quarter-length variants in Garter robes are at Wentworth Wood-house (painted for the 2nd Marquess of Rockingham; see No. 1045) and Welbeck, and the head is also used in portraits of the Duke in military uniform (e.g., in the National Portrait Gallery (625) and in the Scottish National Portrait Gallery (910)); the military pattern was engraved by Spooner and Fisher, the latter as painted in 1760 (Chaloner Smith, p. 490). The type seems to have served as the basis of Nollekens's posthumous bust (1814) of the Duke at Windsor. No. 1009 was certainly painted in Reynolds's studio. It is perhaps the portrait painted for General Keppel, for which apparently two payments (amounting to £76. 18s.) are recorded in Reynolds's Ledgers (Fitzwilliam Museum, vol. I); in his Sitter-book for 1764, on 21 August, Reynolds noted: 'Mr Reynolds has promised Col Keppel to send The D: Cumberland's Picture home this day.' X-ray (1963) revealed extensive alterations in the costume. The Duke appears to have been painted first in robes of state which were altered to the robes of the Garter; the raised right arm, as well as the unorthodox—and illogical—heavy fold of Garter mantle over the shoulder, were presumably painted during this alteration. The Garter robes are painted in a much freer manner than the head, which is revealed by X-ray as rather lightly handled, and possibly more freely than the earlier, underlying, costume. No. 1009 was exhibited at the British Institution in 1827 (149) and 1831 (139).

1010. WILLIAM, DUKE OF CUMBERLAND

Buckingham Palace. 106×71 in., 269,2×180,3 cm.

Full-length, standing, in Garter robes, clasping his sword in his left hand; the plumed hat of the order rests on a table on the left.

In the collection of George IV, recorded in the Council Chamber at Carlton House in 1792. In 1795 it was cleaned and repaired by Simpson (P.R.O., H.O. 73, 23). On 27 August 1810 it was again sent from Carlton House to Simpson 'to be retutch'd and Cleand' (Jutsham, *R/D*, f. 70; see below); recorded in the West Ante-room at Carlton House in 1816 (4: 'A whole length portrait of William, Duke of Cumberland, Sir Joshua Reynolds', measurements given as 107×69 in.); sent at the Regent's instructions to Lawrence on 17 July 1816, without a frame (Jutsham, *R/D*, f. 240); in the inventory of 'Carleton Palace' (4) it is stated to be 'At Sir Thos Lawrence's'. In 1835 it was occupying the place in the Waterloo Chamber ultimately filled by No. 890; later at Buckingham Palace (630).

Literature: Graves and Cronin, vol. I, p. 216; Waterhouse, *Reynolds*, p. 45.

A version of a type perhaps derived from the sitting in March 1758 (see No. 1009). The finest version of the full-length design is probably the one at Chatsworth (Waterhouse, *op. cit.*, pl. 49); payment for this is recorded in Reynolds's Ledgers (Fitzwilliam Museum, vol. I). The Ledger also contains payments for portraits of the Duke for the Earl of Sandwich (a version was formerly at Hinchingbrooke), the Earl of Albemarle, the Princess of Hesse and Princess Amelia; it is conceivable that No. 1010 is the one painted for Princess Amelia. The portrait has at some stage suffered considerably. There is an apparent *pentimento* where the Duke's mantle is tucked into the belt at his waist. It is doubtful if it can ever have been as fine as the version at Chatsworth and it is simplified in detail, both in the figure and the accessories; but it would be difficult to assess the original quality of No. 1010, as Simpson's work on it in 1810 (see above) involved 'bringing to an even Surface and Repg [presumably repairing or repainting] parts that had been Scaled off, Uniting and toneing down the sky in Various Parts Near the Horison, as also Glazeing the face & hands Refreshing [and varnishing] a Capital Portrait of Wm Duke of Cumberland by Sir J. Reynolds' (W.R.A., Geo. 26878–9). It was exhibited at the British Institution in 1813 (138). A version of No. 1010 is at Bramham Park; a small contemporary version belongs to Lord Cottesloe.

1011. GEORGE III WHEN PRINCE OF WALES (*Plate* 89)

Windsor (2531). 50¼×40 in., 127,6×101,6 cm.

Three-quarter-length, standing by a carved table on which rests his coronet, wearing an ermine-lined cloak and the ribbon of the Garter.

Presented to George IV by Reynolds's niece, the Marchioness of Thomond, and received at Carlton House on 5 June 1815: ' . . . His Majesty George The 3d half Length in A Green Velvet Coat Embroiderd with Gold—when Young—not any Frame, by Sir Joshua Reynolds' (Jutsham, *R/D*, f. 347). Recorded in store at Carlton House in 1816 (294); sent to St. James's in 1831.

Literature: Leslie and Taylor, vol. I, pp. 163, 176; Graves and Cronin, vol. I, pp. 355–6; Collins Baker, *Windsor*, p. 266; Waterhouse, *Reynolds*, pp. 45–6; City Art Gallery, Plymouth, *Sir Joshua Reynolds*, 1951 (18).

The Prince of Wales sat to Reynolds at 10 a.m. on 12 January 1759 (Sitter-book at R.A.), probably for this portrait. For some reason, however, it remained on Reynolds's hands until his death, when it passed into the possession of Lady Thomond. The set of the head and the general presentation are strikingly reminiscent of Liotard's pastel of the Prince (Millar, No. 581) and it is possible that Reynolds had to depend to some extent on this earlier portrait. There is a *pentimento* where the cuff originally came higher up the right arm.

1012. THE MARRIAGE OF GEORGE III
(*Plate* 91)

Kew (*Hampton Court* No. 1387). $37\frac{1}{2} \times 49$ in., $95,2 \times 129,5$ cm.

The Archbishop of Canterbury, Thomas Secker, blessing the royal couple at the altar of the Chapel Royal, St James's Palace; the Archbishop is assisted by the Bishop of London, Thomas Hayter. On the left are a group of ladies including the bridesmaids. Behind the King are members of his own family. Two heralds are standing on the left.

Remained in the possession of Sir Joshua Reynolds until his death; sold at his sale at Greenwood's, 16 April 1796 (11), bt. Elwin; sold in Woodburn's sale at Christie's, 12 May 1821 (69), when it was bought in; purchased in 1833 from Mrs. Woodburn by Henry Graves, who later sold it to Queen Victoria or, possibly, to William IV (W. T. Whitley, *Art in England 1821–37* (1930), p. 306).

Literature: Graves and Cronin, vol. I, p. 357; Collins Baker, *Windsor*, p. 267.

Walpole wrote that 'Reynolds has made a sketch of the king's wedding, taken from the music gallery in the chapel' (*Anecdotes*, vol. V, p. 61). The marriage of the King and Princess Charlotte of Mecklenburg-Strelitz took place in the evening of 8 September 1761 and Reynolds's sketch probably gives a fairly accurate, if hurried, impression of the ceremony and the decking of the Chapel Royal. On the left is the canopy under which the King and his bride sat on two state chairs after the ceremony; under or near it are the Maids of Honour and the Ladies of the Bedchamber; behind the bride are the bridesmaids: Lady Sarah Lennox, Lady Caroline Russell, Lady Anne Hamilton, Lady Essex Kerr, Lady Harriet Bentinck, Lady Caroline Montagu, Lady Elizabeth Keppel, Lady Louisa Greville, Lady Elizabeth Harcourt and Lady Susan Strangways. On the right, seated at the back of the Chapel, is the King's mother, Augusta, Princess of Wales; in front of her are the King's brothers and sisters (the Duke of York and Prince William had led the bride into the Chapel) and possibly his aunt, Princess Amelia. In the foreground on the right is William, Duke of Cumberland, who had given away the bride. The King is apparently dressed in a silver costume with the collar of the Garter. The bride wore a very pretty little tiara of diamonds and an 'endless mantle of violet-coloured velvet, lined with ermine'. (Accounts of the ceremony are to be found in, for example, Walpole's letters of 9 and 10 September to Henry Seymour Conway and Mann respectively; *The Gentleman's Magazine*, vol. XXXI (Sept. 1761), pp. 416–17; and *The Annual Register* (vol. IV) for 1761, pp. 211–13.)
No. 1012 was exhibited at the British Institution in 1833 (30).

1013. EDWARD, DUKE OF YORK (*Plate* 95)

Windsor Castle (293). $30\frac{1}{4} \times 24\frac{7}{8}$ in., $76,8 \times 63,2$ cm.

Half-length in naval uniform, his head in profile to the left, wearing the ribbon and star of the Garter and holding a telescope in his right hand.

It is difficult to disentangle accurately the references in the early sources to Reynolds's portraits of the Duke in the royal collection. No. 1013 was probably the portrait of 'the late Duke of York after Sʳ Joshua. Reynolds framed', bought by George IV from Colnaghi on 20 August 1810 for £42 (W.R.A., Geo. 27539); it was received at Carlton House ('A half Length') on 27 August, sent to Simpson to be cleaned on the same day and returned in October (Jutsham, *R/D*, ff. 70, 133; for Simpson's bill see W.R.A., Geo. 26878–9 and below). This was probably the portrait recorded in store at Carlton House in 1816 (286): 'A head of the late Duke of York, in

a naval uniform. Sir Joshua Reynolds', measurements given as 29×24 in., and again in 1819 (307), but the later entry ('Portrait of the late Duke of York in a Naval Uniform. Sir J. Reynolds') gives the measurements as 30×25 in. The portrait at Carlton House was taken to Windsor in April 1829.

Literature: Leslie and Taylor, vol. I, pp. 162, 176; Graves and Cronin, vol. III, pp. 1081–2; Collins Baker, *Windsor*, p. 268; City of Birmingham, Museum and Art Gallery, *Sir Joshua Reynolds*, 1961 (27).

The Duke sat, as Prince Edward, to Reynolds, at twelve o'clock on 29 December 1758 and on 2 and 8 January 1759 (Sitter-books in R.A.); opposite the appointment for the second sitting is a note by Reynolds in the Sitter-book: 'Prince Edwards Cloaths send to Mʳ Toms'.[1] No. 1013 was probably painted from these sittings, but the same type was produced by Reynolds in 1766 (see No. 1014). Reynolds was paid £26. 5s. for a portrait of the Duke (undated entry in Ledgers in the Fitzwilliam Museum, vol. I). The portrait is in a curious condition. There are clear traces of alterations in the uniform, especially in the lay-out of the facings; the Garter ribbon was painted over the waistcoat and some of the concealed part of the star of the order can be seen through the facing of the uniform; and there are signs of minor alterations round the hat and face. The alterations to the uniform were probably carried out in Reynolds's studio after the sitter's rise in rank. The Prince went to sea in 1758 as a midshipman under Lord Howe's command; on 14 June 1759, 'the otherwise indispensable regulation of the service being waved [*sic*]', he was promoted to the rank of post-Captain and appointed to the *Phoenix*, and on 8 April 1761 he was appointed Vice-Admiral of the Blue. In No. 1013 he wears the undress uniform of a Flag Officer and there are apparent traces of alterations to the uniform to record both these promotions. X-ray (1963) revealed that the lower part of the canvas had been severely damaged and that areas of original paint are missing, especially in the lower right corner. This condition perhaps explains Simpson's account of his work on the picture in August 1810 (see above), for which he charged five guineas: 'To Cleaning Restoring the Originality & Repg a $\frac{3}{4}$ Port of the late Duke of York by Sir J. Reynolds.' There are signs in the X-ray of a triangular object, which may be a hat, at the bottom of the design. See Nos. 1014, 1040.

1014. EDWARD, DUKE OF YORK

Buckingham Palace. $30 \times 25\frac{1}{4}$ in., $76,2 \times 64,1$ cm.

Head and shoulders in profile to the left, in a painted oval, in naval uniform with the star of the Garter, holding a horse-whip in his right hand.

It is conceivable that the references given under No. 1013 to a portrait of the Duke by Reynolds in George IV's collection should be connected with No. 1014. Simpson's bill for work done for the Prince of Wales in 1794 includes £1. 6s. for cleaning 'the late Duke of York by Sir Joṣ Reynolds' (P.R.O., H.O. 73, 23). On the other hand, a payment on behalf of the Regent (probably in July 1815) of £13. 2s. to Colnaghi for a 'Portrait of H.R.H.'s The Duke of York, 'Framed' (Jutsham, *PP.*, f. 19) could refer to this portrait. No. 1014 was recorded at Buckingham Palace (637) in 1860 (*V.R. inv.*).

Literature: Graves and Cronin, vol. III, p. 1082.

On 18 July 1766 Reynolds was paid £26. 5s. for the 'Duke of York with the Horsewhip' (Ledgers in Fitzwilliam Museum, vol. I). The head, however, seems to be based on the portrait for which sittings had been given in 1759–8 (see

1. This is Peter Toms, Reynolds's drapery painter.

No. 1013). The uniform in both this and No. 1040 is that of a Flag Officer; it was officially introduced by an order dated 13 July 1767, but there are indications that this new uniform had been coming into fashion for several years before it was made official. A version of No. 1014 was sold at Christie's, 14 March 1924 (27) as a Gainsborough of George III; another, stated to have come from the collection of Havelock Allen, near Durham, was in a private collection in Philadelphia in 1962. The type seems to have been used in an equestrian group, sold at Christie's, 17 June 1929 (107), and on the art-market in New York in 1958.

1015. MARIA, DUCHESS OF GLOUCESTER

Buckingham Palace. 73¾ × 53¾ in., 187,3 × 136,5 cm.

Full-length, seated, resting her right elbow on a ledge and supporting her head on her hand.

Painted for the Duke of Gloucester; bequeathed in 1844 by his daughter, Princess Sophia Matilda (No. 1016), to the Prince Consort, who placed it in his Drawing-Room at Buckingham Palace (Queen Victoria's Journal, 28 December 1844).

Literature: Graves and Cronin, vol. I, pp. 363–4; Waterhouse, *Reynolds*, p. 64; R.A., *King's Pictures* (93).

Exhibited at the Royal Academy in 1774 (214), next to No. 1016; Walpole, who thought No. 1015 'Good, but the figure looks short', stated that both pictures had been painted for the Duke. The Duchess had sat to Reynolds (as Lady Waldegrave) on 29 June 1771 (Sitter-books at R.A.). Payments are recorded of £236. 5s. to Reynolds for 'Duke of Glocester for the Dutchess and Princess Sophia' in February 1779 (Ledgers in Fitzwilliam Museum, vol. II; under 18 January 1779 is a payment of £150 (struck through) for 'The Dutchess of Gloucester Paid').
The condition of No. 1015 is unsatisfactory. Parts of the original surface appear to have disintegrated and there are areas of repaint. The picture had probably begun to give trouble at an early date. Attached to the back is a note by Beechey (dated 30 January 1815) on its condition and recommendations for its treatment in the future. He advised strongly against the use of mastic, copal or any form of oil varnish and recommended the gentlest treatment if the surface was ever to be cleaned.
Small copies of No. 1015 are not uncommon, e.g., sold at Christie's, 11 June 1946 (166) and 10 June 1949 (118); the first of these reappeared at Sotheby's, 25 July 1956 (53). A large copy of No. 1015 in miniature by Richard Crosse was sold at Sotheby's, as Mrs. Siddons, on 31 July 1961 (72). Another miniature by Richard Crosse, probably painted in 1776 and sold at Sotheby's, 25 May 1964 (71), was based on No. 1015 but included a child (probably Princess Sophia Matilda) with a dog.

1016. PRINCESS SOPHIA MATILDA OF GLOUCESTER (*Plate* 97)

Windsor Castle (351). 25 × 30½ in., 63,5 × 77,5 cm.

Lying on the ground with her arm round a Maltese dog.

Presumably painted for the child's parents; bequeathed by her sister-in-law, Mary, Duchess of Gloucester, to Queen Victoria in 1857: 'a picture of the Princess Sophia Matilda with a Dog painted by Sir Joshua Reynolds' (will proved 5 June 1857); recorded in the Corridor at Windsor in 1859 (*V.R. inv.*).

Literature: Leslie and Taylor, vol. II, pp. 76–7; Graves and Cronin, vol. I, pp. 365–6; Collins Baker, *Windsor*, p. 269; Waterhouse, *Reynolds*, p. 64; R.A., *King's Pictures* (90); City of Birmingham Museum and Art Gallery, *Sir Joshua Reynolds*, 1961 (59).

Exhibited at the Royal Academy in 1774 (215); the engraving by T. Watson was published in 1775. Payments are recorded in Reynolds's Ledgers (Fitzwilliam Museum, vol. II): £236. 5s. under February 1779, 'Duke of Glocester for the Dutchess and Princess Sophia'; and £50 under January 1779, 'Duke of Glocester for the Princess Sophia'. It was exhibited at the British Institution in 1813 (111).

1017. HENRY, DUKE OF CUMBERLAND

Windsor Castle (332). 30⅛ × 25¼ in., 76,5 × 64,1 cm. (framed as an oval).

Head and shoulders in Garter robes.

Presumably painted for George IV. Large portraits of the two late Dukes of Cumberland were in the Council Chamber at Carlton House in 1792. 'A Portrait of his Royal Highness the Duke of Cumberland whole length', at £157. 10s., was among the pictures for which payment was outstanding in May 1793 (H.O. 73, 21).[1] Recorded in the West Ante-room at Carlton House in 1816 (1: 'A whole length portrait of the late Duke of Cumberland. Sir Joshua Reynolds', measurements given as 93 × 57 in.). It was described by Pyne (vol. III, *Carlton House*, pp. 18–19) as 'exquisitely finished . . . in a perfect state of preservation'; it was, however, so severely damaged in the fire at Carlton House, 8 June 1824, that only the head was preserved. Recorded at Windsor by 1845.

Literature: Leslie and Taylor, vol. II, pp. 19, 54; Graves and Cronin, vol. I, p. 218; W. T. Whitley, *Artists and their Friends in England 1700–99* (1928), vol. II, pp. 290, 292; Collins Baker, *Windsor*, p. 266; Waterhouse, *Reynolds*, p. 63.

The Duke sat to Reynolds on 13 February 1773 (Sitter-book at R.A.) and the portrait was exhibited at the Royal Academy in 1773 (232). A full-length of the Duchess of Cumberland, who had sat to Reynolds in the same month, was exhibited at the same time (233); it is now at Waddesdon (Waterhouse, *op. cit.*, pl. 146). Northcote records a sitting by the Duke as early as 4 April 1772; and on 19 November wrote that he had been employed by Reynolds in painting the drapery 'from the Duke's own robes put on upon the layman' (Whitley, *loc. cit.*). From T. Watson's mezzotint (*Fig.* 32), published on 20 May 1774, the original can be seen in its entirety; the landscape background contained a view of Windsor Castle from the north. The surface of the surviving fragment is still frizzled from the fire of 1824; but the head appears to be in a reasonable state of preservation, although it was probably considerably repainted when the canvas was cleaned and repaired by Seguier in September 1862 (*V.R. inv.*). A copy of No. 1017 in its original state is in the Freemasons' Hall.

1018. FREDERICK, DUKE OF YORK
(*Plate* 102)

Buckingham Palace. 94½ × 57¾ in., 240 × 146,7 cm.

Full-length, standing in Garter robes, resting his left hand on his sword; the plumed hat of the order rests on a table behind him.

Probably painted for George IV to be hung in the old Throne Room at Carlton House,[2] where it is to be seen in Wild's plate in Pyne (vol. III, *Carlton House*, p. 28; inv. of 1816 (18)); in 1813 it had been sent from Carlton House to the British Institution (Jutsham, *R/D*, f. 132); removed in 1832 to the State Apartments at St. James's, where it hung in the Throne Room.

1. On 18 March 1811 Cutter sold to the Prince Regent for £52. 10s. 'One Picture of the Duke of Cumberland Painted by Sir J Reynolds' (W.R.A., Geo. 26894), which cannot be identified with certainty.
2. On 16 May 1784 the Prince of Wales told his brother 'I am keeping to [*sic*] places in my House, on purpose for Portraits of you & Billy' (W.R.A., Geo. 43646–7; see No. 835). No. 1018 was cleaned for the Prince by Simpson in 1795 (P.R.O., H.O. 73, 23).

Literature: Leslie and Taylor, vol. II, p. 516; Graves and Cronin, vol. III, p. 1083; Waterhouse, *Reynolds*, p. 79; R.A., *King's Pictures* (115).

The Duke sat to Reynolds on 16, 19, 22 and 24 November 1787 and 1, 26 and 29 January 1788 (Sitter-books at R.A.); the portrait was exhibited at the Royal Academy in 1788 (88). It is probable that only the head was painted by Reynolds himself and that the robes were painted by an exceptionally good assistant in the studio. The engraving of the portrait by Jones was published on 18 December 1790. A copy of the head is at Deene Park. No. 1018 was exhibited at the British Institution in 1813, 1826 (160) and 1827 (99).

1019. ALEXANDER MONTGOMERIE, ELEVENTH EARL OF EGLINTON (1726–96)
(*Plate* 96)

Buckingham Palace. 30 × 25 in., 76,2 × 63,5 cm.

Head and shoulders, in a plumed Highland bonnet.

Recorded in store at Carlton House in 1816 (253: 'An unfinished portrait of the Earl of Eglinton. Sir Joshua Reynolds') with a note by Jutsham: 'The Head of this unfinished Portrait was cut out from the Canvas, Framed and sent to Windsor Castle March 13th 1829' (later Windsor inv. No. 336).

Literature: Leslie and Taylor, vol. II, pp. 432, 468; Graves and Cronin, vol. I, pp. 281–2; 45, Park Lane, *Sir Joshua Reynolds*, 1937 (46); Waterhouse, *Reynolds*, p. 75; R.A., *King's Pictures* (88).

Lord Eglinton sat to Reynolds on 24 and 27 March and 3 and 6 April 1784 (Sitter-book at R.A.), probably for a full-length in Highland dress for which Reynolds made a preparatory drawing.[1] A payment by Lord Eglinton to Reynolds of £88. 19s. (? in November 1783) (Ledgers in Fitzwilliam Museum, vol. II) can hardly have been for this portrait if the sittings had not been completed. It is possible that No. 1019 was a preliminary study for the head; but it is equally possible that the full-length was never finished and that it came into the possession of George IV, perhaps already cut down to *c.* 50 × 40 in. No measurements are given of the picture in George IV's inventories before it was cut down in 1829, but in the inventory of 1819 (346) it was valued at £105, the same sum as is set beside Nos. 845, 850 in this Catalogue, for example. At a later date, before 26 July 1865, when Redgrave completed his entry for the picture in the *V.R. inv.*, the canvas had been framed as an oval. At a still later date the area within the oval was overpainted to a slight extent, possibly by Seguier in 1865. The photograph attached to Redgrave's notes shows a much rougher and less finished area under the present sky, *pentimenti* (apparently) round the head and on the sitter's back, and a coat or plaid, also clearly modelled, but much more intelligible—and much more obviously tartan—than the shawl-like garment which the sitter wears at present; the plumes in the bonnet also seem then to have been less clearly defined than they now are. The *pentimenti* which were almost entirely concealed by the overpainting may indicate that No. 1019 is a fragment from the unfinished full-length, and not from a preliminary study of the head. It is perhaps significant that Bone's miniature copy of No. 1019, signed and dated 1787 (Royal Library), shows below the head only the black cravat and a small indication of a collar as if this was all that was intelligible of what Reynolds had finished. A version of No. 1019 belongs to the Earl of Eglinton. An early

1. Recorded by Leslie and Taylor, *op. cit.*, p. 432, as in the possession of Lord Delamere; this may have been the drawing sold in Lady Thomond's sale at Christie's, 26 May 1821 (19).

copy, on the art-market in London in 1935, was later in the possession of Mr. Victor Cazalet.

Cornet in the Scots Guards, 1744; raised the 77th Regiment of Foot, which he commanded in the American War of Independence; Colonel of the 51st Regiment of Foot, 1767–95, and of the 2nd Dragoons, 1795–6; Equerry to the Queen, 1761–9; Deputy Ranger of Hyde Park and St. James's Park, 1766–8.

1020. THOMAS, LORD ERSKINE (1750–1823)
(*Plate* 98)

Windsor Castle (350). 50 × 39¾ in., 127 × 101 cm.

Three-quarter-length, leaning against a table on which are papers and an inkstand; behind, on the right, are bookshelves.

Given to George IV by the sitter. On 7 April 1810 'A Three Quarter Length . . . Lord Erskine' was received from Lord Erskine, without a frame, at Carlton House; on 29 November it was sent to Simpson to be cleaned (Jutsham, *R/D*, ff. 78, 115). Simpson's account, under January 1811, for five guineas for 'Cleaning & Nourishing &c a Portrait of Lord Erskine at half length by Sir J. Reynolds', was paid in January 1812; and in January 1811 J. Smith provided, for £31. 12s., 'A large handsome frame Gilt in burnish Gold' for it (W.R.A., Geo. 26878–9, 26893). The portrait was placed in the Crimson Drawing-Room at Carlton House (No. 13 in inv. of 1816; Pyne, vol. III, *Carlton House*, p. 23, seen in plate) and was removed to the New Corridor at Windsor on 30 April 1828.

Literature: Leslie and Taylor, vol. II, pp. 484–5, 499; Graves and Cronin, vol. I, p. 291; Collins Baker, *Windsor*, p. 269; Waterhouse, *Reynolds*, p. 77.

Erskine, who was Attorney-General to the Prince of Wales, 1783–92, sat to Reynolds on 10, 17, 19 and 21 January and 7 February 1786 (Sitter-book at R.A.) and the portrait was exhibited at the Royal Academy in 1786 (65), and again at the British Institution in 1827 (85). The engraving by J. Jones was published on 6 May 1786 (Chaloner Smith, vol. II, p. 749). The background is bituminous and severely cracked in many places, but the figure appears to be in sound condition. Campbell, in his *Lives of the Lord Chancellors* (vol. VI (1847), p. 709) stated that the best portrait of Erskine is that by Hopner [*sic*] at Windsor.

Youngest son of the 10th Earl of Buchan. Served in the navy and army, but went to the bar (he was called in 1778) and was immensely successful; he secured the acquittal of Lord Keppel (No. 1024) at his court-martial in 1779. A brilliant advocate and orator, he was inordinately vain and, as a politician, unsuccessful. He was a friend of Fox and Sheridan and the Prince of Wales; Lord Chancellor, 1806–7; he was chivalrous in defence of Queen Caroline at her trial.

1021. DAVID GARRICK (1717–79) (*Plate* 94)

Windsor Castle (363). 30¼ × 25¼ in., 76,8 × 64,1 cm.

Inscribed on the back of the canvas by the artist: *David Garrick | aet 52 | 1768 | JR pinx*

Half-length, as Kitely in Ben Jonson's *Every Man in his Humour*, wearing a Van Dyckian costume with his arms folded across his chest.

Stated to have been given by Reynolds to Edmund Burke; it was sold in Burke's sale at Christie's, 5 June 1812 (93), when it was bought by Lord Yarmouth for the Prince Regent; received at Carlton House on 4 [*sic*] June 1812 from Lord Yarmouth (Jutsham, *R/D*, f. 199, '. . . in Gilt Frame') and recorded in store at Carlton House in 1816 (290: 'A head of Mr Garrick, as Kitely.

Sir Joshua Reynolds'); removed to the New Corridor at Windsor on 20 August 1828.

Literature: Leslie and Taylor, vol. I, p. 282; Graves and Cronin, vol. I, p. 350; Collins Baker, *Windsor*, p. 270; Waterhouse, *Reynolds*, p. 59; R.A., *King's Pictures* (92); City Art Gallery, Plymouth, *Paintings by Sir Joshua Reynolds*, 1951 (40); R.A., *European Masters of the Eighteenth Century*, 1954–5 (8); *British Painting in the Eighteenth Century*, Montreal, Toledo, 1957–8 (56).

Garrick sat to Reynolds on a number of occasions; sittings on 17, 20 and 26 May 1767 (Sitter-book at R.A.) could be associated with No. 1021. It was exhibited at the British Institution in 1827 (27). A copy was recorded in the Chéramy collection in Paris in 1908; a copy on the art-market in London in 1905 is now in the National Portrait Gallery (4504); a copy was sold at Sotheby's on 30 October 1957 (70); a sketch-like version, almost certainly a copy, was in the collection of Captain Eric Palmer in 1953. Garrick had revived Ben Jonson's play at Drury Lane on 29 November 1751. The King attended on the second night and the production, which Garrick had prepared with exceptional care, took the town by storm. Garrick's performance as Kitely was one of the triumphs of his career; he made slight alterations to the original text in order to emphasise the character's jealousy, and he dressed the characters in 'old English Manners'. Murphy said of his playing: 'Such was the expression of that various face, that the mixed emotions of his heart were strongly marked by his looks and the tone of his voice'. Garrick's final appearance in the part was at Drury Lane on 25 April 1776. Finlayson's engraving of Reynolds's portrait, published on 1 February 1769, states that it showed the actor in Act II, sc. I, which is set in a hall in Kitely's house and contains four long speeches by Kitely himself: 'Yea, every look, or glance, mine eye ejects, Shall check occasion'.

One of the greatest figures in the history of the English stage and the most popular actor of his day until his retirement in 1776. He and Reynolds were both in Dr. Johnson's circle. Reynolds, who did not like Garrick personally, drafted a 'Character' of the actor in which he described Garrick's obsession with his own reputation and with the impression he was making, in whatever company he was. For the portrait of Garrick by Hogarth see Millar, No. 560.

1022. JOHN MANNERS, MARQUESS OF GRANBY (1721–70) (*Plate* 93)

St. James's Palace. 97 × 82½ in., 246,4 × 209,5 cm.; enlarged on the right in painting.

Full-length, standing, wearing a breastplate with the uniform of Colonel of the Royal Regiment of Horse Guards (blue, with scarlet facings and gold lace), leaning with his left arm on his charger; on the other side of his charger is a negro page; in the background a battle is raging and a detachment of Horse Guards is galloping towards it.

No. 1022 and No. 1027 were perhaps painted for George, 1st Marquess Townshend (d. 1807), who had served with both Generals in the Seven Years War. On 16 July 1810 both portraits were received from Lady Townshend at Carlton House and on 27 August they were delivered to Simpson to be cleaned (Jutsham, *R/D*, ff. 70, 133). Simpson's account, which was settled in January 1812, includes 25 shillings for taking down the portraits at Lady Townshend's residence and £20 'To Cleaning, Nourishing & Varnishing an Equestrian Portrait of the Celebrated Marquis of Granby, Capital by Sr. J. Reyn' (W.R.A., Geo. 26878–9). Wyatt's bill, dated at Lady Day 1811, includes £253 'To enlarging 2 frames for Paintings (Marqs of Granby and Count de Lipe) 5 members . . .' (*ibid.*, 26890–1); it was presumably at this time

that the martial trophies were made for the frames on these two portraits. No. 1022 was in the Crimson Drawing-Room at Carlton House in 1816 (9: 'A whole length portrait of the Marquis of Granby, with a negro holding a horse. Sir Joshua Reynolds'; the portraits can be seen in position in Westall's drawing of the marriage of Princess Charlotte, 2 May 1816 (Oppé, Nos. 646–7)). It was sent to St. James's in November 1830. The two portraits were engraved by S. W. Reynolds in *The Royal Gallery of Pictures* (1840), pp. 16, 32, and, as the selection in this volume is stated to have been made 'from the Buckingham House Gallery', it is possible (but unlikely) that the portraits were for a time at Buckingham Palace. No. 1022 was certainly at St. James's in 1864 (*V.R. inv.*).

Literature: Leslie and Taylor, vol. I, pp. 261–2; Graves and Cronin, vol. I, pp. 383–4; W. E. Manners, *Some Account of the . . . Marquis of Granby* (1899), pp. 150–1; Waterhouse, *Reynolds*, p. 57.

The Marquess had sat to Reynolds on 11, 12, 13 and 14 June 1764 and 6 and 16 May 1766; his horse had an appointment with Reynolds on 3 June 1765 at 11 a.m. (Sitter-books at R.A.). No. 1022 is a replica, almost certainly to a great extent by Reynolds himself, of the portrait exhibited at the Society of Artists in 1766 (137; Walpole's note in *Walpole Soc.*, vol. XXVII (1939), p. 76). The exhibited picture had been painted for the Maréchal de Broglie and can be associated with the payment of £250 'in full July 3ᵈ 1773' for 'Lord Granby with a horse given to [Marshal Broglie]' (Ledgers in Fitzwilliam Museum, vol. II). It is now in the Ringling Museum of Art, Sarasota (*Catalogue* (1949) by W. E. Suida, pp. 317–18). Another repetition is at Trinity College, Cambridge. A number of variants are recorded. A full-length in which the charger is replaced by a cannon is at Belvoir; another was at Stowe; a three-quarter-length version is at Petworth (162).[1] A small oil sketch was in the Lincoln sale at Christie's, 31 March 1939 (47); a less good small version was in the collection of Lord Brassey; a small copy is in the Guildhall and another is at Askham Hall. A copy of the head by H. Hall is at Weston Park. A head and shoulders drawing from this type is in the National Portrait Gallery (1186). The portrait was engraved by J. Watson.[2] The design directly influenced a portrait at Alnwick, attributed to J. B. van Loo, of Algernon, Earl of Hertford. No. 1022 was exhibited at the British Institution in 1813 (130), 1826 (136) and 1827 (154).

Eldest son of the 3rd Duke of Rutland; Lieutenant-General, 1759, and a popular, generous and brave commander. As Commander-in-Chief of the British Forces in Germany in the Seven Years War, he particularly distinguished himself at Warburg on 31 July 1760, when he led a succession of cavalry charges against the French lines. This episode is perhaps commemorated by Reynolds in the background of No. 1022. Prince Ferdinand of Brunswick publicly thanked Lord Granby, 'under whose orders all the British cavalry performed prodigies of valour which they could not fail of doing having his Lordship at their head'.

1023. FRANCIS RAWDON-HASTINGS, SECOND EARL OF MOIRA AND FIRST MARQUESS OF HASTINGS (1754–1826) (*Plate* 101)

Buckingham Palace. 94½ × 58¼ in., 240 × 147,9 cm.

Full-length, standing, in the undress uniform of a Colonel and A.D.C. to the King, holding his hat in his right hand

---

1. This, or a three-quarter-length at Stanway, is presumably the portrait sent on 15 November 1813 from Carlton House to Lord Egremont by desire of Lord Yarmouth and at the Prince Regent's command (Jutsham, *R/D*, f. 140).
2. There is also a small mezzotint of the head of the negro page.

which rests upon his sword; in the background a battle rages in a wooded landscape.

Painted for Frederick, Duke of York. Bought by George IV at the Duke of York's sale at Christie's, 7 April 1827 (107), for £72. 9s. (W.R.A., Geo. 26554); recorded in the inventory of 'Carleton Palace' (605); later at Buckingham Palace (638) and Windsor (3129).

Literature: Leslie and Taylor, vol. II, p. 588; Graves and Cronin, vol. II, pp. 783–5; Waterhouse, *Reynolds*, p. 82; R.A., *King's Pictures* (107); City of Birmingham, Museum and Art Gallery, *Sir Joshua Reynolds*, 1961 (88).

Lord Hastings sat to Reynolds, as Lord Rawdon, on 26 and 28 June and 2, 5, 10 and 12 July 1789 (Sitter-book at R.A.); under 13 July is a note on his uniform: 'Lord Rawdon White Wastcoat single breast a small blue Collar and small Buttons Epaulet white Breeches double breasted Coat Buttons at equal distance.' In May 1790 a payment to Reynolds of £210 is recorded under 'Lord Rawdon' (Ledgers in Fitzwilliam Museum, vol. II). The portrait was exhibited at the Royal Academy in 1790 (94); the engraving by John Jones was published on 1 May 1792. There are signs of alterations by Reynolds to the outline of the hat; there are *pentimenti* in the disposition of the curtain draped in the trees behind the sitter; and the first painting of the sky shows through the trees and most distant part of the landscape. Among newspaper reports on the progress and reception of the portrait (Graves and Cronin, *loc. cit.*) is a report that the head had been finished in two sittings by 26 September 1789 and the rest 'sketched out'. A drawing after No. 1023 by Grimaldi was sold at Christie's, 9 February 1960 (27B); enamel copies (half-length) by Grimaldi, signed and dated 1790 and 1792 are at Windsor. No. 1023 was exhibited at the British Institution in 1813 and 1827 (144).

Soldier and statesman; served with distinction in America and in 1793 commanded the expedition to Brittany. In 1794 commanded reinforcements for the Duke of York in Flanders; Master of the Ordnance, 1806–7, and Governor of Bengal, 1815–22. He was a close friend of the Duke of York, a firm friend and supporter of the Prince of Wales and A.D.C. to the King, 1782–93. In April 1810 the Prince of Wales presented to him the magnificent portrait of himself in Garter robes with a negro page (*Fig.* XIV) which had been exhibited at the Royal Academy in 1787 (90) and is now at Arundel Castle (Jutsham, *R/D*, f. 56; R.A., *The First Hundred Years*, 1951–2 (98)). The Prince is reputed to have said, 'Moira and I are one, we have but one heart and one fate through life between us.'

1024. AUGUSTUS, FIRST VISCOUNT KEPPEL (1725–86) (Plate 100)

St. James's Palace. 94¼ × 58½ in., 239,4 × 148,7 cm.

Full-length, in Admiral's full-dress uniform, standing on the sea-shore and leaning on the fluke of an anchor; in his right hand he holds a paper.

Painted for George IV and recorded in the Ante-room at Carlton House in 1792; the Prince took especial pains in framing his set of naval portraits (i.e., Nos. 849, 851, 1024, 1026). Edward Wyatt's account for work done in 1808 included £135 for 'Three new whole Length Frames made Match for Paintings of Admirals . . .', and £260 'To Carving and Gilding . . . 16 Corners for 4 Frames for Paintings of Admirals . . . Dolphins, Anchors, Coral, Oak &c' (W.R.A., Geo. 26860). Recorded in store at Carlton House in 1816 (279: 'A whole length of Lord Keppell, in an admiral's uniform. Sir Joshua Reynolds'); in the King's Closet at St. James's in 1832.

Literature: Graves and Cronin, vol. II, p. 544; Waterhouse, *Reynolds*, p. 77; R.A., *King's Pictures* (106).

Presumed to have been presented by the sitter to the Prince of Wales. In Reynolds's Ledgers (Fitzwilliam Museum, vol. II) is a payment of two hundred guineas in August 1786, 'Lord Keppell given to the Prince of Wales'. In 1864 (*V.R. inv.*) it was stated that the paper in the Admiral's right hand was inscribed with details of naval operations involving Admiral Barrington, Lord Howe, Lord Hood, Vice-Admiral Milbanke and Admiral Pigot. Of this inscription nothing can be discerned and it was presumably removed during one of the restorations that No. 1024 has suffered. An engraving of the head and shoulders by Scriven was published on 12 March 1814. A half-length copy is at Chequers; a head and shoulders copy is in the collection of Sir A. H. Shafto Adair. No. 1024 was exhibited at the British Institution in 1813.

Son of the 2nd Earl of Albemarle. Entered the Navy in 1735; Admiral of the White and First Lord of the Admiralty, 1782. In 1777, when Commander-in-Chief of the grand fleet, he was court-martialled for allowing the French fleet to elude him, but was acquitted. He was a friend of the Prince of Wales and, for many years, of Reynolds. Reynolds had painted him on many occasions and, in 1749, had gone to the Mediterranean on board Keppel's ship.

1025. LOUIS PHILIPPE JOSEPH ('PHILIPPE ÉGALITÉ'), DUKE OF CHARTRES, LATER DUKE OF ORLÉANS (1747–93)

Buckingham Palace. 93¾ × 58¼ in., 238,1 × 147,9 cm.

Full-length, standing, in Hussar's uniform with the ribbon of the Saint-Esprit, holding his plumed hat in his left hand; behind him is a negro groom holding a charger and in the distance is a castle on a hill.

Painted for George IV; recorded in the West Ante-room at Carlton House in 1816 (7: 'A whole length portrait of the late Duke of Orleans, with a negro holding a horse. Sir Joshua Reynolds'), where it can be seen in Wild's plate (1819) in Pyne, vol. III, *Carlton House*, p. 17. On 27 August 1810 it was sent to Simpson to be cleaned;[1] it returned in October 1810 (Jutsham, *R/D*, f. 70); Simpson's bill includes ten guineas for 'a New Stretching frame, laying down and Secureing, Cleaning & Repg: the Sky of a Most Capital Picture of the late Duke of Orleans Sir J. Reynolds' (W.R.A., Geo. 26878–9). Edward Wyatt's bill for work in 1811 includes £17. 10s. for 'making, richly Carving and Gilding a Coronet . . . for frame' for this portrait (*ibid.*, 26890–1). It was sent for exhibition to the British Institution in 1813 (55) and 1823 (17); on the first occasion the organizers of the exhibition were allowed to keep the portrait 'for the study of the artists attending the British School' after the exhibition had closed (Jutsham, *R/D*, f. 130, *Deliveries*, f. 40; *Letters of George IV*, vol. I, 296). Jutsham wrongly noted in the 1816 inv. that the portrait had been destroyed in the fire at Carlton House, 8 June 1824. It was in fact only severely damaged—'Damaged and nearly distroy'd by Fire'— and it was sent on 2 February 1825 to Lawrence in order that he could copy it (Jutsham, *Deliveries*, f. 70); it was still with Lawrence at his death (Garlick, *Catalogue*, p. 279).

Literature: Cunningham, vol. I, p. 240; Leslie and Taylor, vol. II, pp. 479–86; Law, 1882, p. 36; Graves and Cronin, vol. II, pp. 710–11; A. Britsch, *La Jeunesse de Philippe-Égalité* (Paris, 1926), pp. 416–18; Waterhouse, *Reynolds*, p. 77.

Painted while the Duke was in London in 1785. Reynolds wrote to the Duke of Rutland on 30 May 1785: 'I have begun a whole length of the Duc de Chartres for the Prince of Wales, and the Prince is to sit for him' (*Letters of Sir Joshua Reynolds*, ed. F. W. Hilles (1929), p. 124). On 13 September

1. Simpson had cleaned it earlier, in 1794 (P.R.O., H.O. 73, 23).

1785 Reynolds was paid £262. 1s. for the portrait (Ledger in Fitzwilliam Museum, vol. II). It was eventually handed over to the Prince in March 1786. It was exhibited at the Royal Academy in 1786 (85) and the Duke sat under his portrait at the Annual Dinner at the Academy. Farington (*Diary*, vol. I, p. 16) remembered it: 'a very fine one . . . and a remarkable likeness, which everybody acknowledged who then had an opportunity of comparing it with the original'. The portrait was discovered by Redgrave at Hampton Court; in 1874 (*V.R. inv.*) he wrote that the fire had 'fried up the whole surface and even destroyed some of the canvas—In 1874—it was put into the hands of the restorer to save as much as remained of a very fine work of art.' An impression of the condition in which Redgrave found the portrait can be gained from a photograph (?of 1874) preserved in the inventory clerk's office at Buckingham Palace; the original appearance of the portrait can be judged from J. R. Smith's mezzotint, published on 30 March 1786 (*Fig.* 33) or from the small copy in the Musée Condé, Chantilly. Another small copy, by Drummond, is at Petworth (C. H. Collins Baker, *Catalogue of the Petworth Collection* . . . (1920), pp. 26–7), a small copy by Roqueplan is in the Wallace Collection (603); another is in the Musée Carnavalet; and see No. 1045. Garlick (*Catalogue*, p. 155) assumes that the copy by Lawrence is the small version at Chantilly, which was sold to the Duke of Aumale in 1856 by Evans, who had bought Lawrence's copy at Christie's, 18 June 1831 (107). But the copy was certainly to be of the size of life and a life-size copy, which was with a private collector in London in 1938, was the copy in Lawrence's sale; Evans may himself have painted the little copy which he sold to Aumale. The copy by Lawrence had been bespoken in 1824 for the sum of £525: 'Copy fm the best remaing Materials or Authority, of the late D: of Orleans (by Sir Joshua Reynolds)' (W.R.A., Geo. 27041; *Letters of George IV*, vol. III, 1591); but the archives do not provide evidence that it was finished or paid for by the King. It is possible that a copy had been made for the sitter in 1785/6 (A. Britsch, *op. cit.*). Callet's portrait of the Duke at Versailles (MV. 3909) is apparently based on the design of No. 1025.

Great-grandson of the Regent Orléans and father of King Louis-Philippe. Before the French Revolution he nourished an *anglomanie* and paid a number of visits to London. When he came over with a large party of French men and women in the early summer of 1783, the Prince of Wales disliked him: 'I think he is a great beast; in short, I cannot bear him'; the Duke of York thought that 'By all accounts Monsier de Chartres must be a terrible brute, always drunk and very fond of low company'. Debauched though he was, he had a magnificent presence: Reynolds is said to have observed of him 'that He was in manner the most elegant man He had ever seen.—He had noticed him at Court & remarked that many men appeared graceful when *in motion*, but that the Duke of Orleans was the only man who appeared so when *standing still*' (Farington, *Diary*, vol. I, pp. 249–50). The Duke was regarded with abhorrence in London for his conduct towards Louis XVI. The Prince took No. 1025 down from the walls of Carlton House (Pyne, vol. I, p. 16), but, because of the veneration with which it was regarded by painters, 'occasionally permitted [it] to be studied by artists' (*ibid.*, vol. III, *Carlton House*, p. 19). The Duke was guillotined in 1793; in the previous year he had sold the great Orléans collection of pictures.

1026. GEORGE BRYDGES, FIRST LORD RODNEY (1719?–1792) (*Plate* 99)

St. James's Palace. 94⅜ × 58⅛ in., 239,7 × 147,6 cm.

Full-length, in Admiral's full-dress uniform with the ribbon and star of the Bath, standing on the sea-shore with his hand on the fluke of an anchor. In the distance is a naval engagement.

Stated to have been painted for George IV (Graves and Cronin, *loc. cit.*); recorded in the Ante-room at Carlton House in 1792; see No. 1024. Recorded in store at Carlton House in 1816 (278: 'A whole length of Lord Rodney, with the fleet in the background. Sir Joshua Reynolds'). In the King's Closet at St. James's in 1832.

Literature: Graves and Cronin, vol. II, pp. 840–1; Waterhouse, *Reynolds*, p. 81; R.A., *King's Pictures* (100).

Rodney sat to Reynolds on 2, 5, 9 and 14 May 1788 and 2 March 1789 (Sitter-books at R.A.). The portrait was exhibited at the Royal Academy in 1789 (225). It was engraved by Scriven. A copy at Greenwich was painted by Shepperson who began work on 9 November 1824 on copies of No. 1026 and Nos. 849, 851, and finished them on 14 February 1825; these copies were sent to Greenwich on 9 March 1825 (Jutsham, *Deliveries*, f. 72). Another copy is at Kitley. A miniature copy by Grimaldi (1792) is at Windsor. No. 1026 was exhibited at the British Institution in 1813 1820 (48) and 1827 (182).

Entered the Navy in 1732. Admiral of the White, 1778; Commander-in-Chief of the Leeward Islands and Barbados, 1779. He defeated a Spanish squadron off Cape St. Vincent in 1780 and two years later he defeated the French in the Battle of the Saints. He was a friend of the Prince of Wales, whom he described in a letter to Payne (No. 850) as 'our great, amiable and Royal friend'.

1027. FREDERICK WILLIAM ERNEST, COUNT OF SCHAUMBURG-LIPPE (1724–77) (*Plate* 92)

St. James's Palace. 95½ × 80½ in., 242,6 × 204,5 cm.; enlarged on the right in painting.

Full-length, standing, in dark blue uniform with the ribbon of the Black Eagle of Prussia and holding a stick in his right hand; behind him are cannon, a (?French) standard and a negro page holding a charger.

Perhaps painted for George, 1st Marquess Townshend (*d.* 1807). See No. 1022. Simpson's account, settled in January 1812, included £16 'To Cleaning, Nourishing & Varnishing an Equestrian Portrait of the Count de Lippe Capital by Sir J. Reynolds' (W.R.A., Geo. 26878). No. 1027 was in the Crimson Drawing-Room at Carlton House in 1816 (8: A whole length portrait of Count de la Lippe, with a negro holding a horse, and a piece of ordnance. Sir Joshua Reynolds'). It was sent to St. James's in November 1830.

Literature: Leslie and Taylor, vol. I, pp. 235–6; Graves and Cronin, vol. II, pp. 559–60; Waterhouse, *Reynolds*, p. 55; R.A., *King's Pictures* (108).

The Count sat to Reynolds on 23 October 1764 and 3 and 5 August 1767 (Sitter-books at R.A.). A three-quarter-length version is at Cowdray; Waterhouse also quotes a head and shoulders, signed and dated 1767, in the possession of the Fürst zu Schaumburg-Lippe. In the version at Cowdray the flag is decorated with the French *fleur-de-lis*. A payment of £25, dated 12 August 1767, is recorded in Reynolds's Ledgers (Fitzwilliam Museum, vol. I) under 'Count Le Lippe'. No. 1027 may have been painted, presumably *c.* 1767, as a pendant to No. 1022; the design seems related to Ramsay's late full-length at Badminton of Admiral Boscawen. No. 1027 was exhibited at the British Institution in 1813, 1826 (133) and 1827 (128).

Commander of Artillery under Prince Ferdinand of Brunswick in the Seven Years War; in command, in 1761, of the English troops sent to the defence of Portugal. His mother was a daughter of George I by the Duchess of Kendal.

1028. CHARLES FITZROY, FIRST LORD SOUTHAMPTON (1737–97) (*Plate* 90)

Buckingham Palace. 36 × 28¼ in., 91,4 × 71,8 cm.

Half-length, in the state coat of the 1st Foot Guards, holding his hat under his left arm.

Acquired by George IV; it was received at Carlton House from Colnaghi on 15 May 1822 (Jutsham, *Receipts*, f. 160; 'In a Gilt Frame'; additional No. 597 in the Carlton House inv. of 1816); sent to Windsor (later inv. No. 288) in 1828 or 1829.

Literature: Leslie and Taylor, vol. I, pp. 186, 201; Graves and Cronin, vol. I, p. 316; Waterhouse, *Reynolds*, p. 48; City Art Gallery, Plymouth, *Sir Joshua Reynolds*, 1951 (23).

Lord Southampton sat to Reynolds in 16 January 1760, as Colonel Fitzroy, and on 5 February 1761 Mr. Fitzroy sat to him (Sitter-books at R.A.). No. 1028 should perhaps be connected with the earlier sitting. A second portrait, still in the possession of the family, may be connected with the later sitting. In Reynolds's Ledgers (Fitzwilliam Museum, vol. I) are payments (?1760) of £18. 18s. and £57. 15s. under 'Coll. FitzRoy'. The family still owns also a good second version of No. 1028, with a background of sky. In the printed catalogue (1843) of works of art in the Corridor at Windsor it is stated that George IV had bought No. 1028 in 1818 [*sic*] for forty guineas from Paul Colnaghi and that Colnaghi's son Dominic had purchased it at the sale of the effects of the establishment at which Lord Southampton had been educated and to which he had presented his portrait on leaving. No. 1028 was exhibited at the British Institution in 1827 (172). It was engraved by S. W. Reynolds (1820).

Grandson of the 2nd Duke of Grafton; Ensign in the 1st Foot Guards, 1752, Captain, 1756, and Lieutenant-Colonel, 1758; served in the Seven Years War and was A.D.C. to Prince Ferdinand of Brunswick; Groom of the Bedchamber to George II and George III, 1760–2, Vice-Chamberlain to the Queen, 1768–82, and Groom of the Stole to the Prince of Wales, 1780–97. As an early friend and councellor of the Prince, Southampton 'had only one fault, to be dislik'd by him and a blind attachment to the King'.

1029. THE DEATH OF DIDO (*Plate* 104)

Buckingham Palace. 58 × 94¼ in., 147,3 × 239,4 cm.

Dido, Queen of Carthage, expiring on her funeral pyre.

Bequeathed by Reynolds to his niece, the Marchioness of Thomond; at Lady Thomond's sale at Christie's, 19 May 1821 (72), it was bought by Sir Charles Long at the command of George IV for £735; received at Carlton House on 21 May 1821 (Jutsham, *Receipts*, f. 135) and recorded as an additional No. (581) in the inv. of 1816; later in the Picture Gallery at Buckingham Palace (43).

Literature: J. Northcote, *Memoirs of Sir Joshua Reynolds* (1813), p. 281; Waagen (1838), vol. II, p. 376, (1854), vol. II, p. 24; Leslie and Taylor, vol. II, pp. 326–7; Graves and Cronin, vol. III, pp. 1146–7; Waterhouse, *Reynolds*, p. 72; R.A., *King's Pictures* (498).

Exhibited at the Royal Academy in 1781 (160). According to Leslie and Taylor (*loc. cit.*), Stothard visited Reynolds when he was at work on the picture and saw that Reynolds had built up a pyre of 'billets of wood' over which he had thrown the queen's drapery and on it 'a lay figure in her attitude and dress'. Leslie and Taylor refer to the sitting by

Elizabeth Wateridge on 18 and 23 March 1781 (Sitter-book at the R.A.) as for the figure of Dido. It was exhibited at the British Institution in 1813 (33), 1823 (21), 1826 (110), 1827 (2) and 1833 (19). It was engraved by J. Grozer (1796) and S. W. Reynolds. The surface has been severely marred by bituminous contraction of the paint and the details of the composition are more easily discerned in the engravings or in small copies, i.e., at Helmingham Hall and at Sotheby's, 12 January 1966 (94), with a painted proscenium arch over the design and attributed to Stothard. An enamel copy by Bone, painted for the Prince of Wales in 1804, is at Windsor (2577); a very good small version was sold at Christie's, 28 November 1947 (106); a good version is in the Pennsylvania Museum, Philadelphia; other small versions are recorded.

The figure of Dido is based closely on a figure of Psyche in a passage in Giulio Romano's ceiling decorations in the Sala di Psyche in the Palazzo del Tè at Mantua (E. Wind, '"Borrowed Attitudes" in Reynolds and Hogarth', *Journal of the Warburg Institute*, vol. II (1938–9), pp. 182–3).

Dido had ordered the pyre to be constructed and laid on it a sword belonging to Aeneas, his garments and a portrait of him; in No. 1029 a sword, a shield and a small statue are beside the queen. After Aeneas and the Trojan fleet had set sail (in the distance on the right in No. 1029), she climbed the pyre and stabbed herself with Aeneas's sword. Her sister Anna attempted in vain to staunch the blood; Juno, in pity, sent down Iris from Olympus ('saffron-winged, sparkling like dew and trailing a thousand colours as she caught the light of the sun') to cut a lock of the dying queen's hair and thereby release her spirit (Virgil, *The Aeneid*, bk. IV, trans. by W. F. Jackson Knight (1956), pp. 111–18).

1030. CYMON AND IPHIGENIA (*Plate* 103)

Buckingham Palace. 56⅜ × 67¾ in., 143,2 × 172,1 cm.

The shepherd Cymon, guided by Cupid, feasting his eyes on Iphigenia sleeping beside a stream in a glade.

Bequeathed by Reynolds to his niece, the Marchioness of Thomond, and presented by her to George IV; received at Carlton House on 16 May 1814 (Jutsham, *R/D*, f. 305) and recorded in store at Carlton House in 1816 (222); in 1818 it was sent to Seguier to be cleaned and varnished (Jutsham, *ibid.*, f. 292); later in the Picture Gallery at Buckingham Palace (160).

Literature: Waagen (1854), vol. II, pp. 24–5; Leslie and Taylor, vol. II, pp. 536–7, 538; Graves and Cronin, vol. III, pp. 1143–4; Waterhouse, *Reynolds*, p. 81.

Exhibited at the Royal Academy in 1789 (143); engraved by Haward (1797), S. W. Reynolds and Geller. According to Leslie and Taylor (*loc. cit.*), Seguier refused to clean it when it entered George IV's collection and persuaded the King 'that in attempting to remove [the dirt] we should destroy some of the beautiful glazings'. It was exhibited at the British Institution in 1813 (48), 1826 (87), 1827 (66) and 1833 (39). A very good reduced version, stated to have been in the collection of Thomas Lister, was sold at Christie's, 19 November 1965 (16). A small, partly unfinished, copy by Etty is in the York City Art Gallery (88); a small copy, attributed to Etty, was on the art-market in 1962; an alleged sketch by Reynolds was in a private collection in Avignon in 1946. A good small version was in the Besnard Sale, Charpentier, Paris, 31 May–1 June 1934 (82). An enamel copy by Bone, painted for the Prince of Wales in 1806, is at Windsor (2574).

The story of Cymon and Iphigenia is told by Boccaccio (*Il Decamerone*, Giornata Quinta, Novella Prima). Reynolds may have used Dryden's translation, published in his *Fables*

Ancient and Modern (1700). Cymon ('Fair, Tall', but of 'A clownish Mien') was the son of a Cyprian lord who confined him to his country estates. On a summer morning, carrying 'His Quarter Staff, which he cou'd ne'er forsake', he found in the deep recesses of the grove, by a stream, the sleeping Iphigenia. Looking at her, 'with stupid Eyes And gaping Mouth', he was instantly enamoured of her beauty.

1031. ST. MICHAEL THE ARCHANGEL SLAYING THE DRAGON (*After Guido Reni*)

Hampton Court (1145). 114¼ × 75⅜ in., 289,6 × 191,4 cm.

Presented to George IV by Mary, Marchioness of Thomond; received from her at Carlton House on 25 July 1818 (Jutsham, *Receipts*, f. 36: '. . . in a Gilt Frame'; additional No. 550 in inv. of 1816) and later placed on the Staircase; in September 1833 sent to Hampton Court, where it served for a time as the altarpiece in the Chapel. Later at St. James's Palace.

Literature: Graves and Cronin, vol. III, p, 1243.

A copy, painted in 1750 by Reynolds in Rome, of Guido's altar-piece in S. Maria della Concezione (*Mostra di Guido Reni*, Bologna, 1954 (43)). He records that he began the copy on 30 May and finished it on 10 June (Leslie and Taylor, vol. I, p. 41).

After Sir Joshua Reynolds

1032. PORTRAIT OF THE ARTIST

Buckingham Palace. 30 × 25 in., 76,2 × 63,5 cm.

Head and shoulders, wearing spectacles.

In the collection of George IV. When it arrived at Carlton House from Lord Yarmouth on 4 June 1812 it was 'said to be by Sir J Reynolds . . . from the Collection of Edmond Burke had been presented to him by Sir Joshua' (Jutsham, *R/D*, f. 199); recorded in store at Carlton House in 1816 (284: '. . . after a picture by himself'); later at Windsor (1069).

Literature: Graves and Cronin, vol. II, p. 805.

A contemporary copy of No. 1008.

1033. GEORGE III

Holyroodhouse. 94⅝ × 58⅜ in., 240,3 × 148,3 cm.

Full-length, seated in the Coronation Chair, wearing robes of state and holding the sceptre in his right hand; St. Edward's Crown is on a cushion on the left.

Nos. 1033, 1034 were presumably presented by the sitters to James Graham, 3rd Duke of Montrose, Master of the Horse (see No. 1184); there is an old inscription, *The Duke of Montrose*, on the back of both in chalk; they were sold at Christie's, 21 June 1946 (134) and presented to H.M. King George VI by the 6th Duke of Montrose in July 1946.

Nos. 1033, 1034 are good contemporary copies of the original portraits painted by Reynolds for the Royal Academy, to be shown in 1780 at the first exhibition held by the Academy at Somerset House. The originals are still at the Royal Academy (R.A., *Kings and Queens*, 1953 (238, 249), *Treasures of the Royal Academy*, 1963 (7, 20)). The King had given sittings to Reynolds at Buckingham House on 17, 21, and 26 May 1779 (Sitter-books at R.A.). A large number of copies were distributed as official portraits of the King and Queen. Lawrence made copies for the same purpose from the same prototypes and in 1794 purchased from Lady Inchiquin three pairs of unfinished portraits from Reynolds's estate; he told Farington on 17 April 1794 that he would have to work

on all three pairs. In 1802 Lawrence was requiring assistance to prepare five pairs for official use. (Garlick, *Catalogue*, pp. 85–6). On 28 November 1789 Reynolds had noted that there were five Kings and four Queens in the Academy, and two Kings and one Queen in his house (Ledgers in Fitzwilliam Museum, vol. II). Nos. 1033, 1034 are perhaps more suggestive of Lawrence than Reynolds in quality. The canvas on which No. 1033 is painted appears to have been used first for a different male portrait, of which the head, perhaps the only part to be completed, is clearly visible under the King's left shoulder.

1034. QUEEN CHARLOTTE

Holyroodhouse. 94½ × 58½ in., 240 × 148,6 cm.

Full-length, seated under a canopy, in robes of state, wearing a small crown; her sceptre lies on a cushion in front of her.

See No. 1033. The Queen sat to Reynolds at Buckingham House on 6, 8, 10 and 13 December 1779 and 14 April 1780 (Sitter-books at R.A.).

1035. GEORGE III

Buckingham Palace. 94¼ × 58¼ in., 239,4 × 147,9 cm.

Recorded at Buckingham Palace (1073) in 1877 (*V.R. inv.*).

A good copy of the same pattern as No. 1033; the quality seems perhaps nearer to Lawrence than to Reynolds. See No. 1036.

1036. QUEEN CHARLOTTE

Buckingham Palace. 94 × 58 in., 238,8 × 147,3 cm.

Presumably the pendant to No. 1035; a good copy of the same pattern as No. 1034. Both portraits were recorded at Buckingham Palace in 1909 (p. 138).

1037. GEORGE III

Marlborough House. 93½ × 57½ in., 237,5 × 146 cm.

Recorded at Buckingham Palace (1072) in 1876 with No. 1038 (*V.R. inv.*); the pair was later at York House.

Nos. 1037, 1038 are bad, late versions of Reynolds's state portraits (see No. 1033). On the back of the portrait of the Queen is the name of T. [*sic*] Beckwith, Governor of Barbados. The portraits were probably painted, therefore, for Sir George Beckwith (1753–1823), successively Governor of Bermuda, 1797, St. Vincent, 1804, and Barbados, 1808.

1038. QUEEN CHARLOTTE

Marlborough House. 93½ × 58 in., 237,5 × 147,3 cm.

Recorded at Buckingham Palace (1080) in 1872 with No. 1037 (*V.R. inv.*).

See No. 1037.

1039. GEORGE III

St. James's Palace. 94¾ × 58⅞ in., 240,7 × 149,5 cm.

Full-length, seated in the Coronation Chair, wearing robes of state and holding his sceptre in his right hand.

Recorded in the Throne Room at St. James's in 1863 (*V.R. inv.*).

A good copy of the original in the Royal Academy (see No. 1033); it is possible that it is one of the copies finished under Lawrence's auspices.

1040. EDWARD, DUKE OF YORK

Windsor Castle (469). 25 × 18½ in., 63,5 × 47 cm.

Head and shoulders in profile to the left, in a painted oval, in naval uniform with the star of the Garter.

See No. 1014; recorded at Windsor in 1878 (*V.R. inv.*).

Literature: Graves and Cronin, vol. III, p. 1082; Collins Baker, *Windsor*, p. 268.

No. 1040 appears to be a copy, painted in Reynolds's studio, of No. 1014; X-ray (1963) seemed to indicate that it was of feebler quality than the other two versions or variants of this portrait (Nos. 1013, 1014) and that the canvas had been used earlier for at least the first draft of a different portrait. Reynolds's Ledgers (Fitzwilliam Museum, vol. I) include under 18 July 1766, as well as the payment for No. 1014, £26. 5s. for 'Duke of York for Lord Waldegraves Picture' and the same sum for the 'Duke of York given to Capt Walsingham'.

1041. GEORGIANA, DUCHESS OF DEVON-SHIRE (1757–1806), WITH HER DAUGHTER GEORGIANA (1783–1858), LATER COUNTESS OF CARLISLE

Windsor Castle (384). 44 × 56⅜ in., 111,8 × 148,3 cm.

Three-quarter-length, seated, playing with her baby daughter on her knee.

Painted for George IV; recorded in the inventory of 'Carleton Palace' (687: 'Portrait of the Duchess of Devonshire. Lawrence after Sir J. Reynolds'). On 13 December 1828 Morant submitted a bill for £25. 10s. for a richly ornamented frame 'for a Bishop's ½ length Portrait of the Duchess of Devonshire' (W.R.A., Geo. 26558); Morant's label is still on the frame.

Literature: Graves and Cronin, vol. I, p. 249; Collins Baker, *Windsor*, p. 271.

A very good copy by William Etty after Reynolds's famous picture in the Devonshire collection, exhibited at the Royal Academy in 1786 (166: Waterhouse, *Reynolds*, pl. 267). It had been bespoken from Lawrence in 1825 for the sum of £420 ('Copy of a Picture by Sir Joshua Reynolds of the Duchess of Devonshire & her Child'); Lawrence's receipt for this sum for the picture is dated 27 November 1826 (W.R.A., Geo. 27042, 26691). Redgrave, however, in an undated note in the *V.R. inv.* (March, 1859), states 'I learnt from Etty that he made this Copy when with Sir T. Lawrence'. A writer in the *Art Journal*, January 1855, had stated that Lawrence had consigned the task, given to him by George IV, of copying the Reynolds, to Etty;[1] Etty had, however, not been working with Lawrence since 1808.

Daughter of the 1st Earl Spencer, she married the 5th Duke of Devonshire in 1774. She was celebrated for her 'irresistible manners and the seduction of her society' and had a close and tender relationship with the Prince of Wales. Her daughter married the 6th Earl of Carlisle in 1801.

1042. CHARLES JAMES FOX (1749–1806)

Buckingham Palace. Pastel on paper: 33¾ × 26¼ in., 85,7 × 66,7 cm.

Head and shoulders in a light blue coat.

Drawn for George IV; later at Kew (*V.R. inv.*, 1876, Buckingham Palace No. 523).

On 2 May 1808 William Lane submitted his bill for £52. 10s.

1. I am grateful to Mr. Dennis Farr for this reference.

for 'A Portrait of the late Rt Honble C. J. Fox' and (at an additional sum) for a frame for it; he was paid under a warrant dated 21 July 1808 (W.R.A., Geo. 26856, 89456). No. 1042 is a copy of the head from Reynolds's portrait, exhibited at the Royal Academy in 1784 (108), of which the original is at Holkham and an original repetition at Melbury (Waterhouse, *Reynolds*, pl. 246).

Famous Whig statesman, much disliked by George III but a close friend and adviser of the Prince of Wales at the time of the Regency Crisis of 1788–9 and the Prince's marriage to Mrs. Fitzherbert, which he strongly advised the Prince not to contract.

1043. DAVID GARRICK (1717–79)

Buckingham Palace. 12 × 10 in., 30,5 × 25,4 cm.

Half-length, seated at a table on which he rests his clasped hands.

Recorded at Buckingham Palace (788) in 1876 (*V.R. inv.*).

A small late copy of the portrait exhibited at the Royal Academy in 1776 (241); the best versions are those at Knole and in the collection of the Marquess of Lansdowne.

See No. 1021.

1044. LOUIS PHILIPPE JOSEPH, DUKE OF ORLÉANS (1747–93)

Buckingham Palace. 36 × 23¼ in., 91,4 × 60 cm.

Recorded at Buckingham Palace (838) in 1876 (*V.R. inv.*).

A small later copy, probably painted early in the nineteenth century, of No. 1025.

1045. CHARLES WATSON-WENTWORTH, SECOND MARQUESS OF ROCKINGHAM (1730–82)

Buckingham Palace. 94½ × 58¾ in., 240 × 149,2 cm.

Full-length, standing in Garter robes and holding a paper in his right hand, beside a table on which is the plumed hat of the order; papers and a portfolio lie beneath the table.

Presented to George IV by Lady Rockingham (see below), and recorded in the Council Chamber at Carlton House in 1792. On 12 October 1810 it was sent to Simpson for 'Cleaning Nourishing & Var[nishing]' (Jutsham, *R/D*, f. 72; W.R.A., Geo. 26878–9); recorded in store at Carlton House in 1816 (239: 'A whole length of the Marquis of Rockingham. Sir Joshua Reynolds.'); later at Buckingham Palace (639).

Literature: Graves and Cronin, vol. II, p. 836.

In February 1786 Reynolds was paid £157. 10s. for a portrait of Lord Rockingham 'given to the P. of Wales' (Ledgers, vol. II, in the Fitzwilliam Museum). The original, in the possession of Earl Fitzwilliam, had been painted nearly twenty years earlier: Rockingham sat to Reynolds on 19 and 23 December 1766 and 1 and 2 June 1768 (Sitter-books in R.A.). No. 1045 seems a respectable copy, painted in Reynolds's studio, but unlikely to have been worked on by Reynolds himself. A number of other copies and derivations are known. Fisher's engraving of the original was published on 1 July 1774. No. 1045 was exhibited at the British Institution in 1826 (155), 1827 (150) and 1833 (5).

Leader of the Whig party; Prime Minister, 1765–6 and March–July 1782; Lord of the Bedchamber, 1751–62.

Charles Jean Robineau

Portrait-painter and musical composer. He was French by birth and was in London during the 1780's. He exhibited at the Royal Academy in 1785 and 1788.

1046. GEORGE IV WHEN PRINCE OF WALES

Windsor Castle (969). 24 × 20 in., 61 × 50,8 cm.

Signed and dated: *Robineau | 1787 London*

Full-length, standing in a landscape, holding a cane and wearing the star of the Garter.

Presumably painted for the Prince; recorded in store at Carlton House in 1816 (309; the Carlton House label is still on the back).

The figure is very close to that of the Prince in No. 1050. The vaguely oriental flavour of the buildings in the distance may be an allusion to the Pavilion at Brighton.

1047. GEORGE IV WHEN PRINCE OF WALES

Windsor Castle (1552). 30 × 25¼ in., 76,2 × 64,1 cm.; No. 1047 is a rectangular canvas, but has been for a long time framed as an oval.

Head and shoulders in a red coat with the ribbon and star of the Garter.

Probably painted for John Santhague (No. 1114); bought by Jutsham for George IV at Santhague's sale, 3 October 1821, for twenty-six shillings (Jutsham, *Receipts*, f. 151: '. . . in a Gilt Frame—by Robini'; Carlton House 1816 inv., additional No. 591).

Probably painted *c.* 1787; the type is very close to No. 1046.

1048. KARL FRIEDRICH ABEL (1725–87)
(Plate 136)

Kew (*Hampton Court* No. 938). 30½ × 25¼ in., 77,5 × 64,1 cm.

The signature and date (*C. Robineau 1780*), recorded in 1842, is now indecipherable in detail. It is on the back of the chair behind the sitter.

Half-length, seated at a harpsichord.

In the collection of George IV; recorded in store at Carlton House in 1816 (378: 'A half length of Mr Abel, the musician. Richard Wilson'; the Carlton House 1816 label is still on the back); later at Hampton Court, Kensington and Buckingham Palace.

Literature: Law, 1881, 1898 (813).

The attribution to Richard Wilson in the inventory of 1816 is inexplicable. By 1842 Mrs. Jameson (vol. II, p. 402) had recorded Robineau's signature and the date (W. G. Constable, *Richard Wilson* (1953), p. 65). A version, attributed to Fuseli, has been wrongly identified as a portrait of Haydn (R. Hughes, *Haydn* (1962), p. 87).

Composer and a famous performer on the viol da gamba. A pupil of J. S. Bach at Leipzig and, 1748–58, a member of the court band at Dresden; came to London in 1759, was taken up by the Duke of York and became one of Queen Charlotte's chamber musicians. The Queen owned the famous portrait of Abel by his friend Gainsborough (see above, p. xxi).

1049. THE CHEVALIER DE SAINT-GEORGE
(1745–99)

Windsor Castle (968). 24⅛ × 20 in., 61,3 × 51,1 cm.

Signed and dated: *Robineau 1787*.

Full-length, standing in a landscape, holding a sword; his hat and another sword, belonging to a disarmed adversary, are lying on the ground beside him.

Probably painted for George IV. Recorded in store at Carlton House in 1816 (310; the 1816 label is still on the stretcher and the Prince of Wales's seal is on the back of the canvas).

Presumably painted in London at the same time as No. 1050.

A creole and a celebrated swordsman, athlete and amateur musician; he served in the musketeers, and was 'capitaine des chasses et surintendant de la musique du duc d'Orléans'. He was apparently a favourite with the Prince of Wales and took part in fencing contests before him (e.g., No. 1050).

1050. THE FENCING-MATCH BETWEEN THE CHEVALIER DE SAINT-GEORGE AND THE CHEVALIER D'ÉON (1728–1810)

Windsor Castle (1195). 25⅛ × 30⅛ in., 63,8 × 76,5 cm.

Saint-George fencing with the Chevalier d'Éon, who is in his usual female dress, in front of a group of spectators in an interior at Carlton House; the glazing bars are decorated with the Prince of Wales's feathers. The Prince of Wales, wearing the star of the Garter, stands prominently behind the barrier; the boy in a hat beside him may be one of his younger brothers.

Probably painted for George IV. Recorded in store at Carlton House in 1816 (326; the 1816 label is still on the stretcher).

The fencing-match took place at Carlton House on 9 April 1787 in the presence of the Prince of Wales, several of the nobility, and 'many eminent Fencing Masters of London'. Robineau's picture of the scene was engraved (with slight variations) by V. M. Picot. Domenico Angelo was stated by his son, who performed before the Prince on the same day, to be among the spectators behind the Prince. A contemporary press notice stated that 'nothing could equal the quickness of the repartee, especially considering that the modern Pallas is nearly in her sixtieth year, and had to cope with a young man equally skilful and vigorous' (Henry Angelo, *Reminiscences*, ed. H. Lavers Smith (1904), vol. II, pp. 46, 421). The figure of the Prince was perhaps based on No. 1046. For the Chevalier de Saint-George see No. 1049. The Chevalier d'Éon was a famous French secret agent—and a fine swordsman—who spent much of his life disguised as a woman. It was firmly believed that he was a woman until autopsy after his death revealed the truth.

John Russell

1745–1806. Portrait-painter in pastel and oil, apprenticed to Francis Cotes. He first exhibited, at the Society of Artists, in 1768, and thereafter exhibited regularly and copiously at the Royal Academy. He was Crayon Painter to the King and the Prince of Wales and later to the Duke and Duchess of York.

Russell's statement, 12 January 1793, of money due to him from the Prince, included £26. 5s. for 'Portrait of Mrs Fitzherbert in Crayons. Kit Cat', done in 1791 (P.R.O., H.O. 73, 23). In September 1793 Solomon Hudson was paid £42. 16s. for rich frames and glasses for Russell's pastels of the Prince and Mrs. Fitzherbert which he had made in 1791 (W.R.A., Geo. 26799). The portrait of Mrs. Fitzherbert (*Fig.* XI) was in store at Carlton House in 1816 (382) and was sent to Mrs. Fitzherbert at Brighton by William IV on 5 October 1830. It is now in the possession of Lord Stafford.

1051. GEORGE IV WHEN PRINCE OF WALES
(Plate 131)

Buckingham Palace. 102½ × 71 in., 250,2 × 180,3 cm.

Inscribed: *Painted by J. Russell R.A. Crayon Painter to His Majesty and to His Royal Highness the Prince of Wales, 1791.*

Full-length, standing, in the green uniform of the Royal Kentish Bowmen with the ribbon and star of the Garter, holding a bow and leaning against a statue of Diana on which rests his hat with a regulation black plume. His gold buttons are decorated with the Prince of Wales's feathers and the initials RKB. At the base of the statue are items from an archer's equipment, including a quiver decorated with the Prince of Wales's feathers. In the distance a group of Kentish Bowmen are shooting at the butts.

Probably painted for George IV as a present to the Bowmen or to their founder, J. E. Madocks; in 1894 the portrait was in the possession of H. Madocks. It was purchased by King Edward VII from Lord Colebrooke in 1908.

On 12 January 1793 Russell sent up a statement of money due to him from the Prince of Wales, which included £73. 10s. for a portrait 'as president of the Royal Kentish Bowmen in Oil whole length superior' (P.R.O., H.O. 73, 23). It was exhibited at the Royal Academy in 1792 (182); in the previous year Russell had also exhibited (158) a portrait of the Prince, which may have been the portrait 'in Crayons', done in 1790, for which £21 was owing in 1793. The engraving of No. 1051 by Bartolozzi was published in 1795 with a dedication to the Royal Kentish Bowmen; a half-length variant, engraved by Collyer, was published in 1792. The head is extremely close in type to Russell's pastel, signed and dated 1789, in the Fogg Museum (*Fig.* XII) and to a drawing in the Witt Collection, Courtauld Institute (3671), which is inscribed, perhaps slightly later, as drawn from the life by Russell in 1794 (R.A., *British Portraits*, 1956-7 (660)). This date is impossible to accept as the drawing has every appearance of having been made *ad vivum*. No. 1051 was therefore presumably based on Russell's earlier and smaller portraits. A miniature, related to the pastel, is recorded in the collection of Mrs. Daniel McCarthy, Philadelphia; a copy in pastel of this type is at Antony.
The (Royal) Society of Kentish Bowmen was formed in 1785 and disbanded in 1802. The Prince of Wales became Patron of the Society in 1788 and was elected President in 1789. He regularised the method of scoring, laid down the values for the different rings on the target, and presented the annual trophies.
On behalf of the Surrey Bowmen the Duke of Clarence wrote to his brother on 16 July 1794, hoping that, as Patron of the Kentish Society, he would come to their festivities on 4 August. 'Tho' we must dine in tents yet we shall have venison and turtle, and perhaps for once you may be amused by the naturals of Surrey' (*Correspondence of George Prince of Wales*, vol. II, p. 445).

1052. MARTHA GUNN (1726-1815) *(Plate 133)*

Buckingham Palace. Pastel on paper: 35½ × 27½ in., 90,2 × 69,8 cm.

Signed and dated: *J Russell RA. pinxt 1795.*

Half-length, presumably standing in the sea, in a blue coat and a blue hat lined with scarlet, holding in her arms a naked child; in the background is a bathing-machine belonging to SMOAKER & CO BRIGHTON with two women dipping a girl in the waves.

Presumably executed, with No. 1053, for George IV; by his command the two pastels were sent from Carlton House to Brighton on 27 October 1814 (Jutsham, *R/D*, f. 172: 'Two Paintings in Crayons by Mr Russel—Portraits of Matha Gun & Smoaker—Two Brighton Bathers—Framed & Glazed . . .'); recorded at Buckingham Palace (691) in 1863 (*V.R. inv.*).

Literature: G. C. Williamson, *John Russell* (1894), pp. 60, 159; H. D. Roberts, *A History of the Royal Pavilion Brighton* (1939), pp. 14-17; R.A., *The First Hundred Years*, 1951-2 (378).

Exhibited at the Royal Academy in 1796 (355). W. Nutter's engraving was published on 1 June 1797 with a dedication to the Prince of Wales. A copy of No. 1052 is in the Art Gallery and Museum at Brighton.

The famous 'Brighton Bather' or 'dipper', who presumably worked in partnership with 'Old Smoaker' (No. 1053) and had 'dipped' ladies at Brighton since 1750, when Dr. Richard Russell had begun to publicise the beneficial effects of sea bathing. According to an advertisement of 5 April 1780, Martha Gunn and her colleagues had their headquarters at 3 East Street. By 1815 she had ceased to bathe her customers, but was still to be found on her usual spot on the beach at 6 o'clock every morning. She was something of a favourite at the Pavilion.

1053. JOHN 'SMOAKER' MILES (1721-94)
(Plate 134)

Buckingham Palace. Pastel on paper: 35½ × 27½ in., 90,2 × 69,8 cm.

Signed and dated: *J. Russell RA. pt / 1791*

Half-length, standing by a breakwater with a view of the beach beyond, in nautical dress, raising his hat with his right hand.

Presumably executed, with No. 1052 (q.v.), for George IV; recorded at Buckingham Palace (690) in 1863 (*V.R. inv.*).

Literature: G. C. Williamson, *John Russell* (1894), pp. 61, 160; H. D. Roberts, *A History of the Royal Pavilion Brighton* (1939), pp. 14-17; R.A., *The First Hundred Years*, 1951-2 (366).

Exhibited at the Royal Academy in 1791 (434). There is a possible *pentimento* in the drawing of the right arm.

One of the earliest known 'bathers' of gentlemen at Brighton. A fine swimmer, he was very popular with the Prince of Wales who frequently bathed under his charge. Blunt, sincere and generous, Miles was very popular and at his death the Prince ordered a sum of money to be paid to his widow.

George Samuel

d. 1823(?). Topographical draughtsman and landscape painter in oil and watercolour. He exhibited at the Royal Academy, 1785-1822, and at the British Institution, 1807-23.

1054. A VIEW OF WINDSOR CASTLE

Windsor Castle (3074). 41¾ × 71¾ in., 106 × 182,2 cm.

Signed and dated: *G. Samuel. 1816*

A view of the Castle from the north-west with the River Thames in the foreground.

Purchased in November 1924 from E. Parsons & Sons by Ernest Dunkels, who presented it to Her Majesty the Queen in 1956.

Samuel exhibited views of Windsor at the Royal Academy in 1817 (419: *View of Windsor Castle*) and at the British

Institution in 1818 (260, measurements, perhaps including the frame, given as 86×57 in.). No. 1054 was engraved by T. Sutherland for the frontispiece of vol. I (1819) of Pyne's *History of the Royal Residences*.

Paul Sandby

1725–1809. Landscape painter and draughtsman. His brother, Thomas, was closely associated with William, Duke of Cumberland, when he was Ranger of Windsor Forest, and with his works in the Park and Forest at Windsor and at Virginia Water; and Windsor and its environs had a profound influence on Paul Sandby. For the brothers' work at Windsor the reader is referred to A. P. Oppé, *The Drawings of Paul and Thomas Sandby . . . at Windsor Castle* (1947). Paul Sandby exhibited views of Windsor, at the Society of Artists and the Royal Academy, between 1763 and 1808. He was probably particularly active at Windsor, *c.* 1760–71.

Attributed to Paul Sandby

1055. THE NORTH TERRACE AT WINDSOR CASTLE (*Plate* 87)

Windsor Castle (991). 40×50¼ in., 101,6×127,6 cm.

A view on the terrace, with the west end of Queen Elizabeth's Gallery in the foreground, looking along to Winchester Tower. The figures strolling on the terrace include a group of children, with their attendant, and a young officer.

Recorded at Windsor in 1878 (*V.R. inv.*)·as by 'Van Assam'.

Redgrave records in the *V.R. inv.* that there had formerly been a paper label on the stretcher inscribed: 'View of the North Terrace Van Assam 1792'. Very faint traces of this can still be seen. There is apparently no record of a painter called Van Assam (or 'Van Assen' as it appears at a slightly later date) who could have painted No. 1055, and it is perhaps reasonable to attribute No. 1055 tentatively to Paul Sandby, although very little is known of his work in oil. Apart from the placing of the figures, the composition is almost identical with one of his more finished views of the North Terrace (now in the possession of Her Majesty Queen Elizabeth the Queen Mother; A. P. Oppé, *The Drawings of Paul and Thomas Sandby . . . at Windsor Castle* (1947), *Fig.* 6, p. 19), and is therefore related to drawings at Windsor (*ibid.*, Nos. 1–6). The two little girls, standing beside their attendant, are, moreover, almost identical with two in another drawing at Windsor (*ibid.*, No. 296); they are seen again in Sandby's aquatint, published on 1 September 1776, of *Windsor Terrass looking Westward*. An oil painting in Philadelphia (*Fig.* 34) is almost certainly a pendant to No. 1055 and bears the same close relationship to a finished view, in this case the gouache formerly in the collection of H.R.H. the Princess Royal (*ibid.*, *Fig.* 7, p. 21), to the aquatint of the view looking eastward, published on the same date as the other (above), and to a drawing at Windsor (Oppé, No. 8). The drawings to which the two pictures can be related appear to date from the 1770's and the two pictures may have been the two views of the terrace, looking westward (259) and eastward (260) which Sandby exhibited at the Royal Academy in 1774. It would, of course, be impossible to state that these were not water-colours as the catalogue does not mention the technique in which they were painted.

George Sanders

1774–1846. Portrait-painter in miniature and on the scale of life. A native of Fifeshire, he came to London from Edinburgh in 1805 and had an immediate success. By 1811 he had given up painting miniatures. He has frequently been confused with George Lethbridge Saunders (1807–63). Of the portraits discussed below, that of Byron (No. 1056) is clearly by Sanders; and despite confusing earlier references to the portraits of Keith (No. 1058) and Princess Charlotte (No. 1057), it is unlikely that they are by, or derive from originals by, the younger painter.

1056. GEORGE GORDON, SIXTH LORD BYRON (1788–1824) (*Plate* 258)

Buckingham Palace. 44½×35⅛ in., 113×89,2 cm.

Standing on the shore of a rocky bay; behind him is a youth with a dinghy, presumably belonging to the yacht in the background.

Apparently given by Byron to his mother (*d.* 1811); thereafter with John Murray, but ultimately in the possession of John Cam Hobhouse, later Lord Broughton de Gyfford (*d.* 1869); bequeathed by his daughter, Charlotte, Lady Dorchester, to H.M. King George V in 1914; later at Windsor (2732).

Literature: Sir L. Cust, 'Notes on Pictures in the Royal Collections —XXXI', *Burl. Mag.*, vol. XXVII (1915), pp. 3–7; Collins Baker, *Windsor*, p. 283; R.A., *British Portraits*, 1956–7 (382); L. A. Marchand, *Byron a Biography* (1957), vol. I, p. 178.

Probably painted, or at least begun, in 1807 (see below). Byron had proposed visiting the Highlands in that year and the picture may commemorate the trip by boat to the Hebrides that he was planning. It was finished before he left England in July 1809 and is mentioned in letters to his mother. It may be the picture referred to in a letter of 22 June 1809: 'There is a portrait of me in oil, to be sent down to Newstead soon.' On 24 May 1810 he wrote: 'Did you ever receive a picture of me in oil by *Sanders* in *Vigo Lane*, London? (a noted limner); if not, write for it immediately; it was paid for, except the frame (if frame there be), before I left England.' On 28 June 1810 he again wrote that the portrait had been 'finished and paid for long before I left England'. On 1 July 1810 he wrote: 'I am glad you have received my portrait from Sanders. It does not *flatter* me, I think, but the subject is a bad one, and I must even do as Fletcher [i.e., his valet] does over his Greek wines—make a face and hope for better' (*Letters and Journals*, ed. R. E. Prothero, vol. I (1898), pp. 224, 275, 283, 284).
A copy was on the art-market in London in 1951, possibly one of the two copies which were in existence by 1812 (*Letters and Journals*, vol. II, p. 179). The design was engraved by W. Finden for Moore's *Life* of the poet (1830) and by E. Finden (1834); on the latter engraving the portrait is stated to have been painted in 1807.

Soon after the publication of *Childe Harold's Pilgrimage* in 1812, Byron was presented to the Regent at a ball. Later, in *Don Juan* (Canto XII, lxxxiv) he provided an unforgettable vignette of the Prince at that time: 'A Prince, the prince of princes at the time, With fascination in his very bow . . . A finished gentleman from top to toe'. They 'conversed on poetry and poets' for more than half an hour. In 1814 the Regent was, however, distressed to learn that Byron was the author of lines to Princess Charlotte sympathising with her over her father's faults (J. Richardson, *George IV* (1966), pp. 117–21).

After George Sanders

1057. PRINCESS CHARLOTTE

Windsor Castle (648). 36¾ × 29 in., 93,3 × 73,3 cm.

Half-length, her head turned to the right almost in profile, wearing a royal coronet of an unusual design; painted to be framed as an oval.

Presented to Queen Victoria on her birthday, 24 May 1845, by Leopold I, King of the Belgians (Queen Victoria's Journal, 26 May 1845; MS. Catalogue of Queen Victoria's private pictures &c: 'after Saunders. Portrait of the late Princess Charlotte (½ length) in a green velvet dress & coronet') and placed in the Sitting-room at Windsor.

Literature: Collins Baker, *Windsor*, p. 283.

A copy, painted for Queen Victoria, of the portrait (*Fig.* 35), probably painted in 1816, which is still in the collection of H.M. The King of the Belgians. Leopold I had apparently promised Queen Victoria 'a Copy of poor Aunt Charlotte's Picture by Saunders; I wish it *so* much' (W.R.A., Vic. Y, 92, 10). In sending over the copy the King described the portrait: 'The face is extremely like, and the likest that exists; the hair is a little too fair, it had become also darker' *ibid.*, Y, 71, 65). Queen Victoria was extremely pleased with the picture '. . . & it is admirably copied' (*ibid.*, Y, 92, 25). It was probably of this portrait that Leopold I was thinking when he wrote to Queen Victoria on 29 December 1843: 'Though there are things which are not quite right, however it is more Lady like than Mr. Daw's coarse paintings' (*ibid.*, Y, 70, 27). From these references it is clear that No. 1057 is a copy, but the name of artist and sitter are painted on the back of the canvas and it is of surprisingly good quality for a copy. A copy of No. 1057 in enamel was given to the Prince Consort by Queen Victoria (*V.R. inv.*, Buckingham Palace, No. 1326); on this copy the date of the original portrait is given as 1816. The original is of the same size and format as No. 1057. A good version of No. 1057 belongs to the Marquess of Lansdowne.

1058. GEORGE KEITH ELPHINSTONE, VISCOUNT KEITH (1746–1823)

Windsor Castle (3135). 50 × 40 in., 127 × 101,6 cm.

Three-quarter-length, wearing the robes of the Order of the Bath and clasping his sword in his left hand.

Inscribed later with the identity of the sitter.

Perhaps acquired by William IV. Recorded at Hampton Court in 1849 (*The Stranger's Guide* (801, unattributed); later No. 865); later at Kensington and Buckingham Palace.

Literature: Law, 1881, 1898 (24).

In its present form the design must have been painted after 2 January 1815, when Lord Keith was created G.C.B. Although No. 1058 has always been attributed to Thomas Phillips (e.g., by Law, *loc. cit.*), the head is identical with a type engraved by H. Meyer as after G. Saunders (published in 1812). This engraving shows Keith in naval uniform, wearing the star of the Bath. A version of No. 1058, sold at Sotheby's, 20 June 1951 (39), and now in the National Maritime Museum, had perhaps passed by descent from the sitter's daughter, Margaret. It was attributed to G. L. Saunders. Other versions in robes exist, at three-quarter-length (i.e. in the collections of the Marquess of Lansdowne and of Lord Elphinstone) or head and shoulders (i.e., at Keith Hall); Saunders is in all cases given as the painter of the original, but G. L. Saunders was born in 1807 and

could hardly have evolved this type. It is probable that No. 1058 represents a type for which Keith did not give a fresh sitting, but which was painted to record his elevation in the Order of the Bath; it appears to be the work of a copyist.

See No. 845.

Francis Sartorius

1735–1804. Sporting painter, son of John and father of John Nost Sartorius. He exhibited at the Royal Academy between 1775 and 1790; he also exhibited at the Free Society, 1773–83, and at the Society of Artists between 1778 and 1791.

1059. GEORGE III's CHARGER

Windsor Castle (965). 51 × 40 in., 129,5 × 101,6 cm.

Signed: *Fs Sartorius. Pinxt*

A white charger, wearing saddle and bridle and scarlet saddle-cloth laced with gold, held by a groom in royal livery (scarlet coat, blue waistcoat, all laced with gold) in a wooded landscape with a stretch of water in the distance.

Perhaps painted for George III, but recorded in store at Carlton House in 1816 (432: 'His Majesty's white charger led by a groom in the royal livery. Sartorius'); sent to the King's Lodge on 31 May 1822 (Jutsham, *Deliveries*, f. 35); later at Windsor (965) and Cumberland Lodge.

Probably painted c. 1785. A variant, signed and dated 1786, was in the De la Pole sale at Christie's, 24 February 1922 (14).

1060. TWO COACH HORSES (*Plate* 88)

Buckingham Palace. 40 × 50½ in., 101,6 × 128,3 cm.

Signed: *Fs Sartorius | Pinxt*

A pair of cream horses, wearing state harness, standing in a landscape near a stable; by the stable door is a groom in blue livery.

Perhaps painted for George III, but more probably for George IV. Recorded in store at Carlton House in 1816 (427: 'A pair of cream-coloured horses, harnessed, with a boy at the stable door. Sartorius'); sent to the King's Lodge on 31 May 1822 (Jutsham, *Deliveries*, f. 34); later at Windsor (1673) and Cumberland Lodge.

Presumably the picture exhibited at the Royal Academy in 1789 (392: *A pair of His Majesty's coach-horses*). There appears to be a confused area on the left, where Sartorius may at first have intended to paint a barn or a shed.

John Nost Sartorius

1759–after 1824. Sporting painter, son of Francis Sartorius. He exhibited at the Society of Arts between 1776 and 1783 and at the Royal Academy, 1781–1824.

1061. BARONET WITH SAMUEL CHIFNEY UP

Buckingham Palace. 25¾ × 30¾ in., 65,4 × 78,1 cm.

Signed: *J N Sartorius, pinxt*

Possibly acquired by King Edward VII; recorded in the Billiard Room at Buckingham Palace in 1909 (p. 260).

A derivation from Stubbs's picture of the same subject (see No. 1118).

Johan Jacob Schalch

1723–89. Landscape and animal painter, born in Schaffhausen, who worked in France and Germany. He was apparently in England in the 1750's and in 1761 he exhibited at the Society of Artists three landscapes (96–8) of which one was a view in Richmond Park.

1062. A VIEW OF FROGMORE

Windsor Castle (3136). 29¾ × 40⅝ in., 75,6 × 103,2 cm.

A view across the lake to Frogmore House, with labourers and carts in the foreground.

Presumably acquired by George IV. Recorded in store at Carlton House in 1816 (226: 'A view in Windsor-Park, with a man driving a cart. Johan Jacob Schalck', measurements given as 30 × 40½ in.); later at Buckingham Palace (806).

Nos. 1062–5 were painted *c.* 1760. They therefore probably show Frogmore House and its setting as they were when Sir Edward Walpole lived there and were painted about thirty years before Wyatt converted the house into the 'elegant villa' he designed for Queen Charlotte.

1063. A VIEW OF FROGMORE

Windsor Castle (1499). 29½ × 40⅝ in., 74,9 × 103,2 cm.

Signed: *Johan Jacob Schalch*

A view across the lake to Frogmore House with swans and sheep in the foreground.

Presumably acquired by George IV. Recorded in store at Carlton House in 1816 (227: 'A view in Windsor-Park, with swans, ducks, sheep, and a lodge in the background. Johan Jacob Schalck', measurements given as 30 × 40½ in.).

See No. 1062.

1064. A VIEW AT FROGMORE

Windsor Castle (1486). 29¾ × 40¼ in., 75,6 × 102,2 cm.

A view of the lake with swans on the water in the foreground, the bridge on the left, a small classical temple in the distance and two labourers mowing on a bank on the right.

Presumably acquired by George IV. Recorded in store at Carlton House in 1816 (225: 'A view in Windsor-Park, with swans and a boat in the water, and a chinese bridge. Johan Jacob Schalck', measurements given as 30 × 40½ in.).

See No. 1062.

1065. A VIEW AT FROGMORE

Windsor Castle (997). 30 × 40¾ in., 76,2 × 103,5 cm.

The signature, *Johan Jacob Schalch*, was recorded in 1878 (*V.R. inv.*), but cannot now be discerned.

A view of the lake by moonlight, near the bridge, with sheep on the bank.

Presumably acquired by George IV. Recorded in store at Carlton House in 1816 (224: 'A view in Windsor-Park, by moonlight. Johan Jacob Schalck', measurements given as 30 × 40½ in.).

See No. 1062.

1066. A VIEW AT FROGMORE

Windsor Castle (1135). 19⅜ × 25 in., 49,2 × 63,5 cm.

The signature of the artist is apparently recorded in a later note on the *V.R. inv.*, but cannot now be discerned.

A view of the lake near the bridge, with sheep on a bank and a little temple in the distance.

Presumably acquired by George IV. Recorded in store at Carlton House in 1816 (229: 'Another view in Windsor-Park, with sheep grazing and a Chinese bridge', measurements given as 19 × 24½ in.).

Probably painted at the same period as Nos. 1062–5.

1067. LANDSCAPE WITH FIGURES

Buckingham Palace. 29⅝ × 40¾ in., 75,2 × 103,5 cm.

Signed: *Jacob Schalch. fecit*

A mountainous landscape with a river flowing past ruins and under a ruinous bridge; in the foreground is a woman with children and a dog.

Recorded in the Coffee Room at Kew (Geo. III, *Kew*); taken to Buckingham Palace (1197) in 1877.

Nos. 1067, 1068 may originally have formed part of a set of pictures painted by Schalch for Augusta, Princess of Wales. On 14 July 1759 Schalch signed a receipt for two hundred guineas 'for four Pictures' for the Princess (W.R.A., Geo. 55465). Nos. 1067, 1068 are in particularly fine contemporary English carved frames (H. Clifford Smith, *Buckingham Palace* (1930), p. 227).

1068. LANDSCAPE WITH A RIVER

Buckingham Palace. 29½ × 40¾ in., 74,9 × 103,5 cm.

Signed: *Jacob Schalch.* Redgrave in 1870 (*V.R. inv.*) appears to have read also the date 1755, but this is now indecipherable.

A river running through a rocky valley; a fisherman is seated with a dog in the foreground and cows are on a bank on the left.

Recorded with No. 1067 in the Coffee Room at Kew (Geo. III, *Kew*); taken to Buckingham Palace (1198) in 1877. A very early label on the back of the frame is inscribed: 'Breakfast Room / [over door] from dining room'.

See No. 1067.

Charles Henry Schwanfelder

1773–1837. Animal, sporting and portrait-painter, born in Leeds, where he worked all his life. He exhibited at the Royal Academy between 1809 and 1835 and was Animal Painter to George IV, 1817–21.

1069. THE MALCOLM ARABIAN (*Plate* 260)

Windsor Castle (2320). 48⅜ × 60⅜ in., 122,9 × 153,3 cm.

Signed and dated: *C. H. Schwanfelder / 1814.*

A grey, with dark mane and tail, trotting in a mountainous landscape in which is a group of Arabs.

Presumably painted for George IV. It was received from the painter in July 1814: '. . . A Gray Horse & Landscape the Malcolmn Arabian—by Mr Schwanfelder—in a Gilt Frame the Frame made by Mr Smith' (Jutsham, *R/D*, f. 319); recorded in store at Carlton House in 1816 (408); sent to the King's Lodge on 31 May 1822 (Jutsham, *Deliveries*, f. 33). Later at Stud Lodge (1151).

Presumably the picture exhibited by Schwanfelder at the Royal Academy in 1814 (324: *Malcolm, an Arabian, the property of H.R.H. the Prince Regent*). The Arabian, fifteen hands high and weighing twenty stone, had been foaled *c.* 1805 in the stud of the ruler of the Arabian peninsula, who presented him, as a colt, to the Pasha of Baghdad. Colonel Malcolm, who was present when the Pasha was killed in action, obtained the horse and sent it to England.

1070. PORTRAIT OF A HORSE

Windsor Castle (2318). 28 × 36 in., 71,1 × 91,4 cm.

Signed and dated: *C. H. Schwanfelder | 1814.*

A chestnut horse in a paddock.

Probably painted for George IV. Recorded in store at Carlton House in 1816 (440); sent to the King's Lodge on 31 May 1822 (Jutsham, *Deliveries,* f. 36). Later at Stud Lodge (1167).

There is a slight *pentimento* in the ears, which were originally pricked up and are now laid back.

1071. PORTRAIT OF A HORSE

Windsor Castle (2319). 28 × 36⅛ in., 71,1 × 91,8 cm.

Signed and dated: *C. H. Schwanfelder | 1814.*

A bay horse, standing in a landscape of fields and woods.

Probably painted for George IV. Recorded in store at Carlton House in 1816 (441); sent to the King's Lodge on 31 May 1822 (Jutsham, *Deliveries,* f. 36). Later at Stud Lodge (1160).

Dominic Serres

1722–93. Marine painter. A native of Gascony, he ran away to sea, but was captured by a British frigate and came to England *c.* 1758. He exhibited at the Society of Artists, 1765–8, and at the Free Society, 1761–4, and became a founder member of the Royal Academy (see No. 1210), where he exhibited, 1769–93. He was Marine Painter to George III.

1072. THE ROYAL VISIT TO THE FLEET: I
(*Plate* 81)

Buckingham Palace. 60½ × 96 in., 153,7 × 243,8 cm.

Signed and dated: *D. Serres | 1774.*

George III, on board the *Barfleur,* saluted by the fleet.

The four episodes from the royal visit, Nos. 1072–5, presumably painted for George III, were recorded in the Medal Room at Buckingham House in 1819 (985–8); the pictures were later taken to Windsor and later, probably all on 25 April 1832, to Hampton Court (No. 1072 bears inv. No. 1012) and Kensington.

Literature: (for the set) Law, 1881, 1898 (875).

The royal visit lasted from 22 to 26 June 1773.[1] The King arrived at Portsmouth in the morning of 22 June. At 1.30 p.m. he embarked in a barge and went on board the *Barfleur* of 90 guns at Spithead, where he was received by the Board of Admiralty. At 3.30 he sat down to a table of thirty covers; he re-embarked in his barge at 6 o'clock. In No. 1072 the *Barfleur* is seen surrounded by the barges of the Board of Admiralty, the three Flag Officers and all the Captains. The flag of the Lord High Admiral, the Royal Standard and the Union flag had been hoisted in the *Barfleur* when the King came on board; 'on the sight of which all the ships, except the *Barfleur,* saluted with twenty-one guns each'. On the right of the *Barfleur* in No. 1072 can be seen the *Royal Oak* with the flag of Thomas Pye, Vice-Admiral of the Red, and the *Dublin* with the flag of Lord Edgcumbe as Vice-Admiral

1. There is a full account of the review in the *Annual Register* for 1773, pp. 202–7.

of the Blue. No. 1072 was exhibited at the Royal Academy in 1774 (269: *His Majesty saluted by the Fleet at his arrival on board the Barfleur at Spithead*). A smaller version, also signed and dated 1774, is in the collection of Col. K. E. Savill.
In the Royal United Service Institution is (A35/25) a 'Plan Elevation and Perspective View' in watercolour by Serres (signed and dated 1773) of the ships drawn up for review.

1073. THE ROYAL VISIT TO THE FLEET: II

Buckingham Palace. 60 × 96 in., 152,4 × 243,8 cm.

Signed and dated: *D. Serres. 1775.*

George III, on board the *Augusta* yacht, sailing from Spithead towards St. Helens with the Plymouth Squadron.

See No. 1072; No. 1073 bears Hampton Court No. 1013.

On 25 June 1773 the King sailed in the *Augusta* yacht from Spithead to Sandown Bay. When the yacht arrived at Spithead, Lord Edgcumbe, with his division, got under sail and followed His Majesty. In No. 1073 Lord Edgcumbe is seen leading his squadron with a St. George at the fore to indicate a Vice-Admiral of the White. No. 1073 was exhibited at the Royal Academy in 1775 (288).

1074. THE ROYAL VISIT TO THE FLEET: III
(*Plate* 82)

Buckingham Palace. 60 × 96½ in., 152,4 × 245,1 cm.

Signed and dated: *D. Serres. 1775.*

George III, on board the *Augusta* yacht, returning to Spithead.

See No. 1072; No. 1074 bears Hampton Court No. 1011.

See No. 1073. In No. 1074 the yacht is seen, with the King in the stern, on the return voyage to Spithead in the afternoon and evening of 25 June 1773. The yacht is running before a fresh breeze off the east coast of the Isle of Wight; Culver Cliff is seen in the distance on the left. According to the *Annual Register,* 'In all the processions before-mentioned, both to Spithead and back again, a very great number of yachts, and other sailing vessels and boats, many of them full of nobility and gentry, accompanied the barges, as well as the Augusta yacht, while the King was on board'. On 26 June the King returned to Kew. No. 1074 was exhibited at the Royal Academy in 1775 (289: *His Majesty's return to Spithead*).

1075. THE ROYAL VISIT TO THE FLEET: IV

Buckingham Palace. 60½ × 96½ in., 153,7 × 245,1 cm.

Signed: *D. Serres 177[?5]*

Ships, yachts and small boats; a salute is being fired.

See No. 1072; No. 1075 bears Hampton Court No. 1014.

No. 1075 presumably records an episode during the visit of the King to the fleet on 23 and 24 June 1773 (see No. 1072). Mr. Michael Robinson has suggested that No. 1075 may show the moment on the afternoon of 24 June when, after Vice-Admiral Thomas Pye had been promoted Admiral of the Blue, he kissed the King's hand, hoisted his flag in the *Royal Oak* and was saluted by all the ships present except the *Barfleur.* The *Barfleur* is probably the ship in the background which is not saluting.

1076. A CALM

Buckingham Palace. 17¼ × 25 in., 43,8 × 63,5 cm.

Signed and dated: *D. Serres. 1789.*

A frigate with other vessels becalmed; a ship's boat is pulling towards the spectator.

Recorded at Hampton Court in 1849 (*The Stranger's Guide*, No. 1007; later No. 1046); later at Kensington.

Literature: Law, 1881, 1898 (886).

John Thomas Serres

1759–1825. Topographical and marine painter, son of Dominic Serres, whom he succeeded as Marine Painter to the King. He was recorded as Marine Painter to the Duke of Clarence from as early as 1790. His marriage to Olivia Wilmot was unhappy and resulted in a separation in 1804, but he suffered much from her persecutions and died in debt as a result of her claims.

1077. THE THAMES NEAR LIMEHOUSE
(*Plate* 155)

Kensington Palace. 42 × 60½ in., 106,7 × 153,7 cm.

Signed and dated [*J.T.*] *SERRES. 1790*

Vessels of various kinds on the Thames at Limehouse; the church of St. Anne is seen in the distance.

Recorded at Hampton Court in 1849 (*The Stranger's Guide*, No. 988; later inv. No. 1025).

Probably the picture exhibited at the Royal Academy in 1790 (86: *View on the Thames, looking towards Limehouse church*). The view is apparently taken from near the Timber Yards on the river, slightly below St. Anne's and just below Mr. Bateson's Yard.

1078. THE THAMES AT WINDSOR BRIDGE
(*Plate* 154)

Windsor Castle (2342). 43⅛ × 48 in., 109,5 × 121,9 cm.

Signed and dated: *I.T. SERRES | Pinxt 1798*

A carriage, presumably carrying the King, crossing the old bridge between Windsor and Eton with an escort of cavalry; on the river is a barge with the Royal standard at the stern.

Sold by A. K. Sadgrove at Christie's, 3 July 1886 (177), bt. Parker, from whom it was purchased by Queen Victoria in February 1887 (P.R.O., L.C.1/473, 12, 21, 71).

1079. THE ROYAL YACHT, THE *ROYAL GEORGE*, AT PORTSMOUTH

Buckingham Palace. 37 × 49 in., 94 × 124,5 cm.

Signed and dated: *J.T. SERRES. | 1820*

The *Royal George* off Portsmouth Harbour; the Signal Tower is clearly seen. The yacht flies the Royal Standard, Admiralty Flag and the Red Ensign. The King is apparently on board (? wearing the Garter star and ribbon) with a group of sailors, officers, ladies and gentlemen, among them one wearing the Garter who may be the Duke of York. In the left foreground fisherfolk are selling fish; on the sail of their boat is the name *STAG of Cowes*.

Presumably painted for George IV. It was received at Carlton House from the artist between 16 and 24 February 1821 (Jutsham, *Receipts*, f. 131: '. . . His Majesty's Yacht laying in Portsmouth Harbour—by Mr Serris'); additional No. 580 in the Carlton House inv. of 1816. Sent to the King's Lodge on 27 September 1823, but only for a short time (Jutsham, *Deliveries*, f. 48); later at Hampton Court (1035) and Kensington.

Literature: Law, 1881, 1898 (905); C. M. Gavin, *Royal Yachts* (1932), pp. 106–7.

The *Royal George* of 330 tons, designed by Sir Henry Peake, had been laid down at Deptford in 1814 and launched three years later. In 1822 the King sailed in her from the Thames to the Firth of Forth for his visit to Edinburgh. In 1834 she took Queen Adelaide to Holland. Queen Victoria went in 1842 on her only cruise in her, to Leith; she was not finally broken up until 1905. The Prince Regent had joined the Yacht Club in 1817 and had entered the *Royal George* among the Club's yachts; he made a number of trips off the coast near Brighton.

1080. THE BATTLE OF CAMPERDOWN: I. THE BEGINNING OF THE ACTION

Buckingham Palace. 36⅛ × 48 in., 91,8 × 121,9 cm.

Signed and dated: *J. T. Serres. 1798.*

The British fleet, soon after noon on 11 October 1797, bearing down to attack the Dutch fleet. On the right the *Monarch*, flagship of Vice-Admiral Richard Onslow, is cutting through under the bows of the Dutch Vice-Admiral; in the centre the *Ardent* is bearing down on Admiral De Winter's flagship, the *Vryheid*; nearby in the centre the *Venerable*, Admiral Duncan's flagship, passes through the enemy's lines. On the left is the *Circe* frigate which had been active before the battle in reporting the enemy's movements. The *Triumph*, *Agincourt* and *Monmouth* are nearest to the spectator.

Nos. 1080, 1081 were perhaps in the collection of William IV; they are recorded at Hampton Court (No. 1080 bears later No. 1053) by Mrs. Jameson (p. 418) and in 1849 (*The Stranger's Guide*, Nos. 956, 970) and were later at Kensington.

Literature: Law, 1881, 1898 (892).

The design is identical with that engraved by Ralph Dodd as painted by himself. The engraving was published in March 1798 with an explanatory key on which the above description is partly based. Dodd exhibited at the Royal Academy in 1798 (586) a picture of the battle. It is probable that Nos. 1080, 1081 were copied by Serres from Dodd's engravings.

The battle was fought off Camperdown in the Texel on 11 October 1797 between Admiral, later Viscount, Duncan (1731–1804) and a Dutch fleet under Admiral De Winter; it was fiercely contested, but ended in a conclusive victory for the British and removed the danger of an invasion launched from Holland. The *Monarch* broke the enemy's line at 12.54 p.m.; Vice-Admiral Onslow, in the words of Admiral Duncan, 'bore down on the Enemy's Rear in the most gallant Manner, his Division following his Example'.

1081. THE BATTLE OF CAMPERDOWN: II. THE CLOSE OF THE ACTION

Buckingham Palace. 36¼ × 48 in., 92,1 × 121,9 cm.

Signed and dated: [*J T*] Serres [*1798*]; the signature and date are now very obscure.

The scene on the afternoon of 11 October 1797. The Dutch flagship, the *Vryheid*, is slowly returning the *Venerable*'s fire; on the right is the *Hercules*, a Dutch ship of sixty-four guns, ablaze; and on the extreme left is the *Wassenaar*, which was compelled to strike. In the foreground a British boat is rescuing the sole survivor from a boat that had put off from the *Hercules*.

See No. 1080; No. 1081 bore Hampton Court No. 1064.

Literature: Law, 1881, 1898 (904).

See No. 1080. The design is identical with that engraved by Ralph Dodd as painted by himself. The engraving was published in March 1798 with an explanatory key. The firing ceased at 3 p.m. All the masts on the Dutch flagship had gone by the board and she eventually surrendered, having attempted in vain to force a way through five English ships.

Olivia Serres

1772–1834. Amateur landscape-painter. Daughter of Robert Wilmot, a house-painter, she married J. T. Serres, from whom she was receiving drawing lessons, in 1791. In 1806 she was appointed Landscape Painter to the Prince of Wales and in 1817 she first put forward her claim to be regarded as 'Princess Olive of Cumberland', daughter of Henry, Duke of Cumberland, by Mrs. Payne. Her claim was finally dismissed in 1823 and she died in poverty. She exhibited at the Royal Academy between 1793 and 1808 and at the British Institution, 1806–11.

1082. CLASSICAL LANDSCAPE WITH FIGURES

Windsor Castle (1179). 24¾ × 29¾ in., 62,9 × 75,6 cm.

Fishermen by a river; on the right is a church at the top of a steep cliff.

Nos. 1082, 1083 were presumably presented by the artist to George IV. On 10 December 1807 they were received from her at Carlton House: 'Two Landscapes with Figures—Gilt Frames'. They were sent to Red House (Jutsham, *R/D*, f. 29); in 1816 they were recorded in store at Carlton House (No. 1082 bears the 1816 inv. No. 219).

Nos. 1082, 1083 are pastiches of Richard Wilson.

1083. CLASSICAL LANDSCAPE WITH FIGURES

Windsor Castle (1180). 25 × 29¾ in., 63,5 × 75,6 cm.

A fisherman with a woman and a dog by the side of a lake in a wooded landscape.

See No. 1082; No. 1083 bears the 1816 inv. No. 220.

A companion to No. 1082.

Sir Martin Archer Shee

1769–1850. Portrait-painter. Born in Dublin, he came to London in 1788. President of the Royal Academy, 1830–50; he exhibited there, 1789–1845.

1084. WILLIAM IV (*Plate* 301)

Windsor Castle (171). 106½ × 70½ in., 270,5 × 178,1 cm.

Full-length, standing, in Garter robes with his right hand on his sword and St. Edward's Crown and sceptre beside him; in the distance is a view of Windsor Castle.

Painted for the King.

Literature: M. A. Shee, *The Life of Sir Martin Archer Shee* (1860), vol. II, pp. 37–43; Collins Baker, *Windsor*, p. 286.

Painted in 1833. On 19 September Shee wrote that Lord Wellesley's portrait (No. 1088) had been admired by the King and that Wellesley had communicated to him the King's promise to sit 'to me for his portrait, to be sent to Lord Wellesley in Ireland'. On 7 November Shee went to Brighton and within two or three days began the portrait;

the King gave sittings in one of the State Apartments in the Pavilion. On 10 November Shee wrote to his wife: 'The King sat today for an hour and half; I worked at the rate of a steam engine of forty-horse power, and had the whole court circle in admiration of the progress I had made. The King's favourite daughter, Lady Sidney, came in during the sitting, and exclaimed that it was very like already.' Nine days later he wrote again that everything at the Pavilion was '*couleur de rose*', that the Queen had described the portrait as 'the best by far that had ever been painted of the King' and that he hoped to finish the head soon. The King, at the Queen's request, 'decided that the portrait should be completed as a commission from himself and placed in Windsor Castle'; he promised at the same time to sit for a portrait 'of the same size and class' for Lord Wellesley. The portrait was exhibited at the Royal Academy in 1834 (67) and thereafter placed in the Throne Room at Windsor, where it is still to be seen; C. Turner's engraving of it was published on 2 January 1836. In No. 1084 there are small *pentimenti* in the robes, e.g., on the King's left shoulder. The version at the Royal Academy (see No. 1089) was commissioned by the Academy and exhibited there in 1835 (63; R.A., *British Portraits*, 1956–7 (524)).

1085. QUEEN ADELAIDE (*Plate* 300)

Buckingham Palace. 99¼ × 63¾ in., 252,1 × 161,9 cm.

Full-length, standing, wearing a feathered hat and holding a handkerchief in her right hand; her rich crimson velvet pelisse is trimmed with ermine. In the background is a terrace with a view of a valley and a distant town.

Painted for William IV and set up later on the Principal Staircase at Buckingham Palace (*V.R. inv.*, 1864, No. 221; *Buckingham Palace*, 1909, p. 35).

Literature: M. A. Shee, *The Life of Sir Martin Archer Shee* (1860), vol. II, pp. 89–92; Minutes of the Court of Assistants of the Goldsmiths' Company, 26 February 1836 and 24 November 1837.

Shee received the King's commands to be in attendance at Windsor from 14 May 1836 in order to begin a full-length of the Queen to be placed in the hall of the Goldsmiths' Company; the Court of Assistants of the Company had been informed on 26 February 1836 that the Queen wished to present them with a portrait and had given Shee instructions to this end. By 18 May he had received a second sitting; he thought the 'high approbation' that had been expressed was almost ridiculous in view of the small progress he had made, but everyone, from the King downwards, was anticipating 'a most agreeable likeness'. The Queen, however, presented difficulties as a subject 'beyond anything I could have anticipated'; she 'particularly requests that the picture may not be flattered'. When the portrait was completed, the King was so pleased with its composition and execution that he retained it for himself; Shee was therefore commissioned by the Queen to produce another portrait for the Goldsmiths (M. A. Shee, *loc. cit.*); this second version was completed by 24 November 1837 and is still in their Hall. Queen Adelaide's disbursements, 30 September–31 December 1837 include £766. 10s. to Shee for two full-lengths of herself (W.R.A., Geo. 89746). No. 1085 was exhibited at the Royal Academy in 1837 (68).

1086. HENRY PAGET, SECOND EARL OF UXBRIDGE AND FIRST MARQUESS OF ANGLESEY (1768–1854)

Windsor Castle (193). 106¾ × 70½ in., 271,1 × 179,1 cm.

Full-length, standing, in uniform as General of Hussars,

wearing the ribbon and star of the Garter, the badge of a G.C.B., and the Waterloo Medal.

Painted for William IV and placed in the Waterloo Chamber, where it was recorded in 1837 (*Guide* to the Castle).

Literature: Collins Baker, *Windsor*, p. 287.

Exhibited at the Royal Academy in 1836 (59), when it was stated to have been painted at the command of William IV to be placed in the Waterloo Chamber; it was admired at the exhibition by Princess Victoria (*Journal*, 18 July 1836).
Colonel of the 7th Light Dragoons (Hussars), 1797–1842; served in the Low Countries; commanded the cavalry under Sir John Moore in Spain; and, with skill, heroism and energy, commanded the cavalry and light artillery at Waterloo (see No. 764), where he lost a leg. Lord Steward at the coronation of George IV; Master-General of the Ordnance, 1827, 1846; Lord-Lieutenant of Ireland, 1828–9, 1830–3; Field-Marshal, 1846. Stockmar described him as 'a tall well-made man; wild, martial face, high forehead, with a large hawk's nose . . . A great deal of ease in his manners'.

1087. SIR THOMAS PICTON (1758–1815)

Windsor Castle (210). 50 × 40 in., 127 × 101,6 cm.

Three-quarter-length, standing, in the uniform of a Lieutenant-General, wearing the ribbon and star of the Bath and the badge of the Order of the Tower and Sword of Portugal; he rests his right hand on his sword.

Painted for William IV and placed in the Waterloo Chamber, where it was recorded in 1837 (*Guide* to the Castle).

Literature: Collins Baker, *Windsor*, p. 286.

Exhibited at the Royal Academy in 1836 (54), when it was stated to have been painted at the command of William IV to be placed in the Waterloo Chamber. An engraving of this type was published by C. Turner in 1843. No. 1087 is a posthumous portrait, based by Shee on his earlier portrait, now in the National Portrait Gallery (126), of which an engraving by Easling had been published in November 1810.
Gazetted Ensign in the 12th Regiment of Foot in 1771; commandant and military governor of Trinidad, 1797–1803; appointed in 1810 to command the 3rd Division in the Peninsula; he commanded the 5th Division and the reserve at Waterloo, where he was killed leading a charge by his 2nd Brigade. 'I found him', said Wellington, 'a rough foul-mouthed devil as ever lived, but he always behaved extremely well; no man could do better in different services I assigned to him.'

1088. RICHARD COLLEY WELLESLEY, MARQUESS WELLESLEY (1760–1842)

Buckingham Palace. 101¾ × 70½ in., 258,4 × 179,1 cm.; a small area of canvas has been turned over at the top (*c.* 1¼ in.) and bottom (*c.* ¾ in.).

Full-length, standing in Garter robes as Lord Steward, with his staff in his right hand and wearing round his neck the badge of the Grand Master of the Order of St. Patrick; in the background is a view of Westminster Abbey.

Presented by the sitter to William IV, who placed the portrait at Windsor. Recorded in the Master of the Household's Corridor at Buckingham Palace in 1876 (*V.R. inv.*, No. 552); later moved into the Green Drawing-Room to occupy the position and frame then filled by No. 712. The frame is one of the fine tabernacle frames, probably made for Augusta, Princess of Wales (see Nos. 720, 869); on the frame is written 'Prince's Picture', a possible indication that the frame was used at one time for No. 834.

Literature: M. A. Shee, *The Life of Sir Martin Archer Shee* (1860), vol. II, pp. 35–7.

Exhibited at the Royal Academy in 1833 (154). Lord Wellesley vacated the office of Lord Steward on assuming, for a second time, the Lord Lieutenancy of Ireland. He was entitled to wear the badge of the Order of St. Patrick as having been the Grand Master of the Order in his first term of office as Lord-Lieutenant, 1821–8. Lord Wellesley apparently requested permission to present the portrait to William IV on giving up the office of Lord Steward. He was a patron of Shee and seems to have been responsible for bringing him to the favourable notice of William IV (see No. 1084) who 'agreed in the public admiration which had been expressed' of the portrait of Wellesley (M. A. Shee, *loc. cit.*). There is a variant of No. 1088 by Fortescue Bates at Stratfield Saye.

See No. 916.

After Sir Martin Archer Shee

1089. WILLIAM IV

St. James's Palace. 106½ × 70 in., 270,5 × 177,8 cm.

A copy painted in 1865 by Glasgow for the set of portraits of sovereigns at St. James's Palace (*V.R. inv.*). It was painted, not from No. 1084, but from the version at the Royal Academy.

1090. LLOYD, FIRST BARON KENYON (1732–1802)

Windsor Castle (360). 30 × 25 in., 76,2 × 63,5 cm.

Head and shoulders, wearing robes and collar of the Lord Chief Justice.

Presented to George IV by the second Lord Kenyon and received at Carlton House in April 1829 (Jutsham, *Receipts*, f. 266: 'The half Lenth Portrait of the Late Lord Kenyon in a Gilt Frame . . . I believe was presented by Lord Kenyon to His Majesty through . . . The Duke of Cumberland and sent to N 105 Pall Mall by Mr Seguier, & by him sent to Windsor Castle'). Recorded at Windsor in 1865 (*V.R. inv.*).

An early copy from the three-quarter-length (*c.* 1800), still in the possession of Lord Kenyon, which was formerly attributed to Romney (e.g., J. Steegman, *A Survey of Portraits in Welsh Houses*, vol. I (1957), p. 154) but was engraved by W. Hall (1833) as by Shee. Copies similar to No. 1090 are in the Middle Temple and the National Portrait Gallery (469), the latter made by Davidson in 1839.
Admitted student at the Middle Temple, 1750; K.C., 1780; Attorney-General, 1782–3, 1783–4; Lord Chief Justice of the King's Bench, 1788–1802. A sound and honest lawyer, liked by George III who, as he records, on one occasion (15 March 1800) took him for a long walk 'to show me the place where he meant to build his new house at Kew'.

Henry Singleton

1766–1839. Painter of portraits and subject-pictures; a prolific illustrator of books. In 1780 he exhibited at the Society of Artists; thereafter he exhibited regularly at the Royal Academy between 1784 and 1839 and at the British Institution between 1806 and 1839.

1091. THE MARRIAGE OF GEORGE, PRINCE
OF WALES (*Plate* 171)

Buckingham Palace. 19¼×24 in., 48,9×61 cm.

Signed and dated: *H. Singleton | 1795.*

The Prince, standing before the altar in the Chapel Royal,
St. James's Palace, about to place the ring on his bride's
finger. Behind are the Archbishop of Canterbury, John
Moore, and the Bishop of London, Beilby Porteous. On the
left, under a canopy, is seated George III with, behind him,
the Dukes of Kent (?), Gloucester (?) and York; on the
right is the Queen. Maids of Honour and bridesmaids are
grouped on either side.

Recorded in the collection of Edward VII when Prince of Wales
in 1877 (*A Catalogue of the Works of Art at Marlborough House and at
Sandringham Norfolk belonging to Their Royal Highnesses the Prince and
Princess of Wales* (1877), p. 75).

The disposition of the principal figures is not unlike the
arrangement in Hamilton's sketch of the same subject (No.
827); for artistic reasons, presumably, the attendant figures
are placed between the altar and the King and Queen
whereas Hamilton placed them more to the sides of the
Chapel Royal and behind the King and Queen. The Prince
of Wales, in No. 1091, wears the Garter ribbon with the
collar, which is probably incorrect. The King's costume is
different in the two pictures: Hamilton dressed him in blue
with the collar of the Garter, Singleton in red with the
ribbon and star. Singleton clearly attempted accurate
portraits of many of the figures in his design. Among Singleton's drawings in the British Museum is a study (L.B. 26)
of the head of a cleric, possibly connected with No. 1091.

Thomas Stothard

1755–1834. Book-illustrator, decorative designer and painter
of biblical, mythological, historical, classical and literary
subjects.
In 1807 Hoppner took round to Carlton House Stothard's
Canterbury Pilgrims. The Prince of Wales admired the picture
and accepted the dedication of Cromek's engraving of it
(W. T. Whitley, *Art in England 1800–20* (1928), pp. 126–7).

1092. SIR RALPH ABERCROMBY AT THE
BATTLE OF ALEXANDRIA (*Plate* 230)

Kensington Palace. 44½×60½ in., 107,9×153,7 cm.

Lieutenant-General Sir Ralph Abercromby (1734–1801) lies
on the ground, his wounded thigh bound up, supported
by, on the left, his son, Colonel (later Sir John) Abercromby
(1772–1817) and, on the right, Major-General John Moore
(1761–1809) who holds in his left hand the bridle of Abercromby's horse; immediately behind Abercromby are
Brigadier-General (later Sir John) Stuart (1759–1815) and
Major-General the Hon. George James, later 3rd Earl Ludlow (1758–1842). On the extreme left Lieut.-Col. (later
General) Robert Anstruther (1768–1809) looks down on the
scene; beside him, in a hat, is Major-General John Cradock,
later 1st Lord Howden (1759–1839) and, looking up at
Anstruther, is Major-General Richard Lambart, 7th Earl of
Cavan (1763–1837). In the upper background, by a standard, is Colonel Birch. Between Lord Cavan and the group
round Abercromby are Major-General Hely-Hutchinson
(see No. 987), Brigadier-General (later Sir) Hildebrand
Oakes (1754–1822) and Captain (later Admiral Sir)
William Sidney Smith (1764–1840) with his right arm in a
sling. Standing behind Moore is the young Lieutenant-

Colonel James Kempt (see No. 935); on the extreme right
is Major (later Major-General) James Stirling (*d.* 1834) of
the 42nd Regiment.

Formerly in the possession of Sir James Kempt (*d.* 1854; see No.
935). After his death it probably passed to Sir George Cooper or
General Sir Charles Gore. It seems as if, by 24 February 1855, it
had passed into the possession of Queen Victoria, probably at the
wishes of Kempt or Gore (W.R.A., P.P. Vic. Add. 46). In 1876
it was hanging in Buckingham Palace (462).

Painted, perhaps for Sir James Kempt, soon after the event.
Sir Ralph Abercromby had died on 28 March 1801, seven
days after his victory over the French at Alexandria; a victory gained under his leadership by a regenerated British
Army. Although wounded earlier in the day, Abercromby
did not collapse until the battle was nearly over. An engraving of Stothard's picture by Francis Legat was published on
1 January 1805.[1] Stothard presumably falsified the event in
order to bring into the picture officers not actually present at
the moment when Abercromby sank to the ground. He may
have begun work on the picture early in 1802; a number of
the officers included in it did not return to England until
early in that year. A drawing by Stothard of the head of
Sidney Smith, very close to that in the group, is in the British
Museum (L.B. 144a.).

For Hely-Hutchinson, later 2nd Earl of Donoughmore, who
succeeded to Abercromby's command, and for Kempt, who
was Abercromby's A.D.C., see Nos. 987, 935 respectively.
Abercromby, who had entered the army in 1756, had been
appointed to command the Mediterranean forces in 1800.
His son was an officer of promise and ability, who returned
to England with the official despatches relating the course
of the campaign. Moore, with Oakes as his second-in-
command, had led the Reserve in the battle, in which he
played a leading part and was wounded, and in the earlier
landing at Aboukir. Anstruther, as Quartermaster-General,
greatly distinguished himself in the campaign; he died at
Corunna and was buried beside Moore. Cavan was in command of a Brigade and succeeded Hutchinson after the
latter's return to England; Lord Howden became second-
in-command after Abercromby's death; Stuart commanded
the foreign brigade which played a decisive part in the victory. Smith, who had defended Acre against the French,
commanded the seamen employed on shore and was
wounded in his right arm in the battle; at the close of the
campaign he was praised for his ardour and intrepidity.
Ludlow commanded the 2nd Brigade of Guards in the
battle. The 42nd Regiment particularly distinguished itself
and suffered heavy losses throughout the Egyptian campaign;[2] Major Stirling commanded the Regiment's left
wing and captured a standard. He served fifty-two years in
the Regiment and commanded it throughout the Peninsular
Wars. Col. Birch can perhaps be identified with John Birch,
a Lieutenant in the Royal Engineers at the time of the battle.

Peter Edward Stroehling

1768–after 1826. Portrait-painter, whose works are almost
always below the scale of life. Born in Düsseldorf, he worked
at Paris, Mannheim, Frankfurt, Mainz, Rome, Naples,

1. It was reissued in 1828 by Bowyer and Parkes. From an accompanying
Key I have compiled the description in the picture which gives the ranks
of the sitters at the time of the battle.
2. The *History* of the expedition by R. T. Wilson (1803) particularly
praises the parts played in the battle by Moore, Oakes, Stuart, Ludlow,
Smith and Stirling and the 42nd; and this praise is reiterated in Hely-
Hutchinson's official papers (*ibid.*, vol. II, p. 189).

Vienna, Russia and Berlin. In London he exhibited at the Royal Academy in 1803–4, 1806–7, 1819, 1821, 1823 and 1825–6. Between 1810 and 1820 Stroehling is recorded as Historical Painter to the Prince of Wales.

In the Prince's papers there are many references to portraits by Stroehling of the Prince which were given away. In January 1808 'Portrait of His Royal Highness by Mr Strowling—Gilt Frame' was given to Colonel McMahon (Jutsham, *R/D.*, f. 22);[1] on 7 September 1811 another portrait of the Prince by Stroehling in a gilt frame was given to the Rev. Dr. Jackson (*ibid.*, f. 98); a copy of one of Stroehling's portraits was given by the Prince to Baron Linsingen in August 1812—it had been received from Stroehling four months earlier (*ibid.*, ff. 120, 193); and an equestrian portrait, which had been received from Stroehling in November 1814, was sent to Blücher on 24 November (*ibid.*, ff. 174, 335).

Stroehling was commissioned to paint the Prince as the Black Prince. In July 1811 the artist was lent a drawing of the Black Prince 'to Copy from'. On 21 April 1813 this portrait of the Prince was sent to Stroehling 'to make some alteration in the Plume' (*ibid.*, ff. 88, 132). The portrait was in store at Carlton House in 1816 (391): 'The Prince Regent, as the Black Prince. Mr Stroehling', measurements given as 33 × 25½ in., on copper. It was sent to the King's Lodge on 27 September 1823, 'intended to be given to the Duchess of Gloucester'.

In October 1813 Stroehling delivered a portrait of the Prince 'on Horseback in Hussar Uniform—Gray Horse—in Gilt Frame—the Frame made by Mr Ferrara' (*ibid.*, f. 269). This was in store at Carlton House in 1816 (390, measurements given as 32 × 28 in., on copper) and was given away by George IV on 22 June 1822, apparently to Lady Conyngham as it is still in the Conyngham collection. There are various references in Jutsham's papers (*ibid.*, ff. 102, 138, 146, 351) which may refer to this portrait and to alterations being made to the dress.

Among the additional numbers to the inventory of Carlton House in 1816, No. 604 was 'A Small whole Length Portrait of George The Fourth—in his Coronation Robes—wearing his Crown—with his right Hand resting on the Sceptre—a Crown & Orb on a Cushion', measurements given as 27 × 18 in. It was returned to Stroehling on 3 November 1823 as the King had declined to purchase it (*Deliveries*, ff. 43, 49).

A small full-length of the Duke of Kent was at Carlton House by August 1808, 'Painted by Strowling'; in March 1810 it was lent to the Duke 'to look at' (*R/D.*, ff. 49, 54). It was in store at Carlton House in 1816 (400, measurements given as 24 × 18 in., on copper) and it was sent to the King's Lodge at Windsor on 27 September 1823, when it was the King's intention to present it to the Duchess of Gloucester. Between July and November 1814 portraits by Stroehling of the Tsar on horseback and the King of Prussia on a bay horse were received at Carlton House in gilt frames; on 12 June 1815, on General Bloomfield's orders, they were sent to Mr. Bicknell (*ibid.*, ff. 194, 335). Unframed pictures by Stroehling of two horses, Borodina a grey and Trinidada a bay (with two horses in the background) were included in this receipt and despatch. A picture of 'Ganimede' by Stroehling was in store at Carlton House in 1816 (403, measurements given as 23 × 17 in.). It was given by the King to Sir William Knighton on 26 June 1824.

1. Stroehling had delivered at Carlton House on 4 December 1807 'Two Pictures—Portraits of His Royal Highness The Prince of Wales—Gilt Frames—now in Throne Room—one of these Pictures deliverd To HR Highness Jany 1st 1808', which was presumably the portrait given to McMahon (*ibid.*, f. 29).

In addition to the payments to Stroehling cited under No. 1093, there is a record of a payment to Stroehling through Bloomfield in March 1815 of £1,575, probably in connection with the four pictures sent to Bicknell. The Duke of Kent's accounts include, under 22 August 1814, the payment of £52. 10s. to Stroehling (W.R.A., Geo. 34602, 43262). Farington saw in the Prince Regent's Writing-room at Carlton House, on 26 June 1811, the 'set of small pictures of the Royal Family, excepting the King, by Stroehling painted in a Vanderwerfe manner' (*Diary*, vol. VII, p. 9). For the portrait by Stroehling of Baron Bennigsen, see below, No. 1238.

1093. GEORGE III (*Plate* 237)

Kensington Palace. Copper: 24 × 19 in., 60,7 × 48,3 cm.

Signed and dated: *P. E. Stroehling | Windsor 18th Novembre | 1807*

Full-length standing, with a spaniel at his feet on a terrace overlooking the Quadrangle, with a view of the Round Tower and the statue of Charles II; a carriage with a mounted escort is driving across the Quadrangle. The King wears Windsor uniform with the Garter, the ribbon and star of the order and the badge of the Bath.

Probably (see below) given by George IV to Princess Sophia, after whose death it was acquired by Queen Victoria in 1848 or 1849 (MS. Catalogue of Queen Victoria's private pictures &c.); later at Windsor (804) and Buckingham Palace.

Literature: R.A., *Kings and Queens*, 1953 (240).

Although it was not taken over by George IV, it had apparently been painted for him. A portrait for 200 guineas of 'His Majesty the King' is included in the bill for work done for the Prince by Stroehling. The first item on the bill is dated 1807 and at the end of the bill are Stroehling's signature and the date 1 May 1809 (W.R.A., Geo. 26845–6). The total sum, for fourteen 'Cabinet Pictures' (one a miniature) and their frames, was 3,130 guineas. The sum was paid to Stroehling between 17 July 1807 and July 1810 (*ibid.*, 26847–50, 26862–3, 32293, 34602, 89450, 89456, 89460, 89466, 89467).

1094. QUEEN CHARLOTTE (*Plate* 236)

Kensington Palace. Copper: 23¾ × 18⅞ in., 60,3 × 47,9 cm.

Incised on the back with the names of artist and sitter and as *done at | Windsor 1807*.

Full-length, seated, wearing a light blue wrap and at her breast a jewelled miniature of George III; on her left are her crown, orb and sceptre, resting on a cushion laid on a rich ermine-lined robe; beside her is a small Pomeranian and in the foreground is a smoking urn (?) with a sprig of bay (?); on a ledge behind the Queen is a statue of Britannia and beyond is a view of Windsor Castle from the vicinity of the Queen's Lodge.

Painted for George IV. In December 1807 there were received at Carlton House from Stroehling 'Six Paintings in Gilt Frames—Portraits of Her Majesty—and five Princesses'; they were placed in store in the Throne Room and returned on 27 May 1808 to Stroehling 'To new Frame Varnish and Exhibit—by permission of His Royal Highness' (Jutsham, *R/D*, ff. 24, 31; the 'five Princesses' were Nos. 1095–9). No. 1094 was recorded in store at Carlton House in 1816 (392) and was sent to the King's Lodge on 27 September 1823; later at Windsor (802) and Buckingham Palace.

Literature: R.A., *Kings and Queens*, 1953 (250).

A portrait of the Queen, at 200 guineas, was included in Stroehling's bill for work done for the Prince of Wales (see No. 1093).

1095. PRINCESS AUGUSTA (*Plate* 238)

Kensington Palace. Copper: 24 × 18⅞ in., 61 × 47,9 cm.

Incised on the back with the names of artist and sitter and as *done at | Windsor 1807.*

Full-length, seated, wearing a robe lined with leopard skin. On a classical table are a bowl of fruit and the score of *Rule, Britannia;* the wall behind her is decorated with a classical relief of a ship and there is a view of the sea in the distance. A tambourine, cymbals and other musical instruments are on the floor.

See No. 1094. No. 1095 was recorded in store at Carlton House in 1816 (393); sent to the King's Lodge on 27 September 1823; later at Windsor (807) and Buckingham Palace.

A portrait of Princess Augusta, at 200 guineas, was included in Stroehling's bill for work done for the Prince of Wales (see No. 1093).

1096. PRINCESS ELIZABETH (*Plate* 239)

Kensington Palace. Copper: 24 × 19 in., 61 × 48,3 cm.

Incised on the back with the names of artist and sitter and as *done at | Windsor 1807.*

Full-length, seated, in an ermine-lined robe, holding on her knees a stretched canvas on which she is presumably painting the vase of flowers on a table in front of her; her painting equipment rests on a table at her side. On the floor are scissors and an album of silhouettes; in the background is a relief of Adonis (?).

See No. 1094. No. 1096 was recorded in store at Carlton House in 1816 (394); sent to the King's Lodge on 27 September 1823; later at Windsor (805) and Buckingham Palace.

A portrait of Princess Elizabeth, at 200 guineas, was included in Stroehling's bill for work done for the Prince of Wales (see No. 1093).

1097. PRINCESS MARY (*Plate* 240)

Kensington Palace. Copper: 24 × 18⅞ in., 61 × 47,9 cm.

Signed and dated: *P. E. Stroehling 1807;* and incised on the back with the names of artist and sitter and as *done at | Windsor 1807.*

Full-length, standing, supporting a framed classical relief of the head of George III; painting equipment is on a table beside her and behind her is a chafing-dish under a relief of Cupid.

See No. 1094. No. 1097 was recorded in store at Carlton House in 1816 (395); sent to the King's Lodge on 27 September 1823; later at Windsor (801) and Buckingham Palace.

A portrait of Princess Mary, at 200 guineas, was included in Stroehling's bill for work done for the Prince of Wales (see No. 1093).

1098. PRINCESS SOPHIA (*Plate* 241)

Kensington Palace. Copper: 23⅞ × 19 in., 60,6 × 48,3 cm.

Incised on the back with the names of artist and sitter and as *done at | Windsor 1807.*

Full-length, standing at work on an embroidery frame, looking up at a bust of Minerva; a little spaniel is on a sofa behind.

See No. 1094. No. 1098 was recorded in store at Carlton House in 1816 (396); sent to the King's Lodge on 27 September 1823; later a Windsor (808) and Buckingham Palace.

A portrait of Princess Sophia, at 200 guineas, was included in Stroehling's bill for work done for the Prince of Wales (see No. 1093).

1099. PRINCESS AMELIA (*Plate* 242)

Kensington Palace. Copper: 24⅛ × 18⅛ in., 61,3 × 46 cm.

Incised on the back with the names of artist and sitter and as *done at | Windsor 1807.*

Full-length, standing in a mountainous landscape, striking a lyre which rests on the score of *God Save the King;* a classical sword and helmet lie on the ground behind her.

See No. 1094. No. 1099 was recorded in store at Carlton House in 1816 (397); sent to the King's Lodge on 27 September 1823; later at Windsor (806) and Buckingham Palace.

A portrait of Princess 'Emilie', at 200 guineas, was included in Stroehling's bill for work done for the Prince of Wales (see No. 1093).

1100. AUGUSTUS, DUKE OF SUSSEX

Kensington Palace. Copper: 24 × 18⅛ in., 61 × 46 cm.

Signed: *Stroehling*

Full-length, standing in a mountainous landscape, in the uniform of Colonel of the Loyal North Britons, resting his right hand on his broadsword.

Possibly painted for Queen Charlotte (see below); later in the possession of Princess Sophia, after whose death it was acquired by Queen Victoria in 1848 or 1849: 'Strelling. Small full length portrait of the Duke of Sussex, in the uniform of a Highland Regiment' (MS. Catalogue of Queen Victoria's private pictures &c.); later at Windsor (803) and Buckingham Palace.

Stroehling exhibited a portrait of the Duke of Sussex at the Royal Academy in 1806 (193), the year after the Duke had become Colonel of the Loyal North Britons. No. 1100 is probably the portrait seen in the Green Pavilion at Frogmore in Wild's plate (published 1 June 1817) in Pyne, vol. I, *Frogmore,* pp. 12–13. No. 1100 is not, therefore, likely to be identical with the portrait of the Duke by Stroehling recorded in store at Carlton House in 1816 (401, measurements given as 24 × 18 in.) and sent to the King's Lodge on 27 September 1823. This was apparently to be given to the Duchess of Gloucester; and in her will (proved 5 June 1857) the Duchess left to the Duchess of Kent 'a small full length picture of the Duke of Kent by Strooling and a picture of the Duke of Sussex in a Scotch dress by the same Master also a picture of George the Fourth by the same Master'. The head of the Duke in No. 1100 is of the same type as a miniature by Cosway in the Scottish United Services Museum, Edinburgh.

1101. PRINCESS AMELIA

Kensington Palace. Copper: 22½ × 16¾ in., 57,1 × 41,6 cm.

Signed: *P.E.Stroehling*

Full-length, standing, leaning on a sofa and holding a book in her right hand, beside a table on which are papers and an ink-well. In the background is a mountainous landscape with a castle.

Perhaps originally in the collection of Frederick, Duke of York: on the back of the frame is a label inscribed *Duke of | York.* Recorded at Buckingham Palace (792) in 1876 (*V.R. inv.*); later at Windsor (2411).

Probably painted *c.* 1805, perhaps slightly earlier than No. 1099.

1102. FREDERICA, DUCHESS OF YORK
(*Plate* 243)

Kensington Palace. Copper: 24 × 18¾ in., 61 × 47,6 cm.

Full-length, standing on a terrace in a garden, surrounded by four dogs: a running dog, a gun dog, a Portuguese water dog and a Maltese.

Painted for George IV. Recorded in a store at Carlton House in 1816 (398); sent to the King's Lodge on 27 September 1823; later at Windsor (800) and Buckingham Palace.

Literature: Museum and Art Gallery, Birmingham, *British Embroidery*, 1959 (239).

A portrait of the Duchess of York, at 200 guineas, was included in Stroehling's bill for work done for the Prince of Wales (see No. 1093). The distant lake and woods in the background may be unfinished.

1103. LOUISA, QUEEN OF PRUSSIA
(1776–1810)

Kensington Palace. Copper: 24 × 18 in., 61 × 45,7 cm.

Full-length, standing, apparently as Hebe: holding a jug and cup and with the Prussian eagle at her side with a laurel wreath in its beak. In the background is the Brandenburg Gate.

In the collection of George IV. Recorded in store at Carlton House in 1816 (399); sent to the King's Lodge on 27 September 1823; later at Windsor (799) and Buckingham Palace.

Stroehling exhibited a portrait of the Queen at the Royal Academy in 1803 (227). No. 1103 was probably painted in Berlin; the Brandenburg Gate is surmounted by G. Schadow's Victory group which was removed by the French in 1807 and erected in its present position in 1814.

Daughter of Charles II, Grand Duke of Mecklenburg-Strelitz, and niece of Queen Charlotte; in 1793 she married Frederick William III of Prussia (No. 898). She bore with great courage the sufferings inflicted on her family and herself during the war between France and Prussia.

1104. THE DEATH OF PRINCE LOUIS FERDINAND OF PRUSSIA (*Plate* 244)

Windsor Castle (474). Copper: 30⅜ × 24 in., 71,2 × 60,7 cm.

Inscribed on the back with the name of the artist and the event.

The Prince, on horseback and wearing Prussian uniform with the star of the Black Eagle, engaged with a French hussar; the battle is raging in the distance.

In the collection of George IV; recorded in store at Carlton House in 1816 (402: 'Prince Louis of Prussia engaged with a French hussar. Mr Stroehling.'); sent to Windsor for a short period on 27 September 1823 (Jutsham, *Deliveries*, f. 42).

Prince Louis Ferdinand (1772–1806), the 'Prussian Alcibiades', was son of Prince Ferdinand of Prussia and grandson of Frederick William I. At the battle of Saalfeld, 10 October 1806, he was in command of the advance guard of the Prussian army. His troops were routed and he was killed by *maréchal des logis* Guindet of the 10th Regiment of Hussars.

1105. HENRY PAGET, SECOND EARL OF UXBRIDGE AND FIRST MARQUESS OF ANGLESEY (1768–1854) (*Plate* 245)

Windsor Castle (1379). 36⅝ × 43¾ in., 92,4 × 111,1 cm.

Riding in a rocky landscape on a white charger; a cavalry action is raging in the distance, and cavalry soldiers appear behind Lord Uxbridge. He wears the uniform of Colonel of the 7th Light Dragoons (Hussars) with the Peninsula Medal; his saddle is enriched with tiger skin. On the ground is a shattered cannon decorated with the French imperial eagle.

Presumably painted for George IV and in his possession by March 1814, when it was sent to the artist 'for some alteration by desire of Colonel Bloomfield' (Jutsham, *R/D*, f. 146); on 25 July 1815 it came back from the artist and in May 1816 it was sent to Lord Anglesey (*ibid.*, ff. 232, 351). Recorded in store at Carlton House in 1816 (389); sent down to the King's Lodge on 27 September 1823 (Jutsham, *Deliveries*, f. 47).

Presumably painted in London, perhaps soon after the sitter's return from the Peninsula in January 1809. An engraving of No. 1105 by Meyer was published by Colnaghi on 1 May 1818.

See No. 1086.

1106. FIELD-MARSHAL GEBHARDT VON BLÜCHER (1742–1819)

Windsor Castle (925). 36¾ × 44½ in., 93,3 × 113 cm.

Signed and dated: *Stroehling | 1814.*

Riding in a rocky landscape, wearing Field-Marshal's uniform. He wears the badge of the Iron Cross of Prussia and the ribbons of St. Andrew and St. George of Russia and the Black Eagle of Prussia; his stars include the Black Eagle, Maria Theresa of Austria and St. George of Russia; and he wears the jewelled miniature of George IV which the King gave him in London (see No. 886). Behind him are a trumpeter, mounted troops and an A.D.C.

In the collection of George IV. Received at Carlton House from the artist between July and November 1814 (Jutsham, *R/D*, f. 335: 'Marshall Prince Blucher on Horseback—Gray Horse. Gilt Frame'); recorded in store in 1816 (387); sent to the King's Lodge on 27 September 1823.

Presumably painted for the Prince Regent in London in the summer of 1814.

See No. 886.

1107. MATVEI IVANOVITCH, COUNT PLATOV (1757–1818)

Windsor Castle (1378). 36½ × 44 in., 92,7 × 111,8 cm.

Signed and dated: *Stroehling | 1814*; and inscribed *A | FONTAINEBLEAU | 1814.*

Riding on a white charger in the uniform of a Cossack General with an elaborate silvered plume decorated with a crowned A. Galloping Cossacks and a view of Fontainebleau are seen in the distance. Count Platov wears the badges of the Orders of Maria Theresa, St. George of Russia, St. John of Jerusalem and St. Anne of Russia; the ribbon and star of the Black Eagle of Prussia; and a miniature of George IV in a jewelled setting.

Presumably painted for George IV. Received at Carlton House from Stroehling between July and November 1814 (Jutsham, *R/D*, f. 335); recorded in store at Carlton House in 1816 (388); sent to the King's Lodge on 27 September 1823.

Presumably painted for the Regent in London, at the same time as No. 910, in the summer of 1814. On 16 February 1814 Platov with his Cossacks had reduced Fontainebleau, capturing a general, some cannon and prisoners.

See No. 910.

Gilbert Stuart

1755–1828. Portrait-painter. Born in the colony of Rhode Island, to which his father had emigrated from Scotland. He came to London in 1775 and became a pupil of West. Within a short time he was in successful independent practice. In 1787 he went to Ireland. He returned to America at the end of 1792 or early in 1793.

After Gilbert Stuart

1108. GEORGE WASHINGTON (1732–99)
Buckingham Palace. 35¼ × 28 in., 89,5 × 71,1 cm.

Head and shoulders in black.

Probably acquired by Queen Victoria; recorded at Buckingham Palace (631) in 1876 (*V.R. inv.*).

A copy, of respectable quality, of Stuart's third portrait of Washington, the 'Athenaeum Head', painted at the order of Mrs. Washington in Stuart's studio in Germantown in the summer or autumn of 1796. The unfinished original of this type, kept by Stuart himself, is on loan from the Athenaeum in Boston to the Museum of Fine Arts. It was used by Stuart as the basis of innumerable repetitions and variations of this type which was also close to the head in the previous type, the 'Lansdowne', probably begun in Philadelphia in April 1796; No. 1108, and other derivations, appear to combine features from both types and from the 'Monro-Lennox' type (*c.* 1800–1). Copies of Stuart's portraits of Washington were being manufactured in large quantities by copyists such as Thomas Sully during the nineteenth century (for this problem see J. H. Morgan and M. Fielding, *The Life Portraits of Washington and Their Replicas* (Philadelphia, 1931), especially pp. 223–4, 228–9, 270–311, 324–38, 341–6, apparently without reference to No. 1108).

Commander-in-Chief of the military forces of the colonies in the American War of Independence; first President of the United States, 1789–97.

George Stubbs

1724–1806. Painter of horses, animals, portraits, conversation-pieces and sporting scenes. He worked at first mainly in the north and in Lincolnshire, but by 1760 he was settled in London.

In addition to the pictures still in the royal collection, there was in store at Carlton House in 1816 (426): 'A sorrel, and a chestnut horse, with a black and white dog. Stubbs', measurements given as 60 × 96 in. It was sent to the King's Lodge on 31 May 1822 (Jutsham, *Deliveries*, f. 34) and was at Cumberland Lodge in January 1844. It does not appear to have survived. It may have been a companion picture to the large lost picture by Sawrey Gilpin (see above, p. 45); and is almost certainly the picture described in *The Sporting Magazine* of November 1809 as in the Prince of Wales's collection (Gilbey, p. 229) and as having been painted *c.* 1800. A bill, dated 14 February 1793, addressed to the Prince by Thomas Allwood, is for £110. 16*s.* 0*d.*: 'To Carving & Gilding eight Picture frames of half length size for

sundry Pictures painted by Mr Stubbs. all of one pattern'. The bill is endorsed in Stubbs's hand: 'This is a true Bill—Geo: Stubbs'. (P.R.O., H.O. 73, 17). Allwood's frames are still on the pictures.

1109. GEORGE IV WHEN PRINCE OF WALES (*Plate* 139)
Windsor Castle (2956). 40⅜ × 50¼ in., 102,5 × 127,6 cm.

Signed and dated: *Geo: Stubbs pinx:* | *1791.*

Riding on a chestnut horse, with two small terriers running ahead; the Prince wears the star of the Garter on a dark blue coat. In the distance is a view of Westminster and a stretch of water which is probably the Serpentine rather than the lake in St. James's Park.

Presumably painted for George IV; recorded in store at Carlton House in 1816 (255: 'The Prince of Wales on a chestnut horse'); sent to the King's Lodge on 31 May 1822 (Jutsham, *Deliveries*, f. 33); later at Stud Lodge (1161), Marlborough House and Buckingham Palace.

Literature: Gilbey, pp. 115–16; R.A., *British Art,* 1934 (377), *Commemorative Catalogue* (1935), p. 49, *First Hundred Years,* 1951–2 (111), *Kings and Queens,* 1953 (253).

Probably the portrait of the Prince of Wales exhibited by Stubbs at the Royal Academy in 1791 (91).

1110. WILLIAM ANDERSON WITH TWO SADDLE-HORSES (*Plate* 140)
Windsor Castle (1681). 40¼ × 50⅜ in., 102,2 × 127,9 cm.

Signed and dated: *Geo: Stubbs p:* | *1793.*

Two chestnut saddle-horses belonging to the Prince of Wales with Anderson the groom in royal livery (scarlet with blue collar and cuffs) mounted on the leader. In the background is an extensive prospect of an open landscape and the sea, presumably on the south coast.

Presumably painted for George IV; recorded in store at Carlton House in 1816 (417: 'The Prince's chestnut saddle horses, with Anderson, the groom. Stubbs'); sent to the King's Lodge on 31 May 1822 (Jutsham, *Deliveries*, f. 33); later at Cumberland Lodge.

Literature: Gilbey, pp. 122–3; Shaw Sparrow, *Sporting Artists,* p. 143; R.A., *King's Pictures* (484); Walker Art Gallery, Liverpool, *George Stubbs,* 1951 (54).

William Anderson was helper and hack-groom to the Prince of Wales, 1788–1800; he became head groom in 1804 and, in 1812, Groom of the Stables.

1111. JOHN GASCOIGNE (*d.* 1812) WITH A BAY HORSE (*Plate* 146)
Windsor Castle (1682). 40 × 50¼ in., 101,6 × 127,6 cm.

Signed and dated: *Geo: Stubbs pinxit* | *1791.*

Gascoigne, the groom, approaches the horse with a sieve.

Presumably painted for George IV; recorded in store at Carlton House in 1816 (415: 'A bay horse, with Gascon the groom. Stubbs'); sent to the King's Lodge on 31 May 1822 (Jutsham, *Deliveries*, f. 33); later at Cumberland Lodge.

Literature: Gilbey, p. 122; Shaw Sparrow, *Sporting Artists,* p. 143; Shaw Sparrow, pp. 11–12.

The horse has been recently identified with Creeper, a bay colt, bred by Lord Archibald Hamilton in 1786 (by Tandem out of Harriet) and bought by the Prince of Wales in 1791; in that year he won a subscription purse of sixty guineas at Newmarket and the King's Plate at Lichfield; he was later sold to C. Wilson and ran his last race in 1794. A horse of this name was among the hunters kept by the Prince in Hampshire in 1791–2.

John Gascoigne or Gaskoin(e) was hunting-groom (and later head groom) to the Prince of Wales, 1785–1800, and Clerk of the Stables, 1802–12. According to Mrs. Papendiek, the Prince 'had a seraglio' in the family of Gascoigne at his hunting seat in Hampshire (presumably Kempshott Park, near Basingstoke), 'the brother of the females being raised from groom to the head of the stud stables, and at his death buried with the honours of the Royal liveries' (*Court and Private Life . . .*, ed. Mrs. V. Delves Broughton (1887), vol. I, p. 257).

1112. LAETITIA, LADY LADE (d. 1825) (Plate 143)

Windsor Castle (1685). 40¼ × 50⅝ in., 102,2 × 127,9 cm.

Signed and dated: *Geo: Stubbs pinxit | 1793.*

Riding on a rearing bay horse, with a view of the Round Pond (?) at Kensington behind; she wears a blue riding-habit and high-crowned plumed hat.

Presumably painted for George IV; recorded in store at Carlton House in 1816 (419: 'Mrs Hill, on a chesnut horse. Stubbs'; remains of the 1816 label are on the frame); sent to the King's Lodge on 31 May 1822 (Jutsham, *Deliveries*, f. 34) and to Cumberland Lodge in January 1844.

Literature: Gilbey, p. 125; Shaw Sparrow, *Sporting Artists*, p. 143; R.A., *King's Pictures* (477).

The identity of the sitter is perhaps not precisely established. In the earliest reference to the picture (see above) she is described as Mrs. Hill, but by Redgrave (*V.R. inv.*, 3 February 1873) she is stated to be Lady Lade. The sitter bears a reasonably close resemblance to Reynolds's portrait of Lady Lade, shown at the Royal Academy in 1785 (Water-house, *Reynolds*, pl. 252).

Laetitia Darby, alias Smith, who married, in or before 1789, Sir John Lade, 2nd Bt., was a notorious adventuress. She had been servant in a house in Broad St., St. Giles's, which had an unsavoury reputation. She and her husband were friends of the Prince of Wales (the Prince bought horses from the Baronet); but her appearance in his company at an assembly at Brighton in 1789 caused more respectable ladies, including Lady Elizabeth Luttrell (see No. 797) to leave the room and the town in protest. Lady Lade was famous as whip and horsewoman and regularly hunted at Windsor; her bad language was proverbial.

1113. SIR SIDNEY MEDOWS (1701–92) (Plate 144)

Windsor Castle (1687). Panel: 32½ × 40 in., 82,5 × 101,6 cm.

Signed and dated: *Geo: Stubbs px | 1778.*

Riding on a white horse in a hilly landscape with a lake or river in the background.

Presumably acquired by George IV *c.* 1818; recorded in store at Carlton House in 1819 (355) and as additional No. 546 in the inventory of 1816 ('Portrait of Sir Sidney Meddows—Mounted upon a Grey Horse—Green Coat—& Cocked Hat—Stubbs'); sent to the King's Lodge on 31 May 1822 (Jutsham, *Deliveries*, f. 38); later at Cumberland Lodge.

Literature: Gilbey, pp. 118–19; Shaw Sparrow, *Sporting Artists*, p. 143; Shaw Sparrow, pp. 10–11; R.A., *King's Pictures* (481).

No. 1113 entered George IV's collection later than his other pictures by Stubbs. It was also painted considerably earlier. The signature and date had probably been concealed by the frame since 1824, when Wyatt enlarged a frame, formerly

on the picture of a Rabbi (then attributed to Rembrandt and now at Buckingham Palace), for use on this picture (Jutsham, *Deliveries*, f. 55).

Succeeded his father as Knight Marshal, 1758, and was appointed Deputy Ranger of Richmond Park, 1761. A famous horseman, Sir Sidney worked reguarly in his riding-house for two or three hours a day 'during which time, he either rode or worked in hand 12 horses till within a few days of his death'. The Prince of Wales visited the riding-house while Sir Sidney was there. After his death, his partner, Strickland Freeman, published in 1806 his *Art of Horseman-ship* which embodied his partner's principles. The work was dedicated to the Prince and the copy presented to him by the author is in the Royal Library.

1114. JOHN CHRISTIAN SANTHAGUE (d. 1821)

Windsor Castle (1680). Panel: 35½ × 54 in., 90,2 × 137,2 cm.

Signed and dated: *Geo Stubbs pinxt | 1782.*

Walking at the edge of a lake in a rocky, richly wooded landscape, accompanied by three dogs: an elkhound, a Pomeranian and a (?mongrel) terrier.

Presumably painted for George IV. Recorded in store at Carlton House in 1816 (424: 'Mr Santhagen, with three dogs. Stubbs'; remains of the 1816 label are on the frame); sent to the King's Lodge on 31 May 1822 (Jutsham, *Deliveries*, f. 34) and to Cumberland Lodge in January 1844.

Literature: Gilbey, pp. 119–20; Shaw Sparrow, *Sporting Artists*, p. 143; R.A., *King's Pictures* (497).

The picture is in very bad condition; the panel is split in three places, much original paint has been lost and the surface has been severely rubbed overall. A photograph attached to the sheet (dated 5 February 1873) in the *V.R. inv.* already indicates much of this; on the sheet and in the photograph the cracks are recorded; the photograph seems to show much loss of original paint; and Redgrave described the surface as 'covered with streaky Varnish which should be removed'. Seguier may therefore have caused some of the damage to the painting when he cleaned, repaired and varnished it in September 1873. In 1879 Seguier again repaired and varnished the panel, and parquetted the panel after it had fallen from the wall.

Santhague was a Page of the Backstairs in the Household of the Prince of Wales and Prince Frederick, 1772–80; at the time of his death he was first Page to George IV.

1115. SOLDIERS OF THE TENTH LIGHT DRAGOONS (Plates 141, 145)

Windsor Castle (974). 40¼ × 50⅝ in., 102,2 × 127,9 cm.

Signed and dated: *Geo: Stubbs p: | 1793.*

A mounted sergeant (with his sword at the carry), a trum-peter, a sergeant shouldering arms and a private presenting arms, in a large meadow; in the distance is a village with a river (?).

Presumably painted for George IV; recorded in the Armoury at Carlton House in 1816 (480: 'Two corporals, a private, and a trumpeter, of the 10th Regt of Light Dragoons. Stubbs').

Literature: Gilbey, pp. 113–14; Shaw Sparrow, p. 11; R.A., *British Art*, 1934 (394), *Commemorative Catalogue* (1935), p. 49; R.A., *King's Pictures* (495).

The Prince of Wales was appointed Colonel in command of the 10th Light Dragoons on 19 November 1782. He was always deeply attached to the regiment and its uniform (see Nos. 660, 664). In 1784 its uniform had been changed to that seen in No. 1115, with a pattern composed of strips of braid across the jacket, probably under the influence of continental prototypes. In No. 1115 Stubbs may have been asked to record soldiers mounting guard or their mounted and dismounted order for guard-mounting. In the possession of Field-Marshal Sir Gerald Templer are two pictures (of a sergeant and a private in the regiment) in the manner of Stubbs and perhaps connected with No. 1115.

1116. PORTRAIT OF A GENTLEMAN

Windsor Castle (1684). $40\frac{1}{8} \times 50\frac{3}{8}$ in., 101,9 × 127,9 cm.

Signed and dated: *Geo: Stubbs pinxit | 1791*.

Riding a bay charger, inside a riding-school.

Presumably painted for George IV; recorded in store at Carlton House in 1816 (418: 'Sir William Meadows, on a bay charger. Stubbs'); sent to the King's Lodge on 31 May 1822 (Jutsham, *Deliveries*, f. 34); later at Cumberland Lodge.

Literature: Gilbey, p. 124; Shaw Sparrow, *Sporting Artists*, p. 143.

Formerly (see above) identified as a portrait of Sir William Medows (1738–1813), second son of Philip Medows. Sir William, however, was a soldier (he entered the army in 1756 and became a General in 1798) and in 1791 was serving in India. It is possible that No. 1116 is a portrait of Sir Sidney Medows (see No. 1113) working a horse in his riding-school.

1117. THE PRINCE OF WALES'S PHAETON
(*Plate* 142)

Windsor Castle (1671). $40\frac{1}{4} \times 50\frac{1}{2}$ in., 102,2 × 128,3 cm.

Signed and dated: *Geo: Stubbs pinxit | 1793*

The distant landscape with a large lake may be intended for Virginia Water. The phaeton, gaily painted and upholstered, stands on the right; a tiger-boy raises the shaft to which the two horses are to be harnessed. Samuel Thomas, the Prince's State Coachman, in scarlet coat with gold collar and cuffs, holds one of the horses; the other draws back from the dog Fino (see No. 1124). The horses' blinkers are decorated with the Prince of Wales's feathers.

Painted for George IV. Recorded in store at Carlton House in 1816 (420: 'The Prince's Phaeton, with a pair of black horses, Thomas, the state-coachman, and a boy. Stubbs'); sent to the King's Lodge on 31 May 1822 (Jutsham, *Deliveries*, f. 34), to Cumberland Lodge in 1873, and to Fort Belvedere in March 1936.

Literature: Gilbey, pp. 120–2; Shaw Sparrow, *Sporting Artists*, p. 143; Shaw Sparrow, p. 11; R.A., *King's Pictures* (500); Walker Art Gallery, Liverpool, *George Stubbs*, 1951 (29).

Samuel Thomas (*?d.* 1800/1) was appointed Post-Chaise man in Ordinary to George III in 1767. In 1771 he was appointed Body Coachman to the Prince of Wales; he seems to have held the post until 1800.

1118. BARONET WITH SAMUEL CHIFNEY
(*c.* 1750–1807) UP

Windsor Castle (2957). $40\frac{1}{8} \times 50\frac{1}{4}$ in., 101,9 × 127,6 cm.

Signed and dated: *Geo: Stubbs pinxit | 1791*.

Chifney, in royal colours, riding a bay horse, presumably at the finish of a race; in the background is the rubbing house at Newmarket.

Probably painted for or acquired by George IV and mentioned in his collection in November 1809; recorded in store at Carlton

House in 1816 (413: 'A running horse, at speed, rode by Shifney. Stubbs'); sent to the King's Lodge on 31 May 1822 (Jutsham, *Deliveries*, f. 33); later at Stud Lodge (1166), Cumberland Lodge, Marlborough House and Buckingham Palace.

Literature: Gilbey, pp. 116–17, 229.

A number of versions of this design exist. There are versions at Belvoir and in the Huntington Gallery, San Marino, both signed and dated 1791; another is in the Durdans collection (exh., Ackermann & Son Ltd., March 1966 (3)). One of these was presumably the version exhibited by Stubbs at the Turf Gallery, Conduit Street, in January 1794, and engraved by G. T. Stubbs for the *Turf Review* (pl. XII, published on 20 February 1794). One of the versions was in Stubbs's sale by Coxe, 26–7 May 1807 (78). See also No. 1061.

Baronet, foaled in 1785, was by Vertumnus out of Penultima. He was the property of Sir Walter Vavasour and in 1789 was bought by the Prince of Wales. Thereafter he was ridden by Chifney. In 1791 he won the Oatlands Stakes at Ascot (said to be commemorated in this picture) and, his last race, the King's Plate at Newmarket; he was sold and sent to America (T. H. Taunton in *Portraits of Celebrated Racehorses* (1887), vol. I, pp. 183–4).

Samuel Chifney the elder (for his son, see No. 700) was famous for his 'rush' and for his exquisite hands. He had been employed by Lord Grosvenor, the Duke of Bedford and Thomas Panton before he entered the service of the Prince of Wales. He was involved in the celebrated scandal at Newmarket in October 1791. He had won easily for the Prince on Escape in two races; on 20 October, when he had persuaded the Prince not to bet on him, he came in fourth; but on the following day he won on Escape against heavy odds. The Stewards of the Jockey Club let it be known that no gentleman would start against Chifney on the Prince's horses. The Prince withdrew from the turf and gave Chifney a pension. He was incensed when Chifney published, in 1804, *Genius Genuine*, an explanation of the episode.

1119. HOLLYHOCK (*Plate* 148)

Windsor Castle (2321). $15\frac{1}{4} \times 18\frac{3}{4}$ in., 38,7 × 47,6 cm.

A bay horse, standing in a landscape; behind, near a lake, are a shepherd-boy and girl with a dog and a flock of sheep.

On the back are the remains of an early label, stating that the picture was given to 'M. Monet [?] dans un dernier voyage en Angleterre' in 1766 by Lord Bolingbroke; and that the horse had been painted by Stubbs in London, the background by Vernet, dog and sheep by Boucher. Bought by George IV from Colnaghi on 16 April 1810: 'A portrait of a horse by Stubbs—the Landscape by Vernet—the—Figures by Boucher' (W.R.A., Geo. 27524); recorded in store at Carlton House in 1816 (436); sent to the King's Lodge on 31 May 1822 (Jutsham, *Deliveries*, f. 35); later at Stud Lodge (1145) and Cumberland Lodge.

Literature: Gilbey, pp. 127–8; Shaw Sparrow, *Sporting Artists*, pp. 142–3.

There is nothing inherently improbable in the traditional account (see above) of the picture's early history. Stubbs was working in the 1760s for Frederick St. John, 2nd Viscount Bolingbroke (1734–87). Hollyhock, foaled in 1765, was bred by the Duke of Cumberland by Young Cade out of Cypron and bought at Windsor by Lord Bolingbroke. In 1769, at the second spring meeting at Newmarket, he won the Jockey Club Plate for four-year-olds. He ended his life at Lord Rockingham's stud and died while covering a mare. Stylistically the figures and animals in the background are not impossible for François Boucher, nor is the landscape for

Claude-Joseph Vernet. The picture was engraved by J. Scott for the *Sporting Magazine*, vol. 21 (January 1803), p. 21. The attribution to the three artists appears under the plate and in an accompanying note the original recipient of the picture is called 'Mr. Monnet'.

1120. PUMPKIN WITH WILLIAM SOUTH UP

Windsor Castle (1895). Panel: 32⅜ × 40 in., 82,2 × 101,6 cm.

South, in Lord Foley's colours (blue and white), on a chestnut horse, standing by a mound in a spacious landscape.

Probably acquired by George IV. Recorded in store at Carlton House in 1816 (425): 'A chestnut horse, rode by South. Stubbs'); sent to the King's Lodge on 31 May 1822; later at Stud Lodge (1164) and Cumberland Lodge.

Literature: Gilbey, p. 119.

A smaller version of a design of which the best version (*Fig.* 36), signed and dated 1773, is now in the Rothschild collection at Ascott, Wing. Another, obscurely signed and dated (1775?) and formerly at The Durdans, belongs to the Countess of Halifax. It was probably one of the larger versions which was engraved by G. T. Stubbs (published for the *Turf Review* on 20 February 1794, pl. XIII); but No. 1120 may have been the picture sold in Stubbs's sale by Coxe, 26–7 May 1807 (79). A copy is also in the Darwin Museum, Down House. During restoration, initiated in 1950, it was discovered that No. 1120 had been heavily overpainted. Much of the repaint was removed, but very little of the original paint was found to have survived on any part of the panel. On the back are faint indications of a drawing by Stubbs in chalk of a horse and a cow (?).

Pumpkin, by Match 'em out of Old Squirt Mare, had been bred by John Pratt (foaled in 1769) and was later owned jointly by Lord Foley and Charles James Fox for whom, as well as for the Prince of Wales, South (*b.* 1735) rode. In his twenty-four races he was successful sixteen times. The last race was run in 1776. A different portrait of Pumpkin by Stubbs, painted in 1774, is in the Mellon collection (R.A. *Painting in England 1700–1850*, 1964–5 (274); T. H. Taunton, *Portraits of Famous Racehorses* (1887), vol. I, pp. 125–7).

1121. A BAY HORSE WITH A GROOM
(*Plate* 149)

Windsor Castle (2322). Panel: 22¼ × 28¾ in., 56,5 × 73 cm.

Signed and dated: *Geo: Stubbs pinxit | 1791*. The date is damaged, but this seems the correct reading and not *1761*, as noted in *V.R. inv.* and other sources.

A bay horse, saddled, held by a groom in royal livery (scarlet, gold lace, blue collar and cuffs).

Presumably painted for George IV; recorded in store at Carlton House in 1816 (435): 'A bay horse, saddled, with a groom in the royal livery. Stubbs'); sent to the King's Lodge on 31 May 1822 (Jutsham, *Deliveries*, f. 35); later at Stud Lodge (1156) and Cumberland Lodge.

Literature: Gilbey, pp. 126–7.

1122. A GREY HORSE (*Plate* 151)

Windsor Castle (1683). 40¼ × 50¼ in., 102,2 × 127,6 cm.

Signed and dated: *Geo: Stubbs pinxit. | 1793*.

Walking in a landscape.

Presumably painted for George IV; recorded in store at Carlton House in 1816 (414: 'A grey horse. Stubbs'); sent to the King's Lodge on 31 May 1822 (Jutsham, *Deliveries*, f. 33); later at Cumberland Lodge.

Literature: Gilbey, pp. 125–6; Shaw Sparrow, p. 5.

There is an alteration by Stubbs to the position of the off fore-leg, which was not at first raised so high. The horse has recently been identified tentatively with Grey Trentham, a grey colt bred by the Earl of Egremont in 1788 by Trentham out of a mare by Herod; he is recorded in races, 1791–4; in 1793 he won the King's Plate at Burford and Lichfield and in 1794 he won the King's Plate at Guildford. See No. 1123.

1123. A GREY HORSE (*Plate* 150)

Windsor Castle (1410). 40¼ × 50⅛ in., 102,2 × 127,3 cm.

Signed and dated: *Geo: Stubbs. | pinxit 1793*.

Galloping in a stormy landscape, wearing a bridle.

Presumably painted for George IV; recorded in store at Carlton House in 1816 (416: 'A grey horse, with the head of a bridle. Stubbs'); sent to the King's Lodge on 31 May 1822 (Jutsham, *Deliveries*, f. 33); later at Cumberland Lodge.

Literature: Gilbey, pp. 123–4; Shaw Sparrow, p. 5.

There are slight *pentimenti* in the forelegs and the off hind leg. Stubbs, moreover, at first painted a saddle and girth on the horse which he later painted or rubbed out. The horse is almost certainly the same animal as in No. 1122 and may therefore be a second portrait of Grey Trentham.

1124. FINO AND TINY (*Plate* 152)

Buckingham Palace. 40 × 50 in., 101,6 × 127 cm.

Signed and dated: *Geo: Stubbs | Pinxit 179[?1]*

A Spitz dog, with a small spaniel, standing in a mountainous landscape with the sea or a lake in the distance.

Presumably painted for George IV; recorded in store at Carlton House in 1816 (423: 'Two dogs, Fino and Tiny. Stubbs'); sent to the King's Lodge on 31 May 1822 (Jutsham, *Deliveries*, f. 34); later at Windsor (1227) and Kew.

Literature: Gilbey, p. 114; Walker Art Gallery, *George Stubbs*, 1951 (51).

Possibly the picture—*A Pomeranian dog*—which Stubbs exhibited at the Royal Academy in 1791 (7); the same dog appears in No. 1117.

1125. A ROUGH DOG (*Plate* 153)

Buckingham Palace. 40 × 50 in., 101,6 × 127 cm.

Signed and dated: *Geo: Stubbs pinxit | 1790*.

Lying under a tree in a rocky landscape, with a glimpse of the sea in the distance.

Presumably painted for George IV; recorded in store at Carlton House in 1816 (422: 'A rough dog. Stubbs'); sent to the King's Lodge on 31 May 1822 (Jutsham, *Deliveries*, f. 34); later at Windsor (1221) and Kew.

Literature: Gilbey, p. 114.

Possibly the picture—*A shepherd's dog from the South of France* —which Stubbs exhibited at the Royal Academy in 1791 (275).

1126. A RED DEER BUCK AND DOE (*Plate* 147)

Windsor Castle (1686). 39¾ × 50¼ in., 101 × 127,6 cm.

Signed and dated: *Geo: Stubbs pinx ... | 1792*.

Emerging from a group of trees within a paddock.

Presumably painted for George IV; recorded in store at Carlton House in 1816 (421: 'A buck, and a doe. Stubbs'); sent to the King's Lodge on 31 May 1822 (Jutsham, *Deliveries*, f. 34); later at Cumberland Lodge.

Literature: Gilbey, p. 119; Shaw Sparrow, *Sporting Artists*, p. 143.

In 1790–1 John Brookes had supplied the Prince of Wales with at least fourteen and a half brace of red deer at 50 guineas per brace. A further four brace had been brought from Paris. Brookes was also responsible for taking some of the animals to Bagshot and others to Brighton and Kempshott (W.R.A., Geo. 25508).

Francis Swaine

d. 1782. Painter of marine subjects and landscapes. He exhibited in London, at the Society of Artists and the Free Society, between 1761 and 1783.

1127. THE ENGAGEMENT BETWEEN THE *ARETHUSA* AND *LA BELLE POULE*

Buckingham Palace. 24⅜ × 36½ in., 61,9 × 92,7 cm.

Signed: *F. Swaine.*

The two ships firing at each other in a calm sea under the light of the moon on the night of 17 June 1778.

Recorded, apparently at Hampton Court (673), in 1852; later at Kensington.

Literature: Law, 1881, 1898 (894).

The encounter marked the beginning of hostilities between England and France in the War of American Independence. Admiral Keppel (No. 1024) sailed from St. Helens on 12 June 1778. West of the Lizard he observed, on 17 June, two French frigates reconnoitring the fleet; one of the French ships was conducted to the Admiral. Captain Marshall on the frigate *Arethusa* requested the captain of the other frigate, *La Belle Poule*, to agree to do likewise. The French captain refused and a fierce action began between the two ships and lasted for more than two hours. The *Arethusa* was much damaged; at daybreak *La Belle Poule*, who had suffered the heavier casualties, was towed to safety.

1128. A RIVER LANDSCAPE IN HOLLAND

Hampton Court (340). Panel: 6 × 8 in., 15,2 × 20,3 cm.

The signature and date 1782 are partly concealed under the inventory number.

A fishing boat and a small vessel under sail near a village on a river in Holland.

See No. 1129.

Literature: Law, 1881, 1898 (897); Collins Baker, *Hampton Court*, p. 167.

On the back of the panel is a contemporary inscription: *for | Miss* [?*Bemtland*] | *Thrednedle.* No. 1128 is probably a copy of a seventeenth-century Dutch picture.

1129. SHIPS IN A BREEZE

Hampton Court (339). Panel: 6 × 8⅛ in., 15,2 × 20,6 cm.

Signed: [*F*] *Swaine*; the signature is partly concealed under the inventory number.

A royal yacht, close-hauled in a stiff breeze, with other shipping.

Nos. 1128, 1129 are recorded at Hampton Court in 1849 (*The Stranger's Guide*, Nos. 961, 962).

Literature: Law, 1881, 1898 (895); Collins Baker, *Hampton Court*, p. 167.

Closely based on Willen van de Velde the Younger, with the ships brought up to date.

John Taylor

c. 1745–1806. Landscape-painter, born in Bath, where he worked almost all his life. There is an important reference to him in Smollett's *Humphry Clinker* (1771) as 'a gentleman residing in this place [i.e., Bath], who paints landscapes for his amusement . . . If I am not totally devoid of taste, however, this young gentleman of Bath is the best landscape-painter now living . . .' Smollett's description of his style fits very well Nos. 1130–4 below.

1130. CLASSICAL LANDSCAPE WITH FISHERMEN

Buckingham Palace. 40 × 50⅛ in., 101,6 × 127,3 cm.; painted to be framed as an oval.

Signed and dated: *John Taylor. Invt & Pinxt | 1770.*

An evening landscape with fishermen at their nets in the foreground and a classical temple (?) among trees on the right.

Nos. 1130, 1131 were probably the pair stated to have been presented to George III and placed in the Coffee Room at Kew (Geo. III, *Kew*; George IV No. 1111); No. 1130 is presumably the 'Sun Set' by Taylor recorded in that room; recorded at Buckingham Palace (447) in 1869 (*V.R. inv.*).

1131. LANDSCAPE WITH FIGURES

Buckingham Palace. 39¾ × 50 in., 101 × 127 cm.; painted to be framed as an oval.

Signed and dated: *John Taylor | Invt & Pinxt Bath 1769.*

Figures by a fence in the foreground; in the distance is a castle which strongly resembles Windsor and a town on an estuary with shipping.

See No. 1130 (Geo. III, *Kew*; George IV, No. 1118); recorded at Buckingham Palace (443) in 1869 (*V.R. inv.*).

1132. LANDSCAPE WITH A LARGE TREE
(*Plate* 19)

Buckingham Palace. 40 × 50 in., 101,6 × 127 cm.; painted to be framed as an oval.

Signed and dated: *J Taylor 1780* (initials in monogram).

A boy reclining with a dog under a large tree; in the distance is a herd of cattle near a bridge, and on the right is a group of buildings on a cliff.

Nos. 1132, 1133 are among a group of eighteen pictures, portraits as well as landscapes, which were sent up to Carlton House (where they arrived on 7 February 1822) on offer from Dr. J. Taylor, the artist's son, of Clifton, Bristol; two only were retained and the remainder were sent back to Dr. Taylor on 23 February 1822 (Jutsham, *Receipts*, ff. 154–5, *Deliveries*, f. 30). No. 1132 was recorded at Carlton House (inv. of 1816, later No. 593; the Carlton House label was formerly on the back) and was at Buckingham Palace (614) in 1876 (*V.R. inv.*).

1133. CLASSICAL LANDSCAPE WITH FIGURES

Buckingham Palace. 39¾ × 50 in., 101 × 127 cm.; painted to be framed as an oval.

Signed and dated: *Taylor | of Bath 1793*

Boys and a cow in the foreground of a classical landscape; in the distance is a broad river with a town and groups of classical buildings.

See No. 1132. Recorded at Carlton House (inv. of 1816, later No. 594; the Carlton House label was formerly on the back); at Buckingham Palace (613) in 1869 (*V.R. inv.*).

1134. LANDSCAPE WITH RUINS

Buckingham Palace. Panel: 15 × 10¾ in., 38,1 × 27,3 cm.

Signed and dated: *J Taylor 1776.*

Figures among elaborate classical ruins, with a stream in the foreground.

No. 1134 was among the pictures selected from the group sent to George IV by the artist's son on 7 February 1822 (see No. 1132): 'A Square Picture—Ancient Buildings—with Figures & Cattle' (Jutsham, *Receipts*, f. 155); recorded as additional No. 595 in the Carlton House inventory of 1816. Later at Kew.

James Ward

1769–1859. Engraver and painter, who had worked very successfully in mezzotint as a young man, but turned increasingly to painting genre scenes, animal subjects and portraits. In 1794 he was appointed Painter and Engraver in Mezzotint to the Prince of Wales.

In a series of letters to Sir William Knighton, one of which is dated 21 April 1824, Ward wrote of his early introduction to the royal family, his presentation of the engraving of No. 660 to Queen Charlotte and some of the Princesses. He hoped to be given a room in which he could carry out his work for the King: 'My reflections pointed to the circumstance of Sir Thomas Lawrence engaged proffessionally in Buckingham House, Mr Holloway at Hampton Court, Sir Willm Beechey and the late Mr West in Windsor Castle'. The King had admired two of his cabinet pictures, then belonging to Sir Charles Blunt and Mr. Allnutt. Ward dedicated to George IV his volume of fourteen lithographic drawings of horses (W.R.A., Geo. 26517–26).

1135. MONITOR (*Plate 287*)

Buckingham Palace. 32⅜ × 43⅝ in., 82,2 × 110,8 cm.

Signed and dated: *J WARD (in monogram) RA.1821*

A chestnut horse, standing in a landscape; in the distance two horses are chasing sheep.

Painted for George IV. Recorded at Windsor (829) in 1878 (*V.R. inv.*).

Ward's account of 19 March 1825 includes £105 for 'Portrait of Monitor' (W.R.A., Geo. 26532). The engraving by Ward of No. 1135, chosen as a blood-horse of remarkable strength and activity, was published in April 1823 by Ackerman and Colnaghi; a select proof, retouched by Ward, is in the Royal Library. No. 1135 is probably the picture exhibited by Ward at the Royal Academy in 1825 (22: Monitor, *the property of H.M. King George the Fourth*).

1136. NONPAREIL (*Plate 285*)

Buckingham Palace. Panel: 31½ × 43¾ in., 80 × 111,1 cm.

Signed and dated: *J WARD (in monogram) RA. 1824*

A bay horse standing by a river with, in the distance, a view of Windsor from the north-west and a rainbow in the sky.

Painted for George IV. Recorded at Windsor (828) in 1878 (*V.R. inv.*).

Ward's account of 19 March 1825 included £105 for 'Portrait of Nonpareil' (W.R.A., Geo. 26532). No. 1136 is presumably the picture—Nonpareil, *the favourite charger of his most gracious Majesty King George the Fourth*—exhibited by Ward at the Royal Academy in 1825 (10). Ward's engraving of it, as the King's favourite charger, was published on 1 May 1824.

1137. SOOTHSAYER

Buckingham Palace. 32¼ × 44 in., 81,9 × 111,8 cm.

Signed and dated: *J WARD (in monogram) RA. 1821*

A chestnut, standing in a spacious landscape.

Painted for George IV. Recorded at Stud Lodge (1162) in 1868 (*V.R. inv.*); later at Marlborough House.

Ward's account of 19 March 1825 includes £105 for 'Portrait of Soothsayer' (W.R.A., Geo. 26532). The engraving by Ward of No. 1137, as a celebrated racehorse lately in the King's possession, was published on 20 April 1828; a select proof, retouched by Ward, is in the Royal Library.
A son of Sorcerer out of Goldenlocks, Soothsayer was bred by R. O. Gascoigne in 1808. He won the St. Leger in 1811 and was then sold to Lord Foley; he won his last race in 1813, at Newmarket.

Benjamin West

1728–1820. Painter of portraits, historical, classical and religious subjects. Born in Pennsylvania, he went to Italy in 1760, arrived in England in 1763 and exhibited two pictures at the Society of Artists in 1764. He gained, through the introduction of Robert Drummond, Archbishop of York, the patronage of George III; he was one of the original members of the Royal Academy (see No. 1210); and in 1772 he became Historical Painter to the King. In 1792 West succeeded Reynolds as President of the Royal Academy.
George III conceived (*c.* 1780) the idea of a private chapel at Windsor, to be constructed in Horn Court and to be decorated with thirty-five large canvases by West illustrating the history of revealed religion. While working on the paintings West received £1,000 per annum from the King, but he was informed in the autumn of 1801 that the paintings were to be 'suspended'. The project was abandoned, possibly at the orders of Queen Charlotte. As early as 15 September 1799 (unpublished) Farington had noted 'West not to paint the pictures for the Revelation chamber, only to finish what he has begun'. It was apparently James Wyatt who had conveyed to West the King's instructions not to continue the series (*ibid.*, 5 June 1805). None of the paintings which had been finished were taken over by the Crown; they were returned to West's family and sold at auction in the West sale by Robins, 22–5 May 1829. In West's own statement of his work on this project (Galt, part II, pp. 209–13), the charge for the completed pictures amounted, up to January 1801, to £21,705. Galt claimed that West had been on friendly terms with the royal family for forty years, but Farington, whose copious references are a primary source for West's relations with the King, indicates as early as 1793 that West was not so often seen at Windsor as hitherto.

Thereafter there was a steady deterioration in West's position at court; by 1804 he was 'no longer looked up to' by the royal family (see particularly, *Diary*, vol. I, pp. 18, 225–6, 278–9, vol. II, pp. 134, 167–8, 170–1, 183, 192–3, 243, 280, 281–2, vol. III, pp. 17–18, 33, 37–9, vol. IV, p. 54, vol. VI, p. 93). West succeeded Richard Dalton (d. 1791) as Surveyor of the King's Pictures and from c. 1812 was occupied in making lists of them for the Prince Regent (see inv. Nos. 43, 44 and 46, pp. xvii–xx above).

1138. GEORGE III (*Plate* 108)

Windsor Castle (3124). $100\frac{1}{2} \times 72$ in., $255,3 \times 182,9$ cm.

Signed and dated: *B.West | 1779*

Full-length, standing, in a military coat, wearing the ribbon and star of the Garter and holding a roll recording troop dispositions, headed: *Plans of the Camps of Cox Heath, Warley* [see Nos. 932, 933], *St Edm* [*Port*]*smouth & Plymouth | with a General Return of your Majesty's Forces in Great Britain | Augt 18 1779*. The crown, orb and sceptre are on a cushion behind the King; beside him are his military hat and a blue mantle laced with gold and lined with ermine. In the background is a camp by the sea-shore and ships of the fleet with the *Royal George* firing a salute; on the shore nearer at hand are the King's charger held by a groom[1] in royal livery and a detachment of the 15th Light Dragoons led by Lord Amherst, in the uniform of a General with the ribbon and star of the Bath, and William, 5th Marquess of Lothian (1737–1815), in the uniform of a Major-General with the ribbon and star of the Thistle.

Painted for George III and Queen Charlotte. Recorded with No. 1139 by Pyne, in the King's Audience Chamber at Hampton Court (Pyne, vol. II, *Hampton Court*, pp. 49–50; later inv. No. 494); later at Kensington and Buckingham Palace.

Literature: Galt, part II, pp. 208, 216; Law, 1881, 1898 (318).

The composition is listed by Galt (*loc. cit.*), who states that West was paid £262. 10s. for it. It was exhibited at the Royal Academy in 1780 (116). There are *pentimenti* in the King's left leg and right arm and in Lord Lothian's horse. A small version, which is said to be signed and dated 1775 and in which the King wears a hat, belongs to the Historical Society of Pennsylvania, Philadelphia. The head of the King in No. 1138 is close to those in a signed three-quarter-length in armour in the Cleveland Museum of Art and in a seated three-quarter-length at Broomhall which is identical with that engraved by E. Fisher (published 28 February 1778). The painting commemorates the events of the summer of 1779, in which the King ('I sigh for an action') played an active part. There was a threat of invasion from France and of an attack by the combined fleets of France and Spain. The alarm was at its height in August, when the enemy fleets were in the Channel. Amherst, as Commander-in-Chief, had summoned the militia regiments into the field; in his plan of defence he entrusted to the Dragoons (see above) the patrolling of the coasts of Kent and Sussex under the threat of enemy landings. In 1780 Prince William was serving in the *Royal George* (see No. 1144).

For Lord Amherst, see No. 995. Lord Lothian became a General in 1796; he was Colonel of the 1st Horse Guards, 1777–89, 11th Dragoons, 1798–1813, and 2nd Dragoons, 1813–15; he was appointed Gold Stick in 1777.

1. In the inventory of Hampton Court in 1835 (414) the groom's name is given as Smart.

1139. QUEEN CHARLOTTE (*Plate* 109)

Windsor Castle (3125). $101 \times 71\frac{1}{2}$ in., $256,5 \times 181,6$ cm.

Signed and dated: *Benj. West. | 1779*

Full-length, standing, resting her left hand on a table by a cushion on which rests her crown; a small spaniel sits at her feet. In the background is a view of the south front of Windsor Castle and the Queen's Lodge. On a terrace behind the Queen are her thirteen children to date: Prince Alfred and Princess Amelia were to be born later. The youngest, Prince Octavius, had been born on 23 February 1779; he is in a little phaeton, pulled along by Prince Ernest and pushed by Prince Adolphus; Prince Augustus is playing with a dog; Princesses Mary and Sophia stand by the baby and the eldest Princesses, Charlotte, Augusta and Elizabeth, stand behind. On the right are Prince William in the uniform of a midshipman, with the ribbon and star of the Thistle, and Prince Edward; on the left, in Windsor uniform with the ribbon and star of the Garter, stand the Prince of Wales and Prince Frederick.

Painted for George III and Queen Charlotte. Recorded with No. 1138 by Pyne, in the King's Audience Chamber at Hampton Court (Pyne, vol. II, *Hampton Court*, pp. 49–50; later inv. No. 498); later at Kensington and Buckingham Palace.

Literature: Galt, part II, pp. 208, 216; Law, 1881, 1898 (321); R.A., *King's Pictures* (111).

The composition is listed by Galt (*loc. cit.*,) who states that West was paid £262. 10s. for it. It was exhibited at the Royal Academy in 1780 (130). The figure of Prince Augustus is close to that in No. 1145. There is a *pentimento* in Prince William's left foot. See also No. 1140.

1140. QUEEN CHARLOTTE

Buckingham Palace. $89 \times 55\frac{1}{4}$ in., $226,1 \times 140,3$ cm.

Signed and dated: *B.West.1782*

Full-length, standing, resting her right hand on a table by her crown; a cavalier spaniel sits at her feet. In the background are the Queen's fourteen children to date and a view of the south front of Windsor Castle and the Queen's Lodge.

Presumably painted for the Queen. Placed in the Queen's Bedchamber at Windsor: 'Her Majesty and all the Princes and Princesses. Mr West' (Geo. III, *Windsor*); recorded in the Coffee Room at Buckingham House in 1819 (775); moved to Hampton Court on 17 December 1835 and placed in the Prince of Wales's second room; later at Windsor (470) and Marlborough House.

Literature: Galt, part II, pp. 215, 216.

Galt (*loc. cit.*) records 'a second whole length of Her Majesty, with all the Royal children in the background', for which West was paid £262. 10s. No. 1140 is a repetition of No. 1139, but in reverse. By 1782 the Queen had given birth (on 22 September 1780) to Prince Alfred, who is presumably the baby in the little phaeton in the second version of the design; Prince Octavius is now seated on the front of the carriage. The figure of the Queen is close in type to No. 1142.

1141. GEORGE III AND QUEEN CHARLOTTE

Windsor Castle (816). Panel (oval): $22\frac{3}{8} \times 31\frac{1}{2}$ in., $56,8 \times 80$ cm.

Signed and dated: *B. West | 1789*

Double portrait in profile to the right; the King wears the robes of the Garter.

Probably painted for the Audience Chamber at Windsor (see below); recorded at Hampton Court in 1835 (551); a label on the back states that it had been received from Windsor on 25 April 1832.

Literature: Collins Baker, *Windsor*, p. 306.

The picture does not appear in the list given by Galt (part II, pp. 207–15) of pictures painted by West for the King between 1768 and 1801; but is probably the 'medallion with profiles of their Majesties', painted by West for the embellishment of the canopy in the Audience Chamber at Windsor (Pyne, vol. I, *Windsor*, p. 166). Walpole refers in a letter to Mary Berry, 9 October 1791, to the 'gaudy, clumsy throne, with a medallion at top of the King's and Queen's heads, over their own—an odd kind of tautology, whenever they sit there!' (*Letters*, ed. Mrs. P. Toynbee, vol. XV (1905), p. 78). The composition shows signs of considerable alteration; the two heads were originally much closer and the King was in classical guise, with a laurel wreath and a naked breast.

1142. QUEEN CHARLOTTE WITH CHARLOTTE, PRINCESS ROYAL (*Plate* 114)

Buckingham Palace. 66¼ × 81 in., 168,2 × 205,7 cm.

Signed and dated: *Benj. West | 1776*

Three-quarter-lengths, on a sofa, engaged in tatting a piece of material or embroidery between them; on the table beside the Queen is a bust of Minerva, a sheet of music and papers inscribed [*diseg*] *nio da Raffa*[*ello*]; in the distance are St. James's Park and Westminster Abbey.

Painted for George III and Queen Charlotte and placed in the King's Closet at St. James's (Geo. III, *St. James's*); removed *c.* 1804/5 to Windsor (Geo. III, *Removals*) and placed in the Dining-Room of the Queen's Private Apartments (Legge's lists, 1813, 1816); later at Hampton Court (492) and Kensington.

Literature: Galt, part II, pp. 208, 216; Law, 1881, 1898 (316), *Kensington* (1899), p. 106.

Exhibited at the Royal Academy in 1777 (362). West received £157 for the picture. A drawing by West of the figure of the Queen is at Windsor (Oppé, No. 640). Valentine Green's engraving of No. 1142 was published in 1778; he also engraved a derivation of the Queen from the same source. The face in No. 1142 is very close to No. 1140. A version of the figure of the Queen in No. 1142 is at Broomhall.

1143. GEORGE, PRINCE OF WALES, WITH PRINCE FREDERICK, LATER DUKE OF YORK (*Plate* 110)

Buckingham Palace. 95½ × 65½ in., 242,6 × 166,3 cm.

Signed and dated: *B.West | 1777*

Full-lengths; the Prince of Wales, wearing a state robe with the collar and star of the Garter, rests his left arm on his brother's shoulders; he wears the Garter round his leg and behind him are the plumed hat of the order and the Prince of Wales's crown. The younger Prince wears the robes of the Garter with the collars of the Garter and the Bath.

Painted for George III and Queen Charlotte and placed in the King's Closet at St. James's (Geo. III, *St. James's*); removed *c.* 1804/5 to Windsor (Geo. III, *Removals*) and placed in the Dining-Room of the Queen's Private Apartments (Legge's lists, 1813, 1816); later at Hampton Court (500) and Kensington.

Literature: Galt, part II, p. 208; Law, 1881, 1898 (322), *Kensington* (1899), p. 105.

Exhibited at the Royal Academy in 1778 (330). West received £210 for the picture. Valentine Green's engraving of it was published on 4 November 1779; the head of Prince Frederick was engraved as the frontispiece to Christopher Smart's *Hymns for the Amusement of Children*.

1144. PRINCE WILLIAM, LATER DUKE OF CLARENCE, AND PRINCE EDWARD, LATER DUKE OF KENT (*Plate* 111)

Buckingham Palace. 96 × 65½ in., 243,8 × 166,3 cm.

Signed and dated: *Benj. West | 1778*

Full-lengths; Prince William, wearing a midshipman's uniform with the ribbon, star and mantle of the Thistle, stands by a large globe on which he points to the English Channel; Prince Edward directs his brother's attention to a model of the *Royal George* which rests on a stand decorated with the figure of Britannia, who is partly concealed by a standard on which is displayed the white horse of Hanover.

Painted for George III and Queen Charlotte and placed in the King's Closet at St. James's (Geo. III, *St. James's*); removed *c.* 1804/5 to Windsor (Geo. III, *Removals*) and placed in the Dining-Room in the Queen's Private Apartments (Legge's lists, 1813, 1816); later at Hampton Court (502) and Kensington.

Literature: Galt, part II, pp. 208, 216; Law, 1881, 1898 (324), *Kensington* (1899), p. 107.

Exhibited at the Royal Academy in 1780 (7). West received £262. 10s. for the picture. Valentine Green's engraving of the figure of Prince William from No. 1144 was published on 1 February 1780, when the Prince was serving on the *Royal George*. There are *pentimenti* in the collars of both boys.

1145. PRINCESS AUGUSTA, PRINCESS ELIZABETH, PRINCE ERNEST (LATER DUKE OF CUMBERLAND), PRINCE AUGUSTUS (LATER DUKE OF SUSSEX), PRINCE ADOLPHUS (LATER DUKE OF CAMBRIDGE) AND PRINCESS MARY (*Plate* 115)

Buckingham Palace. 66¼ × 71 in., 168,2 × 180,3 cm.

Signed and dated: *B. West | 1776*

Full-lengths; Prince Ernest and Prince Augustus are pulling along a little cart in which the infant Princess Mary is supported by her elder sister and Prince Adolphus. A small spaniel plays with a ball in front of a toy drum.

Painted for George III and Queen Charlotte and placed in the King's Closet at St. James's (Geo. III, *St. James's*); removed *c.* 1804/5 to Windsor (Geo. III, *Removals*) and placed in the Dining-Room in the Queen's Private Apartments (Legge's lists, 1813, 1816); later at Hampton Court (488) and Kensington.

Literature: Galt, part II, pp. 208, 216; Law, 1881, 1898 (310), *Kensington* (1899), p. 105.

Exhibited at the Royal Academy in 1777 (363). West received £315 for the picture, which must have been painted some months after the birth of Princess Mary on 25 April 1776. Valentine Green's engraving of it was published on 29 September 1778. There are *pentimenti* in the fall of the baby's frock. The figure of Prince Augustus is very close to that in No. 1139. A drawing in the Victoria and Albert Museum (*Fig.* 37) is related to No. 1145, but may be for a different family group.

1146. AUGUSTUS, DUKE OF SUSSEX

Buckingham Palace. 36×27¾ in., 91,4×70,5 cm.

Signed and dated: *B.West.1780*

Three-quarter-length, leaning on a table; in the distance is a view of Windsor Castle.

Formerly in the collection of George, Duke of Cambridge (*d.* 1904) and in his sale at Christie's, 11 June 1904 (117); bought by H.M. Queen Mary in March 1934 from the estate of Sir Augustus FitzGeorge.

Literature: Galt, part II, p. 215.

Stated by Galt (*loc. cit.*) to have been painted for Queen Charlotte; see No. 1169. It was exhibited at the Royal Academy in 1782 (97).

1147. PRINCE ADOLPHUS, LATER DUKE OF CAMBRIDGE, WITH PRINCESS MARY AND PRINCESS SOPHIA (*Plate* 112)

Buckingham Palace. 95½×59 in., 242,6×149,9 cm.

Signed and dated: *B. West | 1778*

Full-lengths: Prince Adolphus and Princess Mary support the infant Princess Sophia on a carved and gilded chair; an ermine-lined royal robe is draped beside them; at their feet are a large retriever (his collar is inscribed ... *W* ... *AMUS*) and a little spaniel; in the background is a view of the gardens at Kew with Sir William Chambers's Great Pagoda.

Painted for George III and Queen Charlotte and placed in the King's Closet at St. James's (Geo. III, *St. James's*); removed *c.* 1804/5 to Windsor (Geo. III, *Removals*) and placed in the Dining-Room in the Queen's Private Apartments (Legge's lists, 1813, 1816); later at Hampton Court (487) and Kensington.

Literature: Galt, part II, p. 208; Law, 1881, 1898 (309), *Kensington* (1899), p. 106; R.A., *British Portraits*, 1956–7 (311).

Exhibited at the Royal Academy in 1780 (17). West received, probably in 1779, £262. 10s. for the picture.

1148. PRINCE OCTAVIUS (*Plate* 113)

Windsor Castle (1522). 50½×40 in., 128,3×101,6 cm.

Signed and dated: *B.West.1783*

Full-length, standing, wearing a large hat and drawing his father's sword from its scabbard; on the floor is a toy horse on wheels, and on the right are the King's hat and sword-belt. In the distance is a view of the Horse Guards.

Recorded in the King's Gallery at Kensington: 'Portrait of Prince Octavius West' (Geo. III, *Kensington*); later at Frogmore—perhaps taken there by Queen Charlotte—and probably the '*Portrait of his Royal Highness Prince OCTAVIUS, when a child*', recorded in the Bow Drawing-Room there (Pyne, vol. I, *Frogmore*, p. 19).

Literature: Collins Baker, *Windsor*, p. 307.

West painted for George III 'a whole-length portrait of Prince Octavius holding the King's sword' and received £73. 10s. for it (Galt, part II, pp. 214, 216); it was exhibited at the Royal Academy in 1782 (93). The engraving by Facius was published by Boydell in 1785. The sword has been identified by Mr. A. V. B. Norman at Windsor (706).

1149. THE APOTHEOSIS OF PRINCE OCTAVIUS (*Plate* 116)

Buckingham Palace. 94¼×60⅜ in., 239,4×153,3 cm.

Signed and dated: *B. West 1783* (the last two digits are very obscure).

Prince Octavius is welcomed in Heaven by his brother Alfred under the protective wings of an angel and watched by two cherubs. On the ground below is a view of Windsor Castle from the south.

Painted for George III and Queen Charlotte and placed in the King's Dressing-Room (B.M. Add. MS. 6391, f. 122) and later in the Wardrobe at Buckingham House (Geo. III, *Buck. Ho.*); in 1804 it was moved from the King's Closet at Buckingham House to the King's State Bedchamber at Windsor (Geo. III, *Removals;* visible in C. Wild's plate in Pyne, vol. I, *Windsor*, p. 161); later at Hampton Court (503) and Kensington.

Literature: Galt, part II, pp. 215, 216; Law, 1881, 1898 (325); W. T. Whitley, *Artists and their Friends in England 1700–99* (1928), vol. I, pp. 309–10.

Painted for the King for £315. It was exhibited at the Royal Academy in 1784 (81). Prince Octavius died on 3 May 1783; his younger brother, who greets him in No. 1149, had died on 26 August 1782. A study for the whole composition (*Fig.* 38) is in the Witt Collection (615); a drawing in the Museum of Fine Arts, Boston (*Fig.* 39), contains studies for the principal figures. In No. 1149 the clouds at the bottom are so thinly painted as to seem unfinished; the angel's left foot (of which there is a *pentimento*) is also very thinly painted.

Sir Robert Strange's engraving of No. 1149 was published in 1786 with a dedication to the Queen. On 5 January 1787 he presented to the King and Queen at Buckingham House, where he had worked on his plate, some fine impressions of the print (Walpole, *Anecdotes*, vol. V, p. 225; Whitley, *loc. cit.*).

1150. ST. PETER DENYING CHRIST (*Plate* 117)

St. James's Palace. 48¾×49 in., 123,8×124,5 cm.

Signed and dated: *B. West | [?1778]*

St. Peter disclaiming Christ, who stands near him with the damsel at the door of the high priest's residence.

Painted as a present for George III; recorded in the Queen's Private Apartments at Windsor in 1813 (Legge's inv.); later at Hampton Court (491).

Literature: Galt, part II, pp. 215; Law, 1881, 1898 (314).

According to West's statement of his work for the King and Queen, 'His Majesty honoured me by accepting' this picture. It was exhibited at the Royal Academy in 1779 (342). Valentine Green's mezzotint of it was published on 1 May 1780. A version is in the church at Thoresby, possibly the picture mentioned by Galt (part II, p. 221). In May 1861 R. Farrier applied for permission to copy No. 1150 (P.R.O., L.C. 1/97, 150).

1151. ST. GEORGE SLAYING THE DRAGON

Kensington Palace. 77×86 in., 195,6×218,4 cm.

Signed and dated: *B. West | 1787.*

The Saint, protecting the princess with his shield, is about to plunge his spear into the dragon; in the distance are spectators on their knees.

Painted for George III for the King's Audience Chamber at Windsor, where it is seen over the fireplace in Pyne's plate (vol. I, *Windsor*, p. 166); later at Hampton Court (496) and Windsor (2528).

Literature: Galt, part II, pp. 213, 217; Law, 1881, 1898 (319).

Painted for George III for £630.

1152. THE DEPARTURE OF REGULUS
(*Plate* 121)

Kensington Palace. 88½ × 120 in., 229,9 × 304,8 cm.

Signed and dated: *BENJAMIN WEST | PINXIT | LONDINI 1769.*

Regulus, in the Senate House at Rome, spurning the pleadings of his family, the Senate and his friends, is about to return to Carthage, possibly in the steps of the Carthaginian envoys. Beyond a colonnade are ships in a large harbour.

Painted for George III and placed in the Warm Room at Buckingham House (Geo. III, *Buck. Ho.*: 'Regulus leaving the Senate of Rome and returning to Carthage. Mr West'). The picture may for a short time have been at Windsor: in the inv. No. 35 above (p. xlix) is a reference, in the Public Dining-Room, to 'Regulus's departure from the Senate house at Rome, on his return to Carthage' (no artist's name is given). No. 1152 was taken to Hampton Court (501) on 18 September 1833.

Literature: Galt, part II, pp. 25–6, 33, 37, 38–41, 45, 207, 216; Law, 1881, 1898 (323); R.A., *The First Hundred Years*, 1951–2 (395).

Painted for George III for £420. According to Galt the King, who was shown the *Agrippina landing with the Ashes of Germanicus*[1] that West had painted in 1766 for Archbishop Drummond, admired it with the Queen and suggested to West 'another noble Roman subject . . . I mean the final departure of Regulus from Rome'; West was commanded to proceed with a sketch, which was submitted to the King who directed West to paint the picture of a size to fill a space in one of the principal apartments (presumably the Warm Room) at Buckingham House; when the picture was finished, West took it to Buckingham House to show to the King and Queen and received the King's instructions to exhibit it at the newly-formed Royal Academy. A little drawing for the design is in West's sketchbooks (No. 3) at the Royal Academy. The picture was shown at the first exhibition, in 1769 (120). Valentine Green's mezzotint of it was published on 14 November 1771. No. 1152 was exhibited at the British Institution in 1824 (143) and 1833 (15).

The picture illustrates the famous moment in the epic story of the Roman Consul, Marcus Atilius Regulus, who in 255 B.C. had been captured by the Carthaginians and sent by them to negotiate an exchange of prisoners or to discuss peace-terms; he urged the Senate to reject these terms, although this meant that he was bound to return to Carthage, captivity and death. According to Galt (*op. cit.*, p. 26) the King read to West 'the subject of my picture' from Livy. The story is, however, only briefly told by Livy in the summary of the lost book XVII of his history. The story is told in much greater detail in the *Punica* of Silius Italicus, who describes Regulus's inflexible fortitude in the face of his two little sons and their fainting mother Marcia. The moral qualities of the hero—'Magnitudo animi et fortitudo'—were cited by Cicero (*De Officiis*, book III, XXVI–VII) and by Horace, as an example of Martial Courage, in his famous ode (book III, ode V).

1153. THE OATH OF HANNIBAL (*Plate* 122)

Kensington Palace. 88¼ × 119¾ in., 229,1 × 304,1 cm.

Signed and dated: *B. West. PINXIT | 1770*

In a large temple, decorated with trophies of arms, standards and statues, the young Hannibal, under his father's aegis

and trampling on a Roman shield and eagle, takes an oath on the altar at the foot of a statue of Jupiter.

Painted for George III and placed in the Warm Room at Buckingham House (Geo. III, *Buck. Ho.*: 'Hannibal swearing enmity to the Romans . . . Mr West'); taken to Hampton Court (490) on 18 September 1833.

Literature: Galt, part II, pp. 45–6, 207, 216; Law, 1881, 1898 (312); R.A., *English Taste in the Eighteenth Century*, 1955–6 (385).

Painted for George III for £420 as a companion to No. 1152. According to Galt (*op. cit.*) 'The painting being finished it was carried to Buckingham-house, and His Majesty, after looking at it with visible satisfaction, said, that he thought Mr. West could not do better than provide him with suitable subjects [i.e., Nos. 1156, 1157] to fill the unoccupied pannels of the room in which the two pictures were then placed.' No. 1153 was exhibited at the Royal Academy in 1771 (209). There are *pentimenti* in the right arm and knee of the statue of Jupiter and in the jug on the right of the ox's head. Valentine Green's mezzotint of No. 1153 was published on 1 November 1773.

The literary source is presumably the opening of book XXI of Livy's *Ab Urbe Condita*. Hannibal's father, Hamilcar, was offering sacrifices before transporting his army to Spain; Hannibal, then nine years old, begged his father to take him with him; Hamilcar, taking him up to the altar, made him swear, with his hand laid on the victim, that as soon as he could he would prove himself the enemy of Rome.

1154. THE FAMILY OF THE KING OF ARMENIA BEFORE CYRUS (*Plate* 119)

Kensington Palace. 41¼ × 54 in., 104,8 × 137,2 cm.

Signed and dated: *B. West. | 1773*

Cyrus, seated at the door of his tent, confronting the aged King of Armenia, his family and followers.

Painted for George III and placed in the Warm Room at Buckingham House (Geo. III, *Buck. Ho.*: 'Relates to the history of Cyrus'); removed to Hampton Court (499) on 18 September 1833.

Literature: Galt, part II, pp. 50, 207, 216; Law, 1881, 1898 (315); R.A., *English Taste in the Eighteenth Century*, 1955–6 (383); Canada and U.S., *British Painting in the Eighteenth Century*, 1957–8 (71).

Painted for George III for £157. 10s. According to Galt Nos. 1154, 1155 were painted to complete the set of heroic subjects painted for the King. The subject has recently been described as Cyrus with the family of Astyages, King of Media; but it in fact illustrates (see Galt, *loc. cit.*) an episode in the story of Cyrus's dealings with the King of Armenia, as told by Xenophon in his *Cyropaedia*, book III, i, 1–37. The King of Armenia had plotted against Cyrus and failed to pay his tribute. He had sent away his younger son, his Queen, his son's wife and daughters and had taken refuge on a hill. His family and treasure were captured by Cyrus and he was compelled to appear before Cyrus on trial, accompanied by his family in their carriages. West illustrates the moment during the dialogue between the King and Cyrus when the King's elder son Tigranes 'stripped off his turban and rent his garments, and the women cried aloud and tore their cheeks, as if it were all over with their father and they were already lost'.

1155. THE WIFE OF ARMINIUS BROUGHT CAPTIVE TO GERMANICUS (*Plate* 120)

Kensington Palace. 41 × 53¾ in., 104,1 × 136,5 cm.

Signed and dated: *B. West. | 1773*

---

1. Exhibited at the Society of Artists in 1768 (175); now in Yale University Art Gallery (G. Evans, *Benjamin West and the Taste of his Times* (Southern Illinois University Press (1959), pl. 1).

The wife of Arminius, with other captives, brought before Germanicus by Segestes.

Painted for George III and placed in the Warm Room at Buckingham House (Geo. III, *Buck. Ho.*); removed to Hampton Court (495) on 18 September 1833.

Literature: Galt, part II, pp. 50–1, 207, 216; Law, 1881, 1898 (313); R.A., *English Taste in the Eighteenth Century*, 1955–6 (395); Rome, *Il Settecento a Roma*, 1959 (663).

Painted for George III for £157. 10s. The episode illustrated by West occurred during the campaigns of Julius Caesar Germanicus in Germany. In A.D. 15 Arminius, chief of the Cherusci, was fighting against Segestes, another tribal chief. Germanicus came to the aid of Segestes. Thusnelda, wife of Arminius and daughter of Segestes, was captured. Segestes presented himself before Germanicus as 'fit mediator for a German people' and interceded for his daughter who was *enceinte*. Germanicus promised safety to his kinsfolk and children. West presumably drew the outline of the story from the *Annals* of Tacitus, book I, 55–8; but Strabo in his *Geography* (book VII, I, 4) describes the captives before Germanicus in more detail, including Segimundus, brother of Thusnelda; Thusnelda's three-year-old son, Thumelius; and Sesithacus, a chieftain of the Cherusci, with Rhamis, his wife. These were presumably included in West's group of captives. According to Galt (*op. cit.*), George III was pleased with the suggestion that West should paint this subject as there was a tradition that Thusnelda was an ancestress of the Hanoverian dynasty. A preparatory drawing belongs to the Pennsylvania Historical Society, Philadelphia.

1156. THE DEATH OF EPAMINONDAS
(*Plate* 123)

Kensington Palace. 87½ × 70⅝ in., 222,2 × 179,4 cm.

Signed and dated: *B. West| 1773*

The dying Epaminondas, outside his tent, supported by his grief-stricken followers.

Painted for George III and placed in the Warm Room at Buckingham House (Geo. III, *Buck. Ho.*); removed to Hampton Court (493) on 18 September 1833.

Literature: Galt, part II, pp. 50, 207, 216; Law, 1881, 1898 (317).

Painted for George III for £315. West had apparently suggested to George III that the subject, 'as a classic subject and with Grecian circumstances', would make a suitable contrast with No. 1167. No. 1156 was exhibited at the Royal Academy in 1773 (304). It was engraved by Valentine Green (mezzotint published on 21 February 1774) and P. Bernard. In the Wakefield Art Gallery is a very much smaller and later picture of this subject by West, but it bears no relation to No. 1156. The design of No. 1156, in broad outline, is influenced by Gravelot's engraving of the same subject in Rollin's *Ancient History*, vol. IV (P. S. Walch, 'Charles Rollin and early Neoclassicism', *Art Bulletin*, vol. XLIX (1967), pp. 123–4.
Epaminondas, a famous Greek general, was mortally wounded in an inconclusive victory over the Spartans at Mantinea in 362 B.C. The story of his death is told, for example, by Diodorus Siculus, *Library of History*, book XV, 86–7, and Cornelius Nepos, *De Excellentibus Ducibus*, XV. He was wounded in the chest by a spear, which broke off, leaving its iron point in his body. Assured that when the spear-point was drawn from his chest he would die, he first asked his armour-bearer if his shield had been saved and, on seeing it

(as in West's rendering of the scene), 'he said, "It is time to die"', and directed them to withdraw the spear-point'.

1157. THE DEATH OF THE CHEVALIER BAYARD (*Plate* 124)

Kensington Palace. 87¼ × 70½ in., 221,6 × 179,1 cm.

Signed and dated: *B. West | 1772*.

The dying Chevalier, clasping his sword, is surrounded by his mourning companions; his adversaries, headed by the Constable of Bourbon and advancing under the Imperial banners, are paying homage to him.

Painted for George III and placed in the Warm Room at Buckingham House (Geo. III, *Buck. Ho.*); removed to Hampton Court (489) on 18 September 1833.

Literature: Galt, part II, pp. 50, 207, 216; Law, 1881, 1898 (311).

Painted for George III for £315. West had apparently suggested the subject to George III as a companion to Nos. 1156, 1167, as it 'would serve to illustrate the heroism and peculiarities of the middle ages'. It was exhibited at the Royal Academy in 1773 (305). Valentine Green's mezzotint of it was published on 21 February 1774. In the Wakefield Art Gallery is a very much smaller, and quite different, picture by West, signed and dated 1797, of the dying Bayard. Pierre Terrail, Chevalier de Bayard, celebrated for his exploits in the service of Charles VIII, Louis XII and Francis I, was mortally wounded in the groin by a shot from an arquebus on 30 April 1524 during the campaigns in Lombardy. His soldiers propped him against a tree, where, with the hilt of his sword at his lips, he recited the Miserere. As he lay dying he received the homage of his adversaries, headed by the Constable of Bourbon who had deserted to the Imperial cause and whom Bayard, with his last breath, pronounced less happy than himself. West could have read of the Chevalier's death in one of the many later editions of the sixteenth-century accounts of his life and deeds.

1158. EDWARD III CROSSING THE SOMME
(*Plate* 125)

Kensington Palace. 54 × 59 in., 137,2 × 149,9 cm.

Signed and dated: *B. West. 1788*.

The English army, led by Edward III, crossing the river and driving back the French forces; the Black Prince appears prominently in the group of mounted soldiers following the English King. The banners flying over the English array include those of the King, Sir John Beauchamp and William de Montacute, 2nd Earl of Salisbury.

Painted for George III and placed in the King's Audience Chamber at Windsor (C. Knight's *Windsor Guide* (c. 1790); Pyne, vol. I, *Windsor*, pp. 166–7); later at Buckingham Palace (477).

Literature: Galt, part II, pp. 214, 217; R.A., *King's Pictures* (503).

Painted for George III for £630. It was exhibited at the Royal Academy in 1792 (66: *Edward IIId passing the river Soame; painted for the Audience Chamber in Windsor Castle*). A small *modello* of the design, signed and dated 1788 and very close in every detail to No. 1158, was with Spink's in 1951 and later with Knoedler (N.Y.); this may be the version of the design listed by Galt, *op. cit.* p. 225.
No. 1158 was recently described as the battle of Crécy (13 August 1346; see No. 1164), but in fact illustrates the crossing of the Somme before the battle. When Edward III reached the Somme he found the bridges had been demolished. A peasant showed him the ford of Blanche Tache below Abbeville, across which the King led his troops

when the tide was low. The French forces on the opposite bank, under Godemar de Faye, were driven back. The standard accounts of the action available to West were in ch. XV of Hume's *History of England* and ch. CXXVII of Froissart's *Chronicle*. According to Froissart, 'The Frenchemen defended so well the passage at the yssuing out of the water, that they had moche to do: the Genowayes dyde them great trouble with their crosbowes; on thother syde the archers of Englande shotte so holly togyder, that the Frenchmen were fayne to gyve place to the Englysshmen'. The English archers are clearly seen in No. 1158.

1159. EDWARD III ENTERTAINING HIS PRISONERS

Kensington Palace. 39⅜ × 60⅛ in., 100 × 152,7 cm.

Signed and dated: *B. West. 1788.*

The King, after his captives had supped with the Prince of Wales, placing a chaplet of pearls on the head of the Sieur de Ribaumont. Behind the King stands Sir Walter de Manny whose banner is seen through the colonnade on the left.

Painted for George III and placed in the King's Audience Chamber at Windsor (C. Knight's *Windsor Guide* (*c.* 1790); Pyne, vol. I, *Windsor*, pp. 168–9; later inv. No. 163).

Literature: Galt, part II, pp. 214, 217.

Painted for George III for £525. A preliminary *modello* of the design was in the Neeld sale at Christie's, 13 July 1945 (174); this may have been the sketch listed by Galt, *op. cit.*, p. 227.

No. 1159 illustrates the banquet at Calais after the forces of Edward III, led by Sir Walter de Manny, had defeated an attempt by the French to recapture the town in January 1349. After the meal the King came into the room to talk with his prisoners. He greeted with particular courtesy Eustace de Ribaumont, with whom he had fought in single combat during the engagement; he placed on his head a chaplet of pearls that he himself had been wearing, released him from his ransom and set him free. The story could have been read by West in ch. XV of Hume's *History of England* and chs. CLI and CLII of Froissart's *Chronicle*.

1160. QUEEN PHILIPPA AT THE BATTLE OF NEVILLE'S CROSS (*Plate* 127)

Kensington Palace. 38¾ × 59¾ in., 98,4 × 151,8 cm.

Signed and dated: *B. West. 1789*

Queen Philippa, her gown and saddle-cloth decorated with the royal arms of England, on horseback at the head of her forces; on the left is the Scottish army with King David II fighting on foot, about to surrender to his captor, John Copland. At the head of the Queen's forces are Henry, 2nd Lord Percy, the Archbishops of Canterbury (John de Stratford) and York (William la Zouche) and the Bishops of Durham (Thomas de Hatfield) and Lincoln (Thomas le Bec). The banners above the Scots army are those of the King of Scots, St. Andrew, Baliol and Douglas.

Painted for George III and placed in the King's Audience Chamber at Windsor (C. Knight's *Windsor Guide* (*c.* 1790); Pyne, vol. I, *Windsor*, pp. 167–8; later inv. No. 165).

Literature: Galt, part II, pp. 213, 217.

Painted for George III for £525. In 1793 West showed at the Royal Academy (74) *Philippa, Queen Consort to Edward III, at the battle of Nevill's Cross, near Durham where David,* *King of Scotland, was made prisoner.* This was probably No. 1160, but Galt lists another version of the subject (*op. cit.*, p. 225) and 'the small sketch' of it (*ibid.*, p. 227).

David II, as an ally of Philip VI of France, had invaded England in an attempt to divert Edward III's attention. At Neville's Cross, near Durham, his army was routed by the northern barons on 17 October 1346 and he was captured. The Queen entrusted the command of the English forces to Lord Percy. According to Hume (ch. XV of his *History of England*), she rode 'through the ranks of her army, exhorted every man to do his duty . . . Nor could she be persuaded to leave the field, till the armies were on the point of engaging.' After lodging the King of Scots in the Tower, the Queen embarked for Calais (see No. 1161). West could also have read Froissart's account of the battle (ch. CXXXVIII of his *Chronicle*), in which special mention is made of the Scottish axes 'sharpe and harde' and the 'great strokes' made with them. These axes are clearly seen on the left of No. 1160.

1161. THE BURGHERS OF CALAIS (*Plate* 128)

Kensington Palace. 39⅜ × 60⅛ in., 100 × 153,3 cm.

Signed and dated: *B. West. 1789*

Queen Philippa interceding with Edward III, before whom lie the keys of Calais with a sword and a captured French flag; of the three figures behind the King, one is the Prince of Wales, another Sir John Beauchamp. Before the King are the captive burghers, attended by citizens and soldiers. One of the banners on the right is that of Sir Walter de Manny.

Painted for George III and placed in the King's Audience Chamber at Windsor (C. Knight's *Windsor Guide* (*c.* 1790); Pyne, vol. I, *Windsor*, p. 168; later inv. No. 167).

Literature: Galt, part II, pp. 214, 217.

Painted for George III for £525. A preliminary *modello* of the design was in the Neeld sale at Christie's, 13 July 1945 (174); this may have been the sketch listed by Galt, *op. cit.*, p. 227. West exhibited a picture of this subject at the Royal Academy in 1788 (89). This may be the picture in Detroit (G. Evans, *Benjamin West and the Taste of his Times* (Southern Illinois University Press, 1959), pl. 50) and the 'second picture' of the subject listed by Galt, *op. cit.*, p. 224.

The famous event illustrated by West took place on 3 August 1347, when Edward III entered Calais after a siege which had lasted nearly a year. West could have looked up the story in ch. XV of Hume's *History of England* or ch. CXLVI of Froissart's *Chronicle*. By the terms of the surrender of the town, Edward III had agreed to spare the inhabitants if six chief burghers of the town should give themselves up 'bare heeded, bare foted and bare legged . . . with haulters about their neckes, with the kayes of the towne'. They were presented to the King outside the gates of the town by Sir Walter de Manny; Edward III determined to have them beheaded, refused to heed Sir Walter's intercession, but finally yielded to his Queen's plea on behalf of the captives.

1162. THE INSTITUTION OF THE ORDER OF THE GARTER

113 × 176½ in., 287 × 448.3 cm.

Signed and dated: *B. West. 1787*

Edward III and the Black Prince, with the Knights of the Garter, kneeling on either side of an altar at which two Bishops (? of Winchester and Salisbury), wearing the badge of the Garter on their vestments, bless the Statutes of the order. The Queen kneels, with other royal and attendant ladies, in front of the altar. In a gallery beyond are spectators including the younger royal children and distinguished captives, such as David Bruce, King of Scotland, whose shields and banners hang from the walls. Along the top of the canvas are painted the arms of the King, Black Prince and the original twenty-four Knights.

Painted for George III for the King's Audience Chamber at Windsor (C. Knight's *Windsor Guide* (c. 1790); Pyne, vol. I, *Windsor*, p. 169; later No. 168). Placed on loan in the Palace of Westminster in 1968.

Literature: Galt, part II, pp. 213, 216; Collins Baker, *Windsor*, p. 306.

Painted for George III for £1,365. It was exhibited at the Royal Academy in 1792 (8: *The first ceremony, when Edward the Third, with the original Knights, instituted the most noble order of the Garter; painted for the Audience Chamber in Windsor Castle*). In 1787 West had exhibited at the Academy (19) 'a finished sketch' of this subject. Galt (*op. cit.*, pp. 220, 226, 227, 229) also lists 'The small picture of the Order of the Garter, differing in composition from the great picture at Windsor', 'Small sketch of the Order of the Garter', 'The second small sketch of the Order of the Garter' and 'Picture of the Order of the Garter'. One of these, presumably, is the small version of No. 1162 in the National Gallery (315; transferred to the Tate Gallery. See M. Davies's catalogue, *British School* (1946), pp. 170–1) which was engraved for *The Vernon Gallery* and shows slight variations from the final design, principally in being simplified and slightly cut off at both sides. Among the spectators in the gallery on the extreme left of No. 1162 is West himself, probably painted for him by Gilbert Stuart. The *Public Advertiser* of 3 August 1787 stated that West had finished some of the large pictures for Windsor Castle, on which he had been long engaged; that in No. 1162 West's portrait was to be introduced at the King's desire; and that West had asked Stuart to paint this for him (W. T. Whitley, *Gilbert Stuart* (1932), p. 64). It has been suggested that Stuart's own likeness appears above that of West.
The Order of the Garter was probably inaugurated on St. George's Day, 23 April 1348. It was associated from very early days with the Chapel of St. Edward and St. George at Windsor, in which West appears to have set his scene. His principal source for the early history of the order was probably Ashmole's work, published in 1672.

1163. EDWARD, THE BLACK PRINCE, RECEIVING KING JOHN OF FRANCE AFTER THE BATTLE OF POITIERS

113 × 177 in., 287 × 449,6 cm.

Signed and dated: *B.West. 1788*

The Black Prince, wearing his feathers in his helmet, stands under a tent to greet the captive king. Shields and weapons, presumably French, lie on the ground before him. The figures around the Prince and his captive wear crests and surcoats or carry banners. Among them are figures probably intended for William de Montacute, 2nd Earl of Salisbury, John, Lord Mohun, Ralph, Earl of Stafford, Sir Jean de Grailly, Captal de Buch, Thomas Beauchamp, Earl of Warwick, and John de Vere, 7th Earl of Oxford.

Painted for George III for the King's Audience Chamber at Windsor (C. Knight's *Windsor Guide* (c. 1790); Pyne, vol. I, *Windsor*, pp. 169–70; later No. 164). Placed on loan in the Palace of Westminster in 1968.

Literature: Galt, part II, pp. 213, 216; Collins Baker, *Windsor*, p. 305.

Painted for George III for £1,365. It was exhibited at the Royal Academy in 1794 (8: *Edward the Black Prince receiving John, King of France, prisoner, after the battle of Poictiers. Painted for His Majesty's Audience Chamber in Windsor Castle*). Galt records (*op. cit.*, p. 226) a 'small picture' of the same subject. The battle of Poitiers had been fought on 19 September 1356, when the Black Prince routed the French army, superior to him in numbers and led by King John. The French King was captured and conducted by the Earl of Warwick to the Black Prince's tent, where his captor treated him with legendary courtesy. West could have read of the battle in ch. XVI of Hume's *History of England* and in ch. CLXII–V of Froissart's *Chronicle*.

1164. EDWARD III WITH THE BLACK PRINCE AFTER THE BATTLE OF CRÉCY

113 × 176 in., 287 × 447 cm.

Signed and dated: *B.West. 1788.*

The King, his surcoat decorated with the royal arms of England, clasps the hand of the Black Prince, at whose feet lies the coronet decorated with the motto and feathers of the blind King of Bohemia who lies dead, near his horses and attendants, at the Prince's feet. The King of Bohemia's white horse stands on the left; beyond is the windmill on the hill from which the King had watched the battle. The figures standing round the King and Prince wear crests and surcoats or carry banners. Among them are figures probably intended for Thomas Beauchamp, Earl of Warwick, Sir John Mohun, Edward Le Despenser (?), Bartholomew, Lord Burghersh, Richard Fitzalan, Earl of Arundel, Roger, Lord Clifford, Sir Miles Stapleton, Sir John Lisle, Sir Nigel Loring, Roger Mortimer, Earl of March, and Sir Thomas Holland.

Painted for George III for the King's Audience Chamber at Windsor (C. Knight's *Windsor Guide* (c. 1790); Pyne, vol. I, *Windsor*, p. 167; later No. 166). Placed on loan in the Palace of Westminster in 1968.

Literature: Galt, part II, pp. 213, 216; Collins Baker, *Windsor*, p. 305.

Painted for George III for £1,365. It was exhibited at the Royal Academy in 1783 (16: *King Edward III embracing his son, Edward the Black Prince, after the battle of Cressy. Painted for His Majesty's Audience Chamber in Windsor Castle*). For a preliminary sketch, see No. 1165.
The Battle of Crécy was fought on 25 August 1346. The French were heavily defeated. The blind King of Bohemia was slain. The Prince of Wales behaved with celebrated valour. According to Hume (in ch. XV of his *History of England*), the King embraced his son after the victory and exclaimed: 'My brave son! Persevere in your honourable cause: You are my son; for valiantly have you acquitted yourself today: You have shown yourself worthy of empire.' In addition to Hume's account of the battle, West could also have consulted Froissart (ch. CXXX of his *Chronicle*). West clearly was at pains to illustrate the motto and badge of the dead King of Bohemia which were adopted by the Prince of Wales in memory of his victory.

1165. EDWARD III WITH THE BLACK PRINCE AFTER THE BATTLE OF CRÉCY

Kensington Palace. 15 × 20½ in., 38,1 × 52,1 cm.

Sold by the executors of Mrs. T. Natt at Christie's, 12 June 1886

(33); bought by Queen Victoria in 1887 (P.R.O., L.C. 1/513,9), and thereafter at Windsor (2167) and Buckingham Palace.

A preliminary sketch for No. 1164, perhaps the 'first sketch' of the battle of Crécy, listed by Galt, part II, p. 227. The main elements in the design are established, but there are differences in detail (e.g., in the position of the Black Prince's horse on the left) between No. 1165 and the final design and almost none of the heraldic detail has yet been worked out. No. 1165 or 1166 could be the sketch of this subject in the West sale by Robins, 22-5 May 1829 (105, measurements given as 14½×24 in.).

1166. EDWARD III WITH THE BLACK PRINCE AFTER THE BATTLE OF CRÉCY
(*Plate* 126)

St. James's Palace. Canvas mounted on panel: 16½×25¾ in., 41,9×65,4 cm.

Signed and dated: *B. West 1789.*

Formerly in the collection of Robert Vernon; sold after his death by Christie's, 21 April 1877 (124); bought by Queen Victoria in 1887 (P.R.O., L.C. 1/513,9) and thereafter at Windsor (2166) and Buckingham Palace.

No. 1166, perhaps the 'Small picture of the Battle of Cressy' listed by Galt, part II, p. 226, is a replica on a small scale of No. 1164 which had been painted in the previous year.

1167. THE DEATH OF WOLFE

Kensington Palace. 60½×96½ in., 153,7×245,1 cm.; there are original additions, made in painting, of *c.* 6½ in. on the left and *c.* 6½ in. on the right.

Wolfe is seen dying in the arms of three officers, in the middle of a group of mourning figures (see below). In the distance on the right are seen the British troops disembarking in the St. Lawrence River and scaling the Heights of Abraham; on the left they are seen overwhelming the retreating French army.

Painted for George III and placed in the Warm Room at Buckingham House (Geo. III, *Buck. Ho.*; Walpole, *Visits*, p. 79); removed to Hampton Court (497) on 18 September 1833.

Literature: Galt, part II, pp. 46-50, 207, 216; Waagen (1854), vol. II, p. 365; Law, 1881, 1898 (320); J. C. Webster, 'Pictures of the Death of Major-General James Wolfe', *Journal of the Soc. of Army Historical Research*, vol. VI (1927), pp. 30-7; W. T. Whitley, *Artists and their Friends in England 1700-99* (1928), vol. I, pp. 281-2; J. C. Webster, *Wolfe and the Artists* (Toronto, 1930), pp. 64-70; C. Mitchell, 'Benjamin West's "Death of General Wolfe" and the Popular History Piece', *Journal of the Warburg and Courtauld Institutes*, vol. VII (1944), pp. 20-33; R.A., *The First Hundred Years*, 1951-2 (59); J. F. Kerslake, 'The Likeness of Wolfe' in *Wolfe, Portraiture and Genealogy* (1959), pp. 17-43.

A second version, painted for the King for £315 in 1771, of the original, signed and dated 1770, which had been exhibited at the Royal Academy in 1771 (210). The original had been bought by Lord Grosvenor; it is now in the National Gallery of Canada, Ottawa (8007; see catalogue of *Older Schools*, ed. R. H. Hubbard, Ottawa and Toronto, 1957, pp. 132-3, for bibliography). The King, according to Galt, had heard of the picture, 'which excited a great sensation', but had been put off buying it by learning that West had dressed the characters in modern military costume. Reynolds had at first urged West to 'adopt the classic costume of antiquity'. The delay enabled Lord Grosvenor to buy the picture, but the King commissioned West to paint a copy for him, to which Nos. 1156, 1157 were later painted

as companion pieces. The picture was extremely popular. Galt lists, apart from the original and No. 1167, five more repetitions[1] and a drawing of the subject (*op. cit.*, pp. 220, 223, 233); other copies are recorded and Woollett's engraving of the original was published by Boydell on 1 January 1776. No. 1167 is slightly larger than the first version; the additions on the sides (see above) contain details not included in the original.

Although West clothed the figures in his picture in modern dress and uniforms, the group round the dying Wolfe is entirely imaginary. The design is crammed with inaccuracies. When Wolfe fell on the Plains of Abraham on 13 September 1759, only three people were present at his death. The figures in No. 1167 have been identified as follows: the surgeon holding a handkerchief to Wolfe's heart is Surgeon Robert Adair; supporting Wolfe on the other side are Captain Hervey Smith or Smyth, an A.D.C., and Colonel Isaac Barré, Deputy-Adjutant; behind Wolfe stand Colonel Williamson and, holding the flag, Lieutenant Henry Browne; the group on the left, from left to right, are Sir William Howe, later 5th Viscount Howe, Lieut.-Col. Simon Fraser, Master of Lovat, Captain Debbieg, Brigadier Robert Monckton, and Colonel Napier (?); on the right stand one of Wolfe's servants and a grenadier. In fact it was probably Lieutenant Browne and not Adair (who was never at Quebec) who attended the dying general; Monckton, at the time of Wolfe's death, was lying severely wounded on the battlefield; the pensive Indian is a totally imaginary figure. It is stated that Brigadier-General James Murray refused to allow West to include him in the design as he had not been near Wolfe at the time of his death, and that at least one officer refused to pay West the £100 which was asked for a place in the composition (R. H. Mahon, *Life of General the Hon. James Murray* (1921), p. 24; A. Doughty, *The Siege of Quebec* (Quebec, 1901), vol. II, p. 314). West's interest in Wolfe is attested by his imaginary portrait of him as a boy; a version, signed and dated 1771, is at Squerryes, with a small version of No. 1167. A small copy, from the private collection of H.M. King George V, is at Buckingham Palace.

1168. A VIEW IN WINDSOR GREAT PARK
(*Plate* 118)

Windsor Castle (2621). 60×84¾ in., 152,4×215,3 cm.

Signed: *BWest.* There may also be a date, but this is now indecipherable and even the signature is hard to read.

In the foreground a peasant's family, squatting in a clearing in Windsor Forest, greet the father of the family on his return with a bundle of faggots; near the peasants' hut are pigs and cattle. Through an opening in the trees is seen a stag-hunt, with George III taking part, and a distant view of Windsor Castle from the south; on a hill to the left is a large building (?Cranbourne Lodge).

Stated to have remained in the painter's possession until his death; sold in the West sale by Robins, 22-5 May 1829 (67). Bought by King Edward VII in 1904 from Colonel Tatham.

Literature: J. T. Smith, *A Book for a rainy Day*, 2nd. ed. (1845), pp. 113-14; *Windsor*, 1922, p. 7.

Almost certainly the picture exhibited by West at the Royal Academy in 1785 (31: *A Landscape representing the country near Windsor*[2]); and also probably one of the two pictures

---

1. The repetition for Lord Bristol is still at Ickworth and is signed or inscribed *B West/1779*; the one for the Prince of Waldeck is now in the University of Michigan; the small copy for the Monckton family is in the University of Toronto.
2. See V. & A., *Cuttings*, vol. I, p. 255.

listed by Galt, vol. II, pp. 227, 230: *The large Landscape from Windsor Forest* or *Picture of the View of Windsor-Castle from Snow-Hill, in the Great Park*. Drawings by West of gnarled trees in Windsor Great Park are recorded: e.g., at Christie's, 14 March 1967 (28), and in the collection of Sir Michael Adeane.

After Benjamin West

1169. PRINCE AUGUSTUS, LATER DUKE OF SUSSEX

Windsor Castle (2583). $36\frac{1}{8} \times 27\frac{3}{4}$ in., $91,8 \times 70,5$ cm.

Formerly in the possession of Princess Sophia (*d.* 1848); bequeathed by her in 1848 (as by West) to Queen Victoria (MS. Catalogue of Queen Victoria's private pictures &c.); recorded at Buckingham Palace (843) in 1871 (*V.R. inv.*).

Literature: Collins Baker, *Windsor*, p. 308.

A contemporary copy or repetition of No. 1146.

Richard Westall

1765–1836. Painter of portraits and subjects of all kinds, who also worked in watercolour and was a very prolific illustrator of books. From 1827 he was in the Household of the Duchess of Kent as drawing-master to the young Princess Victoria. The Princess, when she heard of his death in poverty, wrote of him in her Journal (6 December 1836) as 'a very indulgent, patient, agreeable master'. The Duchess of Kent settled a pension on Westall's sister.

1170. QUEEN VICTORIA AS A GIRL
(*Plate* 302)

Buckingham Palace. $57 \times 44\frac{3}{4}$ in., $144,8 \times 113,7$ cm.

Signed and dated: *R. Westall. 1830.*

Full-length, seated on a bank by a stream in a wooded landscape. She is accompanied by her little terrier Fanny and holds a sketchbook in her left hand.

Painted for the Duchess of Kent and bequeathed by her to Queen Victoria in 1861. Recorded in the Equerries' Room at Windsor (786) in 1878 (*V.R. inv.*).

Literature: Collins Baker, *Windsor*, p. 309.

Westall's preliminary drawing of the Princess, dated 1829, is in the Royal Library (Oppé, No. 643). No. 1170 was exhibited at the Royal Academy in 1830 (64); Finden's engraving of it was published in 1834.

1171. THE WILD HUNTSMAN (*Plate* 296)

Kensington Palace. $29\frac{3}{4} \times 24\frac{3}{4}$ in., $75,6 \times 62,9$ cm.

Signed and dated: *R.W / 1831*

The Wildgrave, his spear raised to kill the stag, is restrained by the hermit; on the Wildgrave's left rides the 'Horseman, young and fair'; on his right the 'Sable Hunter'.

Given to Queen Victoria in 1834 by the Duchess of Kent (MS. Catalogue of Queen Victoria's private pictures &c.); recorded at Windsor in 1862 (1177).

Literature: R.A., *King's Pictures* (476).

Exhibited at the Royal Academy in 1832 (35). The picture illustrates Scott's *Wild Huntsman* (1796), written in imitation of Bürger's *Wilde Jäger*. The Wildgrave, who set out to hunt on a Sunday, is joined in the chase by a fair youth who

beseeches him to exchange the hunt for 'devotion's choral swell' and a dark browed rider who urges him on his reckless course. A white stag is relentlessly pursued to a forest hermitage, where, 'all mild, amid the rout profane', the hermit prays the huntsman not to desecrate it.

1172. THE COTTAGE DOOR; INSTRUCTION

Kensington Palace. Panel: $12 \times 9\frac{3}{8}$ in., $30,5 \times 23,8$ cm.

Signed and dated: *R.W / 1832.*

A child seated at the door of a cottage while her grandmother reads to her.

Bequeathed to Queen Victoria by the Duchess of Kent in 1861; placed in the visitors' rooms at Osborne (515; Osborne *Catalogue* (1876), p. 327).

In 1836 Westall exhibited at the Royal Academy (1) *A cottage girl and her grandmother*, which was admired by Princess Victoria (Journal, 18 July 1836).

Francis Wheatley

1747–1801. Painter of portraits, conversation-pieces, landscapes, country scenes and subject-pictures; he worked for a short time in Ireland.

1173. LORD SPENCER HAMILTON (1742–91)
(*Plate* 80)

Windsor Castle (774). $30\frac{1}{8} \times 25$ in., $76,5 \times 63,5$ cm.

Full-length, standing in a landscape with a stick under his arm.

Presented to George IV by General Lister in 1817: 'A Painting in a Gilt Frame . . . Lord Spencer Hamilton—whole Length . . .' (Jutsham, *Receipts*, f. 25); on 21 May 1818 it was sent to Seguier to be repaired and varnished and in June he was paid one guinea for lining it and making a new stretcher (*ibid.*, *R/D*, f. 292, *PP.*, f. 49). Recorded at Carlton House (inv. of 1816, additional No. 538: '. . . in a Scarlet Coat—Cocked Hat—& Jockey Boots'; in the 1819 inv. (275) it is in store).

Literature: R.A., *British Art*, 1934 (400), *Commemorative Catalogue* (1935), p. 74; Collins Baker, *Windsor*, p. 310; Aldeburgh Festival and City Art Gallery, Leeds, *Francis Wheatley*, 1965 (4).

Presumably painted *c.* 1778. Wheatley exhibited small whole-length portraits of gentlemen at the Society of Artists in 1768 (179), 1774 (322, 323, 324) and 1775 (300, 303) and at the Royal Academy in 1786 (66, 107). A version belonging to Lord Templemore has a less elaborate foreground and landscape background; it may have been painted for Lord Spencer's sister, the 1st Marchioness of Donegal.

Third son of the 5th Duke of Hamilton. Colonel (1782) in the 2nd Foot Guards. On 20 November 1783 he was appointed Gentleman of the Bedchamber to the Prince of Wales. The Duchess of Devonshire wrote in 1782 that the 'first sentiments of [the Prince's] heart were a strong attachment to his Br Prince Frederick, to Cl Lake and Ld Spencer Hamilton, who highly merited his favour'. On one occasion he paid a debt of £500 for which Lord Spencer had been arrested.

Manner of Francis Wheatley

1174. A COUNTRY WOMAN CARRYING HOLLY

Hampton Court (648). $23\frac{1}{4} \times 16\frac{1}{4}$ in., $59,1 \times 41,3$ cm.

Full-length, walking in a landscape, holding a bunch of holly on her head; a lamb walks beside her.

Recorded at Hampton Court in 1869 (*V.R. inv.*); on the back is a label relating to an inventory of 27 July 1852.

Literature: Law, 1881, 1898 (450); Collins Baker, *Hampton Court*, p. 170.

The design is clearly influenced by Wheatley, but the handling is much too bad for the picture to be by Wheatley himself.

Sir David Wilkie

1785–1841. Painter of genre scenes, historical subjects and portraits. Born at Cults (Fifeshire) and trained in Edinburgh, he came to London in 1805 and first exhibited at the Royal Academy in 1806. He visited France in 1814 and 1821. In 1822 George IV was again anxious to acquire one of his humorous genre subjects and expressed a strong dislike of the subject-matter in Wilkie's *Preaching of John Knox* (Cunningham, *Wilkie*, vol. II, pp. 72, 79–80); Wilkie was soon at work on No. 1184. In July 1823 Wilkie succeeded Raeburn as Limner to the King for Scotland.

From 1825 to 1828 Wilkie was on the Continent. In January 1830 he succeeded Lawrence as Principal Painter to the King. He was continued in this office by William IV and Queen Victoria, but it seems that William IV regarded Beechey as his official portrait-painter; Queen Victoria, who sat to Wilkie in October 1837 for a state portrait (see above, p. xlii), never liked his work.

1175. BLIND-MAN'S-BUFF (*Plate* 264)

Buckingham Palace. Panel: 24⅞ × 36⅛ in., 63,2 × 91,8 cm.

Signed and dated: *David Wilkie. 1812*

An excited group of children and young people playing blind-man's-buff in the large room of a public house; the game is watched by an old lady and some small children.

Painted for George IV. Recorded in store at Carlton House in 1816 (213) and in the Upper Ante-room in 1819 (155); it was sent on 27 September 1823 to the King's Lodge, but was only there for a short period; on 17 June 1824 it was again sent down to the King's Lodge (Jutsham, *Deliveries*, ff. 48, 54); later in the Picture Gallery at Buckingham Palace (Mrs. Jameson, *Companion to the most celebrated Private Galleries of Art in London* (1844), p. 67; *V.R. inv.*, No. 428).

Literature: Waagen (1838), vol. II, p. 376; Cunningham, *Wilkie*, vol. I, pp. 339, 347, 350–3, 378–82, 387, vol. III, p. 525; Waagen (1854), vol. II, p. 25; W. T. Whitley, *Art in England 1800–20* (1928), pp. 198, 207, 210; R.A., *British Art*, 1934 (477), *Commemorative Catalogue* (1935), p. 111, *Scottish Art*, 1939 (142), *King's Pictures* (496), *The First Hundred Years*, 1951–2 (257); National Gallery of Scotland, *Ramsay, Raeburn & Wilkie*, 1951 (25), *Paintings and Drawings by Sir David Wilkie*, 1958 (8); R.A., *Sir David Wilkie*, 1958 (24).

The Prince Regent had conveyed to Wilkie, through Benjamin West, a wish that he would paint a picture for him as a companion to No. 685: 'let Wilkie make choice of the subject—take his time in painting it—and fix his own price'. Wilkie apparently settled on the subject of Blind-Man's-Buff; on 18 November 1811 Wilkie wrote to his sister that he was expecting to begin a sketch of this subject, which is presumably the sketch, signed and dated 1811, in the Tate Gallery (M. Davies, *The British School*, National Gallery (1946), pp. 172–3 (No. 921); the sketch was transferred to the Tate Gallery in 1949). The sketch was exhibited at the Royal Academy in 1812 (115). It is not clear whether Wilkie

had begun work on this subject before receiving the command from the Regent. On 19 March 1812 Wilkie reported that he had proceeded with the work, but that a long illness had delayed its completion; he asked permission to exhibit it in an unfinished state at his private exhibition, opening on 1 May 1812 at 87 Pall Mall; it was No. 4 in the catalogue of the exhibition. On 16 March 1813 West reported that the picture would be ready for presentation to the Regent by 25 March; on 24 March he wrote: 'I have frequently seen the picture in its progress to its finish; its subject is a youthful company playing at Blindmans Buff: you will find the subject is supported with that perspicuity every where appropriate to its character—life with mirth and good temper is seen in every group and in every figure'. The picture was at last finished by 2 April, and was exhibited at the Royal Academy in 1813 (148) when it was a great success. The Prince told Wilkie that he was delighted with the picture; it was sent to Carlton House in July 1813 (Jutsham, *R/D*, f. 255.) On 27 September and 29 November he submitted to Colonel McMahon his bill for five hundred guineas (Cunningham, *loc. cit.*; *Letters of George IV*, vol. I, 250, 256, 300, 320, 350). From 19 August 1818 to 2 June 1822 the picture was with Wilkie so that it could be engraved (Jutsham, *ibid.*, f. 300); the engraving by A. Raimbach was published on 1 June 1822 with a dedication to George IV. It was also engraved by Greatbach. In his picture of a wall of his studio, apparently painted for his brother, Wilkie included No. 1175 (Sotheby's, 7 April 1965 (262)).

In the sketch of 1811 the design and details are fully worked out and show very little variation from the finished design.[1] Writing on 28 March 1813, Farington states that Wilkie had considered the picture to be in a finished state 'about three months ago' (i.e., presumably at the end of 1812, when he would have put on the signature and date), but that he found that those who saw it were not much struck with it. He had, contrary to his usual practice, painted it 'without *having models to sit for Him*'; he 'went to work again upon the picture', with the use of models (i.e., presumably in the early months of 1813) and 'greatly improved it' (*Diary*, vol. VII, pp. 160–1). A signed pen and ink sketch (*Fig.* 40) in the National Gallery of Scotland may be earlier than the oil sketch of 1811; there are considerable differences in the left half of the design, which is on a separate (inserted) piece of paper.[2] There are two other studies for the figures in the left half of the design in the National Gallery of Scotland (D. 4746, 4747). In the British Museum is a detailed study by Wilkie for the hands clasping the head of the girl by the settle on the right and studies for a right hand, probably that of the blind man (Binyon, vol. IV, pp. 344 (22), 348 (47, e, g, h)). The oil sketch of part of the right half of the design, formerly in the collection of Mr. F. F. Madan, could be the 'small sketch or copy of part of my picture' which Wilkie sent off to his brother in December 1813 (Cunningham, *op. cit.*, vol. I, p. 387). Two other sketches are recorded (see N. G. of Scotland, *Sir David Wilkie*, 1958 (9, 10, 11)). Two drawings, connected with the early stages of the development of the design, were with Agnew's in 1967. A sheet of studies connected with the design is in the Witt Collection (1763). A good early copy of No. 1175 was sold at Sotheby's, 11 February 1959 (76). No. 1175 was exhibited at the British Institution in 1845 (15) and 1849 (120).

1. A drawing, probably from an early stage in the growth of the design, was in the J. W. Brett sale at Christie's, 8 April 1864 (666).
2. As early as 1812 a writer in the *Examiner* (1812), p. 327, had identified the young man in profile, advancing to the middle of the room, with Mulready.

1176. THE PENNY WEDDING (*Plates* 265, 267)

Buckingham Palace. Panel: $25\frac{3}{8} \times 37\frac{5}{8}$ in., $64,4 \times 95,6$ cm.

Signed and dated: *DAVID WILKIE 1818*.

The interior of a Scottish barn or farm-house (?): two couples are already dancing to the music of a violin and a 'cello; the newly-married couple are taking the floor. The wedding-feast is in progress behind them (a piper stands by the table) and the scene is watched by two main groups of spectators; those on the left are probably intending to join the dance.

Painted for George IV. It was delivered at Carlton House on 26 January 1819 (W.R.A., Geo. 27039; Carlton House inv. of 1816, additional No. 555: 'A Scotch Wedding—consisting of Many Figures'); it was sent on 27 September 1823 to the King's Lodge, but was only there for a short period; on 17 June 1824 it was again sent to the King's Lodge (Jutsham, *Deliveries*, ff. 48, 54); later in the Picture Gallery at Buckingham Palace (inv. No. 430).

Literature: John Grant, *The Penny Wedding* (1836), p. 5; Waagen (1838), vol. II, pp. 376–7; Cunningham, *Wilkie*, vol. II, pp. 9–11, 19, vol. III, p. 526; Waagen (1854), vol. II, p. 25; R.A., *British Art*, 1934 (425), *Commemorative Catalogue* (1935), p. 111; R.A., *Scottish Art*, 1939 (145), *King's Pictures* (499); National Gallery of Scotland, *Ramsay, Raeburn & Wilkie*, 1951 (23), *Paintings and Drawings by Sir David Wilkie*, 1958 (20); R.A., *Sir David Wilkie*, 1958 (20).

At a meeting with the artist in 1813, the Prince Regent expressed to Wilkie his delight with No. 1175 and said that he 'wished me to paint, at my leisure, a companion picture of the same size' (Cunningham, *op. cit.*, vol. I, p. 379). Wilkie probably did not begin to paint the picture before 1818; in fact the subject had been in his mind since at least 1810 (*ibid.*, vol. I, p. 281). On 26 October he wrote to Charles Long that the picture was nearly finished; on 29 October he showed it to the Prince 'who seemed perfectly satisfied with it'; and on 14 November Wilkie informed Long that the picture was finished and ready for delivery to Carlton House and asked if he could exhibit it at the Royal Academy. It was exhibited there in 1819 (153) and was a great success. On 29 November 1819 Wilkie submitted his bill for the picture: £525 for the painting and £20 for 'ornamented gilt Frame for ditto'; he received payment on 10 February 1820 (W.R.A., Geo. 27039, 32645, 35531). The engraving of No. 1176 by James Stewart was published on 16 April 1832 with a dedication to William IV. It was also engraved by Greatbach. The picture was exhibited at the British Institution in 1842 (11) and 1850 (92).

There are a number of drawings for the composition. A drawing in the British Museum (*Fig.* 43, Binyon, vol. IV, p. 343 (19, e)) is probably a first sketch, in which the bridal couple appears to be placed on the right of the design. Three drawings for figures and groups on the left of the design are in the National Gallery of Scotland (D.4751, 4365 (*Fig.* 44), 4359). In the British Museum are drawings of two couples dancing, probably related to No. 1176; a drawing for the left hand of the man holding a plate at the table; a study for the hands of the girl standing on the left while a companion fastens her dress; and a study for the right hand of the girl pulling on her shoe in the foreground (Binyon, *loc. cit.*, p. 343 (19, a, b, c, d)). A drawing in the collection of Mr. Michael Bevan appears to be connected with the couples dancing on the right of the composition. A study of dancing figures, possibly connected with No. 1176, is in the Royal Library (17877 a).

In the catalogue of the Royal Academy exhibition of 1819 the subject is described as a marriage festival of a kind once common in Scotland, at which each of the guests paid a subscription towards the expenses of the feast; the money left over, after the expenses had been paid, helped the newly-married couple to begin keeping house. The Penny Wedding is described in detail in John Grant's volume, *op. cit.*, which he dedicated to Wilkie who had 'immortalized the subject by the splendid effusion of his pencil'. Wilkie's treatment of the theme has obvious points of contact with David Allan's painting of the same subject (*Fig.* 42).

1177. I PIFFERARI (*Plate* 266)

Buckingham Palace. $18\frac{1}{8} \times 14\frac{1}{4}$ in., $46 \times 36,2$ cm.

Signed and dated: *D Wilkie Roma* / *1827*

The *pifferari*, or country musicians, playing before a shrine to the Madonna at which three pilgrims from the country are kneeling.

Bought by George IV; recorded in the inventory of 'Carleton Palace' (640: 'The Pifferari—Calabrian Shepherds playing their Hymns to the Madonna, when arriving with the Pilgrims in Rome'); recorded in 1835 at St. James's Palace (Waagen (1838), vol. II, p. 291); thereafter at Buckingham Palace (432).

Literature: Cunningham, *Wilkie*, vol. II, pp. 414, 454, vol. III, pp. 3, 4, 15–16, 527; R.A., *King's Pictures* (491).

On 27 April 1827 Wilkie wrote from Rome to his brother that he had, after his long illness, 'within the last five months completed two small pictures'; one of them he had already sold, the other was clearly No. 1177. On 1 July 1828, after his return to England, he told Andrew Wilson that the King had bought No. 1177 and No. 1178. To Sir William Knighton he wrote on 30 August 1828: 'Permit me to inform you that the two pictures of Roman Pilgrims, which the King has done me the honour to purchase from me, are now *framed*, and ready to be delivered whenever his Majesty may be pleased to command' (Cunningham, *loc. cit.*). Wilkie's receipt of £420, for 'Two Cabinet Pictures painted for His Majesty', is dated 8 August 1828 (W.R.A., Geo. 26758, 35812). No. 1177 was exhibited at the Royal Academy in 1829 (298); the engraving by H. Roth was published on 1 July 1829.

Wilkie's first visit to Rome had been between November 1825 and February 1826. The two pictures that he was to paint were inspired by what he had seen in the streets of Rome just before Holy Week in the Holy Year, 1825. On 28 November 1825 he wrote to his brother: 'Great doings are expected here in the Holy Week ... Multitudes of pilgrims from all parts of Italy are assembled in the streets, in costumes remarkably fine and poetical ... Each party of pilgrims is accompanied by one whose duty it is to give music to the rest. This is a piper, or pifferaro, provided with an immense bagpipe, of a rich deep tone, the drones of which he has the power of modulating with notes by his fingers, while another man plays on a smaller reed, the melody or tune answering the purpose of the chanter. Their music is religious, and resembles in sound the Scotch bagpipe. In parading the streets they stop before the image of the Virgin, whom they serenade, as shepherds, at this season previous to Christmas, in imitation of the shepherds of old, who announced the birth of the Messiah.' Writing to his sister on 27 December, he described the pilgrims' costumes —the broad cape over their shoulders with the crucifix fastened over the left breast—and their long staves 'topped by a cross' (Cunningham, *op. cit.*, vol. II, pp. 194, 210). Before he was well enough to paint again, Wilkie had amused himself by 'sketching from pilgrims' (*ibid.*, p. 297). A preparatory drawing for No. 1177, signed and dated Rome 1825, is in the collection of Professor I. R. C. Batchelor. The design of No. 1177 is related to David Allan's etching of *The Calabrian Shepherds* for which there are preparatory drawings in the British Museum (L.B. 2), dated 1768, and the National Gallery of Scotland (D.431).

1178. A ROMAN PRINCESS WASHING THE FEET OF PILGRIMS (*Plate* 268)

Buckingham Palace. Panel: 19¾ × 16⅝ in., 50,2 × 42,2 cm.
Signed and dated: *David Wilkie Geneva 1827*.

The princess kneels to wash the feet of two pilgrims; her maid stands behind her with a towel; two more pilgrims are seen behind.

Bought by George IV; recorded in the inventory of 'Carleton Palace' (639); recorded at St. James's Palace in 1835 (Waagen (1838), vol. II, p. 291, identifying the princess as a Princess Doria); thereafter at Buckingham Palace (431).

Literature: Cunningham, *Wilkie*, vol. II, pp. 446, 452–5, vol. III, pp. 3, 4, 15–16, 527.

Wilkie was at Geneva from early June to early September 1827. He began on 20 June to paint 'my Picture of A Roman Princess washing the Pilgrims' Feet'; he finished it on 8 September. On 27 August he wrote to his sister: 'I have nearly completed another picture. It has six figures, and is somewhat more finished than those I did in Rome . . .'; it had been much admired and he had declined two offers for it. In a letter to his brother, 12 September 1827, he described the picture: '. . . a handsome young lady, humbling herself, even to the washing of the feet of a poor pilgrim. What is fortunate—the lady is the favourite figure. Its progress has made a considerable sensation. A young lady I saw by accident that resembled the Princess Doria (the person intended) struck me as a perfect model. Interest was made to get her to sit: jewels and plate were borrowed, and every assistance procured for me that I could possibly want.' On 1 July 1828, after his return to London, he reported that it, with No. 1177, had been bought by the King; by 30 August they were framed and ready for delivery (Cunningham, *loc. cit.*); and on 8 August 1828 he had received £420 for the two pictures (W.R.A., Geo. 26758; for Wilkie's two Italian pictures see also Haydon's *Diary*, ed. W. B. Pope (Harvard University Press), vol. III (1963), pp. 299–300). No. 1178 was exhibited at the Royal Academy in 1829 (224). It was engraved by Greatbach and C. Heath. A drawing by Wilkie, perhaps representing his first idea for the subject, was sold at Sotheby's, 12 February 1964 (120). Another drawing, signed and dated 1826, was on the art-market in London in 1941.

Soon after his arrival in Rome, Wilkie had been fascinated by the multitude of pilgrims from the countryside (see No. 1177). He had been particularly impressed by their entertainment for three nights in the Convent of Sta. Trinita, 'with the previous washing of their feet'; the female pilgrims had 'this kindly office . . . rendered unto them by a sisterhood composed of the first ladies of rank, the princesses of the place' (Cunningham, *op. cit.*, vol. II, pp. 210–11).

1179. THE SPANISH *POSADA*: A GUERILLA COUNCIL OF WAR (*Plate* 269)

Buckingham Palace. 29½ × 36 in., 74,9 × 91,4 cm.
Signed and dated: *David Wilkie. Madrid 1828*.

A guerilla council of war in a Spanish *posada* or inn. Three churchmen, a Dominican, a monk from the Escorial and a Jesuit are seated at a table in close debate with a guerilla in Valencian costume; behind them is the landlady to whom a student from Salamanca, with his lexicon and cigar, is whispering; a *contrabandista* from Bilbao rides in on a mule; a Castilian guerilla stands on the right with his rifle; on the floor are a minstrel dwarf and a goatherd and his sister. Through the open door is a view of the Guadarrama mountains.

Purchased by George IV and recorded in the inventory of 'Carleton Palace' (635: 'The Spanish Posado D. Wilkie'); thereafter at Buckingham Palace (429).

Literature: Cunningham, *Wilkie*, vol. II, pp. 506–7, 509, vol. III, pp. 2, 4, 5, 9–11, 13, 14–16, 505, 527; R.A., *King's Pictures* (483).

Painted, with Nos. 1180, 1181, in Madrid between Wilkie's arrival there in October 1827 and his departure in May 1828. A drawing for the four figures at the table (*Fig.* 41), signed and dated at Madrid, 25 February 1828, is in the National Gallery of Scotland (D.4294). No. 1179 was apparently the earliest of the three pictures painted in Spain. On 25 February 1828 Wilkie wrote to his brother: 'The first I began and completed in the space of ten weeks; and . . . am yet surprised how it has been accomplished. It represents a council of war.' It was admired by artists and connoisseurs in Madrid, among them Washington Irving[1] and Vincente López. On Wilkie's return to England, the King saw his three Spanish paintings and bespoke them for his collection. On 29 December 1828, however, Wilkie told Sir William Knighton that they would be finished about the end of January 1829; on 12 February 1829 Wilkie wrote from Windsor, 'My Spanish pictures have just been submitted, and the approval has been to my satisfaction. The Posada is preferred, as best of all' (Cunningham, *loc. cit.*). It was exhibited at the Royal Academy in 1829 (56). Wilkie's receipt for 2,000 guineas 'for Three Pictures painted for His Majesty (. . . The Posada . . .)' is dated 18 March 1829 (W.R.A., Geo. 26761); in January 1829 he had submitted Collins's bill for £36. 11s. for their frames (*ibid.*, 26575). It was engraved by J. C. Armytage.

1180. THE DEFENCE OF SARAGOSSA (*Plate* 272)

Buckingham Palace. 37 × 55½ in., 94 × 141 cm.
Signed and dated: *David Wilkie. Madrid 1828*.

Agostina Zaragoza, the 'Maid of Saragossa', stepping over the dead body of her husband, is about to put the lighted match to a twenty-four-pounder directed at an attacking column of French troops.

Purchased by George IV and recorded in the inventory of 'Carleton Palace' (636: 'The defence of Saragossa D. Wilkie'); recorded at St. James's Palace in 1835 (Waagen (1838), vol. II, p. 291); thereafter at Buckingham Palace (425).

Literature: Cunningham, *Wilkie*, vol. II, pp. 506–7, 509, 510–11, vol. III, pp. 2, 4, 5, 9–11, 13, 14–16, 505, 527; R.A., *King's Pictures* (480); National Gallery of Scotland, *Paintings and Drawings by Sir David Wilkie*, 1958 (70); R.A., *Sir David Wilkie*, 1958 (36); D. Farr in *Burl. Mag.*, vol. C (1958), p. 440; Arts Council, *The Romantic Movement*, 1959 (376).

Painted, with Nos. 1179, 1181, in Madrid between Wilkie's arrival there in October 1827 and his departure in May 1828. A preliminary sketch in watercolours (*Fig.* 45) in the Blackburn Art Gallery is signed and dated at Madrid, 29 November 1827. In a letter to Andrew Wilson, dated 17 March 1828, Wilkie wrote that he had begun the third of his subjects inspired by the Spanish War of Independence. To his sister he wrote from Madrid on 31 March: 'I am now proceeding with my *third* picture for the season . . . The

1. *Life and Letters*, ed. P. M. Irving (1862), vol. II, p. 224.

Defence of Saragossa . . . This picture all my kind friends wish I could have finished here; but the tour to the south, and my anxiety to have these pictures early in London, prevents me'. It seems, therefore, as if the picture may have been unfinished when Wilkie left Madrid.[1] On Wilkie's return to England the King saw his three Spanish pictures, bespoke them for his collection, and, on 10 September 1828, ordered, through Sir William Knighton, a fourth picture (i.e., No. 1182) to be painted to make up the series. On 29 December 1828, however, Wilkie told Knighton that his 'three Spanish subjects will be completed about the end of January'; on 12 February 1829 he wrote from Windsor, 'My Spanish pictures have just been submitted, and the approval has been to my satisfaction. The Posada is preferred, as best of all, and the fourth picture commanded to be gone on with.' 'Painters', wrote Wilkie a month later, 'appear to like most The Maid of Saragossa'. It was exhibited at the Royal Academy in 1829 (128), when—'a poetic subject, conceived poetically'—it was much admired (Cunningham, *loc. cit.*). Wilkie's receipt for 2,000 guineas 'for the Three Pictures painted for His Majesty (the Siege of Sarragossa . . .)' is dated 18 March 1829 (W.R.A., Geo. 26761, 35812); in January 1829 he had submitted Collins's bill for £36. 11s. for frames for the three pictures (*ibid.*, 26575). S. Cousins's engraving of No. 1180 was published on 1 May 1837. It was also engraved by Greatbach. A small copy of No. 1180 belongs to the Rev. David Rudall.

The defence of Saragossa in the summer of 1808 was one of the most famous episodes in the Spanish insurrection against the French. French forces appeared before the city on 15 June; early in August they were compelled to raise the siege. Wilkie's picture commemorates the desperate moment on 2 July when General Verdier launched a heavy attack on the west and south of the city. Joseph Palafox, leader of the rising in the valley of the Ebro, was present at the Portillo Gate, where the gunners of a small battery had been shot down; as the French closed in, the Maid seized the lighted match from the hand of her dying husband and fired the gun at point-blank range into the French column. Owing to her example, the assault was beaten off; Palafox gave her, on the spot, a commission as sub-lieutenant of artillery. The scene is described by Wilkie in the catalogue of the Royal Academy exhibition of 1829. He states that the battery was placed at the Convent of Sta. Engracia.[2] The Maid's husband is lying dead and his gun is being trained by Palafox and by Father Consolaçion, an Augustinian friar, who served with distinction as an engineer and is pointing along the line of fire with his crucifix. Behind the gun is the priest Boggiero, a tutor to Palafox and another hero of the resistance, writing a despatch, which is to be carried by a pigeon, announcing the heroic resistance of the city. In his letter to his sister from Madrid, 31 March 1828, Wilkie had described the picture: 'capable of a striking and uncommon effect both of composition and colour'; he had also had a sitting from Palafox, 'who looks like a hero, but who, for effect, I represent as a patriot volunteer rather than as a general, and have tried to restore to him some of the youthfulness of which twenty years, and the severities of a French prison, have deprived

1. On 15 April 1828 Washington Irving wrote to his brother from Seville, whence Wilkie was returning to Madrid a few days later, 'He has sketched out on canvas his Defence of Saragossa, in which he has introduced an excellent likeness of Palafox' (see Irving's *Life and Letters*, ed. P. M. Irving (1862), vol. II, p. 253).
2. He may have been misled by hearing of the severe attack on this battery, and its heroic defence, on 4 August. For an account of the siege, see ch. II in section III of C. Oman, *A History of the Peninsular War*, vol. I (1902). Wilkie probably knew C. R. Vaughan's *Narrative of the Siege of Zaragoza* (3rd. ed. 1809); Agostina Zaragoza's heroism is described on pp. 14–16.

him.' The Maid herself was seen by English visitors to Spain. Knighton saw her in 1809 ('about two and twenty, rather pretty, and of a very interesting appearance . . . The courage of this young woman really surpasses all belief'); in the same year Byron saw her in Seville, 'decorated with medals and orders'; he celebrated her heroism at Saragossa in the first canto of *Childe Harold's Pilgrimage*, stanzas 54–9. In 1809 she was serving with her battery in Andalusia.

1181. THE GUERILLA'S DEPARTURE
(*Plate* 270)

Buckingham Palace. $36\frac{1}{2} \times 32\frac{1}{4}$ in., $92,7 \times 81,9$ cm.

Signed and dated: *David Wilkie. Madrid. 1828.*

A Spanish guerilla fighter is taking leave of his Carmelite confessor, before departing to join his confederates; the confessor, watched by a half-naked beggar-boy, is giving the guerilla a light for his cigar.

Purchased by George IV and recorded in the inventory of 'Carleton Palace' (637); at St. James's Palace in 1835 (Waagen (1838), vol. II, pp. 291–2); thereafter at Buckingham Palace (427).

Literature: Cunningham, *Wilkie*, vol. II, pp. 506–7, 509, vol. III, pp. 2, 4, 5, 9–11, 13, 15, 505, 521, 527; National Gallery of Scotland, *Ramsay, Raeburn & Wilkie*, 1951 (31), *Paintings and Drawings by Sir David Wilkie*, 1958 (75); R.A., *Sir David Wilkie*, 1958 (44).

The second of the three pictures of subjects from the Spanish insurrection painted by Wilkie between his arrival in Madrid in October 1827 and his departure in May 1828. In a letter to Andrew Wilson, written from Madrid on 17 March 1828, he stated that he had finished two Spanish subjects (i.e., Nos. 1179, 1181 and begun a third (No. 1180). A preliminary drawing,[1] already close to the final composition, is signed and dated by Wilkie as drawn at Toledo on 27 October 1827, i.e., the day after he had arrived at Toledo on a tour with Washington Irving (*Life and Letters*, ed. P. M. Irving (1862), vol. II, p. 219); another drawing (*Fig.* 46),[2] probably earlier, shows the two principal figures in reverse and does not contain the boy whom Wilkie introduces as a tribute to Murillo. After Wilkie had brought the pictures back to England and they had been bespoken and admired by George IV (see No. 1180), Wilkie was commanded to paint No. 1182 as a companion to No. 1181 in order to complete the series. No. 1181 was exhibited at the Royal Academy in 1829 (403). Wilkie's receipt for 2,000 guineas 'for the Three Pictures painted for His Majesty (. . . the Guerilla's Return [*sic*])' is dated 18 March 1829 (W.R.A., Geo. 26761); in January 1829 he had submitted Collins's bill for £36. 11s. for frames for the three pictures (*ibid.*, 26575). No. 1181 was engraved by J. C. Armytage.

1182. THE GUERILLA'S RETURN (*Plate* 271)

Buckingham Palace. $36\frac{1}{2} \times 32\frac{1}{4}$ in., $92,7 \times 81,9$ cm.

Signed and dated: *David Wilkie London 1830*

The wounded guerilla, on his mule and with his left arm in a sling, is helped by his confessor (see No. 1181) as he returns to his home; a kneeling woman with a bowl of water is preparing to bathe his wounds.

Painted for George IV and recorded in the inventory of 'Carleton Palace' (638); recorded at St. James's Palace in 1835 (Waagen (1838), vol. II, p. 292); thereafter at Buckingham Palace (426).

Literature: Cunningham, *Wilkie*, vol. III, pp. 5, 10, 527; National Gallery of Scotland, *Ramsay, Raeburn & Wilkie*, 1951 (37).

1. It was sold at Christie's, 24 June 1960 (65).   2. *Ibid.* (64).

On 10 September 1828 Wilkie received through Sir William Knighton the King's command to complete his set of three Spanish subjects (i.e., Nos. 1179–81) with a fourth, 'which I propose to paint'; on 12 February 1829 Wilkie wrote to Knighton from Windsor that the King had liked his Spanish pictures: 'and the fourth picture commanded to be gone on with' (Cunningham, *loc. cit.*). It was exhibited at the Royal Academy in 1830 (375). On 2 March 1830 Wilkie had been paid 400 guineas for 'a Painted [*sic*] for His Majesty of the return of the Wounded Guerilla to His Family' (W.R.A., Geo. 26759, 35812); on 5 June 1830 he signed a receipt for £102. 17s. 6d. for frames by Collins for pictures that included No. 1182. No. 1182 was engraved by J. C. Armytage.

1183. GEORGE IV (*Plate* 273)

Holyroodhouse. 110 × 70½ in., 279,4 × 179,1 cm.

Signed and dated: *David Wilkie 1829*. The area in which the signature and date are placed is covered with bituminous cracks and they are not now easy to decipher.

Full-length, standing, with his left hand on a Highland broadsword. The King is in full Highland dress: a bonnet with the three eagle's feathers as worn by a Highland chief; jacket, shoulder plaid and kilt of the royal tartan; and the usual Highland accoutrements, pistols, dirk, sporran and powder-horn. In addition he wears the badge of the Fleece, the ribbon of the Thistle, the stars of the Garter and the Thistle and the Garter round his leg. The Honours of Scotland (Crown, Sword of State and Sceptre) are on the carved throne on the right; above them hangs a Highland targe.

Painted for George IV; recorded in the inventory of 'Carleton Palace' (633), but at Holyroodhouse since December 1831.

Literature: Cunningham, *Wilkie*, vol. III, pp. 10, 21–22, 28, 38, 40, 42–4, 46–7, 51, 528; W. T. Whitley, *Art in England 1821–37* (1930), p. 193.

On 17 August 1822, two days after his entrance (No. 1184), the King held his first Levee at Holyroodhouse. Wilkie was present. 'In compliment to the country, his Majesty appeared in complete Highland costume, made of the royal Stewart tartan, which displayed his manly and graceful figure to great advantage' (R. Mudie's *Account* of the King's visit, quoted in *Visit of George IV to Edinburgh 1822*, Scottish National Portrait Gallery (1961)). According to Lockhart, 'His Majesty's Celtic toilette had been carefully watched and assisted by the gallant Laird of Garth, who was not a little proud of the result of his dexterous manipulations of the royal plaid . . . And he did look a most stately and imposing person in that beautiful dress' (*Life*, Edinburgh edition, vol. VII (1902), p. 58).
Wilkie was subsequently commissioned to paint the King in this costume. On 12 February 1829 (by which time he had prepared a sketch) he wrote to Knighton that, when his Spanish pictures had been submitted to the King, 'all at once I was asked what I was doing about the large one in the Highland dress. I said I was ready to begin it whenever commanded: the reply was, "whenever you please".' By 21 April 1829 he had had three sittings from the King and completed the head: 'I must try the hands, which if they can be made like, I shall be satisfied, and proceed with the rest at home'. On 24 April he reported that he had had another sitting and a further two more were given with the promise of a final one on 26 April. 'His Majesty appears to take a good deal of interest about the picture'. On 8 December 1829 Wilkie referred to the portrait as 'in progress'. On 11 February 1830 he told Knighton, 'I am now working upon the whole-length, for which I have a fine-looking Highlander

for a model, Mr. Seguier . . . encourages me in the whole-length'.[1] After he had sent it to the Royal Academy in April (it was No. 63 in the summer exhibition), Wilkie wrote: 'I have made this the most glazed, and deepest-toned picture I have ever tried, or seen tried, in these times. It is at once a trial of Rembrandt all over,—the dresses, the accoutrements, and throne gold, a dark back-ground,—no white except on the hose and the flesh,—telling as principal lights. The half-length Sebastiano del Piombo at Genoa, gave me a hint for the style and air of the figure.' A drawing in the National Gallery of Scotland (D.2300C., *Fig.* 47) could be the preparatory sketch mentioned above; it shows the King bare-headed and in a jacket of a military style. In the final painting there is much bituminous cracking. Much of Wilkie's original drawing can still be discerned in the costume. There are slight *pentimenti*: the belt was at first slightly lower, the sporran slightly higher.
On 10 April 1830 Wilkie signed a receipt for £525 for the 'Whole Length Portrait of His Majesty, for Scotland' (W.R.A., Geo. 26762). In the same year he painted (for four hundred guineas) the replica for the Duke of Wellington which is now at Apsley House. On 5 June 1830 he was paid £210 by the King 'for painting a Bishop's Half Length Portrait of His Majesty for . . . the Duke of Buccleugh' (W.R.A., Geo. 26763). This was sent early in 1831 to Dalkeith Palace, where the King had stayed during his visit to Edinburgh, and is still in the Buccleuch collection. A frame for No. 1183 was furnished by Francis Collins in 1830 (*ibid.*, 26597). A full-length copy was on the art-market in London in 1946. The original, at the command of William IV, was packed off by sea to Edinburgh on 13 December 1831; before it was placed in Holyroodhouse it was exhibited at the Royal Institution in Edinburgh.
The King's Highland outfit was supplied by George Hunter of Edinburgh, whose account, amounting to £1,354. 18s., is dated 23 September 1822. This included the weapons and jewelry shown in No. 1183, the fine white goatskin sporran, 61 yards of 'Royal Sattin Plaid', 31 yards of 'Royal Plaid Velvet' and 17½ yards of 'Royal Plaid Casemere' (W.R.A., Geo. 29600). The broadsword, dirk, powder-horn and the two belts are still at Windsor.

1184. THE ENTRANCE OF GEORGE IV AT HOLYROODHOUSE (*Plate* 282)

Holyroodhouse. Panel: 49⅝ × 78 in., 126 × 198,1 cm.

Signed: *David Wilkie*. The area on which the signature is written is much disfigured by bituminous cracking and it is possible that Wilkie added a date which is now indecipherable. It is not clear from Redgrave's notes in the *V.R. inv.* (1860) whether or not the date 1829 was visible. On the back of the panel is inscribed in chalk, almost certainly in the artist's hand: *D Wilkie R A / № 2*.

The front of the Palace of Holyroodhouse with a crowd of spectators. The King, accompanied by trumpeters and a page and the Exon of the Yeomen of the Guard, and dressed in the uniform of a Field-Marshal with the ribbon of the Thistle and the stars of the Garter and Thistle, is about to receive the keys of the palace which are offered to him by Alexander, 10th Duke of Hamilton (1767–1852); the Duke, hereditary Keeper of the palace, is in full Highland dress and wears the tartan of the Earls of Arran. On the right of the King, James Graham, 3rd Duke of Montrose (1755–1836), Lord Chamberlain, points towards the entrance of the palace, before which stands George Campbell, 6th Duke

1. Haydon saw the portrait on 22 February 1830 (*Diary*, ed. W. B. Pope (Harvard University Press), vol. III (1963), p. 425).

of Argyll (1768–1839) in full Highland dress ('in his family tartan') as hereditary Master of the Household in Scotland. Behind Argyll the Honours of Scotland are borne on horseback: the Crown by Sir Alexander Keith (d. 1832), Knight Marischal of Scotland, the Sceptre by Lord Francis Leveson-Gower (1800–57) representing the Countess of Sutherland, and the Sword of State by George Douglas, 17th Earl of Morton (1761–1827). On the left, near the entrance to the palace, stands John Hope, 4th Earl of Hopetoun (1765–1823), in his uniform as Captain-General of the Royal Company of Archers, and Sir Walter Scott (1771–1832) 'in the character of historian or bard'.

Painted for George IV and recorded in the inventory of 'Carleton Palace' (634); seen by Waagen (1838, vol. II, p. 292) at St. James's in July 1835; later in the Picture Gallery at Buckingham Palace (69) and the Corridor at Windsor (412).

Literature: Cunningham, *Wilkie,* vol. II, pp. 82, 84–5, 86, 89–91, 96, 103, 104–6, 111, 116, 118, 119–20, 122; vol. III, pp. 9, 10, 25, 28, 30, 37, 42, 43, 44–5, 527; R.A., *British Portraits,* 1956–7 (364); T. S. R. Boase, *English Art 1800–70* (1959), pp. 157–8.

Begun in 1822 but not finished until the end of 1829 or very early in 1830. The King arrived at Holyroodhouse in the afternoon of 15 August 1822. Wilkie witnessed the event: 'I saw the King alight; he had not much colour, but upon the whole was looking well. He was dressed in a field marshal's uniform, with a green ribbon of the order of the Thistle. He was received by the Dukes of Hamilton and Montrose, and a variety of others, who were at the door to meet him; but upon the whole this point, which was capable of producing great effect, was not arranged with sufficient regard to the importance of it.' Although Wilkie might have preferred to record some other episode in the royal visit to Scotland, the King fixed upon this moment 'with all the chiefs of the north on his right and left'. In September 1822 Wilkie returned to London with a number of sketches for the royal picture; on 15 December he showed his sketches to Peel who 'did not think them capable of making a picture'. In the summer of 1823, fired by his appointment as Limner to the King for Scotland, he seems to have set seriously to work upon the picture, but as late as 31 October 1823 he described himself as 'now beginning' it. He had already shown a preliminary sketch to the King, who had ordered him to proceed and 'proposed to sit for his portrait when I have got all the figures laid in, and his own figure sufficiently advanced for that purpose'. Wilkie was at that stage 'in hopes, though it is still an experiment, that with so many objects as it contains, well suited for painting, and with portraits in action, and the associations connected with the scene itself, that I may be able to make it an effective subject'. Until the spring of 1824 Wilkie spent time 'in blottings out and pencillings in' on the picture. Haydon records on 7 February 1824 that Wilkie had been to Windsor with his sketch, but had lost an opportunity of a sitting from the King; two days later Haydon criticized Wilkie's putting the King in jackboots (*Diary,* ed. W. B. Pope (Harvard Univsersity Press), vol. II (1960), pp. 461–2, 463). Later in the year the King gave Wilkie three sittings (*ibid.,* p. 491). Early in September 1824 Wilkie was back in Edinburgh in order to paint the portraits and 'correct' the landscape in it; by 26 September he had finished his studies at the palace, the 'likeness and dress' of Sir Alexander Keith, the mace of the Court of the Exchequer and the regalia, but he had not yet taken the likeness of Scott. In his absence abroad, from July 1825 to June 1828, Wilkie can have done nothing to the picture. By January 1829, however, he was hopeful that he would be free to start work on it once more: 'I think I am able for this, as it is far

on towards completion.'[1] It was shown to the King and 'some directions were given me about the chief figure'. In September 1829 he was again in Edinburgh 'to confirm his own notions' in the picture and on 8 December he was able to report that the picture 'so long interrupted, is now drawing to a close. It is all painted in, and waits only for the toning.' On 11 February 1830 Wilkie told Sir William Knighton that the picture, with No. 1182, was ready to be submitted for the King's inspection. It was shown at the Royal Academy in 1830 (125; with long description in the catalogue). On 2 March 1830 Wilkie signed a receipt for 1,600 guineas for the picture (W.R.A., Geo. 26760, 35813) and on 5 June he signed a receipt for £102. 17s. 6d. for 'rich frames' supplied by Francis Collins for three pictures, including No. 1184; the frame still adorns the picture. The finished painting was engraved by W. Greatbach. Haydon (*op. cit.,* p. 283) noted the changes of style within the picture.

Numerous preparatory drawings for No. 1184 are known. A drawing at Windsor (*Fig.* 49; Oppé, No. 663) is probably an early study for the whole composition. The scene is slightly less crowded; the Duke of Hamilton and Lord Hopetoun are apparently the only principals included at this stage; and the figure of the King is in the more ingratiating position which Wilkie first designed, but which the King told him to alter to something more martial and imposing (Cunningham, *op. cit.,* vol. II, p. 90). In smaller sketches at Windsor (17774–6, 17877b) Wilkie can be seen developing the stance of the King and the figures immediately around him. A sheet of studies at The Binns includes one for the same passage; others were sold at Sotheby's, 8 February 1956 (69) and 12 February 1964 (120). An oil sketch of the King and the figures immediately around him was sold at Sotheby's, 14 July 1948 (129), and is now in the collection of Her Majesty Queen Elizabeth the Queen Mother.[2] A drawing for the figure of the Duke of Hamilton (*Fig.* 55) is in the Ashmolean Museum; a drawing for the Duke of Argyll is at Windsor (*Fig.* 52; Oppé, No. 665).[3] Among studies perhaps made in Scotland in 1824 are a drawing of the exterior of Holyroodhouse (*Fig.* 48; Oppé, No. 662); the drawing in the Ashmolean of the Earl of Morton with the Sword of State; and an oil sketch (*Fig.* 54) at Lennoxlove of the head of the Duke of Hamilton. In 1828 Wilkie produced the *modello* in the Scottish National Portrait Gallery (1040), which anticipates the final design in outline and in many details and is now clearer than the finished picture. It is interesting that there is no trace of Scott in the *modello.* The head of Scott in No. 1184 is clearly based on the same sitting as the portrait in the Parliament Hall, Edinburgh. If that was the portrait painted for Knighton, it was the one being painted as late as December 1828 (Cunningham, *op. cit.,* vol. III, p. 9) and Scott must therefore have been inserted into No. 1184 at a very late stage; but in his *Journal,* under 7 January 1826, Scott states that he had earlier (presumably in 1824) sat to Wilkie for the picture.[4] Many areas of the surface of No. 1184 are now faded or obscured by bituminous cracking; certain passages in the shadows have virtually disappeared, but it is still possible to discern the laboured execution of certain passages (particularly in the portrait heads) and *pentimenti* in some of the principal figures, especially in the King himself. Previous repaintings were removed in 1952–3.

1. From a letter at Windsor to Knighton, 12 May (?1829) it seems that Wilkie was still needing sittings from some of those shown in No. 1184.
2. Exhibited, R.A., *Sir David Wilkie,* 1958 (17).
3. This figure occurs again in a drawing, in the National Gallery of Canada, of visitors arriving at a Drawing Room at Holyrood.
4. Lockhart, *Life* (Edinburgh Edition, vol. X (1903), p. 237) had a low opinion of the portrait of Scott in No. 1184.

The Duke of Hamilton bore St. Edward's Crown at the Coronations of William IV and Queen Victoria and acted as Lord High Steward. He married the daughter and heiress of William Beckford and did much to enrich the famous collections at Hamilton Palace. For the Duke of Argyll, see No. 1188. The Earl of Hopetoun was a distinguished soldier and acted as Gold Stick during the visit. The Duke of Montrose was Lord Chamberlain, 1821–7, 1828–30, and the Earl of Morton was Chamberlain of the Household to the Queen, 1792–1818. Lord Francis Leveson-Gower became in 1846 1st Earl of Ellesmere. For Sir Walter Scott, see No. 913.

1185. WILLIAM IV (Plate 276)

Windsor Castle (177). $106\frac{1}{2} \times 69\frac{3}{4}$ in., $270,5 \times 177,2$ cm.; there is a slightly later addition of *c.* $7\frac{3}{4}$ in. at the top.

Signed and dated 1832.[1]

Full-length, standing, in the robes of the Garter with the collars of the Garter and the Bath and resting his right hand on his sword; the Imperial Crown stands on a table beside him; at the foot of the table is a ship's compass and a breast-plate.

Painted for William IV for the Waterloo Chamber, where Waagen and Sir William Knighton (see above, pp. xxv–vi), for example, saw it in 1835.

Literature: B. R. Haydon, *Diary*, ed. W. B. Pope (Harvard University Press), vol. III (1963), p. 593; Waagen (1838), vol. I, p. 168; Cunningham, *Wilkie*, vol. III, pp. 50–1, 54, 58, 70, 528; Collins Baker, *Windsor*, p. 312.

William IV first sat to Wilkie at the Pavilion, Brighton, on 7 November 1831. On the following day he wrote to his sister that he had had a second sitting: 'all that see the picture seem to think it most promising'; on 28 November he wrote to Knighton that he had been granted all the sittings he had required and that 'the portrait, if I can judge at all, appears to be satisfactory as to likeness, although adapted to the air of a state picture'. On 28 February 1832 he again wrote to Knighton: 'the portrait of the King is all painted in. Seguier did not propose any alteration, but wishes me with glazings to work it up to as much force in colour as possible.' Haydon (*loc. cit.*) had admired the portrait on 16 January 1832. The portrait was exhibited at the Royal Academy in 1832 (71). Wilkie received three hundred guineas for it. A drawing at Windsor (1389: *Fig.* 57)[2] may be one of Wilkie's first ideas for the portrait; an unfinished oil sketch at Penshurst may embody a study from life for the portrait (Walker Art Gallery, Liverpool, *Kings & Queens of England*, 1953 (42), illustrated souvenir, pl. 35). In 1833 a version seems to have been given to the Scottish Hospital. In July 1833 Wilkie reported to Knighton that two copies of the King's portrait were nearly finished, but it is not clear of what design these were copies. A copy of No. 1185, formerly in the Ormond collection, was on the art-market in London in 1954; a version was painted for the University of Oxford and presented by Queen Adelaide, with a companion portrait of herself, in 1838 (Mrs. R. L. Poole, *Catalogue of Portraits*, vol. I (1912), p. 146); and a three-quarter-length version is in Toledo, Ohio. The head is very close to that in the full-length of the King in military uniform, signed and dated as painted at Brighton in 1833, given to the Duke of Wellington by William IV and now at Apsley

1. The signature and date are recorded as *David Wilkie fecit 1832* by Redgrave in 1868 (*V.R. inv.*) on the carpeted step below the King's feet. This area is now, however, so distorted by bituminous contractions that nothing can be read there.
2. Oppé, No. 666; a comparable study is in the collection of Mr. John Woodward.

House (R.A., *Sir David Wilkie*, 1958 (35), illustrated souvenir, pl. 22); and to the head and shoulders portrait in the Scottish National Portrait Gallery (806); this last is close to the portrait at Slane Castle. In studies by Wilkie in the Tate Gallery and at Windsor (17780: *Fig.* 56) for a double-portrait of William IV and Queen Adelaide, the figure of the King is also close to No. 1185. Studies by Wilkie for the collars of the Garter and the Bath (also at Windsor, 17782, 17783; *Figs.* 50, 51) are probably connected with his portrait of the King.

1186. AUGUSTUS, DUKE OF SUSSEX
(Plate 274)

Buckingham Palace. $99\frac{1}{2} \times 64$ in., $252,7 \times 162,6$ cm.

Signed and dated: *DAVID WILKIE f. 1833*

Full-length, standing, in Highland dress, with the Garter round his hose, leaning on a Highland broadsword and holding a chieftain's plumed bonnet in his hand; on a ledge beside him rests a targe and below the ledge is a dead eagle; a Scottish deer-hound sits beside him.

Painted for the Duke of Sussex, who gave it to Queen Victoria on 24 February 1838. On that day the Queen wrote in her Journal that she met the Duke in the Throne Room at Buckingham Palace, 'where he presented me with his full length (size of life) portrait in the Highland dress, painted by Sir David Wilkie'. Placed in the Large Drawing-Room (*Buckingham Palace*, 1841, p. 97), but later set up on the Principal Staircase (*V.R. inv.*, 1864, No. 219).

Literature: Cunningham, *Wilkie*, vol. III, pp. 70, 514, 529.

Cunningham (*loc. cit.*), among the pictures painted by Wilkie early in 1833, mentions 'that first of all modern portraits, for truth of character and harmonious brightness of colour, the Duke of Sussex, as Earl of Inverness, in the costume of a Highland Chief'.[1] Cunningham stated that when it was exhibited at the Royal Academy in 1833 (207) no picture could stand against it; 'it seemed to lighten all around'.[2] An oil sketch for the composition, formerly in the collection of Evan Charteris, and now belonging to Mrs. George Dawnay, shows the Duke wearing his Highland bonnet. A preparatory drawing belongs to the Garrick Club. In September 1954 the Royal Library purchased from a descendant of the artist pen and ink sketches (e.g., *Fig.* 53) for the figure and two sheets of studies of the dead eagle (Nos. 17777–9). In No. 1186 there appear to be substantial *pentimenti* in the outline of the figure and also possibly in the sky.

1187. VICTORIA, DUCHESS OF KENT, WITH PRINCESS VICTORIA AND MEMBERS OF HER FAMILY (Plate 278)

$50 \times 40\frac{1}{4}$ in., $127 \times 102,2$ cm.

The Princess, holding a casket (?) in both her hands, stands beside a table on which are a casket and a purse (?). The Duchess of Kent stands behind the Princess. On the left, under a bust of Edward, Duke of Kent, stands Prince Charles of Leiningen (1804–56) with his hands on his sword; behind the Duchess's left shoulder is Prince Leopold of

1. Haydon, however, records on 26 October 1832 that Wilkie was painting the Duke. 'It was something like Lawrence & Raeburn, & not like himself; and yet fine, but not original' (*Diary*, ed. W. B. Pope (Harvard University Press), vol. III (1963), p. 657). On 31 March 1833 Wilkie was finishing the portrait: 'it looked powerful, but not like' (*ibid.*, vol. IV (1963), p. 69).
2. Wilkie, in a letter to the Duke written on 26 July 1833, reported that No. 1186 had come back from the exhibition and asked if it was to be sent to Kensington Palace (W.R.A., Geo. 48303–4).

Saxe-Coburg, in armour and holding a baton. Another male and two female figures are included in the group. A dog looks up at the Princess in the foreground.

A later inscription on the stretcher states that No. 1187 was bought at Wilkie's sale at Christie's, 25–30 April 1842 (639), for the 9th Earl of Leven and Melville (d. 1876); acquired in 1948 from the Leven and Melville family by Her Majesty Queen Elizabeth the Queen Mother.

Literature: R.A., *Sir David Wilkie*, 1958 (50).

The later inscription (see above) states that the scene represents the Princess with her presents on her thirteenth birthday, i.e., on 24 May 1832; but one in a group of three drawings[1] by Wilkie for this composition bears on the back a contemporary inscription that the Princess is seen, when twelve years of age, in 1831. The earlier date is the more likely, as Prince Leopold, who was in England in 1831, was not here on the Princess's birthday in 1832. No. 1189 is a study for the head of Prince Charles (perhaps the only finished head on the canvas) in No. 1187, but the latter seems to be an unfinished picture rather than a sketch for a larger design. There is apparently no documentation for the picture and no indication as to who commissioned it. In 1837, after Princess Victoria's accession, Wilkie said that the young Queen appeared to recognise him 'as an early friend' and that 'having been accustomed to see the Queen from a child, my reception had a little the air of that of an early acquaintance' (Cunningham, *Wilkie*, vol. III, pp. 227, 229). According to the inscription cited above, the two female figures behind the Duchess of Kent are intended for the Baroness Lehzen (1784–1870), who had become governess to Princess Victoria in 1824 and Charlotte, Duchess of Northumberland (1786–1866), who in 1830 was appointed as the official Governess to the Princess. On Princess Victoria's birthday in 1831 William IV and Queen Adelaide gave a children's ball in her honour.

1188. THE FIRST COUNCIL OF QUEEN VICTORIA (*Plate* 279)

Windsor Castle (414). 59¾ × 94 in., 151,8 × 238,8 cm.; there is a join made by Wilkie c. 14½ in. from the right.

Signed and dated: *David Wilkie f 1838*.

The Queen (1), dressed in white, is seated at the head of the table. In her hand she holds 'the most gracious declaration then addressed by Her Majesty to the Lords and others of the Council then assembled'. She confronts her Accession Council. Before her stands Lord Melbourne (12) with 'a State Paper, which received the first signature of Her Majesty as Queen'; lower down the table are seated, opposite each other, the Dukes of Cumberland (23) and Sussex (28), wearing the insignia of the Garter; the Duke of Wellington (24), also wearing the Garter, hands a pen to the Duke of Sussex; before Sussex lies the 'Declaration of Her Majesty's rightful Accession to the Throne, to be signed by the members of the Privy Council'. Greville (2), as Clerk of the Council, holds the book in which its actions were recorded.

Painted for Queen Victoria and placed by her in the Corridor at Windsor, where it has since remained.

Literature: Cunningham, *Wilkie*, vol. III, pp. 226–7, 229, 233, 235, 237–8, 239, 241–2, 252–3, 254, 531; Collins Baker, *Windsor*, p. 311; R.A., *King's Pictures* (51); National Gallery of Scotland, *Paintings*

1. The drawings are also in the possession of H.M. Queen Elizabeth the Queen Mother.

and Drawings by Sir David Wilkie, 1958 (91); R.A., *Sir David Wilkie*, 1958 (37).

The Queen gave Wilkie a sitting in the Pavilion at Brighton from 12.45 to 1.45 on 17 October 1837. He had gone down in accordance with instructions from the Lord Chamberlain in order to begin work on the new State Portrait; but the Queen 'had heard of a sketch I had made of her First Council'. She 'has commanded a picture of her first Council, and has been telling me who to put in it'. Wilkie asked his sister to send down a canvas from his painting room; he intended to 'paint in her figure from to-day's sitting [when he had perhaps painted the oil sketch, see below], and sketch the group upon it, so as to have it ready for the Saturday's sitting'. On 28 October he wrote again to his sister: 'Her Majesty has been most gracious, appearing to recognise me as an early friend. I proceed with the picture—have painted in her figure on the canvas you sent . . . Her face I have painted, nearly a profile—it is thought like her. She sat today in the dress—a white satin, covered with gauze embroidered—I think it looks well. All here think the subject good, and she likes it herself. Lord Conyngham and Mr. Seguier give me encouragement about it. She appoints a sitting once in two days, and never puts me off.' On 24 October 1837, before leaving the painting room after a sitting, the Queen 'sent for Lord Melbourne to see the Picture, with which he was much pleased . . . a great many Portraits will be introduced into the picture; Lord Melbourne will be painted standing near me'. On 31 October Wilkie was given the last sitting the Queen could manage 'at present'. In her Journal the Queen records sittings on 17, 21, 24, 26 and 28 October. Writing to Collins on 12 November, Wilkie told him of the commission and his progress: 'the Queen . . . is placed nearly in profile at the end of a long table, covered with a red cloth. She sits in a large chair, or throne, a little elevated, to make her the presiding person. This will be a picture of considerable plague in adjusting the persons; but as every one seems keen about the subject, I shall proceed, though I am putting other things at a stand.' The picture took precedence over everything else that Wilkie had in hand; it was *expected* that it should be finished in time for showing at the Royal Academy in 1838. On 1 December the Queen 'Saw Sir David Wilkie's picture of the First Council which he brought to show me the other figures he has sketched in'. By 12 February 1838 Wilkie had received sittings from the Dukes of Sussex (28) and Wellington (24),[1] from the Lord Chancellor (8), Lords Melbourne (12) and Lansdowne (7), Lord John Russell (10) and the Archbishop of Canterbury (22); he had just asked Peel (27) for a sitting. He seems at this stage to be completing the group of the most important figures near the table; the lesser figures may have been added hurriedly and later (Cunningham, *Wilkie*, pp. 226–7, 229, 233, 235, 237–8; *The Girlhood of Queen Victoria*, ed. Viscount Esher (1912), vol. I, p. 230; and the Queen's Journal).

A number of preparatory drawings exist for the picture. A sketch for the whole subject is in the Oppé collection (*Fig.* 59; R.A., *The Paul Oppé Collection*, 1958 (304)); another is at Windsor (*Fig.* 62; Oppé, No. 667); a drawing of the Queen and the group of figures nearest to her (*Fig.* 61), was sold at Sotheby's, 28 January 1959 (42), and is now in the collection of the Earl of Perth. Also at Windsor are studies for the figure of the Queen (Oppé Nos. 668 (*Fig.* 60), 669; the latter shows the Queen very much as in the painting, but with a dog beside her chair) and a study for her right

1. For Wellington's determination to appear in proper costume, see Haydon's *Diary*, ed. W. B. Pope (Harvard University Press), Vol. V (1963), p. 32.

KEY[1]

1. THE QUEEN.

2. Charles Greville (1794–1865). Clerk of the Council, 1821–59.

3. George Byng, later 2nd Earl of Strafford (1806–86). P.C., 1835; Comptroller of the Household, 1835–41; Treasurer of the Household, 1841.

4. William Keppel, 4th Earl of Albemarle (1772–1849). P.C., 1830; Master of the Horse, 1830–4, 1835–41.

5. George Campbell, 6th Duke of Argyll (1768–1839). P.C., 1833; Keeper of the Great Seal, 1827–8, 1830–9; Lord Steward of the Household, 1833–4, 1835–9.

6. Henry Paget, 1st Marquess of Anglesey (1768–1854). P.C., 1827 (see No. 1086).

7. Henry Petty-Fitzmaurice, 3rd Marquess of Lansdowne (1780–1863). P.C., 1806; High Constable of Ireland at the Coronation of George IV, 1821; Lord President of the Council, 1830–4, 1835–41, 1846–52; K.G., 1836.

8. Charles Pepys, later 1st Earl of Cottenham (1781–1851). P.C., 1834; Lord High Chancellor, 1836–41.

9. Henry Grey, Viscount Howick, later 3rd Earl Grey (1802–94). P.C., 1835; Secretary at War, 1835–9.

10. Lord John Russell, later 1st Earl Russell (1792–1878). P.C., 1830; Secretary of State for the Home Department, 1835–9.

11. Thomas Spring Rice, later 1st Baron Monteagle (1790–1866). P.C., 1834. Chancellor of the Exchequer, 1835–9.

12. William Lamb, 2nd Viscount Melbourne (1779–1848). P.C., 1827 (see No. 848).

13. Henry Temple, 3rd Viscount Palmerston (1784–1865). P.C., 1809; Secretary for Foreign Affairs, 1830–4, 1835–41, 1846–51.

14. James Abercromby, later 1st Baron Dunfermline (1776–1858). P.C., 1827; Speaker of the House of Commons, 1835–9.

15. Charles, 2nd Earl Grey (1764–1845). P.C., 1806; K.G., 1831; Bearer of the Sword of State at the Coronation of William IV, 1831.

16. George Howard, 9th Earl of Carlisle (1773–1848). P.C., 1806; K.G., 1837.

17. Thomas, 1st Baron Denman (1779–1854). P.C., 1832; Lord Chief Justice of the King's Bench; Solicitor-General to Queen Caroline at her trial in 1820.

18. Thomas Erskine (1788–1864). P.C., 1831; Chief Justice of the Common Pleas and of the Bankruptcy Court.

19. George Howard, Viscount Morpeth, later 10th Earl of Carlisle (1802–64). P.C., 1835; Chief Secretary for Ireland, 1835–41.

20. George Hamilton-Gordon, 4th Earl of Aberdeen (1784–1860). P.C., 1814.

21. John Singleton Copley, Baron Lyndhurst (1772–1863). P.C., 1826.

22. William Howley (1766–1848). Archbishop of Canterbury, 1828–48.

23. Ernest, Duke of Cumberland and King of Hanover.

24. Arthur Wellesley, 1st Duke of Wellington (1769–1852). P.C., 1807 (see No. 917).

25. George Child-Villiers, 5th Earl of Jersey (1773–1859). P.C., 1830; Lord of the Bedchamber to the Prince of Wales, 1795; Lord Chamberlain, 1830, 1834–5; bore the Queen Consort's sceptre at the Coronation of William IV; Master of the Horse, 1841–6, 1852.

26. John Wilson Croker (1780–1857). P.C., 1828.

27. Sir Robert Peel, 2nd Bt. (1788–1850). P.C., 1812.

28. Augustus, Duke of Sussex.

29. Henry Richard Vassall Fox, 3rd Baron Holland (1773–1840). P.C., 1806; Chancellor of the Duchy of Lancaster, 1835–40.

30. Sir John Campbell, later 1st Baron Campbell (1779–1861). Attorney-General, 1834, 1835–41.

31. James Gascoyne-Cecil, 2nd Marquess of Salisbury (1791–1868). P.C., 1826. Bore the sword called 'Curtana' at the Coronation of Wiliam IV.

32. John Fane, Lord Burghersh, later 11th Earl of Westmorland (1784–1859). P.C., 1822.

33. Thomas Kelly (1772–1855). Lord Mayor of London, 1836–7.

1. This is based on the Key printed with Charles Fox's engraving of No. 1188 (see below). I have only included in the notes about the sitters the dates when they became Privy Councillors and their posts at the time of Queen Victoria's accession.

hand (Oppé, No. 670) which may not be associated with this picture. An oil sketch (*Fig.* 58) of the head of the Queen, as she appears in the painting, is in the collection of Col. William Stirling. It seems that at first Wilkie intended to place the Queen facing the spectator. The drawings for the design as a whole show that he added the figures behind the Queen (2–5) to it after the design had been fairly carefully worked out. At first (*Fig.* 59) the principal figures seem to have been seated at the table; later (*Fig.* 62) Wilkie stood Melbourne and Wellington up, but Cumberland was at this stage apparently at the Queen's left hand. In Lord Perth's drawing (*Fig.* 61) Wilkie was evolving a group on the Queen's left, composed of Lord Cottenham (8), Lord John Russell (10), Melbourne (12) and Lord Denman (17). The picture was exhibited at the Royal Academy in 1838 (60); Wilkie's list (9 April 1838) of the paintings he was sending to the exhibition was sold at Sotheby's, 29 October 1962 (265), and is now in the National Library of Scotland (MS. Acc. 3419); it includes (No. 1 on the list) a detailed description of the picture. Cunningham (*op. cit.*, pp. 241–2) records tactfully the difficulties Wilkie had experienced from sitters who had jostled and intrigued for a place in the design, from those who were placed in the rear but wished to be in the van, from others who modestly took the back though deserving a place in the foreground, and from others who were anxious that justice should be done to their fine looks. In August 1838 Wilkie received the picture back 'to be immediately engraved' by agreement with Moon. Moon published the engraving by Charles Fox in 1846. A copy by Brooks was commissioned by the Lord Chamberlain in 1891 (No. 1191).

The Queen held her Accession Council at Kensington Palace at eleven o'clock on 20 June 1837, a few hours after her Accession. It was held in the Red Saloon and the Queen naturally wore a black mourning dress. Wilkie's record of the scene should be compared with Greville's famous account (*Journal*, ed. H. Reeve (1899), vol. III, pp. 414–17). Wilkie surely recaptured the Queen's 'perfect calmness and self-possession . . . graceful modesty and propriety', but she came intensely to dislike the picture. On 28 February 1838 she spoke with Melbourne 'of Wilkie's picture of the First Council, which I saw this morning and which though a fine picture contains very few good likenesses; Lord Melbourne's is quite detestable and really quite vexes me'. When she was looking at pictures standing in the Corridor on 12 November 1847, she thought it 'one of the worst pictures I have ever seen, both as to painting & likenesses. Everyone was horrified when they saw it yesterday'. Wherever it was hung 'it cannot look well' (Journal).

1189 PRINCE CHARLES OF LEININGEN (1804–56) (*Plate 277*)

Windsor Castle (3057). $20\frac{7}{8} \times 17$ in., $53 \times 43,2$ cm.; in addition, *c.* $\frac{3}{4}$ in. is turned over on the left and *c.* $1\frac{1}{2}$ in. on the right.

Head and shoulders, unfinished.

Stated to have been presented by the artist to the Duchess of Kent and to have been given by her to Queen Victoria (*V.R. inv.*); later at Buckingham Palace (424).

Literature: R.A., *King's Pictures* (84); National Gallery of Scotland, *Ramsay, Raeburn & Wilkie*, 1951 (36), *Paintings and Drawings by Sir David Wilkie*, 1958 (72); R.A., *Sir David Wilkie*, 1958 (33).

The face alone is finished; the cravat is hurriedly indicated. The head is closely related to the figure of the Prince in Wilkie's group of Princess Victoria with members of her family (No. 1187). An unfinished head of the 'Duke of Saxe Leiningen, The head finished', was in the Wilkie sale at Christie's, 25–30 April 1842 (649); it was not in fact sold, but was delivered, presumably to the Duchess of Kent, by Wilkie's sister.

Son of the Duchess of Kent by her first marriage to Ernest Charles, Prince of Leiningen, and half-brother of Queen Victoria. In 1848 he became head of the Department of Foreign Affairs in the German Empire. Queen Victoria mourned him deeply: 'how *impossible it is to realise* the dreadful thought that I shall never see his dear, dear face again in this world'.

1190. ABD-UL-MEJÍD (1823–61), SULTAN OF TURKEY (*Plate 275*)

Buckingham Palace. Panel: $27\frac{5}{8} \times 23$ in., $80,7 \times 58,4$ cm.

Full-length, seated on a richly gilded and upholstered sofa, holding his sword across his knees; round his neck he wears the Order of Glory.

Intended by Wilkie as a present to Queen Victoria; in the Corridor at Windsor in 1859 (*V.R. inv.*, No. 366); later at Buckingham Palace and Osborne.

Literature: B. R. Haydon, *Diary*, ed. W. B. Pope (Harvard University Press), vol. V (1963), pp. 29–30; Cunningham, *Wilkie*, vol. III, pp. 284, 327–8, 330, 340, 345–52, 354–5, 358–63, 532; R.A., *The First Hundred Years*, 1951–2 (307); E. K. Waterhouse in *Burl. Mag.*, vol. XCIV (1952), p. 52; National Gallery of Scotland, *Paintings and Drawings by Sir David Wilkie*, 1958 (115); R.A., *Sir David Wilkie*, 1958 (41).

Wilkie arrived in Constantinople on 5 October 1840. He asked if the Sultan would sit to him for his portrait. The Sultan agreed ('considering that doing so might show his consideration for the Queen of Great Britain'), but difficulties arose and it was not until 12 December that Wilkie had the first sitting in the Sultan's Winter Palace. Wilkie wished to paint the Sultan 'sitting on the throne as Sultan, receiving people presented', wearing the cloak of the Sultan. In his first sitting of about an hour and a half Wilkie 'got the face nearly painted in'. On 14 December, at a second sitting of nearly three hours, Wilkie disposed the Sultan's hands and sword as he desired and painted in the dress; the Sultan expressed a wish to be painted in white gloves and chose a sofa from an adjoining room (Wilkie may first have painted him sitting on a throne or chair). On 19 December Wilkie painted in the diamond hilt of the sword and 'raised it with the hands higher in the picture'; the Sultan 'was most particular about the likeness, which, in the course of sitting, I had to alter variously, the Sultan taking sometimes the brush with colours, and indicating the alteration he wished made'. On 27 December the Sultan gave 'an excellent sitting of two hours' and expressed his desire for a copy of the picture; Wilkie agreed to begin it at once and finish it in London; he made drawings of the sword and canopy. On 29 and 30 December he worked on the head, hand and sword in the copy. The Sultan seemed to have been 'highly pleased' with the portrait and on 3 January 1841 Wilkie had a sitting for the copy ('I thought it became more like than the first'), made drawings of the badge and collar and was presented with a gold and jewelled snuff-box.

The portrait was exhibited at the Royal Academy in 1842 (117). The copy, for which the Sultan paid 200 guineas, may be the one now in the Topkapi Museum. Two studies (one signed and dated) for the painting were in Wilkie's sale, Christie's 25–30 April 1842 (586, 587); a drawing of the same design, signed and dated 1840 and then in the collection of I. C. C. Boyd, was published in lithograph by Joseph Nash in Wilkie's *Sketches in Turkey, Syria and Egypt* (1843), pl. III.

Succeeded his father, Mahmúd II, as Sultan in 1839. A humane and enlightened ruler, he was enfeebled by indulgence in alcohol and the harem and lacked the will to enforce the reforms he promulgated early in his reign. He was much under the influence of the British Ambassador, Lord Stratford de Redcliffe, and was the ally of England and France in the Crimean War.

After Sir David Wilkie

1191. THE FIRST COUNCIL OF QUEEN VICTORIA

Kensington Palace. 60½ × 95 in., 153,7 × 241,3 cm.

Commissioned by the Lord Chamberlain and acquired in 1891 (P.R.O., L.C. 1/552, II, 13).

A copy by Brooks of No. 1188. It was painted to hang in the Nursery at Kensington among the pictures illustrative of Queen Victoria's life and reign (Law, *Kensington* (1899), p. 113, (1903), p. 114) and to be used for exhibition purposes.

George Willison

1741–97. Portrait-painter. A native of Edinburgh, he exhibited at the Society of Artists between 1767 and 1778 and at the Royal Academy in 1771–2. He went to India in 1774. He returned to London in 1781 and later settled in Edinburgh.

1192. MUHAMMAD ALI KHAN, WALAJAH (1717–95), NAWAB OF THE CARNATIC (*Plate* 288)

93 × 57½ in., 236,2 × 146 cm.

Full-length, standing, resting his left hand on his sword; his costume is enriched by a magnificent *kamarband*.

In the collection of George III: recorded in the King's Gallery at Kensington in 1778 ('The Nabob. Willison') and 1818 (340); sent to Hampton Court (155) on 1 November 1833 and sent by H.M. King George V to the Victoria Memorial Hall, Calcutta, in 1920 (*Illustrated Catalogue of the Exhibits*, Victoria Memorial, Calcutta (1925), No. 196).

Literature: Law, 1881, 1898 (362); Sir W. Foster, *A Descriptive Catalogue of the Paintings, Statues, &c., in the India Office* (5th ed., 1924), p. 6; 'British Artists in India, 1760–1820', *Walpole Soc.*, vol. XIX (1931), pp. 78–9; Sir E. Cotton, *A Descriptive List of the Pictures in the Viceroy's Residences . . .* (1936), p. 24.

In February 1775 the Nawab sent two portraits of himself by Willison to London, one for the King (i.e., presumably No. 1192) and the other for the East India Company. The latter is probably the version in the Old India Office collection, now in the Commonwealth Office; this is inscribed with the sitter's titles and the date 1775. A third version of this type, which had been painted in 1774, belongs to the Government of India and is in Viceroy's House, Delhi. A version with a different background was on the art-market in London in 1931 and 1936. One version of the portrait, presumably one of the two sent to London in 1775, was exhibited at the Society of Artists in 1777 (167). A small variant, including members of the Nawab's family, was sold at Christie's, 22 June 1925 (58).

The Nawab succeeded his father in 1749; he was the British candidate for the Arcot succession, but he was a confirmed intriguer and later in his life was in secret negotiation with Tippoo Sultan.

John Wootton

1686(?)–1764. Painter of landscapes and military and sporting subjects. For his earlier pictures in the royal collection, see Millar, pp. 29, 179–83, Nos. 544–55.

Attributed to John Wootton

1193. GEORGE III'S PROCESSION TO THE HOUSES OF PARLIAMENT

Buckingham Palace. 35½ × 53½ in., 90,2 × 135,9 cm.

The King, accompanied by a gentleman and (?) the Queen, in the new Gold State Coach (see below), approaching the Horse Guards with an escort of Household Cavalry, Walking Footmen and Yeomen of the Guard; among the crowd of spectators are two Blue-coat boys and a figure in an Oriental turban. On the left is the Entrance Lodge to the garden of Carlton House; the figures watching the procession from the balcony may be members of the King's family or household.

Acquired by George IV for £84. On 17 January 1822 it was received at Carlton House from Mr. Rickards: 'A Painting—representation of George The Second going in State through the Park . . . by Hogarth' (Jutsham, *Receipts*, f. 154; inv. of 1816, additional No. 592 with the same attribution); it was later at the King's Lodge, Windsor Castle (413) and Buckingham Palace.

Probably painted to record the first public appearance of the Gold State Coach designed by Sir William Chambers and decorated with paintings by Cipriani. On 25 November 1762 'His majesty went . . . to the house of Peers, and opened the session of parliament . . . His majesty went in a new state coach' (*Annual Register*). On 30 November Walpole wrote to Mann: 'There is come forth a new state coach, which has cost 8,000*l.* It is a beautiful object, though crowded with improprieties . . . The crowd to see it on the opening of Parliament was greater than at the Coronation, and much more mischief done'. Iconographically No. 1193 is a sequel, therefore, to Millar, No. 488 (q.v.); on grounds of style it can be reasonably certainly attributed to Wootton in his last years.

Richard Wright

1735–1775(?). Marine painter, stated to have been self-taught, who exhibited in London between 1762 and 1773.

1194. QUEEN CHARLOTTE'S PASSAGE TO ENGLAND (*Plate* 9)

Buckingham Palace. 35⅜ × 50½ in., 89,9 × 128,3 cm.

Signed: *R: Wright Pinx.*

The squadron, under the command of Admiral Lord Anson in the *Nottingham*, escorting Princess Charlotte of Mecklenburg-Strelitz in the *Royal Charlotte* in a rough sea.

In the collection of Queen Charlotte, recorded in the Green Pavilion at Frogmore (Pyne, vol. I, *Frogmore*, pp. 15–16); later at Hampton Court (1001) and Kensington.

Literature: Mrs. Jameson, vol. II, p. 418; Law, 1881, 1898 (889).

Presumably the picture exhibited by Wright at the Society of Artists in 1762 (137: *A View of the Storm when the queen was on her passage to England, painted from a sketch drawn on board the Fubbes yacht*). Anson's squadron consisted of the *Nottingham, Winchester, Minerva, Tartar* and a number of yachts. The Princess arrived at Stade on 22 August 1761. On the following day she went on board the *Royal Charlotte* yacht (formerly the *Royal Caroline*, Captain Peter Dennis). On 28 August the squadron put to sea and, after severe storms which nearly drove them on to the Norwegian coast, reached Harwich on 6 September.

The central part of No. 1194 was incorporated by Wright in the background of Reynolds's portrait of the Duchess of Ancaster who had accompanied the Princess to England (Waterhouse, *Reynolds*, pl. 92 and note).

Johann Zoffany

1733/4–1810. Born near Frankfurt am Main and possibly partly of Hungarian descent. After working in Germany, he went to Italy and, after a period in the service of the Elector of Treves, came to London in 1760. He was in Italy, 1772–9, and in India, 1783–9.

In addition to the works still in the royal collection, there is a record of four portraits by Zoffany in the Bedchamber at Buckingham House (Geo. III, *Buck. Ho.*): 'The Queen's Mother', measurements given as 50 × 40 in.; 'Prince George', measurements given as 50 × 40 in.; 'The Princess Royal', measurements given as 36 × 28 in.; and 'The Prince of Wales and the Bishop of Osnabourgh', measurements given as 19¼ × 15¼ in. The last was probably the picture of the two boys 'as cupids, with a landscape on copper', which Zoffany had exhibited at the Free Society in 1766 (201). It was apparently given by the Queen to Lady Charlotte Finch on 22 October 1765, when she wrote in her diary: 'I staid at Kew. The Queen gave me a Picture in Small size done by Zoffani in Oyl, of the P. of Wales & P. Frederick' (Finch MSS., formerly at Burley-on-the-Hill). The portrait of the Princess Royal may be the portrait of her which was formerly in the Duke of Cambridge's collection and was later on the art-market as by Dance. It is now in Tryon Palace Restoration, South Carolina. The portrait of Prince George may conceivably have been No. 1000, to which Zoffany's name could have been applied in error by the compiler of the Buckingham House inventory.

1195. GEORGE III (*Plate* 24)

Windsor Castle (2924). 64½ × 54⅛ in., 163,8 × 137,5 cm.

Three-quarter-length, seated, in a General Officer's coat with the ribbon and star of the Garter, wearing the Garter round his leg; his hat and sword lie on the same marble-topped gilt carved commode as appears in the background of No. 1199.

Painted, with No. 1196, for the King or Queen Charlotte and first recorded with No. 1196 in the Queen's Gallery at Kensington (George III, *Kensington*: 'His Majesty. Zoffani', with later pencil note: 'gone'); recorded in the Dining-Room at Buckingham House in 1819 (738); removed to Kew in 1834; later at Buckingham Palace (625).

Literature: Manners and Williamson, p. 209; Collins Baker, *Windsor*, p. 326; R.A., *King's Pictures* (62); Arts Council, *Johann Zoffany*, 1960–1 (3).

Painted in 1771 and engraved in 1772 by R. Houston; it was also engraved by Fritzsch (1779) and R. Laurie. It was exhibited at the Royal Academy in 1771 (230: note by

Walpole: 'Very like, but most disagreeable and unmeaning figure'). The chair was first painted by Zoffany at an angle to the picture-plane; the first lines of brass-headed studs on the front of the chair can be seen below the amended position and there are signs of alteration to the back and left side of the chair. A contemporary copy belongs to the Marquess of Zetland; see also Nos. 1197, 1213. In a standing three-quarter-length portrait of the King in the collection of S.K.H. Prince Ernst August, the head is almost identical with No. 1195. There is a poor copy of No. 1195 at Somerset House. Mrs. Mary Knowles's embroidered life-size copy (at Kew) is signed and dated 1771; her embroidered *Self-portrait* shows her at work on a reduced copy of it.

1196. QUEEN CHARLOTTE (*Plate* 25)

Windsor Castle (2925). 64½ × 54⅛ in., 163,8 × 137,5 cm.

Three-quarter-length, seated, in a richly laced dress and a black shawl, leaning on an elaborately carved gilt table with a marble top; a pot of flowers stands at her elbow. On her right wrist the Queen wears a bracelet of pearls in which is set a miniature of George III.

Painted, with No. 1195, for the Queen or George III and first recorded with No. 1195 in the Queen's Gallery at Kensington (Geo. III, *Kensington*: 'Her Majesty. Zoffani', with later pencil note: 'gone'); recorded in the Dining-Room at Buckingham House in 1819 (739); removed to Kew in 1834; later at Buckingham Palace (626).

Literature: Manners and Williamson, p. 209; Collins Baker, *Windsor*, p. 327; R.A., *King's Pictures* (64); Arts Council, *Johann Zoffany*, 1960–1 (4).

Painted in 1771 and engraved in 1772 by R. Houston 'from the Original Picture in the Possession of his Majesty' (Chaloner Smith, vol. II, p. 654; it was also engraved, with a simpler background, in 1772 by R. Laurie, *ibid.*, p. 801); although it must have been painted as a pendant to No. 1195, it was not exhibited at the Royal Academy. There are minor *pentimenti* in the arrangement of the curtains and in the outline of the Queen's head and left shoulder; a fold of drapery at first hung over the marble top of the table. There are indications that the column on the left of the Queen's head was added by Zoffany to the design or strengthened during painting. In a standing three-quarter-length portrait of the Queen in the collection of S.K.H. Prince Ernst August, the head seems closely connected with No. 1196; see also No. 1198. There is a poor copy of No. 1196 at Somerset House; a copy of the head was bought by H.M. Queen Mary at the Egmont sale, Christie's, 24 February 1933 (46), and given to H.R.H. the Duke of York, later H.M. King George VI.

1197. GEORGE III

Buckingham Palace. Oval, copper: 30¾ × 25 in., 78,1 × 63,5 cm.

Head and shoulders, in robes of state with the collar of the Garter.

Bought with No. 1198 by H.M. Queen Mary for the Buckingham Palace Collection.

The head is of the same type as No. 1195; it is of good quality and probably by Zoffany himself.

1198. QUEEN CHARLOTTE

Buckingham Palace. Oval, copper: 30½ × 25⅝ in., 77,5 × 65,1 cm.

Head and shoulders, in robes of state, wearing diamonds in her hair and magnificent jewels on her corsage.

See No. 1197.

The head is of the same type as No. 1196, with slight variations in the jewels; but it seems certainly to be by Zoffany himself.

1199. QUEEN CHARLOTTE WITH HER TWO ELDEST SONS (Plates 26–8)

Windsor Castle (519). 44¼×50⅞ in., 112,4×129,2 cm.

The Queen is seated at her dressing-table. Her profile is seen reflected in the looking-glass on the table; at her knee stands Prince Frederick, later Duke of York, in Oriental costume; she rests her left hand on a boar-hound held by George, Prince of Wales, who carries a spear and wears Roman costume with a plumed helmet decorated with the Prince of Wales's feathers. A drum and standard are on a chair on the left. Through the window is seen a lawn with an ibis (?) upon it, a clipped hedge and ornamental trees. The figure of one of the Queen's ladies is reflected in a mirror in the room beyond.

Perhaps painted for Queen Charlotte, but not apparently recorded in the inventories of her or George III's pictures. By 1794 it was in the possession of the Prince of Wales: in that year Simpson charged three guineas for cleaning it (P.R.O., H.O. 73, 23). In 1806 George Simpson charged three guineas 'To Cleaning a Picture wt the Portrait of her Majesty and their Royal Highnesses the Princes of Wales and York wt a View of a Dressing Room by Zoffani' (W.R.A., 26878). It was in store at Carlton House in 1816 (276: 'The interior of another apartment at Windsor . . . Mr Zoffany'); in the inventory of 'Carleton Palace' (311) the location is altered to 'Kew Palace'.[1] By 1878 it had been altered to 'a room of Buckingham palace' (V.R. inv.). The picture went from Carlton House to Kew.

Literature: Manners and Williamson, pp. 36–7, 210; H. Clifford Smith, *Buckingham Palace* (1930), pp. 86–7; R.A., *British Art*, 1934 (242), *Commemorative Catalogue* (1935), p. 65; Collins Baker, *Windsor*, p. 329; R.A., *King's Pictures* (63), *European Masters of the Eighteenth Century*, 1954–5 (105).

Probably painted c. 1765, perhaps slightly later than No. 1200. The room is almost certainly one of the new rooms on the ground floor of the garden front of Buckingham House. The rather formal vista from the window, the style of the door surrounds and the brick façade (seen against the window reveal) have led Mr. John Harris to this conclusion. The rooms are furnished with some of the Queen's finest possessions. The clock is still at Windsor; its face is signed by Ferdinand Berthoud, its (later) outer face by Vulliamy (1821). The carved and gilt console table in the room beyond is used again by Zoffany in No. 1195. The pictures hanging in the room (reflected in the tall mirror behind the Queen) and in the rooms beyond almost certainly are among those that had very recently been bought from Consul Smith's collection; it is not too fanciful to recognise pictures by Canaletto and (?) Zuccarelli and many of the pictures are in frames of the form associated with Smith. The picture over the door (?a scene from the life of Ulysses or Aeneas) is not in this type of frame and is no longer in the royal collection.

There are slight *pentimenti* in the Queen's head, which was at first either dressed higher or with a different ornament; the carved crown on her chair was at first larger; and there are changes in the fall of lace over the looking-glass and in the fall of the Queen's dress over the cushion and at the feet of Prince George.

1. When the picture was exhibited at the British Institution in 1826 (125), the room was described as in Kew Palace.

1200. GEORGE, PRINCE OF WALES, AND FREDERICK, LATER DUKE OF YORK (Plate 29)

Windsor Castle (517). 44×50⅜ in., 111,8×127,9 cm.

The two children are seen in infant's 'coats', playing with a little spaniel (the younger boy is seated) in an interior at Buckingham House (see below).

No. 1200 is possibly the picture received at Carlton House from Mr. Saxon on 19 June 1809: 'A Painting Containing the Portraits of Their Majestys and His Royal Highness The Prince of Wales and Duke of York—by Zophany . . . recommended by Captain Scott as an Original [sic]' (Jutsham, R/D, f. 97). It was in store at Carlton House in 1816 (275): 'The interior of one of the apartments at Windsor, with the portraits of the Prince of Wales and the Duke of York, when young'; in later Carlton House inventories the location is changed to Kew Palace and Buckingham House. The picture was later at Kew.

Literature: Manners and Williamson, p. 211; H. Clifford Smith, *Buckingham Palace* (1930), p. 88; Collins Baker, *Windsor*, p. 330; R.A., *King's Pictures* (46).

The children can, on the basis of the early references to the picture (see above), probably be identified as the two eldest children of George III and Queen Charlotte and not as Prince William and Prince Edward, a description recorded by Redgrave in 1878 (V.R. inv.). The two children in No. 1200 cannot be reconciled with the portrait of Prince William in No. 1201.[1] No. 1200 was probably painted in 1765; Prince Frederick had been born on 16 August 1763 and his elder brother on 12 August 1762. The room in which they are playing is the Second Drawing-Room or Warm Room at Buckingham House. It can be compared with Stephanoff's plate (1818) in Pyne (vol. II, *Buckingham House*, p. 14), in which the door[2] is exactly identical with that reflected in the mirror over the fireplace in No. 1200. This mirror had already been dismantled by the time of Stephanoff's view; the marble fireplace is now in the State Bedroom at Windsor.[3] The screen was stated by Clifford Smith (loc. cit.) to have been supplied for the Queen's House by William Vile in 1763. The two pictures by Van Dyck, *The Villiers Boys* and the *Three Children of Charles I* (Millar, 153 and 151), are seen in the same frames and positions in Stephanoff's plate and are recorded in the Warm Room in Geo. III, *Buck. Ho.* The painting of the *Infant Christ*, by a follower of Maratti (Levey, 545), was certainly at Buckingham House at this period, but is not recorded in this room. It is possible that Zoffany placed it in No. 1200 (or was instructed to do so) as a suitable devotional piece, above contemporary portraits of the Princes' parents which cannot be identified with any surviving portraits; they have an air of early Reynolds and may be inventions by Zoffany.

1201. GEORGE III, QUEEN CHARLOTTE AND THEIR SIX ELDEST CHILDREN (Plate 32)

Windsor Castle (463). 41¼×50¼ in., 104,8×127,6 cm.

The family, in Van Dyck costumes, is grouped under a colonnade (?) on the edge of a wooded park. The King and his eldest son, George, Prince of Wales (later George IV),

1. When No. 1200 was shown at the British Institution in 1826 (121) the children were described as Prince William (b. 21 August 1765) and Princess Charlotte (b. 29 September 1766), but in the following year (144) the above identification was accepted.
2. Mr. John Harris tells me that this is identical with a design for a door made by George III and given by him to Thomas Worsley to be executed for Buckingham House.
3. Identified by Mr. Geoffrey de Bellaigue.

wear the ribbon (and the King also wears the star) of the Garter; Prince Frederick, later Duke of York, stands between them, wearing the ribbon of the Bath. On the left, playing with a cockatoo, Prince William (later William IV) wears the ribbon of the Thistle; near him sits Prince Edward, later Duke of Kent, with the little spaniel who appeared in No. 1200. Princess Charlotte stands beside the Queen, holding the hand of the infant Princess Augusta, who clasps a teething coral. The Queen wears over her heart a miniature portrait of the King (?). Behind the Queen (her?) crown, orb and sceptre rest on a table.

Recorded in Princess Amelia's Bedroom at Kew (Geo. III, *Kew:* 'The Royal Family Zoffani'); at Windsor in 1862 (*V.R. inv.*).

Literature: Manners and Williamson, pp. 24–6, 211; Collins Baker, *Windsor*, p. 328; R.A., *King's Pictures* (61).

Painted, presumably for George III or Queen Charlotte, early in 1770. Earlom's engraving, dated 29 October 1770, describes No. 1201 as painted in that year (Chaloner Smith, p. 248). Prince William had been made a Knight of the Thistle on 5 April 1770 (it is conceivable that Zoffany added the ribbon of the order to the figure of the Prince after the figure had been painted); Princess Elizabeth, who does not appear in the design, was born on 22 May 1770; and the picture was exhibited at the Royal Academy in 1770 (211), when Walpole described it as 'In Vandyke dresses, ridiculous'. It was again exhibited at the British Institution in 1827 (175). The group formed by the Queen and her two daughters, and the two eldest boys (at three-quarter length), were separately engraved by R. Lowrie. In a possible second plate of Earlom's engraving of No. 1201 (*Fig.* 64) the King's head is turned to the left. There is a *pentimento* where the scalloped edge of the Queen's bodice lies over her skirt. The copies of No. 1201 are normally bad in quality and on a reduced scale, e.g., those sold at Christie's, 6 July 1956 (46) and 14 May 1965 (102), and Sotheby's, 27 November 1957 (146). A small copy, bought by H.M. Queen Mary in 1930 and now at Clarence House, is stated to have been given by Queen Charlotte to the Hon. Miss Neville on her marriage to Sir George Warren. Small figures of the King, the Queen with her daughters, and the eldest Princes in No. 1201 were produced (*c.* 1773) in Derby biscuit porcelain, perhaps on the basis of the groups, modelled by John Bacon in 1772, in the Royal Library (Manners and Williamson, *loc. cit.*; W. B. Honey, 'Royal Portraits in Pottery and Porcelain', *Burl. Mag.*, vol. LXX (1937), pp. 218–29). These figures are very rare. In Zoffany's original sketch for No. 1201 (No. 1202) there are considerable variations in detail from the final design. For the relation of No. 1201 to pictures by Van Dyck in George III's possession, see above, pp. xiv–xv.

1202. GEORGE III, QUEEN CHARLOTTE AND THEIR SIX ELDEST CHILDREN (*Plate* 31)

Windsor Castle (3075). $10\frac{7}{8} \times 16\frac{1}{4}$ in., 27,6 × 41,3 cm.

Formerly in the collection of Camille Groult, Paris; purchased by Her Majesty The Queen in 1957.

Apparently the preliminary sketch in oils for No. 1201. There are minor differences in costume and the positions of the figures between the finished picture and the sketch; in the sketch the figures are livelier and less rigid, the columns are twisted and there is more movement in the curtain.

1203. GEORGE, PRINCE OF WALES, AND PRINCE FREDERICK, LATER DUKE OF YORK (*Plate* 33)

Buckingham Palace. $51\frac{1}{2} \times 79\frac{1}{2}$ in., 130,8 × 201,9 cm. The canvas was originally the same size as No. 1204. When it was placed in its present position, canvas was turned over at the top (*c.* 14 in.) and bottom (*c.* 3 in.), but this canvas was subsequently cut off and destroyed.

Full-lengths, standing in Van Dyck costume, holding hands at the foot of a large tree, beside a ledge on which are some flowers. The elder boy wears the ribbon of the Garter, the younger the ribbon of the Bath.

Nos. 1203, 1204 were presumably painted for George III and Queen Charlotte; they appear on a mutilated page of George III's inventories (invs. Nos. 32–36 on p. xlix above) and it is not certain whether the pictures on this page are at St. James's or Buckingham House. The relevant entries are:]'and Bishop of Osenburg. Zoffany' and]'ss Royal Ditto'. The measurements in each case are given as 70 × 81 in. and with each entry is a note 'F [or T] S^t Js' as if the portraits had come from (or, less likely, were to be removed to) St. James's. They were presumably at Carlton House in 1794, when Simpson charged ten guineas for cleaning them and their frames (P.R.O., H.O. 73, 23). No. 1203 was recorded at Carlton House in 1816 (530); in the inventory of 'Carleton Palace' (528) it was in the Waiting-Room. On 3 May 1826 it was sent to Seguier to be cleaned (Jutsham, *Deliveries*, f. 78). Later at Kew, but by 1841 in its present position over a door in the Throne Room at Buckingham Palace (*Buckingham Palace*, 1841, p. 93; later inv. No. 209).

Literature: Manners and Williamson, p. 210.

Probably painted, with No. 1204, in 1770. The two boys are perhaps slightly older than they appear in the family group (No. 1201). It was exhibited at the British Institution in 1827 (143).

1204. CHARLOTTE, PRINCESS ROYAL, AND PRINCE WILLIAM, LATER DUKE OF CLARENCE (*Plate* 34)

Buckingham Palace. $52\frac{1}{8} \times 78\frac{3}{4}$ in., 132,4 × 200 cm., as at present stretched. When No. 1204 was placed in its present position, canvas was turned over at the top (*c.* $13\frac{1}{2}$ in.) and bottom (*c.* $3\frac{1}{2}$ in.).

Full-lengths, standing on a stone ledge at the foot of a colonnade, beside a basket of flowers, with a dog jumping towards them. The Prince is in Van Dyck costume and holds his sister's hand.

See No. 1203. Recorded at Carlton House in 1816 (531: 'The Duke of Clarence, and the Princess-Royal when young. Mr Zoffany', measurements given as $68\frac{1}{2} \times 79$ in.); in the inventory of 'Carleton Palace' (529) it was in the Waiting-Room. On 3 May 1826 it was sent to Seguier to be cleaned (Jutsham, *Deliveries*, f. 78). Later at Kew, but by 1841 in its present position over a door in the Throne Room at Buckingham Palace (*Buckingham Palace*, 1841, p. 92; later inv. No. 208).

Literature: Manners and Williamson, p. 210.

See No. 1203. Probably painted in 1770. The Prince may be slightly younger than he appears in the family group (No. 1201); and he does not wear the insignia of a Knight of the Thistle, which he was created on 5 April 1770. The placing of the sitters behind the front of the ledge may indicate that the canvas was intended to be placed with the ledge at a certain height above eye level. There is a *pentimento* in the background, where the hanging curtain originally came down to the left of the Princess.

1205. FREDERICK, DUKE OF YORK
(*Plate* 38)

Buckingham Palace. $72\frac{1}{2} \times 60\frac{1}{2}$ in., 184,1 × 153,7 cm.

Signed: *John Zoffany Pinxt.* The canvas is inscribed on the back with the artist's and sitter's names.

Full-length, standing in a landscape in a little military coat (scarlet with blue facings and cuffs) with the ribbon of the Bath, holding his hat in his left hand.

Painted for George III or Queen Charlotte; probably the portrait ('The Bishop of Osnaburgh. Zoffani') recorded in the King's Gallery at Kensington in 1778. Recorded in the Dining-Room at Buckingham House in 1819 (748: 'Full length . . . when young . . .'); moved to Kew in 1834 and to Buckingham Palace (550) in 1860.

Literature: Manners and Williamson, p. 210.

Presumably painted *c.* 1770; the child may be very slightly older than he was when No. 1201 was painted. In the original design the figure was placed beside a large drum and in the lee of a huge suit of seventeenth-century armour decorated with a broad flowing sash and apparently supported on a broad stick. At a very early date these attributes were painted out, probably by Zoffany himself, but they are still to be seen in the replica in the collection of S.K.H. Prince Ernst August (*Fig.* 63) and in a version belonging to Hans Kellermann-Schele, Schellenburg. These versions must, therefore, have been painted, and perhaps despatched, before the alterations were made to the original. In No. 1205 there are also slight *pentimenti* in the sitter's right cuff and in the frill on his wrist.

1206. PRINCE ERNEST, LATER DUKE OF CUMBERLAND (*Plate* 36)

Kensington Palace. $36 \times 27\frac{5}{8}$ in., 91,4 × 70,2 cm.

Full-length, seated on a red cushion, wearing a white frock with a blue sash.

Recorded at Kew in 1861 (P.R.O., L.C. 1/96,27); later at Buckingham Palace (1648).

Presumably painted for George III and Queen Charlotte. The dress is unfinished and there are obvious *pentimenti* in the arrangement of its folds; the naked right foot is also unfinished and so is the right hand which may be holding a shoe. The Prince had been born on 5 June 1771 and it is probable that the portrait was left unfinished when Zoffany left England in the summer of 1772. It is possible that it was at Kensington in 1818 (492: 'Portrait of the Duke of Cumberland when a Child', without attribution; measurements given as $40 \times 38\frac{3}{4}$ in.).

1207. QUEEN CHARLOTTE WITH MEMBERS OF HER FAMILY (*Plate* 30)

Windsor Castle (464). $41\frac{3}{8} \times 50$ in., 105,1 × 127 cm.

The Queen is sitting on a rustic seat in a park-like setting, which may be at Kew, with a stretch of water in the distance. With her left hand she restrains Prince William (later Duke of Clarence), who wears the star of the Thistle; at her knee stands Princess Charlotte, holding a doll. On the Queen's right stands her brother, Prince Charles of Mecklenburg-Strelitz (1741–1816), wearing the ribbon and star of St. Andrew of Prussia; on the extreme right stands her brother Prince Ernest (1742–1814), wearing the ribbon and star of the White Eagle of Poland. Behind the Queen stands Lady Charlotte Finch (1725–1813), holding a baby who touches the Queen's neck.

Probably painted for Queen Charlotte. No. 1207 is, however, not recorded in the royal collection before the reign of Queen Victoria; Redgrave (*V.R. inv.*, 15 October 1862) records it at Windsor and states that it had on the back a label from the time of Callcott's Surveyorship (i.e., 1843–44). It may conceivably have been given by the Queen to one of her brothers.

Literature: Manners and Williamson, pp. 35–6, 210–11; Collins Baker, *Windsor*, p. 332; R.A., *King's Pictures* (65); Castle Museum, Norwich, *English Portraits in the Landscape Park*, 1948 (21).

No. 1207 was exhibited at the Royal Academy in 1773, after Zoffany's departure for Florence (320: *Portrait of her Majesty, in conversation with her two brothers and part of the Royal family*; Walpole added 'And Lady Charlotte Finch'). It must, however, have been painted earlier, at least in part. Prince William and Princess Charlotte are very little older than in No. 1201 and the Princess may have been painted from the same sitting. The baby in Lady Charlotte Finch's arms is probably Princess Augusta. In 1772, the latest year in which Zoffany could have worked on No. 1207, Princess Elizabeth (*b.* 1770) or Prince Ernest (*b.* 1771) would have been the youngest member of the family, but by then Prince William and Princess Charlotte would have been older than they appear here. Walpole's identification of the female figure behind the Queen, sometimes in the past identified as her sister Princess Christiana, must be accepted. There is a *pentimento* in Prince Charles's right leg, which was originally placed in an upright stance nearer his stick; Prince William's right arm and hat are painted over the Queen's draperies and are therefore, in their present position, an afterthought; Lady Charlotte Finch is painted carefully round, and therefore after, Prince William; the back of the seat is painted over the foliage; and there is a *pentimento* in Prince Ernest's left hand and wrist. The figure of the Princess resembles a three-quarter-length of her, attributed to Dance, but possibly by Zoffany, formerly in the collection of the Duke of Cambridge and now in Tryon Palace Restoration, South Carolina.

Prince Charles, the Queen's older brother, succeeded as Duke of Mecklenburg-Strelitz in 1794; for Prince Ernest, see No. 1208. Lady Charlotte Finch, daughter of the 1st Earl of Pomfret, married in 1746 the Hon. William Finch and was the mother of the 9th Earl of Winchilsea (see No. 1211). On 13 August 1762 she was appointed Governess in Ordinary to the infant Prince of Wales; she remained Governess to the royal children until 1792 and was deeply loved by them and by their mother. On 18 October 1808 the Princesses wrote to her of 'The Veneration, Attachment, and Respect which we *feel for* you Dearest Lady Cha . . . nor do we look back to the having been under your care as one of the least of the Mercies of Heaven ' (W.R.A., Geo. Add. 15, 448).

1208. PRINCE ERNEST GOTTLOB ALBERT OF MECKLENBURG-STRELITZ (1742–1814) (*Plate* 37)

Windsor Castle (1536). $49\frac{1}{2} \times 39\frac{1}{2}$ in., 125,7 × 100,3 cm.

Inscribed in chalk on the back of the original canvas: *Mr Zoffanij.*

Three-quarter-length, in Hanoverian military uniform, wearing the ribbon and star of the Polish Order of the White Eagle and leaning against a chair.

Presumably painted for Queen Charlotte. On 12 April 1805 'Portrait of His Highness Prince Ernest . . . Zoffany' was sent to Windsor from the Queen's Apartment at St. James's (Geo. III, *Removals*); it was later among the portraits of her family that the

Queen placed in the Eating-room at Frogmore (Pyne, vol. I, *Frogmore*, pp. 7–8, and plate by Wild (1819), opposite p. 2). It may have been for a time at Hampton Court, but was at Frogmore in 1871 (*V.R. inv.*, as by Ziesenis) and was taken up to the Castle in 1924.

Literature: Manners and Williamson, p. 37; R.A., *King's Pictures* (60).

Presumably painted in 1772 (see below) at the same period as No. 1207 and before Zoffany's departure for Florence. It was exhibited at the Royal Academy in 1773 (321: *A portrait*, identified by Walpole as 'Prince Ernest of Mecklenburg'). There is a slight *pentimento* in the placing of the right hand.

Youngest brother of Queen Charlotte, he was constantly in England. He appears to have left England in the spring of 1772. Writing to George III from Hanover on 8 May 1772 he said: 'the greatest satisfaction I have had since I quitted dear England, has been to see my Regiment, it is still beautifull, and pleases me more than ever'. He was devoted to George III who created him in 1788 a General of Infantry in the British Army.

1209. JOHN CUFF (*Plate* 44)

Windsor Castle (984). $35\frac{1}{4} \times 27\frac{1}{4}$ in., $89,5 \times 69,2$ cm. There is a very early addition of $1\frac{3}{4}$ in. at the bottom.

Signed and dated: *Zoffanÿ pinx / 1772*

Seated at his work-bench polishing a lens, his spectacles pushed up on to his forehead; the tools of his craft are on his bench, to which is fixed a heavy vice, and on the shelves beside him. An assistant stands just behind him.

Presumably purchased by, or painted for, George III or Queen Charlotte. Recorded in Princess Augusta's Bedroom at Kew (Geo. III, *Kew:* 'A Mathematitian. Zoffani'). In the rough draft of this inv., however, No. 1209 appears as 'Mr Cuff—Optician—Zoffany'. It was removed to the New Gallery at Windsor on 20 August 1828; later, for a short period, at Buckingham Palace.

Literature: Manners and Williamson, pp. 34–5, 210; Collins Baker, *Windsor*, p. 335; R.A., *King's Pictures* (504), *British Portraits*, 1956–7 (353); Detroit and Philadelphia, *Romantic Art in Britain*, 1968 (39).

No. 1209 was exhibited at the Royal Academy in 1772 (291) as *An optician, with his attendant.*[1] The optician is identified in the inv. of Kew (see above) as 'Mr Cuff'. When No. 1209 was lent to the British Institution in 1814 (79), the sitter was called 'Mr Cuffs'; at the Institution in 1827 (171) the picture was described as 'Two Old Men'. Redgrave, however (*V.R. inv.*, 6 October 1859), described No. 1209 as 'The Lapidaries' and noted on the stretcher a pencil note (now no longer visible): 'Dollond the Optician in the Strand London'. The portrait has ever since been identified with Peter Dollond, who perfected the achromatic telescope and was Optician to the King and the Duke of York; he was the eldest son of John Dollond. But Peter Dollond was born in 1731 and the old man must be more than forty-two years of age.

Optician, whose shop was 'at the sign of the Reflecting Microscope, exactly against Sergeants' Inn Gate, Fleet St.'; Master of the Spectacle Makers' Company in 1748. He perfected inventions and important improvements in microscopes and in 1744 produced a microscope of brass, mounted on a fixed pillar. He made microscopes for George III and Queen Charlotte.

1. Walpole criticised it: 'Extremely natural, but the characters too common nature, and the chiaroscuro destroyed by his servility in imitating the reflexions of the glasses'.

1210. THE ACADEMICIANS OF THE ROYAL ACADEMY (*Plates* 39, 43)

Windsor Castle (431). $39\frac{3}{4} \times 58$ in., $100,7 \times 147,3$ cm.

The male Academicians, identified in the accompanying Key, are grouped under the lamp that illuminates a life school during the arrangement of the naked model; a younger model is seated in the foreground. Around the walls are placed various casts and on the wall hang portraits of the two female Academicians.

Presumably painted for George III. Recorded in the Upper Library at Buckingham House in 1819 (870: 'The Interior of the Royal Academy. Zoffanii'). On 21 July 1820 it was taken from Buckingham House to Carlton House by command of George IV; on 28 July the frame was sent to Wyatt for re-gilding and the picture to Seguier for cleaning and repairing (Jutsham, *Receipts*, f. 104, *R/D*, ff. 356, 358; *Carlton House*, 1816, additional No. 575); by 1841 it was in the Picture Gallery at Buckingham Palace (99: . . . 'Purchased from the Artist by George the Third'), but by 1859 it was in the Corridor at Windsor (*V.R. inv.*).

Literature: The Literary Gazette, 8 July 1826; Walpole, *Anecdotes*, vol. I, p. xviii, n. by Dalloway; Leslie and Taylor, vol. I, pp. 446–8; Manners and Williamson, pp. 28–34, 211; W. T. Whitley, *Artists and their Friends in England 1700–1799*, vol. I, p. 271; R.A., *British Art*, 1934 (359), *Commemorative Catalogue* (1935), p. 66; Collins Baker, *Windsor*, p. 334; R.A., *King's Pictures* (50), *The First Hundred Years of the Royal Academy*, 1951–2 (28); Waterhouse, *Painting in Britain*, p. 231; M. Levey in *Burl. Mag.*, vol. CI (1959), p. 140.

The scene would be taking place in one of the rooms made available to the young Academy in Old Somerset House. Whitley (*loc. cit.*) prints the account of a visit by Tan-che-qua or Chitqua, the Chinese modeller in the spring of 1771 to the Schools of the Royal Academy, 'where he not only met with a polite reception but had the honour to have his portrait introduced by Mr. Zoffany into a capital picture of the members of that noble institution, which that eminent artist is executing for a great personage'. The 'great personage' was presumably the King, who may understandably have wished to have a picture of the members of his Academy. The picture was exhibited at the Royal Academy in 1772 (290: *The portraits of the Academicians of the Royal Academy*); Walpole stated in his catalogue: 'This excellent picture was done by candlelight; he made no design for it, but clapped in the artists as they came to him, and yet all the attitudes are easy and natural, most of the likenesses strong. There is a print from it' (i.e., the engraving by Earlom, published on 2 August 1773 with a dedication to the King (Chaloner Smith, p. 243)).[1] The group contains all the Academicians of the time, with the exception of Gainsborough and George and Nathaniel Dance; Gainsborough was still working in Bath and it is conceivable that Zoffany's sketch of Gainsborough's head, now in the National Portrait Gallery (3913), was painted with a view to including Gainsborough in the scene. If Zoffany had begun to paint the picture in the spring of 1771, he would have had to expand or alter such original ideas as he had in order to include the three most recent Academicians: Burch (33) and Cosway (35), both elected in 1771, and Nollekens (34), elected in 1772. X-ray (1964), however, reveals no obvious insertions or alterations, but during painting Zoffany enlarged his canvas *c.* $7\frac{3}{4}$ in. on the right, an addition that includes Mrs. Moser (31) and Hoare (36), who must from the first, as foundation members of the Academy, have been intended to appear in the design. Zoffany's original

1. Zoffany was displeased with this print 'as there is no likeness in the heads, and I very much wonder at the success of it' (Whitley, *op. cit.*, vol. I, p. 296).

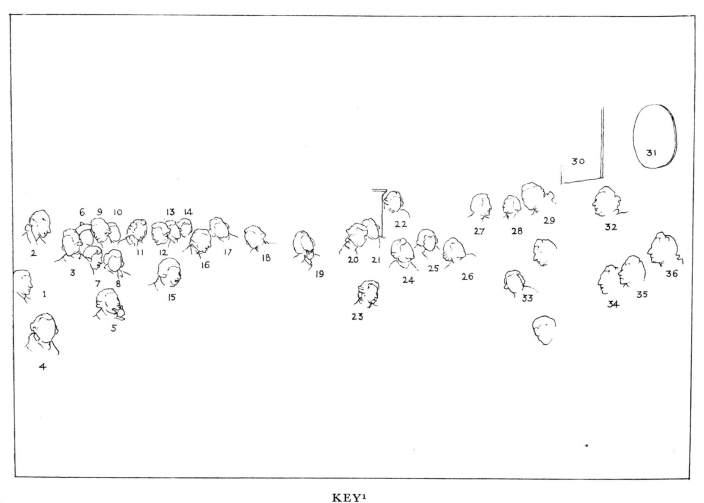

KEY[1]

1. John Gwynn (d. 1786), architect; R.A., 1768.
2. Giovanni Battista Cipriani (1727–85), painter; R.A., 1768.
3. Benjamin West, R.A., 1768, P.R.A., 1792–1820.
4. Johann Zoffany, R.A., 1769.
5. Mason Chamberlin, R.A., 1768.
6. Tan-che-qua, a Chinese artist who came to England in 1769.
7. George Barret (1732(?)–84), R.A., 1768.
8. Joseph Wilton (1722–1803), sculptor; R.A., 1768, Keeper, 1790.
9. Jeremiah Meyer (1735–89), miniaturist; R.A., 1768.
10. Dominic Serres, R.A., 1768, Librarian, 1792.
11. Paul Sandby (1725–1809), watercolour painter; R.A., 1768.
12. Thomas Sandby (1721–98), draughtsman and architect; R.A., 1768, Professor of Architecture.

13. William Tyler (d. 1801), sculptor and architect; R.A., 1768.
14. John Inigo Richards (d. 1810), painter; R.A., 1768, Secretary, 1788.
15. Francis Hayman (1708–76), painter; R.A., 1768, Librarian, 1770.
16. Francis Milner Newton (1720–94), painter; R.A., 1768, Secretary.
17. Sir William Chambers, (1726–96), architect; R.A., 1768, Treasurer.
18. Sir Joshua Reynolds, P.R.A., 1768–92.
19. William Hunter (1718–83), Professor of Anatomy, 1768.
20. Francesco Bartolozzi (1727–1815), engraver; R.A., 1768.
21. Agostino Carlini (d. 1790), sculptor and painter; R.A., 1768, Keeper, 1783.
22. Richard Wilson (1714–82), painter; R.A., 1768, Librarian, 1776.
23. Charles Catton (1728–98), painter; R.A., 1768.
24. Richard Yeo (d. 1779), medallist; R.A., 1768.

25. Samuel Wale (d. 1786), painter; R.A., Professor of Perspective, 1768, and Librarian, 1782.
26. Francesco Zuccarelli (1702–88), R.A., 1768.
27. Edward Penny (1714–91), painter; R.A., 1768, Professor of Painting.
28. Peter Toms (d. 1777), painter; R.A., 1768.
29. George Richard Moser (1704–83), enamellist, R.A., 1768, Keeper.
30. Angelica Kauffmann, R.A., 1768.
31. Mrs. Mary Moser, R.A., 1768.
32. Nathaniel Hone (1718–84), painter; R.A., 1768.
33. Edward Burch (fl. 1771), miniaturist; R.A., 1771, Librarian, 1794.
34. Joseph Nollekens (1737–1823), sculptor; R.A., 1772.
35. Richard Cosway, R.A., 1771.
36. William Hoare (1707(?)–1792), painter; R.A., 1768.

1. The identifications in this Key are taken from one published in 1794 and reproduced in Manners and Williamson, p. 28. A Key was also produced when No. 1210 was shown at the British Institution in 1814. I have provided in the list of sitters no facts for those painters represented in this Catalogue; for the others I have provided only the dates when they became Academicians and when they were appointed to offices within the Academy.

design may have been terminated on the right by the two models. The portraits of the two female Academicians (30, 31) are painted, perhaps both at the same time, over a completed background. There are signs that the head of Bartolozzi (20) was reworked by Zoffany.

Taylor (*loc. cit.*) records that in the Academy's exhibition in 1772 No. 1210 was the picture which 'draw the densest crowd about it'. The writer in the *Literary Gazette* in 1826 records some of the traditions associated with the picture: that the portrait of Hayman (15) 'was not entirely finished from the life' as Hayman was 'of too volatile a temper to afford even a brother academician a fair number of sittings'; and that Zoffany originally determined to poke fun at Wilson's love of the bottle and tobacco by placing on the shelf above his head (22) a tankard of stout and crossed tobacco-pipes under a cover of gold-beater's skin decorated with a plaster cast of the Gorgon's head. Zoffany, who had planned to remove the cover on the eve of the exhibition, apparently relented and, after the exhibition had closed, showed the trick to a select few and then painted out 'this sport of his pencil'. There are signs of alterations at this point in the composition,[1] but X-ray revealed nothing more substantial with which to confirm this tradition.[2] No. 1210 was exhibited at the British Institution in 1814 (163), 1826 (158) and 1827 (147).

In the Royal Academy is an early drawing, after the painting, of the group composed of Hunter (19), Bartolozzi (20), Carlini (21), Catton (23) and Yeo (24); at Windsor is a drawing (Oppé, No. 703), possibly by Huddesford, of eight of the figures in No. 1210, arbitrarily grouped round the figure of Reynolds. At Christie's, 14 March 1952 (230), was sold a group of portrait-drawings, attributed to Charles Grignion, which included heads of Catton, Tan-che-qua, Hunter, Nollekens, Richards, West, Wilton and Yeo. On the backs of the drawings of Catton and Hunter was the slightly later statement that they had been drawn while they were standing to Zoffany; both Richards and Hunter had their hands raised to their chins in the drawings as in the painting.

1211. THE TRIBUNA OF THE UFFIZI
(*Plates* 40–2)

Windsor Castle (349). 48⅝ × 61 in., 123,5 × 154,9 cm.

The figures, connoisseurs, diplomats, travellers and young men on the Grand Tour, are disposed in three groups in the Tribuna; on the left Zoffany himself (4) is showing Raphael's 'Niccolini-Cowper' *Madonna* (45) to Lord Cowper (1) while Mr. Loraine-Smith (5), watched by Lord Mount Edgcumbe (6), makes a sketch from *Cupid and Psyche* (49); on the right a smaller group is examining the Medici *Venus* (53); in the foreground, in front of the famous octagonal table (76), a group, presided over by Sir Horace Mann (20), wearing the ribbon and star of the Bath, discusses Titian's *Venus of Urbino* (47).

The walls of the Tribuna are closely hung with pictures; around the walls are shelves on which small works of art are placed; statues and other pieces stand or lie on the floor; in the foreground are nails, a hammer and pliers, used in framing a picture, and a painter's brushes, palette, easel, knife and maulstick.

1. For the portraits of Wilson and Zuccarelli in No. 1210 see respectively D. Cooper in *Burl. Mag.*, vol. XC (1948), p. 114, and M. Levey, *ibid.*, vol CI (1959), p. 140.
2. A variant of this tradition is recorded by Cunningham (vol. I, p. 160). X-ray reveals minor alterations to the carving on the wall behind Bartolozzi (20) and Carlini (21).

Commissioned by Queen Charlotte and ultimately acquired by the King or Queen Charlotte (see below). Recorded at Kew in 1788 (see below) and in the Upper Library at Buckingham House in 1819 (869: 'The Interior of the Grand Dukes Gallery at Florence'); on 21 July 1820 it was taken from Buckingham House to Carlton House by command of George IV; and on 28 July the frame was sent to Wyatt for regilding and the picture to Seguier for cleaning and repairing (Jutsham, *Receipts*, f. 104, *R/D*, ff. 356, 358; *Carlton House*, 1816, additional No. 574). By 1841 it was in the Picture Gallery at Buckingham Palace (98: '. . . purchased from the Artist by George the Third'), but by 1859 it was in the Corridor at Windsor (*V.R. inv.*).

Literature: The Literary Gazette, 8 and 15 July 1826; Walpole, *Anecdotes*, vol. I, p. xviii, n. by Dalloway, vol. V, pp. 83, 84; Manners and Williamson, pp. 45–64, 211; W. T. Whitley, *Artists and their Friends in England, 1700–1799*, vol. I, pp. 295–6; S. Sitwell, *Conversation Pieces* (1936), pp. 28–30; Collins Baker, *Windsor*, p. 333; R.A., *King's Pictures* (48), *The First Hundred Years of the Royal Academy*, 1951–2 (50); Waterhouse, *Painting in Britain*, p. 231; R.A., *Italian Art and Britain*, 1960 (125); O. Millar, *Zoffany and his Tribuna* (1967).

In the summer of 1772, after the collapse of his plans to go with Sir Joseph Banks on Cook's second expedition to the South Seas, Zoffany decided to go to Italy. According to Farington, Queen Charlotte, when Zoffany told her of this project, 'patronised Him, and procured him letters of introduction to the principal persons there, with a present of £300 for His Journey, and an order to paint for Her the Florence Gallery'. Lord Cowper was asked by the Queen to gain for Zoffany 'every advantage in your power'; and on 13 August 1772 Sir Horace Mann was officially informed that the Grand Duke of Tuscany had asked the Director of the Uffizi Gallery to do everything possible to assist Zoffany in painting his view of the Tribuna in the Gallery. Zoffany began work on the picture in the late summer or early autumn of 1772. By the end of 1773 much of the picture must have been completed; Zoffany at one stage was hoping to finish it by March 1774. He continued, however, to add to it until the end of 1777 and did not leave Florence before April 1778. He had paid a visit to Vienna in the late summer of 1776 and had undertaken important other commissions in Italy and Vienna which delayed his return to London. He was in Parma in 1779 and came home later in the year. Walpole saw the picture in Zoffany's house in London on 12 November 1779.

The Tribuna had been built in the Gallery by Bernardo Buontalenti in 1585–9 as a shrine to contain some of the most precious, exotic and celebrated works of art in the Medici collections. In Zoffany's time the original arrangement of works of art in the room had been altered considerably, but much of the original decoration of the room that has since been destroyed survived and this is recorded by Zoffany with scrupulous accuracy. The three walls that Zoffany tackled in his picture are those on the north-east side of the room: on the left, that is, as you come into the room through the original entrance from the Corridor outside. By the end of 1772 Zoffany appears to have painted a large part of the background of the scene: the three walls hung with pictures (23–44),[1] the shelves running round the room and supporting a collection of small antique and renaissance works of art (e.g., 68–75) and the six principal statues on the floor (48–53). Zoffany, however, did not interpret literally Queen Charlotte's commission and obviously decided to compose *his* Tribuna rather than transcribe accurately what was before his eyes in that section of the Grand Duke's Gallery. He varied the disposition of the objects on the shelves and placed on those in his picture some

1. Numbers in brackets refer to the Key on pp. 156–157.

pieces that were outside his vision. Of the statues, *Cupid and Psyche* (49) had probably never been in the Tribuna and in Zoffany's time seems to have been in the *Seconda Galleria* of the Uffizi. Zoffany made certain alterations as the work progressed to the arrangement on the shelves, but made only one important change in the statues and pictures: X-ray reveals that *Hercules Strangling the Snake* (51) is painted over a slightly taller statue, probably the *Apollino* which has always stood in the Tribuna, and that the place occupied by a picture (37) nearby was originally filled with a smaller picture. That the arrangement of pictures in Zoffany's Tribuna differs to a great extent from the actual disposition of pictures in the room is at once apparent from the inventory of the Uffizi in 1769 and the slightly earlier official drawings of the walls of the room. Zoffany, claiming to be Queen Charlotte's painter, 'had leave to have any Picture in the Gallery or Palace taken down; for you must have observed that he has transported some from the latter place [i.e., the Pitti] into his Tribune'. The list (preserved in the Archivio degli Uffizi) of paintings recorded by Zoffany in his picture states that seven came from the Pitti (24, 25, 33, 38, 39, 40, 43) to be incorporated into his scheme. He retained at least one picture from the actual arrangement of each wall; he was compelled to distort the actual relative scales of the pictures, especially in deciding to include the large pictures by Allori (43) and Rubens (33); his selection is perhaps gayer than what was actually before his eyes; and he was obviously concerned to pay a lavish tribute to the Grand Duke's collection of Raphaels.

'Small figures (portraits) as Spectators' had always formed part of the original scheme for the picture and Zoffany conceived a conversazione of an unusual kind. By the end of 1772 a number of figures had been inserted, of which at least one was later removed and is now only visible in X-ray; and by the middle of February he had composed three main groups of figures. On the left, gazing at the *Satyr* (50) he placed Lord Cowper (1), Lord Plymouth (3) and Valentine Knightley (10), with Charles Loraine-Smith (5) sketching *Cupid and Psyche* (49); on the right, absorbed in the *Venus de' Medici* (53), he grouped Lord Winchilsea (13), the two Wilbrahams (14, 21), Watts (15) and Doughty (16), and in the foreground were three figures—Sir Horace Mann (20), possibly only in draft, Patch (18) and Felton Hervey (17), discussing Titian's *Venus of Urbino* (47), held up for their pleasure by Pietro Bastianelli (11).

Additions were, however, to be made to all three groups. The portrait of Mann was finally inserted on 28 September 1773. Taylor (19) and Gordon (12) were inserted into the group in the foreground, Gordon probably in the summer of 1774. Bruce (22) was added on the right in January 1774; the present head of Lord Winchilsea (13) is several inches lower than it was at first (the original position is clear in X-ray). Late in 1777, when Lord Lewisham (8) and Stevenson (7) were in Florence, they were put into the group on the left, probably at the same time as Richard Edgcumbe (6). At some stage Zoffany was so bold as to insert himself (4), offering Raphael's 'Niccolini' *Madonna* (45) to Lord Cowper; in order to fit this passage in he had to push Lord Plymouth

(3) a pace or two back (X-ray shows his original position under the proffered *Madonna*) and he inserted Sir John Dick (2) admiring the picture.

Everyone who had seen Zoffany at work on the picture in the Gallery was enthusiastic over his patience and skill in representing with such accuracy works of art of such different shapes, sizes and textures. The likenesses in the portraits seem to have been admirable. But the 'best judges' in Florence 'found great fault in the perspective which, they say, is all wrong. I know that he was sensible of it himself, and tried to get assistance to correct it; but it was found impossible, and he carried it away as it was'. It is clear from X-ray that Zoffany intended to paint much more than is now visible of Buontalenti's elaborately patterned floor; X-ray, and the naked eye, can detect the pattern running right through most of the foreground. But Zoffany decided to cover it with mats and with the miscellany of works of art scattered arbitrarily on the floor of the Tribuna around the *Arrotino* (48): Greek, Etruscan, Roman, Egyptian objects and Guercino's *Samian Sibyl* (46) which the Grand Duke had acquired early in 1777. He faithfully records damages to some of these pieces that have since been made good.

The picture was exhibited at the Royal Academy in 1780 (68): *A room in the gallery of Florence, called the Tribuna, in which the principal part is calculated to show the different styles of the several masters*. All who saw it praised Zoffany's industry and imitative skill; but Walpole, for example, thought the idea of the conversazione 'absurd', with 'the flock of travelling boys, and one does not know nor care whom'. Unfortunately the King and Queen were equally shocked by the 'travelling boys'. As late as 1804, 'The King spoke of Zoffany's picture of the *Florentine Gallery* painted for him, & expressed wonder at Zoffany having done so improper a thing as to introduce the portraits of Sir Horace Man—Patch, & others.—He sd. the Queen wd. not suffer the picture to be placed in any of her apartments.' The picture remained, probably for some years, on Zoffany's hands while it was decided what he should be paid for it. His royal patrons, who had apparently paid his expenses in going to Florence and an annual allowance (probably of three hundred pounds), considered that he had unnecessarily protracted his stay in Florence and had worked for other patrons. Official records of payments to Zoffany have not come to light, but from the conflicting statements and traditions it seems unlikely that he was paid more than one thousand pounds for his picture.

By 22 December 1788 the picture was at Kew. 'During this day H.M.y continued a little ticklish & He was obliged to be managed by The Attendants very attentively. He took a dislike to a Picture which hung in his room. It was the School of Florence by Zoffany. He had it immediately off the Nails on the Floor, before He was perceived to be busy with it. The Picture was directly moved into the Next room.' It was exhibited at the British Institution in 1814 (2; lent by Queen Charlotte), 1826 (162) and 1827 (151).

The evidence on which the above account is based is fully set out in O. Millar, *Zoffany and his Tribuna* (1967).

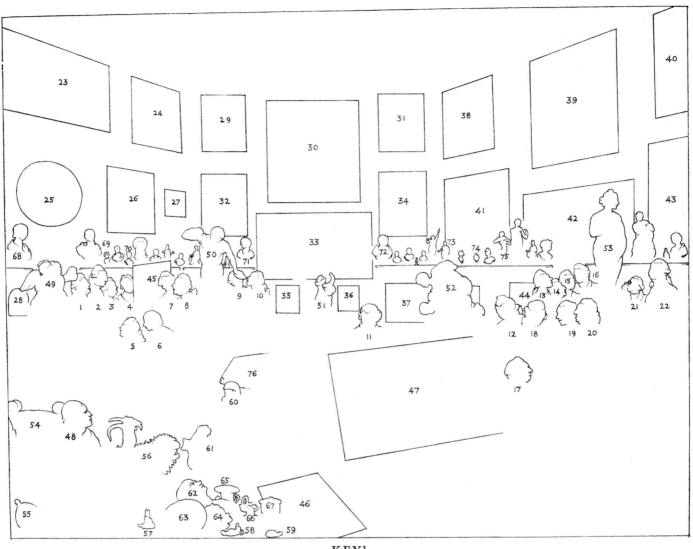

KEY[1]

PORTRAITS

1. George, 3rd Earl Cowper (1738–89), Prince of the Holy Roman Empire. A distinguished collector and devoted lover of Florence. 'I do', wrote Walpole to Mann on 12 November 1779, 'allow Earl Cowper a place in the Tribuna: an English Earl, who has never seen his earldom, and taken root and bears fruit at Florence, and is proud of a pinchbeck principality in a third country, is as great a curiosity as any in the Tuscan collection.' The Earl eventually bought the Raphael, which is now in the National Gallery of Art, Washington. Zoffany is reported to have hawked it round the English visitors to Florence. When Cowper hoped to be given the Garter, he ingratiated himself with George III by finding works of art for him in Italy. On 23 April 1780 he wrote to the King from Florence, offering him the Raphael and a *Self-portrait* of the painter for £2,500; 'Zoffany can inform your Majesty of them, as he has had them in his hands' (*The Correspondence of King George the Third*, ed. Sir J. Fortescue, vol. V (1928), p. 50). In two letters written to Cowper from London, 17 June 1780 and (?late in) 1781, Zoffany writes of his attempts on Cowper's behalf to interest the King in the two pictures (MSS. formerly at Panshanger, now with Lady Salmond).

2. Sir John Dick (1720–1804), Baronet of Braid. British Consul at Leghorn, 1754–76. Robert Adam described him as 'a clever little man . . . with a glib tongue, quick conception and good understanding, esteemed by all for his hospitality, genteel spirits and sweet behaviour'. He is wearing in No. 1211 his badge as a Baronet of Nova Scotia and the ribbon and star of the Russian order of St. Anne of Schleswig-Holstein; he was nominated 'Chevalier' of the order on 25 March 1774 and received the ensigns early in 1775. He was a life-long friend of Boswell.

3. Other Windsor, 6th Earl of Plymouth (1751–99). He was in Florence in January, February and June 1772; Mann said of him: 'the most sweet temper and fat body I ever knew. What a sad prospect at his age, of being immovable before he is thirty.'

4. Johann Zoffany.

5. Charles Loraine-Smith (1751–1835), second son of Sir Charles Loraine, 3rd Bt. He left Florence with Mr. Doughty (16) on 14 February 1773.

6. Richard Edgcumbe, later 2nd Earl of Mount Edgcumbe (1764–1839). A man of musical and artistic tastes, 'a most neat little beau'. He was on his travels in Italy in 1784.

7. Mr. Stevenson, companion to Lord Lewisham (8) on his travels. Sir William Hamilton thought him 'as proper a companion for a young man as any I have ever seen in that situation'.

1. The identifications of the portraits in this Key are based on that provided when No. 1211 was exhibited at the British Institution in 1814 (see below). In at least one portrait (11) this Key can be shown to be wrong.

8. George Legge, Lord Lewisham, later 3rd Earl of Dartmouth (1755–1810). Lord of the Bedchamber to the Prince of Wales, 1782–3; Lord Chamberlain, 1804–10. He embarked on a tour of the Continent with Mr. Stevenson in July 1775. They were in Florence on 2 December 1777. Sir William Hamilton wrote: 'I cannot find the least fault in him, except his outside is a little too fat.'

9. *Called* Joseph Leeson, Viscount Russborough, 2nd Earl of Milltown (1730–1801). His presence in Florence is only reported in the *Gazzetta Toscana* of 8 August 1778, after Zoffany's departure; and the figure does not agree in age or appearance with the portrait by Batoni (1751) in the National Gallery of Ireland.

10. Valentine Knightley (1744–96), of Fawsley. He is probably the Knightley who was in Florence in November 1772; and could well be the Knightley who left Florence in March or April 1773 and took with him to Walpole a bundle of Walpole's letters to Mann.

11. Pietro Bastianelli, a *custode* in the Gallery.

12. Mr. Gordon. The *Gazzetta Toscana* reported on 2 July 1774 that a *sig. Gordon* was in Florence; he was probably identical with *Monsieur Godron Uffiziale Inghilese*, reported in Florence on 13 August 1774.

13. George Finch, 9th Earl of Winchilsea (1752–1826). Gentleman of the Bedchamber, 1777–1812; Groom of the Stole, 1804–12. He was in Florence from December 1772 to late March 1773.

14. Mr. Wilbraham (see No. 21 below).

15. Mr. Watts. He was reported in Florence by Lord Winchilsea on 2 January 1773.

16. Mr. Doughty. He was in Florence in February 1773 and left with Loraine-Smith (5) on 14 February.

17. Hon. Felton Hervey (1712–73), ninth son of the 1st Earl of Bristol. Equerry to Queen Caroline of Ansbach and Groom of the Bedchamber to William, Duke of Cumberland. He was in Florence early in September 1772. His pictures were sold at Christie's on 3 and 4 February 1775.

18. Thomas Patch (see Nos. 977–9 in this Catalogue).

19. Sir John Taylor (d. 1786), created a Baronet in 1778. Recorded in Rome in 1773; perhaps also the Taylor who was in Florence in November 1772.

20. Sir Horace Mann (1706–86). Famous as the friend and correspondent of Horace Walpole. Early in 1738 he was assisting the British Resident at the court of the Grand Duke of Tuscany and in 1740 he succeeded to the post; he stayed at Florence for another forty-six years, as Resident, 1740–65, Envoy Extraordinary, 1765–82, and Envoy Extraordinary and Plenipotentiary, 1782–6. His principal duties were to report on the activities of the exiled Stuarts and to receive English travellers; he was a man of taste who rendered invaluable service to English collectors. He received the Order of the Bath in 1768.

21. T. Wilbraham. The two gentlemen of this name (see above, No. 14) were perhaps two of the sons of Roger Wilbraham of Nantwich: Thomas (b. 1751), George (1741–1813) or Roger Wilbraham (1743–1829). A portrait of Roger bears a resemblance to No. 14; he was an F.S.A. and F.R.S. and owned a fine library of Italian and Spanish books, partly collected on his travels. No. 14 also bears a resemblance to the figure called Mr. Wilbraham in the caricature group by Patch at Floors Castle. The two Mr. Wilbrahams are reported in Florence by Lord Winchilsea (13) between December 1772 and 16 February 1773.

22. James Bruce (1730–94). The famous African traveller; he was in Florence in January 1774. On his return to England he presented to George III the volumes of drawings made during his travels, probably with the assistance, if not actually by, Luigi Balugani (see A. P. Oppé, p. 30).

PAINTINGS

23. Annibale Carracci. *Bacchante.*
24. Guido Reni. *Charity.*
25. Raphael. *Madonna della Sedia.*
26. Correggio. *Virgin and Child.*
27. Sustermans. *Galileo.*
28. Unidentified. Conceivably the old copy (in the Uffizi) of Rembrandt's *Holy Family* in the Louvre; this copy, with an arched-topped frame, is seen in the drawings of the Tribuna (see below).
29. School of Titian. *Madonna and Child with St. Catherine.*
30. Raphael. *St. John.* Zoffany reduces the design on the left and slightly on the right.
31. Guido Reni. *The Madonna.*
32. Raphael. *Madonna del Cardellino.*
33. Rubens. *Horrors of War.*
34. Franciabigio. *Madonna del Pozzo.*
35. Holbein. *Sir Richard Southwell.*
36. Lorenzo di Credi. *Portrait of Verrocchio*; now described as a portrait of Perugino by Raphael.
37. Now attributed to Niccolò Soggi. *Holy Family.*
38. Guido Reni. *Cleopatra.*
39. Rubens. *The Painter with Lipsius and his pupils.*
40. Raphael. *Leo X with Cardinals de' Medici and de' Rossi.*
41. Pietro da Cortona. *Abraham and Hagar.*

Now in the Kunsthistorisches Museum, Vienna.

42. School of Caravaggio. *The Tribute Money.*
43. Cristofano Allori. *The Miracle of St. Julian.*
44. Unidentified. *The Roman Charity.*
45. Raphael. 'Niccolini-Cowper' *Madonna*, formerly at Panshanger and now in Washington.
46. Guercino. *The Samian Sibyl.*
47. Titian. *The Venus of Urbino.*

Of these Nos. 24, 25, 27, 29, 33, 38, 39, 42, 43 and 46 are now in the Pitti; Nos. 25, 32 and 42 are still in the same frames as those painted by Zoffany.

STATUES

48. The *Arrotino* or *Scita Scorticatore.*
49. *Cupid and Psyche.*
50. *The Satyr with the Cymbals.*
51. *Hercules strangling the Serpent.*
52. *The Wrestlers.*
53. *The Venus de' Medici.*

OBJECTS ON THE FLOOR

54. South Italian or Apulian *cratere*, 4th century B.C.
55. Etruscan helmet.
56. The Etruscan Chimera.
57, 58, 59. Roman *lucernae.*
60. Egyptian Ptahmose, XVIIIth dynasty.
61. Greek bronze torso.
62. Bust of Julius Caesar.
63. Silver shield of the Consul Flavius Ardaburius Aspar.
64. Bronze head of Antinous.
65. South Italian *cratere.*
66. Etruscan jug.
67. South Italian *situla.*

Nos. 54, 55, 56, 60, 61, 63, 64, 65, 66, 67 are in the Museo Archeologico in Florence; No. 57 is in the Bargello; and No. 62 in the Uffizi.

OBJECTS ON THE SHELVES
(Many remain unidentified)

68. Bust of 'Plautilla'.
69. Small female head.
70. Head of Tiberius in jaspar, on gold mount of the sixteenth century.
71. Bust of 'Annius Verus'.
72. Bust of an unknown boy, the 'Young Nero'.
73. Bronze figure of Hercules.
74. Small Egyptian figure.
75. Bronze *Arion* by Bertoldo di Giovanni.

No. 75 is in the Bargello; Nos. 69, 70, 74 are in the Museo degli Argenti; No. 73 is in the Museo Archeologico; and Nos. 68, 71, 72 are in the Uffizi.

76. Octagonal table made by Ligozzi and Poccetti, now in the Opeficio delle Pietre Dure in Florence.

Attributed to Johann Zoffany

1212. A BALSAM

Windsor Castle (1383). 36⅛×28 in., 91,8×71,1 cm.

Standing in a large flower-pot within a painted oval.

Recorded in the Private Closet at Kensington in 1818 (561: 'A Balsam. Zoffani', measurements given as 36×32 in.); sent to Hampton Court on 12 September 1838.

Apparently an accurate portrait of the common Balsam (*Impatiens balsamina*) which since the sixteenth century had been very popular in England as a pot plant; No. 1212 shows the plant in its highly cultivated, double-flowered form.[1] The ascription to Zoffany in the inventory of 1818 is so unusual that it may have some sure foundation, but it does not seem to be confirmed by the quality of the picture which is perhaps less vigorously painted than, for example, the flowers in Nos. 1196, 1203, 1204.

After Johann Zoffany

1213. GEORGE III

64×53¾ in., 162,6×136,5 cm.

Three-quarter-length, seated, in a General Officer's coat with the ribbon and star of the Garter.

Probably painted for George III; recorded in the King's Gallery at Kensington in 1818 (359: 'Portrait of His Majesty. Zoffani', measurements given as 64×54 in.); moved to Hampton Court in 1835 and placed in the Prince of Wales's third room (No. 550 in the inv. of 1835: 'After Zoffani'); later at Windsor (466) and Frogmore and sent to York House in October 1924.

An early copy of No. 1195, with variations in the head and in the position of the right hand.

1214. QUEEN CHARLOTTE

Windsor Castle (1553). 30×25½ in., 76,2×64,8 cm.

Head and shoulders.

Recorded at Frogmore *c.* 1872 (*V.R. inv.*).

A derivation, simplified and of no quality, from No. 1196.

Artists Unknown

1215. WILLIAM, DUKE OF CUMBERLAND (*Plate 7*)

Hampton Court (1484). 60½×72½ in., 153,7×184,1 cm.

Riding on a chestnut horse in a red coat of a military cut, over a breastplate; he wears the ribbon of the Garter and the badge of the Bath. Beside him stands an officer in a bright blue coat, with red facings and gold lace; he is perhaps one of the Duke's Orderly Officers and may be an Artillery officer in a form of state dress. There is a view of Windsor and Eton in the background, taken from the high ground to the south of the Castle in Windsor Great Park.

Acquired by George IV. On 26 January 1811 Jutsham entered the receipt at Carlton House of 'A Painting in Gilt Frame Portrait of William Duke of Cumberland on Horseback with Portrait standing on the left side' (Jutsham, *R/D*, f. 147); recorded in store at Carlton House in 1816 (263) and in 1819 (468, with an attribution to Zoffany). Sent to Windsor (452) in October 1823; later at Buckingham Palace.

1. I am very grateful to Dr. E. Launert of the British Museum (Natural History) for this information.

Probably painted *c.* 1755. It is conspicuously better than the equestrian portraits of the Duke in the conventions associated with Morier (e.g., Nos. 943–50) and the sound quality of the heads makes the attribution in 1819 to Zoffany (see above) understandable. It is, however, most unlikely that Zoffany worked on the picture; the heads are perhaps nearer to Brompton or Benjamin Wilson. Henry Angelo records in his *Reminiscences* ((1830), vol. I, pp. 27, 31, 121, vol. II, pp. 139–40) that Brompton on occasion painted the figures on horses by Morier. There are *pentimenti* in the head of the attendant officer and in the horse's tail.

1216. GEORGE III, WHEN PRINCE OF WALES

Buckingham Palace. 30⅛×25⅛ in., 76,5×63,8 cm.

Head and shoulders in a painted oval, wearing the ribbon and star of the Garter.
Acquired by H.M. Queen Mary.

Apparently a derivation from Liotard's pastel (Millar, No. 581) and therefore connected with No. 1011.

1217. GEORGE III

Buckingham Palace. 56¼×46¼ in., 142,9×117,5 cm.

Three-quarter-length, standing with his hat in his left hand.

Recorded at Buckingham Palace (1076) in 1866 (*V.R. inv.*), when it still bore a label stating that it had been brought from Windsor on 25 April 1832.

Apparently of the same type as No. 1218; the pose is slightly reminiscent of No. 774.

1218. GEORGE III (*identity uncertain*)

Windsor Castle (486). Oval: 15⅞×13 in., 40,3×33 cm.

Head and shoulders in a blue coat with the ribbon and star of the Garter.

Recorded at Windsor in 1870 (*V.R. inv.*).

Inscribed on the back as a portrait of Frederick, Prince of Wales, No. 1218 forms part of the same set of royal portraits as Millar, Nos. 634–9; it is possible, however, that it is a portrait of George III and it appears to be of the same type as No. 1217.

1219. AUGUSTA, DUCHESS OF BRUNSWICK, WITH A CHILD

Buckingham Palace. Pastel on paper, mounted on canvas: 29½×23⅛ in., 74,9×58,7 cm., including an addition at the top, which seems original, of 1¾ in. The design was clearly intended to be framed as an oval.

Probably from the collection of H.M. Queen Mary; apparently first recorded in addenda to the 1909 *Catalogue* of Buckingham Palace, p. 216.

Probably painted in London at the same time as No. 869. The child is therefore likely to be Prince Charles George Augustus of Brunswick. No. 1219 is very close in style to Catherine Read.

1220. PRINCESS LOUISA

Windsor Castle (2543)

Pastel on paper: 24×19 in., 61×48,3 cm.

Half-length, holding a Maltese dog in her arms.

Nos. 1220, 1221 were probably drawn for Augusta, Princess of Wales; in 1876 (*V.R. inv.*) the Carlton House, 1816, label was still discernible on the backs of both pastels, identifying them with No. 514 in that inventory: 'Sixteen crayon portraits of the royal family'. They were later at Kew and Buckingham Palace (No. 1220 was No. 520 in *V.R. inv.*).

The two portraits were probably drawn *c.* 1764; formerly attributed to Cotes, they are almost certainly by a less accomplished artist, conceivably Catherine Read.

1221. PRINCESS CAROLINE

Windsor Castle (2542). Pastel on paper: 24¼ × 19 in., 61,6 × 48,3 cm.

Head and shoulders, with flowers in her hair.

See No. 1220 (at Buckingham Palace No. 1221 was No. 518 in the *V.R. inv.*).

See No. 1220.

1222. THE CORONATION OF GEORGE IV

Buckingham Palace. 49¼ × 63⅜ in., 125,1 × 161 cm.

A view looking towards the West End of Westminster Abbey. The figures, from left to right, are: (?) Henry Pelham, 4th Duke of Newcastle (1785–1851), carrying the Curtana; Hugh Percy, 3rd Duke of Northumberland (1785–1847), carrying the second sword; Lord Wellesley (see No. 916); Lord Eldon (see No. 896); the Duke of Devonshire (see No. 895); (?) Edward Legge (1767–1827), Bishop of Oxford; a peer holding his coronet; two pages or officials; the King on whose head the Archbishop of Canterbury (see No. 846) is placing the crown; (?) Bernard Howard, 12th Duke of Norfolk (1765–1842); (?) John Manners, 5th Duke of Rutland (1778–1857), who bore the sceptre with the dove; a Bishop;[1] Prince Leopold of Saxe-Coburg-Saalfeld; Lord Anglesey (see No. 1086); Lord Hill (see No. 988); and the Duke of Wellington (see No. 917).

First offered as a purchase for the royal collection by a Mr. Jones of St. John's Wood in May 1892; Queen Victoria ultimately agreed in October 1892 that it should be purchased for £25 (P.R.O., L.C. 1/570, 69; 571, 17, 133, 150, 152; 589, 1).

Probably the source of the coloured plate inserted in Robert Whittaker's *Ceremonial of the Coronation of . . . King George the Fourth* (1832). At the time of its purchase the picture was attributed to George Dawe, but it scarcely seems good enough to be by him. It is also unlikely that the portraits are *ad vivum*. The heads of Devonshire, the King and Anglesey, for example, are taken from easily recognizable portraits by Lawrence.

1223. FREDERICK, DUKE OF YORK

Windsor Castle (2478). Pastel on vellum: oval, 12 × 9⅝ in., 30,5 × 24,4 cm.

Head and shoulders in the uniform of the Horse Grenadier Guards.

Recorded at Buckingham Palace (737) in 1876. No. 1223 or No. 1224 was presumably the portrait recorded in the Armoury at Carlton House in 1816 (489: 'The Duke of York. (Crayons)', measurements given as 11 × 9 in.); it was later at Kew. The second version was probably the portrait recorded in the Green Dressing-Room at Buckingham House in 1819 (715: 'Small Portrait of His Royal Highness the Duke of York (Crayons)').

1. Possibly Richard Beadon (1737–1824), Bishop of Bath and Wells, or Shute Barrington (1734–1826), Bishop of Durham; or, less likely, Edward Harcourt (1757–1847), Archbishop of York.

Presumably painted *c.* 1785, possibly in Germany, where the Duke was undergoing military training. He had been appointed Colonel of the 2nd troop of Horse Grenadier Guards on 23 March 1782. No. 1223, or No. 1224, may be 'a painting Portrait of His Royal Highness Duke of York framed', which George IV had bought from Colnaghi for £13. 2s. on 19 July 1815 (W.R.A., Geo. 26963); see also No. 1014. Both versions of the design had formerly been attributed to Russell, but they do not seeem sufficiently rich in texture.

1224. FREDERICK, DUKE OF YORK

Buckingham Palace. Pastel on vellum: oval, 12⅛ × 9⅞ in., 30,8 × 25,1 cm.

Head and shoulders in the uniform of the Horse Grenadier Guards.

Almost certainly the portrait recorded in the Armoury at Carlton House in 1816 (489: 'The Duke of York. (Crayons)', measurements given as 11 × 9 in.); later at Kew. Recorded at Buckingham Palace (734) in 1876 (*V.R. inv.*).

A second version, slightly less free in quality, of No. 1223.

1225. FREDERICK, DUKE OF YORK

Buckingham Palace. 98½ × 64 in., 250,2 × 162,6 cm.

Full-length, standing, in Field-Marshal's uniform with the star of the Garter, holding his plumed hat in his right hand. In the background is a view of the Horse Guards.

Formerly in the collection of George, Duke of Cambridge (*d.* 1904); bequeathed by him to the Prince of Wales, later H.M. King George V; later at Frogmore.

The head appears to have been based ultimately on the same type as No. 876. The design presumably dates from *c.* 1820 and could perhaps be attributed to Mather Brown.

1226. AUGUSTUS, DUKE OF SUSSEX

Windsor Castle (1814). 50¼ × 40 in., 127,6 × 101,6 cm.

Three-quarter-length, seated, wearing the Garter and the star of the order and the badge of the Bath and holding his spectacles in his right hand; his left arm rests on an open Latin MS. on a table and other volumes are nearby. The Duke's arms are painted in the upper left corner.

Stated in an inscription on the back to have been bequeathed to Queen Victoria by the Duchess of Inverness (*d.* 1873; but see No. 678); at Windsor in 1874.

Painted at the end of the Duke's life; the head is perhaps connected with the type of the portrait by Rand which was engraved by W. Walker in 1840 (see No. 1006).

1227. WILLIAM FREDERICK, DUKE OF GLOUCESTER

Buckingham Palace. 36¾ × 30¼ in., 93,3 × 76,8.

Half-length, in Field-Marshal's uniform, holding his hat in his hand. He wears the ribbon and star of the Garter, and the badges of the Bath and the Guelphic Order.

Formerly in the collection of the Duke of Cambridge, sold at Christie's, 11 June 1904 (48); it was acquired by Queen Mary and given by her to H.R.H. the Duke of York, later H.M. King George VI.

The type probably dates from *c.* 1815–20.

1228. MARY, DUCHESS OF GLOUCESTER

Windsor Castle (2918), 56×44¼ in., 142,2×112,4 cm.

Three-quarter-length, seated on a sofa, in a black dress and an ermine-lined red robe.

Stated on the back to have been given by the sitter to W. Dee in March 1847 (William Dee was House-Steward and Butler to the Duchess); later in the possession of the Duke and Duchess of Teck at White Lodge, and thereafter in the possession of the Earl of Athlone; later probably in the collection of H.M. Queen Mary. Sent down from Buckingham Palace on 3 July 1928.

Probably painted *c.* 1825–30.

1229. PORTRAIT OF A MAN

Kensington Palace. 30×25 in., 76,2×63,5 cm.

Head and shoulders in black, wearing a small gold chain across his shoulder, the badge of an order on a red ribbon and (?) the ribbon of the Garter.

See No. 678; formerly at Buckingham Palace (417).

The portrait was formerly said to represent Augustus, Duke of Sussex, but it does not bear a wholly convincing likeness to other portraits of the Duke (e.g., No. 828) at this date (*c.* 1812) and the Duke would probably have been shown wearing the star of the Garter.

1230. PORTRAIT OF A PRINCESS

Kew (Hampton Court No. 1371). 30⅛×25 in., 76,5×63,5 cm.

Head and shoulders in a richly laced dress and an ermine-lined robe, wearing very rich jewels in her hair, round her neck and at her breast; a coronet is placed behind her.

In the collection of George IV and recorded in store at Carlton House in 1816 (348: 'A head of her Majesty, when young', measurements given as 30×25 in.; the Carlton House 1816 label is still on the back); later at Buckingham Palace (1165).

Although identified within her lifetime (see above) as a portrait of Queen Charlotte, No. 1230 does not represent her. If an English princess is represented, it is possible that the sitter is Princess Augusta, the eldest of George III's sisters. Cleaning (1966) revealed the coronet (of the type worn by English princesses), which may have been painted out at an early date, because it had been left unfinished. Alternatively the painter himself, before completing the coronet, may have decided to remove it. No. 1230 was recorded at Carlton House next to an alleged portrait of George III when young; this also (Millar, No. 628) was wrongly identified.

1231. PORTRAIT OF A LADY

Windsor Castle (3025). 30¼×25⅛ in., 76,8×63,8 cm.

Half-length, seated, in a lace cap, holding a snuff box in her left hand. In the background is a view of Windsor Castle and the Queen's Lodge from the south.

Purchased for the Royal Library in December 1939 from R. W. Alston.

Probably painted *c.* 1780. At the time of its purchase it was suggested that No. 1231 was a portrait of Mrs. Delany, who was closely connected with Windsor Castle and the royal family and received a 'fine enamelled snuff box' as a bequest from the Duchess of Portland in 1785. The old lady bears, however, no resemblance to Mrs. Delany (No. 975) and is more likely to have been a servant or dependant of the royal family at Windsor. There is a variant of this portrait at Dorney Court, where the sitter was not identified as Mrs. Delany (the two portraits are reproduced by Olwen Hedley, 'Mrs. Delany's Windsor Home', *Berkshire Archaeological Journal*, vol. 59 (1961), p. 52).

1232. BANDITTI DIVIDING THEIR SPOIL

Hampton Court (670). 53×66¾ in., 134,6×169,5 cm.

A party of banditti dividing their spoil over a drum at the mouth of a rocky cave.

Recorded at Hampton Court in 1868 (*V.R. inv.*), but bearing a label indicating that it was in the collection by July 1852.

Literature: Law, 1881, 1898 (212).

Formerly attributed to Salvator Rosa, but painted *c.* 1770 by an English painter influenced, in subject-matter and in style, by J. H. Mortimer.

1233. THE NUBIAN GIRAFFE

32½×27 in., 82,5×68,6 cm.

The giraffe is standing in a landscape of an African flavour, with his two Arab attendants.

In the collection of George IV. Jutsham recorded the receipt at Carlton House on 29 August 1827 'from Mr Hay of The Colonial Office' of 'A Painting, representation of the Cameleopard & Two Portraits of the attendant Arabs. I sent it to The Royal Lodge by desire of Sir William Knighton I put it into a Gilt Frame' (Jutsham, *Receipts*, f. 225); recorded at Windsor in 1878 (*V.R. inv.*). Lent to the Zoological Gardens in 1924.

Painted presumably soon after the arrival of the giraffe (see No. 651) in London on 11 August 1827, or conceivably before its departure from Africa. The two attendants are recognisably those painted by Agasse in No. 651; No. 1233 has, indeed, been attributed to Agasse, but does not seem of sufficiently high quality.

1234. A FLAMINGO

Kew (Hampton Court No. 1462). 49×39¼ in., 124,5×99,7 cm.

Standing in a wooded landscape by a lake.

Recorded at Kensington in 1818 (585: 'A Storck in a Landscape. Zoffani'.); later at Hampton Court and Windsor (1381).

Formerly attributed to Bogdani. It is conceivable that the attribution to Zoffany in the inventory of 1818 represents an error for Bogdani, but No. 1234 is not by Bogdani and may be by Zoffany.

1235. A VIEW OF WESTMINSTER HALL

Kensington Palace. 19½×27¾ in., 49,5×70,5 cm.

A view of Westminster Hall with figures and coaches in Old Palace Yard and a glimpse of St. Margaret's Church and Westminster Abbey beyond.

Bought by the Lord Chamberlain in 1879; formerly at St. James's Palace.

At the time of its purchase, No. 1235 was attributed to Thomas Malton, i.e., presumably Thomas Malton the younger (1748–1804), who exhibited views of Old Palace Yard at the Royal Academy in 1782 (533) and 1796 (863). These may have been watercolours and very little appears to be known of Malton's work in oils. A watercolour, topographically very near to No. 1235, was with Frank T. Sabin in 1963.

1236. A LANDSCAPE WITH FIGURES

Windsor Castle (1138). 20 × 30 in., 50,8 × 76,2 cm.

A lady and gentleman walking with a child beside a lake on which is a small barge, flying a blue ensign, and a sailing boat.

Recorded at Carlton House in 1816 (228: 'A smaller view in Windsor-Park, with figures, and a boatman on a barge'; the 1816 label is still on the stretcher).

Painted *c.* 1760. No. 1236 bore formerly a tentative attribution to Richard Wilson, but is nearer in style to Schalch. The scene is probably on the banks of Virginia Water and it is possible that No. 1236 came into the collection with Schalch's views of Frogmore (Nos. 1062–6).

After Sir Anthony van Dyck

1237. CARDINAL GUIDO BENTIVOGLIO (1579–1644)

Buckingham Palace. 54¼ × 44¾ in., 137,8 × 113,7 cm.

Three-quarter-length, seated, holding a paper in his hands.

Presented to King Edward VII, when Prince of Wales, by John, 1st Lord Savile of Rufford (*d.* 1896) (*Buckingham Palace*, 1909, p. 104).

A three-quarter-length copy, formerly attributed to Reynolds, from the great full-length, painted by Van Dyck in Rome in 1623 and now in the Pitti at Florence (G. Glück, Van Dyck (*Klassiker der Kunst*, Stuttgart, 1931), 180). No. 1237 is clearly an eighteenth-century copy of a portrait that would obviously have fascinated the young Reynolds, but there is apparently no contemporary evidence to associate the copy with him. He was in Florence from 10 May to 4 July 1752 and certainly spent much time in the Pitti.

Peter Eduard Stroehling

1238. LEVIN AUGUST, COUNT BENNIGSEN (1745–1826)

Windsor Castle (2782). Copper: 7⅜ × 6¼ in., 18,7 × 15,9 cm.

Head and shoulders in a painted oval, his head turned to the left in profile; he wears the uniform of the Russian Chevalier Garde with the ribbon and star of St. Andrew of Russia, and the badges of St. George of Russia and of St. John of Malta.

Recorded, before 1860, at Kew; later at Buckingham Palace (721).

Presumably painted *c.* 1810–15.

Hanoverian by birth, Bennigsen entered Russian service in 1773. He was involved in the conspiracy to assassinate Paul I, became General of Cavalry, 1802, and commanded the Russian armies at Eylau and Friedland, 1807; he later held command in the campaign of 1812 and at the battle of Leipzig.

COMPARATIVE ILLUSTRATIONS

1. Sir William Beechey: *George III at a Review*. Victoria and Albert Museum

2. George Chambers: *A View of Greenwich*. Laing Art Gallery, Newcastle

3. J. S. Copley: Sheet of Studies. Museum of Fine Arts, Boston

4. George Dawe: *Ernest I, Duke of Saxe-Coburg-Gotha.*
Coburger Landesstiftung, Schloss Ehrenburg

5. Gainsborough Dupont: *Caroline, Princess of Wales.*
G. W. Leigh, Esq.

6. Thomas Gainsborough: *The Duke and Duchess of Cumberland*. H.M. The Queen

7. Thomas Gainsborough: *The Duke and Duchess of Cumberland.*
British Museum

8. G. Dupont after Gainsborough: *The Eldest Princesses*

9. Thomas Gainsborough: *George III*.
National Museum of Warsaw

10. Thomas Gainsborough: *Prince William, later Duke of Clarence*.
Mrs. Etienne Boegner, Long Island, New York

11. Thomas Gainsborough: *Diana and Actaeon*. Marchioness of Anglesey

12. Thomas Gainsborough: *Diana and Actaeon*. Huntington Library and Art Gallery, California

13. Thomas Gainsborough: *Diana and Actaeon*. Cecil Higgins Art Gallery, Bedford

14. Thomas Gainsborough: Letter to the Secretary of the Royal Academy.
Royal Academy, London

15. E. Hodges after Hoppner: *William IV when Duke of Clarence*

16. Sawrey Gilpin and William Marlow: *The Long Walk*. Mrs. P. Starkey, Radway

17. Sir Thomas Lawrence: *Caroline, Princess of Wales* (?).
Sir Arundell Neave, Bt.

18. Sir Thomas Lawrence: Sketch of a Uhlan with a Charger.
Ashmolean Museum, Oxford

19. Sir Thomas Lawrence: *William IV when Duke of Clarence*.
Trustees of the Goodwood Collection

20. Sir Thomas Lawrence: *Prince George of Cumberland*.
S. K. H. Prince Ernst August

21. Sir Thomas Lawrence: *Frederick, Duke of York.*
Museo de Arte de Ponce

22. W. Say after Place: *Sa'adat Ali Khan, Nawab of Oudh*

23. Allan Ramsay: Study of a Crown. National Gallery of Scotland

24. Allan Ramsay: Sketch of Queen Charlotte with Prince
Frederick (?). National Gallery of Scotland

25. Allan Ramsay: *George IV when Prince of Wales.*
National Gallery of Scotland

26. Alan Ramsay: Sketch for Prince William, later Duke of Clarence (?).
National Gallery of Scotland

27. Allan Ramsay: *Prince George Augustus of Mecklenburg-Strelitz.*
National Gallery of Scotland

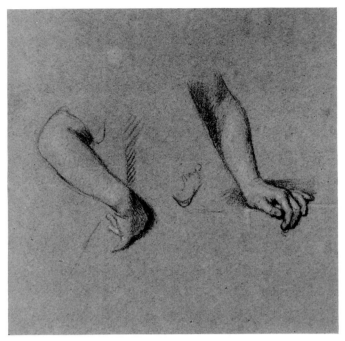

28. Allan Ramsay: Study of the hands of George III.
National Gallery of Scotland

29. Allan Ramsay: Study of the arms of the Prince of Wales.
National Gallery of Scotland

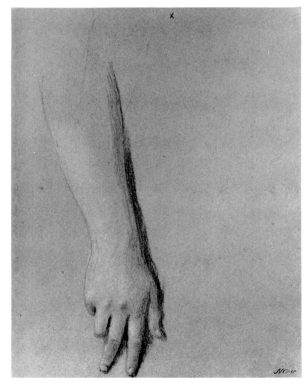

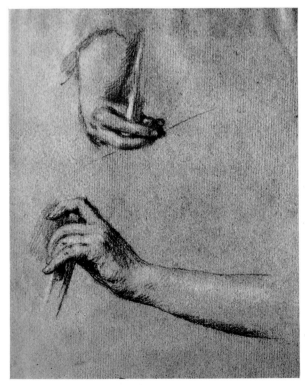

30. Allan Ramsay: Study of the arm of Queen Charlotte.
National Gallery of Scotland

31. Allan Ramsay: Study of hands.
National Gallery of Scotland

32. T. Watson after Reynolds: *Henry, Duke of Cumberland*   33. J. R. Smith after Reynolds: *Louis Philippe Joseph, Duke of Orléans*

34. Paul Sandby: *The North Terrace at Windsor Castle*. Philadelphia Museum of Art

35. George Sanders: *Princess Charlotte*. H.M. The King of the Belgians

36. George Stubbs: *Pumpkin*. Evelyn de Rothschild, Esq.

37. Benjamin West: Sketch for a Group of five Children. Victoria and Albert Museum

38. Benjamin West: *The Apotheosis of Prince Octavius.*
Witt Collection, Courtauld Institute

39. Benjamin West: Sheet of Studies for *The Apotheosis of
Prince Octavius.* Museum of Fine Arts, Boston

40. Sir David Wilkie: *Blind-Man's-Buff*. National Gallery of Scotland

41. Sir David Wilkie: Sketch for *The Spanish Posada*. National Gallery of Scotland

42. David Allan: *The Penny Wedding*. Beaverbrook Art Gallery, Fredericton, New Brunswick

43. Sir David Wilkie: Sketch for *The Penny Wedding*. British Museum

44. Sir David Wilkie: Sketch for *The Penny Wedding*. National Gallery of Scotland

45. Sir David Wilkie: Sketch for *The Defence of Saragossa*. Public Library, Museum and Art Gallery, Blackburn

46. Sir David Wilkie: Sketch for *The Guerilla's Departure*

47. Sir David Wilkie: Sketch of George IV. National Gallery of Scotland

48. Sir David Wilkie: Study for *The Entrance to Holyroodhouse*. Royal Library, Windsor Castle

49. Sir David Wilkie: Sketch for *The Entrance of George IV at Holyroodhouse*. Royal Library, Windsor Castle

50. Sir David Wilkie: Study for the Collar of the Garter. Royal Library, Windsor Castle

51. Sir David Wilkie: Study for the Collar of the Bath. Royal Library, Windsor Castle

52. Sir David Wilkie: Sketch for the Duke of Argyll.
Royal Library, Windsor Castle

53. Sir David Wilkie: Sheet of Studies. Royal Library, Windsor Castle

54. Sir David Wilkie: *Alexander, 10th Duke of Hamilton.*
Duke of Hamilton

55. Sir David Wilkie: Sketch for the Duke of Hamilton.
Ashmolean Museum, Oxford

56. Sir David Wilkie: Sketch for William IV with Queen Adelaide.
Royal Library, Windsor Castle

57. Sir David Wilkie: Sketch for William IV.
Royal Library, Windsor Castle

58. Sir David Wilkie: Study of Queen Victoria. Lt.-Col. William Stirling

59. Sir David Wilkie: Sketch for *The First Council of Queen Victoria*. Miss Armide Oppé and Denys Oppé, Esq.

60. Sir David Wilkie: Sketch for *The First Council of Queen Victoria*. Royal Library, Windsor Castle

61. Sir David Wilkie: Sketch for *The First Council of Queen Victoria*. Earl of Perth

62. Sir David Wilkie: Sketch for *The First Council of Queen Victoria*. Royal Library, Windsor Castle

63. Johann Zoffany: *Frederick, Duke of York*. S.K.H. Prince Ernst August

64. R. Earlom after Zoffany: *George III, Queen Charlotte and their eldest Children*

INDEXES

INDEX OF PORTRAITS

References in roman numerals are to the more important notices in the Introduction. References in roman type are to items in the Catalogue; in heavy type they refer to undoubted portraits of a sitter; in ordinary type they are to items in which earlier, rejected, tentative or suggest identifications are mentioned or discussed.

Abd-ul-Mejíd, Sultan of Turkey, **1190**
Abel, Karl Friedrich, xxi, xxviii, **1048**
Abercromby, Col. Sir John, **1092**
Abercromby, Sir Ralph, **1092**
Aberdeen, George Hamilton-Gordon, 4th Earl of, **1188**
Adair, Robert, **1167**
Adelaide, Queen, xl, **1085**
Adolphus, Prince, *see* Cambridge
Albemarle, William Keppel, 4th Earl of, **1188**
Alexander I, Emperor of Russia, xxxiii, xxxiv, xli, **686, 745, 746, 883**
Alexander II, Emperor of Russia, **748**
Alfred, Prince, **792, 817, 1140, 1149**
Amelia, Princess, daughter of George II, 1012
Amelia, Princess, daughter of George III, xxviii, xxxvi, **670, 712, 840, 855, 881, 1099, 1101**
Amherst, Jeffrey, 1st Lord, **995**
Anderson, William, **1110**
Angerstein, John Julius, xxxvi
Anglesey, Henry Paget, 2nd Earl of Uxbridge and 1st Marquess of, xl, **764, 1086, 1105, 1188, 1222**
Angoulême, Louis-Antoine de Bourbon, Duke of, xxxv, **884, 926**
Anson, Thomas, 2nd Viscount, later 1st Earl of Lichfield, **728**
Anstruther, Lt.-Col. Robert, **1092**
Arcot, Nawab of, **990**
Argyll, George Campbell, 6th Duke of, **1184, 1188**
Augusta, Princess of Wales, **1002, 1012**
Augusta, Princess, *see* Brunswick, Duchess of
Augusta, Princess, daughter of George III, xxiii, **666, 672, 681, 682, 784, 798, 1095, 1139, 1140, 1145, 1201, 1202,** 1207
Augustus, Prince, *see* Sussex

'Baccelli La' (Giovanna Zanerini), xxviii, **769**
Baker, Jane, **696**
Baker, William, **696**
Barré, Col. Isaac, **1167**

Barret, George, **1210**
Barrington, Shute, Bishop of Durham, 1222
Bartolozzi, Francesco, **1210**
Bastianelli, Pietro, **1211**
Bathurst, Henry, 3rd Earl, xxxv, **885**
Beadon, Richard, Bishop of Bath & Wells, 1222
Beatty, William, **762**
Beauclerk, Topham, **689, 690**
Bedford, Francis Russell, 5th Duke of, xxviii, **827, 841**
Bennett, Charles, **829**
Bennigsen, Levin August, Count, **1238**
Bentinck, Lady Harriet, **1012**
Bentivoglio, Cardinal Guido, **1237**
Birch, Col. (?John), **1092**
Bligh, Lt. George, **762**
Bloomfield, Lt.-Col., Benjamin, later 1st Lord, **711**
Blücher, Field-Marshal Gebhardt von, xxxiii, **886, 1106**
Boggiero, Father, **1180**
Bogle, George, 870
Boothby, Sir William, **689, 690**
Bourk (Birch), –, **829**
Brotherton, Col. T. W., 728
Browne, Col. George, 728
Browne, Lt. Henry, **1167**
Bruce, James, **1211**
Bruhl, Miss, **827**
Brunswick, Augusta, Duchess of, xii, **869, 1219,** 1230
Brunswick, Charles George Augustus, Prince of, **869, 1219**
Bunce, William, **762**
Burch, Edward, **1210**
Burke, Walter, **762**
Burton, William Conyngham, **728**
Bute, John Stuart, 3rd Earl of, xiii, xvi
Byron, George Gordon, 6th Lord, xlii, **1056**

Cambridge, Adolphus, Duke of, xxxiv, 721, **788, 867, 878, 1139, 1140, 1145, 1147**
Cambridge, Augusta, Duchess of, **674**

Campbell, John, 1st Lord, **1188**
Campbell, Major, **829**
Canning, George, xxxvi, **887, 927**
Capo D'Istria, John, Count, xxxiv, **888**
Carlini, Agostino, **1210**
Carlisle, George Howard, 9th Earl of, **1188**
Carlisle, George Howard, 10th Earl of, **1188**
Carlisle, Georgiana, Countess of, **1041**
Carnarvon, Elizabeth, Countess of, **827**
Caroline of Ansbach, Queen, xxvii
Caroline of Brunswick, Princess of Wales, xxxii, **768, 827, 874, 1091**
Caroline, Princess, daughter of Frederick, Prince of Wales, xii, **720,** 1221
Casanova, A. Dufay de, **695**
Castlereagh, Robert Stewart, Viscount, later 2nd Marquess of Londonderry, xxxv, **889**
Catton, Charles, **1210**
Cavan, Richard Lambart, 7th Earl of, **1092**
Cawdor, Isabella Caroline, Countess of, **684**
Chamberlain, Mason, **1210**
Chambers, Sir William, **1210**
Charles, Archduke of Austria, xxxiv, **891**
Charles X, King of France, xxxiv, xxxv, **890, 928**
Charles, Prince of Leiningen, xli, **1187, 1189**
Charles, Prince of Mecklenburg-Strelitz, **1207**
Charlotte, Queen, xii, xiii, xiv, xvi, xviii, xx, xxii, xxvii, xxviii, **659, 717, 718, 775, 777, 779, 809–812, 827, 997, 998, 1005, 1012, 1034, 1036, 1038, 1091, 1094, 1139–1142,** 1193, **1196, 1198, 1199, 1201, 1202, 1207, 1214,** 1230
Charlotte, Princess Royal, daughter of George III, **665,** 684, **717, 718, 782, 798,** 840, **1139, 1140, 1142,** 1200, **1201, 1202, 1204, 1207**

165

INDEX OF SUBJECTS

References are to the Catalogue numbers

I. RELIGIOUS SUBJECTS

II. CLASSICAL SUBJECTS

III. HISTORICAL EVENTS: MEDIEVAL

IV. HISTORICAL EVENTS: MODERN

INDEX OF ARTISTS

References in roman numerals are to the pages of the Introduction. References in roman type are to items in the Catalogue; in heavy type they refer to paintings directly associated with a given painter; in ordinary type they refer to entries in which older and rejected attributions are mentioned or tentative attributions put forward, or to entries in which the name of an artist or craftsman otherwise occurs.

ERRATUM: p. 77, no. 916. Lawrence's note to Farington was written on 12 August 1812, not 12 August 1821.